A COMPARATIVE GRAMMAR OF THE GAUDIAN LANGUAGES

WITH SPECIAL REFERENCE TO THE EASTERN HINDI

A COMPARATIVE GRAMMAR OF THE GAUDIAN LANGUAGES

WITH SPECIAL REFERENCE TO THE

EASTERN HINDI

ACCOMPANIED BY

A LANGUAGE-MAP AND A TABLE OF ALPHABETS

A. F. RUDOLF HOERNLE

GYAN

Published by

Gyan Publishing House
5, Ansari Road
Daryaganj, New Delhi-110002
Phone: 011-47034999, 9811692060
E-mail: books@gyanbooks.com

Distribution Network
gyanbooks.com
India, USA, Canada, UK, Australia, France

ISBN : 9788121232654 (PB)
First Published, London, 1880

2nd Impression 2020

Printed at: Gyan Press, Delhi.

A
Comparative Grammar of the Gaudian Languages
Author: A. F. Rudolf Hoernle

A COMPARATIVE GRAMMAR OF THE GAUDIAN LANGUAGES

WITH SPECIAL REFERENCE TO THE

EASTERN HINDI

ACCOMPANIED BY

A LANGUAGE-MAP AND A TABLE OF ALPHABETS

BY

A. F. RUDOLF HOERNLE

LONDON
TRÜBNER & CO., 57 & 59, LUDGATE HILL
1880

TO

KARL STEFFENSEN

PROFESSOR OF PHILOSOPHY IN BASEL

IN

GRATEFUL REMEMBRANCE

OF THE

YEARS OF STUDY PASSED UNDER HIS GUIDANCE

This Volume

IS

DEDICATED.

CALCUTTA, Spring 1880.

PREFACE.

In order to account for the perhaps somewhat unusual arrangement of this book, I must explain, that my original plan was merely to write a Grammar of the Eastern Hindí accompanied by short notes, pointing out its Gauḍian affinities. Gradually these notes grew to such an extent as to change almost entirely the character of the book, which in its present state is rather a comparative grammar of the Gauḍian languages than a simple grammar of the Eastern Hindí. The two subjects have been kept apart as much as possible, so as to enable the reader to use the book ad libitum for the study of either, the Eastern Hindí only, or the Gauḍian generally. For this purpose the comparative matter has been mainly distributed in the paragraphs headed „Affinities" and „Derivation"; the others refer to Eastern Hindí. To further increase the usefulness of the book an index of such Gauḍian words as are explained in the Grammar is in course of preparation and will shortly be published.

The amount of information contained within this volume, is very much more than may appear at first sight. An idea of its extent may be gained by a glance over the index of subjects. Putting aside the information about the Eastern Hindí most of which is original, the book not only goes over nearly the entire ground, covered by the volumes of Mr. Beames' Comparative Grammar, but also adds a not inconsiderable quantity of additional matter, especially in regard to the derivation of Gauḍian grammatical forms from the Prákṛits. It was not easy to compress all this mass of information within one comparatively small volume to which, for various reasons, it was necessary to confine the work. This necessity will account for the perhaps excessive conciseness of diction and the extensive use of abbreviations; an inconvenience for which, I feel, I must crave the indulgence of the reader, but which, by the help of the prefixed list of abbreviations, I hope will prove no serious difficulty.

As regards the sources of my materials for the grammar of Eastern Hindí, in the absence of all literature (except in the Baiswáṛí), I had to rely almost entirely on the information, partly obtained through long personal intercourse with the people, but especially supplied by native scholars or (in a few cases) by Europeans intimately acquainted with the country people. Among the former it gives me great pleasure to acknowledge the very efficient help rendered me by the kindness of Paṇḍit Gopál Bhaṭṭa, Professor of Sanskrit at the Jay Narain's College in Benares, who to a scholarly knowledge of Sanskrit adds an intimate acquaintance of the Vernaculars as spoken by the people, representatives of whom, from every part of India, may be met with in Benares.

As regards the comparative portion of the book, every work that I could think of as bearing on the subject has been consulted. Most of these will be found mentioned in the list of abbreviations. A few works, such as E. Müller on the Jaina Prákṛit, Jacobi's edition of the Kalpasútra, A. Grierson's Maithilí Grammar, unfortunately came into my hands too late to be turned to account. Most of the Prákṛit Grammarians (such as Márkaṇḍeya, Ṣubhachandra, Kramadíṣvara, Trivikrama, Siṃharája etc.) are quoted from MSS. in my possession; but Vararuchi and Hemachandra are generally cited from the excellent editions of Cowell and Pischel respectively.

The publication of this volume, begun in Germany in 1878, has been so long delayed through my absence from Europe, which necessitated the sending out of the proofsheets to India. I fear this had the further evil consequence of many misprints remaining undetected, for which I hope the kind reader will make allowance. I do not think any serious misprint has escaped correction.

R. H.

CONTENTS.

Note: See also „Affinities“ and „Derivation“ in the Index of Subjects, p. 407.

LIST OF ABBREVIATIONS.

A. Gr. = Translation of the Âdi Granth by Trumpp.
A. Mg. = Ardha Mágadhí Prákṛit.
Ap. or *Ap. Pr.* = Apabhraṃṣa Prákṛit.
Ap. Mg. = Apabhraṃṣa Mágadhí Prákṛit.
Ap. Ṣr. = Apabhraṃṣa Ṣauraseni Prákṛit.

B. = Bengálí.
B. H. Dy. = Bate's Hindí Dictionary.
Bh. = Bhojpurí.
Bhag. or *Bh.* = Bhagavatí.
Br. = Braj.
Bs. = Beames' Comparative Grammar of the Modern Aryan languages.
Bs. or *Bw.* = Baiswáṛí.

Cw. = Cowell's edition of Vararuchi's Prákṛita Prakáṣa.

Dk. = Dakshiṇátya Prákṛit.
Dl. = Delius' Radices Pracriticae.

E., in conjunction with other initials, = Eastern; e. g. *E. H.* = Eastern Hindí, *E. Gḍ.* = E. Gauḍian, *E. Rj.* = Eastern Rájpútání.
Eth. = Etherington's Hindí Grammar.

G. = Gujarátí.
Gḍ. = Gauḍian.
Gh. or *Gw.* = Gaṛhwálí.
Gl. = Sg. Goldschmidt.

H. = Hindí; or, in conjunction with other initials, = High; as *H. H.* = High Hindí, *H. B.* = High Bengálí.
H. C. = Hema Chandra's Prákṛit Grammar (ed. Pischel).

J. A. S. B. = Journal of the Asiatic Society of Bengal.
J. G. O. S. = Journal of the German Oriental Society.

K. I. = Kramadíṣvara's Prákṛit Grammar.
Kf. = Kafirí.
Kl. = Kellogg's Hindí Grammar.
Km. = Kumaoní.
Kn. = Kanaují.
Ksh. = Kashmírí.
Kth. = Kaithí.

Ld. = Panjábí Grammar printed in Loodiana.
L. Dh. = Lakshmí Dhara's Shaḍbháshá chandriká.
Ls. = Lassen's Institutiones Linguae Pracriticae.

M. = Maráṭhí; or, in conjunction

with other initials, = Modern; as *M. Gḍ.* = Modern Gauḍian, *M. M.* = Modern Maráṭhí.

M. M. = Max Müller's Sanskrit Grammar.

M. W. = Moniers William's Sanskrit-English Dictionary.

Man. = Student's Manual of Maráṭhi Grammar.

Mcch. = Mṛchchhakaṭiká (ed. Stenzler).

Mḍ. = Márkaṇḍeya's Prákṛit Grammar.

Mg. = Mágadhí Prákṛit.

Mh. = Máhárásh̤ṭrí Prákṛit.

Mh. Ṣr. = Mahárásh̤ṭrí - Ṣauraseni Prákṛit.

Mr. or *Mw.* = Máṛwáṛí.

Ms. = Mason's Páli Grammar.

Mth. = Maithilí.

N. = Naipálí.

N. Gḍ. = Northern Gauḍian.

O. = Oṛíyá; or, in conjunction with other initials, = Old; as *O. H.* = Old Hindí, *O. W. H.* = Old Western Hindí, *O. P.* = Old Panjábí; *O. S.* = Old Sindhí, *O. Gḍ.* = Old Gauḍian.

P. = Panjábí.

Pl. = Pischel's Dissertatio Inauguralis.

Pr. = Prákṛit.

Pr. or *Pers.* = Persian.

Pr. R. = Prithiráj Rasau by Chand Bardáí.

Ps. = Paiṣáchí Prákṛit.

Psh. = Pashtú.

Rj. = Rájpútání.

R. T. = Ráma Tarkavajíṣás Prákṛit Grammar.

S. = Sindhí.

S. C. = Ṣubha Chandra's Prákṛit Grammar.

S. Ch. = Shama Charan's Baugálí Grammar.

S. D. = Sahitya Darpaṇa.

S. Gḍ. = Southern Gauḍian.

S. Gdt. = Sg. Goldschmidt.

S. L. = St. Luke translated into Naipálí.

S. R. = Siṃha Rájá's Prákṛit Grammar.

Skr. = Saṃskrit.

Sn. = Sutton's Oṛíyá Grammar.

Spt. = Sapta Ṣataka (ed. Weber).

Sr. = Saurasení Prákṛit.

St. G. = Stanislas Guyard's Grammaire Palie.

T. D. or *T. Das.* = Tulsí Dás' Ramáyan.

T. V. = Trivikrama's Prákṛit Gramm.

Tr. = Trumpp's Sindhí Grammar.

Ved. = Vedic.

Vr. = Vararuchi's Prákṛit Grammar (ed. Cowell).

W., in conjunction with other initials, = Western; as *W. Gḍ.* = Western Gauḍian, *W. H.* = Western Hindí, *W. Rj.* = Western Rájpútání.

Wb. = Weber's edition of the Sapta Ṣataka (*Spt.*) and of the Bhagavatí (*Bh.*).

GRAMMATICAL TERMS.

abl. = ablative.
acc. = accusative.
act. = active (case or voice or verb).
adj. = adjective.
adv. = adverb or adverbial.
aff. = affix.
auxil. = auxiliary.

c. g. or com. gen. = common gender.
C. R. = Causal Roots.
C. V. = Causal Verb.
cl. = class.
comp. = compound.
Cp. R. = Compound Roots.
cond. = conditional.
conj. = conjunct or conjunction or conjunctive mood.
conj. cons. = conjunct consonant.
cons. = consonant.
constr. = construction.
contr. = contracted or contraction.

D.R. or Dm. R. = Denominative Roots.
dat. = dative.
Db. C. V. = Double Causal Verb.
dem. = demonstrative pronoun.
der. or deriv. = derivative.
dir. = direct.
Dr. R. = Derivative Roots.
du. = dual.

emph. = emphatic.
euph. = euphonic.
exc. = except or exception.

f. or fem. = feminine.
fut. = future.

gen. = genitive or general.

imp. or imper. = imperative mood.
ind. or indic. = indicative mood.
indef. = indefinite or indefinitive.
inf. = infinitive.
instr. = instrumentalis.
inter. or interrog. = interrogative pronoun.
intr. = intransitive.
intr. V. = intransitive Verb.

lg. f. = long form.
loc. = locative.

m. or masc. = masculine.

N. = noun.
n. or neut. = neuter.
nom. = nominative.
num. = numeral.

obl. = oblique.
orig. = original.

P. P. = past participle.
P. R. = Primitive Roots.
part. = participle.
pass. = passive.
pers. = person or personal.
pl. or plur. = plural.
pleon. = pleonastic.
postpos. = postposition.
prec. = precative.
pret. = preterite.
pron. = pronoun or pronominal.

qual. = quality.
qual. pron. = qualitative pronoun.
quant. = quantity.
quant. pron. = quantitative pronoun.

R. = root.
red. f. = redundant form.
refl. = reflexive pronoun.
rel. = relative pronoun.
resp. = respectively.

S. = suffix.
S. R. = Simple Roots.
S. V. = Simple Verb.
sg. or sing. = singular.

sh. f. = short form.
st. f. = strong form.
subst. = Substantive.
suff. = suffix.

tbh. or tadbh. = tadbhava.
term. or termin. = termination.
tr. = transitive.
Tr. V. = Transitive Verb.
ts. = tats. or tatsama.

voc. = vocative.

wk. f. = weak form.

An asterisk (*) prefixed to a word means a conjectural or theoretical form of a word.

INTRODUCTION.

THE LOCAL DISTRIBUTION AND MUTUAL AFFINITIES OF THE GAUḌIAN[1]) LANGUAGES.

Seven languages of the Sanskrit stock are usually enumerated as spoken in North India, viz. Sindhí, Gujarátí, Panjábí, Hindí, Bangálí, Oṛíya, Maráṭhí. Of these H. is commonly said to be spoken over an area of more than 248000 square miles and to be the language of between 60 and 70 millions or fully $^1/_4$ of the inhabitants of India. This statement is true only in a very limited and special sense. It is true if by H. we understand the literary or High-Hindí (including under this term Hindústání or Urdú); but it is quite incorrect if it be understood to imply that only one language is spoken generally by the people inhabiting that area. It is, a priori, extremely improbable and contrary to general experience that one and the same language should be spoken by such large numbers of people over a tract of country so widely extended. As a matter of fact, two entirely different languages are spoken in the so-called Hindí area; one in the western, the other in the eastern half. For the sake of convenience, these two languages will be called in this treatise Western Hindí and Eastern Hindí; but the terms are not altogether good ones, as they give too much of an impression that Western and Eastern Hindí are merely two different dialects of

1) I have adopted the term Gauḍian to designate collectively all North-Indian vernaculars of Sanskrit affinity, for want of a better word: not as being the least objectionable, but as being the most convenient one.

the same (Hindí) language. In reality, they are as distinct from one another, as B. in the east and P. in the west are supposed to be distinct from what is commonly called Hindí. Indeed the likeness between E. H. and B. is much closer than between E. H. and W. H.; and on the other hand, the affinity between W. H. and P. is much greater than between W. H. and E. H. In short W. H. and E. H. have as much right to be classed as distinct languages rather than different dialects, as P., H., and B.

It is impossible at present, accurately to define the limits of the various Gauḍian languages and dialects. It is a subject to which little attention has been paid hitherto. Moreover, it seems probable, that in most cases adjoining languages and dialects pass into each other so imperceptibly, that the determination of the limits of each will always remain more or less a matter of doubt and dispute. At present, we can only fix with certainty the centres of their respective areas. The following remarks and the accompanying map which attempts to show their local distribution, must be understood with this proviso. The area in which H. (commonly so called, i. e. E. H. and W. H.) is spoken, occupies the central portion of North India. It extents in the north to the lower ranges of the Himálaya mountains; in the west to a line drawn from the head of the gulf of Kachchh in a north-easterly direction to the upper Satlaj near Simla; in the south to the Narmadá river or the Vindhyá range of mountains; in the east to a line following the course of the Sankhassí river to its junction with the Ganges and thence in a south-westerly direction to the Narmadá. The H. area is bounded on the north by those of Gw., K., and N.; on the west by P., S., and G.; on the south by the M. area, and on the east by O. and B.

The Gaṛhwálí, Kumaoní and Naipálí are apparently dialects of one great language, the area of which is bounded on the south by that of Hindí, on the east by the upper Satlaj, on the west by the upper Sankhassí, and on the north by the higher ranges of the Himálaya. The Gaṛhwálí is spoken between the Satlaj and

Ganges, the Kumaoní between the Ganges and Gogarí, the Naipálí between the Gogarí and Sankhassí. In the following pages these three dialects will be designated by the collective name of *Northern Gauḍian.*

The area of the Panjábí nearly covers the province from which it derives its name, extending from the Hindí area in the east to the Indus in the west, and from the lower ranges of the Himálaya in the north to the junction of the five rivers in the south. There are apparently two principal dialects of this language; viz. the Multání spoken in the Southern Panjáb about Multán, and the dialect of the Northern Panjáb. P. is spoken by about 12 millions of people distributed over 60000 square miles.

The Sindhí area lies on both sides of the lower Indus. It meets the Hindí area on the east, and that of the Panjábí on the north, and is bounded by the Kela mountains on the west. The language comprises three principal dialects; the Siráikí spoken in the upper Sindh, north of Haiderábád; the Láṛí or dialect of the lower Sindh spoken in the Indus delta and on the sea-coasts; and the Tharelí spoken in the Tharu or desert of Eastern Sindh (see Tr. II). It is spoken by about 2 millions of people and over 90000 square miles.

The Gujarátí area comprises the provinces of Kacch and Gujarát or the country around the gulf of Kambay. The Kacchí is a distinct dialect, and its true affiliation, whether to Sindhí or Gujarátí appears to be still doubtful. Gujarátí has seemingly no marked dialectic divisions. It is spoken over 50000 square miles by about 6 millions of people.

The Maráṭhí area is bounded by the Vindhyá mountains on the north, where it joins that of Western Hindí. At their eastern extremity it meets the Eastern Hindí area, whence the line of demarcation runs in a south-westerly direction to the sea-coast near the city of Goa. There are two principal dialects: the Konkaní and Dakhaní. The former is spoken in the west, in the Konkan or narrow strip of country between the mountains and the sea;

the latter in the north-east in the (so-called) Dakhan or Central India. In the south-east, about Satara and Kolhapur, there is apparently a third variety (Bs. I, 104). Maráṭhí is spoken by about 13 millions of people and over 113000 square miles. It should be observed, that in the neighbourhood of the upper Narmadá Maráṭhí is contignous to Eastern Hindí. One gradually merges into the other, and it is impossible, at present, to say exactly where one begins and the other ends. It is certain, however, that E. H. is spoken about Jabalpur. On its south and south-east, respectively, Maráṭhí has the Drávidian languages, the Kanarese and Telugu.

The Oṛíya area is bounded on the north by the Subanarekhá river and in the west by a line drawn from the sources of that river in a southerly direction to about Ganjam on the east-coast of India. According to Beames (I, 118, 106) it is rapidly supplanting the old non-Aryan dialects, spoken in the vast tract of mountains, lying between its western boundary-line and the eastern limits of the Maráṭhí area. It is spoken by about 5 millions of people over 66000 square miles.

The Bangálí area ist nearly coterminous with the province of Bangál, being bounded by the Eastern Hindí area on the West. Four principal varieties of the language are said to exist (Bs. I, 106); one in Eastern Bangál about Silhet and Tipara, another in Northern Bangál about Dinajpur; one in Southern Bangál about Midnapur and Calcutta, and the principal one in Central Bangál. It is spoken by about 36 millions of people over 90000 square miles.

Within the area of Hindí, as previously defined, many differing dialects are spoken. Their exact number is, at present, uncertain. Eight principal dialectic varieties, howerer, may be distinguished. Namely, beginning in the West; *first*, the dialects of Western Rájpútáná as far as the Aravalli mountains. The principal one is the Márwáṛí or the dialect of the country of the Máṛs, a Rájpút tribe, spoken about Jodhpur and Jaynagar. *Secondly*, the dialects of Eastern Rájpútáná, spoken about Jaypúr and Kotah, on the high lands between the Aravalli mountains and the river Betwá. *Thirdly*, the Braj Bháshá or the dialect of the upper Doáb, spoken on the plains of the Jamná and Ganges, about Agrá, Mathurá, Delhi, etc. It is so called from Vraj „cow-pen", the name of the district round Brindában and Mathurá, the birth-place of Krishṇa. *Fourthly*, the Kanaují spoken in the lower Doáb and Rohilkhaṇḍ. It takes its name from the old city of Kanauj on the Ganges. *Fifthly*, the Baiswáṛí or dialect of the country of the Bais, a Rájpút tribe; spoken to the north of Allahábád. Its district is nearly coterminous with the province of Audh, whence it is also called Avadhí. In a slightly modified form it is also spoken to the south of Allahábád, in Baghelkhaṇḍ, the country of the Baghels, an other Rájpút tribe. *Sixthly*, the dialects of the country lying north and south of Banáras, and spoken to beyond Gorakhpúr and Bettiah in the North and to about Jabalpúr in the South, where their area is contiguous with that of the Maráṭhí. The principal one is the Bhojpúrí, which is current in the central portion of this tract on both sides of the Ganges between Banáras and Chaprá. It takes its name from the ancient town of Bhojpúr, now a small village, near Buxar, and a few miles south of the Ganges[1]). *Seventhly*, the Maithilí or the dialect of the district of Tirhút, spoken about Muzaffarpur and Darbhanga. It is called

---

1) „It was formerly a place of great importance, as the head-quarters of the large and powerful clan of Rajpoots whose head is the present Maharaja of Doomraon and who rallied round the standard of the grand old chief Kuñwar Singh in the mutiny of 1857. Readers of the entertaining »Sair-ul Mutakherin« will remember how often the Mahomedan Soubas of Azimabad (Patna) found it necessary to chastise the turbulent Zemindars of Bhojpur, and how little the latter seemed to profit by the lesson. It is remarkable that throughout the area of the Bhojpurí language a spirit of bigoted devotion to the old Hindu faith still exists, and that the proportion of Mahomedans to Hindus is very small. Rajpoots everywhere predominate, together with a caste called Bábhans (बाभन) or Bhuinhárs (भुइँहार = landleute) who appear to be a sort of bastard Brahmins, and concerning whose origin many curious legends are told." Beames J. R. A. S. vol. III, p. 484 (new series).

so after the ancient city of Mithilá, the capital of Videha or modern Tirhút (Tírabhukti). *Eightly*, the Mágadh or the dialect spoken to the south of the Ganges between Gayá, Patná and Bhágalpúr. It has its name from the old district of Magadh, now better known as Bihár.

These dialects naturally divide themselves into two great groups, according to some very marked peculiarities of pronunciation and inflexion, etc., which will be noted presently. The first group comprises the western dialects; viz. those of W. and E. Rájpútáná, of the Braj and of Kanauj. The second group includes the dialects of Banáras, Tirhút and Bihár. The central dialect of Audh and Baghelkhaṇḍ is of uncertain affiliation. In some points it agrees with the western group (e. g., in having the W. H. past part. in *á* or *ia*, see § 302); but as in most others (e. g., the E. H. future in *ab*) it exhibits the same peculiarities as the eastern dialects, it appears more appropriate to class it, for the present, with the latter. The eastern group of dialects constitutes, what I have called, the Eastern Hindí language; the western group the Western Hindí. The latter language is that which most nearly resembles what is commonly known as Hindí, namely the literary or High-Hindí. This latter is merely a modified form of the Braj dialect, which was first transmuted into the Urdú by curtailing the amplitude of its inflexional forms and admitting a few of those peculiar to Panjábí and Maṛwárí; afterwards Urdú was changed into High-Hindí. The H. H., as distinguished from the Urdú or Hindústání, is a very modern language; but Urdú itself is comparatively modern. It originated during the twelfth century[1]) in the country around Delhi, the centre of the Muhammedan power. In that spot the Braj dialect comes into contact with the Máṛwárí and Panjábí; and there among the great camps (*urdú*) of the Muhammedan soldiery in their

1) The great battle of Pánipat near Delhi was fought A. D. 1192. It put an end to the Hindú and established the Muhammedan empire of Delhi. The last Hindú ruler (*Prithiráj*) fell in the battle.

intercourse with the surrounding populations a mixed language grew up, which, as regards grammar, is, in the main, Braj, though intermixed with Panjábí and Márwáṛí forms, while as regards vocabulary, it is partly indigenous Hindí, partly foreign (Persian and Arabic). For example, the final long *á* of strong masculine nouns, where the Braj has *au* and the Máṛwáṛí *o*, is a bit of Panjábí; again the affix *ne* of the active case is a contribution from Máṛwáṛí[1]). Where the Braj has alternative forms, one only was adopted by the Urdú. Thus Braj forms the future either in *ihauṃ* or in *auṃgau* (1st pers. sg.); Urdú has retained only the latter in the form *úṃgá*, on account (no doubt) of its similarity to the Panjábí *áṃgá*. It was only in the sixteenth century, chiefly in the reign of Akbar, that Urdú was reduced to a cultivated form. With the extension of the Muhammedan power, its use spread over the whole of the Hindí area; but it remained the language of those exclusively who were more immediately connected with that power, either in the army or court or the pursuit of learning; it never became the vernacular of the people. The High-Hindí dates only from the present century. It is an outcome of the Hindú revival under the influence of English Missions and Education. Naturally enough, Urdú, the dominant and official dialect, came to hand in this movement and was *Hinduised* or turned into High-Hindí by exchanging its Persian and Arabic elements for words of native origin (more or less purely Sanskrit). Hence Urdú and High-Hindí are really the same language; they have an identical grammar and differ merely in the vocabulary, the former using as many foreign words, the latter as few as possible.

It appears, then, that there are three different forms of speech current in the Hindí area; viz. the H. Hindí or Urdú, the W. Hindí, and the E. Hindí. The first of these is nowhere the vernacular of the people, but it is the language of literature, of

---

1) The affix of the active case was originally a dative affix, which is in Mṛ. *ṇe*, in P. *ṇúṃ*, in Br. *kauṃ*, see § 371.

the towns, and of the higher classes of the population; and it takes the form of Urdú among Muhammedans and of Hindí among Hindús; though the difference between these two forms is less marked in the mouth of the people than in the books of the learned. On the other hand, both the W. H. and E. H. are vernaculars of the people generally. Their boundary line may be roughly set down at about the 80th degree of E. Longitude. In the area lying to the west of that line and containing about 150000 square miles W. H. is spoken by about 40 millions of people, in some one or other of its above mentioned dialectic forms. Among these the Braj Bháshá is the most important, as it is the best known variety. It is not only the source of the Urdú and, through it, of the modern literary Hindí, but it has itself received some measure of literary cultivation (see pg. XXXV). In this respect, indeed, the Braj occupies an unique position not only in the W. H., but amongst Hindí dialects generally. In the following pages, whenever W. H. simply is spoken of, the Braj, as being its typical form, is especially intended.

The E. H. area, lying to the east of the 80th degree, contains about 100000 square miles and a population of about 20 millions. Among the various E. H. dialects spoken by these people, that of the Banáras district or the Bhojpúrí is the most important. It is the one which is especially referred to in this work by the term Eastern Hindí, and the grammar of which forms more prominently my subject. It must be considered the typical dialect of the E. H.; for it exhibits all the peculiar features of that language in their fullest number and most marked form. This is much less the case with the other E. H. dialects. The more westerly, the Baiswáṛí, in some not unimportant points shows the distinctive marks of the W. H. (see pg. VI). On the other hand the easterly, the Maithilí especially, exhibit unmistakeable similarities to the neighbouring Bangálí and Naipálí. Indeed, I am doubtful, whether it is not more correct to class the Maithili as a Bangálí dialect rather than as an E. H. one. Thus in the formation of the past tense, Maithili agrees very closely with Bangálí, while it differs widely from the E. H., see § 503.

Taking, then, the Braj and the Bhojpúrí as the two typical dialects of the two great W. H. and E. H. groups respectively, and comparing them with each other, without entirely excluding from consideration the others; a number of very marked peculiarities present themselves. These, it will be seen, are so important, especially when considered in their relation to the non-Hindí (i. e., other Gauḍian) languages, that it appears perfectly justifiable to consider the W. H. and E. H. as being as completely distinct languages as the other North-Indian languages are universally allowed to be. The following enumeration of differences is not an exhaustive one. I shall only mention the most important. There are many others which the reader will not fail to note for himself, as he goes through the grammar. I shall arrange them under the following heads: 1) pronunciation, 2) derivation, 3) inflexion, 4) construction, 5) vocables.

Firstly; as to pronunciation: 1) E. H. has a tendency to dentalise cerebral semivowels; thus E. H. often has *r* and *rh* for W. H. *ṛ* or *ṛh*; it has also *r* and sometimes *n* for W. H. *l* (see §§ 16. 29. 30. 31). 2) While sometimes W. H. omits medial *h*, E. H. inserts an euphonic *h* [1]). 3) While E. H. never tolerates, W. H. sometimes adds euphonically an initial *y* or *v* [2]). 4) E. H. has the short vowels *ĕ*, *aĭ*, *ŏ*, *aŭ* which are unknown to W. H. (see §§ 5. 6). 5) E. H. generally prefers to retain the hiatus *aï* and *aü*, while W. H. always contracts them to *ai* and *au* [3]) (see § 68).

Secondly; as to derivation: 1) the strong form of masc. nouns of the *a-base* has in E. H. a final *á*, and of the short form of pronouns a final *e*, but in W. H. a final *au* or *o* (see §§ 47.

1) e. g., E. H., *dihal* he gave, but W. H. *diá* or *diyá*.

2) e. g., E. H., *e me* in this, *o me* in that, but W. H. *yá meṃ*, *vá meṃ*.

3) e. g., E. H., *baïṭhai* he sits, W. H. *baiṭhe*; E. H. *aür* and, W. H. *aur*.

48. 433. 437, 4)[1]). 2) The singular possessive pronoun has in E. H. a medial *o*, but in W. H. *e* or *á* (see §§ 449. 450)[2]). 3) E. H. prefers the weak form in (quiescent) *a* of masculine nouns with an *a-base*, W. H. the strong form in *au* or *o*[3]) (see § 205). 4) E. H. prefers the long form (of subst.) in *avá* or *au*, W. H. that in *ayá* or *ai* (see § 202)[4]). (5.) While W. H. uses, as a rule, only the short form of the pronouns, E. H. has generally also a long form in *na* (see §§ 436. 437,3)[5]).

Thirdly; as to inflexion; and here both as regards declension and conjugation. *As to declension:* 1) E. H. does not possess the active case of the W. H. formed with the affix *ne* (see §§ 370. 371)[6]). 2) The oblique form singular of strong masculine nouns in *á* has in E. H. a final *á*, but in W. H. *e* (see §§ 363, 5. 365, 3. 6)[7]). *Next as to conjugation:* 1) the present tense is made in E. H. by adding the auxiliary participle *lá* to the ancient (Sanskrit) present; in W. H. by adding *gá* or *hai* or *chhai* (see §§ 500. 501)[8]). 2) The past tense is formed in E. H. by means of the suffix *al* or *il*, in W. H. by the suffix *yau* or *yo* (see §§ 502. 505)[9]). 3) The future tense is made in E. H. by means of the suffix *ab* or *ib*, in W. H. by the suffixes *ih* or *as* (or, what need not concern us here, by adding the auxiliary participles *gau* or *go* to the ancient present) (see §§ 508. 509)[10]). 4) While E. H.

---

1) E. H *bhalá* good, W. H. *bhalau* or *bhalo*; E. H. *je* which, W. H. *jau* or *jo*.

2) E. H. *morí* (fem.) mine, but W. H. *merí* or *márí*.

3) e. g., E. H. *baṛ* great, W. H. *baṛau*; E. H. *mor* mine, W. H. *merau*; E. H. *det* giving, W. H. (Mw.) *deto*, E. H. *paṛhal* read, W. H. *paṛhyau*.

4) e. g., E. H. *ram'vá* or *ramau* Rám, W. H *ramayá* or *ramai*.

5) e. g., E. H. *se* or *tavan* he, W. H. only *so*.

6) e. g., E. H. *á kailĕs* he did, W. H. *vá ne kiyau*.

7) e. g., E. H. gen. *ghoṛá kai*, W. H. *ghoṛe kau* of nom. *ghoṛá* horse.

8) e. g., E. H. *holá* he becomes, W. H. *haigá* or *hvaihai* or *hvaichhai*.

9) e. g., E. H. *rahal* he remained, W. H. *rahyau*.

10) e. g., E. H. *karaboṃ* I shall do, W. H. *karihauṃ* or *karasuṃ* (or *karauṃgau*).

possesses the infinitive in *ab* or *ib* in common with W. H., it does not share with it that in *an* (see § 261)[1]).

Fourthly; as regards construction, there is one great difference, that, in the case of the past tense of transitive verbs, E. H. possesses a regular active construction with a proper active past tense, whereas W. H. uses a passive construction with the help of the active case (in *ne*) of the subject; (see §§ 371. 487).

Fifthly; as regards the vocabulary, some of the commonest and most important vocables are altogether different. Thus the (so-called) substantive verb is in E. H. 3. sing. present *báṭai* he is, past *rahal* he was, in W. H. pres. *hai* (or *chhai*), past *tho* (or *ho* or *chho*); again the prohibitive particle is in E. H. *jin*, in W. H. *mat*; again the causative post-position is in E. H. *bade* or *bare for the sake of*, in W. H. *liye*.

These differences are sufficiently radical in themselves, to establish the claim of the E. H. to be considered a distinct language from W. H. But their importance will be seen still more clearly, if we now examine them in their relation to the eastern and western Gauḍian languages; setting aside, for the present those of the north (Naipálí) and south (Maráṭhí). To the east of the combined E. H. and W. H. area are Bangálí and Oṛiya; to the west Panjábí, Gujarátí and Sindhí. On comparing these languages with W. H. and E. H., it appears that B. and O. have in common with the latter all those peculiarities in which it differs from the former; and that P., G. and S. share with the former all (or nearly all) those peculiarities in which it differs from the latter. Thus all the languages of the former class (i. e. E. H., B., O.) show a preference for *n* over *l*; and of *aï* and *aü* over *ai* and *au*; they do not tolerate an initial *y* or *v*; and possess the short *ĕ* and *ŏ*; their short pronouns have a final *e* and their possessive pronouns a medial *o*; most of their pronouns have an alternative long form in *na*, and their masculine nouns of the *a-base*, gene-

1) e. g., E. H. *karab* doing, W. H. *karabauṇ* or *karanauṇ*.

rally, the weak form in *ă*; they have no active case; their oblique form singular of strong masculine nouns in *á* ends in *á*; their past tense is made with *il* and their future tense and infinitive with *ib*; and lastly they construct actively the past tense of transitive verbs. Only in the present tense do B. and O. differ from E. H. in that they form no compound tense like it, but only use the simple ancient present tense; a form which they have in common not only with E. H., but (as will be shown further on, pg. XXXII) with all Gḍ. languages.

The case of W H. in respect to P., G. and S. is precisely similar. They all prefer *ṛ*, *l*, to *r* and *n*; and *ai* and *au* to *aï* and *aü*; in certain cases they make use of initial *y* and *v*, but have no short *ĕ* and *ŏ*; their strong masculine nouns and short pronouns end in *o* [1]); their pronouns have no long form in *na* [2]), and, as a rule, their masculine nouns have the strong form in *o* or *au*; they have an active case made with *ne* [3]), and an oblique form singular in *e* [4]) of strong masculine nouns in *o* (or P. *á*); they make their past tense with the suffix *ya* or *ia*, and an infinitive with *an*; lastly they all construct passively the past tense of transitive verbs. Besides, G. and P., like W. H., form the present tense by adding the auxiliary verb *chhai* or *hai*, and the future by the suffixes *ih* or *as*; and their singular possessive pronouns have, as in W. H., a medial *e* or *á*. In these three points S. follows a way of its own, different, however, from both the others.

Although, therefore, the agreement is not quite perfect within each of the two groups [5]), yet it is complete in the most

---

1) Exc., P. strong masc. nouns end in *á*; G. short pron. end in *e*, exc. *ṣo* who.

2) Exc. relat. pron. *kon* in W. H., P., G., but not in S.

3) Exc., S. and Mw. use no affix with the active case.

4) Exc., G. and Mw. and partially Br. and Kn. in *á*.

5) The agreement is much more complete in the E. than in the W. group. This circumstance is significant, on account of its bearing on the probable history of their respective immigration into and occupation of North-India (see pg. XXXII).

important points. These are the six following, of which the five first are morphological and the sixth syntactical; viz. 1) the form of masculine nouns of an *a-base,* whether weak or strong; 2) the termination of such strong masculine nouns, whether in *á* or *o*; 3) their oblique form singular, whether ending in *á* or *e*; 4) the suffix of the past tense, whether *al* or *ya*; 5) the suffix of the future, whether *ab* or *ih* (or *as*); 6) the construction of the past tense, whether actively or passively. Even in regard to the minor points, the divergences are mostly confined to S., which is the most outlying of the Gauḍian languages.

There are two conclusions which are obviously suggested by that agreement. In the first place; E. H. has evidently a much closer resemblance to B. and O., than to W. H.; and on the other hand, W. H. is much more nearly allied to P., G. and S., than to E. H. Whence it follows, that since B. and O. are accounted separate languages from E. H., and P., G. and S. from W. H., a fortiori E. H. and W. H. must be considered as distinct languages, and not merely as dialects of one and the same. Indeed, the only two points of any importance, in which E. H. agrees with W. H. rather than with B. and O. are; 1) the oblique form singular in *e* of strong masculine adjectives in *á* (see § 386), which adjectives the latter do not possess at all; and 2) the first preterite tense made with the past participle in *ya* or *ia* (see 502. 503), which they form a little differently[1]), but which, strictly, belongs not so much to E. H., as to the intermediate dialect, the Baiswáṛí.

The second conclusion is, that the languages whose affinities have been hitherto discussed, divide themselves into two large groups or two great forms of speech; the one extending over the eastern half of North-India and comprising E. H., B. and O.; the other covering its western half and including W. H., P., G. and S.

---

1) e. g., E. H. *paṛhyoṃ* I read, B. *paṛhiyáchhi*, O. *paṛhiachhuṃ*, but W. H. *paṛhyau*.

These two great forms of speech I designate in this treatise the *Eastern Gauḍian* and the *Western Gauḍian speeches* or groups of languages. The close resemblance of the various members of these two groups among themselves clearly points to a time, when those two forms of speech were nothing more than distinct languages, and what we now know as separate languages, were merely their different dialects.

We have now to consider, what relation the two remaining Gauḍian languages, viz. Maráṭhí and Naipálí, bear to those two great forms of speech, the E. Gḍ. and the W. Gḍ. On examining their affinities with respect to the points discussed above, it will be found, that they each occupy a distinct position, yet so that Maráṭhí is rather more nearly allied to E. Gḍ.; and Naipálí to W. Gḍ. Their position as forms of speech distinct from both E. Gḍ. and W. Gḍ., is founded chiefly on these two facts: 1) that with respect to some of the points, in which E. and W. Gḍ. differ from one another, M. and N. sometimes agree with one, sometimes with the other; and 2) that in some other points they agree with neither, but follow a line of their own.

Thus as regards Maráṭhí, it agrees with E. Gḍ. in the following points: 1) the termination *á* of the strong masculine nouns of the *a-base* (see § 48); 2) the final *á* of their oblique form singular[1]); 3) the formation of the past tense by the suffix *al* (see § 505); and 4) the formation of the future by the addition of the auxiliary participle *la* to the ancient present (see § 509). This last point requires a word of explanation. It will be remembered (see pg. X and VII) that this compound form, which serves in M. as a future, is used in E. H. as a present, and that a similar compound form, made up of the auxiliary participle *ga* and the ancient present, is used in W. H. as a present tense, and in P. (and H. H.) as a future (see § 501). Now these circum-

---

1) e. g., gen. *ghoḍyá chá* of *ghoḍá* horse; *vichvá chá* of *vichú* scorpion; *páṇyá chá* of *páṇí* water.

stances show, that the compound form in *ga* is W. Gḍ., and the other in *la* E. Gḍ.

On the other hand, M. agrees with W. Gḍ. in the following points: 1) the pronunciation generally (see §§ 11. 16. 18); 2) the *o* termination of the short pronouns (see § 437, 3. 4); 3) the absence of the pronouns of a long form in *na*; exc. the interrog. pron. *koṇ* who; 4) the strong form, generally, of masculine nouns of the *a-base* (see § 205); 5) the long form in *ayá* of the same nouns (see § 202); 6) the active case formed with *ne* (see § 371); 7) an infinitive made with the suffix *an* (see § 320); and lastly 8) the passive construction of the past tense (see § 487). It will be observed that of those six characteristics which have been noted as being the most important points of difference between the E. Gḍ. and W. Gḍ., M. agrees with the former in *four*, and with the latter only in *two*. Having regard to this circumstance, M. must be considered to rank with the E. Gḍ. rather than with the W. Gḍ. group. Moreover, of the two points in which M. agrees with W. Gḍ., one is syntactical, while all four points which it has in common with E. Gḍ., are morphological. This shows still more clearly the E. Gḍ. character of M.; for languages are classified according to their morphological characteristics [1]).

Further, the points which are peculiar to M. are the following: 1) its pronunciation of the palatals, as *ts*, *dz*, etc. (see § 11), and its disaspiration of a medial aspirate (see § 145. exc. 2., e. g., *vichú* scorpion for *vichhú*); 2) its possession of a peculiar form of the singular possessive pronoun (see §§ 450. 430, 5) [2]);

1) This is illustrated by an observation which Bs. I, 102 quotes from a native author (Shastri Vrajlal Kalidas in his History of the Gujarati Language pg. 50): „If a native from the North (speaking W. Ḥindi) comes into Gujarat, the Gujarati people find no difficulty in understanding his language; but when people from the South (speaking Maráṭhí) come to Gujarat, the Gujarati people do not in the least comprehend what they say.“ The reason simply is, that although syntacticelly G. does not differ either from M. or W. H., yet in its morphological characters it differs widely from M., while it agrees very closely with W. H.

2) e. g., M. *májhá* mine, but E. Gḍ. *mor*, W. Gḍ. *meran* or *máro*.

3) of a distinct oblique form singular of all nouns (see § 363)[1]); 4) of a peculiar present resembling closely in form that tense which, in common with all other Gḍ. languages, it uses as a preterite subjunctive (see § 501); and 5) of a peculiar conjunctive participle in *ún* (see § 491). For these reasons, as well as because, with respect to the points before referred to, M. is neither decidedly E. Gḍ. nor W. Gḍ., it must be considered to constitute a group by itself. This third group will be called in this treatise, the *Southern Gauḍian speech.*

The case of Naipálí (including Gaṛhwálí and Kumáoní) very much resembles that of Maráṭhí. It agrees with W. Gḍ. in the following points: 1) the final *o* of the strong masculine nouns of the *a-base* (see § 48); 2) the final *o* of the short pronouns (see § 437, 3. 4); 3) the medial *e* of the singular possessive pronouns (see § 450); 4) the preference of the strong form in nouns of the *a-base*; 5) the possession of an active case made the affix *le* (= *ne* of the W. Gḍ., see § 371); 6) the formation of the present by adding the auxiliary verb *chha* to the ancient tense (see § 501); 7) of the past by the suffix *yo* or *iyo* (see §§ 305. 503); and 8) of the infinitive by the suffix *an* (see § 320).

On the other hand, N. agrees with E. Gḍ. in the following points; 1) the pronunciation generally[2]); 2) the final *á* of the oblique form singular of strong masculine nouns of the *a-base* (see § 363)[3]); and 3) the formation of the future by adding the auxiliary participle *lá* to the ancient present tense (as in the M. future and the E. H. present, see pg. X, XIV and § 509); and 4) the active construction of the past tense of transitive verbs (see § 487). Here again it will be observed that of the six important points before mentioned, N. agrees with the W. Gḍ. in *three,* and with the E. Gḍ. in *three;* but while of the former all three, of the

---

1) e. g., *ghará* of *ghar* house; *kaví* of *kavi* poët; *gurú* of *guru* teacher; *ghoḍyá* of *ghoḍá* horse; *vichvá* of *vichú* scorpion; *páṇyá* of *páṇí* water.

2) e. g., often *n* for *l*; short ĕ and ŏ.

3) e. g., gen. sg. *kurá ko* of *kuro* word.

latter only two are morphological characters. It follows accordingly that N. is more closely allied to the W. Gḍ. than to the E. Gḍ. group of languages.

Further, N. stands by itself in the following points: 1) the aspiration, in certain cases, of a medial consonant[1]); 2) the softening, occasionally, of an initial hard consonant[2]); 3) the active affix *le*. These are not very important matters; but taken together with the other fact, that in the six main points N. is divided in its affinity between the W. and E. Gḍ., they show that it must be looked upon as constituting a separate group of its own, which I shall call in this treatise the *Northern Gauḍian speech*. Perhaps the circumstance which brings out most clearly that both M. and N. are really separate forms of speech as well as the W. and E. Gḍ. is this: that, as regards the past tense of transitive verbs, M. agrees morphologically (suffix *al*) with E. Gḍ., but syntactically (passive constr.) with W. Gḍ., while on the other hand N. agrees morphologically (suff. *ya* or *ia*) with W. Gḍ., but syntactically (active constr.) with E. Gḍ.

The result, then, so far arrived at is, that there are *four* great forms of speech, occupying the whole of North-India (viz. N. Gḍ., W. Gḍ., S. Gḍ., and E. Gḍ.). At a former period each constituted a single language. They have gradually broken up into varieties which in the W. Gḍ. and E. Gḍ. have already become distinct languages, while in the N. Gḍ. and S. Gḍ. they are as yet no more than dialects. Further, it has appeared that these *four* great forms of speech naturally divide themselves into *two* greater groups; one comprising the N. Gḍ. and W. Gḍ., the other the S. Gḍ. and E. Gḍ. This circumstance, then, points to a still more remote period in the glottic history of India, when there

1) Apparently only when there was originally a double consonant; e. g., N. *áphu* self, for H. *áp*, Pr. *appá*; N. *ághi* before, for H. *áge*, Pr. *agge*; N. *bálakh* child, for H. *bálak*, Pr. *valakko*; N. *mắjhad* for H. *mắjat*, Pr. *majjanto*, etc.; see S. Luke 1, 17. 24. 41. 11, 39.

2) e. g., root *gar* to do for *kar*.

were only two great varieties of speech current in North India, which divided that country diagonally between them; the one occupying the north-western, the other the south-eastern half. These two greater glottic divisions I shall designate, for reasons to be explained presently, the *Ṣauraseni Prákrit tongue* and the *Mágadhí Prákrit tongue* respectively.

The oldest Prákrit grammar, which we possess (that of Vararuchi, 1st cent. B. C.) enumerates four varieties of Prákrit; viz. the Prákrit proper, the Ṣaurasení, the Mágadhí and the Paiṣáchí. The first of these is commonly called the Mahárásh ṭrí (now Maráṭhí); the Ṣaurasení (now Braj) and Mágadhí (now Bihárí) take their names from the provinces which form the centres of the W. Gḍ. and E. Gḍ. areas respectively; the Paiṣáchí is ascribed by some later Pr. grammarians [1]) to Nepál among other places. Hence it might be thought, that those four ancient Prákrit varieties are coordinate forms of speech and correspond to the four Gauḍian speeches. This view, however plausible at first sight, is certainly erroneous. The whole subject of the relation of the Prákrits, as learned from the old native writers, to the Gauḍians, as known to us by actual experience, is involved in much confusion and obscurity, partly because of the sometimes uncertain, sometimes (seemingly) contradictory statements of those authors, partly on account of the apparent discrepancy in phonological and morphological characters between the Prákrits and the Gauḍians. The most probable account of the matter seems to be the following.

There are in reality only two varieties of Prákrit. One includes the Ṣaurasení and the (so-called) Mahárásh ṭrí. These are said to be the prose and poëtic phases of the same variety, and even this distinction is, probably, artificial. The other is the Mágadhí. The relation of Paiṣáchí to these two varieties may be roughly described as that of Low or Vulgar to High-Prákrit. The latter

1) e. g., by Lakshmídhara in his Shaḍbháshá Chandriká, see Ls. 13.

was used in literature, and never strictly a *spoken* language; it was more or less artificial from the very beginning, and became still more so in course of time. On the other hand, the Low-Prákrit (or Paiṣáchí) was the spoken language of the people; that is, probably in the beginning, of those aborigines, who fell under the domination and influence of the Aryan immigrants, and in whose mouth the Aryan vernacular was distorted into Paiṣáchí. For that name is a term of contempt; the uncouth dialect of the *savages* or *cannibals*, as the Aryans called it. It is ascribed by the native grammarians to the tribes, bordering on the Aryan area in the north (Himálaya, Nepál) and south (Paṇḍya, Dakhan) [1]). Again the most striking feature of the Paiṣáchí is its change of the Aryan *ṇ*, *l* and the sonants into *n*, *ḷ* and the surds respectively, which latter are peculiar to the Dráviḍian languages. According to Caldwell (Cp. Gr. p. 102—105) those languages had originally no sonant mutes. The Dráviḍians, therefore, when adopting Aryan speech, would naturally mispronounce its sonants as surds. All this time, of course, the Aryan immigrants had their own *vernacular*, understanding by that term the spoken language of the people as distinguished from its literary form. Gradually as the aboriginal population were amalgamated by the Aryan immigrants, the peculiarities of its Paiṣáchí speech would naturally die out[2]); and the Aryan vernacular, incorporating whatever in the Dráviḍian speech was capable of assimilation, would remain the sole occupant of the field. This Aryan vernacular is called by the Pr. grammarians the *Apabhraṃṣa* Prákrit, as being in their opinion a corrupted language in comparison with what they considered the purer, the

1) e. g., Lakshmídhara in the Shaḍbháshá Chandriká says: piṣácha-deṣás tu vṛddhair uktáḥ, páṇḍya kekaya váhlíka sahya nepála kuntaláḥ, sudesha bhota gándhára haiva kanojanás tathá. Ls. 13.

2) None of the Gauḍians show any trace of the Paiṣáchí change of sonants into surds though some have the *n* and *ḷ*; nor is any specimen of Paiṣáchí found in the Pr. plays (Ls. 388); the ancient Bṛhatkathá of Guṇádhya is supposed to have been written in a Paiṣáchí dialect (see Pischel Diss. inaug. 32. 33). Pais. clearly died out at a very early period.

literary Prákrit (i. e., the Mh.-Ṣr. and the Mg.). In reality it was merely the illiterate vernacular of the people spoken by the side of the literary Ṣaurasení and Mágadhí, and certainly more ancient than the literary Maháráshṭrí [1]). It follows, then, that the vernacular of the Aryans when spoken by themselves is the Apabhraṃṣa, and when spoken by the aborigines, the Paiṣáchí. The Apabhraṃṣa, however, of the Pr. grammarians exhibits the Aryan vernacular, as it was at a rather later period than that in which it became Paiṣáchí in the mouth of the aborigines [2]). Of the oldest Aryan vernacular (the *Ancient Apabhraṃsa*, as I may call it) which was the contemporary of Paiṣáchí and probably not greatly different from it, we have no record; unless, indeed, it be the Pálí. In order of time, therefore, Pṣ. comes first, next the Ap. Pr., lastly Gḍ,; but in order of descent the series is: Anc. Ap. (or Pálí), Ap. Pr., Gḍ. [3]).

1) Compare e. g. the past part. pass. Ṣr. and early Ap. *kadhido* or *kahido*, Mg. *kadhide* or *kahide*, Mh. *kahio*, later Ap. *kahiu* „said".

2) In the time of the later Pr. gramm., at all events, the knowledge of what Pṣ. really was, had become lost. Though, following old tradition, they all give the rules of Pṣ.; yet when they treat of its relation to the Ap., they are constantly confounding the two, and sometimes even invent an altogether new signification for Pṣ., making it equivalent to certain (more or less pure Skr.) styles of Ap. (e. g., R. T. in Ls. 23. & Exc. 6). — The chronological succession of the Pr. gramm. is still far from settled (see Pl. Diss.), but Hemachandra in the 12th century A. D., is probably the earliest grammarian, who mentions the Ap., while the first who notices the Pṣ. is Vararuchi in the 1st cent. B. C. (see Cw. VI), if not earlier. From this fact, however, it must not be concluded, that no Ap. existed in the time of Vararuchi. For the Ap. Pr. (even as known by H. C.) has some older forms than the Mh. Pr., and the latter is already treated of by Vararuchi. The reason of his omitting all mention of any Ap. was probably, that he intended to treat merely of the high or literary Pr. varieties; and, of course, there would be a literary Pṣ. Pr. variety, whenever the aborigines had to deal with High-Prákrit.

3) Paiṣ. or Pál. or Anc. Ap. *kathito*, Ap. Pr. *kadhido* or. *kahido*, W. Gḍ. *kahio* or *kahyo said*; Pṣ. *rutito*. Anc. Ap. *rudito*, Ap. *roïdo*, W. Gḍ. *roïo* or *royo wept*; Pál. *gamito*, Ap. Mg. *gamide* or Ap. Ṣr. *gamido*, E. Gḍ. *gaïl* or *gelá* or W. Gḍ. *gaïo* or *gayo*.

I have spoken of the Apabhraṃṣa or Aryan vernacular. But it must not be supposed that it was everywhere identical. The Aryan immigration gradually extended over an area, too wide to remain the home of one single form of speech. Accordingly the term Apabhraṃṣa must be understood to be the collective name of several Aryan vernaculars, spoken in various parts of North India. It is invariably used in this sense by Pr. grammarians. They always define it to mean the language of *„the Abhíras and other similar people"*[1]), i. e., briefly, of the lower orders, which constitute the mass of the population everywhere. In their enumeration of the various Ap., each of the provincial *languages* (as we now call them) occurs; e. g., Abhírí (Sindhí, Marwáṛí), Âvantí (E. Rájpútání), Gaurjarí (Gujarátí), Báhlíká (Panjábí), Ṣaurasení (W. Hindí), Mágadhí or Práchyá (E. Hindí), Odrí (Oṛíyá), Gauḍí (Bangálí), Dákshiṇátyá or Vaidarbhiká (Maráṭhí) and Saippalí (Naipálí?)[2]).

It will be noticed that in the above list the same Ṣaurasení and Mágadhí Prákrits are enumerated by the Pr. grammarians as Apabhraṃṣas or vernaculars, which they elsewhere treat of as literary or High-Prákrits. On the other hand, it will be noted that the (so-called) Mahárâshṭrí Prákrit does not occur in this list at all; nor, indeed, is it found in any list of Apabhraṃṣas or vernaculars. This shows plainly that the Mh. Pr. was not looked upon as the *vernacular* of any people, and that it did not take its name from the Mahárâshṭra (or Maráṭha) country. Indeed, it is doubtful, by what right that name is given to the particular form of Pr., which commonly bears it. In the oldest Pr. grammar of Vararuchi it is never so called, except once in-

---

1) Thus L. Dh. in the Sh. Ch.: *apabhraṃṣas tu bhâshá syád abhírádigiráṃ chayaḥ* (Ls. 12). The Abhírs, or Ahírs as they are now called, are a tribe, members of which are found in every part of North-India. They are cowherds by profession, but are considered by the natives to be a „good" (Aryan) caste, a sort of inferior Rájpúts.

2) See the lists of K. I. and R. T. in Ls. 18. & Exc. 5. 7.

cidentally at the end of the chapter on Ṣaurasení[1]). Again it is to be remarked that the great grammarians of the West and South, Hemachandra, Trivikrama and Ṣubhachandra, who must have been familiar with the living Maráṭhí vernacular, avoid the name altogether. The dialect in question is called by them simply *the* Prákrit. They, probably, felt that the name was misleading. It is only in the Pr. grammarians of the East, Kramadeṣvara, Márkaṇḍeya, Lakshmídhara, Rámatarkavágíṣa, etc., that the name Mahárásḥṭrí is distinctly given to the dialect and connected with the Mahárásḥṭra country[2]). This goes far beyond what is justified by Vararuchi's incidental use of the term. The probability is that they misunderstood his meaning. For he seems to use the term not as a *proper name*, but as a laudatory or descriptive expression, meaning „the Prákrit of the great kingdom" (i. e., of the famed country of the Doáb and Rájpútáná, see note 1 on p. XXV) and therefore the *principal* Prákrit. According to this view the term Mahárásḥṭrí is not far from synonymous with what we now call Western Hindí. At all events, whatever interpretation may be given to the term, there can be no doubt that, as a matter of fact, the dialect so called *is* Western Hindí, and has no one point in common with Maráṭhí, in which the latter differs from Western Hindí (or W. Gauḍian generally). Thus the Mh. Pr. past participle is made with *ia* (or *ya*) as in W. H., not with *al* as in M., the future is made with *iha* as in W. H., not with the auxiliary participle *la* as in M.; and the same is true, as will be shown afterwards (p. XXVII), in regard to the termination of masculine nouns with an *a-base* and to the oblique form or genitive singular. Thus in

---

1) After finishing his remarks on the Ṣr., he says: „the rest of that dialect is like the Mahárásḥṭrí" (*ṣeshaṃ mahárásḥṭrivat* Vr. 12, 20); whence it is rightly concluded that by the name Mh. he refers to that Pr. dialect, which he had before treated of simply as *the* Prákrit.

2) Thus K. I. or rather his commentator: „the Prákrit of the Mahárásḥṭra country is the principal Prákrit" (*prákṛtam mahárásḥṭradeṣíyaṃ prakṛshṭabhásháṇam*); in Ls. 17.

four out of the five important morphological points Mh. Pr. agrees with W. H., and not with M.; the remaining point (the strong form of masculine nouns of an *a-base*), being common to both W. H. and M., is of no account in the question. It appears, then, that the Mh. Pr. is merely a particular form of ancient W. H., or rather since W. H. has become a distinct language in more recent times, of W. Gḍ. And Ṣr. Pr., as its name indicates (Ṣú-rasena being nearly the same as Braj), is another form of the same. Together they represent tho old W. Gḍ. speech. This fact is indicated by the peculiar manner of their use in the Pr. plays. For they are not employed as the languages of different peoples, but of different kinds of composition, Mh. for poetry, the Ṣr. for prose[1]).

It has been already remarked that Pr. grammarians enumerate among the Apabhraṃṣas or vernaculars a Mágadhí and a Ṣauraseni Apabhraṃṣa. The two great Pr. varieties, the Mágadhí and the Ṣauraseni-Máhárásḥṭrí, are simply the high or literary forms of these two low or Apabhraṃṣa ones. They are, probably, to some extent artificial; yet there can hardly be a doubt — as the following comparison will show — that they have retained the leading peculiarities of the two vernaculars, of which they are the refinements.

The fact that these two vernaculars, the Mg. Ap. and the Ṣr. Ap., have furnished both the substratum and the name for the two great High-Pr. varieties, proves that they were the two leading vernaculars of North-India, typical of all the others. Accordingly we find that Pr. grammarians (as Márkaṇḍeya, etc.) arrange the eastern dialects in a great group around the Mg. Pr. as their type. Among those which they name as its members, the following are the most important: the Mágadhí, Arddhamá-

1) Thus Viṣvanátha Kavirája in the Sahityadarpana says: „noble and educated women, speaking in prose, are to use Ṣr., but Mh. in speaking in verse“ (see Ls. 35).

gadhí, Dákshiṇátyá, Utkalí, and Ṣábarí [1]). Mágadhí is the speech of modern Bihár and (western) Bangál, and corresponds generally to the present Bangálí (incl. of the E. H. dialects, the Mágadh and Maithilí). Arddhamágadhí is described as a mixture of Mágadhi and Ṣaurasení (or Máhárásh ṭrí) [2]); it follows that it must have been spoken to the west of Mágadhí, that is, in the Banáras district; it corresponds, therefore, to the Bhojpúrí or the E. H. *proper*. Dákshiṇátyá is the speech of Vidarbha, the modern Berár [3]) and adjoining districts. It corresponds, therefore, to the Dakhaní, one of the principal dialects of the present Maráṭhí, and thus to this language generally [4]). Utkalí is the speech of what is now called Orissa, and corresponds to the modern Oríyá. Ṣábarí is the name of the dialect spoken in the country lying between that occupied by Dákshiṇátya on the one side and Mágadhí and Utkalí on the other (about the town of Ratnapur and the Mohar mountains). It will be seen, then, that the Mg. group of the Pr. grammarians consists of what we call now the Bangálí, Eastern Hindí, Oṛíyá and Maráṭhí languages, at a time when, probably, they were still dialects only of one great speech. Or, in other words, the old Mg. group includes both (what I call) the eastern and southern Gaudian speeches. Accordingly I have given to the two combined the name of the *Mágadhí Prákrit tongue*.

In like manner, the same grammarians arrange the western dialects in a great group around the Ṣr.-Mh. Pr. as their type.

---

1) So R. T. in the Prákrit Kalpataru; see Ls. 21.

2) Mḍ. quotes a saying of Bharata, that it is like Sr. (*saurasenyá adúratvád iyam eva arddhamágadhí iti bharata;* 12th pada, fol. 49); and K. I. 12 (see Ls. 17. 393) connects it with the Mh. (*máhárásh ṭrímiṣrárddhamágadhí*). The description of E. H. as Arddhamágadhí, i. e. half mágadhí, is a very good one; for E. H. has affinities with both Bangálí (= Mágadhí) and Western Hindi (= Máhárásh ṭrí-Ṣaurasení).

3) So in the S. D.: *dákshiṇátyá vaidarbhí* (see L. 36. 20).

4) Dákshiṇátya is used to the present day in North India as a synonym for Maráṭhí; e. g., Maráṭhí Bráhmans are generally known only as Dákshiṇátya Bráhmans.

The most important members of this group are the Máháráshtrí, Ṣauraseni, Âvantí, Práchyá, and Sakkí. The Máháráshṭrí and Ṣaurasení together represent W. Hindí; but as the future in *ih* is peculiar to Mh., and the fut. in *is* to Ṣr. (see Ls. 353, 4.), and on the other hand the Br. and Kn. have the fut. in *ih*, but Mw. the fut. in *as* (or *is*), it appears that Mh. corresponds to Br. and Kn., to which may be added Eastern Panjábí, while Ṣr. corresponds to Mw., and also to G. as having the same future in *as* (or *is*)[1]). Âvantí is the speech of Ujjain and Eastern Rájpútáná. Práchyá, as its name indicates, is the most eastern member of the group and, probably, corresponds to Baiswáṛí[2]). Sakkí is, probably, the speech of Sindh and the Western Panjáb[3]). Thus it appears that the Mh.-Ṣr. group consists of what we now call Western Hindí, Gujarátí, Panjábí and Sindhí. To these, for reasons previously stated, Naipálí must be added. In other words, the Mh.-Ṣr. group represents the Western and Northern Gauḍian speeches; and accordingly I have called the two combined the *Ṣauraseni Prákrit tongue*.

1) Ṣúrasená is the name of the country about Mathura or of the Vraj; but it must be remembered that Ṣr. and Mh. are with the Pr. grammarians not exactly the names of local, but of prose and poetic dialects. Vararuchi (or Kátyáyana, the author of the Vártikas on Páṇini, see Pl. 12), in whose Pr. grammar the term Mh. first occurs, lived according to Hindú tradition about 56 B. C. at the court of the „great king" Vikramáditya (see Cw. VI), whose dominions included the whole of N. W. India. The principal „speech of that great country" or Máháráshṭrí, as Vr. calls it, was taken by him, and after him by all Pr. grammarians, as *the* standard Prákrit.

2) Práchyá is explained in the S. D. as being equivalent to Gauḍí (*práchyá gauḍiyá*, see Ls. 36) or, apparently, Bangálí. But, on the other hand, Md. makes Práchyá to be an offshoot of Ṣaurasení (*práchyásiddhiḥ ṣaurasenyáḥ* 10th páda, fol. 47); while, according to Daṇḍí (see Ls. 33), the Gauḍí follows the Mg. type. Besides, in another place, in a list of Apabhraṃṣas, both Md. and R. T. (see Ls. Exc. 7) distinguish the Práchá from the Gauḍí. If, then, the Gauḍí is of the Ṣr. type, it can hardly be anything else than the Baiswáṛí, the intermediate dialect between E. Gḍ. and W. Gḍ.

3) Sakkí is apparently the language of the Sakas (lat. sacae, Scythians) who overran W. India and were defeated in a great battle by Vikramáditya. In Sindh, many names of villages and towns contain the name Saka; e. g., the town Sakkar on the Indus.

Mg. Pr., then, coincides with S.-E. Gḍ. and Ṣr. Pr. with N.-W. Gḍ. in their geographical limits. It remains to be shown that they do so philologically also. It must be remarked *in limine*, 1) that the particulars noted by the Pr. grammarians with respect to the various Apabhraṃṣas are extremely scanty and, for the most part, only phonological. From this it may be justly concluded — what, indeed, is probable a priori — that the Aps. did not materially differ from their respective High-Pr. forms in their great morphological and phonological features; 2) that the silence of the Pr. grammarians as to any particular peculiarity, now found in modern vernaculars, does not necessarily prove its non-existence in their time; for they note only those peculiarities of Pr., which they could, satisfactorily to themselves, trace to a Skr. origin; all others they simply left unnoticed as being deṣya (see p. XXXVII); 3) that the dialect which is treated of by Pr. gramm., such as Hemachandra, simply as Apabhraṃṣa, probably occupied in the western division a position analogous to that of the other which is spoken of simply as Prákrit; i. e., one is *the* Apabhraṃṣa as the other is *the* Prákrit[1]). But, as in the case of *the* Pr., so also in the case of *the* Ap. it must, no doubt, be understood, that its rules, unless where the contrary is expressly stated, extend to all other Aps. also.

We now proceed to the examination. Of the already mentioned six important characteristics, the syntactical one (regarding the construction of the past tense) must be at once set aside. The Pr. grammarians never refer to this point at all; and from Pr. writings very little evidence is to be obtained on the subject;

1) With Mḍ. this chief Ap. is called Nágarápabhraṃṣa; he expressly connects it with the Mh.-Ṣr., *the* Pr. of the western division (*nágaraṃ tu máhárásht̤rísaurasenyoḥ pratisht̤hitaṃ*); e. g., respecting conjugation: *atra cha kareï dhareï ityadau tasya svaraṣeshatvaṃ mahárásht̤ryáṣrayeṇa karedi dharedi ity ádau datvaṃ ṣaurasenyáṣrayeṇa mantavyam* (17th páda, fol. 53. 55); its identity with W. Gḍ. is shown by the fact, that Mḍ. gives the characteristic W. Gḍ. possess. pronouns *merá, terá*, to the Nág. Ap. (*tvadíye teraṃ, madíye meraṃ* 17th páda, fol. 56).

though what little there is makes in favour of my theory (see § 371). There remain, then, the five morphological points. In regard to these, there is a striking coincidence between the evidence of Pr. gramm. and plays on the one hand, and the result of our enquiry concerning the difference of Mg. and Ṣr., on the other. Thus, *firstly*: Pr. gramm. state that nouns with an *a-base* end in *o* in Ṣr. P., but in *e* in Mg.; our enquiry shows that in W. Gḍ. and N. Gḍ. they end in *o* (or *au*), but in S. Gḍ. and E. Gḍ. in *á*, which vowel appears to be a modification of the Mg. *e* (see §§ 47. 48). *Secondly:* according to the Pr. gramm., the Western (cf. note on pg. XXVI) Ap. Pr. has a genitive singular (= oblique form, § 366) in *ahe*, the Mg. Pr. in *áha*; according to our enquiry W. and N. Gḍ. have an oblique form in *e*, the S. and E. Gḍ. in *á*; here *e* is a modification of *ahe* and *á* of *áha* (see § 365, 1. 6). *Thirdly;* from our enquiry it appears that W. and N. Gḍ. use almost exclusively the strong form (in *o*) for *a-bases*, while as to S. and E. Gḍ., it is used almost exclusively in M., much less in E. H. and very little in B. and O. (see § 205). Now the existence of special rules in Pr. gramm. about the use of the strong form (in *ao* = Skr. *akaḥ*) in the Mh. and Ap. Pr., and its common occurrence in Pr. literature (see Ls. 288. 460. 475. Wb. 69) prove its extreme frequency in the great Mh.-Ṣr. vernacular. As to the other great vernacular, the Mg., there is only the scanty evidence of Pr. literature; and from this it would appear that the strong form was very frequent in the southern Mg. vernaculars, the Ṣakarí, Ṣabarí and, by analogy, Dákshiṇátyá (cf. Ls. 431), but rare in the northern, the Arddhamágadhí (cf. Ls. 413, 7). There is, then, a sufficiently close agreement in this case also. *Fourthly;* in Gḍ. the past participle passive is used to make the past tense active. According to our enquiry, the N. and W. Gḍ. use the past participle in *ia* or *ya*, and the E. and S. Gḍ. a past participle in *al*. Now Pr. gramm. state that the past participle in *ia* is peculiar to the Mh.-Pr. (Vr. 7, 32. Ls. 363). As to the Mg. Pr. they give no general rule; but in the few cases, where the past participle is expressly noted, it ends in *ḍa* (see Vr. 11, 15), and from another rule on the nominative it would appear incidentally, that generally the past participle ended in *ida* (Vr. 11, 11. cf. Ls. 396, 4. 6. 400, 3 and H. C. 4, 260. 302). From Pr. literature it appears further, that in the Low-Mágadhís *d* and *ḍ* were apt to be changed into *l* (see Ls. 412. 423). Here again, considering the scanty evidence, the agreement is sufficiently striking[1]). *Fifthly*, our enquiry shows that N. and W. Gḍ. use a future in *ih* or *as*, but E. Gḍ. in *ab* or *ib*. The latter is simply the future participle passive used in an active sense, precisely as E. Gḍ. employs the participle past passive to form an active past tense (see § 487). The W. Gḍ. future in *ih*, however, is also used in E. H. (see § 509); and it is to be noted that both future forms are promiscuously used in it in the sense of the imperative (or precative) and the future (§§ 498. 508, note). Now according to the Pr. gramm., the future in *ih* or *iss* is peculiar to the Mh.-Ṣr. Pr. (H. C. 3, 166—170. 4, 275), and from Pr. literature it appears that the Mh. form in *ih* was used in Mg. also (see Ls. 413. 434); while the future in *ab* was confined to the lowest kinds of Mg. (Ls. 422; देव्व *you will give*). The latter future form was evidently considered very low. I know, indeed, only of that *one* instance of its admission into Pr. literature; but under the circumstances, it is sufficient to establish the agreement in question[2]).

1) It is quite possible that while the High-Mg. had the termination *ida* (or *iḍa*) the Low-Mg. vernaculars generally changed it into *ila* (or *ala*), but that the latter was considered by the Pr. Paṇḍits (supposing that the change of *d* or *ḍ* to *l* had already taken place in their time) altogether too vulgar to be frankly admitted into literature, excepting a few rare cases, such as *kale* for *kade* or *kaḍe* „done". Though it is also possible that the universal change of the termination *ida* into *ila* may have taken place after their time.

2) The compound forms of tenses (e. g., the M. future) which constitute another morpholog. character, afford us no help here. These curious formations are neither found in the Pr. gramm. nor in Pr. liter. Either they were considered too vulgar to be noticed, or more probably

As regards the morphological characters, then, my contention that E. and S. Gḍ. together correspond to the old Mg. Pr., and W. and N. Gḍ. together to the old Ṣr. Pr. appears to be fully borne out, considering the kind and amount of evidence, that is available on the subject. It now remains to examine the phonological characters which, according to the Pr. grammarians, distinguish the Mg. Pr. from the Ṣr.-Mh. Of these the following four are the most important. Mg. changes 1) *s* into *ṣ* (Vr. 11, 3. H. C. 4, 288); 2) *r* into *l* (H. C. 4, 288); 3) *j* into *y* (Vr. 11, 4. H. C. 4, 292); and 4) *ksh* into *sk* (Vr. 11, 8. H. C. 4, 296). As to the change of *s, r, j* into *ṣ, l, y* respectively see §§ 16. 18. 20. As to the change of *ksh* into *sk*, according to the Pr. gramm., *ksh* changes in Mh.-Ṣr. Pr. into *kkh* (Vr. 3, 29. H. C. 2, 4), but exceptionally also into *chchh* (Vr. 3, 30. H. C. 2, 17). Now according to the analogy of all similar changes (e. g., of *st* into *tth* or *ṭṭh* Vr. 3, 11. 12), *kkh* presupposes a form *sk*, and *chchh* a form *ṣch*. It follows of necessity that at some period of the Indoaryan vernacular *ksh* must have been pronounced sometimes as *sk*, sometimes as *ṣch*. But the link between these two forms *sk* and *ṣch* is *ṣk*; for the Mg. speaking people, according to their custom of turning *s* into *ṣ*, would pronounce *sk* as *ṣk*, and the palatal *ṣ* of the latter would gradually palatalize the conjoint *k* into *ch*, making *ṣch*; finally *ṣch* would change into *chchh*. Now in the change of *ksh* into *kkh* there are *two* steps; viz. 1) *ksh* into *sk*, 2) *sk* into *kkh*; but in the change of *ksh* into *chchh* there are *four* steps, viz. 1) *ksh* into *sk*, 2) *sk* into *ṣk*, 3) *ṣk* into *ṣch*, 4) *ṣch* into *chchh*. It is plain that if these changes proceeded, on the whole, *pari passu*, the Mg. speaking people would have got only as far as *ṣk*, when the Mh.-Ṣr. speakers had already arrived at *kkh*. Now this is almost exactly what Vararuchi states

they did not exist at all at that time, i. e. 6 or 7 centuries ago. It appears that the verb *as* „to be“ was the only verb used enclitically in Pr. times, and that the employment of the verb *achh* „to be“ and the participle *gá* „gone“ and *lá* „come“ in this manner is of later date.

to have been the case in his time; viz. Mh.-Ṣr. had *kkh*, but Mg. had *sk*. Here *sk* must be, probably, interpreted as *ṣk* by the general rule regarding the change of sibilants in Mg.[1]) (cf. Ls. 398). But the form *ṣk* was only a passing step in the phonetic evolution, the end of which has been reached long since, and now for some centuries already *ksh* is pronounced *chchh* or *chh* (see § 36). As the change of *s* into *ṣ* is general in B., partial in M., and rare in E. H. (see § 20), it is, accordingly, found that in most old tadbhava words B. and M. have *chh* for *ksh*, but E. H. has *kh* or even *h*[2]). The rule is not quite strict; nor, indeed, has it ever been so; for many instances exhibiting the Mg. change of *ksh* to *chchh* occur already in the Mh.-Ṣr. Pr. (see Vr. 3, 30).

Thus it appears from philological considerations not less than geographical ones, that, at some former period of its history, North India was divided between two great forms of speech, which I call respectively the *Ṣauraseni tongue* and the *Mágadhi tongue*. Roughly speaking, their areas occupied, one the northwestern, the other the southeastern half of North-India. Their boundary line coincided with that which now divides the areas of the N. and W. Gḍ. from those of the S. and E. Gḍ. speeches. But there is reason to believe that at a still earlier period the limits of the Mg. area extended further towards the North West. For 1) the following morphological characters of the Mg. tongue are found in different parts of the Ṣr. area; a) the termination *á* of the strong masculine nouns with an *a-base* in P. and, to a certain extent, in Br. and Kn.; b) the termination *á* of the obli-

1) Pr. literature, apparently, has no example of *sk* or *ṣk* (cf. Ls. 408-428); but it has numerous examples of *ṣṭ*, where H. C. gives *sṭ* (see Cw. 181). H. C. and T. V. have the conjunct *ḥk* with the *jihvámúliya visarga* for *s*, except in the case of *preksh* „to see", where, curiously enough, all the steps are actually given: viz. *prekshate* and *peskadi* (or *peṣkadi*) in T. V. 3, 2. 34 and *peṣchadi* or *pechchhaï* in T. V. 3, 2 32 (cf. H. C. 4, 295. 297).

2) e. g., B. *káchhe* „near", „at", E. H. *káhī̃* (Skr. *kakshe*); or B. *máchhi*, M. *máṣi*, E. H. *mákhí* (or *máchhí*) „fly" (Skr. *makshiká*); or B. *dachhin*, M. *daṣin*, E. H. *dakhin* (or *dachhin*) „south" or *dáhin* „right" (Skr. *dakshiṇaḥ*).

que form singular in G., M., E. R. and, again to some extent, in Br. and Kn.; c) the genitive affix, which is not only in E. Gḍ. (*kai, kar, er, ar*), but also in Br. and Kn. (*kau*) and probably in M. (*chá* or old M. *chiyá*) a modification of the Pr. *kario* (Skr. *kṛtaḥ*), while G., P. S., and, probably, Mw. use one of a different origin (see § 377); d) the compound future in *lá* (or *lo*) which is possessed by N. and E. R. by the side of the Ṣr. future in *ih* (see § 509, 4); e) the past participle in *al* which is found in E. R., in as much as it is contained in the enclitic *lá* of the compound future, which is a curtailment of the past participle *ailá* „come" (see § 509, 4). Again 2) there occur in the Ṣr. area the following phonological characters of the Mg.: a) the change of *l* to *n* is found in N. (in the compound future see § 509, 4) and in G. and P. (in the active affix *neṃ, núṃ*, see § 375); b) the change of *l* to *r* is found also in S. (see § 16, also § 14 on *ñ*). It is also worth noting that the Pr. writers themselves supply indications of the partially Mg. character of E. R. and G.; the latter (called Abhírí), though generally classed with the Ṣr. group, is once included by R. T. in the Mg. (see Ls. Exc. 3); and as to E. R. or Âvantí see Ls. 417. 419 [1]).

Generally speaking, it will be observed, that the Mg. characteristics, beginning with a very few and isolated traces in the far West, increase in number, as we proceed towards the East, till at last at the present frontier of the E. and S. Gḍ. areas they predominate so as to constitute the Mg. tongue. These circumstances seem to disclose the fact that sometime in the remote past the Mg. must have reached up to the extreme western frontiers and been the only language of North India; but that in course of time it gradually receded more and more towards the South and East

---

1) Still the general character of the Âvantí or E. R. is Ṣaurasení; thus Mḍ. calls it expressly „a mixture of Mh. and Ṣr." (*ávantí syán maháráshṭrísaurasenyos tu saṃkarát, anayoḥ saṃkaráḍ ávantí bháshá siddhá syát* 11th páda fol. 47[b]); and afterwards he says that Báhlíkí is allied to it (*ávantyám eva váhlíkí* ibid. fol. 48[a]); see also Ls. 435. 436.

before the advancing tide of the Ṣr. tongue, .leaving, however, here and there in the deserted territories traces of its former presence. What the eastern and southern frontiers of the Mg. may have been in those early times, when it reached to the far West of India, it is impossible to say. Very probably, as it receded before the Ṣr., it may have conquered fresh territories in the South and East which had not been before occupied by any Aryan tongue. The head-quarters of the Ṣr. tongue, whence it gradually spread toward the North-East and East, appear to have been in western Rájpútáná. It is possible, in some measure, to trace the direction and extent of its advancing tide. Thus a) traces of its past participle in *ia* are found as far east as in B. and O. (see §§ 305. 503), but not in M.; b) traces of its oblique form in *e* are found as far east as in the Bh. and M.; c) traces of its future in *ih* are found as far east as in Bh. It will be seen, that the tide is fullest in the West (especially in Sindh, the Panjáb and Western Rájpútáná), but gradually grows weaker and narrower as it advances eastward, mainly following the course of the broad valley of the Ganges, and working itself like a wedge into the Mg. area, which overlaps it on its southern and northern banks, in the E. R., G. and N., in which the Mg. relics are most noticeable.

From these indications it would appear that the Mg. tongue is the older of the two; that is, that its occupation of North India preceded the developement and extension of the Ṣr. Perhaps this may be taken to point to the fact that two great immigrations of people of the Aryan stock into India took place at different periods, both speaking essentially the same language, though in two different varieties. For there can be no doubt that the two varieties, the Mg. and the Ṣr., whatever their differences may be, are essentially the same language, of which the Sanskrit variety, being its literary or high form, preserves on the whole the oldest phase. Thus one of the most striking points of identity is the ancient Skr. present tense active, which is preserved to the present day in all Gḍ. languages of North-India alike (see § 474)[1]). Even in those cases where the outward shape or grammatical use of a particular form widely diverged, the original unity can be traced by easy and natural steps. Thus as to outward shape, the E. Gḍ. future in *ab* or *ib* can be traced back (see § 314) to the ancient participle future passive in *tavya* (or *itavya*), and the E. and S. Gḍ. past tense in *al* or *il* to the ancient past participle passive in *ta* (or *ita*), which, in an other direction, has given rise to the N. and W. Gḍ. participle in *ia*. These two instances are also examples of a change in grammatical use. For in E. Gḍ. the two participles, which had originally a passive sense and indeed have it still in S. and W. Gḍ., are used to form active tenses, viz. the participle future passive in *itavya* to form the future active in *ab* or *ib*, and the participle past passive in *ita* to make the past active in *al* or *il*. Here the intransitive verbs, the „passive" of which naturally becomes a „middle voice", afford the connecting link (see §§ 303, note. 309. 371. 487).

We have traced the Mg. tongue back to the extreme western frontiers of North India. Beyond that line lie the areas of the Pashtú and Káfirí languages. They immediately adjoin that of the present Panjábí. Trumpp in his essays on those two languages[2]) has called attention to their many affinities with the Gauḍians. Among these there are some with both of the principal varieties of Gḍ., the N.-W. Gḍ. or Ṣr. and the S.-E. Gḍ. or Mg. But what is, perhaps, more remarkable than the mere fact of their affinity is that, in some of the oft-mentioned great test-points, they — and more especially the Pashtú — exhibit decided Mg. characteristics. Thus a) the masculine strong form of *a-bases* ends in Pashtú with *ai*, corresponding to E. and S. Gḍ. *á*, Mg. Pr. *aë*; b) the past participle ends with *alai* (strong form) or *al* (weak form)

---

1) Modern M. is an exception in using this old pres. tense as a habitual past; but old M. retains it as a present tense.

2) See J. G. O. S. vol. 20 pg. 377 and vol. 21 pp. 10 ff. 23.

corresponding to (strong form) *alá* in M. and (weak form) *al* in E. H.[1]); c) the Káfirí has a compound future made with the enclitic participle *la*, just like the M. future and the E. H. present[2]); d) the auxiliary verb has in Pashtú an initial *ś*, like the initial *s* of M., which is a modification of the E. Gḍ. *chh*[3]); e) Pashtú like M. has a double set of palatals, viz. *ch* and *ts*, *j* and *dz*. Lastly f) Pashtú has the dative affix *lah*, like the M. *lá*, and the dative affix *ratah*, like the E. H. *baṭe* or *bare*.

It would appear from this, that the Mg. Pr. and the Pashtú and Káfirí were once in close connection, perhaps one language; and that, at some time in the remote past, they became separated by the Ṣr. Pr. tongue, like a wedge, cleaving them asunder and gradually pushing the Mg. farther and farther away towards the east.

Accordingly four periods may be distinguished in the linguistic history of India. First, when the Mg. tongue, in some form, was the only Aryan vernacular in North India. Secondly, when the Ṣr. tongue existed there beside the Mg. Thirdly, when these were broken up, each into two speeches, the W. and N. Gḍ. and the E. and S. Gḍ. Fourthly, when these four speeches were subdivided into the several Gḍ. languages. The last period is that now prevailing. As to the date of the first period we know nothing. The earliest Pr. grammar of Vararuchi (1st cent. B. C. or earlier) already discloses, in the second period, the two great

---

1) e. g., weak form Psh. *kṛal* = E. H. *kayal*, B. *karil* = Ap. Mg. **karide*, Skr. *kṛtaḥ*; and strong form Psh. *kaṛalai* = M. *kelá* (for *kaïlá* — *karilá*) = Ap. Mg. **karidae*, Skr. *kṛtakaḥ*. — The other, i. e. the Ṣr., form of the past part. also occurs in Psh. It ends in *a quiescent* (weak form) or in *ai* (strong form), precisely as in W. and N. Gḍ.; e. g., weak form Psh. *kaṛ* or *kṛah* „done", O. H. *kar* or *kari* = Ap. Pr. *kariŭ*, Mh. Pr. **kario*, Skr. *kṛtaḥ*; strong form Psh. *kaṛai* = Bs. *kará* or Br. *karau* or *karyau* = Ap. Pr. *kariaŭ*, Mh. Pr. **kariao*, Skr. *kṛtakaḥ*. But it should be remembered that the E. Gḍ., too, has both part., to make the first and second preterites, see §§ 503. 505.

2) e. g., Kf. 3. sg. *balále* „he will say" = M. *bolel*, E. H. *bolailá*.

3) e. g., Kf. *śi* „he is" = M. *ase*, O. *chhe* or *achhe*, B. *chhe* or *áchhe*.

divisions of the Ṣr. and Mg. in occupation of North India. The earliest Gḍ. literature exhibits the third period already existing; for in the Western Gauḍian poët Chand (end of 12th cent. A. D.) W. H., P. and G. are indistinguishable; in the Southern Gauḍian poëts Námdeva and Dnándeva (end of 13th cent. A. D.) M. is seemingly separate; in the Eastern Gauḍian poët Bidyápati (middle of 14th cent. A. D.[1]) B. and E. H. are as yet one language. The later Gḍ. writers of the 15th, 16th and 17th cent. (as the W. Hindí Kabír, the E. Hindí Tulsí Dás, the Bangálí Kabi Kankan, the Oriya Upendro Bhanj, the Maráṭhí Tukarám, the Gujarátí Narsingh Mehta; see Bs. I, 82—96) show the modern division of the Gḍ. languages already existing.

Note. I believe, it will be found on closer examination of the W. H. that its two dialects, the Mw. and Br., must, in reality, be classed as two different languages of the W. Gḍ. group, in the same sense as P. and G. For Mw. and Br. differ from each other in the same degree, as either of those two from P. and G. Thus in declension: 1) the termin. of the obl. form sg. of strong masc. nouns of the *a-base* is *á* in Mw., but *e* in Br.; here Mw. agrees with G., but Br. with P.; e. g., Mw. *ghoṛá ro*, G. *ghoḍá no* „of a horse"; Br. *ghoṛe kau*, P. *ghoṛe dá*; 2) Mw., like S., uses no active case-affix; but Br. has *neṃ*, corresponding to P. *nai*; e. g., Mw. *ghoṛai*, G. *ghoḍáe*, „by a horse"; Br. *ghoṛe neṃ*, P. *ghoṛe nai*. In conjugation: 1) Mw., like G., forms the fut. ind. with the suff. *as*, but Br. with *ih*; e. g., Mw. *karasí*, G. *karaṣe* but Br., *karihai* „he will do"; 2) the auxiliary verb has *chh* in Mw. and G., but *h* in Br. and P.; e. g., Mw. *chhai*, G. *chhe* „he is"; Br. and P. *hai*; etc.

---

1) Or, according to Beames (Ind. Antiquary Febr. 1873), middle of the 15th cent.

Table of Affinities.

Literary.	High = Vernaculars = Low.					Semi-aryan.
		Ancient Sansk.				
Class. Skr.	Páli		Anc. Ap.			Pais.
	Mh.-Ṣr., Mg.	Ap. Mg.		Ap. Ṣr.		
		E. Gḍ.	S. Gḍ.	W. Gḍ.	N. Gḍ.	
	H. B., H. H., etc.	O., B., E. H.	M.	W. H., P., G., S.	N.	Urdú.

EASTERN HINDI LITERATURE.

As regards E. H. literature, there is very little to be said. In the E. H. proper or the Bhojpúrí there is, apparently, no literature whatever, either prose or poetry. All my inquiries on this subject have been alike fruitless. I have heard people say, that there are a few poems in the more easterly dialects of the E. H., as the Maithilí. But I suspect the reference was to the well known religious songs of Bidyápatí and others of the Vaishṇava school. These, however, belong to the earlier period, in which E. H. was not yet separate from B. The only specimens of literature of the strictly E. H. period are the writings of Tulsí Dás, especially his great work, the Rámáyan, a Hindí version of the well known story of Ráma, though not by any means a translation of Válmíki's famous Sanskrit work of the same name. The language of Tulsí Dás, however, is not E. H. proper or Bhojpúrí, but the Baiswárí, which is a dialect formed by a mixture of W. and E. H. (see pp. V. VI). Tulsí Dás was a native of Hájipúr, a village near the celebrated hill of Chitrakúṭa in the state of Riwá, about 50 miles S. E. of the town of Bandá in Bandelkhaṇḍ. He lived from 1541 to 1624. Once he made a journey to Brindaban (and Delhi?); but for the most part he lived in Benares as minister of the Rájá of that town. For some more, mainly legendary particulars of his life, see Garcin de Tassy's histoire de la litterature Hindouie vol. 3, pp. 235—244, where also some other less known works of his are enumerated.

All the other celebrated Hindí poëts wrote in some dialect of W. H., generally Br. or Kn. The oldest of them is Chand Bardaí, who was a native of Lahore, but lived at the court of Prithíráj, the last Hindú ruler of Delhi, at the end of the 12th cent. He is the author of the Prithiráj Rasau, an epic poem recounting the exploits of that monarch. He belongs, however, strictly speaking, to the pre-Hindí period, when W. H. was not as yet separate from P. and G. Next to him come Kabír of Benares in the second half of the 15th cent., the author of the Ramainis and Ṣabdas. After him are Súr Dás of Mathurá, Nabhájí and Keshava Dás of Bijapúr, the authors respectively of the Súrságar, the Bhaktamálá and the Rámchandrika, etc. They flourished in the 16th cent., during the reigns of Akbar and Shah Jehan, the Augustan age of North India. Then follow Bihárí Lál of Ambir near Jaipúr, the author of the Satsai, and Lál Kavi from Bandelkhaṇḍ, the author of the Chhatra Prakaṣ, in the 17th cent. For further particulars as to the lives and works of all these poets, see the respective articles in Garcin de Tassy's hist. de la litt. Hind. They all were natives of Western Hindústán, except Kabír, whose sect (the Kabír-panthís) still numbers most of its adherents in the E. H. area. He was born in or near Benares, and died and is buried in Magahar near Gorakhpúr in the Benares district. Yet his writings are certainly not in E. H., but in W. H. The fact is strange and has not, I think, been sufficiently noticed. Though he afterwards became a Hindú and even the founder of a Hindú sect, he was brought up originally by his Muhammedan foster-father in his own religion; and apparently he spent some part of his life in or near Delhi at the time of the emperor Sikandar Lodi. Perhaps one or both of these facts may be the reason of the peculiarity.

THE TERMS TATSAMA, TADBHAVA, etc.

The term *tatsama* means lit. „the same as it" or *Sanskritic*. It denotes properly those Gauḍian words which have retained exactly the same form as they were in Sanskrit; e. g., E.H. *bhrátá* „brother", *rájá* „king". But practically it includes all words which have been reintroduced into the Gḍ. directly from the Skr., though in the process they have undergone slight phonetic changes, analogous to, but not so thorough as those which have been suffered by the tadbhava words (see §§ 40 ff.); e. g., E. H. *chhamá* „forgiveness", for Skr. *kshamá;* E. H. *ágyá* „command", for Skr. *ájñá;* E. H. *bisnu* „Vishṇu", for Skr. *vishṇuḥ;* E. H. *kripá* „mercy", for Skr. *kṛpá;* E. H. *karam* „work", for Skr. *karma;* E. H. *putar* „son", for Skr. *putraḥ*. These might be called *semitatsamas*.

The term *tadbhava* means lit. „having the same nature as it" or *Prákritic*[1]). It denotes those Gḍ. words which, though the same in substance as in Skr., are considerably different in form. Practically it includes all those words which have come into Gḍ. from the Prákrit, and not from the Skr. In the E. H. these

1) Pr. Gramm. distinguish two kinds of tadbhavas; thus S. R. (fol. 1ª) *saṃskṛtabhaváḥ cha dvidhá, sáddhyamánasaṃskṛtabhaváḥ siddhasaṃskṛtabhaváḥ cheti*; i. e. „there are two kinds of words which have the same nature as in Sanskrit; viz. those which must be shown to be so, and those which are admittedly so." It is not quite clear, however, wherein the distinction exactly consists, as no examples are given. Probably such forms are referred to, as *rái* and *ratti* „night" (H. C. 2, 88), both for Skr. *rátriḥ*. The latter (*ratti*) is a *siddha tadbhava*, for its identity with the Skr. *rátriḥ* is *evident* and follows from the *general* rules (viz. H. C. 2, 79. 1, 84); but the former (*rái*) is a *sáddhyamána tadbhava*, because its identity *must be established* by a *special* rule (viz. H. C. 2, 88). It will be seen that the distinction is analogous to what in Gḍ. I have a distinguished as semitatsamas from the proper tadbhavas (as *putar* and *pút* „son"), or to Beames' distinction of *late* and *early tadbhavas* (see Bs. I, 13—17). But our „semitatsamas" or „late tadbhavas" are not identical with the Pr. Gramm. *siddha tadbhavas;* for the former *ex hypothesi* have not come through the Pr. at all, but are directly resuscitated from the Skr. at various periods. For this reason, and because they are clearly nearer in form to the pure tats. than to the pure tadbh., I have preferred to class them as a subdivision of tats. rather than (as Bs.) of tadbh.

words are generally obtained from the A. Mg.; but sometimes from the Ṣr. Thus compare the following prákritic words with the above list of sanskritic ones: E. H. *bhái* „brother" for A. Mg. *bháïe;* E. H. *ráy* „king" for A. Mg. *láyá* or *láá;* E. H. *khet* „field" for A. Mg. *khettaṃ* (Skr. *kshetram*); E. H. *dáhin* „right" for Pr. *dáhiṇaṃ* (Cw. 100. Skr. *dákshiṇam*); E. H. *án* „order" for Mg. *aññá* (H. C. 4, 293); E. H. *kánh* „krishṇa" for A. Mg. *kaṇhe* (Skr. *krishṇaḥ*); E. H. *kisán* „husbandman" for A. Mg. *kisáṇe* (Skr. *kṛsháṇaḥ*); E. H. *kám* „work" for A. Mg. *kamme;* E. H. *pút* „son" for A. Mg. *putte;* etc. It should be remembered that the Gḍs. are not descended from the high or literary (Mh.-Ṣr. and Mg.) Pr., but from the low vernacular or Ap. (Ṣr. and Mg.) Pr. This fact explains, why some Gḍ. tadbhava words show a higher state of preservation than that observed in the corresponding words of the High-Pr.; for, in some instances, the latter had suffered a greater amount of decay than those of the Low-Pr. Generally speaking, the Low-Pr. is more tenacious of medial consonants than High-Pr. (see Ls. 396. 457). Thus E. H. *ráti* „night", Ap. (Mg.) Pr. *lattí* (cf. H. C. 4, 330), but High-Mh. Pr. *ráí* (Vr. 3, 58, but also *ratti*); E. H. *kháïl* „eaten", Ap. (Mg.) Pr. *kháïda*, but Mh. Pr. *kháïo.* Sometimes the more and the less perfect forms exist side by side; as E. H. *gaïs* (= *gaï* + *s* „thou wentest"), for Ap. (Ṣr.) Pr. *gaïu si* or *gaïdo si* or *gamido si* (Páli *gamito si*, High-Mh. Pr. *gao si* or *gado si*) and E. H. *gailés* or *gaïlés* „thou wentest", for Ap. (Mg.) Pr. *gaïda si* or *gamide si.* Hence, in some cases, it will always be doubtful whether a particular form must be considered as prákritic or sanskritic. Thus E. H. has both *nair* (or *nayar*) and *nagar* „town"; the former is clearly a tadbhava for A. Mg. *ṇayalam* or *ṇaalam*; but the latter may be either a tatsama for Skr. *nagaram* or a tadbhava for Ap. Mg. *ṇagalam.*

Native grammarians add the *deṣya*, as a third division, to the tatsama and tadbhava [1]). The term deṣya means lit. „belonging

---

1) Thus S. R. (fol. 1ª) *iha prákṛtaṣabdás tridhá, saṃskṛtasamás saṃskṛtabhavá deṣyáṣ cheti;* i. e. „there are three kinds of Prákrit words, viz. the same as Skr., of like nature as Skr., and provincial (or country born)."

to the country", i. e., *provincial* or perhaps *aboriginal*. They designate by this name all those words which they are unable to derive satisfactorily to themselves from some Skr. word and, therefore, consider to have had their origin in the country (i. e., *rure* or *provincia*). In what way exactly they suppose them to have originated is not clear; namely whether borrowed from the aborigines, or invented by the rustic Aryans themselves in post-sanskritic times (Beames I, 12), or so corrupted by their common parlance from a Skr. original as to make them unrecognisable. The last seems to me the most probable, to judge from the sentiment of modern Paṇḍits on the subject. The results of modern research tend towards diminishing the number of these deṣya words, by discovering, through means unknown to native grammarians, their real origin and tracing them back to Pr. and Skr. In so far, they make in support of the opinion of those grammarians. But the question, as to whether they are or are not Aryan, is by no means decided thereby. A word may be Prákritic or Sanskritic, and yet may not be Aryan. Whatever non-Aryan elements there may be in the Indo-aryan languages, they must have been incorporated in the earliest times; i. e., at the period, when Paiṣáchí and the Ancient Apabhraṃṣa were spoken by the subject aborgines and their Aryan conquerors respectively, and when old Sanskrit was the Aryan high language; a period which was anterior to that of what is now commonly called (classical) Sanskrit.

Natives distinguish between the *ṭheṭh* or *gáṃvárí* and the *khaṛí* or *nágarí bháshá*. Ṭheṭh means *genuine* or *pure* and gáṃvárí means *rustic* or *vulgar* (from *gáõ* = *gráma* „village"); again khaṛí means *standard* and nágarí *urban* or *cultivated* (from *nagar* „town"). The relation of these two bháshás is analogous to that of English or rather of the South-German dialects as spoken in the towns or by the educated and the same as in the mouth of the village peasantry. The difference exist mainly in the pronunciation and in the vocabulary. Thus, in the ṭheṭh bháshá the auxiliary verb is pronounced *báṛai* or *bárai*, but in the khaṛí bháshá *báṭai*. Again in the latter, tatsama and even Urdú words are much more frequently employed than in the former which is almost entirely destitute of them. The specimens of E. H. appended to this grammar, being written by a Paṇḍit, are rather in the khaṛí than in the ṭheṭh bháshá.

FIRST SECTION. ON LETTERS AND SOUNDS.

1. CHAPTER. THE ALPHABET.

1. The E. H. is commonly written in the *Kaithí* (कैथी or कइथी) alphabet. Its name is derived from Káyath (Skr. कायस्थ), the designation of the writer-caste among the Hindús. Though it has a general resemblance to the modern Devanágarí, there are but few of its letters, which do not exhibit some points of difference; indeed, as will be seen by a reference to the table, all the vowels, and the consonants *kh, ch, jh, bh, d, dh* and *r* differ entirely in the two alphabets; and the horizontal top-line is omitted by the Kaithí in all letters alike[1]). It will be further noticed, that in Kaithí the consonants *k* and *ph*, *p* and *dh*, *r* and *l* very closely resemble each other, being distinguished in each case merely by the addition of a hook or curve to the latter; again, that there is only one sign for each of the following groups of Nágarí letters: 1) 𑂢 (properly = *n*) for the nasals ङ *ṅ*, ञ *ñ*, ण *ṇ*, न *n*; 2) 𑂮 (a combination of *s* and *ṣ*) for the sibilants स *s*, ष *ṣ*, श *sh*; 3) 𑂥 for the labials ब *b* and व *v*; 4) ज (properly = *j*) for the palatals ज *j* and य *y*; and also that of the two forms of *ch* one is very much like to one of the two forms of *dh*, the other to one of the two forms of *y*. For the vowels Kaithí has only four fundamental signs: 𑂃 *ă*, 𑂅 *ĭ*, 𑂇 *ŭ*, 𑂉 *e*. The others

1) Sometimes a series of lines is first ruled across the page, and the letters are afterwards hung on to them. These lines must not be confounded with the top-line of the Devanágarí, and in native writing the two are easy to distinguish.

are distinguished by diacritical marks, as shown in the table. In Manuscripts the initial *í* and *ú* are rarely distinguished from *ĭ* and *ŭ* or the medial *ú* from *ŭ*. It will be seen that altogether the Kaithí alphabet has only *twenty nine* distinct signs. It is used in printing as well as in writing; but owing to the preponderance of H. H., which has adopted the Devanágarí, the latter is much more common in books. I shall adopt it in this work also, as the more generally known of the two.

2. *Affinities.* Four principal types of alphabet are used in North-India; the Kaithí, the Bangálí, the Oṛíyá and the Gurmukhí. The Kaithí is the most widely spread; it is used in writing not only in Eastern, but also, slightly modified, in Western Hindústán, Maráṭhá and Gujarát. In G. and sometimes in E. H. it is adopted also in print. The Bangálí, Oṛíyá and Gurmukhí are used in Bangál, Orissá and the Panjáb respectively, in writing and printing. The Gurmukhí probably takes its name from being originally used in committing to writing the oral traditions of the Sikh Gurus (Nának, etc.). The general likeness of these four types to one another as well as to the older Kutila and Gupta is unmistakeable, though their exact relation among themselves, their origin and age are matters not as yet fully elucidated. For some account of them see Bs. I, 54 ff. Besides these, there are two sub-types much in use in the area occupied by the Kaithí, to which they are the most nearly related. These are the Nágarí or Devanágarí and the Mahájaní or Koṭhíwál. The first is an improvement, the second a corruption of the Kaithí or of its more ancient original. The exact meaning of the term Devanágarí (divine city alphabet) is uncertain; but it suggests its being, as it certainly is, a caligraphic (polished or sacred) writing. The Mahájaní (mercantile) is, as its name implies, the shorthand writing of the merchants and bankers, their *Koṭhíwál* or *office-writing*; and is still commonly used by them. The Devanágarí, on the other hand, is the type adopted for printing in Hindí and Maráṭhí; and as it is exclusively taught in the schools, it

will probably in course of time entirely supersede the Kaithí; perhaps not altogether an advantage, as it can be written with less rapidity and ease than its rival.

1. VOWELS.

3. The E. H. possesses fifteen vowels; a *neutral* and fourteen distinct ones. The latter consist of seven pairs, each containing a short and a long one. They are ·; *ă*, *á*; *ĭ*, *í*; *ŭ*, *ú*; *ĕ*, *é*; *ŏ*, *ó*; *aĭ*, *aí*; *aŭ*, *aú*. Five of these, the neutral vowel and the short *ĕ*, *ŏ*, *aĭ*, *aŭ* are, according to the usual view, unknown to the Sanskrit phonetic system, and therefore have no place in the native grammatical scheme of sounds and characters. But in order to avoid the inconvenience of two different sounds being denoted by the same sign, I have ventured to introduce into the E. H. alphabet, used in this treatise, five new characters. For the short *ĕ*, *ŏ*, *aĭ*, *aŭ* I shall adopt the Gurmukhí or Bangálí forms of the ordinary Nágarí signs, which differ from the latter merely in having a serpentine form (ॆ and ै) instead of a slightly curved one (े and ै). For the neutral vowel I shall adopt a dot (·) placed after the consonant in the same manner as a stroke (ा) is placed after it to denote the long *á*; in transliterating I shall use the *apostrophe*. Accordingly the signs of the fifteen E. H. vowels are as follows:

Initial: — अ *ă* आ *á* इ *ĭ* ई *í* उ *ŭ* ऊ *ú* ऎ *ĕ* ए *é* ऒ *ŏ* ओ *ó* ऐ *aĭ* ऐ *aí* औ *aŭ* औ *aú*
Noninit.: · — ा ि ी ु ू ॆ े ॊ ो ै ै ौ ौ

Note: The neutral vowel requires no initial form, as it never occurs in the beginning. The short *ă* has no non-initial form, as it is inherent in the consonant, which could not be pronounced without it. When it is necessary to indicate the mere consonant, an oblique stroke, called the *viráma* or *stoppage*, is appended to the consonantal sign; thus क *kă*, but क् *k*. The manner of writing the non-initial signs may be seen from the following examples; क· *k'*, क *kă*, का *ká*, कि *kĭ*, की *kí*, कु *kŭ*, कू *kú*, कॆ *kĕ*, के *ké*, कॊ *kŏ*, को *kó*, कै *kaĭ*, कै *kaí*, कौ *kaŭ*, कौ *kaú*.

4. The neutral vowel is the shortest possible vocal utterance, and very obscure in its character. It may be compared to the English *u* in *but*; but it is shorter and more indistinct; like the vowel in the final syllables *ble* or *tre*, as in *amiable, centre*. It resembles the Hebrew *Sh'va mobile*; just as *ĕ* is like the Hebrew *Khateph Segol*, and *ŏ* like the Hebrew *Khateph Qamez*.

5. The five special E. H. vowels are principally met with in the following places:

a) the neutral vowel is pronounced: 1) often in rustic speech, at the end of a word, instead of the *quiescent ă* (see § 24), as घर॒ *ghar' house*, for घर् *ghar*; and 2) in the penultimate of any word having more than two syllables and ending in a heavy one; as घर॒वा *ghar'vá house*; घोड़॒वा *ghŏṛ'vá horse*; कर॒तों *kar'tõ if I did*; पढ़॒लों *paṛh'lõ I read*, etc. A compound consisting of two polysyllabic words is treated as if the words were distinct.

b) the short *ĕ, ŏ, aĭ, aŭ* occur 1) always in the antepenultimate; e. g., बेटिया *bĕṭiyá daughter*; परोसिया *parŏsiyá neighbouring*; लोट॒वा *lŏṭ'vá vessel*; बोलावत् *bŏlávat calling*; 2) optionally in the genitive affixes के *kĕ* and कै *kaĭ* as घर् के *ghar kĕ of the house* (see § 372); 3) in the short pronominal forms in ह् (see § 433), as जेह् कर् *jĕh kar of which* (but जे कर् *jé kar*); 4) in the conjugational suffixes एस् *ĕs*, एन् *ĕn* and ऐं *aĭ̃* (see §§ 504. 506); as कर॒तेस् *kar'tĕs* (if) *thou didst*; पढ़॒लेस् *paṛh'lĕs he read*; रह॒लेस् *rah'lĕs thou remainedst*; कर॒तेन् *kar'tĕn* (if) *they did*; पढ़॒लेन् *paṛh'lĕn they read*; कर॒तैं *kar'taĭ̃* (if) *they did*; पढ़॒लैं *paṛh'laĭ̃ they read*; 5) in the suffix ए *ĕ* of the conjunctive participle (§ 490), as कहे के *kahĕ kĕ having said*; 6) in some frequently used words, as औरु *aŭr* or औ *aŭ and* (see § 26).

6. *Affinities.* The short vowels (they are not diphthongs) *ĕ* and *ŏ* must have existed in Pr. already; thus before conjuncts, as in पोट्टा (or पिट्टा for निद्रा Vr. 1, 12), पोट्टं (for नीडं Vr. 1, 19), सेच्चं (for शैत्यं Vr. 1, 35), सेज्जा (for शय्या Vr. 1, 5), सेव्वा, ऐक्कं (for सेवा, एकं Vr. 3, 58), etc.; and मोत्ता (for मुक्ता Vr. 1, 20), जोव्वणं (for यौवनं Vr. 1, 41), तेल्लोक्कं (for त्रैलोक्यं Vr. 3, 58), etc.

See Ls. 145. 149. Cw. XVIII. Their existence, however, is, I believe, nowhere distinctly noticed by Pr. Gramm., except in the Ap. Pr. by H. C. (4, 410) and T. V. (3, 4. 68), कादिस्थैदोतोरु उच्चारलाघवम्। i. e., after consonants ĕ and ŏ are usually pronounced short. — Both the short vowels ĕ, ŏ, aĭ, aŭ and the neutral vowel are peculiar to E. Gḍ. The subject, however, has been as yet little attended to by Gḍ. Grammarians. As regards the short vowels, B. shows the short ĕ, e. g., in एक् ĕk *one*, and short ŏ in गोम् *gŏm wheat*, बोले *bŏle he speaks*, etc. Oṛiyá, generally, follows the example of B. (see Bs. I, 69). It is usual, apparently, to substitute ă for ŏ in *writing*; thus B. गम्, बले; the same as occasionally in E. H. (see § 26). It is probable, that originally all Gḍ. languages possessed ĕ and ŏ; S. has still preserved the ĕ in some cases, but ordinarily it reduces ĕ to ĭ, and always ŏ to ŭ (see Tr. X—XIII). The other W. Gḍ. languages always substitute ĭ and ŭ for ĕ and ŏ (as to ĕ and ŏ in P. see Ld. 4); even the E. Gḍs. do so occasionally, see § 26 (cf. S. Ch. 330). The Psh. has both ĕ and ŏ (see Tr. J. G. O. S. XXI, 33—35). — In B. the final of the weak adjectives, is pronounced like ŏ, e. g., बड *bŏrŏ great*; but it must not be confounded with the real ŏ which is a shortening of ओ ó, while this ŏ is a modification of अ ă; as shown by O., which pronounces ă; e. g., बड *bără*. E. H. agrees with the W. and S. Gḍs. in dropping the vowel ă at the end of all words; see § 24. On the other hand, both the Psh. and Kf. still retain it (see Tr. J. G. O. S. XXI, 33. XX, 393). — In tatsamas with a conjunct य् or व् before the final अ, the latter is commonly pronounced, as योग्य *yogya worthy*, तत्व *tatva substance*.

Note: The elision of a medial neutral vowel produces a conjunct consonant. Consequently in H. H. and in M. a conj. cons. is sometimes written, as H. H. बिन्ती *binti* for बिनऽती *bin'tí petition*, H. H. दुल्हा *dulhá* for दुलऽहा *dul'há bridegroom*, M. राम्या *rámyá* for रामऽया *rám'yá Rám*, or घोड्या *ghoḍyá* for घोडऽया *ghoḍ'yá of a horse* (obl. form). It would be well, if this system of phonetic spelling were carried out uniformly.

7. The E. H. does not possess the four vowels ऋ *ṛi*, ॠ *ṛí*, ऌ *lṛi*, ॡ *lṛí* of the Skr. phonetic system. Even in Skr. they occur rarely and are more or less artificial. In Pr. they had already disappeared; consequently they could not well survive in the modern Gḍ. In Hindí certainly, whether E. or W., they are never *pronounced*. In H. H. it is customary to *write* ऋ *ṛi* in tats. words; but in *speaking* the syllable रि *ri* or even इर् *ir* is always substituted; thus Skr. अमृत् *ambrosia* is always pronounced *amrit* (अम्रित्) or *amirt* (अमिर्त्); Skr. कृपा *favor kripá* (क्रिपा) or *kirpá* (किर्पा). Perhaps it would be well to follow the example of the old Prákrit Grammarians and apply their system of phonetic spelling to our modern H. H. also. In any case it is incorrect to enumerate these four vowels or any of them as parts of the Hindí phonetic system.

8. *Nasalization.* In E. H. a vowel is pronounced in many words with a nasal tone, precisely as *n* or *m* in such French words, as *compensation*. This tone is indicated by the symbol (ँ), called the *arddhachandra* (*halfmoon*); the tone itself is called *anunásika* (*co-nasal*); see § 23. I shall transliterate it by a *circumflex*. It generally occurs with a long vowel, rarely with a short one or with the semivowels य् and व्; e. g., रहन्तों *rah'tô*, लेइँ *leî*, कोइँ *koî*, हौंठ् *hôṭh*, नींद् *nîd*, or चललँ *chalalã*, कुअँर् *kuãr*, कुआँरि *kuãri*, जाँय् *jãỹ*, जाँव् *jãṽ*.

9. *Derivation and affinities.* The anunásika generally (except occasionally before ह् and स्, see § 67) indicates the elision of a consonant, i. e., of a nasal, when it occurs between two vowels (§§ 127. 128), and of the first part of a conjunct when it stands before a consonant (§ 149). The first case alone occurs in later Pr.; neither of them in earlier Pr. or in Skr.; both are common in all Gḍs.; see § 23.

2. CONSONANTS.

10. The E. H. possesses *thirty five* consonants. They consist of twenty consonants proper or *mutes*, five *nasals*, nine *semi-*

vowels and one *sibilant.* They may be further classified according to the organ of utterance into gutturals, palatals, cerebrals (or *múrdhanya*), dentals, labials, and according to the degree of audibility into *surd* or hard and *sonant* or soft ones; as exhibited in the following table.

	Consonants proper				Nasals	Semivowels		Sibilants
	surd or hard		sonant or soft		sonant	sonant or soft		surd
	unasp.	aspir.	unasp.	aspir.	unasp.	unaspirate	aspirate	unasp.
guttural	क् *k*	ख् *kh*	ग् *g*	घ् *gh*	ङ् *ṅ*	—	ह् *h*	—
palatal	च् *ch*	छ् *chh*	ज् *j*	झ् *jh*	ञ् *ñ*	य् *y*	—	—
cerebral	ट् *ṭ*	ठ् *ṭh*	ड् *ḍ*	ढ् *ḍh*	ण् *ṇ*	ड़् *ṛ*	ढ़ *ṛh*	—
dental	त् *t*	थ् *th*	द् *d*	ध् *dh*	न् *n*	र् *r* or ल् *l*	र्ह् *rh* or ल्ह् *lh*	स् *s*
labial	प् *p*	फ् *ph*	ब् *b*	भ् *bh*	म् *m*	व् *v*	—	—

11. The E. H. palatals are pronounced like the English. Natives, generally good judges in such matters, do not seem, as far as I could learn from them, to have observed any difference between them. I believe the same is the case in B. and O. On the other hand, it has been often observed, that the W. H. palatals are rather more dental than the English; i. e., rather more like *ts, dz*[1]). This is probably true of all W. Gḍ. palatals; excepting, perhaps, Sindhí[2]). In M. they are distinctly semidental, and are pronounced as *ts*, *ts* + *h*, *dz*, *dz* + *h*[3]). It appears, therefore, that the E. Gḍ. palatals are more distinctly and truly palatal than the W. and S. Gḍ. This seems to have been noticed already by the Pr. Grammarians. It is noticeable that both the true palatals and the semidentals occur in Psh. and Kf.[4]). In M.,

1) Thus, e. g., Kl. 11.

2) See Tr. 14. His meaning is not quite clear; he seems to identify them at the same time with the „common Indian" (that is, apparently, the W. Gḍ.) and with the English palatals.

3) The true palatals occur also; but apparently only in tatsamas and before palatal vowels; cf. Bs. I, 72.

4) See Tr. J. G. O. S. XX, 393. XXI, 20. 23.

छ् is almost universally pronounced and written स् or (generally before palatal vowels) श्; e. g., M. रीस् *bear*, E. H. रीछ्; M. सूरी *knife*, E. H. छूरी; M. माशो *fly*, E. H. माछो (see Bs. I, 218). In Mw., both च् and छ् are pronounced (but not usually written) स्; e. g., Mw. सक्को *wheel* for E. H. चक्को; Mw. साग् *buttermilk* for E. H. छाछ् (see Kl. 14, 25). Also G., S., P. and B. pronounce (and write) occasionally छ् as श्; e. g., G. शो *who* for S. छा (see § 438, 6); B. काशे or काछे *near* (Bs. I, 218); S. सो for Mth. छो *we are*, P. सन् for N. छन् *they are*.

Note: Both the true reading and the true meaning of the Pr. Gramm. rule, however, are doubtful. Vr. 11, 5 (MS., see Cw. 89) has चवर्गस्य स्पष्टता तथोच्चारणः, which is explained by Bhámaha चवर्गो यथा स्पष्टस् तथोच्चारणो भवति i. e. „the palatals are so pronounced as to be *distinct*". My MS. of Mḍ. (12th páda, fol. 48[b]) reads चययोरुपत्तय: स्यात्। यकारागम:। य्चिरं। य्मात्र॥ If the examples can be trusted, the true reading would seem to be चपयोर् उपरि य: स्यात् i. e. „*ya* is to be written above (i. e., as first part of a conjunct) the palatals and labials; this *ya* is an (inorganic) addition; e. g., *ychiraṃ* long, *ymáa* (?)" [1]). My MS. is a Nágarí copy of one in Oṛiyá characters, in which य् and प् and again त्र् and रि would closely resemble each other. K. I. 3 (in Ls. 393) reads यपचवर्गयुक्ता मनागुच्चार्या:, which would yield a sense similar to that of Mḍ[s]. rule: „the labials and palatals in conjunction with *ya* are slightly pronounced"; or, perhaps, rather: „*ya* in conj. with l. and p. is slightly pron." This is confirmed by the example given in the rule on the Vocative (Mḍ. 12, 22, fol. 49[a]); see § 48, note.

12. The cerebrals are pronounced by striking the tip of the tongue against the centre of the hard palate, the dentals by striking it against the edge of the upper teeth. It has been a matter of much controversy, whether or not the former are originally Aryan sounds. They constitute a prominent feature of the Drávidian languages, whilst among the Aryans they are peculiar

---

1) *ymáá* mother (*mátá*) or illusion *máyá*?

to India. Hence it has been commonly assumed that they are an importation from the former. This, however, is by no means certain. I am inclined to agree with the opinion of Beames (I, 232—234), that cerebrals of some kind belong to the original stock of the Aryan phonetic system. It is a well known fact that the (so-called) dentals of all the Aryan languages of Europe, especially of England, when referred to the standard of the Indo-aryan (true) dentals are not real dentals at all, but cerebrals of more or less purity. They are formed by striking the tip of the tongue against the anterior part of the hard palate or the gum of the upper teeth; and therefore are semi-cerebrals. To natives of India, whose ears are quick in detecting differences of pronunciation, they sound like real cerebrals and in transliterating English words, they always represent our dentals by cerebrals, as डैरक्टर् *director*, सार्टिफिकेट् *certificate* (cf. § 21). The pure dentals, therefore, are as peculiar to the Indoaryan languages as the pure cerebrals and might with equal reason be adjugded non-aryan. It is far more probable that the original Aryan sound was a semicerebral (if not a pure cerebral) which has in India only, for reasons peculiar to that country, varied in two directions so as to become the true cerebral and the true dental respectively. It is deserving of notice as making for this view, that the old Indoaryan (Sanskrit) cerebral र् and ण् have also been dentalised in various parts of India. The truth seems to be, that the whole class of original Aryan cerebrals has been undergoing in India a process of gradual decerebralisation. The first to be affected were the consonants proper and ल् which had already in Skr. times become to a great extent dentals [1]. The next was the semivowel र् which was dentalised in the times of Mg. Pr. Finally the nasal ण् became dental in the comparatively modern times of Gḍ. As the dentals

---

1) The old (Vedic) Skr. still preserves the old Aryan cerebral ड़. Cp. vedic मृड *gracious* with Skr. मृदु *gentle*; also R. मृड् or मृड़् with मृद्; नट् with नृत्; नड् with नर्द्, etc.

are softer and smoother sounds than the cerebrals, it may be supposed that the enervating climate of the great North Indian plain was, at least, one of the causes determining that process. On the other hand, it is quite natural also, that in those forms of the Indoaryan languages which were current among the common people, i. e., the Prákrits and Gauḍians, the original Aryan cerebrals should to a great extent have not only stood their ground, but even been more intensely cerebralized. For most of those people belonged to or, at all events, were most in contact with the aboriginal Dráviḍian population whose language, like their own, possessed the cerebrals. It is noticeable, that just as in Skr. times the old Aryan semicerebral consonants were often made fully cerebral, so in Pr. times in many cases the old (semidental) न्[1]) is cerebralized to ण्, and in Gḍ. times by the side of the old semicerebral र् a fully cerebral ड़् has been formed. — It may be added as some evidence against the Dráviḍian theory of the cerebrals, that though the Gḍ. languages have now been for centuries under the influence of Arabic and Persian, yet none of the sounds peculiar to the latter have been imported into them (see § 21).

13. The nasal ङ् ṅ, I believe, never occurs in E. H., except in conjunction with a following consonant of its own class, as अङ्गिया *aṅgiyá bodice.* The others may occur by themselves. The ञ् ñ and ण् ṇ, both initial and medial, are occasionally heard in the more vulgar (*ṭheṭh*) forms of E. H.; thus ञाही॑ *ñáhí̃ no,* अगिञा *agiñá fire,* णारसिंघ् *ṇarsiṅgh manlion,* णाराँण *ṇáraiṇ Náráyan,* पाणी *páṇí water.* But in the higher forms of E. H. they are always changed to न् n, as नाही॑ *náhí̃,* नरसिंघ् *narsiṅgh*, etc.; even in tatsama words with an original ण् ṇ, as कारन् *káran cause* for Skr. कारण *karaṇa.* Hence the Kaithí alphabet has no special signs for ञ् ñ and ण् ṇ; and following its practise, I also shall limit myself in this work to the use of न् n. When any of the five

1) The Europeo-aryan *r* and *n* are semicerebral or semidental.

nasals are used as the first part of a conjunct, they are always indicated by a dot placed over the preceding consonant; as पंक् *paṅk mire*, अंत् *ant end*. This dot is commonly called *anusvára*, but it must not be confounded with the real Skr. anusvára which does not exist in E. H. (see § 23).

14. *Affinities.* The two nasals ङ् and ञ् (as non-conjuncts) had already been lost in the Mh.-Sr. Pr. (T. V. 1, 1. 1. H. C. 1, 1). The latter (ञ), however, is expressly mentioned by Pr. Grammarians (Vr. 10, 9. 10. T. V. 3, 2. 37. 3, 4. 61. H. C. 4, 293, 294. 392), as occurring in Mg. Pr. (and also in Ap. and Ps. Pr.), where the Skr. conjuncts न्य् *ny* and ण्य् *ṇy* change to ञ्ञ् *ññ*. Agreeably with this, ञ् occurs in E. Gḍ. (especially in the respective *ṭheṭh bháshás*) before or after the palatal vowel (इ) or semivowel (य); thus E. H. अगिञा *fire* for अगिनिया, Mg. Pr. अगिणिए (see Ls. 244 अगिणी), Skr. अग्निकः; ञाहीँ *not* for न्याहीँ = ने + आहीँ (ने for न or ना, as in B., see S. Ch. 331); B. आगिञा *order* (see S. Ch. 10) for (O. H.) आगिना (Skr. आज्ञा). So also in N. थाञि *at, by* S. Lk. 10, 29. 40 (H. थेँ) for Ap. Pr. थाणि or थाणे, Skr. स्थाने; लिञा *taken* (S. Lk. 19, 8) for W. H. लीना (= लिन्ना)[1]). S. which generally follows E. Gḍ. phonological practices (cf. §§ 16. 18) keeps even more closely to the Mg. precedents; thus S. पुञ *virtue*, Mg. Pr. पुञ्ञं, Skr. पुण्यं; S. थञ *woman's milk*, Mg. Pr. थञ्ञं, Skr. स्तन्यं; S. व्रञे *goes*, Mg. Pr. वञ्ञइ (H. 4, 294), Skr. व्रज्यते (§ 18); S. मञे *heeds*, Mg. Pr. मञ्ञइ, Skr. मन्यते, etc. In these instances the E. H. follows the old Ardhamágadhí which has न्न् *nn*[2]) (see Wb. Bh. 402. 403); thus E. H. पुन् *virtue*, A. Mg. Pr. पुन्नं; E. H. बनै *is made*, A. Mg. Pr. वन्नइ; E. H. मानै *heeds*, A. Mg. Pr. मन्नइ. It is noticeable, that S. has also preserved the guttural nasal ङ् (Tr. XVI. XVIII), as अङ्

1) Apparently it inserts even an inorganic ञ् after इ; as डराञा *feared* for डराइआ (डराया); थिञा *was* for थिआ; रुपिञा *money* for रुपिआ; see S. Lk. 19, 21. 23. 24. Such forms as रुपिञा *money*, अगिञा *order*, however, I have heard also in *ṭheṭh Panjábí*.

2) The Mh.-Sr. Pr. has ण्ण् *ṇṇ* for ण्य् *ṇy* (cf. H. C. 1, 66. 2, 159); but न्न् *nn* for न्य् *ny* (cf. H. C. 2, 25. 44. 1, 243. 3, 58—61, etc.).

aṅu body, मङणु *maṅaṇu ask* (E. H. मांगना); and apparently O. too (see Sn. 18), as केङु *keṅu who*, जेङु *jeṅu which*. This would seem to indicate, that perhaps ङ् also was not quite extinct in Mg. Pr., though I believe that it is not mentioned as present by any Pr. Gramm. I do not know of any instance of its occurrence in E. H. and B. As regards ण् and न्, every ण् changes to न् in Ps. Pr. (Vr. 10, 5. H. C. 4, 306); vice versa, every *medial* न् and optionally every *initial* न् become ण् in all other Prs. (H. C. 1, 228. 229. T. V. 1, 3. 52. 53). Agreeably to this, ण् is found as a medial in all Gḍ. languages, and as an initial occasionally in ṭheṭh Hindí. It is, however, now confined more or less to the ṭheṭh or low forms of the Gḍs. In Urdu, H. H., H. P. and H. B., especially, ण् (even when originally existing in Skr.) has uniformly given way to न्[1]). Thus E. H., etc. पाणी, M. पाणीँ *water*, Pr. पाणिअं (Vr. 1, 18), Skr. पानीयम्, but H. H., etc. पानी; E. H. णारैण् or नारैन *Náráyaṇ*, Mg. Pr. णारायणे or नारायणे, Skr. नारायणः, H. H. नारैन् or नारायन्. As regards म्, it is uniformly preserved in the earlier Pr.; in later Pr. it is in a few cases elided, nasalizing the following vowel, as जउँणा *Jamna* for Skr. यमुना (H. C. 1, 178. T. V. 1, 3. 11). In the Gḍs. this practice is rather common, see §§ 23. 127.

15. E. H. possesses four new consonants, which do not exist in the Skr. phonetic system; the semivowels ऱ् *r*, ऱ्ह् *rh*, ल्ह् *lh* and ड़्ह् *ṛh*. The ऱ् *r* is a pure dental like ल्, which explains their facile interchange (§ 80. 110); ऱ्ह् and ल्ह् are their respective aspirates, pronounced as *r* + *h* and *l* + *h*, as बर्है *barhai grows*, कोल्हू *kolhú*

1) Ps. Pr. possesses only न्; the other Prs., as a rule, only ण्. The high Gḍs., then, follow the Ps. It is a curious coincidence, that the area of the modern Ps. practice is nearly coterminous with the area of direct Mohammedan, i. e., foreign influence; see Introd. — Vr. 2, 42 does not yet admit any option in the change of the initial न्; it is allowed only by the later Gramm. H. C. and T. V., who moreover do not admit the change of न् to ण् at all, if it is the resultant of a Skr. conjunct, as Pr. नाओ (not णाओ) for Skr. न्यायः This circumstance — unless Vr's silence as to the option be merely an oversight — would seem to indicate the commencement of the modern Ps. practice.

sugarmill. The ढ़्, pronounced ṛ + h, as बुढ़िया *buṛhiyá old woman,* is the aspirate of ड़ which is a pure cerebral, and, therefore, is equivalent to the Skr. र् r. For the latter is said by Skr. Grammarians to be a cerebral, not a dental[1]). In fact, it is not, as commonly supposed, the cerebral ड़ ṛ which is the new letter, but the dental र् r. The old Skr. र has assumed a new sound, while its old one is represented by ड़. To avoid the inconvenience of diacritical marks, I shall adopt the Gurmukhí form ड़ for ड़ and ढ़ for ढ़, and the Gurmukhí cerebral र for the Skr. cerebral र्. The aspirates र्ह् rh and ल्ह् lh are single sounds in the same sense as ढ़् ṛh; all three are in certain cases interchangeable with ढ् ḍh, precisely as र्, ल् and ड़ with ड् ḍ.

16. *Affinities.* Vedic Skr. has a cerebral ळ् ḷ and ळ्ह् ḷh, which in certain schools take the place of an original medial ड् ḍ and ढ् ḍh (see M. M. 4). These complete the series of the semivowels. In genealogical order they follow thus: from ड् and ढ् arise (cerebral) ळ् and ळ्ह्, then Skr. or W. Gḍ. (cerebral) र् or ड़ and ढ़, then (dental) ल् and ल्ह्, finally E. Gḍ. (dental) र् and र्ह्. Most words which in W. H. contain a non-initial ल्, have in E. H. an र्, as O. H. फर् *fruit* for W. H. फल्; E. H उरहै *it grows up* for W. H. उलहै. Indeed the affinity between these two sounds is so close and the transition so easy that E. Hindús seem to be hardly conscious of saying र् instead of ल्. This proves, *firstly,* that the E. H. र् is a pure dental sound, and *secondly* that it is more modern than ल्, of which it is, in fact, a comparatively recent modification[2]). Hence it follows that wherever E. H. has its

1) The Skr. र् is, perhaps, not a full cerebral, but a semicerebral, like the English so-called dentals; only in so far, can the modern full cerebral ड़ be called a new sound.

2) It existed, however, already in the A. Mg. of the Bhagavatí (see Wb. Bh. 393). It may be noted, that while the Mg., treated of by H. C., has ल् for र (H. C. 4, 288), द् for त् (H. C. 4, 260. 302), and ध् or ह् for थ् (H. C. 4, 267. 302), the Mg. of the Bhag. has, precisely like E. Gḍ., र् for ल्, elides द्, and uses only ह् (cf. Wb. Bh. 410. 428. 429), e. g., in H. C. कलेदि, in Bhg. करेइ, in E. H. करै *he does*; in H. C. धाराध or धाराह, in Bhg.

dental ड़, there must have been formerly a ल़. This exactly agrees with what, the Pr. Gramms. tell us, was the case in their time. They say (see H. C. 4, 288. T. V. 3, 2. 36 and the examples in Vr. 11, 8. 10. 12. 13), that Mg. Pr. changes every Skr. ड into ल़, that is, it turns the cerebral ड into the dental ल़. The E. H. has gone a step further and has converted every dental ल़ into dental ड़; e. g., Skr. रात्रिः *night*, Mg. Pr. लत्ती, E. H. ड़ात्; Skr. नरः *man*, Mg. Pr. नले, E. H. नड़. There are, however, a few exceptions, as E. H. लेड़ुरी for Mg. Pr. *लंड़ुलिआ (with pleonastic लिआ = डिका) = Skr. रुड्, E. H. लड़ै *he quarrels*, Mg. लडइ, Skr. रटति (see § 110). These bear out the statement of the Pr. Grammarians. But further, that dentalizing process of E. H. is still at work in the present day, turning most W. H. ड़ (= Skr. cerebral ड) into dental ड़, as E. H. तोड़ै *he breaks* for W. H. तोड़ै; and occasionally the intermediate (Mg. Pr.) ल़ is still preserved, as in the W. H. pleonastic suffix डा which is in E. H. ला and ड़ा; e. g., W. H. छेड़ो *goat*, E. H. छेली or छेड़ी (Skr. छागी, Ap. Pr. छायडिआ), or W. H. नाड़ो *watercourse*, E. H. नाली or नाड़ी [1]). Again the very same process, by which the E. H. has already changed all *dialectic* Mg. Pr. ल़ into (dental) ड़, it applies in the present day to all non-initial *original* (Skr.) ल़ also; as Skr. फलं *fruit*, Mg. Pr. फलं, E. H. फड़; Skr. कदलकः, Mg. Pr. कयलए or केलए, E. H. केड़ा. Initial *original* ल़, it is true, are exempted, as Skr. लंबः *long*, Mg. लंबे

जाणाइ, in E. H. जानइ *you know*. It appears, then, that the change of ड to ल़ belongs to the most ancient period of Mg., and that the present phonetic state (of ड़ for ल़) existed already in the Mg. period of the Bhag. In the phonological part of the present work, however, I shall generally give the *ancient* Mg. equivalents (with ल़) of E. H. words; for this reason, more than any other, to keep before the student's mind the fact of the change of the Skr. ड to E. H. ड़, through Mg. ल़!

1) Apparently in these exceptional cases the ल़ was already present in Skr.; cf. the Skr. pleon. suff. ल and ड़; and Skr. नड or नल, Ved. नळ *tubular reed, bone, artery*, etc., whence perhaps नड़ *man*; and Skr. नाडी or नाली *watercourse*, whence, perhaps, नाड़ी *water*.

or लम्मे (see § 18), E. H. लाग (W. H. लंबा), yet the tendency to the change is shown in the occasional substitution of ण् or न् in the place of ल्, as in the pleonastic suffixes णा or ना for ला (e. g., अपणा or अपना *own*, cf. M. अपला); a substitution which is still more common in B. and O. (see Bs. I, 75); for the cerebral ण् contains the sound of *r*, being somewhat like *rn*. Again the trustworthiness of the Pr. Gramms. is shown by their noting the remarkable agreement of S. with E. H., on which point see below. Thus Mḍ. and R. T. say, that S. which is called the *páṣchú* dialect, is distinguished by the interchange of *l* and *r*[1]). It is also noticeable that in the Kaithí alphabet, proper to E. H., the sign for the dental *r* (र) is different from that originally used for the Skr. cerebral *r* (ਰ) and still preserved in the Gurmukhí for the P. cerebral *r*; it is, in fact, a slight modification of the original sign for ल (ल) made by omitting the semicircular stroke (ਰ), and improved into the modern Devanágarí (र). According to the Pr. Gramm. the change of र् to ल् does not obtain in the Mh.-Sr. Pr.; i. e., the latter does not change the cerebral into a dental. This agrees with the fact that to the present day in W. Gḍ. (i. e., W. H., P., G., excl. Br. and S.) ऱ् is more or less distinctly cerebral; and accordingly they do not interchange their ल् and ऱ्, nor have they a cerebral ड़् *ṛ*[2]), but on the other hand they possess a cerebral ळ् *ḷ*. The same is true of the S. Gḍ., which like its original, the Dk. Pr. (Ls. 415), follows the W. Gḍs. (i. e., Mh.-Sr. Pr.). In fact their system of semivowels is very much the same still as in (Vedic) Skr. P. shows a tendency to change its cerebral ळ् to ड़्, and rarely its ल् to ऱ्; hence, probably, its ऱ् is not fully cerebral. S., on the other hand, agrees with E. H. in

---

1) Mḍ. पाश्चाया रेफव्यत्ययेन (18th páda, fol. 56); and R. T. पाश्चात्यता स्याद्र् रलपर्ययेण (Ls. Ap. 5).

2) Their ड् is always *ḍ*, not *ṛ*; and their *r* is equivalent to ड़् *ṛ*; whence, e. g., W. H. बड़ेला *wild hog*, probably written for बर्हेला = वर्हेला from Skr. वराह + pleon. ला; W. H. गंडाड़् or मंडाड़् for Skr. मार्जार:.

every respect; it has the dental ड़् and cerebral ड़, the interchange of ल् and ड़्, and no ळ्; so also Br., except that it does not usually interchange ल् and ड़्. N. and B., again, agree with E. H. in the dental ड़् and cerebral ड़, and the want of ळ्; and though they do not interchange ल् and ड़्, they have the analogous change of ल् to ण् or न्. The same is the case with O., except that it possesses the ळ्; this is strange; I suspect that its ळ् is not a pure cerebral; for sometimes it has both ळ् and ल्, e. g., गोल and गोळ *ball*; sometimes it has ल्, where the W. Gḍs. have ळ्, e. g., G. टळवुँ, M. टळणें, but O. टलिबा *to confound*. To sum up: W. Gḍ. (excl. S.) and S. Gḍ., like the Mh.-Sr. Pr., keep the cerebral ड़्; but E. Gḍ. and N. Gḍ. dentalize it, like the Mg. Pr.; S., like the old Páṣchá, follows the E. Gḍ. practice.

17. In E. H. the semivowels य् and व् are never *organic*, but always *euphonic*, i. e., either simply inserted, or produced by sandhi in order to prevent a hiatus. Thus जीयै *he lives* for जी + ऐ (Pr. जीअइ); खायल् *eaten* for खाइल् (Pr. खाइदे); जाय् के *having gone* for जाइ के; जाँयँ् *they may go* for जा + एँ; again लेवै *to take* for लेऐ; रोवल् *he wept* for रो + अल्; घोड़ःवा *horse* for घोड़ःआ; जाँवँ् *I may go* for जाओँ, etc. It follows that they can never occur at the beginning of a word. It should be remembered, however, that in Kaithí, व् is always written for ब्, and य् not uncommonly for ज्. Whenever such apparently organic य् or व् occur initially, they must be pronounced ज् or ब् respectively; as योग् or जोग् *jog worthy*; संयुत or संजुत् *sañjut joined*; वात् or बात् *bát word*; वाटै or बाटै *báṭai he is*; संवत् or संबत् *sambat year*. This applies even to tatsamas as यात्रा *játrá pilgrimage*, आचार्य *ácháraj preceptor*. The sound of ब् is very peculiar; it is neither distinctly *b* nor *v*; of the two it is nearer to *b*; but in many cases it is difficult to say which it is. This is especially the case in the *ṭheṭh bháshá*; in the khaṛí bháshá, it is, as a rule, distinctly *b*. The same remarks apply to B. and O. — Nor does an *organic* य् or व् ever occur in the middle of a word; it is always vocalized and commonly combined with the adjacent vowels, as नारैन्

or नाराइन *Náráyan* (Pr. नारायणो); देओदारु *pine* (Pr. देवदारु). This applies also to tatsamas, as देवता *deota* (देओता) *idol.* In tatsamas it is the usual, though not the universal practice to write य् and व्; but the Pr. Grammarians' practice of phonetic spelling would be greatly preferable; and for clearness' sake I shall observe it in this work.

18. *Affinities.* This subject is involved in some obscurity. According to the Pr. Gramm. an initial य् always changes to ज् in the Mh.-Sr. Pr. (Vr. 2, 31. H. C. 1, 245. T. V. 1, 3. 74), but in the Mg. Pr. it not only remains unchanged, but even ज् (whether initial or medial) changes to य् (H. C. 4, 292. T. V. 3, 2. 39. cf. Vr. 11, 4. K. I. 5 in Ls. 393); e. g., Skr. योजनम्, Sr. जोअणं, Mg. योअणं. But not only is the modern E. and S. Gḍ. practice precisely the reverse of that of Mg., and the same as that of Mh.-Sr.; but even in the contemporary (Mg.) Pr. literature the Sr. Pr. almost uniformly prevails; e. g., in the Bhagavatí (see Wb. Bh. 394; also Ls. 406. 411. 425). It seems impossible to admit that the Pr. Grammarians should have deliberately foisted on a language, and that in some cases probably their own vernacular, a rule the opposite of which they knew to be the truth. And it seems to be an equally impossible supposition — it is, indeed, as just stated, contradicted by the Pr. literature —, that a revolution so complete in the pronunciation of Mg. should have taken place within the last few centuries, as the accustomed interpretation of their rule would involve. Yet if the य्, which they mention, is understood in the sense of the ordinary semivowel *y*, there seems no escape from one or other of these two improbable alternatives. The solution of the difficully appears to me to be the admission of the fact, that in the old Mg. Pr. times there must have existed an obscure sound, intermediate between *y* and *j*, and doing duty for both these two; precisely analogous to the obscure sound which took the place in Pr. of the two sounds *v* and *b* and which still exists in E. H. (§ 17). These two obscure or neutral sounds I shall call the *semiconsonants* य्

and ब़. The palatal semiconsonant *y* still appears to exist here and there in isolated cases. It has been noticed by Beames to occur in the Panjáb [1]). But from the Pr. Gramm.' statement, it is probable that it once universally prevailed in the Mg. Pr. The two cases, of य़ and ज़ on the one side and of व़ and ब़ on the other, are closely analogous and serve to elucidate one another. The existence of such *semiconsonants* य़ and व़ is, apparently, nowhere expressly noted in the Pr. Gramm.; but it follows almost of necessity from the fact, that side by side with them Pr. possesses an *euphonic* य़ and व़ [2]). The latter are very common in modern Gḍ., and are pronounced precisely like our ordinary semivowels *y* and *v*; whence it follows, that the organic य़ and व़ must have had in Pr. more of a real consonantal character, and are, in fact, semiconsonants, i. e., neutral sounds between the full semivowels and the full consonants [3]). It is this semiconsonant व़,

---

1) „The Hindi holds fast the correct pronunciation (of ज़), but Panjabi rather finds it a stumbling-block. When a Panjabi says मझ *majh* "a buffalocow" the sound he produces is something very odd. It might be represented by *meyh*, a very palatal *y* aspirated; perhaps in German by *möch*, or rather, if it may be so expressed, with a medial sound corresponding to the tenuis *ch*" (Bs. I, 71). It is probably the sound, given to *g* (as in *lebendig*) in the Rhenish Provinces.

2) Thus K. I. 1, 45. कुचिद्यत्वं वा ॥ गअणं गयणं वा ॥ 46. कुचिद् वत्वं वा । सुहओ सुहवो वा ॥ i. e. sometimes (when a consonant is elided) an euphonic *y* or *v* is inserted, as *gayaṇaṃ* for *gaaṇaṃ* (Skr. *gagaṇam*), *suhavo* for *suhao* (Skr. *subhagaḥ*). Again H. C. 1, 180. अवर्णो यश्रुतिः; and T. V. 1, 3. 10 यश्रुतिः । नयरं ॥ in the place of an elided consonant between the vowels *ă* or *á* an euphonic *y* is pronounced; as *nayaraṃ* (Skr. *nagaram*), etc. Mḍ. 2, 2. has अनादावत्र् अदितो वर्णौ पठितव्यौ । यकारवदिति पाठशिक्षा ॥ (MS. fol. 8ᵃ). — See also Wb. Bh. 399.

3) The Pr. Gramm. themselves note a distinction in the sound of the two sets; thus T. V. 1, 3. 10 calls the euphonic *y* लघुप्रयत्नतरयकार „pronounced with smaller effort"; in the same rule among the examples of the euphonic य़ the Pr. णयणं *eye* for Skr. नयनं is given; this would have no sense, unless the organic (Skr.) य़ was pronounced in Pr. differently from the euphonic य़. Again य़ and व़ are in Pr. sometimes *vocalized* and, by combination with the adjacent vowels, form ए and ओ; this

which according to the Pr. Gramm. is sometimes *substituted* for a single medial Skr. प् or ब्, but as a rule *elided*, both in Mh.-Sr. and in Mg. Pr.[1]). They give no rule as to the substitution of the semicons. व् for an initial or a conjunct Skr. ब्; whence it may be concluded, that in the Mh.-Sr. Pr. the latter remained unchanged. This conclusion, indeed, is indirectly supported by the fact that the Skr. conj. म्ब् *mb* does not change in the Mh.-Sr. Pr. into म्म् *mm*, as it would do according to Vr. 3, 8, if it were pronounced in Pr. म्व् *mv* with the semicons. व्[2]). Thus Skr. जम्बु°, Pr. जम्बु° or जंबु° (Spt. 192); Skr. निम्ब°, Pr. णिम्ब° or णिंब° (Spt. 252); Skr. अम्बु°, Pr. अम्बु or अंबु (Spt. A. 32); Skr. बिम्बं, Pr. बिम्बं or बिंबं (Spt. 208); also Pr. अम्बं or अंबं (Vr. 3, 53, for Skr. आम्रं);

---

occurs, as a rule, in declension and conjugation, and it will be observed, that the य् and व् thus treated are always the euphonic semivowels; thus Skr. शयति of शि + अति is Pr. शेदि, Skr. भवति of भू + अति is Pr. होदि, Skr. तन्वी of तनु + ई is Pr. तणुई, etc.; on the other hand, the organic semiconsonants य् and व् are not vocalized, but as a rule elided; thus Skr. नयनं is Pr. णअणं (T. V. 1, 3. 8); Skr. लावण्यं is Pr. लाअण्णं (T. V. 1, 3. 8). In short, the euph. semivowels य् and व् are treated like vowels; but the semiconsonants य् and व् like consonants. Again note the change of Skr. छाया to Pr. छाहा (Vr. 2, 18).

1) Vr. 2, 15 पो वः *v takes the place of p*; H. C. 1, 237. T. V. 1, 3. 61 बो वः *v takes the place of b*; Vr. 2, 2 °पयवां प्रायो लोपः। Md. 2, 2 प्रायः °पबयवां लोपः (MS. fol. 8[a]) „*as a rule v etc. are elided*". These rules are given on Mh., but they apply to Sr. and Mg. too (by H. C. 3, 302. 286). It is noticeable, that they do not apply to the Ap. Pr., which possesses the full consonant ब्; thus H. C. 4, 396 अनादौ स्वरादसंयुक्तानां कखतथपफां गघदधबभाः „*medial single p, ph etc. become b, bh etc.*".

2) While conjuncts consisting of a semivowel with an antecedent nasal are assimilated in Pr. (Vr. 3, 2. 3), those consisting of a consonant with an antecedent nasal are not. Hence the second part of the conjunct in the examples must be pronounced ब् *b*, not व् *v*; otherwise the forms ought to be जम्मू, etc.; as, indeed, they were probably in Mg. The rule Vr. 3, 3 does not apply to the consonant ब *b*, but only to neutral व्; the example लोद्धओ for Skr. लुब्धकः does not prove that it does, as ब् would be assimilated, in any case, by the analogy of the rule Vr. 3, 1.

Skr. चुम्बति *he kisses,* Pr. चुम्बइ or चुंबइ (H. C. 4, 239). On the other hand, it is very probable, that both the initial and the conjunct Skr. ब् were pronounced in the Mg. Pr. as the semiconsonant व्. For the following reasons: *firstly,* while the W. and S. Gḍ., the descendants of the Mh.-Sr. Pr., show, like the latter, the cons. ब् in the place of the Skr. conjunct म्ब्, the E. Gḍ., the descendant of the Mg. Pr. (and S. which generally follows E. Gḍ. practices, cf. § 16), shows म् which postulates in Mg. a conjunct म्म्[1]) and hence the pronunciation म्व् for Skr. म्ब्; thus Skr. जम्बुः, Mh.-Sr. जम्बू, M. जाँबू, G. जांबु, but E. H., B., O. जाम्, S. जामु, Mg. *जम्मू; Skr. निम्बः, Mh.-Sr. णिम्बो, W. H., M., G. नीँब्, but E. H., B., O. नीम्, Mg. *निम्मे; Skr. निम्बूकः, Mh.-Sr. णिम्बूओ, W. H., M., G. निम्बू, but E. H., B., O. नीमू, S. निमु or लिमु, Mg. *निम्मूए; Skr. लम्बः, Mh.-Sr. लम्बो, W. H. लम्बा, but E. H. लाम्, Mg. *लम्मे; Skr. आम्रम्, Mh.-Sr. अम्बं, W. H., P. अम्ब, M. अम्बा, G. आँबो, but E. H., B., O. आम्, S. आमो (also अम्बु), Mg. *अम्मं; Skr. ताम्रम्, Mh.-Sr. तम्बं, W. H., P. ताँबा, M. ताँबें, G. ताँबुं, but E. H., B., O. ताम् or तामा, S. टामो, Mg. *तम्मं (cf. Ls. 246); in Skr. कम्बलः *blanket,* Mg. *कम्मले, E. H. कम्मल् (cf. § 143 exc.) the original Mg. *म्म् is preserved; Skr. सम्बुध्यते, Mg. *सम्मुज्झइ, E. H. समुझै[2]). *Secondly,* while E. Gḍ. (and Br.) possesses the initial semiconsonant व्, the other Gḍ. languages have either the semivowel व् or the consonant ब् (see Bs. I, 252. Kl. 11. 13) at the beginning of words. *Thirdly,* while the Gurmukhí (i. e. Panjábí) and Gujarátí alphabets possess two separate signs for *v* and *b*, the Kaithí (incl. Devanágarí), Bangálí and Oṛiya have only one, namely ब्, to denote both sounds *v* and *b*, and hence, for distinction's sake, they place a dot *under* (E. H. ब़) or *over* (O. बं) it when it has the sound of *v*; as E. H. राब़न् *Rávan,*

1) The Mg. semicons. व् seems to have a tendency to change to म्, e. g., Mg. माहणा for वाहणा (Skr. ब्राह्मणा); Mg. वेसमणा for वेसवणा (Skr. वैश्रवणा); see Wb. Bh. 414. 415; also see § 134.

2) In the last instance सम्मु° the assimilation म्म् appears to be common to all Gḍs.: cf. Bs. II, 108. H. समझौती, G. समजुतो, M. समजूत्.

कवन् *karan who*; but वचन् *bachan word,* वन् *ban wood*[1]). On the whole the case appears to stand thus: In Mh.-Sr. Pr. the Skr. semivowel व् and consonant ब् remain unchanged at the beginning of words, but become the semiconsonant व् in the middle. On the other hand, in Mg. they are pronounced as the semicons. व् in every case whether initial or medial. In E. Gḍ. the Mg. initial semicons. व् has a tendency to be hardened into the consonant ब्, and the Mg. medial semicons. व् has a tendency to be softened into the semivowel व् and vocalized and combined with the adjacent vowels; thus Skr. बुध्यते, Mg. वुज्झइ, E. H. बूझै *he knows*; Skr. शपथम्, A. Mg. सवहं, E. H. सोह. The case of य् and ज् is precisely analogous. It is the semiconsonant य्, to which the Pr. Gramm. rule refers[2]). From this rule it appears, that just as the semiconsonant व् was pronounced in Mg. Pr. for both the Skr. semivowel व् and consonant ब्, so the semicons. य् was pronounced in it for both the Skr. semivow. य् and cons. ज्; and that, again, in every case, both in the beginning and middle of a word. Moreover, just like the Skr. conjunct म्ब् *mb* is pronounced in Mg. म्व् *mv* and changed to म्म् *mm*, so the Skr. conjunct ञ्ज् *ñj* is in Mg. pronounced *ञ्य् *ñy* and becomes ञ्ञ *ññ*[3]). Once more: as the Bangálí and Oṛiyá alphabets have only one character for both *v* and *b*, so they have only one sign for both sounds *y* and *j*, and hence, for distinction's sake, they place a dot (B. य़) or hook (O. यृ) *under* the य् when it has the sound

1) This proves, that the semicons. व् was felt to be more like *b* than *v*; for otherwise the dot would be used, when it signified *b*; as indeed it is in Devanágarí, the alphabet of W. H. and M., where ब् (i. e. व or dot *within* व) signifies *b*.

2) Thus Vr. 11, 4 जो यः *y takes the place of j*; H. C. 4, 292. T. V. 3, 2. 39 जद्ययां यः *y takes the place of j, dy and y.*

3) Thus H. C. 4, 293. T. V. 3, 2. 37 न्यण्यज्ञञ्जां ञ्ञः *ññ takes the place of ñj* etc.; as अञ्ञली for Skr. अञ्जली, धणञ्ञए for Skr. धनञ्जयः, पञ्ञले for Skr. प्राञ्जलः *straight*; none of these words, I believe, have survived in the modern Gḍs.; nor do I happen to know any other instance in B. or O.; in S., perhaps, there is मिञ्ञु *marrow* for Skr. *माज्ञ° (see Tr. XXVII).

of y[1]). On the other hand the Gurmukhí and (in this case also) Kaithí have two séparate signs for y and j, just as in the case of v and b[2]). Finally as in the case of the Mg. semicons. व़, so here too the Mg. init. semicons. य़ has been hardened in the modern E. Gḍ. into the full consonant ज़, and the Mg. medial semicons. य़ is softened into the semivowel य़, vocalized and combined with the adjacent vowels; thus Skr. जानाति *he knows*. Mg. याणइ, E. H. जाने; Skr. रजनी *night*. Mg. रयणी, E. H. रइनि or रैनि. To judge, however, from the evidence of the A. Mg. Pr. of the Bhagavatí, where *ry* and *rj* as a rule appear as *yy*, but *j* remains unchanged (see Wb. Bh. 394. 389), and from the fact that the Kaithí has separate signs for y and j, it is possible, that the A. Mg. never possessed the *single* semicons. य़, but only the double semicons. य्य़, following in the former respect the Mh.-Sr., in the latter the Mg. In any case, in its modern representative, the E. H., the semicons. य़, whether single or double, has become a full consonant. — This theory of the semicons. य़ is confirmed

1) This shows again that the semicons. य़ was in Mg. Pr. more like j than y. — It is noticeable that Bhámaha in his Comm. on Vr. 11, 4 does not use the term स्थाने (he says जकारस्य यकारो भवति), which he employs in all other sútras where an actual phonetic change is enjoined; thus on Vr. 11, 3 he says षकारसकारयोः स्थाने शकारो भवति; and so even on Vr. 11, 7 र्यकारर्जकारयोः स्थाने य्यो भवति i. e. *yy for rj and ry*. Now in the Bhagavatí *rj* and *ry*, as a rule, change into *yy*, but *j* does not change (Wb. Bh. 394. 389). This curious coincidence would seem to show, that the difference in Bhámaha's terminology, if it was intentional, was meant to indicate, that in the case of j the change was one in *writing* only, but in the case of *rj* and *ry* it was one both in *writing* and *pronunciation*. In other words: in Bhám'. time the semicons. य़ had already hardened into the full cons. ज़, though it was still written य़ (as in modern B. and O.), but the double य्य़ was still both written and pronounced as semicons. The latter would naturally hold out longer. In modern E. Gḍ., however, it too has hardened to ज्ज़.

2) It may be remarked, however, that in Kaithí, too, a dot is placed under य़, when it signifies an *organic* y in tatsama words; thus सत्य़ *true*; which shows, that formerly य़ (without dot) signified j, the Pr. substitute of the Skr. organic y.

by and elucidates the treatment of the Skr. conjunct ज्ञ् *jñ* in Pr. and Gḍ. According to the Pr. Gramm. ज्ञ् changes to ण्ण् *ṇṇ* in Mh.-Sr.[1]) (H. C. 2, 42. T. V. 1, 4. 37. Vr. 3, 44), to ञ्ञ् *ññ* in Mg. (H. C. 4, 293. T. V. 3, 2. 37) and to न्न् *nn* in the A. Mg. (Wb. Bh. 402. 403). The Gḍs. show no trace of the form ञ्ञ् *ññ*, but have always न् *n* or ण् *ṇ*; as Skr. राज्ञी *queen*, Pr. रण्णी or रन्नी, E. H. रानी or राणी, N. रानी, M. G. P. S. राणी; Skr. यज्ञोपवीतं *sacrificial thread*, Pr. *जण्णोविअं or जन्नोविअं (cf. Vr. 4, 1), G. जनोइ, E. H. जनउ (for जनोउ see § 26. 122), M. जनवे", S. जणयो, W. H. जनेउ; Skr. आज्ञा *order*, Pr. आणा (Vr. 3, 55) or आना, H. आन्; Skr. संज्ञा, Pr. सण्णा or सन्ना, H. सान् *sign*; Skr. विज्ञापिका, Pr. विण्णत्तिआ or विन्नत्तिआ, H. बिनती *respectful information, petition*; Skr. संज्ञाप्तिका, Pr. सण्णत्तिआ or सन्नत्तिआ, H. सनती *instead* (lit. *killing*)[2]). If ज्ञ् was pronounced as a semicons. (य्), it would easily be assimilated to the succeeding nasal. Besides from the form न्न् *nn* it appears, that this palatal semicons. य् had a tendency to pass into the dental class. There are, however, traces in Pr. of another modification of ज्ञ्, beside that into ण्ण् or न्न्. The Skr. base राज्ञ *king* becomes in Ps. Pr. राचिन (Vr. 10, 12) and in the later Mh. Pr. राइण (H. C. 3, 50—55. K. I. 237. 238. Cw. 45. Ls. 315). The latter presupposes a Sr. form *राजिण or *राज्जिन or Mg. *रायिञ. Here, evidently the conjunct ज्ञ् has been dissolved into जिण or जिन, which the Ps., as usual, changes to चिन. On the same principle the E. H. word सइन् or सैन् *hint* (also S., see Tr. XXXIV) is formed from the Pr. *सइणा or *सजिणा, Skr. संज्ञा[3]). Instead, however,

1) They state, however, that ज्ञ् of the R. ज्ञा *know* always becomes ज् (Vr. 8, 23); this is born out by Gḍ., which has जान्; they also say that ज्ञ् of derivatives of the R. ज्ञा *optionally* becomes ज्ज् (H. C. 2, 83. T. V. 1, 4. 82. Vr. 3, 5); but Gḍ. shows no trace of this.

2) Also देवान् or देवाना *mad*, Pr. दइवण्णू (H. C. 2, 83) or *दइवन्नू, Skr. दैवज्ञः (lit. *inspired*); and बीन् or बीना *seeing*, Pr. *विण्णू or *विन्नू, Skr. विज्ञः (lit. *knowing*); these two words, however, are probably introduced from the Persian, which accounts for their metaphorical meaning.

3) H. has both सान् and सैन् *hint*, but only रानी *queen*, not रैनी; probably to avoid confusion with रैनी *night* for Skr. रजनी.

of ञ् being elided, it generally appears in the modern Gḍ. either as ग् *g* (E. and W. Gḍ.) or ड् *d* (S. Gḍ.). This can be naturally explained, if the original ञ् be supposed to have been at first pronounced as the semicons. य्. The latter, as already stated, has a tendency to pass into the dental class, but it passes even more easily into the guttural; i. e., original ज्ञ becomes गिन or दिन. Next the nasal was suppressed and the two hiatus-vowels of गिश्र contracted to ग्य. This is still the common practice to the present day in regard to tatsamas in P. and H.; e. g., P. गिश्रान्, H. ग्यान् *knowledge* for Skr. ज्ञानं; P. श्रागिश्रा, H. श्राग्या *order* for Skr. श्राज्ञा; but it must have existed already in the Ap. Pr., as evidenced by the modern H. जग्ग् or जाग् *sacrifice*, which presupposes an Ap. Pr. form जग्गं in which the conjunct ग्य् *gy* has become subject to the ordinary Gḍ. laws on the treatment of conjuncts (see § 144. 147. 150); so also the S. सर्वग्गु *omniscient* for *सर्वग्यु (Tr. XXXII). — In G. tatsamas °गिन° is changed to ग्न्य *gnya*; and M. has द्न्य *dnya* for °दिन°; e. g., Skr. ज्ञान is in G. *gnyán*, in M. *dnyán*. It is usual, however, to retain in writing the Skr. conjunct ज्ञ् *jñ* in the place of the modern awkward triple nexus. — It has been already noted, that traces of the insertion of the euphonic semivowels य् and व् are already found in Pr. The practice is far more general in Gḍ.; in E. H., especially, these euph. letters are regularly employed in the formation of the *long* form of nouns (see § 203).

19. E. H. does not possess the two sibilants श् *ṣ* and ष् *sh* of the Skr. phonetic system. Even in tatsama words they are always pronounced as स् *s*, as शिव *siu* (सिउ) *Ṣiva*. Already in the A. Mg. Pr., the original of E. H., they had uniformly given way to the latter (see Wb. Bh. 393. 415. Ls. 411). In writing the symbols श् and ष् are commonly used; but they are always pronounced *s* and *kh* respectively (as खुश् *khús happy*, pers. خوش), and, in fact, are the E. H. (Kaithí) signs of those two sounds. To avoid misunderstanding, however, I shall employ in this work the usual Devanágarí characters स् *s* and ख् *kh*.

20. *Affinities.* The sound of ष् had been already lost in all Prs.; that of श् in the Mh.-Sr. and that of स् in the Mg. (Vr. 2, 43. 11, 3). Accordingly none of the Gḍs. have ष्, the E. Gḍ. (exc. E. H.) has no स्, W. and N. Gḍ. no श्. S. Gḍ. and E. H., follow, like their prototypes (the A. Mg. and Dk. Pr.), the example of the Mh.-Sr. and have, as a rule, no श्. In other words, like their respective originals, E. Gḍ. (excl. E. H.) pronounces all three Skr. sibilants alike as *ṣ*; W., N., S. Gḍ. and E. H. as *s*. In H. H., however, and in the other literary forms of W. Gḍ. both ष् and श् are sounded in tatsamas, but alike as palatal *ṣ*; thus शिव and विष्णु are *ṣiva* and *viṣṇu*. — In *writing*, the character ष्, more or less modified in the different alphabets (see the *table*), is preserved in all Gḍs., and used as a symbol of ख् *kh*. Similarly E. Gḍ. uses श्, and W. and N. Gḍ. स्, and S. Gḍ. स् and श् indifferently, as a symbol for their *one* sibilant. In the literary or high forms of the various Gḍs., the use of all three *characters* स, श, ष (not of their sounds), has been reintroduced; chiefly in tatsamas; in tadbhavas, owing to an imperfect knowledge of their derivation, they are sometimes wrongly employed by native writers.

21. Such foreign sounds as do not occur in the E. H. phonetic system, are assimilated in the following manner:

1) The semigutturals (arabic) ق *q*, خ *kh*, غ *gh* and ح or ه *ḥ* become respectively the pure gutturals क्, ख्, ग् and ह्; as कौल् for قول *agreement*, खाली خالی *only* or *empty*; गरिब् غریب *poor*; हाल् حال *state*; हर् هر *every*.

2) The semipalatals (arabic) ذ *ż*, ز *z̈*, ض *ẑ*, ظ *z̤* become pure palatal ज्; as कागज् (O. H. कागद्) کاغذ *paper*; जास्ती زیادتی *more* (see Bs. II, 54); जिमिदार् زمیندار *landholder*; जामिन् ضامن *surety*; जाहिर् ظاهر *manifest*.

3) The semicerebrals (english) *t* and *d* become pure cerebral ट् and ड् respectively; as कलकटर् *collector*, लाड् *lord*.

4) The semidentals ط *t* and (sibilants) ث *ṡ*, ص *ṣ* and ش *sh* become pure dental त् and स् respectively; as तैयार् طیار *ready*; साबित् ثابت *proved*; साहिब् صاحب *master, sir*; खुस् خوش *happy*.

5) The semilabial ف *f* becomes pure labial फ़, pronounced *ph*, not *f* as in W. H.; e. g., फैदा *phaidá* for فايدہ *faidá profit.*

6) The spirants ع *a* and (sometimes) و *v* are dropped, and if they were medial, the hiatus-vowels are contracted; as मालूम् for معلوم *known*, माफिक् for موافق *like.*

3. THE VISARGA AND ANUSVÁRA.

22. The E. H. does not possess the *Visarga* (:) or unmodified sibilant (see M. M. 4) of the Skr. phonetic system. Already in Skr. the visarga had ceased to be pronounced in certain cases and was assimilated either to the preceding vowel or to the following consonant. In Pr. this became the universal practice (cf. Ls. 142. 229. 230). It follows that none of the Gds. can possess the visarga; on the contrary, they further subject the assimilated vowel or consonant of the Pr. to the disintegrating action of their own laws. Thus compare the following examples: Skr. अन्योऽपि *also another,* A. Mg. Pr. अन्ने वि, E. H. अनउ or अनौ; Skr. यशोवान् *glorious,* A. Mg. Pr. जसोवंते or जसवंते, E. H. जसवंत्; Skr. दुर्बलः *weak,* Mg. दुब्बले, E. H. दूबर्; Skr. निश्चिन्तः *thoughtless,* Mg. निच्चिंते, E. H. निचीत्; Skr. निस्तारयति *he pours off,* Mg. नित्थालइ, E. H. नियारै; Skr. निष्फलं *fruitless,* Mg. निप्फलं, E. H. नीफल; Skr. अग्निः *fire,* Mg. अग्गी, E. H. आगि; Skr. दुःखं *pain,* Mg. दुक्खं, E. H. दुख्; Skr. अन्तःकरणं *conscience,* Mg. अंतक्करणं, E. H. अंतकरन्; Skr. निष्कालयति *expels,* Mg. निक्कालइ, E. H. निकालै; Skr. निश्वासः *breath,* A. Mg. निस्सासे, E. H. निसास्. It will be seen from this, that the spelling with a visarga (as दुःख्, अंतःकरण्), affected by Hindi purists (especially foreign lexicographers), is indefensible. A sound, which had disappeared in Pr. already, could not have survived in Gd. As a matter of fact, no Hindú pronounces or writes [1]) it, even in tatsamas; they say *dukh* not *duḥkh,* and *antakaran* not *antaḥkaraṇ.* The latter is even

1) I have seen a native writer use the visarga to indicate a sonant final *a*, as करबः *karaba* (*you will do*); the practice, however, is not to be commended; as little as the use of the anusvára to indicate *nasalization* (§§ 23. 8); both are abuses of the Skr. symbols.

sometimes pronounced *antkaran*, where the *quiescence* of the *ă*, which could not be unless the *ă* were final (see § 41), clearly proves the absence of a visarga.

23. The E. H. does not possess the *Anusvára* (·) or unmodified nasal (M. M. 4) of the Skr. phonetic system. The anusvára should be carefully distinguished from the *anunásika* (ँ). The former is a separate sound (like the visarga or like any vowel or consonant), while tke latter is merely the nasalization of a sound. If the breath is emitted wholly through the mouth, the *pure* sounds, whether vowels or consonants[1]), are produced; if a part only be thus emitted, while the rest is allowed to escape simultaneously through the nose, a nasalized sound, whether vowel or consonant[1]), is produced; if the breath is expelled wholly through the nose, the mouth being shut, a pure nasal sound (unmodified by any organ of speech in the mouth) is the result. The latter is the anuswára, which, therefore, is called by native Grammarians *násikya*, because pronounced in the nose only. The second group, the nasalized sounds, are called by them anunásika or *co-nasals*, because they are pronounced through both mouth and nose *at the same time*. The pure nasal, monopolising as it does the whole of the breath, cannot be pronounced *together with*, but only *after* an other sound. Hence it is called by the native Gramm. anusvára, i. e. *after-sound*. — Now any sound, whether vowel or consonant, may be nasalized, except र् *r*, स् *s* and ह् *h*[2]); but only five of these, when thus nasalized, are written with separate letters; viz. the nasal consonants or, briefly, the *class-nasals*, ङ् *ṅ*, ञ् *ñ*, ण् *ṇ*, न् *n*, म् *m*. The nasalization of the rest (i. e. य्, ल्, व् and the vowels, which I shall call, briefly, the *anunásika*) is indicated by the sign (ँ), called *arddhachandra* (halfmoon); thus लँ् *l̃*, यँ् *ỹ*, वँ् *ṽ*, आँ *ā̃*, ईँ *ī̃*, ऊँ *ū̃*, etc. (§ 8). The pure nasal (or anusvára) is denoted by the sign (·), called *bindu* (dot);

1) Modified in the mouth, according to the organ of speech, into gutturals, palatals, etc.

2) In Skr. also श् *ś* and ष् *sh*; and in Gd. also ड़ *ṛ*.

thus अं *ám* is the vowel *á succeeded* by a nasal tone, while अँ *ã́* is the nasalized vowel *á*. The latter is but *one* sound; the former are two successive sounds. The two cases, therefore, are quite distinct. — The anusvára has the nearest affinity to the class-nasal म् *m*; the latter is formed by a momentary, the former by a prolonged contact of the lips. — As to the use of these three kinds of nasals (the class-nasals, the anusvára and the anunásika) in Skr., Pr. and Gḍ. respectively, the following *general* laws may be laid down. *Firstly*, as regards the nasal in the *body of the word*. 1) In Skr.: a) a nasal standing before स् *s* (श्, ष्) and ह् *h must* be the anusvára; b) before any consonant proper it *must* be the respective class-nasal; c) before nasals, semivowels and vowels it must be one of the three, ण् or न् or म् (cf. M. M. 5. 7. 59. 60). 2) In Pr.: a) a nasal standing before स् (Mg. श्) *must* be the anusvára; b) before ह् and any cons. proper it *may* be either the anusvára or the respective class-nasal; in the latter case ह् changes to घ् (H. C. 1, 264. T. V. 1, 3. 86); c) before nasals, semivowels and vowels ण्, न् and म् remain, as a rule, unchanged[1]); but occasionally न् before म् may be changed to anusvára, while before vowels it may become व् with or without anunásika or be elided[2]) (cf. ad a. b., Vr. 4, 17. H. C. 1, 29. 30. T. V. 1, 1. 47. 48; ad c., Vr. 3, 2. 3. 43. 44. 53. 2, 3. T. V. 1, 4. 78. 79. 37. 48. 49. 3, 2. 37. 44. 3, 3. 3. 1, 3. 11. H. C. 2, 42. 56. 61. 78. 79. 1, 23. 4, 397. 1, 178). 3) In Gḍ.: a) the nasal is never anusvára under any circumstances; b) before स्, ह्, and any cons. proper it *may* be either anunásika or the respective class-nasal; if anunásika, the preceding vowel is almost universally lengthened; if class-nasal, ह् becomes घ्; c) before semivowels

---

1) Unless the conjunct is dissolved; as Skr. अम्लिका *tamarind*, Pr. अमल्लिआ, H. इमली (see § 167).

2) Occasionally न् before vowels is changed to anusvára or anunásika in Pr.; as Skr. गृहाणि *houses*, Pr. घराइं or घराइँ (H. C. 3, 26. T. V. 2, 2. 31), M. घरेँ.

and vowels it is often changed to anunásika, in which case the hiatus-vowels are generally contracted. Compare the following examples: *ad a. b*) Skr. हंसः *goose*. A. Mg. हंसे, E. H. हाँस् or हन्स् ; Skr. सिंहः *lion*. A. Mg. सिंहे or सिङ्घे (or सिंघे), E. H. सीँह् or सीँघ् or सिङ्घ् (or सिंघ् § 13); Skr. पङ्कः *mud*, Mg. पंके or पङ्के, E. H. पाँक् or पङ्क् (or पंक् § 13); Skr. अञ्जनम् *eyesalve*, Sr. अंजणं or अञ्जणं, E. H. आँजन् or अञ्जन्; Skr. कण्टकः *thorn*, Mg. कंटए or कण्टए, E. H. काँटा or कण्टा; Skr. चन्द्रः *moon*, Mg. चंदे or चन्दे, E. H. चाँद् or चन्द्; Skr. कम्पति *he trembles*. Mg. कंपइ or कम्पइ, E. H. काँपै or कम्पै; *ad c*) Skr. पुण्यम् *virtue*, A. Mg. पुण्णं or पुन्नं, E. H. पुन्; Skr. मन्यते *he heeds*. Mg. मन्नइ, E. H. मानै; Skr. गम्यते *it passes*, Mg. गम्मइ, E. H. गमै; Skr. जम्बुलः *roseapple*, Mg. जम्बुले or *जम्मुले (§ 18), E. H. जामुन्; Skr. अम्रम् *mango*, Mg. अम्बं or *अम्मं (§ 18), E. H. आम्; Skr. जन्मयते *is born* (Den. R.), Mg. जम्मइ (H. C. 4, 136), E. H. जामै or जमै; Skr. भ्रमरकः *bee*, Ap. भवँरउ, E. H. भौँरा; Skr. कमलम् *lotus*, Ap. कवलं, E. H. कवल्; Skr. कुमारः *prince*, Mg. कुमाले or कुमले (H. C. 4, 302. 1, 67), E. H. कुअँर् or कुअर्; Skr. स्थाने *at* (a place), Mg. थाणे or (Ap.) थाणि, E. H. थेँ; Skr. पञ्चत्रिंशत् *thirty five*, Mg. पण्णतीसा or पणतीसा (cf. H. C. 2, 174. 43), E. H. पैँतीस् (for पवँतीस्). There are a few exceptions; 1) in Pr.: *α*) occasionally the anusvára is optionally dropped, in which case the preceding vowel is generally lengthened (Vr. 1, 17. 4, 16. H. C. 1, 28. 29. T. V. 1, 1. 46. 48); *β*) occasionally an anusvára is substituted for a consonant proper forming the first part of a conjunct (Vr. 4, 15. H. C. 1, 26. T. V. 1, 1. 42); *γ*) the nasal preceding a consonant proper which is not *ásanna* (T. V. 1, 1. 47), i. e., between which and itself another consonant has been dropped, *must* be anusvára (H. C. 1, 25. T. V. 1, 1. 41); *δ*) a nasal, preceding ह् by transposition, remains, as a rule, unchanged; very rarely it is elided and the preceding vowel lengthened (Vr. 3, 8. 32. 33. H. C. 2, 74. 75. T. V. 1, 4. 67—70. H. C. 2, 73. T. V. 1, 4. 64). 2) In Gḍ.: *α* and *β*) the Pr. practice is retained and extended, only substituting anunásika for anusvára; *γ*) in this case also anunásika is substituted for anusvára; *δ*) either ह् is elided and the preceding vowel lengthened or the conjunct is dissolved. Compare the following examples: ad *α*) Skr. विंशतिः *twenty,* Pr. वीसा, E. H. बीसु; Skr. सिंहः *lion,* Pr. सीहो or सिंहो, E. H. सीहु or सीँहु, etc. (see above); Skr. मांसम् *flesh,* Pr. मासं or मंसं, E. H. मासु or माँसु or मन्सु; Skr. संहरति *he collects,* Pr. संहरइ or सहरइ (T. V. 3, 1. 133), E. H. सहरै; Skr. सम्मुखे *before,* Pr. संमुहे or समुहे, H. सामहे or समुहे or सौँहीँ; Skr. पठन् *reading,* Mg. पढंते, E. H. पढ़तु; Skr. संस्थः *together with,* Mg. संथे or सत्थे, E. H. साथु; ad *β*) Skr. वक्रम्, Pr. वंकं, E. H. बाँकु; Skr. अश्रुकम् *tear,* Pr. अंसुअं, E. H. आँसू; Skr. सत्यम् *true,* Pr. सच्चं, E. H. साँचु; Skr. निद्रा *sleep,* Pr. णिद्दा, E. H. नीँदु, etc. (see § 149); ad *γ*) Skr. पङ्क्तिः *row,* Pr. पंती, E. H. पाँति; ad *δ*) Skr. चिह्नम् *sign,* Pr. चिण्हं (H. C. 2, 50), E. H. चीन्हु or चिनहा; Skr. ब्राह्मणः *Bráhman,* Mg. बम्हणे, E. H. बामनु or बमहनु; Skr. कृष्णः *krishna,* Mg. कण्हे, E. H. कानु or कनहु (as in कानपुर *Cawnpúr* and कनहैया लालु *Kanhaiyá Lál*); Skr. अस्मे, A. Mg. अम्ह, E. H. हम् *we*; Skr. कुष्माण्डः, Mg. कोहले, E. H. कोहरु; Skr. युष्म°, Pr. तुम्ह°, E. H. तोहरा *your.* *Secondly*; as regards the nasal म् *at the end of a word*: 1) in Skr. a) before consonants it *may* become anusvára or the respective class-nasal; b) before vowels it remains म् (M. M. 29). 2) In Pr. a) before consonants it *must* become anusvára; b) before vowels it generally becomes anusvára or remains unchanged; but it may occasionally become anunásika or be elided (Vr. 4, 12. 13. H. C. 1, 23. 24. T. V. 1, 1. 39. 40. Ṣ. C. 1, 1. 39. 40. H. C. 3, 25. T. V. 2, 2. 30). 3) In old Gḍ. it becomes anunásika if preceded by a long vowel, and is elided if preceded by a short one; this is on the whole preserved by M., G. and S.; in the other modern Gḍs., as in H., B., etc., it is always elided. Compare the following examples: Skr. फलं त्रोटयति or फलन्त्रोटयति *he breaks fruit,* Pr. फलं तोडेइ, E. H. फरु तोँडै; Skr. फलं लभते or फलल्ँभते *he takes fruit,* Pr. फलं लहइ or लेइ, E. H. फरु ले; Skr. फलमवहरति *he gathers fruit,* Mg. फलं अवहलइ or फलमवहलइ, E. H. फरु (ओहरै); Skr. दधि *curds,* Pr. दहिं or दहिँ or दहि; Skr. दधिकम्, Pr. दहिअं, M. दहीँ, E. H. दही. This induction clearly proves two things. *Firstly*; that in the main a gradual attenuation of the nasal has taken place. The nasal consonant of the Sanskrit becomes anusvára in Pr., and anunásika in Gḍ., and finally drops of altogether[1]). In one instance, however, a consolidation of the nasal has taken place; namely the Skr. anusvára before स् and ह् has become in Pr. a nasal consonant before ह्, and in Gḍ. before both स् and ह्. *Secondly,* that Gḍ. possesses no anusvára. This fact has been much obscured by the objectionable modern practice of writing and printing the anusvára, instead of the anunásika, as मैं *I* for मैँ, होंठ् *lip* for होँठ्, etc. The correct practice, which is still generally followed by natives of the old school in their writing and printing[2]), is to use the anusvára, just as in Skr. (M. M. 5. 59), only when the full nasal consonant ought to be written and *must be pronounced.* Here, of course, the *dot* is not the real anusvára, but merely a sort of stenographic sign for the class-nasal, used for the sake of more expeditious writing and not affecting the pronunciation in any way. The anunásika, on the other hand, is used whenever a vowel is to be pronounced with a nasal tone. Thus natives write and pronounce either चाँद् *chā̃d* or चंद् *chand,* but not चांद्. It would be well, to revert generally to this older and more correct practice. In the present work the distinction will be carefully observed.

2. *CHAPTER.* EUPHONIC PERMUTATION OF LETTERS.

1) IN PRONUNCIATION AND INFLECTION.

VOWELS.

24. If any word ends in a short अ *ă,* that अ *ă* becomes *quiescent,* that is, it is not pronounced; and such a word may practically be considered as one ending in a consonant. The

1) H. C. (4, 411) and T. V. (3, 4. 67) have a rule on the Ap. Pr. which seems to indicate such an *attenuation* of the final nasal (anusvára); म्रिन्दोऱ् अन्ते। पदान्ते वर्तमानस्य म्रिन्दोऱ् अपभ्रंशे उच्चारलाघवं भवति प्रायः॥ i. e. the anusvára at the end of a word is usually pronounced *slightly.*

2) In writing the anunásika commonly appears as two dots (˙·), the second being merely an abbreviation of the semicircle (˘).

quiescent *ă* will, for the sake of clearness, be indicated in this work by the *viráma* (cf. § 3, note). Thus बाघ् *bágh tiger* (not *bágha*); बात् *bát word*; चलत् *chalat walking*; होइब् *hoïb we shall be.*

Exception. It is always pronounced in the 2nd pers. plur. in conjugation; thus होइब *hŏïba you shall be* (not *hoïb*), बाट *báṭa you are* (not *báṭ*).

25. An antepenultimate आ *á* is always made अ *ă* which with a following इ *ĭ* or उ *ŭ* optionally, yet generally, combines to ए *ai* and औ *au*. Antepenultimate ई *í*, ऊ *ú*, ए *e*, ओ *ŏ* are shortened whenever followed by a consonant (excl. *euphonic* य् and व्). Thus रम्वा *ram'vá* long form of राम् *rám Ráma*; गिध्वा *gidh'vá* of गीध् *gídh vulture*; घोर्वा *ghor'vá* of घोरा *ghorá horse*; बेट्वा *beṭ'vá* of बेटा *beṭá son*; मिट्का *miṭ'ká* of मीटा *míṭá sweet*; नउवा *naŭvá* or नौआ *nauá* of नाऊ *náú barber*; भइया *bhaïyá* or भैया *bhaiyá* of भाई *bhái brother*; बतिया *batiyá* of बात् *bát word*; सुत्लों *sut'lõ* 1st pr. sg. pret. of सूतब् *sútab to sleep*; खइबों *khaïbõ* or खैबों *khaibõ* 1st pr. sg. fut. of खाइब् *kháïb to eat*; करउतों *karaŭtõ* or करौतों *karautõ* 1st pr. sg. pret. conj. of कराइब् *karáïb to cause to do* (for करावत्तों *karáv'tõ*, see § 34); but पीयतों (if) *I drank*; छूअलों or छूवलों *I touched* (see § 65).

Exception. The long vowel of a transitive (or causal) root is never shortened; e. g., मार्लों *már'lõ I killed* of मारब्, caus. of मरब् *to die.*

Note: There are traces of this law in Pr.; e. g., Ap. Pr. तइसो for *ताइसो (H. C. 4, 403. T. V. 3, 3. 10) = Mh. तारिसो, Skr. तादृशः *such.*

26. The short ऐ *ĕ* and ऐ *aĭ* are sometimes reduced to इ *ĭ*, and short ओ *ŏ* and औ *aŭ* to उ *ŭ*; or, more often, all four to अ *ă*. Thus: बेटिया *bĕṭiyá* or बिटिया *biṭiyá daughter*; कहे *kahĕ* or कहि *kahi having said*; गैलेन् *gailĕn* or गैलन् *gailan they went*; गैलैं *gailãĭ* or गैलँ *gailã they went*; लोटिया *lŏṭiyá* or लुटिया *luṭiyá brass vessel*; परोसिया *parŏsiyá* or परसिया *parasiyá neighbouring*; जनोउ *janŏu* or जनउ *janaŭ brahmanical thread*; औ *aŭ* or अ *a and*; औरु *aŭr* or अरु *ar and*; मुमाखी or मौंमाखी *honey-bee*; चवालिस् or चौंवालिस् *forty four*, etc.

Note: There are traces of this law in Pr.; e. g., वेश्रणा or विश्रणा *pain* (Vr. 1, 34); सणिच्छरो *saturday* for Skr. शनैश्चरः, E. H. सनीछर् (H. C. 1, 149. cf. Vr. 1, 38); सत्तुत्तरसयं *one hundred and seven* for Skr. सप्तोत्तरशतम् (Wh. Bh. 427); अन्नुन्नं or अन्नुन्नं *mutual* for Skr. अन्योन्यम् (H. C. 1, 156); सुंडो *drunk* for Skr. शौण्डः (Vr. 1, 44); Ap. कवणु *who* (H. C. 4, 395. cf. 4, 408) for केवणु = केवडु (lit. *of what sort*, see § 438, 2).

27. A final anunásika is often omitted; thus तूँ *tú̃* or तू *tú* *you*; तैँ *taĩ* or तै *tai* *thou*; मैँ *maĩ* or मै *mai* *I*; मेँ *mẽ* or मे *me* *in*; नाँहीँ *nā̃hī̃* or नाँही *nā̃hí* *not*; जानीँ *jánī̃* or जानी *jání* *we know*, etc.

28. To avoid the *hiatus* of two contiguous vowels, य् *y* is inserted after आ *á*, ई *í*; and optionally व् *v*, after ऊ *ú*, ओ *o* and ए *e*. But neither य् nor व् can be inserted, if the second vowel be इ *ĭ* or ई *í*; in this case the hiatus, as a rule, remains, though अइ *aï* may and ईइ *íï* must be contracted to ऐ *ai* and ई *í* respectively, if they are followed by a heavy syllable. Thus: खिया + अल् = खियायल् *khiyáyal it was eaten*; जा + ए = जाये *to go*; पी + अब् = पीयब् *píyab to drink*; पी + ऐ = पीयै *píyai he drinks*; again चूवत् *chúvat* or चूअत् *chúat dripping* from चू + अत्; चूवै *chúvai* or चूऐ *chúai it drips* from चू + ऐ; रोवत् *rovat* or रोअत् *roät weeping* from रो + अत्; रोवै *rovai* or रोए *roai he weeps* from रो + ऐ; लेवै के *levai ke* or लेऐ के *leai ke to take* from ले + ऐ. But खा + ई = खाई *kháí he shall eat*; खा + ईला = खाईला *kháílá we eat*; पी + ईला = पीईला *píílá we drink*; चू + ई = चूई *chúí it will drip*; चू + ईला = चूईला *chúílá we drip*; बोई *boí he will sow*, बोईला *boílá we sow*; देई *deí he will give*, देईला *deílá we give*; again खइबै *khaïbai* or खैबै *khaibai we shall eat* from खा + इबै; पीबै *píbai we shall drink* from पी + इबै; खाइब् *kháïb we shall eat* from खा + इब्; पीइत् *piït* (if) *we drank* from पी + इत्; चूइबै *chúïbai* and चूइब् *chúïb we shall drip*; बोइबै *boïbai* and बोइब् *boïb we shall sow*; लेइत् *leït* (if) *we took* from ले + इत्.

Exception 1. The suff. ई (3. pr. sg. fut. ind.) may optionally combine with a preceding ई to ई; thus पी + ई = पीई *píí* or पी *pí he will drink*; जी + ई = जी *jí* or जीई *jíí he will live*.

Exception 2. The initial अ of the suffs. of the fut. ind. (viz. अब्यों etc.), of the pres. part. (अत्) and of the pret. conj. (viz. अतों etc.) combines with a preceding आ or ए, and with ओ of the verb हो *to become* to आ, ए, ओ respectively; thus खा + अब्यों = खाब्यों *khábõ I shall eat*; दे + अब्यों = देब्यों *debõ I shall give*; हो + अब्यों = होब्यों *hobõ I shall be*; खा + अत् = खात् *khát eating*; दे + अत् = देत् *det giving*; हो + अत् = होत् *hot being.*

SINGLE CONSONANTS.

29. र् *r* is generally substituted for ड़् *ṛ*; thus E. H. तोरै *he breaks* for W. H. तोड़े; E. H. जोरै *he joins* for W. H. जोड़े; E. H. बारी *garden* for W. H. बाड़ी; E. H. जोरू *wife* for W. H. जोड़ू; E. H. नारी *artery* for W. H. नाड़ी, etc. Sometimes also ह् *rh* for ढ़् *ṛh*; as E. H. बार्है *bárhai he grows* for बाढ़े (W. H. बढ़े); E. H. गार्है *gárhai he beats into form* for W. H. गाढ़े.

30. र् *r* is almost universally substituted for a non-initial ल् *l*; thus E. H. फर् *fruit* for W. H. फल्; E. H. गारी *abuse* for W. H. गाली; E. H. चरै *he walks* for W. H. चले; E. H. डारै *he throws* for W. H. डाले; E. H. करिया *black* for कलिया, etc.; but never रोग् for लोग् *people*, etc.

Exception. The ल् of the suff. अल of the past tense *never* changes; e. g., गयल् *gone*, not गयर्; पढ़लों *I read*, not पढ़रों.

31. ल् *l* and न् *n*, if initial, are sometimes interchanged; thus ल् for न् in लीला *dark blue* or नीला (Skr. नील); and न् for ल् in नोन् *salt* or लोन् (Skr. लवण, cf. Vr. 1, 7); नंगोट् *waistcloth* or लंगोट् (Skr. लिङ्गपट्टः, Mg. लिंगवट्टे) [1]).

32. ह् *h* may be dropped; 1) always final, thus जेह् कै or जे कै *of whom*; ओह् कै or ओ कै *of that*; एलह् or एल *aila you came*; करतह् or करत *karata* (if) *you did.* 2) sometimes medial (see § 126); as ताँ or तहाँ *there*, काँ or कहाँ *where*, जाँ or जहाँ *wheresoever*, मे or मेँ or माहीँ *within*; के or (O. H.) काहीँ *towards*; मराठा or मरहठा *a Maráthá*; सगा *full brother* for *सगहा (see § 120); दिवा *day* for *दिवहा (see § 134, note).

---

1) Not from नंग, Skr. नग्न *naked*, as Bs. I, 248; the original इ of लिंग° is preserved in the ए of B. नेंगुटि.

33. A medial व् *v*, followed by इ or ई, is always elided; and further इ (but not ई) combines with a preceding आ *á* (or अ *ă* by § 25) to ए *ai*; thus पाव् + इबो॑ (= प + इबो॑) = पैबो॑ *I shall find*; आव् + इबे = ऐबे *thou wilt come*; खियाव् + इबह् = खियैबह् *you will cause to eat.* But पाव् + ई = पाई *he will find*; आव् + ई॑ = आई॑ *we come*; खियाव् + ईला = खियाईला *we cause to eat.*

34. A medial य् *y* or व् *v*, containing a *neutral* vowel (see § 5, a), are vocalized to इ *i* and उ *u* respectively, and optionally combine with a preceding अ *ă* (or originally आ *á* by § 25) to ए *ai* or औ *au*. Thus गयल् + ऐस् (= गय॑लेस् *gay'lés*) = गइलेस् *gaïlés* or गैलेस् *gailés thou wentest*; पिया + अल्यूँ (= पियय॑ल्यूँ *piyay'lyú̃*) = पियइल्यूँ *piyaïlyú̃* or पियैल्यूँ *piyailyú̃ I could be drunk*; कराव् + अतो॑ (= करव॑तो॑ *karav'tõ*) = करउतो॑ *karaütõ* or करौतो॑ *karautõ* (if) *I caused to do*; चराव् + अलेस् (= चरव॑लेस् *charav'lés*) = चरउलेस् *charaülés* or चरौलेस् *charaulés he caused to walk.*

35. *Affinities.* There are instances of this change in Pr.; thus आइरिओ or आयरिओ = Skr. आचार्यः (H. C. 1, 73); केलं for *कइलं for कयलं = Skr. कदलम् (H. C. 1, 167); बोरं for *बउरं for *बवरं = Skr. बदरम् (H. C. 1, 170); ओसरइ for *अउसरइ for अवसरइ = Skr. अपसरति (H. C. 1, 172); पाउरणं = Skr. प्रावरणम् (H. C. 1, 175); उसहो or वसहो = Skr. वृषभः (H. C. 1, 133); also in inflexion as जेदि = *जइदि = Skr. जयति; होदि = *हउदि = Skr. भवति, etc.; see § 18, note 3, p. 18).

COMPOUND CONSONANTS.

36. क्ष् *ksh* is always pronounced and written छ् *chh*; thus छोटा *chhoṭá small* (Skr. क्षुद्रकः?); छत॑री *chhat'rí a chhatri* (Skr. क्षत्रियः); छमा *chhamá forgiveness* (Skr. क्षमा *kshamá*).

37. ज्ञ् *jñ* is always pronounced and generally written ग्य् *gy*; as ग्यान् *gyán knowledge* (Skr. ज्ञान *jñana*); आग्या *ágyá command* (Skr. आज्ञा *ájñá*).

38. ंह् *ṃh* is always pronounced and generally written ंघ् *ṅgh* (or ङ्घ *ṅgh*); as संघ् *saṅgh collection* (Skr. संहः *saṃhaḥ*); संघात् *saṅghát collection* (Skr. संहातः *saṃhataḥ*); सिंघ् *siṅgh lion* (Skr. सिंहः); सिंघासन *siṅghásan thron* (Skr. सिंहासनम्), etc. (see § 159).

39. ंस् *ṃs* is always pronounced and written ंस् *ns* (i. e. न्स *ns*, cf. §§ 13. 23); as बंस् (or बन्स्) *bans race* (Skr. वंशः *vaṃṣaḥ*); बंसीधर् (or बन्सीधर्) *bansidhar a name* (lit. *flute-holder*, Skr. वंशीधरः *vaṃṣidharaḥ*); हिंसा (or हिन्सा) *hinsá slaughter* (Skr. हिंसा *hiṃsá*); हंस् (or हन्स्) *hans goose* (Skr. हंसः *haṃsaḥ*), etc. (see § 159).

Note: It has become the fashion in modern times, to resuscitate the writing of ञ and ंह्; but the practice of the older, native school is more correct and preferable.

2) IN DERIVATION [1]).

a) CHANGES OF FINAL SOUNDS.

40. *In limine,* it should be observed, that Skr. and Pr. nouns pass into Gḍ. in the form of the nominative singular, the final sound of which undergoes the following changes:

41. A *visarga* or *anusvára* is dropped, and a preceding अ becomes quiescent; thus E. H. पुतर् *son* (a tats.) for Skr. पुत्रः; E. H. कवि *poët* for Skr. कविः; E. H. गुरु *teacher* for Skr. गुरुः; E. H. परगट् *manifest,* Skr. प्रकटम्; E. H. बन् *forest,* Pr. वणं (Vr. 4, 12), Skr. वनम्; E. H. सै or सय् *hundred,* Mg. सदं (Wb. Bh. 427), Skr. शतम्; E. H. खेत् *field,* Pr. खेत्तं (H. C. 2, 17 छेत्तं), Skr. क्षेत्रम्; E. H. बारि *water,* Pr. वारिँ or वारिं or वारि (cf. H. C. 3, 25), Skr. वारि; E. H. मधु *honey,* Pr. मधु or मधुँ or मधुं (cf. H. C. 3, 25), Skr. मधु, see § 23.

42. Pr. masc. or fem. आ or अ becomes quiescent अ; thus E. H. नीँद् *sleep,* Ap. निद्द (H. C. 4, 418), Pr. णिद्दा (Vr. 1, 12), Skr. निद्रा (fem.); E. H. बाह् *arm* (also बाँह्), Ap. बाह (H. C. 4, 329). Pr. बाहा (H. C. 1, 36. 4, 329), Skr. बाहा (fem.); E. H. बात् *word, event,* Pr. वत्ता (Vr. 3, 24), Skr. वार्त्ता (fem.); E. H. राय् *prince,* Ap. राय (H. C. 4, 402), Pr. राया (H. C. 3, 136) or राआ (Vr. 5, 36), Skr. राजा (masc.).

43. Pr. masc. or fem. ई or इ becomes इ or quiescent अ; thus E. H. दीठ् or दीठि *sight,* Ap. दिट्ठि (H. C. 4, 330) or Pr. दिट्ठी

1) This list of sandhi-laws lays no claim to completeness, a quality unattainable in the present state of our knowledge of Gḍ. derivation; but it contains, perhaps, all the more important and more general phenomena.

(H. C. 1, 128), Skr. दृष्टिः (fem.); E. H. बहिन् or बहिनि *sister*, Ap. बहिणि (H. C. 4, 351) or Pr. बहिणी (H. C. 2, 126), Skr. भगिनी (cf. § 132, note); E. H. आग् or आगि *fire* (fem.), Pr. अग्गी (Vr. 5, 18. fem.), Skr. अग्निः (masc.); E. H. आँख् or आँखि *eye* (fem.), Ap. अक्खि (cf. H. C. 4, 396), Pr. अच्छी (Vr. 4, 20. fem.), Skr. अक्षि (neutr.); E. H. मुन् or मुनि *sage*, Ap. मुणि (cf. H. C. 4, 341) or Pr. मुणी (cf. H. C. 3, 125), Skr. मुनिः (masc.); E. H. बिहफै or बिफै *thursday*, Pr. विहप्फई (H. C. 1, 138), Skr. वृहस्पतिः (masc.); E. H. ज्ञान् or ज्ञानि *sage*, Pr. ज्ञाणी, Skr. ज्ञानी (masc.).

44. Pr. masc. or fem. ऊ or उ becomes उ or quiescent अ; thus E. H. तरु or तरु *tree*, Ap. तरु (H. C. 4, 370), Pr. तरू (H. C. 1, 177), Skr. तरुः (masc.); E. H. पाँसु *rib*, Pr. पंसू (H. C. 1, 26), Skr. पर्शुः (masc.); E. H. तन् or तनु *body*, Ap. तणु (H. C. 4, 401) or Pr. तणू (cf. Vr. 5, 18), Skr. तनुः (fem.); E. H. पतोहू or पतोहु *daughter-in-law*, Pr. पुत्तवहू (cf. Spt. 122), Skr. पुत्रवधूः; E. H. सास् or सासु *mother-in-law*, Pr. सासू (Spt. 339), Skr. श्वश्रूः.

45. Pr. masc. ए or इ becomes ऐ *ě* or इ or quiescent अ; thus E. H. माग् *road*, Mg. मग्गि or मग्गे (Mchh. 96, 20), Skr. मार्गः; E. H. नर् *man*, Mg. नलि or नले (H. C. 4, 288), Skr. नरः; E. H. काम्, Mg. कम्मि or कम्मे (Wb. Bh. 420. masc.), Skr. कर्म (neutr.); E. H. करत् *doing*, Mg. कलंति or कलेंति or कलेंते (Mchh. 108, 18), Skr. कुर्वन्; E. H. रखल् or रखिल् *kept*, Mg. लक्खिदि or लक्खिदे (Mchh. 112, 6), Skr. रक्षितः. Also in locatives; as E. H. लाग् or लागि *till*, Ap. लग्गि or लग्गे (H. C. 4, 334), Skr. लग्ने; and in conjunct participles, as E. H. कह् or कहि or कहे *kahě having said*, A. Mg. कहे (see Wb. Bh. 435) or Mh. कहिअ, Skr. कथित्वा (see § 490, 491).

46. *Affinities.* The termin. ए or इ is Mg. Pr.; the Mh.-Sr. is ओ and Ap. उ (H. C. 4, 332) and both become in W. Gd. उ or quiescent अ; in O. H. and especially in S. the Ap. उ is still preserved; thus W. H. नर्, O. H. and S. नरु (Tr. 33) *man*, Ap. नरु (H. C. 4, 362) or णरु (K. I. 9) or Pr. नरो or णरो (H. C. 1, 229); W. H. काम्, S. कमु (Tr. 33) *work*, Ap. कम्मु, Pr. कम्मो (Vr. 4, 18); W. H. माग्, O. H. मागु, S. मगु *road*, Ap. मग्गु (H. C. 4, 357), Pr. मग्गो (Vr. 3, 50); Kn. करत्, Br. करतु *doing*, Ap. करंतु,

Sr. करंतो or करेंतो. — It will be observed that just as Mh.-Sr. ओ is reduced to Ap. उ, so Mg. ए is reduced to इ. This is expressly stated by Vr. 11, 10. K. I. 12 (cf. Ls. 393. 402) and Md. 12, 20 (fol. 49[a]) सो पुंस्यदेदितो। पुंसि सौ परे अकार एदितौ स्याताम्। i. e., masc. nouns in ă have a nom. sing. in e or i. The form in इ (like that in उ) was probably Ap. Mg. It only occurs exceptionally in the Bhag. (see Wb. Bh. 416). H. C. (4, 287) and T. V. (3, 2. 30) do not notice it; which, perhaps, shows that Ap. Mg. इ was pronounced like short ए ĕ (cf. H. C. 4, 410. and see § 6). — In the Gds., especially in their literary forms, the final इ and उ generally become quiescent, and hence are omitted in *writing*, and thence again have come to be practically identical with quiescent अ. — Occasionally E. H. has Ap. Sr. forms; as घाव् *wound*, Ap. घाउ (H. C. 4, 346), Sr. घाओ, Skr. घातः.

47. Pr. masc. अए becomes आ; thus E. H. घोरा *horse*, Mg. घोडए, Skr. घोटकः; E. H. भला *good*, Ap. भल्ला (H. C. 4, 351), Mg. भल्लए, Skr. भद्रकः; E. H. घरा *pitcher*, Mg. घडए, Skr. घटकः.

48. *Affinities.* The term. अए is Mg.; the Mh.-Sr. is अओ, and Ap. अउ; the latter contracts in the W. and N. Gd. to ओ or (Br.) औ; thus Br. घोड़ौ, भलौ, घड़ौ; Mw., G., S., N. घोड़ो, भलो, घड़ो; only P. forms an exception in having the E. H. term. आ, and hence it has got into Urdú and H. H.; thus P., U., H. H. घोड़ा, भला, घड़ा. Again M., B. and O. have आ like E. H. It will be seen, then, that while E. and S. Gd. have आ, W. and N. Gd. have ओ or औ; again Mg. Pr. has अए, Mh.-Sr. Pr. has अओ; hence it may be concluded, that the E. and S. Gd. termin. आ is a modification of the Mg. Pr. अए, while the W. and N. Gd. ओ or औ is a modification of the Mh.-Sr. अओ. The Ap. Pr. has both अओ and अउ (H. C. 4, 332). Probably the Br. औ is a contraction of the Ap. अउ; as Ap. भल्लउ, Br. भलौ *good*; while the Mw., G., S., N. ओ is a contraction of the Ap. अओ, by the quiescence of अ; as Ap. भल्लओ, Mw., G., S. भलो (i. e. भल्लओ). The Ap. Mg. form, corresponding to the Ap. Sr. अउ, would be अइ (cf. § 46); this is still preserved in the Psh. ए (Tr. J. G. O. S. XXI, 37), as Psh. तले *talai bottom*,

E. H. तड़ा or तला, S. तलो, Ap. Mg. तलइ or तलए, Ap. Sr. तलउ or तलश्रो, Skr. तलकः; but the Psh. has also occasionally the E. Gḍ. form आ; as Psh. लगिआ *applied*, P. लगिआ, Bs. and H. H. लगा, Ap. Mg. लग्गिअइ or लग्गिदए, Skr. लग्नकः (lit. *लगितकः), Ap. लग्गिअउ, Br. लग्यौ, Sr. लग्गिअओ, S. लगिओ or लगो. The Psh. ऐ *ai*, then, corresponds to Br. औ *au*; being contractions of (Ap.) Mg. अइ *aĭ* and Ap. (Sr.) अउ *aŭ* respectively; on the other hand, E. and S. Gḍ. आ corresponds to W. and N. Gḍ. ओ, being contractions of the Mg. अए and Sr. अओ respectively, by the quiescence of अ. It appears, then, that the termin. आ is distinctly Mg., and merely a (comparatively modern) modification of the old Mg. ए; and not, as it is usually assumed, of the old Sr. ओ. There are, however, some traces of the term. आ in Pr.; moreover, they seem to be distinctly connected with Mg. Pr. *Firstly*: Vr. (11; 17) expressly gives शिआला as a Mg. by-form of शिआले *jackal* (E. H. सियाड़). *Secondly*: Vr. (11, 13) and K. I. (Ls. 393) state that the Mg. vocative ends in आ, and Mḍ. (12, 21. 22. fol 49[a]) adds also ए, as चेलए or चेलआ (E. H. चेड़ा) *oh! disciple*[1]). That is, the nom.

1) Vr. 11, 17 शृगालस्य शिआला शिआले शिआलका:॥ and Mḍ. 12, 21 एदोतौ सम्बोधने प्रायः।पुंसि सम्बोधने एदोतौ स्यातां।हे वअंसे।हे वअंसो।प्रायो ग्रहणात्। हे गोमिका।हे भट्टिदालाआ॥ i. e., the voc. of masc. nouns in *ă* ends in *e* or *o*, as, *he voaṃse, he voaṃso* (Skr. वयस्य); and Mḍ. 12, 22 आदाक्षेपे। पुंसि सम्बुद्धौ अकाद आ स्याद् आक्षेपे। अले ले च्चेलआ। चकारात्। च्चेलए। च्चेलओ॥ i. e., the voc. of masc. nouns in *ă*, in the sense of rebuke, ends in *á*; also in *e* and *o*. Neither H. C. nor T. V. give these rules in their chapter on Mg; but they have an allusion to the voc. in आ in their chapt. on the Ap. (H. C. 4, 330. T. V. 3, 4. 1); e. g., ढोल्ला मइँ तुहुँ वारिआ मा करु दीहा माणु; this is Bs. ढोला मैँ तूँ के बारा मत् कर दीहा मान् i. e., lit. boy! I have forbidden you, do not make long sulkiness!; again बिट्टीए मइँ भणिअ तुहुँ मा करु वंकी दिट्ठि, = Bs. बेटी मैँ भनि तूँ के मत् कर बाँकी दीठ् i. e., lit. daughter! I have told you, do not make a coquettish look. It is to be noted, that K. I. (16. 18. cf. Ls. 450) gives both आ and ए as the termin. of the voc. in Ap. Pr. In the present day, E. H. has a voc. in आ, but W. H. in ए; as E. H. हे चेड़ा, W. H. हे चेले *oh disciple*. This, perhaps, explains the silence of H. C. and T. V. as to the Mg. nom. and voc. in आ; they have relegated it into their chapt. on Ap., in which as, perhaps, indicated in H. C. 4, 447

sing. in ए is used in Mg. as voc., and the form in आ is but a slightly worn down by-form of the nom. (as usual with Pr. voc., cf. H. C. 3, 38. T. V. 2, 2. 42 [1]). The latter form, which was at first (in Mg.) confined to the voc.-nom., is in Gḍ. extended to the nom. generally. *Thirdly*: H. C. gives several instances of a nom. in आ in the Ap. Pr.; e. g., भल्ला हुआ तु मारिआ बहिणि महारा कंतु। (4, 351); this is A. Mg. Ap.; the corresponding Sr. Ap. is in कंतु महारउ हलि सहिए निच्छइं रूसेइ जासु। (4, 358); the former is Bs. (a kind of semi E. Gḍ., see Introd.) भला हुआ तु मारा बहिन् गोरा काँत्, i. e., it has happened well, sister, that my husband has killed; the other is Br. (W. H.) काँत् मेरौ सहेली निहचै रूसे जासु i. e. surely friend! with whom my husband is angry [2]).

49. Pr. masc. इए and उए become ई and ऊ respectively; thus E. H. तेली *oilman,* Mg. तेल्लिए (cf. H. C. 2, 98), Skr. तैलिकः; E. H. माली *gardener,* Mg. मालिए, Skr. मालिकः; E. H. बहिनोई (W. H. भौनाई) *sister's husband,* Mg. बहिणिवइए, Skr. भगिनीपतिकः; E. H. नाती *grandchild,* Pr. नत्तिओ (H. C. 1, 137), Skr. नप्तृकः; E. H. भाई *brother,* Pr. *भाइओ (cf. H. C. 1, 137), Skr. भातृकः; again E. H. बिछू *scorpion,* Mg. विंछुए (Vr. 1, 15. 3, 41, T. V. 1, 4. 18), Skr. वृश्चिकः; E. H. लड्डू *a kind of sweetmeat,* Mg. लड्डुए, Skr. लड्डुकः; E. H. गोहूँ *wheat* (H. H. गेहूँ), Ap. Mg. गोहुँवे (cf. H. C. 4, 397), Mg. गोहुमे, Skr. गोधुमः.

50. *Affinities.* These contractions into ई and ऊ are common to all Gḍs.; but in W. and N. Gḍ. they arise from the Mh.-Sr. termin. इओ and उओ respectively; as W. H. तेली, Sr. तेल्लिओ; W. H. माली, Sr. मालिओ; W. H. भौनाइ, Sr. भामिणिवइओ (cf. H. C. 1, 190); W. H. बिछू, Skr. विंछुओ; W. H. लड्डू, Sr. लड्डुओ; W. H. गोहूँ, Sr. गोहुमो. But M. and S. have भाऊ *brother,* Dk. भाउए or भाउओ

and T. V. 3, 4. 71, rules of various Ap. dialects would seem to be mixed up (see also Ps. IX).

1) The voc. in Mh.-Sr. Pr. is either like the nom. हे चेल्लो or worn down हे चेल्ल; so in Mg. either like nom. हे चेल्ले, or worn down हे चेल्ला.

2) It is also like P., which shares the nom. in आ with E. Gḍ., भला होइआ जो मारिआ बहिन् मेरा काँत्।.

(H. C. 1, 131); नातू *grandson*, Pr. नत्तुश्रो (H. C. 1, 137). This contraction as well as those noted in the following paragraphs, may be explained by the apparently Pr. tendency of lengthening the antepenultimate इ (see Wb. Bh. 438) and उ; while at the same time the final ए and श्रो have a tendency in the Ap. to be shortened to इ and उ (see § 46), and in Gḍ. to be cast off altogether (see § 45); thus Mg. तेल्लिए, Ap. *तेल्लिइ, *तेल्लीइ, Gḍ. तेली, Sr. तेल्लिश्रो, Ap. तेल्लिउ, *तेल्लीउ, Gḍ. तेली; or Mg. लड्डुए, Ap. *लड्डुइ, *लड्डूइ, Gḍ. लड्डू, Sr. लड्डुश्रो, Ap. लड्डुउ, *लड्डूउ, Gḍ. लड्डू (cf. § 65, note). There are some traces of this contraction in Pr.; thus Pr. पवासू *traveller* (T. V. 1, 2. 48) or पावासू (H. C. 1, 44. T.V. 1, 2. 10) or पावासुश्रो (H. C. 1, 95) = Skr. प्रवासी (or प्रवासकः); Pr. सव्वण्णू *omniscient* (H. C. 1, 56) for *सव्वण्णुश्रो (= Skr. सर्वज्ञकः); and other words in ण्णू.

51. Pr. fem. इश्रा and उश्रा become ई and ऊ respectively; thus E. H. घोड़ी *mare*, Pr. घोडिश्रा, Skr. घोटिका; E. H. माटी *earth* (W. H. मिट्टी), Pr. मट्टिश्रा (H. C. 2, 29), Skr. मृत्तिका; E. H. लाठी *club*, Pr. लट्ठिश्रा (cf. H. C. 1, 247), Skr. यष्टिका; E. H. मउसी *mother's sister*, Pr. माउसिश्रा (H. C. 1, 134. 2, 142), Skr. मातृष्वसृका; E. H. माई *mother*, Pr. *माइश्रा (see § 63), Skr. मातृका; again E. H. पतोहू *son's wife*, Pr. पुत्तवहुश्रा (cf. Spt. 35), Skr. पुत्रवधुका; E. H. बालू *sand*, Pr. वालुश्रा, Skr. बालुका.

52. *Affinities.* Here all Gḍs. agree; as do also all Prs. But M. has माऊ *mother*, Pr. माउश्रा (H. C. 1, 131), Skr. मातृका. The steps of change are probably these (see § 42); Pr. घोडिश्रा, Ap. घोडिश्र (H. C. 4, 330) or *घोडीश्र, Gḍ. घोड़ी; Pr. वालुश्रा, Ap. वालुश्र or *वालूश्र, Gḍ. वालू, etc.

53. Pr. neut. श्रश्रं, इश्रं and उश्रं become श्रा, ई and ऊ respectively; thus E. H. सोना *gold*, Pr. सोण्णश्रं (cf. Spt. 194) or सुवण्णश्रं (cf. H. C. 1, 26), Skr. सुवर्णकम्; E. H. तामा *copper*, Mg. *तम्मश्रं (see § 18) or तम्बश्रं (cf. Vr. 3, 53), Skr. ताम्रकम्; E. H. लोहा *iron*, Pr. लोहश्रं, Skr. लोहकम्; again E. H. घी *clarified butter*, Pr. घिश्रं (cf. Spt. 22), Skr. घृतम्; E. H. पानी *water*, Pr. पाणिश्रं (Vr. 1, 18), Skr. पानीयम्; E. H. दही *curds*, Pr. दहिश्रं, Skr. दधिकम्; E. H. मोती

pearl, Pr. मोत्तिअं, Skr. मौक्तिकम्; again E. H. आँसू *tear*, Pr. अंसुअं (cf. H. C. 1, 26), Skr. अश्रुकम्; E. H. जू *yoke*, Pr. जुअं, Skr. युगम्; E. H. आलू *potato*, Pr. आलुअं, Skr. आलुकम्.

54. *Affinities*. As regards the forms in आ, B., O. and also P. agree with E. H.; thus B., O., E. H. तामा, P. ताँबा. M. has एँ; as ताँबेँ. The M. nouns are neuter, but the corresponding E. Gḍ. ones are masc.; compare the masc. forms in § 47. In Mg. Pr. neuter nouns either end in अअं or (becoming masc.) in अए (cf. Wb. Bh. 416. Ls. 399). From the Mg. अअं or with the favorite euph. य्, अयं, which form still occurs occasionally in O. H., arises the contracted M. एँ. From the Mg. masc. अए arises probably the E. Gḍ. आ. On the other hand, the corresponding termin. in G. is उँ or उ; as ताँबुँ or ताँबु; in Mw. ओँ or ओ, as ताँबोँ or ताँबो; in Br. औँ or औ (or also आ); in S. ओ, as टामो. The forms with anunásika are neuter, those without it are masculine. These W. Gḍ. forms have arisen from the Ap. (Sr.) Pr., which has the neut. termin. अउँ (H. C. 4, 354. T. V. 3, 4. 26). This contracts in W. H. to औँ or ओँ, and is shortened in G. to उँ. By dropping the final anunásika, the neuters would, naturally, become masc., through identity of termination; see § 48. This masculinizing tendency is seen already in the Ap. Pr., where the neut. termin. अं sometimes becomes masc. उ (Ls. 460. 476. H. C. 4, 331. 445; as m. जलु *water* for n. जलं, cf. H. C. 4, 395), and similarly neut. अउँ would become masc. अउ. As regards the forms in ई and ऊ, they are alike in all Gḍs., except in M., which adds a final anunásika (as पाणीँ *water*, आँसूँ *tear*) and treats them as neuters, while the other Gḍs., having dropped the original anunásika, treat them as masculines.

b) CHANGES OF MEDIAL SOUNDS.

α) SINGLE VOWELS.

55. अ *becomes* इ *or* ई; rarely; thus E. H. पिंजरा *cage*, A. Mg. पंजलअं (cf. Spt. 225), Skr. पंजरकम् (also पिंजरकम्? M. W. 572, 3); E. H. फिरफिर *splashing*, Skr. कर्करम्; E. H. सुमिरन् *memory*, A. Mg.

सुमलणां (cf. H. C. 4, 426), Skr. स्मरणाम् ; E. H. पिचोतर्से *one hundred and five,* A. Mg. पंचुत्तरसयं (cf. Wb. Bh. 427), Skr. पंचोत्तरशतम् ; E. H. चिरई *sparrow,* Pr. चडइग्रा (cf. H. C. 4, 445?), Skr. चटकिका; E. H. खियावै *he feeds,* Pr. खयावइ, Skr. खादयति (*खदापयति); E. H. छिन् *moment,* Pr. छणो (H. C. 2. 20), Skr. क्षणः ; E. H. फिटकरी *alum,* Mg. *फट्टिक्कालिग्रा (or *फिट्टिक्कालिग्रा cf. H. C. 4, 177), Skr. स्फटिकाणिका; E. H. निनानबे *ninety nine,* Pr. *नवाणवुई, Skr. नवनवतिः (see § 397); E. H. छियालिस् *forty six* for O. छयालिस् (see § 152). Especially before ह; as E. H. छिहत्तर् *seventy six,* Mg. छहत्तलि (cf. Wb. Bh. 426), Skr. षट्सप्ततिः ; E. H. छिलोतर्से *one hundred and six,* A. Mg. छलुत्तलसयं (cf. Wb. Bh. 425), Skr. षडुत्तरशतम् ; E. H. लिहल् *taken,* Mg. *लहिदे [1]), Skr. लब्धः (*लभितः); E. H. दिहल् *given,* Skr. दत्तः ; E. H. लिहिस् *thou tookst,* O. H. लिहेस्, Ap. Pr. *लहिग्रसि, Skr. लब्धोऽसि (*लभितोऽसि); E. H. लिहिन् *they took,* O. H. लिहेन्, Ap. Pr. *लहिग्रहिं, Pr. *लहिग्रंति, Skr. लब्धाः सन्ति (in active sense); E. H. दिहिस् *thou gavest,* दिहिन् *they gave*; E. H. किहिस् *thou didst,* O. H. किहेस् for *कएस्, Ap. *करिग्रसि, Skr. कृतोऽसि [2]); E. H. किहिन् *they did.* Again ई in तीसी *flax,* Skr. ग्रतसी (cf. § 172).

Note: W. H. गिने *he counts,* Pr. गणइ (H. C. 4, 358), Skr. गणयति; W. H. छिमा *forgiveness,* Skr. क्षमा; W. H. पिछलो or पछिलो, Ap. Pr. पच्छिल्लउ (Skr. पश्चकः); but E. H. गनै, छमा and पाछिल् or पछिला.

56. ग्र *becomes* उ *or* ऊ; very rarely; as E. H. पुग्राल् *straw,* Skr. पलालो; E. H. मूछ् (also मोंछ्, see § 57) *mustache,* Pr. मंसू (H. C. 2, 86 or *मंछू? cf. H. C. 1, 265), Skr. श्मश्रु; E. H. खुजली *itch,* Ap. Pr. *खज्जुडिग्र (Skr. खर्जूः).

Note: W. H. उंगली *finger,* Pr. ग्रंगुलिग्रा (cf. H. C. 4, 333), Skr. ग्रङ्गुलिका; O. H. सुगन् *bird* (Chand), Ap. Pr. सगुणु, Skr. शकुनः; but E. H. ग्रंगुरी, सगुन्.

---

1) cf. Spt. 146 लहिऊण = Skr. *लभित्वा or लब्ध्वा; and P. past part. लइग्रा.

2) Regarding the forms लिहल्, लिहिस्, लिहिन्, किहिस्, etc. see §§ 307. 501. 503.

57. अ *becomes* ए, ऐ, ओ or ए, ऐ, ओ; rarely; E. H. मेहरू (or मेहरी or मेहरारू) *woman*, Pr. महिला (Spt. 48), Skr. महिला; E. H. केवारू (or केवारा) *door*, Pr. कवाडो, Skr. कपाटः; E. H. चोँच *beak*, Pr. *चंचू, Skr. चञ्चुः; E. H. मोँछ *mustache* (see § 56), Pr. मंसू (H. C. 2, 86), Skr. श्मश्रु; E. H. सेँध *hole* (in a wall), Pr. संधी (cf. H. C. 4, 430), Skr. सन्धिः; and others see § 148.

58. इ *becomes* अ; rarely; E. H. ऐतना *this much*, Mg. एत्तिलए (cf. H. C. 2, 157), Skr. इयतकः, cf. S. एतिरो, G. एटलो; E. H. तेतना *so much*, Mg. तेत्तिलए, Skr. तावत्तिकः; E. H. जेतना *how much soever*, Mg. जेत्तिलए, Skr. यावत्तिकः; E. H. केतना, Mg. केत्तिलए, Skr. कियत्तिकः; E. H. लंगोटू *waistcloth*, Mg. लिंगवट्टे, Skr. लिङ्गपट्टः; E. H. धरती *earth*, Mg. धलित्तिआ, Skr. धरित्रिका; E. H. पोरसा *fathom*, A. Mg. पउलिसअं (cf. H. C. 1, 111. 4, 287), Skr. पौरुषकम्; and optionally E. H. परखै or परिखै *he examines*, Mg. पलिक्खइ, Skr. परीक्षते; E. H. °अलू or °इलू *suffix of past part.*, Mg. इदे, Skr. इतः; e. g., E. H. पढलू or पढिलू *read*, Mg. पढिदे, Skr. पठितः; E. H. °अबू or °इबू *suffix of infinit.*, Ap. इव्वं (K. I. 50. Ls. 468), Skr. इतव्यम्; e. g., E. H. पढबू or पढिबू *to read*, Ap. पढिव्वं, Skr. पठितव्यम्.

Note: Also W. H. गहरू *deep*, Pr. गहिरं (H. C. 1, 101), Skr. गभीरम्; W. H. बहरू *dumb*, Pr. बहिरो (H. C. 1, 187), Skr. बधिरः; W. H. कलेसू *trouble*, Pr. किलेसो (H. C. 2, 106), Skr. क्लेशः; W. H. हरसू *joy*, Pr. हरिसो (H. C. 2, 105), Skr. हर्षः; W. H. बरसू *rain, year*, Pr. वरिसं, Skr. वर्षम्; W. H. फरसू *touch*, Pr. फरिसो (cf. H. C. 4, 182), Skr. स्पर्शः. But E. H. गहिरू, बहिरू, किलेसू, हरिसू, बरिसू, फरिसू. The Pr. form एत्तिलं or (in some MSS.) एत्तिल्लं is probably a curtailment of एत्तिअलं, composed of एत्तिअ and pleon. suff. ल (or ल्ल), and curtailed just as Ap. इव्व from Mh.-Sr. इअव्व, e. g., Ap. पढिव्वं for Sr. पढिअव्वं.

59. इ or ई *becomes* उ or ऊ; very rarely and optionally; E. H. पहरू or पहरी or पहरा *watchman*, Mg. पहली, Skr. प्रहरी; E. H. बुंदी or बिंदी or बुंदा or बूँदू *drop*, Pr. बिंदू (cf. H. C. 1, 34), Skr. बिन्दुः.

Note: Compare Pr. पवासू (H. C. 1, 44) for Skr. प्रवासी *sojourner*.

60. उ *becomes* अ; rarely; thus E. H. आपनू or आपुनू *own*, Pr. अप्पुल्लं (H. C. 2, 163), Skr. आत्मीयम् (or आत्मभवम्), cf. M. आपला,

G. द्रापणो; E. H. पतोहू *son's wife*, Pr. पुत्तवहू, Skr. पुत्रवधूः; E. H. उउगनू *stars*, Mg. उडुगणो (cf. H. C. 1, 202), Skr. उडुगणाः; E. H. कुटकी *a kind of medicine*, Pr. *कटुकिआ, Skr. कटुकिका; E. H. ठथा *troop*, Pr. *तुत्थअं, Skr. यूथकम्; E. H. सामहूँ or समहूँ *in front of*, Ap. सम्मुहहु, Skr. सम्मुखे (H. H. साम्हने); optionally कपूत or कुपूत *bad son*, Mg. *कुपुत्त, Skr. कुपुत्रः; also E. H. बूँदू or बुंदा *drop*, Mg. विंदुए, Skr. विन्दुकः.

Note: Also W. H. उंगलो *finger*, Pr. अंगुलिआ, Skr. अंगुलिका; W. H. बिजली, Pr. विज्जुलिआ (Vr. 4, 26), Skr. विद्युत्; W. H. कूकरू *dog*, Pr. कुक्कुरो, Skr. कुक्कुरः; W. H. जाँबनू *roseapple tree*, Pr. जंबुलो, Skr. जम्बुलः; W. H. समके *he understands*, Pr. संबुज्झइ, Skr. सम्बुध्यते; Mw. कणू or कुणू *who* (see § 438, 2); but E. H. अंगुरी, बिजुरी, कुक्कुर, जामुन, समुके, कौनू. As regards E. H. आपनू *own*, the change of उ to अ, and लू to नू appears already in Pr. अप्पणयं (H. C. 2, 153. 4, 350) = E. H. अपना, see § 111.

61. उ *and* ऊ *become respectively* इ *and* ई; very rarely; as E. H. तनिक *small*, Pr. तणुक्कं, Skr. तनुकः; फिनू or फुनू or पुनू *again*, Pr. पुणो or पुणु (H. C. 4, 343), Skr. पुनर्; E. H. बाई (fem.) *wind*, Pr. वाऊ (masc.), Skr. वायुः (or वातिः masc.); बुंदी (fem.) *drop*, Pr. विंदू (masc.), Skr. विन्दुः.

62. उ *becomes* ए; very rarely; as फेफरा *lungs*, Skr. पुप्फुसः.

63. ऋ *becomes* इ; very rarely; thus E. H. किसान *husbandman*, A. Mg. *किसाणो, Skr. कृषाणः; E. H. गीध *vulture*, Mg. गिद्धे (Md. 1, 31), Skr. गृध्रः; E. H. माई *mother*, Mg. माइआ (Wb. Bh. 178. cf. H C. 1, 135), Skr. मातृका; E. H. भाई *brother*, Mg. *भाइए, Skr. भ्रातृकः; E. H. भतीजा *brother's son*, Mg. *भत्तिज्जए, Skr. भ्रातृजकः.

Note: None of these words are mentioned in the exceptional lists of H. C. I, 128—144. T. V. 1, 275—291. Vr. 1, 28—30, enjoining this change instead of the regular one of ऋ to अ (H. C. 1, 126. Vr. 1, 27), exc. माईणं gen. pl. for Skr. मातॄणाम् (H. C. 1, 135); but Md. gives गिद्धो and Bh. माइय°; and it is plain from the general form of the words, that in all of them the change of ऋ to इ must have taken place in Pr. already. In H. C. 1, 128 we find किसिओ for कृषितः as an analogy for किसाणो; and in 1, 137 नत्तिओ and नत्तुओ for नप्तृकः as an analogy for भाइओ and भाउओ (H. C.

1, 131) = भ्रातृकः; and in 1, 135 गाइहरं for मातृगृहं as an analogy for भत्तिज्जो = भ्रातृज्ञः.

64. ओ *becomes* ए; very rarely; as गेहूँ or गोहूँ, Pr. गोहुमो, Skr. गोधुमः; but only W. and H. H.; the E. H. only गोहूँ.

65. *Short vowels become long*; very rarely; E. H. ढीला *loose*, A. Mg. सिढिलए (cf. Vr. 2, 28. H. C. 1, 215), Skr. शिथिलकः; E. H. पूरु or पुरु *town*, Pr. पुरं, Skr. पुरम्. Comp. H. C. 1, 113 मूसलं, E. H. मूसरु for Skr. मुसलम; especially in the verbal roots पी *drink*, सी *sew*, चू *leak*, छू *touch*, मू *die*, बो *sow*, नो *bow*, भो *roam*; e. g., E. H. पीयै, Pr. पिअइ, Skr. पिबति; E. H. चूऐ, Pr. चुअइ (H. C. 2, 77), Skr. श्चोतति.

Note: This is a very common change in M., made for the purpose of compensating the shortening of the ultimate; as M. हत्तीण *she-elephant* for Pr. हत्थिणी; and it may explain the origin of the modern long termin. आ, ई, ऊ (§§ 47—49); e. g., E. H. घोरी *mare* for घोरिअ = Pr. घोडिआ, etc. It is, also, very common as the result of the elision of part of a conjunct, see § 147.

66. *Long vowels become short*; 1) regularly in the first part of a compound; thus E. H. पनसारु *watering place*, Pr. पाणिअसाला (or perhaps Ap. *पाणिसाला, eliding अ as in इवं for इअवं see § 58, note), Skr. पानीयशाला; E. H. पनचक्की *watermill*, Pr. पाणिअचक्किआ, Skr. पानीयचक्रिका; E. H. फुलवारी *flowergarden* (for फूलवारी), Pr. *फुल्लवाडिआ, Skr. फुल्लवाटिका; E. H. अधपका *half-ripe* (for आधपका), Mg. अद्धपक्कए, Skr. अर्धपक्वकः; E. H. नदीया *name of a town in Bengal* (for नादीया), Mg. नअदीयए, Skr. नवद्वीपकः; E. H. मुमाखी *honey-bee* (for मौमाखी), Mg. महुमक्खिआ, Skr. मधुमक्षिका, etc. 2) rarely otherwise; thus E. H. दिया *lamp* (also दीया and दोवा), Mg. दीयए (or *दियए cf. H. C. 1, 101 पलिविअं = प्रदीपितं), Skr. दीपकः; also in semitats. as E. H. पखान् *stone*, Skr. पाषाणः; E. H. पताल् *hades*, Skr. पातालम्; E. H. मुरछा *swoon*, Skr. मूर्छा; and see also § 25, as E. H. दुबरा *weak* from दूबरु, Mg. दुव्वलए, Skr. दुर्बलकः, etc.; and § 146, as E. H. सब् *all* for *साब्, Mg. सव्वे, Skr. सर्वः, etc.

67. *Vowels are nasalized*; often optionally before ह and स; as E. H. मुँह or मूँह or मुह *mouth, face*, Mg. मुहं (H. C. 4, 300),

Skr. मुखम्; E. H. मेँह् or मेह् *rain*, Mg. मेहे (cf. H. C. 1, 187), Skr. मेघः (lit. cloud, ?); E. H. सोँह् or सोह् *oath* (fem.), A. Mg. सवहे (cf. H. C. 1, 179), Skr. शपथः; E. H. छाँह् *shade*, Pr. छाही (H. C. 1, 249) or छाहा (Vr. 2, 18), Skr. छाया; E. H. बाँह् or बाह् (fem.) *arm*, Pr. बाह or बाहा (H. C. 4, 329), Skr. बाहा (fem., but बाहुः masc.); E. H. माँहै or माँहो or माहो *within*, Ap. मज्झहिं, Skr. मध्ये; E. H. खाँसी or खासी *cough*, Pr. खासिआ (cf. H. C. 1, 181), Skr. कासिका; E. H. हाँसी or हासी *laughter*, Pr. हासिआ (cf. H. C. 3, 105), Skr. हासिका; E. H. घाँस् or घास् (fem.) *grass*, A. Mg. घासे, Skr. घासः (masc.), etc.; rarely otherwise; as E. H. पाँव् or पाव् *foot*, Ap. पाउ, Sr. पाओ, Skr. पादः; E. H. कूआँ or कूआ or कूवाँ or कूवा *well*, Ap. कूवउ or कूवँउ (cf. H. C. 4, 397), Skr. कूपकः; sometimes ह् is elided after nasalization, as E. H. जाँयँ or जाँइँ *they go* (for जाँहिँ), Ap. जाहिं (cf. H. C. 4, 382), Pr. जंति (H. C. 4, 388), Skr. यान्ति.

Note: In Ap. Pr., too, व् is sometimes nasalized; as Ap. जिवँ or जेवँ *how* (see H. C. 4, 397), E. H. ज्यूँ; Ap. तिवँ or तेवँ *thus*, E. H. त्यूँ.

β) VOWELS IN CONTACT.

68. The *hiatus* of vowels is treated in three ways: 1) the two contiguous vowels may be contracted or expanded partly by the ordinary Skr. rules of *sandhi*, partly by special Gḍ. rules given below §§ 71 ff. Or 2) they may be separated by an *euphonic* semivowel (§ 28), and the dissyllable, formed thereby, sometimes again contracted (§ 34). Or 3) they may be left in hiatus. On the whole, the third case is less usual, than the two others; even in E. H.; but certainly in Gḍ. generally; for sometimes, when E. H. preserves the hiatus of the Pr., other Gḍs. make sandhi; thus E. H. कइसन् *of what kind*, but W. H. कैसा, M. कसा, for Ap. Pr. कइसो (H. C. 4, 403); or E. H. गइल् *he went*, but M. गेला, Mg. *गमिदे; or E. H. खाइल् *eaten*, but M. खाल्ला, Mg. खाइदे.

69. The semivowels, which may separate contiguous vowels,

are generally य् or व्, rarely ह्. About the use of य् and व् see § 28. Examples of an inserted euphonic ह् are probably; E. H. घटिहा or घटिया *inferior*; E. H. छूहै or छूवे or छूए *he touches*; E. H. दिहल् *given* for दे + अल् (probably by analogy to लिहल् *taken*, cf. § 307); E. H. दिहिस् *he gave* for दि + इस्, and किहिस् *he did* for कि + इस् (analogous to लिहिस् *he took*, see § 307); E. H. पहिचान् *cognizance* for पइचान् (Pr. परिचिअणं, Skr. परिचयनम्?); E. H. °अनिहार् *a suffix of agency*, Ap. Pr. अणिअअउो (see § 321); E. H. अहा *a pleon. suff.*, Mg. अयए, Skr. *अककः (§ 208); E. H. आहट् or आवट् *a suffix of abstract nouns*, Pr. अअवट्टो (see § 288). There is, apparently, one instance of an euphonic ल्; viz. E. H. दिलोतरसो or दियोतरसो *one hundred and two* (made analogously to तिलोतरसो 103, चलोतरसो 104, छिलोतरसो 106); see §§ 394. 397.

70. *Affinities*. All three semivowels य्, व् and ह् are already used in this way in Prákrit. Thus य् is especially mentioned by H. C. 1, 180. T. V. 1, 3. 10. Ṣ. C. 1, 3. 5 and apparently both य् and व् by K. I. 1, 45. 46 (in Ls. Ap. 41). About ह् there is no rule; but it occurs apparently in the words फलिहो, निहसो, चिहुरो, छाहा, etc. (for स्फटिक, निकष, चिकुर, छाया) mentioned in Vr. 2, 4. 18. H. C. 1, 186. 249. They not unfrequently occur in Pr. literature; especially in Mg.; thus in the Bhagavatí (see Wb. Bh. 397. 409. 411. 415); also in the Saptaṣataka (see Wb. Spt. 28. 29. 45); see also Ps. X.

71. Gd. *sandhi* is made in two ways; 1) by *contracting* the two vowels, or 2) by *expanding* the second. By *expansion* I mean the change of ए or इ to य *ya*, and of ओ or उ to व *va*. Peculiar Gd. contractions are: अ or आ with इ to ऐ; अ or आ with उ to औ; इ with अ to ऐ or ए or ई or इ; उ with अ to औ or ओ or ऊ; ए with अ or इ or उ or ए to ए; ओ with अ to आ. See in detail § 73, etc.

72. Expansion-sandhi is not unknown in Skr.; but it affects the first vowel; thus ए, ऐ, ओ, औ become respectively अय्, आय्, अव्, आव्, and in certain cases इ or ई and उ or ऊ become इय् and उव् (see M. M. 53); e. g., gen. sing. रै-अस् = रायः; नौ-अस् =

नावः ; धी-अस् = धियः ; लू-अस् = लुवः. In Pr. there are traces of the Gd. expansion; thus ओ or उ to व in पवट्ठो or पओट्ठो or पउट्ठो = Skr. प्रकोष्ट (Vr. 1, 40); आवज्जं for *आओज्जं or आउज्जं = Skr. आतोद्यम् (H. C. 1, 156); उ or ऊ to व in सोअमल्लं for *सोवमल्लं for *सोउमल्लं = Skr. सौकुमार्यम् (Vr. 1, 22); दुअल्लं for *दुव्वल्लं or दुऊलं = Skr. दुकूलम् (Vr. 1, 25); ओहलो for *उवहलो (cf. H. C. 1, 173) for उऊहलो = Skr. उदूखलः (H. C. 1, 171); सोमालो for *सुवमालो for सुउमालो = Skr. सुकुमारः (H. C. 1, 171). I do not recollect any example of ए or इ to य. Also the contraction of इ + अ to ए and उ + अ to ओ is found in Skr.; as in gen. sg. अग्नि-अस = अग्नेः ; मधु-अस् = मधोः. Here the change is commonly explained as a *guṇa* of the final इ or उ; but it may be, as in Pr. and Gd. it undoubtedly must be, explained as an expansion of इ and उ to अय् and अव् and contraction of the resultant dissyllable अय and अव to ए and ओ; as *अग्नयः = अग्नेः ; *मधवः = मधोः. Instances of this change in Pr. are not uncommon; thus वेइल्लं for *वयइल्ल for विअइल्लं = Skr. विचकिलम् (H. C. 1, 166); कणेरो for *कणयारो for कणिआरो = Skr. कर्णिकारः (H. C. 1, 168); एण्हिं for *अयण्हिं for इआणिं = Skr. इदानीम् (H. C. 2, 134. Ls. 129); एत्तिअं for *अयत्तिअं for *इअत्तिअं = Skr. इयत्तिकम् ; केत्तिअं for *कयत्तिअं for *किअत्तिअं = Skr. कियत्तिकम् (H. C. 2, 157); एद्दहं for *अयद्दहं for *इअद्दहं = Skr. *इयादृशम् (i. e. *इयत् + दृश or ईदृश ; cf. Wb. Spt. 59); केद्दहं for *कयद्दहं for *किअद्दहं = Skr. *कियादृशम् (or कीदृश) H. C. 2, 157. Again ओ for *अव for उअ = Skr. उत (H. C. 2, 172); cf. ओहरइ for अवहरइ = Skr. अवहरति (H. C. 1, 172); पोरो for *पवरो for *पूअरो = Skr. पूतरः (H. C. 1, 170); पोप्फलं for *पवप्फलं for *पूअप्फलं = Skr. पूगफलम् (H. C. 1, 170); सोणारो for *सवंणारो for *सुअणारो for सुवणारो = Skr. सुवर्णकारः (Spt. 194. H. C. 1, 26), etc. An instance of the change of अ + इ to ऐ in Pr. is ऐ for अइ = Skr. अयि (H. C. 1, 169); but the Pr. tendency is to produce and retain the hiatus अइ, अउ, आउ, as दइच्चो = Skr. दैत्यः (H. C. 1, 151), पउरो = Skr. पौरः (H. C. 1, 162), पाउरणं = Skr. प्रावरणम् (H. C. 1, 175), etc. Somewhat analogous are in Skr. स्वैरम् for स्वईरम्, प्रौढः for प्रऊढः, etc. (M. M. 19).

73. अ or आ *with* अ or आ *becomes* आ ; as E. H. इहाँ *here*,

Ap. Pr. एहहं, Skr. ईदृशे (scl. स्थाने, see § 467); E. H. तोहार् *yours* (W. H. तुम्हारो), Ap. Mg. *तुम्हअलिए or *तुम्हकलिए or तुम्हक्केले (cf. H. C. 2, 99. 147. 4, 422), Skr. युष्माकम्; E. H. खात् *eating*, Mg. खाअंते, Skr. खादन्; E. H. सउँध् (fem.) *bad odour*, Pr. *सडिअअंधी, Skr. *शटितगन्धिः (cf. H. C. 4, 219); E. H. राउत् *name of a caste*, Mg. *लाअउत्ते, Skr. राजदूतः; E. H. लोहार् *blacksmith*, Mg. लोहआले, Skr. लोहकारः; E. H. चमार् *leather-worker, shoemaker*, Mg. चम्मआले, Skr. चर्मकारः; E. H. परिवा *first day of a lunar fortnight*, Mg. पडिवआ (Vr. 4, 7), Skr. प्रतिपत्.

Exception. Sometimes व् is inserted; as in the nominal long forms, e. g., रमन्वा *Ráma* for Mg. लामआह, Skr. रामकस्य (see § 369, 2); sometimes य्, as in रैन् or रयेन् *night*, Mg. लअणी, Skr. रजनी.

74. इ *or* ई *with* इ *or* ई *becomes* ई; as E. H. पी or पीई *he will drink*, Pr. पिइहिइ, Skr. पास्यति (*पिविष्यति), W. H. पीहै = Pr. *पिइहइ; E. H. पीबो *I shall drink*, Ap. Pr. पिइव्वउं, Pr. पिइअव्वम्हि, Skr. पातव्य° (*पिवितव्य°), see § 309.

75. उ *or* ऊ *with* उ *or* ऊ *becomes* ऊ; as E. H. दूना *twofold*, Mg. दुउणए (cf. H. C. 1, 94), Skr. द्विगुणकः.

76. *Affinities.* There are some examples of the preceding contractions in Pr.; as Ap. अम्हारा (H. C. 4, 345) = *अम्हअरिओ or *अम्हकरिओ, Mh. अम्हक्केरो (H. C. 2, 147), Skr. अस्माकम् (lit. *अस्मकृतः), H. H. हमारा, E. H. हमार्, W. H. हमारो (Br.) or म्हारो (Mw.) *our*; Pr. खाइ or खाअइ (H. C. 4, 228), Skr. खादति, E. H. खाय् *he eats*; Pr. राउलं or राअउलं (Vr. 4, 1), Skr. राजकुलम्, E. H. राउर्, W. H. राउल् *a title of honor*; Pr. भाणं or भाअणं, Skr. भाजनम् (H. C. 1, 267) *vessel*; Pr. सोणार° (Spt. 194) for सुवण्णआर°, Skr. सुवर्णकार°, E. H. सोनार् *goldsmith*; Pr. कुम्भारो or कुम्भआरो (Vr. 1, 4), Skr. कुम्भकारः, E. H. कोँहार्, W. H. कुम्हार् *potter*; Pr. पावालिआ for पआवालिआ (Spt. 162), Skr. प्रपापालिका *guardian of a well*; again ऊआसो for *उउआसो for उववासो (H. C. 1, 173, see § 34), Skr. उपवासः, E. H. उपास् (perhaps a semi-tatsama) *fasting*, etc. See Wb. Spt. 32. But as a rule, Pr. prefers to preserve the hiatus; see Wb. Bh. 408. Skr. has similar laws, see M. M. 14. 52.

77. अ *with* इ *becomes* ऐ, *if antepenultimate, but* ऐ *or* अय *aya*

or अय् *ay, if penultimate, optionally*; as E. H. गयल् or गइल् or गैल् *gone*, Mg. गमिदे (see §§ 307. 109), Skr. गतः, W. H. गयौ, P. गइआ, Ap. Pr. *गमिअउ; E. H. भयल् or भइल् or भैल् *been*, Mg. *भविदे (see § 307), Skr. भूतः, W. H. भयौ, P. होइआ, Ap. Pr. भविअउ or हविअउ (cf. H. C. 4, 401); E. H. कय् or कै *having done* for कइ, W. H. करि, Ap. Pr. करि (H. C. 4, 357), Pr. करिअ (H. C. 1, 27), Skr. कृत्वा; E. H. पइठै or पैठै *he enters*, Pr. पइट्ठइ (cf. H. C. 4, 444), Skr. *प्रविष्टति (see § 352); E. H. खइलों or खैलों *I ate*, Mg. खाइदऽम्हि, Skr. खादितोऽस्मि (see § 487); E. H. गइलों or गैलों *I went*, Mg. गमिदऽम्हि, Skr. गतोऽस्मि; E. H. तइसन् or तैसन् *such*, Ap. Mg. तइसिल्ले (see § 111), A. Mg. तारिसे (H. C. 4, 287) or तादिसे (Ls. 115), Skr. तादृशः.

Exception. The termin. ऐ and ऐं of the 3. pr. sg. and pl. pres. and of the gen.-affix कै are *always* thus contracted; e. g., E. H. चलै *he walks* (not चलइ or चलय्), Pr. चलइ, Skr. चलति; E. H. करैं *they do*, Ap. करहिं (H. C. 4, 382), Pr. करंति, Skr. कुर्वन्ति; E. H. कै *of* (lit. *done by*) = O. H. करि, Ap. *करिउ or *करिओ or केरो (H. C. 4, 422), Skr. कृतः. In the oblique form of the singular and in *postpositional* locatives अइ becomes generally ए or ई; as E. H. भले obl. form of भला *good*, O. H. भलहि, Ap. Pr. भल्लह, Skr. भद्रस्य (see § 365, 6. 367, 4); E. H. पाछैं or पाछै or पाछें or पाछे *after*, G. पाछी, Ap. Pr. पच्छइ (H. C. 4, 334. 420; for पच्छहि, see § 367, 4) or पच्छहिं (§§ 367, 5. and 378), Skr. पश्चे; E. H. आगे *before*, Ap. Pr. अग्गइ (H. C. 4, 391), Skr. अग्रे; E. H. माहैं or माहें (cf. § 67) *within*, S. मंझे, Ap. Pr. मज्झहिं or मज्झहि, Skr. मध्ये; E. H. पाहें *near, by side of*, Ap. पक्खहिं, Skr. पक्षे; E. H. लागे or लगे *with, for, till*, M. लागीं, Ap. लग्गहि, Skr. लग्ने.

78. अ *with* उ *becomes* औ, *if antepenultimate, but* औ *or* अव *ava or* अव् *av, if penultimate, optionally*; thus E. H. चौथ् or चवथ् or चउथ् *fourth*, Mg. चउत्थे (Wb. Bh. 425), Skr. चतुर्थः; E. H. चौथा or चउथा *fourth*, Mg. चउत्थए (cf. Wb. Bh. 425), Skr. चतुर्थकः; E. H. औध् or अवध् *the province of Oudh*, also अजुधा (W. H. अजुध्या *semitats.*), Mg. *अयुढा or *अजुडा, Skr. अयोध्या; E. H. रौरा or रउरा *a honorific title, you* (cf. § 25), Mg. लाउलए (cf. Vr. 4, 1), Skr. राजकुलकः; E. H. ऐकलौता or ऐकलउता (or अक° or °टा) *only-born son*, Mg. एक्कल्लउअए

(cf. Wb. Bh. 439) or °ऌए (cf. H. C. 2, 165. Vr. 12, 5), Skr. एकलपुत्रकः; E. H. जेठौत् or जेठउत् *son of husband's elder brother*, Mg. जेट्ठउत्ते (cf. Wb. Bh. 315), Skr. ज्येष्ठपुत्रः.

Exception. The termin. औँ or ओँ of the 1st pr. sg. pres. is always thus contracted; e. g., E. H. करौँ or करोँ *I do*, Ap. करउँ (cf. H. C. 4, 385), Pr. करमि, Skr. करोमि; Ap. Pr. सउ *hundred* is in E. H. सो beside सौ, सव्, सउ; Skr. शतम्. In the *postpositional* locatives अउ becomes ऊ; as E. H. पाछू *behind*, Ap. Pr. पच्छहुं, Skr. पश्चे, etc.; see § 367, 5.

79. *Affinities.* In Pr. अइ and अउ generally remain in hiatus, but sometimes become ए and ओ; thus देव्वं and दइव्वं *fate* (H. C. 1, 153), Skr. दैवम्, but E. H. दैव्; Ap. केहो *of what kind* for *कइहो or *कादिहो, Skr. कीदृशः (cf Ls. 455); Pr. केलं for *कइलं or कयलं (H. C. 1, 167), Skr. कदलम्, also E. H. केरा *plantain*; again Pr. लोणं for *लउणं or लवणं *salt* (H. C. 1, 171), Skr. लवणम्, also E. H. लोन् or नोन्; Pr. चोव्वारो or चउव्वारो *shed, court* (H. C. 1, 171), Skr. चतुर्वारः, but E. H. चौबारू; Pr. चोत्थो or चउत्थो (H. C. 1, 171), but E. H. चौथ्. Only in one exceptional case अइ becomes ऐ, viz. Pr. ऐ for *अइ = Skr. अयि (H. C. 1, 169). These remarks refer to the Mh.-Sr. and Ap. (Sr.) Pr.; perhaps the Mg. even more strictly preserved the hiatus; for thus it may be explained why *on the whole* the E. and N. Gḍ. have ऐ and औ, while the W. and S. Gḍ. have ए and ओ and occasionally even modify ए to आ (just as the Mg. nom. sing. term. ए; see §§ 47. 48), or exceptionally (shortened) to अ; thus E. H., B., O., also M. चौथा, N. (also Br.) चौथो *fourth*, but G., S., Mw. चोथो; E. H., B., O., N., also M. चौदा or चौदह् *fourteen*, but Mw., G. चोद (or चौद), S. चोडहँ; again E. H. गैल् *gone*, but M. गेला; E. H. कैल् *done*, but M. केला; E. H. भैल् *been*, but M. झाला (for *हैला, *ह्याला); E. H. खैलोँ *I ate*, M. खालोँ; E. H. ऐलोँ *I came*, M. आलोँ; E. H. तैसन् *such*, M. तसा. The contraction of the Ap. Pr. loc. term. अहिं to ईँ is quite regular in M.; see Man. 28, 2. 3; as M. घरीँ *in a house*, Ap. घरहिं (K. I. 12, 27. in Ls. 451. see § 367, 5), Skr. गृहे; M. पासीँ *by the side of*, Ap. Pr. पासहिं (cf. H. C. 2, 92),

Skr. पार्श्वे; M. आठी" *for* (affix of dative), Ap. Pr. अट्ठहिं (cf. H. C. 2, 32), Skr. अर्थे; M. ठाई" *in* (Man. 127), Ap. ठाणहिं (cf. H. C. 4, 16), Skr. स्थाने, etc.

80. अ *with* ई *or* ऊ *becomes* ऐ *or* अय् *and* औ *or* अव् *respectively*; *optionally*; as E. H. कनहई or कनहै or कनहय् *kanhai* (krishṇa); E. H. घडऊ or घडौ or घडव् *pitcher*, redundant forms of कान् or कनहा (W. H. कान्हू) and घडा, see § 356.

81. अ with ए, ओ, see § 97.

82. आ *with* इ *or* ई *and with* उ *or* ऊ *remains in hiatus*; thus E. H. खाइब् *we shall eat*, Ap. खाइव्वा (scl. ऽम्ह), Pr. खाइअव्वाऽम्हो, Skr. खादितव्याः स्मः (with active sense, see § 309); E. H. खाई *he will eat*, Pr. खाहिइ (H. C. 4, 228), Skr. खादिष्यति (W. H. खाहै = Pr. *खाहइ); E. H. माई *mother*, Mg. माइआ (see § 61), Skr. मातृका; E. H. बाई *wind* (see § 61); E. H. राउर् *you*, Mg. लाउले (cf. Vr. 4, 1), Skr. राजकुलः; E. H. नाऊ *barber*, Mg. नाविए or ण्हाविए (cf. H. C. 1, 230), Skr. नापितः.

Exception. The suff. उ of the 2nd pr. sg. imper. combines with आ to औ; as E. H. जौ *go thou*, Ap. जाउ (cf. H. C. 4, 387. Ls. 467), Skr. याहि; E. H. खौ *eat thou*, Ap. खाउ, Skr. खाद. A final इ or उ optionally becomes य् and व्; as E. H. खाय् or खाइ *having eaten*, Ap. खाइ (cf. H. C. 4, 439), Pr. खाइअ, Skr. खादित्वा; E. H. जाय् or जाइ *having gone*, Ap. जाइ, Pr. जाइअ, Skr. यात्वा; E. H. जाँयँ or जाँइँ *they go*, Ap. जाहिं (cf. H. C. 4, 382), Pr. जांति, Skr. यान्ति; again E. H. घाव् or घाउ *wound*, Ap. घाउ (H. C. 4, 346), Pr. घाओ, Skr. घातः; E. H. पाव् or पांव् or पाउ or पाँउ *foot*, Ap. पाउ, Skr. पादः; E. H. राव् or राउ *a title of nobility, prince*, Pr. राउ (as if Skr. राजः); E. H. खावँ *I eat*, Ap. खाउं (cf. H. C. 4, 385), Pr. खामि or खाअमि, Skr. खादामि; sometimes also penultimate इ or उ; as E. H. खायल् or खाइल् *eaten*, Mg. खाइदे, Skr. खादितः; E. H. रावर् or राउर् *you* (see above).

83. इ *with* अ *becomes* ए; as E. H. डेढ़ or देढ़ *one and a half*, for *दिअड्ढ, Mg. दिवड्ढ (Wb. Bh. 190. 411, and § 416); sometimes optionally; as E. H. नियर् or नेर् *near*, Mg. निअडं, Skr. निकटम्; when final, ए is shortened to ऐ or इ, as E. H. करे or करि *having*

done, Mg. कलिअ (H. C. 4, 302), Skr. कृत्वा; E. H. चल्यो॑, O. H. चलेउँ, Ap. *चलिअउं (see § 505), Pr. चलिअऽम्हि, Skr. चलितोऽस्मि.

Exception. The nominal termin. इअ contracts to ई; as E. H. पानी *water*, Pr. पाणिअं; see § 53. 49. 50.

84. उ *with* अ *becomes* ओ; as E. H. सोँधा *sweet scent*, Mg. सुअंधए (cf. Spt. 13), Skr. सुगन्धकः.

Exception. The nominal termin. उअ contracts to ऊ; as E. H. आँसू *tear*, Pr. अंसुअं; see § 53. 49. 50.

85. *Affinities.* Both the above contractions are not uncommon in Pr.; thus Pr. लेइ *he takes* for *लिहइ or लहइ (H. C. 4, 335), Skr. लभते, E. H. ले (cf. E. H. past part. लिहल्); Mg. ओज्झाए (cf. H. C. 1, 173) *magician* for *उअज्झाए or उवज्झाए, Skr. उपाध्यायः, E. H. ओझा; Mg. होंति for *हुअंते or हुवंते (cf. H. C. 3, 180), Skr. भवन्, E. H. होत्, etc. (see § 72). They are common alike to all Gḍs.

86. इ *or* उ *with* आ *become* इया *and* उवा; *optionally*; the insertion of य् is usual, that of व् unusual; thus E. H. हिया or हिआ *heart*, Pr. हिअअं, Skr. हृदयम्; E. H. बियाह् *marriage*. Mg. विआहे, Skr. विवाहः; E. H. पियास् *thirst*, Pr. पिआसा (cf. H. C. 4, 434) or पिवासा (Wb. Bh. 274), Skr. पिपासा; E. H. पुआल् or (rarely) पुवाल् *straw*, Pr. *पलाली, Skr. पलाली; and regularly in the nominal long forms, as घोरिया or (rarely) घोरिआ *mare*; जोरुआ or (less usually) जोरुवा *wife*, see §§ 195. 199.

Exception. In the nominal short forms, इआ and उआ are always contracted to ई and ऊ respectively; see § 51.

87. इ *with* उ *or* ऊ *becomes* इयु *and* इयू; *optionally*; the hiatus is more usual; as E. H. सिउ or सियु *Śiva*, Ap. सिउ, Pr. सिओ, Skr. शिवः; E. H. पिऊ or पियू *sweetheart*, Ap. पिअउ, Pr. पिअओ, Skr. प्रियकः.

88. उ *with* इ *or* ई *remains in hiatus*; as E. H. सुइया *needle*, Pr. सूइआ, Skr. सूचिका; E. H. सुई *parrot*, Pr. सुइआ, Skr. शुकिका.

89. इ *or* उ *with* ए *or* ओ; see § 98.

90. ई *or* ऊ *with* अ; see § 97.

91. ई *with any other vowel inserts* य्; as E. H. धीया *daughter*,

Pr. धीआ (Vr. 4, 33), Skr. धीदा or दुहिता; E. H. सीया *Sítá*, Pr. सीआ, Skr. सीता (semitats.); E. H. पीउ *drink thou*, Ap. पिउ (see § 65), Pr. पिव, Skr. पिब; E. H. पीवै *he drinks*, Pr. पिअइ (H. C. 4, 10), Skr. पिबति; E. H. पीयों or पीवों *I drink*, Ap. पिअउं (cf. H. C. 4, 385), Pr. पिअमि, Skr. पिबामि.

92. ऊ *with* आ, इ *and* ई *remains in hiatus*; as E. H. धूआँ *smoke*, Ap. धूवँउ (cf. H. C. 4, 397), Pr. धूमओ, Skr. धूमकः; E. H. चूइहैं *they will leak*, Ap. चुइहहिं (cf. § 65), Pr. चुइहंति, Skr. श्चोतिष्यन्ति; E. H. भूइँ *earth*, Ap. भूविँआं (cf. H. C. 4, 397), Pr. भूमिआ, Skr. भूमिका; E. H. सूई *needle*, Pr. सूइआ, Skr. सूचिका.

93. ऊ *with* ए, ऐ, ओ *and* औ *becomes* ऊवे, ऊवै, ऊवो, ऊवौ; *optionally*; the hiatus is more usual; as E. H. चूए or चूवै *it leaks* (W. H. चूए or चूवे), Pr. चुअइ (H. C. 2, 77), Skr. श्चोतति; E. H. चूओं or चूऔं or चूवों or चूवौं *I leak*, Ap. चुअउं, Pr. चुअमि, Skr. श्चोतामि.

94. ए *or* ओ *with* अ, इ *and* उ; see § 97. 98.

95. ए *or* ओ *with a long vowel remain in hiatus*; less usually व् is inserted after ओ; as E. H. लेई *he will take*, Pr. लहिहिइ, Skr. लप्स्यते (*लभिष्यति); E. H. होई *he will be*, Pr. होही (H. C. 2, 180) or होहिइ (H. C. 4, 388), Skr. भविष्यति; E. H. बोऐ or बोवै *he sows*, Pr. ववइ, Skr. वपति; E. H. बोओं or बोऔं or बोवों or बोवौं *I sow*, Ap. ववउं, Pr. ववमि, Skr. वपामि.

96. ऐ *or* औ *with any vowel insert* य् *and* व्; *optionally*; the insertion of य् is usual, but not that of व्; as E. H. भैयन् or भइयन् के (see § 77) *of brothers*, Pr. भाइआण, Skr. भ्रातृकाणाम्; E. H. भैया or भइया *brother*, Mg. भाइआह, Skr. भ्रातृकस्य (see § 369, 2); E. H. नौअन् or नउअन् को (see § 78) *of barbers*, Pr. नाविआण, Skr. नापितानाम्; E. H. नौआ or नौवा or नउआ or नउवा *barber*, Mg. नाविआह, Skr. नापितस्य; E. H. नौई *he will bow*, Pr. नविहिइ or नमिहिइ (cf. H. C. 4, 158), Skr. नमिष्यति; E. H. नौओं *I bow*, Ap. नवउं, Pr. नवमि, Skr. नमामि; E. H. नौएँ or नौवैं *they bow*, Ap. नवहिं (H. C. 4, 367), Pr. नवंति, Skr. नमन्ति.

97. अ *before or after a long vowel is often elided*; *before*; E. H. सुआर् *cook*, A. Mg. सूअआले, Skr. सूपकारः; E. H. फुलेल् *scented oil*, Pr. फुल्लएल्लं, Skr. फुल्लतैलम्; *after*; E. H. सीर् or सीयर् *cold, damp*, Pr. सीयलं (cf. H. C. 4, 343. Spt. 53), Skr. शीतलम्; E. H. पीर् or

पीयर् *yellow,* Pr. पीअलं (H. C. 1, 213), Skr. पीतलम्; E. H. सूर् or सूअर् *hog,* A. Mg. सूअले, Skr. शूकरः; E. H. थोर् or थोरा *little* (W. H. थोडा), Pr. थोअडं or थोअडअं (cf. H. C. 2, 125), Skr. स्तोकम् or स्तोककम्. But never in conjugation; e. g., E. H. पीयत् *drinking,* Mg. पिअंते, Skr. पिबन्; E. H. बोअत् *sowing,* Mg. ववंते, Skr. वपन्.

Note: पीयत्, बोअत्, etc. are not real exceptions; for their ई, ओ, etc. are merely subsequent Gd. lengthenings (cf. § 65); nor होत् *being,* देत् *giving,* लेत् *taking,* for these are not contractions of हो-अत्, etc., but of Mg. Pr. हुवंते, लहंते, देंते (cf. H. C. 4, 307).

98. इ *or* ए *and* उ *or* ओ *after a vowel often become* य *ya or* य् *y and* व *va or* व् *v respectively*; thus E. H. गयल् or गइल् *gone* (see § 77); E. H. धय् *having put* for धइ, Ap. धरि, Pr. धरिअ, Skr. धृत्वा; E. H. खायल् or खाइल् *eaten* (§ 82. exc.); E. H. पाय् *having found* for पाइ, Ap. पावि, Pr. पाविअ, Skr. प्राप्य; E. H. चूय् *having leaked* for चूइ or चूऐ, Pr. चुइअ, Skr. श्चुतित्वा; E. H. होय् *he is,* Pr. होइ (H. C. 1, 9) or हवइ (H. C. 4, 60), Skr. भवति; E. H. होय् *having been* for होइ or होऐ, Pr. हविअ (H. C. 4, 271), Skr. भूत्वा; E. H. कोयर् or कोइर् *cuckoo* (W. H. कोइल्), Mg. कोइले, Skr. कोकिलः; E. H. नारियर् *cocoanut* (W. H. नारियल्), Mg. नालिएले, Skr. नारिकेलः; O. H. आयसु *order* (in Tulsídás), Ap. आएसु, Pr. आएसो, Skr. आदेशः; E. H. चवथ् or चउथ् *fourth* (see § 78); E. H. घाव् or घाउ *wound* (see § 82. exc.); E. H. जाँवूँ *I go,* Ap. जाउं, Pr. जामि (H. C. 2, 204), Skr. यामि.

Exception. The suff. इ of 3[d] pers. and उ of 2nd pr. sg. pres. and imper. is always dropped after the roots ले, दे; thus ले *he takes,* Pr. लेइ (H. C. 4, 238, see § 85); E. H. दे *he gives,* Pr. देइ (H. C. 4, 238), Skr. ददाति; E. H. दे *take thou,* Ap. देउ, Skr. देहि. Again the nominal term. Mg. इए and उए (or Sr. इओ, उओ) are contracted to ई and ऊ; see § 49; the expansion of final ए (or ओ) to य or व would naturally tend to lengthen the preceding इ and उ; and the resultant अ after ई and ऊ, would drop off, by § 97; e. g., तेल्लिए, तेल्लिय or तेल्लीअ, तेली *oilman.*

γ) SINGLE CONSONANTS.

99. Medial single consonants in E. H are of two kinds, *original* and *resultant.* The former are those which have passed as such into E. H. either from the (A. Mg.) Pr.; as in the tadbh. E. H. सगल् *whole,* A. Mg. सगले, Skr. सकलः; E. H. पड़िवा *first day of a lunar fortnight,* Pr. पडिवआ, Skr. प्रतिपत्; or from the Skr.; as in the tats. E. H. राजा *king,* Skr. राजा, or in the semitats. E. H. क्रिपा *mercy,* Skr. कृपा. The latter are those which have arisen either from the *simplification* (§ 143) of a conjunct consonant by eliding one, as in the tadbh. E. H. पाती *letter,* Pr. पत्तिआ, Skr. पत्रिका; E. H. माथा *head,* Mg. मत्थए, Skr. मस्तकः, or in the semitats. E. H. पिथी, Skr. पृथ्वी; E. H. अजुधा, Skr. अयोध्या; or from the *dissolution* (§ 138) of a conjunct by inserting a vowel; as in the tadbh. भगत् *devoted,* Ap. *भकतु, Skr. भक्तः, or in the semitats. जतन् *effort,* Skr. यत्नः. Tatsama single consonants, whether original or resultant, may, of course (as in Skr.), be of any kind, whether surd or sonant, aspirate or unaspirate; they never suffer any further change in E. H.; for sone doubtful exceptions see §§ 102. 129. Tadbhava *resultant* single consonants, too, as may be seen from the examples in §§ 138, 143, may be of any kind; but the tadbh. *original* can only be sonants, never surds, because already in Pr. every original single surd cons. has been made sonant, if it be not wholly elided (cf. § 101). Both tadbhava classes, the resultant and the original, are liable to further changes in E. H. These may be of five kinds: 1) sonant consonants proper (i. e. cerebrals and dentals) are *softened* to semivowels (ड़ or ऱ् or ल् and ढ़ or ऱ्ह or ल्ह) cf. §§ 102—115; 2) aspirate consonants proper (except palatals and cerebrals) may be *reduced* to the simple aspirate (ह्), cf. §§ 116—120; 3) semivowels (viz. य् and व्) and the nasal (म्) may be vocalized (इ and उ), cf. §§ 121. 122; 4) semivowels (viz. व्, ल्, ऱ्, ह्) and nasals (viz. म् and न्) and occasionally double consonants (viz. क्क्, म्म्, न्न्, त्त्, व्व्, प्प्) may be elided, cf. §§ 123—128 and 151—157; and 5) semi-

vowels (viz. ग् and ब्) may be hardened, cf. § 129. Besides, there are isolated instances of changes of a miscellaneous kind. See in detail § 97, etc.

100. *Affinities.* All these five kinds of changes exist in Pr. already; but modified partly in character, partly in frequency. Thus in Pr. they affect as a rule (exceptions see § 116, note. § 145, exc. 2. and § 142) only *original* single consonants; in E. H. also *resultant* ones. Again 1) in Pr. surds are softened to sonants, in E. H. sonants to semivowels; e. g., *orig.*, Skr. कर्पटकः *cloths*, Mg. कप्पडए, E. H. कपरा; Skr. कथितः *said*, Mg. कधिदे, E. H. कहिल् or कहल्; *result.*, Skr. कपर्दिका, Mg. कवड्डिआ (cf. H. C. 2, 36), E. H. कौरी, W. H. कौड़ी. This rule refers only to cerebrals and dentals, which alone are capable of the change. But something analogous takes place in the case of the other classes; thus in Pr., labials (प् or ब्) are softened to व् (H. C. 1, 231. 237); in E. H., व् is *vocalized*; e. g., Skr. शपथः *oath*, A. Mg. सवधे or सवहे, E. H. सौंह् (for सउह्); in Mg. Pr. for gutturals (क्, ग्) and palatals (च्, ज्) is substituted the euphonic य् (cf. Wb. Bh. 397); in E. H., य् is vocalized; e. g., Skr. नागरम् *town*, Mg. नयलं, E. H. नैर्; Skr. रजनी *night*, Mg. लयणी, E. H. रैनि. There are, however, traces of these changes in Pr. already, see §§ 35. 105. 109, note, etc. Then 2) in Pr., aspirate consonants are changed to sonant aspirates or reduced to the simple aspirate ह् (see H. C. 4, 267. 302. Wb. Bh. 410); E. H. allows only the simple aspirate and occasionally extends the rule to resultant aspirates; e. g., Skr. कुरुथ *you make*, Mg. कलेध or कलेह, E. H. करह्; Skr. पत्ते, Ap. पक्खहिं, E. H. पाहीँ (for पाखीँ). Traces of its extension to resultants, however, occur in Pr. also, see § 116, note and Wb. Bh. 410. Again 3) in Pr., य् and व् are sometimes vocalized (§ 35); in Ap. Pr. also म् (see § 122, note); but in E. H. the process is far more common; see examples above (No. 1). Next 4) in Pr., unaspirate consonants proper and य् and व् only are elided (Vr. 2, 2. H. C. 1, 177); E. H extends the practice occasionally to र्, ल्, ह्, म्, न्, though traces of the latter exist in Pr. also (see §§ 125, note. and 127, note).

Lastly 5) in Mh.-Sr., initial द् is always hardened to त्; E. Gḍ. extends this practice to both initial द् and ब् (see § 17), even when they become the initial of a syllable by the dissolution of a conjunct; e. g., Skr. कार्यम्, E. H. कारज्; Skr. पर्वतः, E. H. परबत्. As to the Gḍs., they all agree generally in regard to the four last kinds of changes. With respect to the first, the E. and S. Gḍ. agree; but W. and N. Gḍ. do not change ट् to त्, but elide it; and have a tendency to preserve ड् or change it to ड़्, but not to ऱ्.

101. With regard to tadbhava original consonants proper, the following may be stated *generally*. In Mg., as in Pr. generally, क् and ग् were usually elided; exceptionally क् was changed to ग् (H. C. 1, 177. cf. 4, 396); च् and ज् were, as a rule, elided (not mentioned at all in E. H. 4, 396; one exception in H. C. 1, 177); ट् and ड् were never elided, but ट् softened to ड् (H. C. 1, 195); in Mg. (but not in Pr. generally, cf. H. C. 1, 177) त् and द् were not elided, but त् softened to द् (H. C. 4, 260. 302. cf. 4, 396); in the later Mg., however, (as in Pr. generally, cf. H. C. 1, 177) द् must have been, as a rule, elided, except in the past part. pass. and in a few other words; in the Mg. of the Bhagavatí, indeed, there appears to be no difference between Mg. and the ordinary Pr. (cf. Wb. Bh. 398. 428. 433); but E. H. (and E. Gḍ. generally) agree with the Pr. Gramm. statement, as above modified (see § 109). In Mg., as in Pr. generally, प् and ब् are softened to ब् (H. C. 1, 231. 237). Again in Mg., as in Pr. generally, ख् and घ् were, as a rule, reduced to ह् (only a few exceptions in H. C. 1, 187. 188. cf. 4, 396); छ् and झ् were always left unchanged (being not mentioned in H. C. 1, 187. 4, 396); and ठ् was always changed to ढ्, but ढ् left unchanged (H. C. 1, 199). In Mg. (but not in Pr. generally H. C. 1, 187) थ् was changed to ध्, and ध् optionally reduced to ह् (H. C. 4, 267. 302. cf. 4, 396). In Pr. generally, फ् was always changed to भ्, and भ् optionally reduced to ह् (H. C. 1, 236. 187. cf. 4, 396). Thus it follows, that E. H. can possess only the following tadbh. orig. cons. proper,

to which it applies its own laws of phonetic change. Of unaspirates: exceptionally ग्; regularly ड़्; in the past part. and exceptionally in other words ट्; regularly व्. Of aspirates: exceptionally ख्; regularly ड़्, फ् and ह्; optionally थ् and ग्. The unaspirates च् and त् are never present; in words like E. H. पचै *it rots,* बजै *it sounds* (§ 143) they are resultant, owing to a doubling (च्च्, ज्ज्) in Pr.

aa) Softening.

102. क् *becomes* ग्; *rarely*; 1) original; thus E. H. काग् *crow,* Ap. कागु, Skr. काकः (but usually कवा, Mg. काए, or कौवा (for *कववा), Mg. काश्रए); E. H. साग् *vegetable,* Ap. सागं, Skr. शाकम्; E. H. सगड़् *cart* (W. H. सगड़्), A. Mg. सगडं (cf. Wb. Bh. 248), Skr. शकटम्; E. H. सगड़् *whole,* Ap. सगलं, Skr. सकलम्; E. H. सगुन् *bird,* Ap. सगुणु, Skr. शकुनः; E. H. ऐग्यारह् *eleven,* Ap. *एगारह (cf. H. C. 1, 177), Skr. एकादश; E. H. परगट् *manifest,* Skr. प्रकटम् (semitats.). — 2) *resultant*; thus E. H. बिगत् or बेगत् *individual,* Skr. व्यक्तः; E. H. मुगति *salvation,* Skr. मुक्तिः; E. H. भगत् *devotee,* Skr. भक्तः; E. H. भगति *faith,* Skr. भक्तिः; E. H. भगताई *devotedness* (cf. § 220) = Skr. भक्तता; E. H. रगत् *blood,* Skr. रक्तम्. Not always; as E. H. चकड़् *wheel,* Ap. Pr. चक्कं (cf. H. C. 4, 398), Skr. चक्रम्; E. H. बकरी *she-goat,* Ap. बक्किश्र, Skr. बक्किका.

Note: Probably in most or all of these words, the change took place in Pr. already; for it is expressly mentioned by Pr. Gramm. to occur in exceptional cases; see H. C. 1, 177. cf. 4, 396; as Pr. एगो, Skr. एकः, Pr. श्रागारो, Skr. श्राकारः, etc. (cf. Ls. 202); and in Gḍ., too, it occurs only as an exception. As a rule क् is elided in tadbh., both in Pr. and Gḍ.; and in tats. it remains unchanged.

103. ट् *becomes* ड़् *or* ड़्; *very rarely*; always resultant, as E. H. निबाड़ै or निबाड़ै *he accomplishes* for *निबाटै, Pr. निव्वट्टइ or निव्वट्टइ, Skr. निर्वर्त्तयति; E. H. पेड़् or पेड़् *tree* for *पेट् (see § 148), Pr. पट्टो, Skr. पत्री (?).

104. ड् *becomes* ड़् *or* ड़्; *as a rule*; ड़् *is more usual*; 1) original; thus E. H. कपड़ा or कपड़ा *cloths,* Mg. कप्पडए, Skr. कर्पटकः; E. H. केवाड़ा or केवाड़ा *door* (§ 57), Mg. कवाडए, Skr. कपाटकः;

E. H. घरै or घड़ै *he fashions,* Pr. घडइ (H. C. 1, 195), Skr. घटयति; E. H. चिरई *bird* (cf. § 55), Pr. चडइआ, Skr. चटकिका, H. H. चिड़िया; E. H. तोरै or तोड़ै *he breaks,* Pr. तोडइ or तोडेइ, Skr. त्रोटयति; E. H. नरू or नड़ू *a kind of reed,* Mg. नडे (cf. H. C. 1, 195), Skr. नटः; E. H. परै or पड़ै *he falls,* Pr. पडइ (Vr. 8, 51), Skr. पतति; E. H. परिवा *first day of a lunar fortnight,* Pr. पडिवआ (Vr. 4, 7), Skr. प्रतिपद्; E. H. परोस् *neighbourhood* (cf. § 122), A. Mg. पडिवासे or पडिवेसे, Skr. प्रतिवासः or प्रतिवेशः; E. H. पापरू or पापड़ू *cake,* Mg. पप्पडे, Skr. पर्पटः; E. H. बारी or बाड़ी *garden,* Pr. वाडिआ, Skr. वाटिका; E. H. भरू or भड़ू *large boat,* Mg. भडे (cf. H. C. 1, 195), Skr. भटः (?); E. H. लरिका or लड़िका *boy,* Mg. *लडिक्कए from Skr. लट (cf. § 252. 334. 353), H. H. लड़का; E. H. लरै or लड़ै *he quarrels* (*makes uproar*), Mg. लडइ, Skr. रटति (cf. § 110, exc.); E. H. सरै or सड़ै *it rots,* Pr. सडइ (Vr. 8, 51), Skr. शटति; generally in the E. H. *pleonastic suffixes* ड़ or र, ड़ा or रा, आड़ or आरू, आड़ा or आरा, Ap. Mg. डे, डए, अडे, अअडए (cf. H. C. 4, 429. 430); thus E. H. गोरू or गोड़ू *foot, leg,* Ap. गवडु (cf. H. C. 4, 397), Pr. गमडो, Skr. गमः (lit. going); E. H. थोरू or थोड़ू *little* (cf. § 97), Ap. Mg. थोअडे, Skr. स्तोकः; E. H. ठोकरा or ठोकड़ा *small piece,* Ap. Mg. *ठोक्कडए (cf. H. C. 2, 125), Skr. स्तोकः; E. H. चमरा or चमड़ा *leather,* Ap. Mg. चम्मडअं, Skr. चर्म; E. H. बछरू or बछड़ू *calf,* Ap. वच्छडउ, Skr. वत्सः; E. H. सैकरा or सैकड़ा *a hundred,* Ap. Mg. सयक्कडअं, Skr. शतकम्; E. H. जेठरा *eldest,* Ap. Mg. जेट्ठडए, Skr. ज्येष्ठः; E. H. पछिवारू or पछिवाड़ू or °वारा *hindmost,* Ap. Mg. *पच्छिवअडे or °वअडए or पच्छिमअडे or °मअडए, Skr. पश्चिमकः; E. H. पछारी or पछाड़ी (scl. रस्सी) *hind-rope* (for tying horses' hind-legs), Ap. पच्छअडिआ, Skr. पश्चक°; E. H. अगारी or अगाड़ी *fore-rope,* Ap. अग्गअडिआ, Skr. अग्रक°, etc. — 2) resultant; thus E. H. कौरी or कौड़ी *cowrie,* Pr. कवड्डिआ (H. C. 2, 36), Skr. कपर्दिका, etc.

105. ड़ *becomes* ल्; *only original*; very rarely; thus the E. H. pleonastic suffix ल् or ला, Ap. Mg. डे or डए (cf. H. C. 4, 429), e. g., E. H. परल् or °ला *ulterior,* Ap. Mg. परडे or °डए, Skr. परः; E. H. मोटल् *fat,* Ap. Mg. *मोट्टडे or *मुट्टडे, Skr. मूर्त्तः; E. H. माउली *mother,* Ap. Mg. *माउडिआ, Skr. मातृका, etc.; also otherwise, as

E. H. छिलोतर्‌नै or °सो, Ap. Mg. *छुडुत्तरसयं or *छलुत्तरसयं (cf. Wb. Bh. 426), Ap. Sr. *छुडुत्तरसउ, Skr. षडुत्तरशतम्.

Note: This change is not uncommon in Pr., see Vr. 2, 23. H. C. 1, 202; in such cases E. H. optionally, but usually changes ल् to र्; as Skr. षोडश *sixteen*, A. Mg. सोलस (Wb. Bh. 426), E. H. सोरह् or सोलह्; Skr. तडाकः *tank*, Ap. तलाउ (cf. H. C. 1, 202), E. H. तराउ or तराव् or तलाव्; Skr. नडम् *a kind of reed*, Pr. नडं or नलं (H. C. 1, 202), E. H. नर् or नल् or नड्; Skr. नाडिका *stalk*, Pr. नाडिआ or नालिआ (H. C. 1, 202), E. H. नारी or नाली or नाडी.

106. ड् *becomes* न्; *only original*; very rarely; thus E. H. तवन् or तउन् or तौन् *that* (lit. *of that kind*), Ap. तेवडु (H. C. 4, 407) or *तेवडो, Pr. तेद्दहो (cf. H. C. 2, 157), Skr. तादृशः (see § 438, 2); E. H. जवन् or जउन् or जौन् *which* (lit. *of which kind*), Ap. जेवडु (H. C. 4, 407), Pr. जेद्दहो, Skr. यादृशः; E. H. कवन् or कउन् or कौन् *who* (lit. *of what kind*), Ap. कवणु (H. C. 4, 395) or केवडु (H. C. 4, 408), Mg. केवडिय° (Wb. Bh. 422), Pr. केद्दहो, Skr. कीदृशः (see § 26, note); cf. also E. H. मुघडा or मुघना *mouth* (of a horse, etc.) from घोथ् *mouth*.

107. त् *becomes* ड् *or* र्; *very rarely*; always resultant; as E. H. सरसठि or सडसठि or सतसठि *sixty seven*, Pr. सत्तसट्ठी (cf. Wb. Bh. 426), Skr. सप्तषष्टिः.

108. द् *becomes* र्; *very rarely*; always original; thus गगरी *waterpot*, Pr. गग्गरिआ (cf. Vr. 2, 13), Skr. गद्गदिका; E. H. सत्तर् *seventy*, Pr. सत्तरी (H. C. 1, 210. Wb. Bh. 248) for *सत्तदी, Skr. सप्ततिः; E. H. °रह् *ten*, Pr. °रह (Vr. 2, 14) or °रस (Wb. Bh. 426), Skr. दश; e. g., E. H. बारह *twelve*, Pr. बारह (H. C. 1, 219) or बारस (Wb. Bh. 425), Skr. द्वादश.

Note: This change, also, is old Pr.; I know no strictly modern example.

109. द् *becomes* ल्; *only original*; always in the E. H. suffix of past part. इल् or अल्, Mg. इदे (cf. H. C. 4, 260. 302. Vr. 11, 11), Skr. इतः; e. g., E. H. गइल् or गेल् or गयल् *gone* (see § 77); E. H. भइल् or भैल् or भयल् *been* (see § 77); E. H. धइल् or धैल् or धयल् *put*, Mg. धल्लिदे (cf. H. C. 1, 36. धरिश्रो Spt. 241), Skr. धृतः; E. H. कइल्

or कैल् or कयल् *done,* Mg. *कलिदे, Skr. कृतः (see § 307); E. H. खाइल् or खायल् *eaten* (see § 82. exc.); E. H. पाइल् or पायल् *found* (cf. §§ 33. 123), Mg. पाविदे (cf. H. C. 4, 387. पाविश्र), Skr. प्राप्तः; E. H. श्राइल् or श्रायल् *come,* Mg. श्राविदे, Skr. श्राप्तः; E. H. पढल् or पढिल् *read,* Mg. पढिदे, Skr. पठितः; E. H. चरल् or चरिल् *walked,* Mg. चलिदे, Skr. चलितः, etc.; rarely otherwise; e. g., E. H. सल् *hundred,* A. Mg. *सदं, Skr. शतम्.

Note: This change is especially Mg., e. g., कले, गले or कदे, गदे (in Md. 12, 28. optional with कडे, गडे, Vr. 11, 15), Skr. कृतः, गतः; Mg. केलश्रं (Sak. 37, 13) for *कलिश्रश्रं, Skr. कृतकम्; A. Mg. ईलिशे for *ईदिशे, Skr. ईदृशः (cf. Lss. 417. 423); rarely in Pr. generally, as Pr. पलित्तं (H. C. 1, 221), Skr. प्रदीप्तम्, E. H. पलीत् *a light, candle;* Pr. पलिलं (H. C. 1, 212) for *पलिदं, Skr. पलितम्, E. H. पलिल् or पलल् *mud;* Pr. श्रलसी (H. C. 1, 211) for *श्रदसी, Skr. श्रतसी, E. H. श्रलसी *linseed.*

110. ल् *becomes* र्; *as a rule;* see §§ 16. 30; thus E. H. नर् *man,* Mg. नले (H. C. 4, 288), Skr. नरः; E. H. राय् *king,* Mg. लाया (H. C. 4, 302), Skr. राजा, etc.

Exceptions. E. H. लेजुरी *cord,* (Ap.) Mg. *लंजुडिश्रा, Skr. रज्जूः; E. H. लरै or लडै *he quarrels* (S. रडे), Mg. लडइ, Skr. रटति (cf. लटति or लडति); but E. H. रारि or राडि *quarrel* (noisy contention), Mg. लाडो, Skr. राटिः; E. H. डालै or डारै *he throws,* Mg. *डालेइ or दालेइ, Skr. दारयति (also दालयति); E. H. भूलै or भूरै *he forgets,* Ap. Mg. *भवलेइ or *भमलेइ, Skr. भ्रमरयति (?); E. H. गलियावै or गरियावै *he abuses* and गाली or गारी *abuse,* cf. § 142; E. H. निकालै or निकारै *he ejects,* cf. § 115, note; E. H. चलोतरसै *one hundred and four,* Mg. चुलुत्तरसयं (§ 397), Skr. चतुरुत्तरशतम्; E. H. सम्हालै or सम्भालै *he supports,* cf. § 120; E. H. चालिस् *forty,* Mg. चत्तलीसा (Wb. Bh. 426), Skr. चत्वारिंशत्; E. H. डाला *branch,* Mg. डालश्रं (cf. H. C. 4, 445), Skr. दारकम्.

111. ल् *becomes* न्; *sometimes;* in the E. H. pleonastic suffix न् or ना, Mg. ल्ल or ल्लए; e. g., E. H. जामुन् *roseapple-tree,* A. Mg. *जम्मुल्ल (see § 18) or जम्बुल्ल, Skr. जम्बूलः; E. H. एतना *so many,* Mg. एत्तिलए (cf. H. C. 2, 157) or Ap. Mg. एत्तुलए (cf. H. C.

4, 408), Skr. इयत्तिकः; E. H. तेतना *so many,* Mg. तेत्तिलए or तेत्तुलए, Skr. तावत्तिकः; E. H. जेतना *as many,* Mg. जेत्तिलए or जेत्तुलए (H. C. 4, 407), Skr. यावत्तिकः; E. H. केतना *how many,* Mg. केत्तिलए or केत्तुलए, Skr. कियत्तिकः; E. H. आपन् or आपुन् or अपना or अपुना *own,* Mg. अप्पुल्लं or अप्पुल्लग्रं (cf. H. C. 2, 163), Skr. आत्मीयम् or °यकम्; E. H. अइसन् or ऐसन् *of that kind,* Ap. Mg. *अइसिल्ले (cf. H. C. 4, 403. 2, 164. Wb. Bh. 437) or *अइसुल्ले (cf. H. C. 4, 429), Skr. ईदृशः; E. H. तइसन् or तैसन् *of that kind,* Ap. Mg. *तइसिल्ल or *तइसुल्ले, Skr. तादृशः; E. H. जइसन् or जैसन् *of whichever kind,* Ap. Mg. *जइसिल्ले or *जइसुल्ले, Skr. यादृशः; E. H. कइसन् or कैसन् *of what kind,* Ap. Mg. *कइसिल्ले or *कइसुल्ले, Skr. कीदृशः, see also § 31.

Note: There are a few optional examples of this change in Pr.; see H. C. 1, 256. 257; as णंगलं or लंगलं, Skr. लङ्गलम् *plough.*

112. ण् *becomes* न्; *as a rule*; see § 13; thus E. H. पानी (or *theṭh* पाणी) *water,* Mg. पाणिग्रं (H. C. 1, 101), Skr. पानीयम्, etc.

113. ठ् *becomes* ड़्; *very rarely*; only resultant; thus E. H. कोड़् *leprosy* for *कोठ्, Pr. कुट्ठं (or कोट्ठं cf. H. C. 1, 116 or कोड्ढं?), Skr. कुष्टम्; E. H. रूड़् *angry,* Mg. लुट्ठे (or लुड्ढे?), Skr. रुष्टः; E. H. अड़तिस् *thirty eight,* Mg. अट्ठतीसा (Wb. Bh. 426), Skr. अष्टत्रिंशत्.

Note: This change is possibly Pr.; as the Skr. conjunct ष्ट has a tendency to change to ड्ढ in Pr.; see § 114.

114. ढ् *becomes* ड़् *or* ह्; *as a rule*; ड़् *is more usual*; thus 1) original; E. H. कमड़ा or कोँड़ा *a kind of gourd,* Mg. कमढए (cf. H. C. 1, 199), Skr. कमठकः; E. H. मड़ा or महा *shed,* Mg. मढए (cf. H. C. 1, 199), Skr. मठकः; E. H. मड़ी *small temple,* Pr. मढिग्रा, Skr. मठिका; E. H. पड़ै *he reads,* Pr. पढइ, Skr. पठति; E. H. पीड़ा *stool,* Mg. पीढए, Skr. पीठकः. 2) resultant; E. H. काड़ै or काहै *he draws,* Pr. कड्ढइ (H. C. 4, 187), Skr. कर्षति (lit. *कृष्यति); E. H. बेड़ै *he encloses,* Pr. वेड्ढइ (Vr. 8, 40) or वेड्ढइ (H. C. 4, 51), Skr. वेष्टते or वेष्टयति; E. H. बड़ै *he grows,* Pr. वड्ढइ (Vr. 8, 44), Skr. वर्धते; E. H. बड़ई or बहइ or बरहइ (cf. § 138) *carpenter,* Mg. वड्ढइए, Skr. वर्धकिकः; E. H. बूड़ा *old man,* Mg. वुड्ढए (cf. H. C. 1, 131), Skr. वृद्धकः; E. H. बूड़ी *old women,* Pr. वुड्ढिग्रा (cf. H. C. 1, 131), Skr. वृद्धिका; E. H. डेड़् or देड़् *one and a half,* Mg. दिवड्ढे (Wb. Bh. 190), Skr. अर्धद्वितीयः

(see § 416); E. H. अड़ाई *two and one half,* Pr. अड्ढअइअ, Skr. अर्द्धतृतीया (see § 416); E. H. साढ़े *one half more,* Pr. सड्ढ°, Skr. सार्द्ध°.

115. ह् *becomes* ल्ह्; *very rarely*; only original; E. H. कुल्हाड़ा *axe,* Mg. कुढालए (cf. H. C. 1, 199), Skr. कुठारकः; E. H. कुल्हाड़ी *small axe,* Mg. कुढालिआ, Skr. कुठारिका; E. H. कोल्हू *mill* (*for making sugar or oil*), Mg. कुढले, Skr. कुठरः (a post round which the mill stone moves).

Note: E. H. दुलहा *bridegroom,* दुलही or दुलहिन् *bride* (spelled H. H. दुल्हा, दुल्हिन् see § 6, note) are Mg. दुल्लहए, दुल्लहिआ (cf. H. C. 4, 338. Ls. 227. 228), Skr. दुर्लभकः, दुर्लभिका (lit. *difficult to obtain, dear*), not Skr. उद्वोढा, उदूढा (as Bs. I, 271. 245). And E. H. निकालै is Pr. निक्कालइ or निक्कालेइ, Skr. निष्कालयति (of R. कल्; perhaps caus. or denom. of कृ), not Pr. निक्कड्ढइ, Skr. निष्कर्षति (as Bs. I, 354). As to कोल्हू, the Mg. कुढले might be कुडुले in Ap. Mg. (cf. vulgar B. कुडूल् *axe* for Mg. कुढाले, see Bs. I, 270), and thence (eliding ल्) कुडुए, कुडू or कोल्हू (cf. §§ 49. 125); there is Skr. कुठारुः, Mg. कुढालू *tree* (*post?*), which might also produce कोल्हू. An instance of this change in Pr. is अंकोल्ल° for *अंकोल्ह° (H. C. 1, 200; cf. पल्लट्टइ and पल्हत्थइ H. C. 4, 200), Skr. अङ्कोठ°.

bb) Reduction.

116. ख् *and* घ् *become* ह्; generally when original; as E. H. मुह् or मुंह् *mouth,* Pr. मुहं (H. C. 2, 164), Skr. मुखम्; E. H. मेह् or मेँह् *rain,* Mg. मेहे (cf. H. C. 1, 187), Skr. मेघः, etc.; sometimes when initial in a compound; as E. H. पोहर् *father's family,* Pr. पिउहरं (H. C. 1, 134) for *पिउघरं, Skr. पितृगृहम्; E. H. नैहर् *wife's mother's family*; E. H. देहर् *idol temple,* Pr. *देअघरं, Skr. देवगृहम्; 2) rarely when resultant; as E. H. रहै *he lasts, stays* for *रखै, Mg. लक्खइ, Skr. रक्ष्यते (pass.); E. H. पाहीँ *by the side of* for *पाखीँ, see § 74. exc.; O. E. H. कहूँ or काहूँ *by the side of* for *कखूँ or *काखूँ, Ap. *कक्खहुं, Skr. कक्षे (cf. § 378, 3).

Exceptions. Sometimes ख् remains unchanged; probably either to avoid confusion, as in E. H. लिखल् *written,* not *लिहल्, Mg. लिहिदे (cf. H. C. 1, 187 लिहइ), to distinguish from E. H. लिहल् *taken* for *लहल्, Mg. लहिदे; or to suit analogy, as in E. H.

सुख् *pleasure* (Pr. सुहं H. C. 1, 187) like दुख् *pain*, Pr. दुक्खं (H. C. 2, 72); but generally words with ख् are tats.; as E. H. सखी *friend*, etc.

Note: The change of original ख् and घ् to ह् is Pr. (H. C. 1, 187); there are also examples of ह् for resultant ख् and घ्; as Pr. दाहिणो or दक्खिणो (H. C. 2, 72), Skr. दक्षिणः, E. H. दाहिन् *right*, but दखिन् or दक्खिन् *south*; Pr. दुहं or दुक्खं (H. C. 2, 72), Skr. दुःखम्, E. H. only दुख् *pain*; Pr. दीहो or दिग्घो (H. C. 2, 91), Skr. दीर्घः *long*, E. H. *deest*.

117. झ् *becomes* ह्; *very rarely*; only resultant; E. H. माँहि॰ or माही॰ *amidst* for *माझी॰, Ap. Pr. मज्झहिं, Skr. मध्ये.

Note: Probably ह् represents the Mg. semiconsonant य् = ज्, as in Pr. छाहा for Skr. छाया (Vr. 2, 18), see § 18.

118. ढ् *becomes* ह्; *very rarely*; only original; E. H. पहिल् or पहेल् *first*, Ap. Mg. *पढइल्लें, Mg. पढमिल्ले (Wb. Bh. 437), Skr. प्रथमः; E. H. पहार् or पहाड़् *mountain-range*, Ap. Mg. *पढिअअडे, Skr. प्रथितकः (lit. *spread out*); E. H. पहारा or पहाड़ा *the multiplication table*, Ap. Mg. *पढिअअडए, Skr. पथितकः (with pleon. उक, see § 217); the ह् is absorbed just as in B., O., H. H. पढ़ा *read*, Mg. पढिअए, W. H. पढ़्यौ, Ap. पढिअउ.

Note: The root पृथ् or प्रथ् shows this change in Pr. already; e. g., Pr. पुढवी or पुहवी or पुहुवी (H. C. 1, 216. 88. 131), Skr. पृथिवी or पृथ्वी *earth*, O. H. पुहुमि; Pr. पिहं or पुहं beside पिधं or पुधं (H. C. 1, 188), Skr. पृथक्; Pr. पिहुलं, Skr. पृथुलम् *full* (Spt. 313). But perhaps there was an Ap. form पध॰. The only other instances of the change of ढ् to ह् which I know, are the Pr. पिहडो or पिढरो, Skr. पिठरः *pot* (H. C. 1, 201) and the G. and S. कुहारो *axe*, Pr. कुठारो (H. C. 1, 199), see Bs. I, 270 and § 115. Perhaps also in Pr. काहावणो or कहावणो (H. C. 2, 71) for *कड्ढावणो, Skr. कार्षापणः or कर्षापणः; cf. Pr. कड्ढइ = Skr. कर्षति (H. C. 4, 187). All Gds. have पहेल॰, S. पेहेरो॰, see § 401.

119. ध् *becomes* ह्; always when original; as E. H. कहै *he speaks*, Mg. कहेदि or कधेदि (H. C. 4, 267. 302), Skr. कथयति; E. H. साह् *a title of merchants*, Pr. साहू (H. C. 1, 187), Skr. साधुः; E. H.

ब्रहिर् *deaf,* Mg. बहिले (cf. H. C. 1, 187), Skr. ब्रधिरः; E. H. दही *curds,* see § 53; also when initial in a compound; as E. H. गोह् *lizard, aligator,* Pr. गोहो, Skr. गोधिः; E. H. गोहूँ *wheat,* see § 64; 2) very rarely when resultant; as E. H. काँहार् or का॑हार् *porter,* Mg. खंधग्राले (cf. H. C. 2, 4 or *कंधग्राले, cf. H. C. 2, 5), Skr. स्कंधकारः.

120. भ् *becomes* ह्; always when original; as E. H. गुहै *he strings,* Pr. गुहइ or गुभइ (H. C. 1, 236), Skr. गुफति; E. H. सौरी or सहरी *a kind of fish,* A. Mg. सहलिग्रा (cf. H. C. 1, 236), Skr. शफरिका; E. H. सोहै *it looks well,* Pr. सोहइ (H. C. 1, 187), Skr. शोभते; E. H. गहिर् *deep,* Mg. गहिले (cf. H. C. 1, 101), Skr. गभीरः; E. H. ग्रहीर् *herdsman,* Mg. ग्राहीले, Skr. ग्राभीरः; also when initial in a compound, as E. H. मुत्ताहल् *pearl,* Pr. मुत्ताहलं (H. C. 1, 236) for *मुत्ताभलं, Skr. मुक्ताफलम्; E. H. कटहल् *jackfruit,* Mg. *कंटग्रहले, Skr. कण्टकफलः; E. H. सुहाग् *good fortune,* Pr. सुहग्गं (cf. H. C. 1, 160), Skr. सौभाग्यम्; 2) rarely when resultant; as E. H. कुँहार् or कोँहार् *potter,* Mg. कुम्भाले or कुम्भग्राले (cf. H. C. 1, 8), Skr. कुम्भकारः; E. H. सम्हालै or सम्भालै *he supports,* Mg. सम्भालेइ, Skr. सम्भारयति; E. H. सगा *full brother* for *सगहा or *सगभा, Mg. सगब्भए, Skr. सगर्भकः; also optionally, as E. H. जीह् or जीभ् *tongue,* Pr. जीहा or जिब्भा (H. C. 2, 57), Skr. जिह्वा.

Note: Words with original भ् are tats. or semitats., as E. H. सुभाव् or सुभाउ *disposition,* Skr. स्वभावः, Pr. सहावो (H. C. 1, 187).

cc) Vocalisation.

121. य् *becomes* इ *and combines with the adjacent vowels;* thus 1) य *ya* to इ, as E. H. बिगत् *individual,* Skr. व्यक्तः (semitats.); 2) ग्रय *aya* to ऐ or ए, as E. H. सै or से *hundred,* A. Mg. सयं, Skr. शतम्; E. H. समै or समे *time,* A. Mg. समये, Skr. समयः; E. H. उदै or उदे *rising,* Skr. उदयः (semitats.); E. H. नैर् or नेर् *town,* Mg. नयलं (cf. H. C. 1, 180), Skr. नगरम्; E. H. नैन् or नेन् *eye,* Mg. नयणं (H. C. 1, 180), Skr. नयनम्; E. H. रैन् or रेन् *night,* Mg. लयणी (cf. H. C. 4, 401), Skr. रजनी; E. H. पैँता *foot of a bed,* Mg. पायंतए (cf. H. C. 3, 134) or पयंतए, Skr. पादान्तकः or पदान्तकः; 3) इय *iya* to ए, as E. H. पछेँत् *backyard,* Ap. Mg. *पच्छिग्रंते or पच्छिमंते, Skr. पश्चिमान्तः, etc.; cf. § 77.

122. व् *becomes* उ *and combines with the adjacent vowels*; thus 1) व *va* to उ, as E. H. सिउ or सिव *Śiva*, A. Mg. सिवे, Skr. शिवः; E. H. देउ or देव *god*, Mg. देवे (cf. H. C. 1, 177), Skr. देवः; E. H. नेउ or नेव *foundation*, Mg. नेवे, Skr. नेमः; 2) वि *vi* to उ, as E. H. नौंई *he will bow* for *नउंई, Pr. नविहिइ or नमिहिइ (cf. H. C. 4, 158), Skr. नमिष्यति; E. H. हौवों or हौंग्रों *I am* for *हउग्रों, Ap. हविग्रउं, Pr. हविग्र म्हि, Skr. भूतोऽस्मि; E. H. नौग्रा or नउग्रा *barber*, see § 96; E. H. जनउ or *जनोउ *sacrificial thread*, Pr. *जन्नोग्रविग्रं (see p. 23 and H. C. 1, 101), Skr. यज्ञोपवीतम्; 3) ग्रव *ava* optionally to ग्रौ; as E. H. ग्रौर् or ग्रउर् *and*, Mg. ग्रवलं, Skr. ग्रपरम्; E. H. कौन् or कउन् or कवन् *who*, see § 106; E. H. कौरी *a kind of shell* (see § 103); E. H. सौती *wife*, Pr. सवत्तिग्रा (cf. Spt. 78), Skr. सपत्निका; E. H. भौंरा *humble-bee*, Ap. भवँरउ (cf. H. C. 4, 397), Skr. भ्रमरकः; E. H. पठौतों or पठउतों *if I send*, Ap. *पट्ठवंतउं, Pr. पट्ठवंतऽम्हि or पट्ठावंतऽम्हि (cf. H. C. 4, 37), Skr. प्रस्थापयन्नस्मि; sometimes to ग्रो; as E. H. सोँह् *oath*, see § 100; E. H. कोँहड़ा *a kind of gourd*, see § 114; sometimes to ऊ; as E. H. लून् or लोन् or नून् or नोन् (see § 31) *salt*, Pr. लोणं or लवणं, Skr. लवणम्; E. H. भूलै or भूरै *he forgets*, Ap. Mg. *भवँलइ or *भमलेइ, Skr. भ्रमयति; 4) इव *iva* to ग्रो; as E. H. ग्रहिनोई, see § 49; or to ऊ, as E. H. पछूत् *back-yard*, Ap. पच्छिवंतु, Skr. पश्चिमान्तः; E. H. ग्रगूग्रा or ग्रगुग्रा *leader, guide*, Ap. Mg. *ग्रग्गिवँग्रए, Skr. ग्रग्रिमगकः; 5) इवा or इवे to ग्रो; as E. H. परोस् *neighbourhood*, see § 104; E. H. परोसै *he distributes*, A. Mg. पलिवेसइ, Skr. परिवेषयति; 6) ग्राव *áva* optionally to ग्रौ; as E. H. महौत् or महाउत् or महावत् *elephant-driver*, Ap. महावँत्तु, Skr. महामात्रः, etc.; cf. § 34. 78.

Note: It will be seen from some of the above examples, that Skr. प् is in Pr. व् (H. C. 1, 231), in Gd. उ; and Skr. म् in Ap. Pr. म् or वँ (H. C. 4, 397), in Gd. उँ or उ. Traces of these changes are found in Pr.; as Pr. लोणं or लवणं, Skr. लवणम् (Vr. 1, 7), E. H. लोन् *salt*; Pr. ग्रोज्काग्रो or उवज्काग्रो, Skr. उपाध्यायः, E. H. ग्रोका *magician*; Ap. पढउं (cf. H. C. 4, 385) for *पढविँ, Pr. पढमि or पढामि, Skr. पठामि, E. H. पढौं or पढों *I read*, see § 497, 2.

dd) Elision.

123. व् *before* इ (*or* ई) *is elided*; *as a rule* (cf. § 33); *only original*; thus E. H. ऐकइस् *twenty one* (W. H. एकीस्), A. Mg. एक्कवीसा (Wb. Bh. 426. H. C. 1, 28), Skr. एकविंशतिः; E. H. बाइस् *twenty two*, A. Mg. वावीसं (Wb. Bh. 425) or वावीसा (Wb. Bh. 426. T. V. 1, 4. 79), Skr. द्वाविंशतिः; E. H. तेइस् *twenty three*, A. Mg. तेवीसं (Wb. Bh. 425) or तेवीसा (H. C. 1, 165), Skr. त्रयोविंशतिः; E. H. पचीस् *twenty five* for *पचइस्, A. Mg. *पंचवीसं or °सा (cf. Wb. Bh. 425), Skr. पञ्चविंशतिः; E. H. सताइस् *twenty seven*, A. Mg. सत्तावीसा (H. C. 1, 4), Skr. सप्तविंशतिः; E. H. अठाइस् *twenty eight*. A. Mg. अट्ठावीसा (Wb. Bh. 426), Skr. अष्टाविंशतिः; E. H. ओनइस् *nineteen* (W. H. उनीस्), A. Mg. ऊणवीसा or एकूणवीसा (Wb. Bh. 426), Skr. ऊनविंशतिः or एकोनविंशतिः; E. H. भइल् *been*, पाइल् *found*, आइल् *come*, see § 109; E. H. पठइबों or पठैबों *I shall send*, Ap. *पट्ठविवउं or *पट्ठाविवउं, Pr. पट्ठाविअव्वऽम्हि, Skr. प्रस्थापितव्योऽस्मि; E. H. पठाई *he shall send*, Pr. पट्ठाविहिइ, Skr. प्रस्थापयिष्यति; E. H. पठइलों or पठैलों *I have sent*, Mg. पट्ठाविदऽम्हि, Skr. प्रस्थापितोऽस्मि, etc. The resultant व्, being always hardened (see § 129) is never elided.

Exception. A few exceptions, see § 122.

Note: In the numerals all Gds. elide व्, exc. M., G. and S.; thus 21 M. एकवीस्, G. एकवीश् (S. एकीह); 22 M. बावीस् or बेवीस्, G. बावीश्, S. बावीह; 23. M. तेवीस्, G. त्रेवीश्, S. ट्रेवीह; 25 M. पंचवीस्, G. पचीश्, S. पंजवीह or पंजीह, etc.

124. र् (= Mg. ल्) *before* इ *is elided*; *sometimes*; only original; thus E. H. कय् *having done* for *कइ, O. H. करि, Mg. कलिअ (H. C. 4, 302) or Mh. करिअ (H. C. 4, 272), Skr. कृत्वा; E. H. धय् *having placed* for *धइ, O. H. धरि, Mg. धलिअ, Skr. धृत्वा; E. H. कै *suffix of genitive* for *कइ, O. H. करि, Mg. *कलिअ or *कलिए, Skr. कृतः; E. H. पै *upon*, Ap. Mg. पलि, Mg. पले, Skr. परे; E. H. पै *however*, Mg. पलि or पले, Skr. परम्; E. H. धइल् *placed* and कइल् *done*, see § 109; E. H. अइसन् or ऐसन् *such* (see § 111), Ap. Mg. *अइसिल्ल (cf. H. C. 4, 403), A. Mg. एलिस° or Mh. एरिस° (H. C. 1, 142), Skr. ईदृश°; E. H. कइसन् or कैसन् *of what kind*, Ap. Mg. *कइसिल्ल (cf. H. C. 4, 403), A. Mg. केलिस° or Mh. केरिस° (H. C. 1, 142), Skr. कीदृश°;

E. H. तइसन् or तैसन् *of this kind,* Ap. Mg. *तइसिल्लु, A. Mg. तालिस° or तारिस° (H. C. 4, 287), Skr. तादृश°; E. H. जइसन् or जैसन् *of which kind,* Ap. Mg. जइसिल्ले, A. Mg. जालिस° or जारिस° (Wb. Bh. 422), Skr. यादृशः; E. H. सा *like,* A. Mg. सलिअए or सरिअए, Skr. सदृशकः (see § 292).

Note: Pr. has an instance of the elision of ल् before इ in बइल्लो *bull* (H. C. 2, 174), Skr. बलिवर्दः.

125. ल् *after* उ *is elided; rarely;* only original; thus E. H. पुआल् *straw,* Pr. *पुलालो, Skr. पलालो (cf. Skr. पुलाक); but perhaps for पवाल् or पावाल् = Pr. पाअवालो, Skr. पादपालो *litter, bed of straw;* E. H. केँचुवा or केँचवा *earth-worm,* Mg. किंचुलए, Skr. किञ्चुलकः; E. H. कोल्हू *sugar-mill,* see § 115.

126. ह् *before or after* इ *is elided; sometimes;* thus in the E. H. suffix of 3. pers. sg. fut. ई (for *इई), Pr. इही or इहिइ, Skr. इष्यति; e. g., E. H. होई *he will be,* Pr. होही (H. C. 2, 180) or होहिइ (H. C. 4, 388), Skr. भविष्यति; E. H. हँसी or हसी (§ 67) *he will laugh,* Pr. हसिहिइ (H. C. 3, 157), Skr. हसिष्यति; E. H. ऐँ (for *अइँ) suffix of 3. pers. pl. pres., Ap. Pr. अहिं, Pr. अंति, Skr. अन्ति; e. g., E. H. करैँ *they do,* Ap. करहिं (H. C. 4, 382), Pr. करंति (H. C. 4, 376), Skr. कुर्वन्ति; E. H. हँसैँ or हसैँ *they laugh,* Ap. हसहिं, Pr. हसंति (H. C. 3, 142), Skr. हसन्ति; E. H. ऐँ or एँ or ईँ suffix of locative (see § 77. exc.), Ap. अहिं (K. I. 12, 27), Skr. ए; e. g., E. H. पाछैँ or पाछेँ *behind,* Ap. पच्छहिं, Skr. पश्चे; E. H. ए suff. of the obl. form sing. of adj. (see § 386), O. H. अहि, Ap. Pr. अहे, Skr. अस्य; e. g., E. H. मीठे *sweet,* O. H. मीठहि, Ap. मिट्ठहे, Skr. मिष्टस्य; E. H. ईँ suffix of 1. pers. pl. pres., Pr. इम, Skr. आमः (§ 497, 4); e. g., E. H. हसीँ *we laugh,* Pr. हसिम, Skr. हसामः; E. H. ले *he takes,* Pr. लेइ (H. C. 4, 238) for *लिहइ or लहइ (H. C. 4, 335), Skr. लभते; E. H. लेँ *they take,* Pr. लेहिं (H. C. 4, 387) for *लिहंति or लहंति (H. C. 4, 341), Skr. लभन्ते; E. H. बिफै or बिहफै *thursday,* Pr. विहप्फई (H. C. 1, 138), Skr. बृहस्पतिः, see also § 32. Sometimes otherwise; as E. H. मो (कहू) *of me,* Ap. Pr. महु (H. C. 4, 379), see § 430, 1.

Note: In W. H., औ or ओ suffix of 2. pers. pl. pres., Ap.

अहु (H. C. 4, 384), Skr. अथः, see § 497, 5; e. g., W. H. माँगो or मांगो *you ask*, Ap. मग्गहु (H. C. 4, 387), Skr. मार्गयथः; also W. Gd. ओं or ओ or अँ or एँ suff. of the obl. form pl., Ap. Pr. अहुं or अहं or अहिं, Skr. आनाम्, see § 365, 7; e. g., Br. नरौं, H. H. नरों, S. नराँ or नरें *men*, Ap. णरहुं or णरहं or णरहिं, Skr. नराणाम्; S. ऊँ suffix of 1. pers. pl. pres., Ap. अहुं (H. C. 4, 386), Pr. अमु (H. C. 3, 155), Skr. आमः, see § 497, 4; e. g., S. हलूँ *we go* (Tr. 314), Ap. चलहुं, Pr. चलमु, Skr. चलामः. About the elision of ह् in Ap. Pr. see Ls. 484; also Pr. सरिआहँ (H. C. 4, 300) for *सरिहाहँ, Skr. सदृशाणाम्, E. H. सा, see § 124.

127. म् *before* इ *and before or after* उ *is optionally elided*; often; generally with anunásika; thus E. H. गोसाईं or गोसामी *monk*, Ap. गोसामिउ, Skr. गोस्वामिकः; E. H. साईं or सामी *master*, Ap. सामिउ (H. C. 4, 409), Skr. स्वामिकः; E. H. कुअँर् or कुअर् or कुवर् *prince*, Ap. Pr. कुवँरु or कुमरु (cf. H. C. 4, 397. 1, 67), Skr. कुमारः; E. H. कुआँर् or कुवार् or कुमार् *youth, prince*, see p. 29; E. H. कुआँरी or कुवारी or कुमारी *virgin, princess*, Ap. कुवँारिआ or कुमारिआ, Skr. कुमारिका; E. H. भूईं or भूमी, Pr. भूमिआ, Skr. भूमिका; E. H. धूआँ or धूवाँ *smoke*, Ap. धूवँउ or धूमउ, Skr. धूमकः; E. H. कोँई or कोई *waterlily* or *jackfruit*, Pr. कुमुइआ (cf. H. C. 2, 182), Skr. कुमुदिका; E. H. सोँहैं or सोँहीं *in front of*, Ap. Pr. समुहहिं (cf. H. C. 1, 29) or संमुहहिं (see § 126), Pr. संमुहम्मि, Skr. सम्मुखे; E. H. रोँऊँ *hair of the body*, Mg. लोमे, Skr. रोम; E. H. रोआँ or रोवाँ *hair of the body*, Mg. लोमअं, Skr. रोमकम्. Rarely without anunásika; as E. H. गइल् or गैल् *gone*, see § 77.

Note: Four instances of the elision of म् before उ are mentioned by H. C. 1, 178 (Vr. 2, 3); Pr. जउँणा, Skr. यमुना *Jamná*; Pr. चाउँडा, Skr. चामुण्डा *Durga*; Pr. काउँओ, Skr. कामुकः *a certain plant*; Pr. अणिउँतयं, Skr. अतिमुक्तकम् *a certain shrub*. None of these occur in E. H.; here they are tats. or semitats.; e. g., E. H. जमुना, not tadbh. *जौन्; perhaps to distinguish from जौन् *foreigner*, Pr. जवणो, Skr. यवनः, as in E. H. जौनपुर् *Jaunpur*, Skr. यवनपुरम्. In Pr. म् before इ might become व् by H. C. 4, 397; and such व् too, would be elided in E. H. by § 123.

128. *न् before or after इ or before उ; with or without anunásika*; very rarely; thus 1) original, as E. H. ठाउँ or ठाउ or ठावँ or ठाव् *place, residence*, Ap. ठाउ (H. C. 4, 332) or ठाणु (H. C. 4, 362), Pr. ठाणं (H. C. 4, 16), Skr. स्थानम्; E. H. थे॑ *from* for *थाइँ (N. थाञि), Ap. थाणि, Pr. थाणे (cf. H. C. 4, 16), Skr. स्थाने, W. H. also ते॑, तई॑, ताई॑; E. H. बाँसुरी *flute*, Pr. वंसणालिग्रा, Skr. वंशनालिका; 2) resultant, as in the E. H. conjunct न्ह for O. H. निन, cf. §§ 18, p. 24. 139, note. 141.

Note: E. H. has also ठाम्, besides ठावँ, ठाउँ; and this rather points to a Pr. word ठामु, ठामं (cf. § 127); H. C. has थामं (H. C. 4, 267), perhaps Skr. स्थामन्.

ee) Hardening.

129. *य् and व् become ज् and ब्*; only resultant; thus E. H. काज् *work*, Pr. *कारिज्जं (cf. H. C. 2, 67), Skr. कार्यम् (or semitats.?); E. H. अचारज् *teacher*, A. Mg. *आचारिज्ज, Skr. आचार्यः (or semitats.?); E. H. अचरज् *wonderful*, Pr. अच्छरिज्जं (H. C. 2, 67), Skr. आश्चर्यम्; E. H. चउबिस् or चौबिस् or चवबिस् *twenty four*, Pr. चउव्वीसं (cf. H. C. 3, 137. Wb. Bh. 425. 426), Skr. चतुर्विंशतिः; E. H. छबिस् or छब्बिस् *twenty six*, A. Mg. छव्वीसं (Wb. Bh. 425), Skr. षड्विंशतिः; E. H. परबत् *mountain*, Skr. पर्वतः (semitats.); E. H. पुरुब् *eastern*, Pr. पुरुव्वं (Ls. 183), Skr. पूर्वम्.

ff) Miscellaneous.

130. *ड् or ढ् become ग् or ड् or ड़्*; in E. H. घड़ै or गढ़ै *he fashions*, Pr. घडइ or गढइ (H. C. 4, 112), Skr. घटते; E. H. बिगरै or बिगड़ै *it is spoilt, destroyed*, Pr. विगढइ or विघडइ, Skr. विघटते; also भ् or फ् *becomes ब् or प्*; as E. H. परसै *he touches*, Pr. फरिसइ (H. C. 4, 182), Skr. स्पर्शयति (denom.); E. H. अबरक् *talc*, Skr. अभ्रकम् (semitats. cf. § 132).

131. *क् or ग्, ट्, प् and ब् become optionally घ्, ठ्, फ् and भ् respectively*; in E. H. परघट् or परगट् *manifest* (see § 102); E. H. पहिलौठा or पहिलौटा *firstborn*, Mg. *पढमिल्लउट्टए (see § 118), Skr. प्रथमपुत्रकः; E. H. फुन् or पुन् *again*, Ap. पुणु (H. C. 4, 343), Skr. पुनर्; E. H. सभ् or सब् *all*, Mg. सव्वे, Skr. सर्वः.

Note: In the seventies the aspirate is produced by the

suppression of the neutral vowel: E. H. एखत्तर् *seventy one* for एक॑हत्तर्; E. H. पछत्तर *seventy five* for पच॑हत्तर्; E. H. सतत्तर् *seventy seven* for सत॑हत्तर्; E. H. अठत्तर् *seventy eight* for अठ॑हत्तर्.

132. *Aspiration is transferred*; in E. H. अखरख् or अखरक् *tale*, Skr. अक्षरकम् (semitats.); E. H. हमार् or हमरा *our* (H. H. हमारा), Ap. Pr. अम्हारा (H. C. 4, 345), see § 73; E. H. फुआ *father's sister* for *पिउहा, Pr. पिउच्छा or पिउसिआ (H. C. 2, 142), Skr. पितृष्वसा; also E. H. फुफी; E. H. फुप् *flower*, Pr. पुप्फं (H. C. 2, 53), Skr. पुष्पम्; E. H. उखारै or उखाड़ै *he plucks up* for *उकाढ़ै, Pr. उक्कड्ढइ (cf. H. C. 4, 187), Skr. उत्कर्षति; E. H. निभाए or निबाहै *he accomplishes*, Pr. निव्वाहेइ, Skr. निर्वाहयति; E. H. म्हैँस् *buffalo*, cf. § 177.

Note: There are instances in Pr.; as बहिणी or भइणी *sister* (H. C. 2, 126), Skr. भगिनी, E. H. बहिनि; Pr. गढइ or घडइ *he fashions* (H. C. 4, 112), Skr. घटते, E. H. गढ़ै or गाढ़ै or गडै or गाडै (§ 130). It is frequent in S.; as पंध्राँ or पंद्रहं *fifteen*, also M. पंधरा; S. इहो *this* for *इन्हो; उहो *that* for *उन्हो (§ 438, 4); खाँ *from* for *कहाँ, खे *to* for *कहे (§ 375); चाल्हारो *forty* for *चालीहारो; पांहू or पान्हू जो *own* for *पानह जो (§ 451).

133. *Consonants are transposed*; in E. H. पहिरै *he puts on* (clothes) for *परिहै, Mg. *पलिहइ or *पलिधइ or *पलिधेइ (cf. Cw. 99, 21), Skr. परिदधाति; E. H. चहुँप and पहुँचै *he arrives*, Pr. पहुच्चइ (H. C. 4, 390, 419), Skr. पर्याप्यते (Mg. पय्यावचइ); also कोच् or कोचर् and चोक् or चोकर् *mud* (Skr. चिक्किल); नखलौ and लखनौ *Lucknow*; बिराम् and बिमार् *sick* (persian بیمار); also W. H. रहस् and हरस् *merriment*, E. H. हरिस् see § 58; H. H. डूबै, E. H. बूडै *he sinks*, Pr. वुड्डइ (H. C. 4, 101), Skr. ब्रुडति (i. e. मज्जति).

Note: Also in Pr.; as वाणारसी (Wb. Bh. 412. H. C. 2, 116), Skr. वाराणसी, E. H. बनारस् *Benares*; Pr. अलचपुरं (H. C. 2, 118), Skr. अचलपुरम्, E. H. अलवर् (for *अलअउरं) *Alwar*; Pr. मरहट्ठं (H. C. 2, 119), Skr. महाराष्ट्रम्, E. H. मरहठ् or मराठ् *Marâṭhâ*, see § 32; Pr. द्रहो (H. C. 2, 120), Skr. ह्रदः, E. H. दह् *deep water*; Pr. हलिआरो or हरिआलो (H. C. 2, 121), Skr. हरितालः; E. H. हरियार् *green*; Pr. हलुअं (for हलुकं) or लहुअं (H. C. 2, 122), Skr. लघुकम्, E. H. हलुक्, H. H. हलका *light*.

134. *Consonants are interchanged*; viz. 1) व् and न्, in E. H. निनानबे *ninety nine*, Pr. *नवाणावइ, Skr. नवनवतिः; 2) व् and म्, in E. H. चिकनावट् *clayey soil*, Pr. चिक्कणावमट्टो, Skr. चिक्कणाकमृत्तिः; and vice versa in E. H. पुहुमि *earth*, Pr. पुहुवी (H. C. 1, 131), Skr. पृथ्वी; E. H. पिरथमी *earth*, Skr. पृथिवी (semitats.); 3) स् and ह्, in E. H. केहरी or केसरी *lion*, A. Mg. केसलिए (cf. H. C. 4, 335. Wb. Bh. 255), Skr. केशरिकः.

Note: The latter in Pr. optionally, in दह or दस *ten* (H. C. 1, 262), Skr. दश, E. H. दस or दहैं; Pr. दिवहो or दिवसो *day* (H. C. 1, 263. Wb. Bh. 378), Skr. दिवसः, E. H. दिवा or दिवस (see § 32); Pr. °दहं (H. C. 2, 157) or °रिसं (H. C. 1, 142. Wb. Bh. 422) or रिश्चं (for रिहं cf. H. C. 4, 300 and § 126, note), Skr. दृशं *like*, E. H. °इस (in तइसन् § 124); Pr. °हत्तरि (Wb. Bh. 426) *seventy*°, Skr. °सप्तति:, E. H. °हत्तर्. The change of व् to म् is not uncommon in B., O. and G.; e. g., O. करिवि or करिमि *I shall do* (Sn. 28), O. केमन्त् *how* for *केवन्त्: B. कमन् *how* = Ap. Pr. केयडु; G. चुमालीश *forty four* = E. H. चौवालिस्; W. H. समा *one and a quarter* = E. H. सवा (§ 416). For examples in Ap. Pr., see H. C. 4, 401. 396 and § 122, note.

135. *Consonants are interpolated*; viz. द् in E. H. पन्दरह् *fifteen*, Pr. पणरह (H. C. 2, 43) or पन्नरस (Wb. Bh. 426. H. C. 3, 123), Skr. पञ्चदश; again र् in E. H. करोर् or करोड़ *ten millions*, Ap. क्रोडि (cf. H. C. 4, 399), Mg. कोडी (Wb. Bh. 427), Skr. कोटिः; E. H. सराप् *curse*. Ap. Pr. *स्रापु (H. C. 4, 399), Skr. शापः (semitats.); again य् in E. H. ऐयारह्, Pr. *एगारह or एक्कारस (Wb. Bh. 424), Skr. एकादश; E. H. ऐक्यावन् *fifty one*, Pr. *एक्कावण्णं, Skr. एकपञ्चाशत्; E. H. ऐक्यासी *eighty one*, Pr. *एक्कासीई (cf. Wb. Bh. 426), Skr. एकाशीतिः; E. H. ऐक्यानबे *ninety one*. Pr. *एक्काणावइ, Skr. एकनवतिः; E. H. निन्यानबे or निनानबे *ninety nine*, see § 134.

Note: E. H. has a word कोरी or कोडी, but it means *score, twenty* (see § 405). — Perhaps E. H. ऐग्य° and ऐक्य° stand for ऐगय° and ऐक्कय, Skr. एकक°. — Occasionally र् is interpolated in Ap. Pr., see H. C. 4, 399; as व्रासु or वासु, Skr. व्यासः *Vyása*.

δ) CONJUNCT CONSONANTS.

136. Medial conjunct consonants in E. H. are of two kinds, original and resultant. The former are those which have passed as such into E. H. from the Pr., as in the tadbh. पक्का *ripe*, A. Mg. पक्कए, Skr. पक्वकः; E. H. पत्थर् *stone*, A. Mg. पत्थले, Skr. प्रस्तरः; E. H. सत्तर् *seventy*, A. Mg. सत्तरि, Skr. सप्ततिः; E. H. निकम्मा *worthless*, A. Mg. निक्कम्मए, Skr. निःकर्मकः; E. H. कान्ह् *krishna*, Mg. कण्हे, Skr. कृष्णः; or from the Skr., as in the semitats. बिस्वास् *belief*, Skr. विश्वासः, E. H. ग्रिहस्त् *householder*, Skr. गृहस्थः. The latter are those which have resulted either a) from the contraction of contiguous vowels, as in the tadbh. चल्यों *I walked*, Ap. *चलिअउं, Pr. चलिअऽम्हि, Skr. चलितोऽस्मि, or in the semitats. आग्या *order*, P. आगिआ, O. H. आगिना, Skr. आज्ञा; or b) from the suppression of an intermediate vowel, as in the tadbh. बिन्ती *petition* for बिनती, Pr. विणत्तिआ, Skr. विज्ञाप्तिका; E. H. दुल्हा *bridegroom* for दुलहा, Mg. दुल्लहए, Skr. दुर्लभकः; E. H. बिस्वा *a measure of land* (the 20. part.), Ap. Mg. वीसवंए or वीसमए, Skr. विंशमकः; E. H. गधा *ass* for गदहा, Mg. गद्दहए, Skr. गर्दभकः; E. H. बर्हेला *hog* for बरहेला, Ap. Mg. *वराहिल्लए, Skr. वराहः, etc. These latter are not uncommon in the *khaṛi* E. H., though very rare in the *theṭh* (e. g., in the numerals एखत्तर् *seventy one*, सयत्तर् *seventy seven*, etc., see § 131, note); in H. H. they are the rule (see § 6, note). Of the resultant conjuncts, those arising from the suppression of a vowel may be of any kind, strong, mixed or weak [1]), homogeneous or heterogeneous; but those arising from the contraction of vowels must be heterogenous and either mixed or weak. Neither kind of resultant suffers any further change in E. H. As to the original conjuncts, the tatsamas may be of any kind, but the tadbhavas can only be either homogeneous (as क्क्, त्त्, त्थ्, म्म्, etc.) or such as consist of a consonant proper preceded by a nasal (as ङ्क्, ञ्ज्, न्त्, etc.) or of ह् following a nasal or semivowel (as

1) These useful terms of classification I have adopted from Beames I, 281.

न्ह्, म्ह्, ल्ह्, र्ह्, ळ्ह् = ऌ्); for these are the only conjuncts tolerated in Pr. (see § 137). Both original classes, the tadbh. and tats., are, as a rule, liable to further change in E. H. This may take place in three ways: 1) they may be *dissolved* by the interpolation of a vowel (अ, इ or उ, §§ 138—142); or 2) they may be *simplified* by eliding one consonant (see §§ 143—150); or 3) they may be *elided* altogether (see §§ 151—157). There are, also, isolated changes of a miscellaneous kind (see §§ 158—166).

137. *Affinities.* These three kinds of changes exist in Pr. also; thus the conj. is *dissolved* in Pr. सलाहा (H. C. 2, 101), Skr. श्लाघा, E. H. सराह *praise*; Pr. सिरी (H. C. 2, 104), Skr. श्री, E. H. सिरि *prosperity*; Pr. दुवारं (H. C. 2, 112), Skr. द्वारम्; E. H. दुवारु *door.* Other examples see § 142. The conjunct is *simplified* in Pr. ईसरो or इस्सरो (Vr. 3, 58), Skr. ईश्वरः, E. H. ईसरु *lord*; Pr. वासा (H. C. 2, 105) for *वस्सा, Skr. वर्षा, E. H. °वास् *rain* (cf. § 283); see also § 150. The conj. is *elided,* either undissolved, as in Pr. राई or रत्ती (H. C. 2, 88), Skr. रात्रिः, E. H. राति *night*; or after dissolution, as in Pr. रअणं (Vr. 3, 60) for रतणं, Skr. रत्नम्, E. H. रतन् *gem*; see also § 157. The former kind of elision is not uncommon in E. H. (see § 151—156); the latter is exceptional, both in Pr. and E. H. (see §§ 141. 142). — Generally speaking, however, the treatment of conjuncts is this, that while Skr. admits almost any kind of them, homogeneous or heterogeneous, Pr. makes them, as a rule, homogeneous, and E. H. further reduces them to single consonants either by dissolution or by the elision of one. The only heterogeneous conjs., tolerated by Pr., are those consisting of a nasal or anusvára preceding a consonant proper (see H. C. 2, 92. 1, 30; e. g., संझा or सञ्झा, Skr. सन्ध्या, E. H. साँझ् *evening*), or of ह following a nasal (see H. C. 2, 74. 75; e. g., Pr. कण्हो, Skr. कृष्णः, E. H. कान्ह् *krishna*; Pr. बम्हणो, Skr. ब्राह्मणः, E. H. बाम्हन् *bráhman*) or ल् (see H. C. 4, 26. 200. 2, 76; e. g., पल्हत्थइ (cf. Wb. Bh. 409), Skr. *पर्यस्तयति, E. H. पल्थै *he turns over*). In the Ap. Pr. also the conjunct of a cons. proper with a following र may occur (see H. C. 4, 398. 399;

e. g., Ap. प्रिउ or पिउ, Skr. प्रियः *beloved*; Ap. व्रासु or वासु, Skr. व्यासः *Vyása*); in E. H., however, this kind of conj. is as a rule dissolved; see § 138. 185. 186.

aa) Dissolution.

138. अ *is interpolated*; *often*; E. H. इमली *tamarind*, Mg. अमलिआ (cf. Wb. Bh. 377) for Pr. *अनिलिआ (cf. H. C. 2, 106), Skr. अम्लिका; E. H. सुदरसन् *beautiful*, A. Mg. सुदरिसणो (cf. H. C. 2, 105), Skr. सुदर्शनः; E. H. दरसन् *interview, visit at a shrine*, Pr. दरिसणं, Skr. दर्शनम्; E. H. बरही *peacock*, A. Mg. बरिहिए (cf. H. C. 2, 104 but cf. Ls. 142), Skr. बर्हिकः; E. H. परामरस् *consideration*, A. Mg. परामरिसे (cf. H. C. 2, 105), Skr. परामर्शः; E. H. सुकर् or सुकल् *white*, Pr. सुक्किलं (H. C. 2, 106), Skr. शुक्लम् (or शुक्रम्); E. H. अमरा *mango*, Pr. अम्बिरअं (cf. H. C. 2, 56), Skr. आम्रकम्; E. H. अमल् *sour*, Pr. अम्बिलं (H. C. 2, 106. Wb. Bh. 415), Skr. अम्लम्; E. H. मुरख् *stupid*, A. Mg. मुरुक्खे (cf. H. C. 2, 112), Skr. मूर्खः; E. H. मुरछा *swoon*, Skr. मूर्छा (semitats.); E. H. अचरज् *wonderful*. कारज् *work*, अचारज् *teacher*, see § 129; E. H. बरहई or बढ़ई or बढ़ई *carpenter* (see § 114); E. H. बमहन् or बामन् *bráhman*, Mg. बम्हणे (H. C. 2, 74), Skr. ब्राह्मणः; E. H. कनहैया or कन्हैया *Krishna*, Mg. कण्हए (cf. H. C. 2, 75), Skr. कृष्णकः; E. H. सहस् *thousand*, Ap. Pr. सहसं, Skr. सहस्रम्; E. H. चकर् *wheel*, बकरी *she-goat*, see § 102, etc. Very commonly in semitats., as E. H. परबत् *mountain* (§ 129), Skr. पर्वतः; E. H. किरपा *mercy*, Skr. कृपा; E. H. किरति *praise*, Skr. कीर्त्तिः; E. H. जनम् *birth*, Skr. जन्म; E. H. रतन् *gem*, Skr. रत्नम्; E. H. जतन् *effort*, Skr. यत्नः; E. H. बिगत् *individual*, रगत *blood* (cf. H. C. 2, 10 रत्त°), भगत् *devotee*, भगति *faith*, भगताई *devotedness*, मुगति *salvation*, see § 102; E. H. बरकि *but*, Pers. बल्कि (بلکه).

139. इ *is interpolated*; *sometimes*; thus E. H. अगिनि or अगनि or आगि *fire*, Pr. अगिणी (Ls. 244) or अगणी (H. C. 1, 102) or अग्गी (Vr. 5, 18), Skr. अग्निः; E. H. मिसिर् or मिसर् *a bráhman family-name*, A. Mg. *मिसिरे (but मीसे *mixed* Wb. Bh. 173. H. C. 2, 170), Skr. मिश्रः; E. H. आइल् or आवल *come*, पाइल् or पावल् *attained*, see § 109; E. H. बिरिछ् *tree*, Skr. वृक्षः; E. H. सइन् *sign*, see § 141.

Note: The E. H. conjunct ग्य *gya*, O. H. गिन *gina* is to be explained by this rule; e. g., E. H. राग्यो, O. H. रागिनो, Skr. राज्ञो; see §18, pp. 23. 24.

140. उ *is interpolated*; *rarely*; thus E. H. पुरुब्, W. H. पुरब्, Pr. पुरुव्वं (Ls. 183) or पुरवं (H. C. 4, 323 or पुरव्वं?), Skr. पूर्वम्; E. H. सुरुन् *top, point,* but सोँग् *horn* and साँग् *spear*, Pr. सिंगं or संगं (H. C. 1, 130), Skr. शृङ्गम्; see also § 187.

141. *Dissolved consonants are treated like original single ones*; thus क् becomes ग् (cf. § 102); e. g., in E. H. बिगत्, रगत्, भगत्, etc.; see § 138; ग् is elided (cf. § 101); e. g., in E. H. सइन् or सैन् *sign*, Pr. *सइणा or *सग्गिणा, Skr. सञ्ज्ञा, cf. Pr. राइणा (H. C. 3, 51) for *राग्गिणा, Ps. Pr. राचिञा (H. C. 4, 304), Skr. राज्ञा; द् becomes ल् (cf. § 109) or is elided (cf. § 101); e. g., in E. H. अइलों or आयों *I came*, Mg. आविद्ऽम्हि or आविअऽम्हि, Skr. आप्तोऽस्मि, etc.; व् is elided (cf. § 123); e. g., in E. H. पइलों or पायों *I obtained*, Mg. पाविद्ऽम्हि or पाविअऽम्हि, Skr. प्राप्तोऽस्मि; न् is elided (cf. § 128); e. g., in the E. H. conjunct °ग्य° for O. H. °गिन°, see § 139, note.

Note: The participial examples, as अइलों, पायों, etc. and Pr. तविओ (H. C. 2, 105), Skr. तप्तः, are scarcely quite apposite, as their इ is a *connecting* (suff. इ + त), not a *dissolving* vowel.

142. *Affinities.* Examples of dissolutions are not uncommon in Pr. Probably many of the above instances, though not recorded by Pr. Gramm., existed in Pr. already. In some cases the dissolving vowel has been changed in E. H.; as in E. H. दरसन् for Pr. दरिसणं; other examples see in §§ 138—140. Other examples, in which E. H. has preserved the Pr. dissolving vowel, are: Pr. सारंगं (H. C. 2, 100), Skr. शार्ङ्गम्, E. H. सारंग् *bow*; Pr. वरिसं, हरिसो, फरिसो, see § 58, note. Some more Pr. examples, see in H. C. 2, 101—114. Vr. 3, 60—66; most of them do not seem to have survived in E. H. In one case, apparently, E. H. does not dissolve, but simplify; Pr. गरिहा (H. C. 2, 104), Skr. गर्हा, but E. H. गारी or गाली *abuse* = A. Mg. *गलिहआ or *गर्हिआ, Skr. गर्हिका; but it dissolves in गरियावे or गलियावे *he abuses* for *गरिहावै, A. Mg. *गलिहावइ or Pr. *गरिहावइ, Skr. गर्हयति (or den. गर्हापयति). Pr. examples of

the treatment of dissolved cons. are: 1) *elision* of cons. proper in रयणं or रअणं *gem* (Vr. 3, 60. H. C. 2, 101) for *रतणं, Skr. रत्नम्, E. H. *deest* to distinguish from E. H. रयन् or रैन् *night*; Pr. वइरं *thunderbolt* (H. C. 2, 105) for *वजिरं, Skr. वज्रम्, E. H. *deest* to distinguish from बैर् *enmity*, Pr. वइरं (H. C. 1, 152), Skr. वैरम्; but E. H. बजर् (semitats.); Pr. सुइलं *white* (H. C. 2, 166 or सुकिलं), Skr. शुक्लम्, E. H. *deest*; Pr. तविश्रो *hot* (H. C. 2, 105) for *तविदो, Skr. तप्तः, E. H. *deest*, but it has तात् = Pr. तत्तो; Pr. पउमं *lotus* (Vr. 3, 65) for *पदुमं, Skr. पद्मम्; E. H. *deest*; Pr. राइणा *by a king* for *रातिणा (see § 141), etc.; 2) *retention* in अगणी *fire* by H. C. 1, 177; 3) *doubling* in सुक्किलं *white* (H. C. 2, 106), Skr. शुक्लम्, E. H. सुकल्; Pr. पुरुव्वं *forward* (Ls. 183) or पुरवं (H. C. 4, 323), Skr. पूर्वम्, E. H. पुरुब् or पुरब्[1]); 4) *reduction* of aspirate in सुहमं (H. C. 2, 101) or सुहुमं (H. C. 2, 113. 1, 118. Wb. Bh. 406. 410) for *सुखुमं, Skr. सूक्ष्मम्.

bb) Simplification.

143. *The first consonant is elided*; as a rule; thus क् in E. H. सकै *he can*, Pr. सक्कइ (H. C. 4, 86), Skr. शक्नोति; E. H. सूखा or सूका *dry*, A. Mg. सुक्खए or सुक्कए (cf. H. C. 2, 5. Wb. Bh. 289—291); ग् in E. H. माग् *road* (see § 45); E. H. बाघ् *tiger*, Mg. वग्घे (cf. H. C. 2, 90), Skr. व्याघ्रः; च् in E. H. पचै *it is digested*, Pr. पच्चइ, Skr. पच्यते; E. H. माछी *fly*, Pr. मच्छिआ (H. C. 2, 17), Skr. मक्षिकाः; ज् in E. H. आज् *to-day*, Pr. अज्ज (H. C. 1, 33), Skr. अद्य; E. H. बूझै *he understands*, Pr. बुज्झइ (H. C. 4, 217), Skr. बुध्यते; ट् in E. H. टूटै *it breaks*, Pr. तुट्टइ (H. C. 4, 230), Skr. त्रुट्यति; E. H. पीठि *back*, Pr. पिट्ठी (H. C. 1, 35), Skr. पृष्ठम् or Ved. पृष्ठिः; ड् in E. H. कोडो or कौड़ी, see § 104; E. H. बढै *it grows*, see § 114; त् in E. H. बात् *event*, *word*, Pr. वत्ता (H. C. 2, 30), Skr. वार्त्ता; E. H. हाथ् *hand*, A. Mg. हत्थे, Skr. हस्तः; द् in E. H. गदहा *ass*, see § 136; E. H. दूध् *milk*, Pr. दुद्धं (H. C. 2, 89), Skr. दुग्धम्; प् in E. H. छपय् or छपै *a kind of verse*, Mg. छप्पये (cf. H. C. 2, 77), Skr. षट्पदः; E. H. बाफ् *steam*, Mg. बप्फे (cf. H. C. 2, 70), Skr. बाष्पः; ब् or व् in E. H.

---

1) सुक्किलं and पुरव्वं seem to be correct readings; as shown by the E. H., which has ब् for व्व, not for व् (cf. § 129).

सव्र् *all,* A. Mg. सव्वे (cf. H. C. 3, 58), Skr. सर्वः; E. H. जीभ् *tongue,* Pr. जिब्भा (H. C. 2, 57), Skr. जिह्वा; र्‍ in E. H. पालकी *a palanquin,* Pr. पल्लंकिश्रा (cf. H. C. 2, 68), Skr. पर्यङ्किका or पल्यङ्किका; ञ् in E. H. पचास् *fifty,* Pr. *पंचासं (see § 397), Skr. पञ्चाशत्; ण् in E. H. सान् *sign,* Pr. सण्णा (H. C. 2, 83), Skr. संज्ञा; E. H. कटहल् *jackfruit,* see § 120; न् in E. H. श्रान् *other,* Mg. श्रन्ने (H. C. 3, 58. Wb. Bh. 403), Skr. अन्यः; E. H. हसत् *laughing,* A. Mg. हसंत (cf. H. C. 3, 181), Skr. हसन्; म् in E. H. काम् *work,* see § 45; ल् in E. H. पलटै *he turns over,* Pr. पल्लट्टइ (H. C. 4, 200), Skr. पर्यस्तयति (den.); ष् in E. H. पूस् *the month December-January,* A. Mg. पुस्से or पूसे (cf. Vr. 3, 58), Skr. पुष्यः. Sometimes in foreign words; as E. H. बाकि *but* for बल्कि, Pers. بلکه; E. H. बाटे *for the sake of* for वास्ते, Ar. واسطی (?).

Exception. Rarely both cons. are retained; as E. H. पक्का or पका *ripe, thorough,* पत्थर् or पाथर् *stone,* निकम्मा *useless,* see § 136; E. H. चक्का or चका or चाका *wheel,* Pr. चक्कश्रं (H. C. 2, 79), Skr. चक्रकम्; E. H. सच्च् or सच् or साच or साँच् *true,* उच्च् or ऊँच् *high,* see § 149, 2; E. H. बच्छा or बछा (§ 145, exc. 2) or बच्चा or बचा *young,* Mg. बच्छए (cf. Vr. 3, 40), Skr. वत्सकः; E. H. पट्टा or पटा *title-deed,* Mg. पट्टए, Skr. पट्टकः; E. H. सत्तर् *seventy,* see § 108; E. H. गिद्ध् or गीध् *vulture,* see § 63; E. H. कम्मल् *blanket,* see p. 20; As a rule, when the first is a nasal; thus E. H. पंक् (i. e. पङ्क् § 13) or पाँक् *mud,* and other examples, see p. 29; cf. also § 149.

144. *The second consonant is elided*; only य्, व् and optionally ह्; thus य in E. H. पाधा *teacher* (cf. § 173), Skr. उपाध्यायः; E. H. श्रवध् *Oudh* (cf. § 78), Skr. अयोध्या; E. H. मधि *within,* Skr. मध्ये; E. H. परा़ग् *Allahabad* for *पर्याग्, Skr. प्रयागः; E. H. परोजन् *necessity* for *पर्योजन्, Skr. प्रयोजनम्; E. H. पराचित् *penance* for *पर्याचित्, Skr. प्रायश्चित्तम् (all semitats.). Again व् in E. H. चूमै *he kisses,* Mg. चुम्वइ (cf. H. C. 4, 239), Skr. चुम्वति; E. H. श्रनरा *mango,* श्रमला *sour,* see § 138; H. H. जामुन् *rose-apple,* see § 111; E. H. लाम् *long,* Mg. लम्वे, Skr. लम्बः; E. H. समुझै *he understands,* Mg. सम्बुझाइ, Skr. सम्बुध्यते, and others, see § 18, p. 20; E. H. पिरथी *earth* (also पिरथमी see § 132), Skr. पृथ्वी (semitats.). Again ह् in बामन् or

ब्राम्हन् or ब्रमहन् *Bráhman*, कान् or कान्ह् *krishna* (e. g., in कानपुर् *Cawnpore*), see § 136; E. H. सून् *daughter-in-law* for *सुन्हू, Pr. *सुण्हुश्रा or *सोण्हुश्रा (cf. Vr. 2, 47. H. C. 1, 261), Skr. स्नुषा (or *स्नुषुका; cf. Pr. माउश्रा for माता, § 52); E. H. समालै or सम्हालै or सम्भालै *he supports*, see § 120; E. H. पलगै *he turns over*, see § 137; E. H. कोलू or कोल्हू *sugar-mill*, see § 115; E. H. गाली *abuse* for *गाल्ही, see § 142.

Exception. Rarely न् is elided before ह्; as E. H. जोहै *he regards, looks*, Pr. जोण्हइ (cf. H. C. 2, 75), Skr. *ज्योत्स्नयति (denom. R.).

145. *The remaining consonant is treated like an original single one*; thus ड् as a rule becomes ड़् or र्; e. g., in E. H. कौरी or कौड़ी *cowrie*, see § 104; ल् as a rule becomes र् (§ 110) as in E. H. गारी or गाली *abuse*, see § 142; ल् sometimes becomes न्, as in E. H. आपन् *own*, see § 111; ण् always becomes न् (§ 112), as in E. H. कान् *ear*, Mg. कण्णे, Skr. कर्णः; E. H. सान्, श्रान् see § 143; कान्, सून् see § 144; ढ् as a rule becomes ढ़् or ह्, as in E. H. बढ़ै *he grows*, see § 114; व् always becomes ब् (§ 129), as in E. H. सब् *all*, see § 143; for a few rare cases, see §§ 103. 107. 113. 116. 117. 119. 120. Otherwise it remains unchanged; as E. H. चकी or चक्की *wheel*, Pr. चक्किश्रा, Skr. चक्रिका; E. H. लाज् *shame*, Pr. लज्जा, Skr. लज्जा; E. H. साठि *seventy*, Pr. सट्ठी, Skr. षष्टिः; E. H. रात् *night*, see p. 14; E. H. हाथी *elephant*, A. Mg. हत्थिए, Skr. हस्तिकः; E. H. आधा *half*, Mg. अडए (cf. H. C. 2, 41), Skr. अर्धकः; E. H. बाप् *father*, Pr. बप्पा (Mchh. 119, 5), Skr. वप्रा; E. H. घाम् *heat*, Mg. घम्मे, Skr. घर्मः (cf. H. C. 4, 327); and other examples in §§ 143. 144. 146. 147. 148.

Exception 1. Sometimes ड् and ढ् preceded by a nasalized vowel remain unchanged; as E. H. मूँडै *he shaves*, मोँढा *stool*, see § 149.

Exception 2. Sometimes aspirates are disaspirated; thus ख् in E. H. परकै or परखै *he tests*, see § 58; घ् in E. H. महंग् *high-priced*, M. महग्घे (Spt. 169), Skr. महार्घः; ध् in E. H. काँदा or काँधा *shoulder*, A. Mg. खंधए (cf. H. C. 2, 4), Skr. स्कन्धकः; छ् in E. H. अचरज् *wonderful* for *अछरज्, see § 129; E. H. बचा or बछा *young*, see § 143. exc.;

E. H. पचतावै or पछतावै *he repents,* Pr. पच्छत्तावइ, Skr. पश्चात्तापयति (denom.); E. H. पूचूँ or पूछूँ *beard,* see § 56; E. H. चाहै or छाहै *he desires,* Pr. उच्छाहइ (cf. H. C. 2, 21), Skr. उत्साहयति (denom.); ठ् in E. H. अरतिस् or अठतिस् or अठ्ठतिस् *thirty eight,* see § 113; E. H. अरतालिस् or अठतालिस् or अठ्ठतालिस् *forty eight,* Pr. अट्ठअत्तालीसं (or अठयाले Wb. Bh. 426), Skr. अष्टचत्वारिंशत्; E. H. अठसठि or अरसठि *sixty eight,* Pr. अट्ठसट्ठी, Skr. अष्टषष्टिः; ढ् in E. H. बडा *great* for *बड्डा, Mg. वड्डए (or वड्ढ° Vr. 1, 27), Skr. वृद्धकः; E. H. बेड् *enclosure* for *बेड्ढ, Mg. वेड्ढे (cf. Vr. 8, 40), Skr. वेष्टः; E. H. गरै or गडै or गड्डै *he fashions,* बिगरै or बिगडै *it is spoilt,* see § 130.

Note: There are traces of this disaspiration in Pr., as सुक्कं or सुक्खं *dry* (H. C. 2, 5), see § 143; Pr. पल्लट्टइ (H. C. 4, 200 for *पल्लट्ठइ) or पल्हत्थइ *he turns over,* see §§ 137. 143; Pr. विंचुओ (H. C. 2, 16) or विंछुओ (Vr. 3, 41), E. H. बिच्छू or बीछू, M. विंचू (Man. 36); Pr. उट्ठो (cf. H. C. 2, 34), see § 149, 2; it is quite the general rule in M., and less so in B. and O.; thus M. हात् *hand,* B., O., E. H. हाथ् (§ 143); M. हाती *elephant,* B., O., E. H. हाथी (§ 145); M. साँज् *evening,* B., O., E. H. साँझ् (§ 149, 1); M. साँद् *hole in a wall,* E. H. सेँध्, see § 57; M., B., O. सीडी *ladder,* E. H. सीढी, Pr. *सिड्ढी, Skr. श्रेढी (?); M., B. साडे $2^1/_2$; M. दीड, B. देड् $1^1/_2$; B. आटत्रिश्, M. अडतीस् or अठतीस् 38; B. आटचल्लिश् 48; M. वडा *great,* वेडा *enclosure,* etc. (see Bs. I, 273). It is worth noting also, that the old Mg. has स्ट, स्त, श्च for ष्ट, स्थ् and च्छ (see H. C. 4, 290. 291. 295); e. g., Mg. कोस्टागालं, Skr. कोष्ठागारम्; Mg. उवस्तिदे, Skr. उपस्थितः; Mg. पुश्चदि, Skr. पृच्छति, etc.

146. *The preceding vowel remains short; sometimes;* thus always in E. H. अत् suffix of part. pres.. Mg. अंते (cf. H. C. 3, 181), Skr. अन् (अन्त°); e. g., E. H. होत् *being,* Mg. होंत (cf. H. C. 3, 180), Skr. भवन्; E. H. करत् *doing,* Mg. कलंते (cf. H. C. 4, 431) or कलेंते, Skr. कुर्वन्, etc.; always E. H. पच् *five,* Pr. पंच, Skr. पञ्च in composition; e. g., E. H. पचीस् *twenty five,* see § 123; E. H. पचपन् *fifty five,* Pr. *पंचपन्नं, Skr. पञ्चपञ्चाशत्; sometimes otherwise; as E. H. दुख् *pain,* see § 116, note; E. H. गभिन् *pregnant,* Pr. गब्भिणा (cf. H. C. 1, 208), Skr. गर्भिता; E. H. सकै, पचै, छपर्, सत्र्, पालकी,

पलटै, सच्, see § 143; E. H. समुकँ, पलथै, see § 144; E. H. बँऊ, see § 114; always in the *antepenultimate* (cf. § 25); thus E. H. आम्, but अमरा *mango*, see § 138; E. H. दूबर्, but दुबरा *weak, thin*, see § 22; E. H. उतरै *he descends*, Mg. उत्तलइ, Skr. उत्तरति; E. H. गदहा, पलटै, see § 143; E. H. अमला, पलथै, see § 144; and others.

Note: Similarly M. has अत् suff. of 3. pers. pl., Pr. अंति, Skr. अन्ति (§ 497, 2 f.); as M. चलत् *they were in the habit of going*, Pr. चलंति, Skr. चलन्ति; both M. and B. have the part. suff. अत् or इत्, but पंच्॰ in comp.; e. g., M. पंचवीस्, B. पंचिश्, E. H. पचीस्.

147. *The preceding vowel becomes long; as a rule*; thus अ in E. H. आठ् *eight*, Pr. अट्ठ, Skr. अष्ट; E. H. रानी *queen*, see p. 23; E. H. साथ् *with*, Pr. सत्थं, Skr. संस्थम्, etc.; इ in E. H. भीख् or भीछ् *alms*, Pr. भिक्खा (cf. Wb. Bh. 197. Spt. 312) or भिच्छा (Spt. 163. cf. H. C. 2, 17. 19), Skr. भिक्षा; E. H. रीछ् or रीख् *bear*, Pr. रिच्छो or रिक्खो (H. C. 2, 19), Skr. ऋक्षः; E. H. दीठि *sight*, see § 43; E. H. सीथ् *boiled rice, indigo*, Pr. सित्थं (H. C. 2, 77), Skr. शिक्थम्; E. H. तीनि or तीन् *three*, Pr. तिण्णि (H. C. 3, 121), Skr. त्रीणि, etc.; उ in E. H. सूत् *thread*, Pr. सुत्तं (H. C. 4, 287), Skr. सूत्रम्; E. H. ऊन् *wool*, Pr. उण्णा, Skr. ऊर्णा; E. H. मूठ् *fist*, Pr. मुट्ठी (H. C. 2, 34), Skr. मुष्टिः; E. H. पूत् *son*, Mg. पुत्ते, Skr. पुत्रः, etc.; ऐ in E. H. सेज् *bedding*, Pr. सेज्जा (see § 6), Skr. शय्या; E. H. पेड् *lump*, Pr. पेण्डं (Vr. 1, 12), Skr. पिण्डम्; E. H. ऐँचा *crooked*, Pr. *ऐंचअं, Skr. अञ्चितकम्; E. H. एक् *one*, Pr. ऐक्कं (cf. H. C. 2, 99), Skr. एकम्, etc.; ओ in E. H. पोठ् *hip*, Mg. *पोट्ठे, Skr. प्रोथः; E. H. बोलै *he says*, Pr. बोल्लइ (H. C. 4, 2), Skr. वदति; E. H. पोथी *book*, Pr. पोत्थिआ (cf. Vr. 1, 20), Skr. पुस्तिका, etc. See other examples in §§ 143—146.

148. *The preceding vowel becomes* ए *or* ओ; *rarely*; thus अ in E. H. लेजुर् or लेजुरी *cord*, see § 110. exc.; सेँध् *hole in a wall*, see § 57; E. H. पेड् *tree*, see § 103; E. H. बेँगन् *egg-plant*, Mg. वंगणे, Skr. वङ्गनः; E. H. एड़ी or एडी *heel*, Pr.?, Skr. अंह्रिः; E. H. ऐँचा *crooked*, see § 147; E. H. केकरा or केकडा *crab*, Mg. कक्कडए, Skr. कर्कटकः; E. H. केँचुरी or केँचुली *skin of a snake*, Pr. कंचुलिआ (cf. H. C. 2, 25), Skr. कञ्चुलिका; again E. H. मोँछ् or मूँछ् *moustache*,

चोँच् *bill,* see § 57. Again इ in E. H. मकेला *middle,* A. Mg. मज्झिल्लए (Wb. Bh. 437), Skr. मध्यः; E. H. केँचुवा *earth-worm,* see § 125; E. H. छेद् *hole,* Pr. छिड्डं (Wb. Bh. 174. Spt. 146), Skr. छिद्रम्; E. H. सेम् *bean,* Pr. सिम्बा, Skr. शिम्बा. Again उ in E. H. कोपै *he is angry,* Pr. कुप्पइ (H. C. 4, 230), Skr. कुप्यति; E. H. कोढ् *leprosy,* see § 113; E. H. कोख् *belly,* Pr. कुक्खी, Skr. कुक्षिः; E. H. सोँठ *ginger,* Pr. सुंठी, Skr. शुण्ठिः.

Note: The change of अ to ए or ओ is probably to be explained by a transfer of the succeeding vowel इ or उ into the preceding syllable. Similarly the ए in the E. H. मेहरू *woman* (see § 57) and in the Bs. अहेस् *thou art,* O. H. अहसि is formed.

149. *The preceding vowel is nasalized;* 1) as a rule after the elision of a nasal; thus आ in E. H. जाँघ् *leg,* Pr. जंघा, Skr. जङ्घा; E. H. बाँझ् *barren woman,* Pr. वंझा, Skr. वन्ध्या; E. H. साँझ् *evening,* Pr. संझा (H. C. 2, 92), Skr. सन्ध्या; E. H. चाँद् *moon,* see p. 29; E. H. डाँडी *footpath,* Pr. डंडिआ (cf. H. C. 1, 217), Skr. दण्डिका; E. H. भाँडा *pot,* Mg. भंडए (cf. H. C. 4, 422. 12), Skr. भाण्डकः; E. H. काँपै *he trembles,* see p. 29; etc. Again ई in E. H. मीँजै *he rubs,* Pr. मिंजइ, Skr. मृञ्जति; E. H. सीँचै *he irrigates,* Pr. सिंचइ (H. C. 4, 239), Skr. सिञ्चति, etc. Again ऊ in E. H. सूँड *elephant's trunk,* Pr. सुंडा, Skr. शुण्डा; E. H. मूँडै *he shaves,* Pr. मुंडइ (H. C. 4, 115), Skr. मुण्डति. Again ए and ओ in E. H. सेँध्, एँचा, बेँगन्, etc., and चोँच्, मोँछ्, see § 148. 2) Sometimes otherwise; thus आ in E. H. आँखि *eye,* see § 43; E. H. माँगै *he requests,* Pr. मग्गइ (H. C. 4, 230. Spt. 71), Skr. मार्गयति; E. H. आँच् *flame* (fem.), Pr. *अच्ची, Skr. अर्चिः; E. H. साँच् *true,* Pr. सच्चं (cf. H. C. 2, 13), Skr. सत्यम्; E. H. साँप् *serpent,* A. Mg. सप्पे, Skr. सर्पः, etc. Again ई in E. H. ईँख् or ईख् *sugar-cane,* Pr. इक्खू (H. C. 2, 17), Skr. इक्षुः; E. H. ईँट् or ईट् *brick,* Pr. इट्टा (H. C. 2, 34), Skr. इष्टा; E. H. भीँत् or भीत् *wall,* Pr. भित्ती, Skr. भित्तिः; E. H. नीँद् or नीद् *sleep,* see § 42. Again ऊ in E. H. ऊँख् or ऊख् *sugarcane,* Pr. *उक्खू or उच्छू (H. C. 2, 17. Vr. 1, 15), Skr. इक्षुः; E. H. मूँग् *a kind of pulse* (fem.), Mg. मुग्गे (cf. Vr. 3, 1), Skr. मुद्गः (masc.); E. H. ऊँच् *high,* Pr. उच्चं (cf. H. C. 1, 154), Skr. उच्चम्; E. H. ऊँट् *camel,* Pr. उट्टो (H. C. 2, 34), Skr. उष्ट्रः. Again ए

in E. H. केँकरा or केकरा *crab*, see § 148. Again ओ in E. H. होँठ् or होठ् *lip*, A. Mg. ओट्ठे (cf. Spt. 22), Skr. ओष्ठः.

150. *Affinities.* 1) The general law of the treatment of conjuncts may be stated thus: Pr. elides the first of the (Skr.) conj. and doubles the second; Gḍ. (exc. S. and P.) elides the first of the (Pr.) conj. and doubles (i. e. lengthens) the preceding vowel; e. g., Skr. भक्तम् *boiled rice*, Pr. भत्तं (H. C. 4, 60. Wb. Bh. 214), E. H., W. H., B., O., M., G. भात्, S. भतु; Skr. सप्त *seven*, Pr. सत्त (cf. H. C. 3, 123), E. H., etc. सात्, S. सत, P. सत्त; Skr. अष्ट *eight*, Pr. अट्ठ (cf. H. C. 3, 123), E. H., etc. आठ्, S. अठ, P. अट्ठ; Skr. रात्रिः *night*, Pr. रत्ती (H. C. 2, 79), E. H., etc. राति or रात्, P. रत्त, S. रति. S. usually preserves the short vowel, and P. the conjunct. 2) Sometimes Pr. exhibits the Gḍ. process; especially when one of the conj. is स् (or श् or ष्); e. g., Pr. लासं (H. C. 2, 92) for *लस्सं (cf. H. C. 1, 84), Skr. लास्यम्, E. H. लास् *dance*; Pr. ईसरो (H. C. 2, 92) or इस्सरो (Vr. 3, 58), Skr. ईश्वरः, E. H. ईसर् *lord*; Pr. वीसा (H. C. 1, 28) or वीसई (Ls. 320), Skr. विंशत् or विंशतिः, E. H. बीस् *twenty*; Pr. सीसं (H. C. 2, 92), Skr. शीर्षम्, E. H. सीस् *head*; Pr. वासा (H. C. 2, 105), Skr. वर्षा, E. H. *वास् *rain* (in झपास् *violent burst of rain*, see § 283), etc.; also otherwise, as Pr. आणा *command* for *अण्णा, see p. 23; Pr. दीहो or दिग्घो *long*, see § 116, note, etc.; see Ls. 274. 3) Sometimes in Pr. the preceding vowel optionally becomes ए or ओ; see H. C. 1, 85. 116. Vr. 1, 12. 20; e. g., Pr. बेल्लं or बिल्लं, Skr. बिल्वम्, E. H. बेल् *wood-apple*; Pr. पोक्खरो, Skr. पुष्करः, E. H. पोखर् *pond*; Pr. पोत्थओ, Skr. पुस्तकः, E. H. पोथा; Pr. मोग्गरो, Skr. मुद्गरः, E. H. मोगर् *mallet*, etc. 4) Sometimes in Pr. the first of the conj. becomes a nasal, analogous to the nasalization of the preceding vowel in Gḍ.; see § 158, note. 5) Sometimes in Pr. the second of the conj. is disaspirated, see § 145. exc.

cc) Elision.

151. क्र् *is elided*; *very rarely*; in E. H. चौधरी *headman, chief* for *चव° (§ 69), *चक्र°, A. Mg. चक्कधरिए, Skr. चक्रधरिकः (lit. discus-holder; from °रिन् + क).

152. च् *is elided*; *rarely*; in E. H. चौवालिस् or चउआलिस् *forty four* (B. चोयाल्लिश), A. Mg. चोयालोसा (Wb. Bh. 426), for Pr. *चउचत्तालोसा (cf. Ls. 259 on च = अ), Skr. चतुश्चत्वारिंशत्; E. H. छियालिस् *forty six* (cf. § 55), Pr. *छचत्तालीसा, Skr. षट्चत्वारिंशत्; E. H. तेँतालिस् (O. तेयालिश), A. Mg. तेआलोसा (H. C. 2, 174 or तिंयाले Wb. Bh. 425) for *तेचत्तालोसा, Skr. त्रयश्चत्वारिंशत्.

Note: In composition the र् of चतुर् and ष् (or ट्) of षष् (or षट्) are, as a rule, assimilated, but sometimes elided; thus ass. in चउद्दह (H. C. 1, 171 for चतुर् + दश) or चउव्वारो (H. C. 1, 171 for चतुर् + वार्); again छप्पओ (H. C. 2, 77 for षट् + पद) or छम्मुहो or छंमु° (Vr. 2, 40. H. C. 1, 25. 30 for षट् + मुख), छग्गुणो (Ls. 240 for षट् + गुण). But el. in चउगुणो (H. C. 1, 171 for चतुर् + गुण) or चउवीसं (H. C. 3, 137 for चतुर् + विंशति), चउमुहु (H. C. 4, 331 for चतुर् + मुख); again छहत्तरि (छ + हत्तरि for षट् + सप्तति) or छद्दिसिं (Wb. Bh. 426. 234 for षट् + दिशो). Hence the above mentioned num. may be derived from the Pr. forms: चउचत्त° or (eliding च, see § 101) चउअत्त°; छचत्त° or छअत्त°; and similarly तिचत्त° or तिअत्त° (Skr. त्रिचत्वारिंशत्).

153. त् *is elided*; *sometimes*; in E. H. आउ and आन् *suff. of abstract nouns* for Ap. Pr. अत्तउ or अत्तणु, Pr. अत्तं or अत्तणं or अअत्तं or अत्तणं, Skr. त्वम् or त्वनम्, see § 227; E. H. चारि *four* for *चआरि, A. Mg. चत्तारि (Wb. Bh. 425. H. C. 3, 122), Skr. चत्वारि; E. H. चालिस् *forty*, see § 110. exc.; E. H. बयालिस् *forty two*, A. Mg. बायालोसं (Wb. Bh. 426) for *बाअत्तालोसं, Skr. द्वाचत्वारिंशत्; E. H. चवालिस् or चौवालिस् or चउआलिस् *forty four* (cf. § 26) and E. H. छियालिस् *forty six*, see § 152; E. H. सैँतिस् *thirty seven* (O. सइँतिश) for सयँ° or सअँ°, A. Mg. सत्ततीसं (Wb. Bh. 426), Skr. सप्तत्रिंशत्; E. H. सैँतालिस् *forty seven* for सयँ° or सअँ°, A. Mg. *सत्तअत्तालोसं, Skr. सप्तचत्वारिंशत्; E. H. रोअब् or रोइब् *to weep*, Pr. रोत्तव्वं (H. C. 4, 212. Vr. 8, 55 or रोइअव्वं Spt. 258 or Ap. Pr. रोइव्वं), Skr. रोदितव्यम्; E. H. मियाँ *friend* (a respectful address), Mg. मिअए or मित्तए (cf. Wb. Bh. 398. Vr. 3, 58), Skr. मित्रकः; or after simplification, in E. H. धाई *wet-nurse*, Pr. धाइआ or *धातिआ or धत्तिआ (cf. H. C. 2, 81), Skr. धात्रिका; E. H. दाई *foster-mother*, *wet-nurse*, Pr. *दातिआ or दत्तिआ, Skr. दात्रिका (lit. giver, scl. of nourishment); E. H. दाऊ

appellation of a father or elder brother (lit. giver of sustenance), Mg. *दातुए or *दत्तुए (cf. H. C. 3, 44), Skr. दातृकः; E. H. भाई *brother*, Mg. *भातिए or *भत्तिए, and E. H. माई *mother*, Pr. *मातिआ or *मत्तिआ, see § 63; E. H. बाय् *he is* for *बाइ, Pr. वत्तइ, Skr. वर्त्तते.

154. प्प् *is elided; very rarely*; in E. H. चउआ or चउपा *fourfooted*, Mg. चउपाए or चउप्पाए (see § 152, note), Skr. चतुष्पादः; E. H. चौअन or चउअन् *fifty four* (M. चौपन्न), Mg. *चउपन्नं or *चउप्पन्नं (see § 152, note), Skr. चतुःपञ्चाशत्.

155. व्व् *is elided; rarely*; optionally in E. H. ए *suffix of the oblique infinitive*, for *अए or *इए for *अव्वे or *इव्वे, Ap. *इव्वहे (see §§ 308. 365, 6), Pr. इअव्वस्स, Skr. इतव्यस्य; e. g., E. H. चलै or चलब्बे (cf. § 129) *to go*, Ap. चलिव्वहे, Pr. चलिअव्वस्स, Skr. चलितव्यस्य; E. H. खाये (for *खाइए) or खाइब्बे or खाब्बे *to eat*, Ap. खाइव्वहे, Pr. खाइअव्वस्स, Skr. खादितव्यस्य.

156. न्न् *is elided; rarely*; in E. H. पैँतिस् *thirty five* (O. पइँतिश, B. पयँत्रिश for पअँ°), A. Mg. पन्नतीसं or पणतीसं (Wb. Bh. 425), Skr. पञ्चत्रिंशत्; E. H. पैँतालिस् *forty five* for पन्नअत°, A. Mg. पन्नचत्तालीसा (Wb. Bh. 425 or पणयालीसं), Skr. पञ्चचत्वारिंशत्; E. H. पैँसठि *sixty five*, A. Mg. *पन्नसट्ठी, Skr. पञ्चषष्टिः.

157. *Affinities.* In Pr. also, there are a few examples of the elision of a conj.; thus some instances of म्म् see in § 152, and of त्त् in § 153; others of त्त are, Pr. राई or रत्ती *night*, Skr. रात्रिः (H. C. 2, 88. Vr. 3, 58), but E. H. राति; Pr. काऊण *having done* (Vr. 4, 23) for *कातूण or *कत्तूण (cf. Vr. 10, 13), Skr. कृत्वा (or *कृत्वानं), E. H. *deest*; Pr. काअव्वं (Spt. 229) *what is to be done*, Mg. कायव्वं (Wb. Bh. 398) or कादव्वं (Vk. 67) *to be done* for *कातव्वं or *कत्तव्वं, Skr. कर्तव्यम्, E. H. *deest* (it forms करब्.); Pr. वअस्सअअ° (Spt. A 53) *companionship*, Skr. वयस्यकत्व°. An instance of क्क् is Pr. तेलोअं or तेल्लोक्कं *the three worlds* (Vr. 3, 58), Skr. त्रैलोक्यम्, E. H. *deest*; and of ग्ग्, Mg. नियंथे *devotee* (Wb. Bh. 397) or निग्गंथे, Skr. निर्ग्रन्थः, E. H. *deest*. See also Wb. Bh. 398. Ls. 273. 274.

dd) Miscellaneous.

158. क्क्, ग्ग्, ग्घ्, क्ख्, च्छ् *become* ङ्क्, ङ्ग्, ङ्घ्, ङ्ख्, ञ्छ् *respectively*; thus क्क् in E. H. कंकर् *limestone*, Pr. *कक्करं, Skr. कर्करम्; E. H. कंकरोल्

a kind of gourd, Ap. Pr. कक्कडुल्लु (cf. H. C. 4, 429), Skr. कर्कट:[1]); again ग्ग् in E. H. नंग् *naked,* A. Mg. नग्गे (cf. Wb. Bh. 185. H. C. 2, 78), Skr. नग्नः, and in its derivatives as नंगा, नंगो *naked,* नंगाई *nakedness,* etc.; again क्ख् in E. H. पंख् *wing,* A. Mg. पक्खे (cf. Wb. Bh. 427. H. C. 2, 106), Skr. पक्षः, and in its derivatives पंखा, पंखी *fan,* पंखरी or पंखड़ी *flower-leaf* (Ap. पक्खडिआ), पंखी *bird* (from Skr. पक्षिन्)[2]); again ग्घ् in E. H. महंग् *high-priced,* see § 145. exc. 2; again च्छ् in E. H. पंछी *bird,* Pr. पच्छिओ, Skr. पक्षिकः (from पक्षिन् + क), and in its cognates पंछाला *tail of a paper-kite* (Ap. *पच्छअउउ) from Skr. पक्ष *tail*[3]).

Note: There are instances of this change in Pr.; as Pr. वंकं, Skr. वक्रम्, E. H. बांक् *crooked*; Pr. अंसू, Skr. अश्रु, E. H. आँसू *tear*; Pr. मंसू, see § 56: Pr. पुंछं, Skr. पुच्छम्, E. H. पूँछ् *tail*; Pr. पंसू, see § 44; Pr. मंजारो, Skr. मार्जारः, E. H. मंजार् *cat,* etc., see H. C. 1, 26. Vr. 4, 15; but E. H. बिच्छू or बीछू *scorpion* (M. विंचू) for Pr. विंछिओ or विंचुओ (H. C. 2, 16), Skr. वृश्चिकः.

159. ंस् *and* ंह् *become* न्स् *and* ङ्घ; *always*; thus ंस् in E. H. हन्स् or हाँस *goose,* see p. 29; E. H. मन्स् or माँस् or मास् *flesh,* see p. 30; E. H. हिन्सा *slaughter,* see § 39, etc.; again ंह् in E. H. सिंघ् or सीँघ् *lion,* see p. 29; E. H. संघार् *collection,* Pr. संघारो or संहारो (H. C. 1, 264), Skr. संहारः, etc.

Note: The change of ंह् to ङ्घ् is optional in Pr. already, see H. C. 1, 264. As to the spelling of ंह् and ंस्, see §§ 38. 39; and of ंघ् see § 13.

160. ङ्क् *and* ङ्ख् *become* ङ्ग् *and* ङ्ख्; *rarely*; thus ङ्क् in E. H. कंगाल् (i. e., कङ्गाल्, see § 13) *destitute,* Mg. *कंकाले (i. e., कङ्काले, see H. C. 1, 30), Skr. कङ्कालः (lit. skeleton, see Bs. I, 98); E. H. कंगन् *bracelet,* Pr. कंकणं (Spt. 68). Skr. कङ्कणम्; E. H. पलंग् *bed,* Mg. पल्लंके (cf. H. C. 2, 68), Skr. पर्यङ्कः; E. H. पलंगरी or पलंगड़ी *small bedstead,* Ap. पल्लंकडिआ, Skr. पर्यङ्किका; E. H. पाँग् or पाँक् *mud,* see p. 29; E. H.

1) But E. H. ककरी or ककड़ी *cucumber,* Pr. कक्कडिआ, Skr. कर्कटिका.

2) Also regularly पाँख्, पांखा, पाँखी, cf. § 149.

3) पंछी and पंछाला might be corruptions for पुंछी, पुंछाला, from Pr. पुंछं, see note.

पाँगा *salt* (obtained from sea-mud), Mg. पंकए, Skr. पङ्कतः; E. H. पंगति *row* (cf. §§ 102, 2. 138, usually पाँति p. 30), Skr. पङ्क्तिः; E. H. बाँगर् *high ground*, Ap. वंकडं, Skr. वक्रम् (lit. *curved*); again ञ्च् in E. H. कुंजी *key*, Pr. *कुंचिआ, Skr. कुञ्चिका.

161. ल्ल् *and* न्न् *become* ल्ह् *and* न्ह्; *optionally*; thus ल्ल् in E. H. काल् or काल्ह् *yesterday* or *to-morrow*, Pr. कल्लं (H. C. 2, 186. Spt. 46), Skr. कल्यम्; E. H. चील् or चील्ह् *kite*, Mg. चिल्ले, Skr. चिल्लः; E. H. चीलर् or चील्हर् *louse*, Ap. चिल्लडु, Skr. चिल्लः; E. H. पेलर् or पेल्हर् *testicle*, Ap. पेल्लडं (cf. H. C. 4, 143 पेल्लइ), Skr. पेलम्, etc. Again न्न् in Bs. दीना or दीन्ह *given*, A. Mg. दिन्ने (cf. Wb. Bh. 402) or दिण्णे (H. C. 4, 302), Skr. दत्तः; Bs. कीन् or कीन्ह् *done* (Ap. Pr. किन्नउ H. C. 4, 329 ?), Skr. कृतः; Bs. लीन् or लीन्ह् *taken* for *लिन्न्, Skr. लब्धः; E. H. इन् or ऐन् or O. H. ऐन्हि suffix of 3. pers. pl. for *एन्नि or *इअन्नि, Pr. इअंति, Skr. इतन्ति (see §§ 497, 6. 503); e. g., E. H. पढिन् or पढेन् or O. H. पढेन्हि *they read* for *पढिअन्नि, Pr. पढिअंति, Skr. *पठितन्ति (denom.); E. H. चलेन् or O. H. चलेन्हि *they walked* for *चलिअन्नि, Pr. चलिअंति (Skr. चलिता भवन्ति), etc.

Note: In Pr. पल्लत्थं (H. C. 2, 68) and पल्हत्थं (H. C. 4, 258), Skr. पर्यस्तम्; Pr. एण्हिं (Vr. 4, 33) for एण्हिं (Ls. 129), Skr. इदानीम्.

162. स्थ् *becomes* स्त्; *rarely*; as E. H. गिरहस्त् *husbandman, householder*, Mg. °हस्ते (cf. H. C. 4, 291), Skr. गृहस्थः (semitats.), and its derivative गिरहस्ती *husbandry*.

163. ण्ड् *becomes* न्ड् *or* न्न्; *rarely*; E. H. गन्ना or गन्डा or गाँडा *sugarcane* (lit. having joints), Mg. गंडए, Skr. गण्डकः; E. H. गंडेरी or गंडेरी *joint of sugarcane*, Ap. गंडइल्लिआ, Skr. गण्डक°.

164. क्क् *becomes* त्त्; *very rarely*; E. H. कुत्ता *dog* (G. कुतर्), Ap. कुक्कुरु, Skr. कुक्कुरः (usually E. H. कूकर् or कुक्कुर्); and its derivative E. H. कुतरू *puppy*.

165. त्य् *and* ध्य् *become* त्त् *or* त् *and* ड् *or* ध् *respectively*; *very rarely*; thus E. H. नित्त् or नित्, A. Mg. नित्ते (cf. Wb. Bh. 414), Skr. नित्यः; E. H. मधि, O. H. मडि, Skr. मध्ये; but see § 144.

166. च्च् *and* त्त् *become* ड् *and* ग्य्; *always in semituts.*; see §§ 36. 37.

c) CHANGES OF INITIAL SOUNDS.

a) VOWELS.

167. अ *becomes* इ; *rarely*; E. H. इमली or अमली *tamarind* (cf. § 138), Mg. अमलिआ (cf. Wb. Bh. 377), Skr. अम्लिका.

168. आ *becomes* अ; *sometimes*; thus E. H. अचारज् *teacher*, Skr. आचार्यः (§ 129); E. H. अचार् or आचार् *conduct*, Skr. आचारः; E. H. अग्या or आग्या *command*, Skr. आज्ञा (all semitats.).

169. ए *becomes* अ; *rarely*; E. H. अकेला *solitary*, A. Mg. एक्कल्लए (cf. H. C. 2, 165) or *एक्किल्लए, Skr. एकलकः.

170. ए *becomes* इ; *sometimes*; as E. H. इग्यारह् or ऐग्यारह् *eleven*; इक्यावन् or ऐक्यावन् *fifty one*, see § 135; and other compounds of एक.

171. ए *and* ओ *become* य *and* व *respectively*; *sometimes*; thus ए in E. H. यक् or ऐक् or एक् *one*, Mg. एक्के (Wb. Bh. 424), Skr. एकः; E. H. यह् or ऐह् (or ई) *he, this*, Ap. एह or एहु (H. C. 4, 362), Skr. ईदृशः; again ओ in E. H. वह् or ओह् (or ऊ) *he, that*, Ap. *एवेह or *एवेहु (see § 438, 1. 5), Skr. *एवादृशः (= एवंविधः); E. H. वनइस् or ओनइस् *nineteen*, see § 123; and other compounds of ऊन; cf. § 98.

172. अ *is elided*; *sometimes*; thus E. H. भीतर् *within*, A. Mg. अब्भिंतरे (Wb. Bh. 206), Skr. अभ्यन्तरम्; E. H. भीजै *he is afflicted with grief*, Pr. *अब्भिज्जइ, Skr. अभ्यर्द्यते (pass. of अर्द्); E. H. भीजै *he is wet*, Pr. *अब्भिज्जइ, Skr. अभ्याद्रर्यते (denom. of आर्द्र *wet*); E. H. झाड़ै *he sweeps*, Pr. *अज्झाडुइ, Skr. अध्यर्दयति (caus. of अर्द्) or Skr. अध्याटयति (caus. of अट् *roam*, cf. Pr. झाटइ H. C. 4, 161); E. H. झंगा *upper garment*, A. Mg. अज्झंगए, Skr. अध्यङ्गकः; E. H. झंगिया *child's vest*, Pr. अज्झंगिआ, Skr. अध्यङ्गिका; E. H. रहट् or अरहट् *water-wheel*; E. H. तीसी *flax*, see §§ 55. 109, note.

Note: Such elisions occur especially in A. Mg.; see Wb. Bh. 405, as रयणी, Skr. अरत्निः, etc.

173. उ *is elided*; *sometimes*; thus E. H. चाहै *he desires*, see § 145, exc. 2; E. H. बैठै or बइठै *he sits*, Pr. उवविट्ठइ, Skr. *उपविष्टति.

(denom. of उपविष्ट, cf. Ap. Pr. बइट्टउ H. C. 4, 444, see § 352); E. H. पै *upon*, see § 124; E. H. पाधा *teacher*, see § 144.

Note: For such elisions in Ap. Mg. see Wb. Bh. 406; e. g., पोसह्, Skr. उपवसथ, etc.

β) SINGLE CONSONANTS.

174. त् *and* द् *become* ट् *and* ड्; *rarely*; thus त् in E. H. टूटै or तूटै *it breaks*, Pr. तुट्टइ (H. C. 4, 230), Skr. त्रुट्यति; E. H. टट्टू or तट्टू *pony*, Mg. *तट्टुए (cf. H. C. 3, 44. 1, 131), Skr. तर्कुकः (of R. तृ; cf. तुरग *horse*); E. H. टीकू or टीका (fem.) *sectarian mark on the forehead*, Skr. तिलकः (masc.), cf. § 125; E. H. ठोँठू or ठोरू *beak* for *टोरू, Pr. तोंडं (Vr. 1, 20), Skr. तुण्डम्. Again द् in E. H. डीठ् or दीठ् or दीठि *sight*, see § 43; E. H. डाढी or दाढी *beard*, Pr. दाढिआ (cf. H. C. 2, 139), Skr. दंष्ट्रिका (also दाढिका); E. H. डाढ़ or दाढ़ *tooth, tusk*, Pr. दाढा (H. C. 2, 139), Skr. दंष्ट्रा; E. H. डारू or डाल् or दाल् *branch* (fem.), A. Mg. दाली, Skr. दारी; E. H. डारा or डाला *branch*, A. Mg. *दालए or *डालए (cf. H. C. 4, 445. Ap. डालइं), Skr. दारकः; E. H. डारी or डाली *branch*, A. Mg. दालिआ, Skr. दारिका; E. H. डेढ़ or देढ़ or डेवढ़ or देवढ़ *one and a half*, see § 114.

Note: Instances in Pr. are; Pr. डोला or दोला, Skr. दोला, E. H. डोरू or दोरू *cord*, whence E. H. डोला or दोला, डोली or दोली *a swing, a dooly*, Pr. डोलओ or डोलिआ or द°, Skr. दोलकः or दोलिका; Pr. डड्ढो or दड्ढो, Skr. दग्धः, E. H. डाढा *burnt. fire* (Skr. दग्धकः?); Pr. डरो or दरो, Skr. दरः, E. H. डरू or दरू *fear*; Pr. डाहो or दाहो, Skr. दाहः, E. H. डाह् *malice, jealousy* and दाह् *burning*; Pr. डब्भो or दब्भो (Wb. Bh. 293), Skr. दर्भः, E. H. डाभ् *kusa-grass*; Pr. डसइ, Skr. दशति *he bites*, E. H. डसै; Pr. डट्ठो or दट्ठो, Skr. दष्टः *bitten, oppressed*, whence perhaps E. H. डाट् *threat*, डाटै or डाँटै *he threatens*; see H. C. 1, 217. 218; but E. H. दहै *it burns*, Mg. दहइ (cf. Wb. Bh. 155), Pr. डहइ (H. C. 1, 218), Skr. दहति; E. H. डंभ् *arrogance*, Pr. डंभो or दंभो, Skr. दम्भः.

175. क्, ट्, ड् *become* ख्, ठ्, ढ्, *respectively*; *very rarely*; thus क् in E. H. खाँसी *cough*, Pr. कासिआ (or खासिआ? cf. H. C. 1, 181),

Skr. कात्तिका; E. H. ठोर् *beak* for *टोर्, see § 174; E. H. ठेँकुना *bug*, Pr. ढंकुणग्रो (S. C. 1, 3. 130), Skr. मत्कुणाकः.

Note: Pr. examples are: खप्परं (H. C. 1, 181), Skr. कर्परम्, E. H. खपर् *skull, tile*; Pr. खोलग्रो (H. C. 1, 181), Skr. कोलकः, but E. H. कोला *nail*; again Pr. छुच्छं or चुच्छं or तुच्छं (H. C. 1. 204), Skr. तुच्छम्, E. H. छूछ् *mean*; again Pr. कडिलो or जडिलो (H. C. 1, 194), Skr. जटिलः, E. H. *deest.*

176. भ् *becomes* ह्; *rarely*; E. H. हाँड़ or भाँड़् *pot*, A. Mg. भंडि (Wb. Bh. 274), Skr. भाण्डः.

Note: In Pr. होइ (H. C. 4, 60), Skr. भवति, E. H. होय् *he is.*

177. *Aspiration is transferred*; E. H. म्हैस् or भैँस् or महिस् or बहिस् *buffalo*, A. Mg. महिसे, Skr. महिषः, see § 178; E. H. भूखा *hungry* for *बुहुखा, Mg. बुभुक्खिए (or भुक्खे Wb. Bh. 290?), Skr. बुभुक्षितः; E. H. भभूति or भभूति *ashes of cowdung*, Skr. विभूतिः (semitats.); E. H. भाप् or भाफ् or बाफ् *steam*, see § 143; E. H. फूप् or फूफ् *flower*, see § 132.

178. म् *becomes* व्; *very rarely*; in E. H. बहिस् or महिस् *buffalo*, see § 177. 134.

Note: In Pr. वम्महो (Vr. 2, 39), Skr. मन्मथः, E. H. *deest.*

179. ल् *becomes* न्; *very rarely*; E. H. नोन् or लोन् *salt*, Pr. लोणं (H. C. 1, 171), Skr. लवणम्, see also §§ 31. 111.

Note: In Pr. णाहलो, Skr. लाहलः, E. H. नाहर् *tiger*; Pr. णंगलं *plough*, णंगूलं *tail*, Skr. लाङ्गलम्, लाङ्गूलम्, but E. H. लांगल् and लाँगूल्, see H. C. 1, 256.

180. न् *becomes* ल्; *very rarely;* E. H. लोल् or नील् *dark-blue* (§ 31), A. Mg. नीले (Wb. Bh. 160. H. C. 3, 32), Skr. नीलः; E. H. लूरी or नूरी *a kind of parrot;* E. H. लीमू or नीमू *lime-tree* (S. लिमु or निमु), see p. 20.

Note: In Pr. लिम्बो or निम्बो (H. C. 1, 239), Skr. निम्बः; but E. H. नीम् *Nimb-tree.*

181. य् *and* व् *become* ज् *and* ब् *respectively;* always; thus य् in E. H. जतन् *effort*, Skr. यत्नः (semitats): E. H. जोग् *worthy*, Mg. योग्गे (cf. Vr. 3, 2), Skr. योग्यः; E. H. जानै *he knows*, Mg. याणाइ (cf. Wb. Bh. 394, note) or याणादि (H. C. 4, 292), Skr. जानाति (see

pg. 22); etc.; again E. H. बात्, see § 143; E. H. बाजै or बजै *it is sounded*, Pr. वज्जइ (H. C. 4, 406), Skr. वद्यते, etc.; also as initial of the second of a compound; as E. H. पुरबासी *citizen*, Skr. पुरवासी (semitats); see § 17.

182. स् *becomes* छ्; *very rarely;* E. H. छोँचै or सोँचै *he sprinkles*, see § 149.

Note: In Pr. छत्तवण्णो (Vr. 2, 41), Skr. सप्तपर्णः; E. H. *deest.*

183. ह् *is prefixed; very rarely;* E. H. होँठ् *lip*, see § 149.

Note: Frequently in S.; as एडो or हेडो *so large*, ओडो or होडो *so large*, एतिरो or हेतिरो *so many* (Tr. 224), एकु or हेकु *one* (Tr. 157), इति or हिति *here* (§ 468, a). Sometimes in B. and M., as B. एथा or हेथा *here*, ओथा or होथा *there* (§ 468, a); M. इकडे or हिकडे *hither* (§ 468, b).

184. *Consonants are elided;* only in alliterative phrases; thus र् in रोटी ओटी *meal* (lit. bread, etc.); or ख् in खाना आना *dinner;* very commonly प्, as पानी आनी *water;* आस् पास् *close by;* उलट् पुलट् *topsy-turvy;* अछतावै पछतावै *he repents deeply;* etc.

γ) CONJUNCT CONSONANTS.

185. अ *is interpolated;* often; thus E. H. नहान् *bathing*, Ap. Pr. णहाणु (H. C. 4, 399), Skr. स्नानम्; E. H. नहाय् *he bathes*, Pr. णहाइ (H. C. 4, 14), Skr. स्नाति: E. H. नहाटै *he flees*, Pr. *णहट्टइ, Skr. *स्नस्तयति (denom. of part. स्नस्त); E. H. परोहन् *carriage*, Ap. प्रवहणं (cf. H. C. 4, 398) or Pr. पवहणं (Mchh. 109, 18), Skr. प्रवहणम्; E. H. परघट or परगट् *manifest*, see § 102; E. H. परगास् *clearness*, Ap. Pr. प्रगासु (cf. H. C. 4, 398), Skr. प्रकाशः; E. H. परगासै *he displays*, Ap. Pr. प्रगासइ or पगासेइ, Skr. प्रकाशयति; E. H. परसन् *pleased*, Ap. Pr. प्रसण्णु, Skr. प्रसन्नः; E. H. परोहा *leathern waterbucket*, Ap. Pr. प्रवहउ or प्रवाहउ (cf. H. C. 1, 68), Skr. प्रवहकः or प्रवाहकः; E. H. सराहै *he praises*, Pr. सलाहइ (cf. H. C. 2, 101), Skr. श्लाघते; E. H. सराहन् *praise*, Pr. सलाहणं, Skr. श्लाघनम्; E. H. सरेस् *glue* (lit. *adhesion*), A. Mg. सिलेसे (cf. H. C. 2, 106), Skr. श्लेषः (or Pers. سریش *sirish*?); E. H. मलान् *faded*, Pr. मिलाणं (H. C. 2, 106), Skr. म्लानम्; and in semitats; as E. H. सलोक् *verse*, Skr. श्लोकः (Pr. सिलोओ H. C. 2, 106.

Ls. 183); E. H. परोजन् *necessity*, परागु *Allahabad*, पराचित् *penance*, see § 144.

Note: In Pr. सलाहा (H. C. 2, 101), Skr. श्लाघा, E. H. सराह् *praise*.

186. इ *is interpolated; sometimes;* thus E. H. तिरपन् *fifty three*, Ap. Pr. * त्रिपण्णं (cf. H. C. 4, 398), Skr. त्रिपञ्चाशत्; E. H. तिरसठि *sixty three*, Ap. Pr. *त्रिसट्ठी, Skr. त्रिषष्टिः; E. H. तिरिका or त्रिका *triad*, see § 408; E. H. गिरहन् *eclipse*, Ap. Pr. ग्रहणं, Skr. ग्रहणम्; E. H. पिलही *spleen*, Pr. *पिलहिआ, Skr. प्लीहिका; E. H. गिलानि *fatigue*, Pr. *गिलाणी (cf. H. C. 2, 106), Skr. ग्लानिः; E. H. तिरिया *woman*, Ap. Pr. *त्रिआ, Skr. स्त्रिका.

Note: In Pr. सिणेहो (Wb. Bh. 405. Ls. 182) or सणेहो or नेहो (H. C. 2, 102), Skr. स्नेहः, E. H. सिनेह् or सनेह् or नेह् *love;* Pr. सिरी (H. C. 2, 104), Skr. श्री, E. H. सिरि *prosperity;* Pr. किरिआ (H. C. 2, 104), Skr. क्रिया, E. H. किरिया *oath;* Pr. किलेसो (H. C. 2, 106) *trouble*, see § 58, note.

187. उ *is interpolated; rarely;* thus E. H. सुमिरन् or सुमरन् *recollection*, Ap. Pr. सुमरणु (H. C. 4, 426. cf. 4, 74), Skr. स्मरणम्.

188. *The first consonant is elided; always;* thus E. H. भीतर् *within* for अभीतर्, A. Mg. अब्भिंतरं (§ 172), Skr. अभ्यन्तरम्; E. H. भीजै, काढै, कंगा, कंगिया, for अभीजै, स्काढै, स्कंगा, स्कंगिया, see § 172; E. H. छमा *forgiveness* for *च्छमा, Skr. क्षमा, see §§ 36. 191; E. H. छाहै *he desires* for *च्छाहै, see § 173.

Exception. ग्य् remains, as E. H. ग्यान् *knowledge*, Skr. ज्ञानम्, see § 191; in the *khaṛi bhâshâ* optionally also र् following a cons., as प्रगट् or परगट् *manifest*, § 185.

Note: In Pr. also; as a rule, see H. C. 2, 89. Vr. 3, 50; thus Pr. झाणं (H. C. 2, 26), Skr. ध्यानम्; Pr. झाओ or धाओ for *ज्झाओ or ढाओ (H. C. 2, 27), Skr. ध्वजः; Pr. छमा or खमा for *च्छमा or *क्खमा (H. C. 2, 18 gives छमा in the sense of *earth* and खमा as *patience* or *forgivenes;* but in E. H., the latter does not exist, and the former means *forgiveness* or *patience*), Skr. क्षमा; Pr. ठाणं or थाणं for *ट्ठाणं or *त्थाणं (H. C. 4, 16), Skr. स्थानम्; etc.; but A. Mg. apparently has occasionally स्न्; as स्नाण° (Wb. Bh. 315. 319),

Skr. ध्यान°; or स्कूसित्रा (Wb. Bh. 295), Skr. ग्रध्यूषित्वा, etc.; see Wb. Bh. 389. 390.

189. *The second consonant is elided;* only ह्; thus E. H. नाऊ *barber*, A. Mg. ण्हाविए or नाविए (cf. H. C. 1, 230), Skr. नापितः (or *स्नापिकः).

Note: In Pr. नेहो (H. C. 2, 102) for *णइहो (not for *स्नेहो as in H. C. 2, 77), Skr. स्नेहः, E. H. नेह् *love, oil;* Pr. निढं (H. C. 2, 109) for *णिहढं, Skr. स्निग्धम्, E. H. *deest.*

190. *अ or इ is prefixed to स् preceding any consonant; only in semitats;* thus E. H. अस्तुति or इस्तुति *praise*, Skr. स्तुतिः; E. H. अस्नान् *bathing*, Skr. स्नानम्; E. H. असनेह् *love*, Skr. स्नेहः; E. H. इस्तरी *woman*, Skr. स्त्री; or in foreign words, as E. H. अस्कूल् or इस्कूल् *school*; E. H. इस्पंज् *sponge*; etc.

Note: A curiosity is the E. H. अचपल् *restless* for Skr. चपलः

191. *ज् and ज्ञ् become ङ् and ग्न्*; only in semitats; see §§ 36. 37. In tadbh. ज्ञ् becomes ण्; e. g., E. H. ज्ञानी or ज्ञान् *sage*, Pr. णाणी (H. C. 2, 83. Vr. 3, 5), Skr. ज्ञानी; but as a semitats. it is E. H. ग्यानी.

SECOND SECTION. ON SUFFIXES AND ROOTS.

FIRST CHAPTER. SUFFIXES.

192. The E. H. suffixes may be divided into two great classes, which I shall call the *pleonastic* and the *derivative*. The former are those, by the addition of which the meaning of a noun is not changed, thus पट् and पटा *board*, आगि and अगिया *fire*, चाम् and चमरा *leather*, मीठ् and मिठका *sweet*, etc. The latter are those which change the meaning of a noun. These may be subdivided into two classes; the *primary* and *secondary*. The former are those which are added to (verbal) roots and form primary bases; e. g., R. खा *eat*, खाऊ or खानिहार् *eater, glutton;* हँस् *laugh*, हँसी *laughter;* बढ् *grow*, बढ्ती *growth*, etc. The latter are added to the bases

of nouns and form secondary bases; as बूढा *old*, बुढापन् *old age*; हलुक् *light*, हलुकई *lightness*; बंगाल् *Bengal*, बंगाली *a man of Bengal*; भेड़् *ram*, भेड़ी *ewe*; etc.

Note: The pleon. suff. are called by Pr. gramm. स्वार्थे or स्वार्थिक (cf. H. C. 2, 164. 429); and the deriv. suff., भवे (cf. H. C. 2, 163). — In Skr., the primary suffixes are called *kṛt* and the secondary *taddhita*. The pleon. suff., as being added to nouns only, would belong to the taddhita class.

193. *Affinities.* In Pr. it had already become customary, and is now almost the rule in E. H. (and Gḍ. generally) to augment verbal roots (called *dhâtus* in Skr.) by the denominative suffix आपि (Pr. आवि or आव, E. H. आव् or आ) and nominal bases (called *prâtipâdikas* in Skr.) by the pleonastic suffix क (Pr. and E. H. अ). It is the coalescence of the original (Skr.) krit or taddhita suffixes with this radical or basic increment, that — besides the usual effect of phonetic decay — accounts for the difference, which, in many cases, appears between them and their modern representatives; thus Skr. वृद्धि *growth* from R. वृध् and suff. ति, but E. H. बढ़ति of R. बर्धाप् and suff. ति (cf. § 325); or Skr. उच्चता *height* from base उच्च and suff. ता, E. H. उचाई from base उच्चअ and suff. इआ (= उच्चक-तिका cf. § 223). — Many of the Skr. suffixes, however, have been long since disused both in Pr. and E. H. *as suffixes;* though, of course, they may be met with in E. H. words (especially in tatsamas) as *nominal terminations* and variously modified by the effect of phonetic laws; thus the Skr. suff. नि, in E. H. मुनि *sage*, Skr. मुनि; suff. मन् in E. H. करम् (tats) or काम् (tadbh) for Skr. कर्मन्; suff. त्रि, in E. H. धरती *earth* for Skr. धरित्री; or in E. H. रात् *night*, Skr. रात्रि; etc. These will not be noticed in the following lists. Most of the other Skr. suff., which are still used as such in E. H., are expressly mentioned also by Pr. grammarians.

1) PLEONASTIC SUFFIXES.

194. The E. H. pleonastic suff. may be divided into two groups, the elementary forms of which are: 1) क or अ and 2) ड

or ˷ or ल or न. Their other forms are reduplications or combinations of these.

First Group.

195. Set. Masculine.

1. आ, ई, ऊ; or इउँ.
2. अक्, इक्, उक्; or अक्क्, इक्क्, उक्क्.
3. अका, इका, उका; or अक्का, इक्का, उक्का.
4. अवा, इवा, उवा; or अवाँ, इवाँ, उवाँ.
5. अकवा, इकवा, उकवा; or अक्कवा, इक्कवा, उक्कवा.
6. औवा, इयवा [1]), उअवा [1]); or औवाँ, इयवाँ [1]), उअवाँ [1]).

Feminine.

1. ई, ई, ऊ; or इउँ.
2. अक्, इक्, उक्; or अक्क्, इक्क्, उक्क्.
3. अकी, इकी, उकी; or अक्की, इक्की, उक्की.
4. इया, इया, उवा; or इयाँ, इयाँ, उवाँ.
5. अकिया, इकिया, उकिया; or अक्किया, इक्किय, उक्किया.
6. इयवा [1]), इयवा [1]), उअवा [1]); or इयवाँ [1]), इयवाँ [1]), उअवाँ [1]).

Note: Observe in adding these suffixes, that their initial vowel always supersedes the final vowel of the word. A long antepenultimate is shortened (see § 25). The semivowels य् and व् may or may not be inserted after इ, उ and औ (cf. § 28); e. g., उवा or उआ, इया or इआ.

196. The first set may be added to either subst. or adj. The forms thus made I shall call their *strong forms;* those without the suff. their *weak forms.* The suff. आ (m.), ई (f.) are added to nouns in अ (*quiescent*). As to adj., all may take them; thus m. साँच् or साँचा *true;* f. साँच् or साँची; or m. मीठ् or मीठा *sweet,* f. मीठ् or मीठी; but the strong form is generally used with fem., while with masc. the weak form is rather the more common. In the case of subst., the usage is more or less fixed; some occurring only in the

---

1) Sometimes pronounced ईवा, ऊवा or ईवाँ, ऊवाँ; contracted like औवा for *अववा § 203; and see §§ 83. 84. exc.

weak form, others only in the strong, while many again may be used in both; on the whole those in the weak form preponderate in E. H., as compared with W. H. Thus m. घरू *house* (not घरा), f. बात् *event* (not बाती); m. घोरा (or घोड़ा) *horse*, f. घोरी *mare* (not घोरू); but m. पट् or पटा *board*, f. भेड़ or भेड़ी *sheep*, etc. The suff. ई and ऊ (both *gen. com.*) are added to nouns in इ and उ respectively; but in most cases, at present, only one of the two forms exists. Thus adj. occur only in the strong form, as भारी *heavy*, गरू *heavy*, हलू *light, slow* (not भारि, गरु, हलु). Subst. as a rule, have either the one or the other; e. g., माली *gardener*, हाथी *elephant*, बालू *sand* (not मालि, हाथि, बालु); on the other hand आगि *fire*, मुनि *sage*, गुरु *teacher* (not आगी, मुनी, गुरू). There are, however, a few examples of the existence of both forms; as ज्ञानि or ज्ञानी *sage*, बहिनि or बहिनी *sister*, पतोहु or पतोहू *son's wife*, etc. See also §§ 42—53.

197. The suffix इउँ (*com. gen.*) can be added to adj. in ई only; as m. f. भारी or भरिउँ *heavy*. The form in इउँ I shall call the *uncontracted*, that in ई the *contracted*.

198. The second, third and fifth sets can be added to adj. of the weak form only. The forms made by the two former I shall call their long forms. Those in का, की or क्का, क्की contain the suff. आ, ई of the first set and are, therefore strong, while those in क् or क्क् are weak. As a rule, the strong long forms only are used in E. H. Thus m. मिठ्का or मिठक्का, f. मिठ्की or मिठक्की, of मीठ् *sweet*; छोट्का, छोट्की or छोटक्का, छोटक्की, of छोट् *small*; भरिका, भरिकी or भरिक्का, भरिक्की *heavy*, of *भारि (only used in the strong form भारी, § 196); हलुक् or हलुक्क् (gen. com.) or हलुका, हलुकी or हलुक्का, हलुक्की *light*, of *हलु (only in the strong form हलू § 196). In a few cases the long form alone exists; as तनिक् or तनिका *small*, of *तनु (see § 61); रचिक् *small*. As to the forms in अकवा, etc. of the fifth set, see § 199.

Exception. There are a few subst. with the suff. क्, का, as भिछुक् *beggar* beside भिछू; बालक् (or बालका) *child* beside बाल् and बाला; छोकरा *boy*, छोकरी *girl* beside छोरा, छोरी, from *छोक् or

*छो° (= Skr. शाव°, Pr. छाव° Vr. 2, 41) with the pleon. suff. रा, री superadded. — Such nouns as लरिका *boy* (H. H. लड़का), बेठिका or बेठिक् *seat* (H. H. बैठक्), etc. contain not the pleonastic, but the derivative suff. का (see §§ 252. 334).

Note: The forms in क्का, क्की have the accent on the syllable immediately preceding it; as मिठक्का *miṭhákkā*, भरिक्का *bharíkkā*, हलुक्की *halúkkī;* but the others on the first syllable; as हलुक्क् *hálukk*, हलुका *hálukā*, छोटन्की *chhŏṭ'kī*, etc.

199. The fourth set may be added 1) to any subst. of the weak form, 2) to any adj. of the weak long form; in the latter case resulting in the fifth set. The forms thus made will be called, in the case of subst., their *long*, in the case of adj., their *redundant* forms. The suff. अवा (m.), इया (f.) are added to nouns in अ, and the suff. इया and उवा (both gen. com.) to nouns in इ and उ respectively. Thus, *subst.*, m. घर् or घरन्वा *house;* f. बात् or बतिया *event;* m. घोरा (wk. f. घोर्) or घोरन्वा *horse;* f. घोरी (wk. f. घोर्) or घोरिया *mare;* m. माली (wk. f. मालि) or मलिया *gardener;* f. बालू (wk. f. *बालु) or बलुवा *sand;* f. आगि or अगिया *fire;* m. गुरु or गुरुवा *teacher*, etc. Again *adj.*, m. हलुक् or हलुकवा *light;* f. हलुक् or हलुकिया; m. छोटन्का (wk. f. छोटक्) or छोटन्कवा *small;* f. छोटक्की (wk. f. छोटक्क्) or छोटक्किया.

Note: Bs. II, 40 and Bates H. Dict. 67 give the form उआ for अवा; and Bates 58. इअ for इया. If these be not merely inaccurate spellings, they must be considered as local peculiarities.

200. The sixth set can only be added to subst. of the weak form. The forms thus made, I shall call their *redundant* forms. The suff. m. औवा, f. इयवा (or ईवा) are added to subst. in अ, and c. g. इयवा and उअवा (or ऊवा) to subst. in इ and उ respectively. Thus m. घर् or घरौवा *house;* f. बात् or बतियवा (or बतीवा) *event;* m. घोरा (wk. f. घोर्) or घोरौवा *horse;* f. घोरी (wk. f. *घोर्) or घोरियवा *mare;* m. माली (wk. f. *मालि) or मलियवा (or मलीवा) *gardener;* f. बालू (wk. f. *बालु) or बलुअवा (or बलूवा) *sand;* f. आगि or अगियवा *fire;* m. गुरु or गुरुअवा *teacher*. The suff. औवा and उअवा may be con-

tracted to औ; e. g., घोरौवा or घोरौ; बलुअवा or बलौ. The suff. औवा may be also contracted into अऊ; as घोरौवा or घोरऊ.

Note: The contracted suff. औ always takes the accent; as घोरौ *ghŏraú*, not *ghórau*.

201. All these suff. are, generally speaking, very commonly employed. The sixth set, however, is very vulgar. As a rule, they change in no way the meaning of the word. Occasionally, those of the fourth and sixth sets may imply contempt or affection or smallness, and those of the second and third sets the comparative degree (see § 388).

202. *Affinities.* The existence of these sets of pleonast. suff. in the various Gḍ. languages has been hitherto but little observed by grammarians; if, at least, we exclude the first, which is very common in them all. It consists, in E. and S. Gḍ., of आ, ई and ऊ; in N. and W. Gḍ. of ओ (or औ), ई and ऊ; see §§ 49—54. As to the others, I have not been able to learn whether or not they exist in N. and W. Gḍ.; excepting the W. H. In this latter and in E. and S. Gḍ., some of them certainly do occur; whether or not all do, it is impossible to say at present. The fourth set is in B. (m.) आ, ए, ओ contracted for E. H. अवा, इया, उआ; as B. रामा, E. H. रमवा *Rám;* B. हरे, E. H. हरिया *Harí;* B. शंभो, E. H. संभुआ *Sambhú;* (f.) B. ई contracted for E. H. इया; as B. राधी, E. H. रधिया *Rádhá,* etc. There are, however, many anomalies[1]). See S. Ch. 71. 72. In M. the fourth set has (m.) अया for E. H. अवा and (f.) ई for E. H. इया; as M. राम्या (for रामन्या cf. § 6, note), E. H. रमन्वा *Rám;* Mg. दुर्गी, E. H. दुर्गिया *Durgá.* See my V[th] Essay on Gḍ. Gramm. in J. B. A. S. XLIII, 36. The W. H. has अया, ऐया, अई, ऐ for E. H. अवा, औवा, अऊ, औ of the fourth and sixth sets respectively; e. g., W. H. कन्हया, कन्हैया, कन्हई, कन्है *krishna*[2]);

---

1) E. g., sometimes इ migrates into the preceding syllable, as in B. काशे or केशे for E. H. कसिया *káṣí* (abbreviated for *káṣináth*).

2) By way of illustration compare तलैया *pond* = Mg. तलायये = Skr. तडाककः of तडाक, with कन्हैया = Mg. कण्हयये = Skr. *कृष्णाककः of कृष्ण.

गड्ढिया, गड्ढैया, गड्ढई, गड्ढै *pit;* etc. In H. H. these pleonastic forms, being more or less vulgar, are not usually employed; but there are a few exceptions, such as बछवा *calf,* कड़वा or कड़ुवा *bitter;* etc.

203. *Derivation.* The original of all these suff. is the suff. क which is sometimes employed in Skr. to form diminutives, as पुत्रकः *little son,* but is more often merely pleonastic. In Pr. it is still more extensively used in the latter way; see Vr. 4, 25 in Cw. 140. H. C. 2, 164. Ls. 258. Wb. Spt. 69. 70; especially in the Ap. Pr.; see H. C. 4, 429. 430. Ls. 341. 475. E. H. employs it, in some cases (cf. § 204), even more frequently than Pr. In the latter the suff. क generally becomes अ, but sometimes remains unaltered. The latter is especially the case in Ps. Pr. (cf. H. C. 2, 164), in Sr. and Mg. Pr. (K. I. 12, 1 in Ls. Ap. 50. cf. Ls. 378. 396), and in Ap. Pr. (K. I. 13, 3 in Ls. 449. 457). The Mg. Pr., moreover, — particularly in its lower types — has not only a tendency to retain क्, but even to prolong the preceding vowel [1]), thus making the suff. आक, ईक, ऊक Md. 12, 16; cf. Wb. Bh. 348. Ls. 431) [2]). In one case, Mg. shortens the preceding आ and compensates it by doubling क्; viz. in हडक्के *heart* (Md. 12, 13. Vr. 11, 6. K. I. 11, 8 in Ls. 393), for *हडाके, Skr. हृदयकम्, Ps. हितअकं (Vr. 10, 14) or हितपकं (H. C. 4, 310), but Mh. हिअअअं (cf. H. C. 2, 164). Further the suff. क is sometimes *reduplicated* in Pr., thus making it अअ (for कक, H. C. 2, 164. 4, 430) [3]) or in Mg. कअ or आकअ,

---

1) Thus in the Mchh. the Mg. form केलाक is much more common than its alternative केलअ. It may be remarked, that since the natural tendency in Pr. is to elide hard consonants, the effort to retain them would tend either to their being doubled or to the lengthening of the preceding vowel.

2) Md. 12, 16 के दीर्घो वा । कप्रत्यये परे पूर्वो दीर्घो वा स्यात् ॥ i. e. „the vowel preceding the suff. क may optionally be long". The MS. reads पूर्वादीर्घो (?); the example is: लाउआके। लाउपाके (?).

3) The example in H. C. 2, 164 is बहुअअं, E. H. बहुअवा.

ईकश्र, ऊकश्र. Thus in Mg. the suff. क may have the following forms (in the nom. sing. incl. final of base): 1) श्रए, इए, उए by elision of क्; 2) श्रके, इके, उके or श्राके, ईके, ऊके by retaining क्; 3) श्रकए, इकए, उकए or श्राकए, ईकए, ऊकए by reduplicating the suff. and retaining क्; 4) श्रश्रए, इश्रए, उश्रए by reduplicating the suff. and eliding क्. In E. H., the first Pr. set is either *contracted* to श्रा, ई, ऊ (cf. §§ 47. 49. 98, exc.), or separated (by inserting य् or व् § 69) into श्रवा, इया, उवा [1]); the result being the 1st and 4th E. H. sets. Exceptionally the Pr. hiatus is retained in E. H. इउँ, which is apparently the same as the Ap. Pr. termination इउं. The second Pr. set becomes in E. H. either श्रक्, इक्, उक् (cf. § 45) or श्रक्क्, इक्क्, उक्क् by doubling क् and shortening the preceding vowel; thus forming the E. H. 2nd set. The third Pr. set again is in E. H. either *contracted* to श्रका, इका, उका and श्रक्का, इक्का, उक्का, or *separated* into श्रकवा, इकवा, उकवा and श्रक्कवा, इक्कवा, उक्कवा; thus producing the E. H. 3[d] and 5th sets. Finally the fourth Pr. set becomes in E. H. श्रौवा (contracted for *श्रव-वा, cf. § 34), इयवा (or इश्रवा or contr. ईवा § 83, exc.), उश्रवा (or उववा or contr. ऊवा § 84, exc.) by inserting य् or व्; thus constituting the E. H. 6th set. E. g., Skr. घोटकः *horse,* Mg. घोउए or (gen.) घोउश्राह (§ 369, 2), E. H. घोरा or घोर-वा; Skr. *घोटककः, Mg. (gen.) घोउश्रश्राह, E. H. घोरौवा (for *घोरववा); or Skr. मिष्टकः *sweet,* Mg. मिट्ठए or मिट्ठके or मिट्ठाके, E. H. मीठा or मिठक् or मिठक्क्; Skr. *मिष्टककः, Mg. मिट्ठकए or मिट्ठाकए, E. H. मिठका or मिठक्का or मिठकवा or मिठक्कवा; etc. Similarly in the feminine: 1) Pr. इश्रा and उश्रा = H. H. ई and ऊ (§ 51) or इया and उवा; 2) Pr. *श्रकी, *इकी, *उकी [2]) or श्राकी, ईकी, ऊकी = E. H. श्रक्, इक्, उक् or श्रक्क्, इक्क्, उक्क् (§ 43); 3) Pr. श्रकिश्रा, इकिश्रा, उकिश्रा or श्राकिश्रा, ईकिश्रा, ऊकिश्रा = E. H. श्रकी, इकी, उकी or श्रक्की, इक्की, उक्की or श्रकिया, इकिया, उकिया or श्रक्किया, इक्किया, उक्किया; 4) Pr. *इश्रश्रा, *उश्रश्रा [2]), (= *इकका, *उकका) = E. H. इयवा, उश्रवा (or उववा). Thus Skr.

1) For an explanation of the final श्रा of these forms see §§ 365, 1. 369, 2.

2) When क् is retained or the suff. reduplicated, the fem. appears to have been formed irregularly.

मृत्तिका *earth,* Mg. मट्टिआ (cf. II. C. 2, 29), E. H. माटी or मटिया; Skr. *मृत्तिकका, Mg. मट्टिअआ, E. H. मटियवा; or Skr. मिष्टा or मिष्टिका *sweet,* Mg. मिट्ठा or मिट्ठिआ, E. H. मीठ् or मीठी or मिठिया; Skr. *मिष्टको, Mg. मिट्ठको or मिट्ठाको, E. H. मिठकू or मिठक्कू; Skr. *मिष्टकिका, Mg. मिट्ठकिआ or मिट्ठाकिआ, E. H. मिठकी or मिठक्की or मिठकिया or मिठक्किया; etc.

204. *Origin.* The original of the suff. क I am inclined to believe to be the past part. pass. कृत *done* for the following reason. There are two main elements क and उ or ल. Each of them exists in a twofold use, as a pleonastic or a derivative suffix. It will be shown, that the latter (उ or ल) in its two uses is essentially the same element and has the same origin (Skr. दृश्र), see §§ 218. 244. 248. 251. The same, probably, is true of the former (क) also. It will be shown in §§ 280. 338 that the suff. क — as a derivative one, at least — has originated from the part. कृत; and in § 377, that the genitive affix क has the same origin.

205. *Origin of the pleonastic forms.* Skr. possesses bases in अ, इ and उ. The declension of the bases in इ and उ is intricate; at least, as they form a very small minority, it was much less familiar, than that of the अ-bases. Hence the custom sprang up in Pr., of adding the suff. क to the इ- and उ-bases, in order to turn them into अ-bases; and from habit, it was extended to the अ-bases themselves; thus tending to produce a uniform kind of declension. We shall observe (§ 347) a similar levelling tendency of Pr. in regard to the treatment of the verbal roots whereby the diversity of the Skr. conjugation was reduced to a uniform pattern. In E. H., this uniformity of declension has become an established fact. In the meanwhile, however, the result of the Pr. habit of adding the suff. क was, to produce a double set of forms of the same meaning; the *weak* forms in ए, इ॰, उ॰, and the *strong* in (Mg.) अए, इए, उए. This must have been felt to be inconvenient. In Gḍ., therefore, the custom grew up of using only one set; and in the struggle for existence, thus ensuing between the two

sets, the hardier one (i. e., that of the *strong* forms), will naturally survive. The tendency to extinction of the weak forms is, indeed, unmistakeable in Gḍ. In E. and W. H., the weak forms in इ and उ (probably from having suffered longest the addition of the suff. क) are altogether extinct in adj., and, to a considerable extent, in subst. also. The case of the weak form in अ, in W. H., is not very different from this. But the E. H. has more nearly preserved the older, i. e. Pr., stage, particularly in regard to adj.; though it also shows signs of the same general tendency, in preferring strong fem. in ई and strong long forms in का, की (see §§ 196. 198). — Another reason for the frequent addition of the suff. क in Pr. was its preference (common to all popular languages) for the use of diminutives. This habit continued in Gḍ., in whose more uncultivated forms, like the E. H., it is very marked. But as the Pr. strong (or diminutive) forms in अए, इए, उए, in their contracted Gḍ. forms आ, ई, ऊ, had been generally substituted in Gḍ. in the place of the (more or less) extinct Pr. weak (or non-diminutive) forms, Gḍ. was obliged to distinguish its diminutive (but, in vulgar speech, pleonastic) forms by some new device. Accordingly य् and व् were inserted in the Pr. strong terminations, and thus were produced the long termin. अवा, इया, उवा of the E. H. The excess of this popular tendency is exhibited in the reduplication of those forms in the redundant terminations औवा, इयवा, उअवा.

Second Group.

206.	Set.	Com. gen.	Masc.	Fem.
	1.	अड़्	अड़ा	अड़ी
	2.	आड़्	—	—

The forms of com. gen. are weak, the others containing the suff. आ, ई of the 1st set 1st group are strong. As to the way of adding them, see § 195, note.

207. These suff. are sometimes added to adj. or subst. of the weak form: Thus: अड़् in गडड़् or गड़् *fort*, from गड़् *enclosure*; अड़ा in गडड़ा (or गड्ढा), from गाड or गडा *cavity*; m. बउरड़ा, f. °ड़ी, from बउर् or m. बउरा, f. °री *mad* (W. H. बावल् or बावला); m.

मिरकटहा, f. °ही *feeble* (also मिरकुटहा), from मरकट् *monkey* (?); again अाह् in m. f. बउराह् *mad.*

208. *Derivation.* These suff. are closely allied to those of first group. Their original is the Skr. pleon. suff. क, the क् of which is elided in Pr. and replaced in Gd. by ह् (see § 69). Thus we have in Mg. Pr. (in the nom. sg., and incl. of the final अ of the base) अए (i. e. अकः), in E. H. अह् (for अहे); or adding pleon. अ (= क, i. e., doubling क) we have Mg. m. अअए, E. H. अहा, Mg. f. अइआ, E. H. अही, In Mg. the vowel, preceding क, may be lengthened, m. आके, f. आकी, or (eliding क्) आए, आई; whence, inserting ह्, arises E. H. m. f. आह् (= आहे, आही). E. g., Skr. गर्तकः, Mg. गड्डके or गड्डए, E. H. गडह् or गड्ढ; Skr. वातुलकः, Mg. वाउलाके or वाउलाए, E. H. बउराह्; or Mg. m. वाउलकके or वाउलअए, E. H. बउरहा, f. Mg. वाउलइआ, E. H. बउरही. By way of illustration compare E. H. घटिहा *inferior, low-priced*, Mg. घट्टिअए, Skr. घट्टितकः.

Third Group.

209. Set.		Com. gen.	Masc.	Fem.
1)	a.	अर् or अड़्	अरा or अड़ा	अरी or अड़ी
	b.	— —	अरू or अडू	अरू or अडू
2)		एर् or एड़्	एरा or एड़ा	एरी or एड़ी
3)		ओर् or ओड़्	ओरा or ओड़ा	ओरी or ओड़ी
4)		अल् or अर्	अला or अरा	अली or अरी
5)	a.	एल् or एर्	एला or एरा	एली or एरी
	b.	ईल् or ईर्	ईला or ईरा	ईली or ईरी
	c.	इल् or इर्	इला or इरा	इली or इरी
6)	a.	ओल् or ओर्	ओला or ओरा	ओली or ओरी
	b.	ऊल् or ऊर्	ऊला or ऊरा	ऊली or ऊरी
	c.	उल् or उर्	उला or उरा	उली or उरी
7)	a.	अन्	अना	अनी
	b.	उन्	उना	उनी

The forms with ड़् are properly W. H., and are rarely used in E. H. (see § 29). Most of the forms with ल् may be, and commonly are pronounced with र् (see § 30); some, however, have always ल्, others always र्. All forms of com. gen. are weak, the others containing the pleon. suff. of the 1st set 1st group are strong. The forms अड़ॅ or अड़ू, contracted from Ap. Pr. अडउ = *अडकः, are properly W. H., and occur only exceptionally in E. H. As to the manner of adding them, see § 195, note.

210. The first set occurs in subst. and adj.; often; thus m. गठड़ or गठरा, f. °री, of गाठ् (or गठा) *bundle;* चमरा, of चाम् *leather;* चीकड़ (or कीचड़), of चीक् (or कीच्) *mud* (cf. § 133); खब्बोड़, of खब्बू *glutton;* टुकरा, f. °री, of टूक् (Skr. स्तोक) *piece;* पटरा, f. °री, of पट (or पटा) *board;* पलंगरा, f. °री, of पलंग् *bedstead;* बछरा, f. °री or m. f. बछरू *calf, colt,* of बछ् (or बछा) *young;* भूखड़, of भूख् (or भूखा) *hungry;* भुलकड़, of भूलक् *forgetful;* मोटरा, of मोट् *bundle;* मेहरारू, of मेहर् *woman;* etc. Sometimes the original word is disused; as सैकरा *a hundred,* of *सैक् (A. Mg. सयक्क, Skr. शतक); टोकरा *basket,* of *टोक्; थोड़ or थोरा, f. °री *little,* of *थो (Pr. थोअ, Skr. स्तोक, cf. § 97); छोकरा or छोरा *boy* and छोकरी or छोरी *girl,* of *छोक् or *छो (see § 198 exc.); छेरा, f. छेरी *goat,* of *छे (Mg. छाय, Skr. छाग); अगारी *front,* of *आगा (Skr. अग्र); पछारी *back,* of *पाछा (Skr. पश्चा); पहाड़ *mountain* and पहारा, *multiplication-table,* of *पहा (Skr. प्रथित *extended,* see § 118); etc. See also § 104.

211. The second and third sets occur in subst. and adj.; very rarely; thus बछेरा *colt,* बछेरी *filly,* of बछ् (or बछा) *young;* घनेड़ or घनेरा, f. °री, of घन् *much;* गडोरा, of गाड् (or गडा) *pit.*

212. The fourth set occurs in subst. and adj.; often; thus मोटल् or मोटला, f. °ली, of मोट् (or मोटा) *fat;* जेठरा, f. °री, of जेठ् (or जेठा) *eldest;* रसरा, f. °री, of *रस्स् or रस्सा *cord;* मुहरा *vanguard,* मुहरी *cuff, bore of a gun,* of मुह् *mouth;* हथल् or हथरी, of हाथ् or हथा *handle;* सुतला or सुतरा, f. °री *string,* of सूत् *thread;* परला, f. °ली, of पार् *beyond;* etc. Sometimes the original word is disused; as अगला, f. ली *former,* of *आग (Skr. अग्र; Ap. Pr. अग्गलउ H. C. 4, 341); मउली *mother,* of M. माऊ, E. H. माई (Skr. मातृ, cf. § 63).

213. The fifth and sixth sets occur in subst. and adj.; rarely; thus the 5th set in पतील् or पतीला or पतिला, of पात् *pot, pan;* खपरेल्, of खपड़ (or खपरा) *tile* (see § 175, note); मुरेला, of मोर् *peacock;* सपेला, of साप् *snake;* अधेला, of आध् *one half;* पइला, of पाय् *a quarter;*

अकेला or इकेला, of एक् *one, solitary*. The 6th set in सपोला, of साप् *snake;* कंकरोला, of ककर् (or ककरी) *gourd;* बतोला, of बात् *talk;* बँसुली or बँसुरी *flute*, of बाँस् *bamboo* (see § 128); बाँकुरा *swaggerer*, of बाँक् *fop;* etc. Sometimes the original word is disused; as in अगिला *foremost*, of आग् (Skr. अग्र); मकेला or मकिला or मकोला *middle*, of *माक् (Skr. मध्य); पछिल् or °ला *last*, of *पाछ् (Skr. पश्च); पहिल् or °ला *first* (cf. § 118).

214. The seventh set occurs in pronouns and sometimes in nouns; thus pron. अइसन् *of this kind*, तइसन् *of that kind;* कइसन *of which kind*, जइसन् *of which kind*, of *अइस्, *तइस्, etc.; see §§ 111. 456—458; एतना, f. °नी *this much*, ओतना, f. °नी *that much;* तेतना, f. °नी *so much;* केतना, f. °नी *how much;* जेतना, f. °नी *as much*, of एत्, तेत्, etc.; see §§ 111. 452—454; आपुन् or आपन् or अपुना or अपना, f. °नी *own*, of *आप् (Skr. आत्मीय), see § 111; तवन्, f. तउनी *he, that;* कवन्, f. कउनी *who;* जवन्, f. जउनी *which*, of *तेव्, *केव्, *जेव्, see §§ 106. 438, 2. Again nouns: छौना, f. छौनी *young of an animal*, from *छौ, see § 210; थुथना, f. °नी, of थोथ् *mouth of an animal;* जामुन्, of जाम् *rose-apple*, see § 111.

215. None of these suff. alter the meaning of the word; though sometimes they restrict it to some particular application; as बछ् or बछा is *any young animal*, but बछरा is a *calf* or *colt* and बछेरा a *colt;* मकेली or मकोली a *kind of carriage of middling size;* मिठरी a *particular kind of sweetmeat;* etc. Sometimes, they imply smallness, as मुरेला a *peachick;* सपोला a *young snake;* अँखरी a *wink*, lit. a small आँख् or *eye*. Sometimes, again, they express likeness, in which case they are more properly to be considered derivative suff., see §§ 241. 245; thus तमरा *a certain jewel of copper color* (lit. *like* ताम् or *copper*); ललरी *a false stone resembling a* लाल् or *ruby;* पातुर् or पतुरा *thin, weak*, lit. *like a* पात् or *leaf*. Sometimes both; thus पुतरा or पुतला, f. °री or °ली *idol, doll*, lit. *a little* or *like a* पूत् *son;* चीलर् or चील्हर् *louse*, lit. *a small* or *like a* चील् *hawk.* — It should be remarked, however, that in the nouns in री or ली which imply smallness, as गठरी, पलंगरी, पटरी, टुकरी, टोकरी, मोटरी, पतोली, सुतली, रसरी, etc. (cf. §§ 210. 213), that quality is denoted by the gender

(cf. §§ 256. 257), not by the suffix; for their corresponding masculines always imply largeness; e. g., गठरा *large bundle*, गठरी *small bundle*, etc.

216. *Affinities.* All Gd. languages possess this group of pleon. suff., see Bs. II, 115—122. As to S., especially, see Tr. 71. 77—79; as to M. see Man. 34. 113. 114. Their forms do not materially differ in any of them from those in use in E. H. But S. has always एरो for एलो; M. has sometimes ड् for ड़् (§ 217), and S. sometimes ड़् for ल्, as in लिखंदड़ु *writer* from लिखंदो, but generally लु, as डिठलु *seen* from डिठो (Tr. 71). Here S. uses the pleon. लु or ड़ु to turn part. into adj.; in the same way G. uses लो (Ed. 113) and M. एला (e. g., मेला *part.* or मेलेला *adj. dead*, Man. 63, 2. 64, 2). For the same purpose Mw. uses डो and N. को, though more in the manner of an affix; e. g., Mw. लिख्यो *part.* and लिख्योडो *adj.*, N. लिख्यो or लिखियो *part.* and लिख्याको *adj. written*.

217. *Derivation.* All these pleon. suff. occur in Pr. (H. C. 2, 164. 165. 166. 173); more especially in Mg. Pr. (Wb. Bh. 437) and Ap. Pr. (H. C. 4, 429. 430). Here (in the Ap. Mg.) they have, in the nom. sg. and incl. of the final of the base, the following forms: 1) m. अडे, f. अडी (H. C. 4, 431) or, with the pleon. suff. अ added, m. अडए, f. अडिआ. These change into the first E. H. set, m. f. अड़् or अर् and m. अड़ा or अरा, f. अड़ी or अरी; e. g., Ap. Mg. गंठडे (Skr. ग्रन्थ H. C. 4, 120), E. H. गठर्; Mg. गंठडए, E. H. गठरा; Mg. गंठडिआ, E. H. गठरी. 2) The same, with the pleon. अ added to the base of the word, m. अअडे, f. अअडी and m. अअडए, f. अअडिआ. These, by inserting य् (§ 69) and contracting अय to ए (§ 121), result in the E. H. second set, m. f. एड़् or एर् and m. एड़ा or एरा, f. एड़ी or एरी; or by inserting व् (§ 69) and contracting अव to ओ (§ 122) result in the E. H. third set, m. f. ओड़् or ओर् and m. ओड़ा or ओरा, f. ओड़ी or ओरी; e. g., Ap. Mg. घणअडे or घणयडे, E. H. घनेर्; Ap. Mg. वच्छअडए or वच्छयडए, E. H. बछेरा; Ap. Mg. वच्छअडिआ or वच्छयडिआ, E. H. बछेरी; again Ap. Mg. गड्डअडए or गड्डवडए (Skr. गर्त H. C. 2, 35), E. H. गडोरा. 3) Mg. m. अल्ले or अले, f. अल्ली or अली or, with pleon. अ added, m. अल्लए or अलए, f. अल्लिआ

or अलिआ. These produce the E. H. fourth set, m. f. अल् or अर् and m. अला or अरा, f. अली or अरी; thus Mg. नवल्ले *new* (H. C. 2, 165. Skr. नव), E. H. नवल्; Mg. एक्कल्लए (H. C. 2, 165. Skr. एक) *solitary*, E. H. इकला or इकरा; Mg. एक्कल्लिआ, E. H. इकली or इकरी; again Mg. पोअलए *yellow* (H. C. 2, 173. Skr. पीत), E. H. पोला or पोरा (§ 97); Mg. अंधलए *blind* (H. C. 2, 173. Skr. अन्ध), E. H. अंधला or अंधरा; Mg. पत्तलं *dish* (H. C. 2, 173. Skr. पात्र), E. H. पत्तल् or पत्तर्; Mg. विज्जुलिआ *lightning* (Ls. 2, 194. H. C. 2, 173. Skr. विद्युत्), E. H. बिजुली or बिजुरी; Ap. Mg. अग्गलए *anterior* (cf. H. C. 4, 141. 444. Skr. अग्र), E. H. अगला. 4) Mg. m. इल्ले or इले, f. इल्ली or इली or, with pleon. अ added, m. इल्लए or इलए, f. इल्लिआ or इलिआ. These constitute the E. H. fifth set, m. f. एल् or ईल् or इल् and m. एला or ईला or इला, f. एली or ईली or इली; thus Mg. m. मज्झिल्लए or मज्झिलए *middle* (Wb. Bh. 437. Skr. मध्य), E. H. मझेला or मझिला; Mg. f. मज्झिल्लिआ or मज्झिलिआ, E. H. मझेली or मझिली; Mg. पढमिल्ले (Wb. Bh. 437. Skr. प्रथम), E. H. पहेल् or पहिल् (§ 118); again Mg. तेत्तिलए (cf. H. C. 2, 157 see §§ 58. 111), E. H. तेतना, G. तेटलो, S. तेतिरो; Mg. f. तेत्तिलिआ, E.H. तेतनी, G. तेटली, S. तेतिरी; again Mg. पत्तिल्लअं or पत्तिलअं *dish, vessel* (Skr. पात्र), E. H. पतीला or पतिला, etc. 5) Mg. m. उल्ले or उले, f. उल्ली or उली or, with pleon. अ added, m. उल्लए or उलए, f. उल्लिआ or उलिआ. These give rise to the E. H. sixth set, m. f. ओल् or ऊल् or उल्, and m. ओला or ऊला or उला, f. ओली or ऊली or उली; thus Ap. Mg. m. मज्झुल्लए *middle* (Skr. मध्य), E. H. मझोला; Ap. Mg. f. मज्झुल्लिआ, E. H. मझोली; Mg. मुहुल्लअं (cf. H. C. 2, 164. Skr. मुख), E. H. मुहरा *vanguard*; Mg. हत्थुल्लिआ (cf. H. C. 2, 164. Skr. हस्त) *handle*, E. H. हथुरी or हथरी; Mg. अप्पुल्ले (see §§ 60. 111), E. H. आपुन् or आपन्; Ap. Mg. तेत्तुलए (cf. H. C. 4, 435., see §§ 58. 111), E. H. तेतना; etc. 6) with pleon. अ added, m. णए, f. णिआ, n. णअं. These become the E. H. seventh set, m. ना, f. नी; thus Mg. अप्पणए (§ 60, note), E. H. अपना; Mg. अप्पणिआ, E. H. अपनी. I believe this is the only example of the pleon. suff. ना in Pr. A comparison with E. H. shows: 1) that the Pr. अप्पणअं (H. C. 2, 153) stands for * अप्पुणअं = अप्पुल्लअं (H. C. 2, 163); and 2) that the न् of this set is a substitute for an original ल्

(or ल्ल्), as in E. H. तामुन् (see § 111). Further a comparison of the various sets tends to show, that the Pr. suff. इल्ल, इल and उल्ल, उल are modifications of original forms एल and ओल, and that the latter are contractions of अयल and अवल, formed, by the insertion of य् and व्, from अअल and, by the prefixion of the pleon. अ, from the simple suff. अल. The latter (अल) itself is, probably, a mere modification of अड, through the common interchange of ड् and ल् (H. C. 1, 202); as shown by the S. विज्जुडी *lightning* for Pr. विज्जुली [1]). As to the origin of अड, see § 218. Of the change of अड to अड़, now almost universal in W. Gd., there are apparently a few examples in Pr.; viz., Pr. दीहरं or दीहं *long* (H. C. 2, 171. Skr. दीर्घ), E. H. दीरू *a long while ago;* Pr. बाहिरं or बाहिं *external* (H. C. 2, 140. of Skr. बहिस्), E. H. m. f. बाहिरू, m. बाहिरा, f. °री. For it should be remembered that the old Pr. र् is a cerebral (= ड़्, see § 15), not (like the E. H.) a dental. The Skr. suff. ल and र (i. e. ड़), sometimes (espec. in later Skr.) used pleonastically, are, no doubt, identical with the corresponding Pr. ones. — The Skr. pleon. suff. ट (as in कर्कः or कर्कटः or कर्कटकः *crab,* Pr. कक्कुडो or कक्कुडओ, E. H. कें॑करू or कें॑करा) is probably a hardening of the Pr. suff. ड, and adopted into Skr. in the ancient period of the Ps. Pr. With this would seem to agree the fact, that Psh. and, occasionally, S. possess a diminutive suff. ओटै or उटै (Tr. 77. Bs. II, 122). There are a few nouns of apparently similar formation in H.; but they may well be compounds; e. g., चमोटा *a strip of leather* = Skr चर्म + पत्रिका; बाम्हनेटा *young bráhman* = Pr. बम्हण + विट्टओ (*bráhman's son*); हिरणोटा *fawn* = हिरण + पुत्र. B. has आटे (S. Ch. 100) and M. ट (Man. 114).

218. *Origin.* The original of these pleon. suff. I believe to be the Skr. suff. (properly a noun) दृश *like,* which is added both to nouns and pronouns. In Pr. it appears as दह; e. g., in एदहं (H. C. 2, 157) = Skr. ईदृशम् (lit. *इयादृश = इयत् + दृश); and in

1) Thus: Skr. मध्यक° (or मध्यम°), Mg. *मज्झअडे = *मज्झअले = *मज्झयले = *मज्झोले = मज्झिल्ले or मज्झिले, E. H. मफेल् or मफिल्.

Ap. Pr. it occurs as डो or डु; e. g., in एवडो or एवडु (H. C. 4, 407) = Skr. *एवाद्दृशः (from Ved. इवत् or Skr. एवम्). These Ap. forms डा and डु are, evidently, contractions for *डहो and डहु resp., where ड् would easily arise from the Skr. द् (just as Pr. इ from Skr. द्‌ H. C. 2, 36. 37) and °अह्° would be suppressed, as e. g. in S. इत्ते or इत्थे *here* = Ap. इत्तहे (H. C. 4, 436., see §§ 468, a. 469). And the Ap. suff. डो and डु, being once established, would be treated in their further evolutions precisely as any other suff., and thus produce all the alternative sets, enumerated in § 209. Their initial ड् would be (as usual) liable to change to ट् or ड़्, ल् or ऱ्, and न्. In the Gḍ. pronouns it actually has undergone all these changes; see §§ 104. 105. 106. 438, 2. 4. 454. — In confirmation of this theory, it is to be remarked: 1) that as shown in § 215, the original meaning *like* of the suff. ड or ल may still be traced in some words; 2) that a suff., meaning *like*, would easily come to be used diminutively and thence pleonastically, as may be seen in such English words as *such* and *such-like, kind* and *kindly*, or in the German *froh* and *fröhlich*, *krank* and *kränklich*; the intermediate *diminutive* sense is more often preserved in S. and M. (see Bs. II, 117. 118); 3) that such a suff. may easily become a *derivative* one; as in the English *kingly*, i. e., *like a king* or *belonging to a king*, or in the German *tödlich*, i. e., *full of death*, *mortal*, *peinlich*, i. e., *full of pain*. Accordingly, as will be shown in §§ 241. 245. 249., all these pleon. suff. occur also as derivative ones in Pr. and Gḍ.; 4) that in M. the suff. sometimes have the forms ढा, ढो (for डा, डो), which have preserved the original ह् of the Ap. Pr. *इहो, *डहो, as in M. तेवढा (Man. 125) for Ap. Pr. तेवडु.

2. SECONDARY DERIVATIVE SUFFIXES.

219. The secondary derivative suff. may be divided into eighteen groups. Of these the eleven first consist of suff. which already existed as such in Pr., the remaining seven contain those which have become such in Gḍ., but were full nouns in Pr.

First Group.

220. Set. 1. Fem. अई. Set. 2. Fem. आई.
Both, containing the suff. ई of § 196., are strong forms. As to the manner of adding them, see § 195, note.

221. These suffixes are used to derive abstract nouns from adjectives. Weak and long forms take the first, strong forms the second set. Thus अई, in हलुअई *lightness*, of हलुक *light*; ठंढई *coldness*, of ठंढ *cold*; सधुअई *simplicity*, of सधुआ *simple*; भरियई *heaviness*, of भरिया *heavy*; etc. Again आई, in भलाई *goodness*, of भला *good*; बड़ाई *greatness*, of बड़ा *great*; मिठाई *sweetness*, of मीठा *sweet*; गोलाई *roundness*, of गोला *round*; etc.

222. *Affinities.* These suff. exist in all Gḍs., though in M. they appear to be considered as non-indigenous and introduced from Hindí (see Man. 112). As to S. see Tr. 58. In P. the suff. is occasionally added also to the long form of adj. in आ, not only (as in E. H.) to that of adj. in ऊ. That long form ends (as in W. H. see § 202) in अया, and अया is vocalized to इआ (cf. § 121); thus बड़ा *great*, lg. f. बड़या, whence बड़िआई *greatness* (see Ld. 13. Bs. II, 79). The आ in such forms is anomalous for अ, as will be seen by a reference to § 221; unless we suppose the base to have been the redundant, not the long form of the word. W. H. and H. H., too, have the anomalous आ; but E. H. has regularly अ; e. g., W. H. गरुआई, but E. H. गरुअई *heaviness.* The H. H. often superfluously adds आई to tats. or semitats., which contain already the identical suff. ता; as H. H. कोमलताई *comeliness*; योग्यताई or जोगताई *worthiness*, etc.

223. *Derivation.* The original of these suff. is the Skr. taddhita ता (fem.), in Pr. दा or आ (Vr. 4, 22. H. C. 2, 154). With the pleon. क superadded, it is Skr. तिका, Pr. दिआ or इआ or, incl. of the final अ of the base, अइआ, and Gḍ. अई (§ 51). And with pleon. अ (= क) added to the base we have Pr. अअइआ, contracted in Gḍ. आई. Thus Skr. मिष्टता or *मिष्टतिका, Pr. मिट्ठइआ, E. H. मिठई; and Skr. *मिष्टकतिका, Pr. मिट्ठअइआ, E. H. मिठाई; again Skr. *साधुकतिका, Pr. साधुअइआ, E. H. सधुअई; etc. This derivation is

illustrated by E. H. अढाई *two and a half,* which is contr. from Mg. अड्ढअइआ (cf. Wb. Bh. 425. H. C. 1, 101 and § 416), Skr. अर्धतृतीया.

Second Group.

224. Set. 1. Masc. आउ or आव्. Set 2. Masc. आन्. Both sets are weak forms. As to the manner of adding them, see § 195, note.

225. These suff. are used to derive abstract nouns from a very small number of adj., expressive of dimension; viz., ऊँचाउ or ऊँचाव् or ऊँचान् *height*, of ऊँचा *high;* गहिराउ or गहिराव् or गहिरान् *depth*, of गहिरा *deep;* ओँडाउ or ओँडाव् or ओँडान् *depth*, of ओँडा *deep;* चोराउ or चोराव् or चोरान् *breadth, width*, of चोरा (H. H. चौडा) *broad, wide;* लम्बाउ or लम्बाव् or लम्बान् *length*, of लम्बा *long*. The forms in आन् are properly and generally masc.; but are sometimes used as fem.

Note: There are also the ordinary forms in आई (§ 229); as ऊँचाई, गहिराई, लमाई, etc.

226. *Affinities.* These suff. are not strictly E. H., but introduced from the W. H.; and occur in all W. Gds. See Bs. II, 80. 81. Tr. 59. In S. they are fem., in G. neuter, and in P. masc. The fem. gender in S. is a Gd. formation, like that of the suff. पी, पणी §§ 228. 230. The tendency of abstract nouns is to become fem.; also in Mg. Pr. there is fem. त्ता or neut. त्तं for Skr. neut. त्वम्, see Wb. Bh. 437. S. appears to have occasionally आइणि for आणि, the former of which, probably, stands for अयाणि and is to be explained like the P. इआई for आई, see § 222. In S. the suff. आणि may be used with any adj. expressing an inherent quality; as अछाणि *whiteness*, काराणि *blackness*, वडाणि *greatness;* etc.

227. *Derivation.* The originals of these suff. are the Skr. (neut.) taddh. त्व or (vedic) त्वन (cf. Wb. Spt. 68. 69). They become in Pr. (nom. sg.) त्तं or त्तणं (Vr. 4, 22. H. C. 2, 154) or, incl. of the final अ of the base, अत्तं or अत्तणं or (eliding त्त, see § 153) अत्तं or अत्तणं (see Spt. A. 52. वअस्सअएणा = Skr. वयस्यकत्वेन) or in Ap. Pr. अउ or अअणु (cf. H. C. 4, 331). Now the Ap. form अउ or, with pleon. अ added to the base, अअउ contracts in H. to आउ or आव्;

and the Ap. form अअणु contracts to H. आन्. E. g., Skr. उच्चकत्वम् *height*, Pr. उच्चअत्तं or उच्चअत्तं, Ap. उच्चअउ, E. H. ऊँचाउ or ऊँचाव्; again Skr. *उच्चत्वनम्, Pr. उच्चत्तणं or उच्चअणं, Ap. उच्चअणु, E. H. ऊँचान्. S. has, apparently, preserved the त्त in मुखित्तणु[1]) *duty of a* मुखी *headman* (Tr. 61), but not in चोकिराटु *boyhood*, which is probably a comp. of चोकर् and वटु (Ap. for Skr. वृत्तम्).

Third Group.

228.	Set.	Masc.	Fem.
	1)	a. प्पा b. प् or पा	—
	2)	a. प्पन् b. पन् or पना	पनी

The suff. in आ and ई are strong, the others are weak forms. Those with प्प् are added to weak, those with प् to strong bases; but पना, पनी to either.

229. These suff. are used to derive abstract nouns from subst. or adj. The forms प्पन् or पन्, however, are those commonly employed. Thus प् in बुड्ढाप् *old age*, of बूड्ढा *old;* प्पा or पा in बुड्ढापा *old age*, छोटप्पा or छोटापा *smallness*, of छोट् or छोटा *small;* मोटप्पा or मोटापा *fatness*, of मोट् or मोटा *fat;* रँडप्पा *widowhood*, of राँड् *widow;* etc.; प्पन् or पन् in बडप्पन् or बडापन् *greatness* (cf H. C. 4, 437), of बडु or बडा *great;* सुधापन् *simplicity*, of सूधा *simple;* गरुप्पन् or गरून्पन् *heaviness*, of *गरु or गरू *heavy;* बालकपन् *childhood*, of बालक् *child*, etc.; पना or पनी in छोटन्पना *smallness;* लुचन्पना or लुचन्पनी *profligacy*, of लुच् *profligate;* ज्ञानन्पनी *knowingness, knowledge*, of ज्ञान् (Skr. ज्ञानी § 191) *knowing;* पातीपना *profligacy*, of पाती *profligate*, etc.

Note: Exceptionally the suff. appears to be added to a verbal root, as in खुजलापन् *itching*, from खुजलाव् *to itch;* but in reality it is added to the noun *खुजला (cf. M. खाजरा Man. 115) *itch*, which, however, is now used only as a fem. खुजली.

230. *Affinities.* These suff. occur in all Gḍs.; though they seem to be less common in B. and O., than in the others

---

1) It is more probably the Ap. Pr. suff. त्तणु (see H. C. 4, 422, 20); viz., Ap. मुखित्तणु scl. वटु.

(see Bs. II, 73). M. has पण् n., पणा m. (Man. 112); S. प fem., पो m.; पाई f., पी f., पणु m., पणो m. (Tr. 59—61); G. पो m., पण् m., पणुँ n. (Ed. 14); P. पा m., पुण् or पुणा m. (Ld. 13., e. g., उचक्कपुणा *business of a* उचक्का *pickpocket*); B. has पन् m., पना or (Bs. II, 71) anomalously पाना; O. has पण् m., पणिआ f. (e. g., भाँउपणिआ *roguery*). B. and O. have more commonly मि (or आमि); as लुचामि *profligacy*, भांडामि *roguery*, ढिलामि *laziness* of ढीला, see Bs. II, 77.

231. *Derivation.* The originals of these suff. are the Skr. (neut.) taddh. त्व or (vedic) त्वन (see § 227). They become in Ap. Pr. (nom. sg.) प्पं or प्पणं (H. C. 4, 437. Ls. 460) or, with pleon. अ added, प्पअं or प्पणअं. The Ap. प्पं and प्पअं become in E. H. प् and प्पा or पा respectively; and the Ap. प्पणं and प्पणअं become E. H. प्पन् or पन् and पना, whence E. H. makes fem. पनी. Thus Skr. वृद्धत्वम्, Ap. वुड्ढप्पं (cf. H. C. 1, 131), E. H. बुढाप्; Skr. *वृद्धत्वकं, Ap. वुड्ढप्पअं, E. H. बुढप्पा or बुढापा; Skr. *वृद्धत्वनम्, Ap. वुड्ढप्पणं, E. H. बुढप्पन् or बुढापन्; Skr. *वृद्धत्वनकम्, Ap. वुड्ढप्पणअं, E. H. बुढापना or बुढापनी; etc. The आ in the E. H. forms आपा, आपन् might be the usual result of the simplification of the conjunct प्प्, but is more likely to be the strong termination of the base, as shown by the M., which changes that आ to ए, as भलेपण् *goodness* (Man. 112) for E. H. भलापन्; i. e., M. adds पन् to the strong form भले = भलय = Pr. भल्लअ = Skr. भद्रक. In the B. and O. मि the प् has been apparently softened to म्.

Fourth Group.

232.	Set.	Com. gen.	Fem.
	1)	वंत् or वत्	वंती or वती
	2)	मंत् or मत्	मंती or मती

The forms of com. gen. are weak, the others are strong. Strong masc. forms (ac वंता, etc.) do not exist.

233. The weak suff. are used to derive *possessional* adj. from subst. of the weak form. Thus वंत् or वत् in धनवंत् or धनवत् (m. f.) *wealthy*, of धन् *wealth*; भगतवंत् or °वत् *faithful*, of भगत् *faith*; सोगवंत् or °वत् *sorrowful*, of सोग् *sorrow*; पुनवंत् or वत् *virtuous*, of

पुन् *virtue;* जयवंत् or वत् *victorious*, of जय् *victory;* मानवंत् or °वत् *proud*, of मान् *pride;* भागवंत् or °वत् *fortunate, excellent*, of भाग् *fortune, excellence*, etc. Again मंत् or मत् in सिरिमंत् or सिरिमत् (m. f.) *excellent*, of सिरि *excellence;* हनुमंत् or °मत् *monkey*, of हनु *jaw;* भक्तिमंत् or °मत् *devoted*, of भक्ति *devotion;* पुनमंत् or °मत् *virtuous*, of पुन् *virtue;* etc.

234. The strong fem. suff. are commonly used to derive abstract nouns from their respective possessional adj., as धनवंती *wealthiness*, of धनवंत् *wealthy;* सोचवंती *thoughtfulness*, of सोचवंत् *thoughtful*, of सोच् *thought*, etc.; see §§ 256. 257.

235. *Affinities.* These suff. exist in all Gds., exc. S. See Bs. II, 106. As to M. see Man. 114. H. H. and the H. Gds. generally are fond of using the tats. forms, m. वान्, f. वती; as रूपवान् *beautiful*, f. रूपवती; धनवान् *wealthy*, f. धनवती; दयावान् *merciful*, f. दयावती, etc. In E. H., however, as distinguished from H. H., the tats. forms do not occur, except in a few proper names, as भगवान् *God*, भगवती *the goddess Gauḍi*, etc.; हनुमान् *the monkey-god*, etc. S. has the suff. वानु m., वानी f. (Tr. 76. 99), as m. सीलवानु, f. सीलवानी, E. H., m. f. सीलवंत् or °वत्; H. H. m. सीलवान्, f. सीलवती *amiable*. This S. form has in exceptional cases crept into the other Gds.; as H., M., G. गाड़ीवान् or गाडीवान् *coachman* (see Man. 113. Ed. 14).

236. *Derivation.* The originals of these suff. are the Skr. taddh. वत् and मत्, which become in Pr. वंत and मंत (Vr. 4, 35. H. C. 2, 159). Whence in the Mg. nom. sg. m. वंते and मंते, f. वंती and मंती; in E. H. m. f. वंत् and मंत् (§§ 43. 45) or वत् and मत् (§§ 143. 146). Or with pleon. ञ added, in Mg. f. वंतिञा and मंतिञा, E. H. वंती and मंती or वती and मती (§ 51). Thus Skr. m. धनवान्, Mg. धणावंते, E. H. धनवंत् or °वत्; Skr. f. धनवती, Mg. धणावंती, E. H. धनवंत् or °वत्; again Skr. f. *धनवत्तिका, Mg. धणावंतिञा, E. H. धनवंती or °वती (scl. वृत्ति *condition*). The S. वानु, f. वानी, though, probably, ultimately connected with the Skr. suff., are independent of the Pr. m. वंते, f. वंती; for they exist also in Pers., and there are no forms मानु, मानी in S., corresponding to Pr. मंते, मंती.

Fifth Group.

237. Set. 1) Com. gen. आइत् (§ 82). Masc. अइता or ऐता. Fem. अइती or ऐती (§§ 25. 77)

The suff. of com. gen. is a weak, the others are strong forms.

238. These suff. occur only with a very few subst. from which they are used to derive possessional adj.; and from the latter abstract nouns are derived by means of the fem. strong form (see § 257). Thus ढलाइत् *shield-bearer*, ढलइती or ढलैती *office of sh.°*, from ढाल् *shield;* बरछाइत् *spearsman*, of बरछा *spear;* कड़खाइत् *warrior-bard*, of कड़खा *war-song;* लिंगाइत् *a ling-worshipper*, of लिंग *phallus;* चरचाइत् *talker*, of चरचा *talk;* नताइत् *kinsman*, of नाता *kin;* कराइत् or करइता or करैता *the name of a very poisonous snake*, of कारा or काला *black;* डकाइत् *robber* and डकइती or डकैती *profession of robbery*, of डाका *robbery;* बहुताइत् (fem.) *abundance*, of बहुत् *much.*

239. *Affinities.* These suff. are properly W. Gḍ., more especially S., whence they have exceptionally passed (mostly in technical terms) into the other Gḍs. In S. they are: 1) m. एतो, f. एती (for *अइतो, *अइती) added to weak bases, as पुट्रेतो *having a son*, of पुट्रु son (base पुट्र, Skr. पुत्र); and 2) m. आइतो, f. आइती added to strong bases, as वाराइतो *opportune*, of वारो *time* (base वारा = वारअ, Skr. वारक). P. has occasionally the form ऐँत् or ऐँदू (see Bs. II, 102).

240. *Derivation.* These suff. may have been originally connected with those of the fourth group. For in Vr. 4, 25. H. C. 2, 159 the Pr. originals इत or इत्त are mentioned in close connection with वंत and मंत. The latter, incl. of the final अ of the base, would be 'अवंत and अमंत or (eliding व् and म्) अअंत, or (inserting य्, § 69) अयंत, or (vocalizing य्, § 121) अइंत, or (again detaching the अ of the base) इंत. Thus Pr. माणइंतो or माणइत्तो *proud* (H. C. 2, 159) would be = माणयंतो = माणअंतो, माणवंतो = Skr. मानवान्. With pleon. अ added to the suff., they are Pr. m. अइत्तओ, f. अइत्तिआ; S. m. एतो, f. एती. Or with pleon. अ added to the base, Pr. m. अअइत्तो, f. अअइत्ती, E. H. m. or f. आइत्; and with pleon. अ added to both the base and suff., Pr. m. अअइत्तओ, f. अअइत्तिआ; S. m. आइतो, f. आइती; E. H. m. अइत्ता or ऐता, f. अइती or ऐती. — There are, however, a few

words of a similar form, such as चढ़ाइत् or चढ़इता or चंढ़ता *rider, trooper*, दंगाइत् or f. दंगइती or दंगैती *quarrelsome*, अकड़ाइत् *swaggerer*, etc., which seem to require a different explanation. They are clearly *primary* derivatives of the Rs. चढ़् *mount*, दंग् *quarrel*, अकड़् *strut;* viz., probably, part. pres. of the denom. verbs चढ़ाव्, दंगाव्, अकड़ाव् (see §§ 349. 352). The suff. of such part. would be in Skr. आपयन्, in Pr. आवेंतो or आवंतो. The latter would change to आअंतो, आयंतो, आइंतो or आइन्तो, and in Gd. आइत्. Possibly the first mentioned derivatives, also, are to be explained in this way, as denominative participles, instead of possessional adj. This is the explanation suggested by Ls. 289. 290. It is favored by the fact that both examples in Vr. 4, 25., viz., रोसाइंतो *angry* and पाणाइंतो *alive*, end in आइंतो with long *á*. Those in H. C. 2, 159., viz., कव्वइन्तो *poëtical* and माणइन्तो *proud*, indeed, end in अइन्तो with *ă*; but this need be no objection; as Pr. may, optionally, shorten the denom. suff. आव to अव, see H. C. 4, 37. Wb. Spt. 65.

Sixth Group.

241.	Set.	Com. gen.	Masc.	Fem.
	1)	आल् or आर्	आला or आरा	आली or आरी
	2)	आलु or आरु	आलू or आरू	आलू or आरू

The forms of com. gen. are weak, the others are strong. As to the manner of adding them, and the use of the alternative forms with लू and रू, see § 195, note.

242. These suff. are used to derive possesional adj. from subst. In some cases, the word has been restricted to some particular secondary meaning. Thus the first set in तोँदाल् or तोँदार् or m. °रा, f. °री *pot-bellied*, of तोँदु *belly;* रसाल् *sugar-cane* or *mango-tree* (lit. *juicy*), of रस् *juice;* पखाल् f. or पखारा or °ला m. *a large double water-bag of leather carried across a bullock's back, with one half suspended on each side of it* (lit. *two-sided*), of पाख् *side;* रेताला *sandy*, of रेत् *sand;* दुधार् or दुधाल् *milch-cow*, of दूध् *milk* (M. दुधालू), etc. Again the 2nd set in दयालु or दयालू m. or f. *merciful*, of दय् (Skr. दया) *mercy;* लजालु or लजालू *bashful*, of लाज् *shame;* perhaps also झगड़ालू *quarrelsome* of झगड़ा *quarrel;* but see §§ 308. 312.

Note: In some words the suff. is probably pleonastic (cf. § 209), as in मेहरू or मेहरारू *woman;* घड़ी or घड़िया f. or घड़ियाल् or घरियार् m. *clock, gong.* In others, where the suff. exists only with रू, it is probably of a different kind, as in चिन्हारू *acquaintance,* etc.; see §§ 272. 273.

243. *Affinities.* These suff. occur only as an exception in the E. Gḍ. and P., but are very common in S. and W. Gḍ.; especially the second set. M. has, as a rule, ळू, sometimes रू; thus केसाळू or केसाड़ू *hairy,* खेळाडू *frolicsome,* see Man. 114. G. also has ळू; as रेताळू or रेताळ *sandy,* S. has लू or रू, like E. H., and sometimes ड़ू (Tr. 66. 69); as धणारू *herdsman,* जवालू (*wheat*) *mixed with barley;* साज़ाड़ू *right-handed.* P. has ळू or लू; as उन्नाळा *woollen,* कसाला *distressed;* see Bs. II, 90—94.

244. *Derivation.* The originals of these suff. are the Pr. suff. आल and आलु (Vr. 4, 25. H. C. 2, 159). They occur, however, especially the latter, in Skr. also. The suff. आल becomes in Mg. (nom. sg.) m. आले, f. आली and, with pleon. अ added, m. आलए, f. आलिआ, whence arise the E. H. first set m. or f. आरू or आल् and m. आरा or आला, f. आरी or आली. E. g., Skr. रसालः, A. Mg. रसाले (cf. H. C. 2, 159), E. H. रसाल् or रसारू; Skr. दुग्धाला, Mg. दुद्धाला or °ली, E. H. दुधाल or °रू; Skr. *तुन्दालकः (cf. तुन्दिल M. W. 378, 2), Mg. तोंदालए (cf. H. C. 1, 116), E. H. तोँदारा; f. Skr. *तुन्दालिका, Mg. तोंदालिआ, E. H. तोँदारी. The suff. आलु becomes in Mg., nom. sg., m. or f. आलू and, with pleon. अ added, m. आलुए, f. आलुआ, whence the E. H. second set, m. or f. आलु and m. or f. आलू. E. g., Skr. दयालुः, Mg. दयालू (cf. H. C. 2, 159), E. H. दयालु or °रु; Skr. लज्जालुका, Mg. लज्जालुआ (H. C. 2, 159), E. H. लजालू or °रू. As to the origin of the suff. आल and आलु, they are probably derivatives of the Skr. suff. दृश *like;* see § 251.

Seventh Group.

245.

Set.	Com. gen.	Masc.	Fem.
1)	अइल् or अइरू	ऐला or ऐरा	ऐली or ऐरी
2)	इल् or इरू	इला or इरा	इली or इरी
3)	अउल् or अउरू	औला or औरा	औली or औरी
4)	उल् or उरू	उला or उरा	उली or उरी

The forms of com. gen. are weak, the others are strong. In the two first sets ल् is commonly used, in the two others र्; for the rest see § 195, note.

246. These suff. are used to derive possessional adj. from subst. Sometimes the word is restricted to some particular meaning. The first and third sets are those commonly used. Thus the 1st set in दंगइल् m. or f. *quarrelsome*, of दंगा *quarrel;* गंठैला, f. °लौ *knotty*, of गाँठ् *knot;* पनैला, f. °लौ *swampy*, of पानी *water;* पथरइल् m. or f., or पथरैला, f. °लौ *full of stones*, of पथर् *stone;* डँकैला *having a sting*, of डाँक् *sting;* खपरइल् *a tiled house*, of खपरा *tile;* बोफइल् *beast of burden*, of बोफ् *load;* दुधइल् *milch-cow*, of दूध् *milk;* etc. Again the 2nd set in रेतिला, f. लौ *sandy*, of रेत् *sand;* बोफिल् *loaded*, of बोफ् *load;* etc. Again the 3d set in पथउर् m. or f., or पथौरा, f. °रौ *full of stones*, of पथर् *stone;* डँकउर m. or f., or डँकौरा, f. °रौ *having a sting, a wasp*, of डाँक् *sting;* रसउर् m. or f., or रसौरा, f. °रौ *juicy*, of रस् *juice;* घमौरी or घमौली *prickly heat*, of घाम् *warmth;* बकौला *hood* and बकौलौ *green caterpillar*, of बाँक् *a bend;* etc. Again the 4th set in पातुर *moth*, of पात् (Skr. पत्र) *wing;* पातुर् or पतुरौ *prostitute*, of पात् (Skr. पात्र) *vessel;* पातुर् *weak* (H. H. पतला; lit. *leaf-like*), from पात् *leaf;* बाउर् or बउरा, f. °रौ *mad* (H. H. बावला), of बाय् *wind* (lit. *inflated*). Occassionally, the suff. expresses relation generally, as in बनैला, f. °लौ *wild, savage*, of बन् *a wood;* घरैला, f. °लौ *tame*, of घर् *house;* कखौरी or कखौलौ *tumour in the armpit*, of काख् *armpit*.

247. *Affinities.* These suff. exist in all Gds., but in the W. and S. Gd. they have an initial ए or ई for ऐ, and ओ or ऊ for औ, and in H. H. also अ for इ or उ. The M., G. and O. have ळ्, and S. often र् for ल्. Thus W. H. एलौ or ईलौ, H. H. एला or ईला or अला, M. एळा or ईळा, G. एळो or ईळो, S. एलो or एरो, ईलो or ईरो, इरु (Tr. 67). The interchange of र् and ल्, however, occasionally occurs in all Gds., and, indeed, already in Pr. (see § 248). Thus H. H. गँठीला, W. H. गँठीलौ *knotty;* W. H. घमोलौ, M. घमोळी *prickly heat;* H. H. पतला *thin*, रेतला *sandy;* etc.; further examples see in Bs. II, 95—101.

248. *Derivation.* The originals of these suff. are the Pr.

suff. इल्ल and उल्ल (Vr. 4, 5. H. C. 2, 159) or, with the pleon. अ added to the base, अइल्ल and अउल्ल or, with pleon. अ added to the suff., इल्लअ, अइल्लअ, उल्लअ, अउल्लअ, whence the E. H. suffixal forms regulary arise. Thus E. H. पथरइल् = A. Mg. पत्थलइल्ले; E. H. पथरैला = A. Mg. पत्थरइल्लए; E. H. पथरउर् = A. Mg. पत्थलउल्ले; E. H. पथरोरा = A. Mg. पथलउल्लए; E. H. पतुरी = A. Mg. पत्तुलिआ, etc. From the Pr. these suff. were probably adopted into the Skr. as taddh. with *one* ल्; thus इल् in Skr. ग्रन्थिल *knotty;* उल् or ऊल in वातुल or वातूल *gouty;* ओल in गण्डोला *raw sugar*, etc. The Pr. taddh. इर (H. C. 2, 145. Vr. 4, 25), which occurs also in Skr., may, perhaps, be identified with the Pr. इल्ल (or इल), by the interchange of ल् and र् (see § 110); in S. it occurs as इड़ (see § 247); but E. H. has no suff. इर, except as an alternative of इल. — As to the origin of the suff. इल्ल and उल्ल (probably from Skr. दृश), see § 251.

Eighth Group.

249. Set.		Com. gen.	Masc.	Fem.
1)	a.	एर् or एड़्	एरा or एड़ा	एरी or एड़ी
	b.		एरू or एड़ू	एरू or एड़ू
2)	a.	ओर् or ओड़्	ओरा or ओड़ा	ओरी or ओड़ी
	b.	औंर् or औंड़्	औंरा or औंड़ा	औंरी or औंड़ी

The forms of com. gen. are weak, the others strong. Those with ड़ are properly W. H. As to the way of adding them, see § 195, note.

250. These suff. are used to derive possessional adj. from subst.; but the derivatives are few in number and always restricted to some particular meaning. Thus the first set, in सपेरा or सपेड़ा *snake-catcher*, of साप् *snake;* कटेरा *palings*, of काँटा *thorn;* पखेरू *bird*, of पाख् *wing*. The second set in लरकोरा or लड़कोड़ा *parents*, of लरिका *child;* पखौरा *shoulder-blade*, of पाख् *side;* हथोरा or हथौरा *hammer*, of हाथ् *handle;* करोरा *tax-gatherer*, of कर् *tax*, etc.

251. *Affinities and Derivation.* I believe these suff. and their derivatives are, strictly, W. Gd., and only introduced into the E. H. from the W. H. To this group belong the suff., S. इड़्यो (Tr. 70) and M. आडूया (Man. 113); e. g., S. पेरिड़्यो *walker*, of पेर् or पैर् *foot*, वाटाडूया *guide*, of वाट *way*. — On comparing

this group with the sixth and seventh, it will be seen, that there are, in each, identical suff. containing ल् or ड़् or ड़्; thus, sixth group, E. H. आलु or आलू, M. आड़ु or आड़ू, S. आड़ु or M. आड; seventh and eighth groups, E. H. एला or ऐला or एड़ा, M. एड़ा; E. H. ओला, औड़ा, W. H. ओला or ओड़ा, M. ओड़ा. Further, on comparing these with the third pleonastic group (§ 209), it will be seen that the suffixes in the two classes are identical. Hence it appears probable, that they have the same origin and are derived from the Skr. suff. दृश, as explained in § 218. Skr. दृशकः would, in Ap. Pr., become डिहउ, whence, eliding ह् and contracting the hiatus-vowels, the forms ड़्यो and ड़्या would arise, as contained in S. इड़्यो and M. आड़्या. The initial vowels of the latter must be accounted for by the addition of the pleon. अ to the base, just as in pleon. एड़ा, एला, इला, etc. (see § 218). — That the Skr. suff. दृश *like* would easily lend itself to derive possess. adj., may be seen from the German *peinlich*, i. e., painful, or from the English *lively*, *prickly*, *sprightly* = full of life, pricks, spirit.

Ninth Group.

252.	Set.	Com. gen.	Masc.	Fem.
	1)	ई	—	इकी
	2)	इक्	इका	इनि or इनी

The suff. इक् and इनि are weak, the others strong forms. As to the manner of adding them, see § 195, note.

253. These suff. are used to derive adj. expressing, in a general way, possession or relation from subst. The first set is the one commonly used; sometimes in its long form इया (see § 199). Thus, 1st set in संगी or सबती *friend*, *companion*, of संग् or संघत् *companionship*; बारी or कुनही *enemy*, of बार् or कुनह् *enmity*; बकवादी or बतोलिया or बतुनिया *a talkative person*, of बकवाद् or बतोला *talk*; सुखी *happy*, of सुख् *happiness*; दुखी *miserable*, of दुख् *pain*; धनी *wealthy*, of धन् *wealth*; तेली *oilman*, of तेल् *oil*; माली *gardener*, of माल् or माला *garland*; धोबी *washerman*, of धोब् (§ 311) *washing*; हथौटी or हथौटिया *craftsman*, of हथौटी *handicraft*; बहेलिया *huntsman*, of बाह् *shooting*; गडेरिया *shepherd*, of गड् *fold*, etc. And हिन्दुई *belonging to*

a Hindú of हिन्दू *Hindú:* मराठी *bel. to a Maráṭhá* of मराठा *Maráṭhá* (man or country); अंग्रेज़ी *English* of अंग्रेज़ *Englishman* or *England*, etc. Again the 2nd set in धनिक् or धनिका, f. °की *wealthy*, of धन् *wealth*, etc.

254. Derivatives in ई are gen. com., when used adjectively; but when used as subst., they form a fem. in इनि or इनी, on which see the next group (§ 256). Thus बंगाली भाखा *Bangáli language:* बहिरी तिरिया *foreign woman;* but बंगालिनि or बंगालिनी *a woman of Bangál,* बहिरिनि or बहिरिनी *a woman of a foreign country.*

255. *Affinities and Derivation.* These suff. exist in all Gḍs.; see Bs. II, 83—89., where examples will be found. — The original is the Skr. taddh. suff. इक; in Mg. (in the nom. sg.) इए or इके (or इक्के § 203, footnote 1) or, with pleon. अ added, इकए; whence E. H. ई or इक् or इका. Thus Skr. धनिकः, Mg. धणिए or धणिके or धनिकए, E. H. धनी or धनिक् or धनिका. Skr. महाराष्ट्रिकः, Mg. मरहट्टिए (cf. H. C. 1, 69. 2, 119), E. H. मराठी (cf. § 32). In the latter and in similar words, the original suff. may also have been the taddh. ईय; practically it makes no difference, as Skr. ईय would be Mg. ईए, E. H. ई. As to the origin of the fem. suff., see §§ 256—262.

Tenth Group.

256. Set. 1) Fem. — ई Set. 2) Fem. इनि or इनी
3) „ आइन् or आइनी „ 4) „ — आनी

The suff. इनि and आइन् are weak, the others strong. As to the manner of adding them, see § 195, note; but observe that the final ऊ of a base is not elided, but changed to उ; हिन्दुइनि or हिन्दुइनी *a Hindú woman* of हिन्दू *Hindú.*

257. These suff. are used to derive feminine from masc. nouns; and it may be remarked, that, with inanimate objects, the fem. generally expresses diminutiveness, while in many other cases it forms abstract nouns. Thus डंगरी *hillock*, of डाँगर् *hill;* बनी *copse*, of बन् *wood;* बाँसी *flute* (lit. *small piece of bamboo*), of बाँस् *bamboo;* गोली *bullet, globule,* of गोला *ball;* डोरी *string* of डोरा *rope;* चोली

bodice, of चोला *waistcoat*, etc. Again सोचवंती *thoughtfulness*, of सोचवंत् *thoughtful;* रखवारि *guarding or guardianship*, of रखवारु *guardian;* ढलैती *shieldbearership*, of ढलाइत् *shieldbearer;* चिन्हारि *acquaintance*, of चिन्हारु *an acquaintance;* पढ़निहारि *reading* or *readership*, of पढ़निहारु or °रा *reader;* etc.

258. The first set may be used with any adj. or subst. in आ. Thus adj.; साँची *true*, of m. साँचा; बाँकी *crooked*, of m. बाँका; मीठी *sweet*, of m. मीठा; भूखी *hungry*, of m. भूखा; बड़ी *great*, of m. बड़ा, etc. Or subst., छोरी or छोकरी or लरिकी *girl*, of छोरा or छोकरा or लरिका *boy;* बेटी *daughter*, of बेटा *son;* काकी *paternal aunt*, of काका *paternal uncle;* नानी *maternal grandmother*, of नाना *mat. grandfather;* बकरी or छेरी *she-goat*, of बकरा or छेरा *he-goat;* घोरी *mare*, of घोरा *horse;* भेड़ी *ewe*, of भेड़ा *ram;* कुकरी *hen*, of कुकरा *cock;* etc. Occassionally the corresponding masc. in आ is not in use (cf. § 196); as सोनारि *fem. goldsmith*, of *सोनारा or सोनारु m.; चमारि f. *leather-worker*, of *चमारा or चमारु m.; कोँहारि, f. *potter*, of *कोहारा or कोँहारु m.; कहारि, f. *porter*, of *कहारा or कहारु m.; सुतारि, f. *carpenter*, of *सुतारा or सुतारु m.

Note: In a few cases the long form in इया (see § 199) is exclusively used; as in कुत्तिया fem., of कुत्ता *dog;* डिब्बिया *small box*, of डिब्बा *box*, बुढ़िया *old woman*, of बूढ़ा *old man;* but the short forms कुत्ती, डिब्बी, बूढ़ी also occur.

259. The second set can be added only to subst. in अ or ई or ऊ, expressing animate objects; never to adj., except when used substantively. Thus in अ; persons; सोनारिनि or °रिनी f. *goldsmith*, of सोनारु m.; चमारिनि or °रिनी f. *leather-worker*, of चमारु m.; गोवालिनि or गुवा° or ग्वा° f. *cowherd*, of गोवाल् m.; घटवालिनि *ferry-woman*, of घटवाल् m., etc. Or animals; पतुरिनी f. *moth*, of पातुरु m.; बाघिनि or बघिनी *tigress*, of बाघ् *tiger;* सीँघिनि or सिँघिनी *lioness*, of सीँघ् *lion*. Again in ई; persons; परोसिनि or °सिनी f. *neighbour*, of परोसी m.; बैरागिनि or °गिनी f. *ascetic*, of बैरागी; मालिनि or °नी f. *gardener*, of माली m.; धोबिनि or °नी *washerwoman*, of धोबी m.; कोढ़िनि or °नी f. *leper*, of कोढ़ी, etc. Or animals; हाथिनि or हथिनी f. *elephant*, of हाथी m. Again in ऊ; नउइनि or नउइनी f. *barber*, of

नाऊ m.; पहरुइनि or °नी *watchman's wife*, of पहरू, etc.; see § 256. Occasionally the masc. is not in use, as बहिनि or बहिन् or बहिनी *sister* (masc. भाई *brother*).

260. The third and fourth sets are confined to some particular words, as पँड़ाइन् or °नी *wife of a* पाँड़ा *a kind of brâhman*; चौबाइन् *woman of the* चौबे *caste*; दुबाइन् *woman of the* दूबे (m.) *caste*; ठकुराइन् *lady* of ठाकुर् *lord, chief*; चौधराइन् *wife of a* चौधरी *headman*; पंडियाइन् *wife of a* पंडा *priest*; गुरुआइन् *wife of a* गुरु *teacher*; पंडिताइन् *wife of a* पंडित् *scholar*; बनियाइन् *woman of the* बनिया *trader-caste*; पुरोहितानी *wife of a* पुरोहित् *family priest*.

Note: These suff. are used even with foreign words, as मेहतरानी or मेहतराइन् *wife of a* मेहतर् (pers. مهتر) *sweeper*; सईसिन् *wife of a* साईस् (arab. سيس) *groom*. — With names of castes or professions the fem. signifies either the wife of a man of the caste, or any woman of that caste, or any woman following that profession.

261. *Affinities.* These suff. occur in all Gḍs. But P. and W. H. have अन् and अनी after nouns in अ; thus E. H. सेठिनि *wife of a* सेठ् *merchant*, W. H. सेठन्, P. सेठन् or सेठनी, S. सेठिणि or सेठिणि or सेठिणी; but E. H. कोरिनि *wife of a* कोरी *weaver*, W. H. कोलिन्, P. कोलिन्, S. कोरिणि or °रिणी (Tr. 99—102. Ld. 13, 41. 42). M. has ईण् as सेठीण्, कोळीण्, वाघीण् (*tigress*), see Man. 24. G. has एण् or अण्, as कोळण् or कोळेण्, वाघण् or वाघण्, धोबण् or धोबेण् (*washerwoman*), see Ed. 26, 9. B. has इनी or अनी or आनी, as वाघिनी, धोबानी, कामारनी (*a fem. blacksmith*), see S. Ch. 36. 40. 41. For further examples, see Bs. II, 163—170.

262. *Derivation.* The original of the E. H. suff. ई is the Skr. taddh. इका, which becomes in Pr. इआ, and is contracted in E. H. to ई, as explained in § 203. It is, in fact, identical with the pleon. fem. ई of the 1st set, 1st group. — The original of the E. H. second set is the Skr. taddh. इनी or, with pleon. क added, इनिका, in Pr. इणी or इणिआ, E. H. इनि or इनी; thus Skr. base मालिन्, m. माली, Mg. माली, E. H. *deest* (*मालि); fem. Skr. मालिनी, Mg. मालिणी, E. H. मालिनि; or with pleon. अ added, Skr. मालिकः

(i. e., मालिन् + क), Mg. मालिए, E. H. माली; fem. Skr. मालिनिका (i. e., मालिनी + का), Mg. मालिणिश्रा, E. H. मालिनी. It should be observed that, while in the case of the fem. E. H. preserves both the weak form मालिनि and the strong form मालिनी, on the other hand in the masc. it has only the strong form माली, but not a weak form *माल् or *मालि (see § 196). Again E. H. सोनार् has two fem., सोनारी and सोनारिनि or °रिनी; the former is = A. Mg. सोणआलिश्रा, Skr. सुवर्णकारिका fem. of सुवर्णकारकः pleon. for °कारः; but the latter is = A. Mg. सोणआलिणी or °लिणिश्रा = Skr. सुवर्णकारिणी or (pleon.) °रिणिका, fem. of सुवर्णकारी (base °कारिन्). The latter masc. form exists in E. H. only in the weak form सोनार्, not in the strong सोनारी; though E. H. सोनार् might and probably does also stand for the A. Mg. सोणआले, Skr. सुवर्णकारः. It is not necessary to assume an anomaly in this and similar words as to the use of the fem. suff. इनि in E. H.; but it appears to be anomalously employed in such words as बाघिनि *tigress* from m. बाघ्, for which fem. form there is no foundation in Skr., which has m. व्याघ्रः, f. व्याघ्री. — The E. H. suff. आइन् arises in various ways. Thus in चौबाइन् it arises from Pr. चउव्वेइणी, Skr. चतुर्वेदिनी; in पँडाइन् and पंडियाइन् it is added anomalously to पाँडा, पंडिया, Mg. पंडिअए, Skr. पण्डितकः, etc. — The E. H. suff. आनी is a tats. for Skr. आनी, as in Skr. इन्द्राणी *wife of Indra.* — The E. H. रस्सी *string* is a regular fem. of the E. H. m. रस्सा, which is derived from the Skr. masc. रश्मिः or pleon. रश्मिकः (or रश्मकः of रश्मन्, see M. W. 835, 1); not *vice versa*, the E. H. masc. रस्सा formed from the E. H. fem. रस्सी (as Bs. II, 149), which would be an unique anomaly.

Eleventh Group.

263. Com. gen. अव्. Masc. आ or अवाँ. Fem. अइँ.
The form अव् is weak, the others are strong. As to the manner of adding them see § 195, note.

264. These suff. are used to derive ordinal numbers from the cardinals, with the exception of the four first and the sixth, which are formed differently (see §§ 269. 401). Thus m. or f. पंचव्,

m. पचा or पचवाँ, f. पचईं *fifth*, of पंच् *five*; m. f. दसव् or m. दसा or दसवाँ, f. दसईं *tenth*, of दस् *ten*; m. f. बारहव् or m. बारहवाँ, f. बारहईं *twelfth*, of बारह् *twelve*, etc. They are added pleonastically to the following: दुसरा or दुसरव् or दुसरवाँ *second*, of दुइ *two*; तिसरा or तिसरव् or तिसरवाँ *third*, of तीनि *three*; चौथा or चौथव् or चौथवाँ *fourth*, of चारि *four*; छठा or छठव् or छठवाँ *sixth*, of छ *six*; बीसा or बीसव् or बीसवाँ *twentieth*, of बीस् *twenty*, etc.

265. *Affinities.* These suff. exist in all Gds., with very slight differences: thus B. m. आ, f. ईँ (S. Ch. 195); M. अवा, f. अवी, n. अवेँ or (from 19th) आवा, आवी, आवेँ (Man. 42. 44); H. H. अवाँ, f. अवीँ; W. H. अवोँ, f. अवीँ; P. अवाँ or अमाँ, f. अवीँ or अमीँ (Ld. 82—85); G. (and O. H.) अमो, f. अमी, n. अमुँ (Ed. 48); S. ओँ, f. ईँ; e. g., B. पाचा, f. पाचईँ; M. पाँचवा, f. पाँचवीँ, n. पाँचवेँ, but विसावा, f. विसावीँ, n. विसावेँ *twentieth*; W. H. पाँचवोँ, f. पाँचवीँ; P. पंजवाँ or पंजमाँ, f. पंजवीँ or पंजमीँ; G. पांचमो, f. पाँचमी, n. पाँचमुँ; S. पंजोँ, f. पंजीँ.

266. *Derivation.* The original of these suff. is the Skr. taddh. म or, with pleon. क added, मक; whence nom. sg. (incl. the final अ of the base) अमकः, f. अमिका, Mg. अमए, f. अमिआ, Ap. Mg. अवँए, f. अविँआ (cf. H. C. 4, 397), E. H. अवाँ or (contracted, after eliding म् or व्) आ; f. अईँ (cf. §§ 33. 47. 51). Thus Skr. पञ्चमकः, Ap. Mg. पंचमए or पंचवँए, E. H. पचा or पचवाँ; f. Skr. पञ्चमिका, Ap. Mg. पंचमिआ or पंचविँआ, E. H. पचईँ. The M. form आवा may be a contraction of the Skr. अतितमकः; e. g., विंशतितमकः, Mg. वीसइअमए (cf. Wb. Bh. 476); or it may have arisen by adding the pleon. अ to the base and be = Skr. *विंशकमकः, Mg. *वीसअमए. In the latter case the addition of the suff. आवा would be pleonastic, as the Skr. विंश itself means *twentieth*; but so it is in E. H. and all other Gds. in चौथवाँ, छठवाँ, बीसवाँ, etc., the regular forms being चौथा, छठा, बीसा, etc.

Improper Suffixes.

267. The suffixes of the following groups are in reality curtailed nouns, and their derivatives modified compounds. This appears from the following facts: 1) that in some cases the base

does not exist in E. H.; e. g., कों॑हार् *potter* of *कों॑ह् (Skr. कुम्भ, E. H. कुंभ्); कं॑हार् *porter*, of *कं॑ह् (Skr. स्कन्ध, E. H. काँध्); रोंआसा *lachrymose*, of *रोंद् (Skr. रोद); 2) that the various suff. (exc. आहट्) are, severally, found only in a very small number of words; 3) that the terminations of their derivatives are not recognised as suff., and their etymology in many cases unknown to all but Skr. scholars.

Twelfth Group.

268. Com. gen. स् or सर्. Masc. सरा. Fem. सरी.
The forms of com. gen. are weak, the others strong.

These suff. are extremely rare, and occur only in numerals; thus m. f. दूसर्, m. दुसरा, f. °री *second* (lit. *twice removed*, i. e., from Nro. 1), of दुइ *two*; m. f. तीसर्, m. तिसरा, f. °री *third* (lit. *thrice moved*, i. e., from Nro. 1), of तीन् *three*; m. चौस् or चउस् or f. चौसरी *a field four times tilled* (lit. *four times moved or turned*).

270. *Affinities.* This curious formation of the second and third ordinal numbers is confined to the E. and S. Gd. and H. H. The W. Gds. have the regular ordinal forms: O. H. दूजौ or दूजो; P. दूजा or दूत्रा = Pr. दुइज्जश्रो or दुइश्रओ (H. C. 1, 94. 209); S. ब्रीओ or ब्रीजो, G. बोजो, Pr. विइअओ (H. C. 1, 94) or बीअओ (H. C. 1, 248) or विइज्जओ (H. C. 1, 248); again W. H. तीजौ or तीजो, P. तीआ or तीजा, S. ट्रीओ or ट्रीजो, G. तीजो, = Pr. तइअओ (H. C. 1, 101) or तइज्जआ (cf. H. C. 4, 339). But H. H. and M. दूसरा, तीसरा.

271. *Derivation.* The original of these suff. is the Skr. past part. pass. सृतः *moved*, in A. Mg. सलिए or सलिअ, which in Gd. becomes सर् by the successive quiescence of the final अ and इ (cf. §§ 45. 302), and स् by the elision of र् (cf. § 124). Similarly the E. H. सरा is = A. Mg. सलिअए, Skr. सृतकः; and f. सरी = A. Mg. सलिइआ, Skr. सृतिका. E. g., Skr. *द्विस्सृतः (i. e., द्विः + सृत), A. Mg. दूसलिए, E. H. दूसर्.

Thirteenth Group.

272. Set.	Com. gen.	Masc.	Fem.
1)	अर् or र्	अरा or रा	अरी or री
2)	आर्	आरा	आरी

The forms of com. gen. are weak, the others strong. As to the manner of adding them, see § 195, note.

273. These suff. are used to derive adj. expressing (genitive) relation from subst. or pronouns; but they occur very rarely. Thus in the possessive pron.; m. f. हमार् or m. हमरा, f. °री *our* (lit. *of us*), of हम् *we*; m. f. तोँहार् or m. तोँहरा, f. °री *your* (lit. *of you*), of तोँह् *you*; m. f. मोर् or m. मोरा, f. °री *mine*, of *मो *I*; m. f. तोर् or m. तोरा, f. °री *thine*, of *तो *thou*. Again in nouns; e. g., m. f. गँवार् or m. गँवरा, f. °री *rustic, vulgar*, of गाँव् *village*; m. f. चिन्हार् or m. चिन्हारा *an acquaintance* (lit. *of a mark, marked*), f. चिन्हारी *acquaintance*; भिखार् *beggar*, of भीख् *alms*; perhaps also हथियार् *tools, weapons*, of हथिया *small handle*; m. घसियारा, f. °री *grassier*, of घसिया (or घास्) *grass*; भठियारा, f. °री *innkeeper*, of भठिया (or भट्ठी) *hearth, inn* (Skr. भ्रष्ट).

274. *Affinities and Derivation.* These suff. are identical with the gen. affixes कर्, करा, करी, see § 377, where their derivation will be fully explained. The full suffix कर् still exists in the M. गांवकर् *villager* (Man. 113), खोडकर् (H. खोडिल्) *mischievous*, of खोड् (Man. 114); चिपलुंकर् *a man of Chiplun* (Bs. II, 181), etc. The curtailed suff. अर्, आर्, etc. are employed in B. and O. as their ordinary gen. affixes; as O. घरर् *domestic* or *of a house*, of घर् *house*. H. H. has हमारा *our*, तुम्हारा *your*, गँवार् *villager*.

Fourteenth Group.

275.

Set.	Masc.	Fem.	Masc.	Fem.
1)	आर्	—	आरा	आरी
2)	—	आरिनि	आरी	आरिनी
3)	कार्	—	कारा	कारी

The forms in आ and ई are strong, the others weak. As to the manner of adding them, see § 195, note.

276. These suff. are used to derive nouns, expressing „workers of something". They are of a limited number. Thus the 1st set in सोनार्, f. सोनारी or °रिनि or °रिनी *goldsmith*, of सोना *gold*; कोँहार्, f. °री or °रिनि or °रिनी *potter*, of कुम्भ् *pot*; कहार्, f. °री or °रिनि or °रिनी *porter*, of काँध् *shoulder*; चमार्, f. °री or °रिनि or °रिनी *leather-worker*, of चाम् *leather*; सुतार्, f. °री or °रिनि or °रिनी *carpenter*, of सूत् *thread*; अंधार् or अंधियार् or अंधारा, f. °री, or अंधियारा m.,

f. °ऱी *dark* or *darkness*, of अंधा *dark*. The 2nd set in पुजारी, f. पुजारिनि or °रिनी *worshipper*, of पूजा *worship*. The 3d set in छुटकारू or °रा or °री *deliverance*, of छुटा *delivered*.

277. *Affinities and Derivation.* The original of these suffixes is the Skr. noun कार or कारिन्; e. g., Skr. कुम्भकारः or °री, Mg. कुंभआले or °ली or कुंभाले or °ली, E. H. कोँहारू (cf. § 120); Skr. पूजाकारिकः (i. e., °रिन् + क), Mg. पूजआलिए, E. H. पुजारी, N. पूजाड़ारि, (S. Lk. 1, 5). These and similar words occur in all Gḍs. As to the fem., see § 259.

Fifteenth Group.

278.	Set.	Com. gen.	Masc.	Fem.
	1)	क्	का	की
	2)	कै	—	—

The forms of com. gen. are weak, the others strong.

279. These suff. are used to derive adj. expressing relation from a subst. Thus काठक् or काठकै or काठका, f. °की *wooden*, of काठ् *wood*; घरकै or घरका, f. °की *domestic*, of घर *house*; बनकै or बनका, f. की *wild*, of बन् *forest*; etc.

280. *Affinities and Derivation.* These suff. are identical with the common genitive affixes; and their derivatives are really genitives of the respective bases. This can be seen from the fact that all the various Gḍ. gen. aff. may be used in this way; thus M. चा in M. घरचा *domestic* (Man. 113. Bs. II, 110), in S. गोठेचो *of the same village*, of गोठु; वेड्होचो *of the jungle*, of वेड्हि (Tr. 91); again Konkaní ला in M. तेथला *of that place*, of तेथेँ *there* (Man. 113); again G. णो in S. चोराणो *thievish*, of चोरु *thief*, or वातूणो *oral*, of वातु *mouth* (Tr. 72. 73); again H. का in M. बोलका *eloquent*, of बोल् *word* (Man. 107), मारका *given to beating*, of मार् *beating* (Man. 115), पाटिलकी *office of a* पाटिल् *village accountant* (Man. 113); in P. पिउका *paternal*, of पिउ *father*; in S. हारिका *relating to a* हारी *peasant* (Tr. 71); again Mw. रो in M. खाजरा *itch-producing*, of खाज् (Man 115); and, of course, each in its own language. — As to the origin of all these affixal forms see § 377. — The vowel ए before चो in S. is not (as Bs. II. 110)

the inflected termination of the noun; for the obl. form of गोठु is not गोठे but गोठु; similarly of वेन्ठि it is not वेन्ठी, but वेन्ठि (Tr. 123. 128); but all these long vowels in S., viz. ए in एचो, ई in ईचो, आ in आपो or आकू (Tr. 70), ऊ in ऊपो, ओ in ओको (Tr. 71), have probably arisen by the suff. being added to the strong form (in अय or इय or अव or उव, contracted to ए, ई, etc.), just as in M. भलेपण् *goodness*, of भला + पण् (see § 231).

Sixteenth Group.

281.	Set.	Masc.	Fem.
	1)	—	आस्
	2)	आसा	आसी

The form आस् is weak, the others are strong. As to the way of adding them, see § 195, note.

282. Of these suff. the first set is used to derive subst., expressing „desire of anything", and the second set to derive adj. meaning „desirous", from an other subst. The number of such derivatives, however, is small. Thus f. निँद्रास् *desire to sleep, sleepiness*; m. निँद्रासा, f. °सी *sleepy*, of नीँद्र *sleep*; ऊँघास् *sleepiness*, °सा m., °सी f. *sleepy*, of ऊँघ् *sleep*; मुतास् f. *desire to make water*, °सा m., °सी f. *desirous of d^to^*, of मूत् *urin*; हगास् *desire to stool*, °सा m., °सी f. *desirous of d^to^*, of हग *excrement*; चुदास् f. *lasciviousness*, °सा m., °सी f. *lascivious*, of चोद् *copulation*; पेटास् *gluttony*, of पेट् *belly*; कटासा m., °सी f. *inclined to bite, snappish*, of काट् *bite*. Sometimes the base is not in use, as in रोआस् f. *inclination to weep*, रोआसा m., °सी f. *tearful*. In a few words the suff. has come to signify abstract nouns, as मिठास् f. *sweetness* (lit. *desire* or *tendency to be sweet*), of मीठ् *sweet*; ऊँचास् f. *height*, of ऊँच् *high*; जुड़ास् *coldness*, of जुड़् (H. H. जूड़) *cold*.

283. *Affinities and Derivation.* These derivatives are found also in W. H. and P. (see Bs. II, 82). In the other Gds. the (so-called) suff. is probably better preserved in its nominal form. It is merely a curtailment of the nouns बाँस् or बाँछ (fem.) *desire* = Skr. वाञ्छा, and बाँसा or बाँछा *desirous* = Skr. वाञ्छकः, as may be seen from the alternative form चुदबाँसा *libidinous*. In

the suff., व् is elided and the hiatus-vowels contracted to आ. Thus Skr. निद्रात्राङ्का, Pr. निद्दवंका, E. H. निँदास्; Skr. रोदनाङ्ककः, Mg. लोग्रवंकए or लोग्रग्रंकए, E. H. रोग्रासा. The change of ह् to स् is very common in M. and Mw., and, though less so, in P., whence it has sometimes passed into the other Gds. (see § 11. Bs. I, 218). — Shakespear's (H. Dict.) identification of the suff. with the Skr. noun आशा *hope* is not tenable; neither is the theory of their connection (as Br. II, 81) with the Skr. desiderative. The latter is true only of E. H. पियास् f. *thirst* = Skr. पिपासा, Pr. पिश्रासा, and E. H. पियासा m., °सी f. *thirsty* = Skr. पिपासितकः m., °तिका f. (not, as Bs., Skr. पिपासुकः, which would be H. पियासू). It exactly corresponds to E. H. भूख् f. *hunger* = Skr. बुभुक्षा, Pr. बुहुक्खा, and E. H. भूखा m., भूखी f. *hungry* = Skr. बुभुक्षितकः m., °तिका f. — The two words झपास् f. and झटास् m. *violent burst of rain* do not belong to this group, but are compounds of झप् or झट् *quick* and Pr. वासा f. or वासं n. *rain* (see H. C. 2, 104), = Skr. वर्षा and वर्षम्.

Seventeenth Group.

284.	Set.	Fem.	Fem.
	1)	आहट् or आवट्	औटी
	2)	आवत्	औती

The forms in ई are strong, the others weak. As to the manner of adding them, see § 195, note.

285. The first set is used to derive abstract nouns from adj. The form आहट् is the one commonly employed. Thus सचाहट् or सचावट् or सचौटी *truth, truthfulness,* of सच् or सचा *true* (= सचाई § 220); मिठाहट् *sweetness,* of मीठ् *sweet;* गरमाहट् *warmth,* of गरम् (Pers. گرم) *warm;* खराहट् *purity,* of खरा *pure;* तिताहट् *bitterness,* of तीत् or तीता *bitter;* चिकनाहट् *smoothness,* of चिकना *smooth;* रुखाहट् *roughness,* of रूख् *rough;* कडुआहट् *bitterness,* of कडुआ *bitter,* etc.

286. The first and second sets occur in a few words, which are derived from subst., and express relation generally; as चमरावत् or चमरावट् *perquisites of a man of the* चमार् *caste;* बपौती *patrimony,* of बाप् *father;* सगौती *flesh, animal food,* (probably) of सगा *kin, related* (= Skr. सगर्भ *of the same origin,* hence *animal* as opp. to *vegetable*

(cf. § 120); हिनौती *humility, supplication*, of हीनू *destitute*; हथौटी *handicraft, dexterity*, of हाथू *hand*.

287. *Affinities.* These derivatives are properly W. Gd. and have been introduced into the E. H. from the W. H. In the latter and in P. they are very common; also in S., which has the contracted forms आटु or आतु (or अतु) or आठो (probably for *आटो), all masc., see Tr. 60. 62. 68. 74.; e. g., चोकिराटु *boyhood*, of चोकरु; डिअणयातु *debtor*, of डिअणो *debt*; भर्यतु *porter*, of भरो *load*; पाणयाठो *damp*, of पाणी *water*, etc. Also occasionally in M.; as रानवट् *belonging to a desert*, of रान् (Man. 113), or contracted to ईट् (= *आवट्) as in रागीट् *angry*, of राग् (Man. 114).

288. *Derivation.* The originals of these suff. are the Skr. nouns वृत्ति fem. or वृत्त neut., and वार्त्ता fem. or वार्त्त neut.; all meaning *condition, state, mode of life, earnings*, etc. (see M. W. 957. 958). The two former become in Pr. वट्टी or वट्टं (H. C. 2, 29), the two latter वत्ता (or वट्टा) and वत्तं (H. C. 2, 30). Next Pr. वट्टी or वट्टा and, with pleon. अ added, वट्टिआ become in H. वट् and वटी, or, with pleon. अ added to the base, आवट् and औटी (contracted for अवटी or अउटी, cf. § 78, for आवटी, § 25) or, with इ substituted for व् (see § 69), आइट्. Similarly Pr. वत्ता or वत्तिआ become in H. आवत् or औती. Thus Skr. *सत्यकवृत्तिः, Pr. सच्चअवट्टी or सच्चअवट्टिआ, E. H. सचावट् or सचौटी; again Skr. चर्मकारकवृत्तिः or °वार्त्ता, Pr. चम्मआरअवट्टी or °वत्ता, E. H. चमरावट् or °वत् (for *चमारावट्, cf. § 25). The S. m. आटु arises similarly from the Skr. neut. वृत्तम्. — Those suff. which form adj., as S. आतु, M. अवट्, arise from the Skr. m. वृत्तः or वार्त्तः, Pr. वट्टो or वत्तो. Thus E. H. गुबरौता or टा *a beetle found in old cow-dung*, from गोबर + वृत्तकः *living in gobar* or *cow-dung*. — In the E. H. चिकनावट् or °वत् (fem.) *clayey soil*, there is probably an exchange of म् and व्, see § 134, 2; E. H. also चिकनी माटी. — The suff. of this group should be carefully distinguished from those of the fifth group (§ 322) which are primary, and have an altogether different origin. Practically they are often confounded, and the dental त्, which is proper to the primary group, given to the secondary, the proper cons. of which is ट्; and *vice versa*.

Eighteenth Group.

289. Com. gen. सू. Masc. सा. Fem. सी.
The form सू is weak, the others are strong.

290. These suff. occur in a very few nouns, which more or less distinctly imply „likeness". Thus आपुस् f. (H. H. आपस्) *kindred* (lit. *like self*); especially in the phrase आपुस् में *among themselves*, of आपु *self*; पैसा m. *a copper coin, the fourth part of an anná*, of पाइ or पाई *a pice* (lit. *like the páda or quarter of a weight of gold*, cf. M. W. 564); पनसा m., पनसी f. *insipid* (lit. *like water*), of पानी *water*; m. ऐकसा, f. °सी *similar, identical* (lit. *like one*), of ऐक् *one*.

291. *Affinities*. These suff. exist. in all Gds. in the above mentioned words (cf. Bs. II, 330). — In M. they may be added, as a pleon. or dimin. suff., to any adj. in the following forms: m. सा, f. सी, n. सें or, less curtailed, com. gen. सर्; e. g., काळसर्, c. g. *blackish*, of काळा *black*; m. लहानसा, f. °सी, n. °सें *littleish*, of लहान् *little* (Man. 114). For the same purpose m. सो, f. सी are used in W. H. (H. H. सा, सी), but as an affix, not as a suffix; that is, the adj., to which they are added, is itself inflected; thus H. H. ऊँचा सा पहाड़ *a rather high mountain*, नीली सी चिड़ियाँ *rather blue birds*, बड़े से घोड़े *rather large horses* (see Kl. 91)[1]. — In W. H. and H. H. the same aff. is also commonly employed to express resemblance; as मेरी सी दशा *a condition like mine*; मुझ सा पापी *a sinner like me*; पंडित् की सी बोली *speech like that of a paṇdit* (examples of Kl. 91. Eth. 58). In E. H. सा, सी are not employed as affixes; in their place it uses ऐसन् *such* with subst. (e. g., हाथी ऐसन् *like an elephant*, आदमी ऐसन् *like a man*) and ऐक् *one* or ऐसन् *such* with adj.; as छोट् ऐक् (usually spelled छोटेक्) or छोट् ऐसन् *rather little* (cf. German *etwas klein*); थोरेक् or थोर् ऐसन् *rather few, some few*; बहुतेक् or बहुत् ऐसन् *rather many*.

---

1) The examples are from Kl. The aff. never denotes *intensity*, as Kl., Eth. (H. Gr. 48) and Bates (H. Dict. 740) state. It expresses the English *rather*, not *very*. It has no connexion with the Skr. सम *like*, still less with the Skr. suff. शस् *fold* (as Kl. 91, a). Bates gives the correct derivation.

292. *Derivation.* The original of these suff. is the Skr. सदृश *like*, as evidenced by the E. H. use of ऐसन्, which is the same as Skr. ईदृश (§§ 111. 458). Skr. सदृशः becomes in A. Mg. सरिसे (Wb. Bh. 422, cf. H. C. 1, 142) or सरिए (cf. H. C. 4, 300 for सरिहे, with ह as in तेहूहं H. C. 2, 157 or in तेहु = *तइहु H. C. 4, 402 = Skr. तादृशः). The latter becomes in Gd. *सरिश्र, *सरि, whence M. सर् or, by eliding र् (cf. Ap. तइसो H. C. 4, 403 = Skr. तादृशः, see § 124) and dropping इ, E. H. स. Similarly Skr. m. सदृशकः = A. Mg. सरिसए or Ap. Mg. *सइश्रए, contracted *सइश्रा or (dropping इ and contracted) E. H. सा; fem. Skr. सदृशिका, A. Mg. सरिसिश्रा, Ap. *सइइश्रा, E. H. contracted *सइई or सी. Precisely similar are E. H. भा or भया or भइश्रा *been* = Mg. भविश्रए, Skr. भूतः; E. H. गा or गया or गइश्रा, Ap. Mg. गइश्रए, Skr. गतः; E. H. का (§ 278) = S. कयो = Ap. कइश्रउ, Skr. कृतः, see § 307; E. H. स् or सर् = A. Mg. सरिए, Skr. सृतः (§ 268). — The E. H. use of ऐकू may be compared with its analogous use in the indefinite numerals (§ 425), as दस् ऐकू *about ten, some ten.*

Nineteenth Group.

293. Com. gen. वार् or वाल्. Masc. वारा or वाला.
Fem. वारी or वाली and वारिनि or वालिनि.

The forms in आ and ई are strong, the others weak.

294. These suff. are used to derive nouns implying possession or relation generally, from subst. Thus गोवार् or गोवाल् c. g. or गुवारा or °ला m. or गुवारी or °ली or गुवारिनि or °लिनि f. *cow-keeper, cowherd*, of गो *cow*; घटवार् or °वाल् c. g., °वारी or °ली or °रिनि or °लिनि f. *wharf-keeper, wharfinger*, of घाट् *landing-place*; नाश्रोवारा or °ला m., °री or °ली f. *boat-keeper, boat-man*, of नाश्रो *boat*; m. कपड़ावारा or °ला, f. °री or °ली *cloth-keeper, cloth-merchant*; दिल्लीवारा or °ला m., °री or °ली f. *belonging to or native of Delhi*, etc. Even with foreign words; as बकसुवारा or °ला m., °री or °ली or °रिनि or °लिनि f. *box-keeper, pedlar.*

295. *Affinities.* These suff. are not properly E. or S. Gd., but W. Gd., whence they have been introduced into E. H., B. (see S. Ch. 88, cf. 154; spelled m. उयाला, f. उयाली; e. g., B. टूपिउयाला *holding or wearing a* टूपि *cap*) and M. (see Man. 113, 2; e. g.,

दूधवाला *milkman*). In W. Gd. they are very commonly used. S. has वारो m., वारी f. (Tr. 76, 36); e. g., घरवारो *owner of a house*; G. has वाळो m., वाळी f. (Ed. 14); e. g., दुधवाळो, टोपीवाळो.

296. *Derivation.* The original of these suff., certainly in the two first examples, probably in all, is the Skr. noun पाल *keeper* or, with pleon. क added, पालक. Thus Skr. m. गोपालः or °लकः, f. °लिका, Mg. m. गोवाले or °लए, f. °लिआ, E. H. m. गोवार or °रा, f. °री. Practically, however, these suff. are confounded with the primary suff. वाला, °लो (in अनेवाला, °लो), see § 315. — The fem. in लिनि is probably an anomalous formation, see §§ 259. 262; though it might be referred to a Skr. base पालिन्.

3. PRIMARY DERIVATIVE SUFFIXES.

297. The primary derivative suffixes may be divided into eight groups, traces of all which already existed, more or less distinctly, in Pr.

First Group.

298. Com. gen. अत्. Masc. अता. Fem. अती (or अति).
The forms in आ and ई are strong, the others weak. The masc. strong form is not much used in E. H., except in the oblique form अते, as an adv. part., see § 488.

Note: Observe, in adding these suff., that य् is inserted after ई, and optionally व् after ऊ and ओ; and अ is elided after आ and ए and after R. हो *be*.

299. These suff. are used to derive the participle present from any root. Thus हसत् *laughing*, of R. हस् *laugh*; पढ़त् *reading*, of R. पढ़् *read*; पीयत् *drinking*, of R. पी *drink*; चूअत् or चूवत् *dripping*, of R. चू *drip*; रोअत् or रोवत् *weeping*, of R. रो *weep*, etc. But खात् *eating*, of R. खा *eat*; देत् *giving*, of R. दे *give*; होत् *being*, of R. हो *be*, etc. The fem. in इ is only used as a component part of the pret. conj.; as करतिस् (f.) *thou didst*, of करति + स्; see § 507.

300. *Affinities.* These suff. exist in all Gds., with very slight modifications; thus B. इत् (only in the obl. f. इते, S. Ch. 148);

O. *अंत् (only in the obl. f. अंत, Sn. 28): H. H. m. अता, f. अती; W. H. m. अतु (Br.) or अतो (Mw.), f. अती: P. m. अदा or अंदा, f. अदी or अंदी (Ld. 24), N. अदो, f. अदी; S. अंदो or इंदो, f. अंदी or इंदी (Tr. 268. 269); G. m. अतो, f. अती, n. अतुँ (Ed. 113, 53); M. c. g. अत or m. अता, f. अती, n. अतें (Man. 63. 73); O. H. m. अंतो or अंत् (Kl. 222. 240. 241). The O. has also उ (e. g., करु *doing*, Sn. 28).

301. *Derivation.* The original of these suff. is the Skr. krit अत् (or अन्त); in Pr. अंत (Vr. 7, 10. H. C. 3, 180. 181), or occasionally in Sr. Pr. अंद (H. C. 4, 261. cf. Ls. 362). Hence nom. sg. Mg. m. अंत, f. अंती (H. C. 3, 182) or, with pleon. अ added, m. अंतए, f. अंतिआ; and E. H. m. f. अत् or m. अता, f. अती (cf. §§ 143. 146). Thus Skr. m. हसन्, f. हसन्ती; A. Mg. हसंत, f. हसंती; O. H. m. f. हसंत्; E. H. हसत्; again Skr. *हसन्तकः, A. Mg. हसंतए, E. H. हसता; fem. Skr. *हसन्तिका, A. Mg. हसंतिआ, E. H. हसती. — The S. अंदो, P. अंदा, N. अदो, Gw. अदो or अंदो (Kl. 215) are similarly derived from the Sr. Pr. अंदओ. — The O. उ has, perhaps, arisen from अन्तु (or अंतु) by the elision of न्? (see § 153). — The E. H. खात् is = Mg. खंते or खाअंते (cf. H. C. 4, 228); E. H. देत् = Mg. देंत (cf. H. C. 2, 206. 4, 379) = *दअंते, Skr. ददत् (or *ददन्तः); E. H. होत् = Mg. होंत (cf. H. C. 3, 180) or हवंत or भवंत (cf. H. C. 4, 60), Skr. भवन्.

Second Group.

302. Set.	Com. gen.	Masc.	Fem.	Masc.	Fem.
1)	इल् or अल्	—	इलि or अलि	इला or अला	इली or अली
2)	इअ or इ	अ	इ	आ	ई

The forms in आ and ई are strong, the others weak. The masc. strong forms in ला are not much used, except in the obl. f. इले or अले, as adv. part., see § 488. The forms with इल° are peculiar to the Maithilí and Magadh in the eastern, and the forms (m.) अ or आ, (f.) इ or ई to Baiswári in the western part of the E. H. area. The latter (Bs.) dialect does not use the first set at all; the other E. H. dialects use both, see § 303.

Note: Observe, in adding the suff. beginning with इ, that य्

is inserted after आ and ई, and optionally व् after ऊ and ओ; before those beginning with इ neither ग् nor व् is inserted.

303. These suff. are used to derive the past participle from any root. Thus हसल् or हसिल् *laughed*, of R. हस् *laugh*; पढल् or पढिल् *read*, of R. पढ् *read*; पीयल् or पीइल् *drunk*, of R. पी *drink*; चूअल् or चूवल् or चूइल् *dripped*, of R. चू *drip*; रोअल् or रोवल् or रोइल् *wept*, of R. रो *weep*; खाइल् or खायल् *eaten*, of R. खा *eat*, etc. The derivatives of the second set, and those of the fem. अलि are never used by themselves, but only as component parts of the pret. indicat. (exc. in Bs), see §§ 502. 504, thus हस्यौं *I laughed*, of हसिअ + उँ; खाइस *thou eatest*, of खाइ + स्; again हसलिस् (f.) *thou laughedst*, of हसलि + स्, etc. But in Bs. हसा m., हसी f. *laughed*; पढा m., पढी f. *read*; खाया m., खाई f. *eaten*; etc.

Note: This part. is used *passively* in the formation of the passive voice, but *actively* in that of the pret. tense active.

304. *Exception.* The following part. pass. are formed irregularly: R. कर् *do*, P. P. 1) कइल् or कयल् or कैल्, or 2) किइअ° or किहि° or Bs. कया or किया *done*; — of R. धर् *place*, P. P. 1) धइल् or धयल् or धैल् or 2) धइअ° or धिहि° or Bs. धया; also regularly धरिल्, धरा, etc. *placed*. — R. मर् *die*, P. P. 1) मुइल् or मुअल् or 2) मुइअ° or मुइ° or Bs. मुआ; also regularly मरिल्, मरा *died*, etc. — R. जा *go*, P. P. 1) गइल् or गयल् or गैल् or 2) गइअ° or गइ° or B. गया *gone*; also regularly जाइल् or जायल् (§ 479. exc.); — R. हो *be*; P. P. 1) भइल् or भयल् or भैल् or 2) भइअ° or भइ° or Bs. भया or भवा *been*; also regularly होइल् or होयल् (§ 479. exc.). — R. दे *give*, P. P. 1) दिहल् or 2) दिइअ° or दिहि° or Bs. दया or दिया *given*. — R. ले *take*, P. P. 1) लिहल् or 2) लिइअ° or लिहि° or Bs. लया or लिया *taken*. — R. आव् *come*, P. P. 1) आइल् or आयल् or 2) आइअ° or आइ° or Bs. आया or आवा *come*. — R. पाव् *obtain*, P. P. 1) पाइल् or पायल् or 2) पाइअ° or पाइ° or Bs. पाया or पावा *obtained*.

305. *Affinities.* The second set occurs in all Gds., exc. M.; but the first set in the E. Gd. and S. Gd. only. Thus 1) both sets; in B., wk. f. इल् (only in the obl. f. इले as a cond. part.,

S. Ch. 148), and wk. f. इय (only in the obl. f. इया as past part. and in the pret. tense, S. Ch. 148. 144), or st. f. आ m., ई f. (only in the pass. sense and to form the pass. voice, S. Ch. 148. 142); in O., st. f. इला (e. g., पडिला *fallen*, Sn. 29) or wk. f. इल् (only in the obl. f. इले as a condit. part., Sn. 28); and wk. f. इ (as past part., Sn. 28) or इअ (only in the pret. tense, Sn. 30), or st. f. आ m., ई f. (as past part., Sn. 30; and in the pass. voice, Sn. 39). — 2) Only first set; in M., st. f. अला or इला m., अली or इली f., अलें or इलें n. (Man. 63. 64. 67. 68, note; e. g., सुटला or सुटिला = E. H. छुटल् or छुटिल् and M. सोडिला or सोडला = E. H. छोड़ल् or छोड़िल्). — 3) Only second set; in O. H. (Chand), wk. f. इय् (= Mg. इए, इअ) or इव् (= Ap. एउ) or st. f. एव् (= Ap. इअउ), see Kl. 213. 215.; in H. H., st. f. आ m., ई f.; in W. H., st. f. यौ or यो m., ई f.; in P., st. f. इआ m., ई f. (Ld. 24); in G., st. f. यो m., ई f., युं n. (Ed. 113. 50); in S., wk. f. इउ or इअ or इ (Tr. 289), or st. f. इओ or यो m., ई f. (Tr. 271. 289); in N., wk. f. इअ or ए or इ, or st. f. यो m., ई f. In all W. Gds. the P. P. is used in the pass. sense only, see § 487. — It is worth noting, that both sets exist in *Pashtú* (see Tr. J. G. O. S. XXIII, 116); e. g., wk. f. *kaṛ* or *kṛah* (= कृतः); st. f. *kaṛai* (= कृतकः); and wk. f. *kṛal* (= *करितः, B. करिल्), st. f. *kaṛalai* (= *करितकः, O. करिला). Trumpp distinguishes the weak and strong forms as part. pret. and part. perf., but these names, being the same in import, do not explain the difference.

Note: Some Gds. add. a pleon. suff. to the past part. in order to make it more of the nature of an adj.; viz., M. adds ला (Man. 63. 64), G. लो (Ed. 50. 113), S. लु or ड़ो (Tr. 272. 69), Mw. ड़ो (Kl. 209, 393), N. को (see § 216). The term. of the part. suffers various modifications before these suff., which may be seen from the following examples: M. पढ़लेला, G. पढ़ेलो, S. पढ़िअलु or पढ़िअड़ो, Mw. पढ़्योड़ो or पढ़ोड़ो, N. पढ़्याको *read*, from the resp. part. M. पढ़ला, G. पढ़्यो, S. पढ़िओ, Mw. पढ़्यो, N. पढ़्यो.

306. *Derivation.* The original of these suff. is the Skr. krit त or, with the connecting vowel इ added, इत. The addition of इ is very common in Pr., even with such roots, as do not take

it in Skr. (see Vr. 7, 32. H. C. 3, 156. Ls. 363. Wb. Spt. 65. Wb. Bh. 432. 433). In Gḍ. it has become almost universal; though there are a very few exceptions, as P. दिट्ठा or डिट्ठा *seen* (Pr. दिट्ठओ, Skr. दृष्टकः), but also regularly देखिआ (Ld. 66); G. दीठो *seen*, पेठो *entered* (Pr. पइट्ठओ, Skr. प्रविष्टकः); S. डिठो *seen*, पेठो *entered*, लधो *obtained* (Pr. लद्धओ H. C. 3, 134., Skr. लब्धकः), and some others, see Tr. 273—279. Ed. 50.— The suff. इत becomes in Pr. either इद् which is the older form preserved in Sr. (H. C. 4, 269), Mg. (see Vr. 11, 11. H. C. 4, 291. 292) and old Ap. (H. C. 4, 396), or इअ which is the later form of the Mh. (Vr. 7, 32. H. C. 3, 156) the A. Mg. (Wb. Bh. 433) and the later Ap. (e. g., हसिउ H. C. 4, 396. = Mh. हसिओ; Ap. धज्जिउ H. C. 4, 439 et passim; compare the treatment of the similar suff. इतव्य = Ap. इएव्वु H. C. 4, 438). The (older) Mg. form इद् further changes in E. and S. Gḍ. to इल and अल (§ 109). The only instances of this change of द् to ल् in Mg. are: कल्ले for कदे (H. C. 4, 290. Skr. कृतः) *done*, गल्ले for गदे (H. C. 4, 302. Skr. गतः) *gone*, and मल्ले for मदे (cf. Ls. 423. Skr. मृतः) *died*[1]) and, moreover, they are confined to the lower (or Ap.) types of Mg. (e.g., the Ṣábarí[2]) and Avantí, Ls. 417). This tendency of the Ap. Mg. has become the general rule in its descendants, the E. and S. Gḍ.; though side by side with the special Ap. Mg. forms in इल they have preserved also the general later (A. Mg., Mh., Ap. Sr.) Pr. forms in इअ. There are, then, the following forms, in the nom. sg.: 1) Mg. m. इदे, f. इदा, and, with pleon. अ added, m. इदए, f. इदिआ; these result in the E. H.

1) It is commonly supposed (Ls. 412. Bs. I, 238) that द् first changed to ड् and then to ल्; and it is true that Vr. 11, 15 gives the three Mg. forms कडे, गडे, मडे; but Mḍ. 12, 28 gives them only as alternatives besides कदे, गदे, मदे. Seeing that the general tendency of the languages of the Mg. class is towards dentalisation (see §§ 15. 16), it seems more probable, that द् changed at once to (dental) ल्, than that it first became cerebral ड्, and then reverted to the dental ल्.

2) It may be remarked, that O. which is closely allied to the Ṣábari (see p. XXIV) preserves the three forms कल् *done*, गल् *gone*, मल् *died*.

m. इल् or अल्, f. इलि or अलि or इल् or अल्; and m. इला or अला, f. इली or अली. 2) Mg. m. इए, f. इआ, and, with pleon. अ added, m. इअए, f. इइआ, whence the E. H. m. f. इअ or (dropping अ) इ, and m. इआ or (suppressing इ) आ, f. इई or (contracted) ई. E. g., Skr. चलितः walked, Mg. चलिदे, E. H. चलिल् or चलल्; or A. Mg. चलिए (Wb. Bh. 215) or Ap. चलिउ, O. H. चलिय् or चलिव्[1]), E. H. चलिअ or चलि, Bs. चलि or चल (chala). Again Skr. चलितोऽस्मि I walked, A. Mg. चलिए म्हि or चलिअ म्हि, Ap. चलिअउं (see § 503, 1. a), E. H. चल्यौं. Again Skr. चलितोऽसि thou walkedst, A. Mg. चलिए सि or Ap. a) चलिअसि or b) चलिअहि (see § 503, 1. b), N. a) चल्येस् or चलिस्, E. H. चलिस्, S. b) चलिएँ. Again Skr. चलितकः walked, Mg. चलिदए, E. H. and M. चलला or चलिला, O. चलिला; or A. Mg. चलिअए, P. चलिआ, Bs., H. H., B., O. चला; or Mh. चलिअओ, Ap. चलिअउ, O. H. चलेव् or चलिओ or चल्यो, W. H. चल्यौ or चल्यो, S. चलिओ or चल्यो, G. and N. चल्यां.

307. *Affinities and Derivation of the Exceptional Forms.* Cognate forms are denoted by identical letters. 1) R. खाद् eat; Skr. (a and c) खादितः or (b and d) खादितकः, Mg. (a) खाइदे or (b) खाइदए or A. Mg. (c) खाइए or (d) खाइअए, E. H. (a) खाइल् or (b) खइला or Bs. (c) खाइ or (d) खाया (for *खाइआ), B. and O. (a) खाइल् or (b) खाइला or (c) खाइ or (d) खिया (for *खया = *खइआ, see below गिया gone, cf. Sn. 40), M. (b) खाल्ला (Man. 80), H. H. (d) खाया, P. (b) काह्दा (with euphon. ह्, § 69) or (d) खाया (Ld. 66); again Ap. Pr. (b) खाइदउ or (d) खाइअउ, Mw. and G. (b) खाधो (for *खाह्दो or खाहिदो with euph. ह्, as in P.), W. H. (d) खायौ or खायो. — 2) R. लभ् take; Skr. (α) लब्धः or (β) लब्धकः, Pr. (α) लद्धो (H. C. 3, 134) or (β) लद्धओ, S. (β) लधो (Tr. 278); or Skr. (a) *लभितः or (b) *लभितकः, Mg. (a) लहिदे or (b) लहिदए or A. Mg. (c) लहिए or (d) लहिअए, E. H. (a) लिहल् or (b) लिहला or (c) लिहि (in the pret. tense, cf. § 502 exc., for *लहि) or Bs. (d) लेवा (contr. for लइआ with euph. व्, cf. § 69, Kl. 224) or लया or लिया (like गिया gone), B. (a) निल् (in the past tense and

1) M., as usual (§ 65, note), changes इउ or इव् to ईव्; e. g., बाँधीव् *bound* or *built*, from R. बाँध् *bind* (see Man. 107. 114).

condit. part., S. Ch. 190), or (d) लिया (S. Ch. 190), O. (a) नेल or (b) नेला or (d) नेया (Sn. 36), M. (b) ल्याला (Mn. 80), H. H. (d) लिया, P. (d) लइग्रा or लिग्रा (Ld. 66) or (b) लीता (perhaps contr. for a Ps. Pr. form *लइतए or *लहितए, or made after दित्ता *given*, Ld. 66); again Ap. Pr. (b) लहिदउ or (d) लहिग्रउ, W. H. (b) Mw. लीदो (contr. for *लइदो) or लीधो (contr. like काधो *eaten*, Kl. 213) or लीनो or लीन्हो (with न् or न्ह् for द् or ध्, cf. H. C. 1, 208 गञ्जिग्राणो = Pr. *गञ्जिग्रदो = Skr. गर्जितः, Pr. ग्रणिउँतयं = Pr. *ग्रदिउग्रयं = Skr. ग्रतिमुक्तकम्) or (d) लेवो (for *लइग्रो) or Br. (d) लयो or लियो, G. (b) लीधो (as in Mw., Ed. 50). — 3) R. दध् *give* (substitute for दा or धा); Skr. (α) हितः (for *धितः) or (β) हितकः, Ap. (α) °हिदु (H. C. 4, 446) or (β) °हित्तउ (H. C. 4, 395), Gḍ. *deest*; again, formed strictly analogous to the P. P. of R. लग्, Skr. *दधितः, Mg. (a) *दहिदे or (b) *दहिदए or A. Mg. (c) *दहिए or (d) *दहिग्रए, E. H. (a) दिहल् or (b) दिहला or (c) दिहि (in the past tense, for *दहि) or Bs. (d) देवा (Kl. 224) or दया or दिया, B. (a) दिल् (in the past tense and cond. part., S. Ch. 190) or (d) दिया (S. Ch. 190), O. (a) देल or (b) देला or (d) देया (Sn. 36), M. (b) दिला (Man. 80), H. H. (d) दिया, P. दित्ता (perhaps for Skr. दत्त, or formed like लीता *taken*, cf. Ld. 66); again Ap. Pr. (b) *दहिदउ or (d) *दहिग्रउ; W. H. (b) Mw. दीदो or दीधो or दीनो or दीन्हो or (d) दयो or Bs. (d) दयो or दियो, G. (b) दीधो (Ed. 59). — 4) R. धृ *place*; Skr. धृतः, Gḍ. *deest*; or Skr. *धरितः, Mg. (a) धलिदे or (b) धलिदए or A. Mg. (c) धलिए (cf. H. C. 1, 36. धरिग्रो) or (d) धलिग्रए, E. H. (a) धइल् or धरिल् or (b) धइला or धरिला or (c) धइ or धरि or Bs. (c) धर or (a) धरा, B. and O. (a) धरिल or (b) धरिला or (d) धरा, M. (b) धरला, H. H. (d) धरा, P. (d) धरिग्रा; again Ap. Pr. (b) धरिदउ or (d) धरिग्रउ, W. H. (d) धर्यो or धर्यो, G. (d) धर्यो, S. (d) धरिग्रो or धर्यो. — 5) R. कृ *do*; Skr. (α) कृतः or (β) कृतकः, Ap. (α) किदु (H. C. 4, 446) or (β) किग्रउ (H. C. 4, 371), S. (β) किग्रो (Tr. 277); again Skr. *करितः, Mg. (a) कलिदे or (b) कलिदए or A. Mg. (c) कलिए or (d) कलिग्रए or Ap. (d) किग्रा (H. C. 4, 396; see H. H. below), E. H. (a) कइल् (§§ 109. 124) or (b) कइला or (c) किहि (in the pret. tense, § 502 exc., with euph. ह, for *किइ = कइ = करि, formed after लिहि *taken*, दिहि *given*) or Bs. कर् or (d) करा, B. and O. (a) करिल् or (b) करिला (in the past tense and condit. part., S. Ch. 144. 148. Sn. 27) or (d) करा (S. Ch. 148. Sn. 39), M. (b) केला (for *कइला, Man. 80), H. H. (d) किया (for *कया = कइया, see S. below, formed after दिया *given*, लिया *taken*, गिया *gone*), P. (d) कीता (perhaps for *कइतए, like लीता *taken*, q. v., Ld. 66); again Ap. Pr. (b) करिदउ or (d) करिअउ or कियउ (H. C. 4, 378 = कइअउ, see below W. H.), W. H. (b) Mw. कीदो or कीधो or कीनो or कीन्हो (formed like लीदो, etc., q. v., Kl. 213), or (d) कर्यो or (d) Br. कर्यौ or कियो (for *कयौ = कइऔ, see below S.), G. (b) कीधो (Ed. 50) or (d) कर्यो, S. (d) कयो (for *कइओ, Tr. 277) or (b) कीतो (see above P.). — 6) R. गम् *go*; Skr. (*α*) गतः or (*β*) गतकः, Mg. (*α*) गदे or गडे or (*β*) गदए or गडए, O. (*α*) गल् or (*β*) गला (in the pret. tense and condit. part., Sn. 34); or Skr. (a) *गमितः, Pali (a) गमितो (Ms. 131), Mg. (a) गमिदे or (b) गमिदए or (c) गमिए or (d) गमिअए (cf. Wb. Bh. 405 गमेयाए = *गमिअयाए = *गमितकया), or Ap. (d) गया (H. C. 4, 376. see H. H. below), E. H. (a) गइल् or (b) गइला or (c) गइ (in the pret. tense, § 502 exc.) or Bs. (d) गगा (= गइआ, see below P.) or contr. गा (Kl. 225), B. (a) गेल् (in pret. tense and cond. part., S. Ch. 144. 148) or (d) गिया (S. Ch. 148, for गया, see below P.), M. (b) गेला (Man. 80), H. H. गया (= गइआ), P. गइआ or गिआ (Ld. 66); again Ap. Pr. (d) गमिअउ or गइअउ or contr. गयउ (H. C. 4, 422. 20., see W. H. and above P.), W. H. (d) Br. गयौ or Mw. गयो or गीयो (Kl. 213.? गियो?), G. (d) गयो (Ed. 50 or गयलो Ed. 83., see § 216), N. गयो. — 7) R. भू *be*; Skr. भूतः, Pr. हूओ (H. C. 4, 64), Gd. *deest*; or Skr. *भवितः, Mg. (a) भविदे or (b) हविदे or (c) हुविदे (cf. H. C. 4, 60) or (d) भविदए or (e) हविदए or (f) हुविदए or (g) भविए or (h) हविए (cf. H. C. 4, 401 परिहविअ° = परिभूत°) or (i) हुविए or (k) भविअए or (l) हविअए or (m) हुविअए, Ap. (m) हुआ (H. C. 4, 351, for हुइआ, see below H. H., and compare Ap. मुआ and मुइआ), E. H. (a) भइल् or (d) भइला or (g) भइ or भय् (§ 123) or (h) हउ or हो (in the pres. tense, § 514, 3, for *हवि, § 122) or Bs. (k) भवा or भया (= भइआ) or contr. भा, B. (b) हइल (in the condit. part., S. Ch. 144. 148) or (l) हइया (S. Ch. 148), O. (c) होइल् or (f) होइला

(in the pret. tense and condit. part., Sn. 35) or (i) होइ (Sn. 35) or (m) हुआ (Sn. 66, see H. H. below), M. (e) झाला (Man. 80, for *ह्याला or *हइला), H. H. (m) हुआ (for हुइआ, see P. and Km. below), P. (m) होइआ (Ld. 26); again Ap. Pr. (k) भविअउ or (l) हविअउ or (m) हुविअउ, W. H. (k) Br. भवौ (for *भव्यौ) or भयौ (= भइऔ) or contr. भौ or Km. भवो or भयो or भो (Kl. 205) or (l) Mw. ह्वियो (suppressing अ between हवि°) or ह्वयो (? Kl. 236) or (m) हुवो or हुयो (Kl. 210, for हुइओ) or contr. हो (Kl. 200), G. (l) हवो (Ed. 69) or (m) होयो (Ed. 69), S. (m) हुओ (Tr. 298, see H. H. above), N. (k) भयो (= भइओ), Km. (m) हुइओ (Kl. 2, 237), Gw. (m) होयो (Kl. 236). — 8) R. मृ *die*; Skr. मृतः, Mg. (*α*) मदे or (*β*) मए (Wb. Bh. 156) or (*γ*) मडे (Vr. 11, 15) or Mh. मुओ (Spt. 144 et passim), O. (a) मल्; or Skr. *मरितः, Mg. (a) मलिदे or (b) मुलिदे or (c) मलिदए or (d) मुलिदए or (e) मलिए or (f) मुलिए or (g) मलिअए or (h) मुलिअए, Ap. (f) मुइअ (H. C. 4, 367. 419., eliding ल् = र्, § 124) or contr. (h) मुआ (H. C. 4, 442., see H. H. below), E. H. (a) मरिल् or (b) मुइल् or (c) मरिला or (d) मुइला or (e) मरि or (f) मुइ or (g) Bs. मरा or (h) मुआ, M. (e) मेला (Man. 80, for *मइला), H. H. (h) मुआ (for मुइआ, see Ap. Mg. above); again Ap. Pr. (g) मरिअउ or (h) मुरिअउ or contr. मुअउ (H. C. 4, 442, for *मुइअउ, see Ap. Mg. above and W. H. below), W. H. (g) मर्यौ or मर्यो or (h) मुऔ or मुओ (for *मुइओ), G. मुवो (Ed. 50), N. (g) मरियो or मर्यो, S. dto. — 9) R. आप् *come* and प्राप् (= प + आप्) *obtain*; Skr. आप्तः or प्राप्तः, Pr. अत्तो or पत्तो (cf. H. C. 4, 332), Gd. *deest*; or Skr. *आपितः or *प्रापितः, Mg. (a) आविदे or (b) आविदए or (c) आविए (cf. H. C. 4, 387 पाविअ, and see Ap. below) or (d) आविअए, E. H. (a) आइल् or (b) अइला or (c) आइ or आय् or (d) Bs. आया (cf. § 423), B. (a) आइल् (in the pret. tense and cond. part., S. Ch. 188. 189)[1]), M. (b) आला (Man. 80, for *आइला), H. H. (d) आया (for आइआ), P. (d) आइआ; again Ap. Pr. (c) आविउ or आइउ (H. C. 4, 422) or (d) आविअउ (cf. H. C. 4, 432 Bombay Ed. आउइओ = आविओ?), W. H. (d) आयौ or आयो (for आइओ), N. आयो. The forms of प्राप् are strictly analogous throughout.

1) The other B. forms आसिल°, etc. are derived from the R. आइस् = Pr. आविस् = Skr. आविश् *enter* (आ + विश्).

Third Group.

308. Set.	Com. gen.	Masc.	Fem.
1)	इब् or अब्	* इबा or * अबा	इबि or अबि
2)	आय् or आव्	आवा	अवाई or आई or आवट्
3)	अब्बू or आबू	—	—
4)	अवइया or अइया	—	—
5)	अवार् or अवाल्	अवारा or अवाला	अवारी or अवाली
6)	आरु or आलू	—	—

The forms of the fourth set are redundant (§§ 200. 202); of the others those in आ, ई and ऊ are strong, the remainder are weak. — The forms with initial इ are not commonly employed, except with Rs. in आ and causal or denom. Rs. in आव् (or आ by § 33). — The masc. strong forms of the first set are never used, exc. in the obl. form इबे or अबे or (by elision of ब्) contr. ए. — The suff. आवट् is sometimes wrongly spelled आहट्, owing to a confusion with the suff. आहट् of § 284.

Note: Observe in adding these suff., 1) that in the first set the initial अ is elided after Rs. in आ, ए and R. हो *be*, and इ after Rs. in ई; 2) that before the suff. of the second and fourth sets, the termin. आव् of caus. and den. Rs. is elided, and final radical आ and ए are shortened. For the rest see § 298, note.

309. *Meaning.* These suff. are used to derive 1) part. fut., both pass. and act., and 2) verbal nouns, both of act and agency, from any root. Originally their derivatives were part. fut. *passive* only; but in the neuter gender they naturally came to express verbal nouns of act and thus were used as the (so-called) infinitive; for *the "it is to be done" of a thing* is equal to *the "doing" of a thing.* Next the pass. sense was dropped, as in the case of the past part. pass. (§ 301, note), and the part. used actively (e. g., in the formation of the fut. tense act. cf. § 509, 3); and thus it came to express verbal nouns of agency. The latter process was facilitated by the addition of pleon. suff., see § 314. With some intrans. verbs, as होव् *to be*, the part. fut. pass. ne-

cessarily has an active sense; and this may have led the way to the general practice of using this part. *actively*.

310. The first set is used to form the part. fut. or the inf. Thus हसब् or हसिब् *what is to be laughed at* or *to laugh*, of R. हस् *laugh*; पढब् or पढिब् *what is to be read* or *to read*, of R. पढ् *read*; करब् or करिब् *what is to be done* or *to do*, of R. कर् *do*; छूअब् or छूहब् or छूइब् *what is to be touched* or *to touch*, of R. छू *touch*; बोअब् or बोवब् or बोइब् *what is to be sown* or *to sow*, of R. बो *sow*. But खाइब् or खाब् *what is to be eaten* or *to eat*, of R. खा *eat*; कराइब् or कराब् *what is to be caused to be done* or *to cause to do*, of C. R. कराव् *cause to do*; पीयब् or पीब् *what is to be drunk* or *to drink*, of R. पी *drink*; देब् or देइब् *what is to be given, debt* or *to give*, of R. दे, *give*; होब् or होइब् *what is to be, future, possible* or *to be*, of R. हो *be*. Thus मो के or मो से ऊ काव् बाटै *by me that is to be done*, or actively मैं करबों (= करब + उँ) *I shall do*. The fem. in इ is used only as a component part of the fut. tense act., as करबिस् (fem.) *thou wilt do* for करबि + स्, cf. § 509, 3.

311. The second set is used to form *nouns of act*. Thus अवाई *coming*, of R. आव *come*; जवाई *going*, of R. जा *go*; खवाई *eating*, of R. खा *eat*; सुझाव् or सुझाइ or सुझावट् *seeing*, of R. सूझ् *see*; सिचाव् or सिचाई or सिचावट् *irrigation*, of R. सींच् *irrigate*; डोलाव् or डोलाई or डोलावट् *movement*, of R. डोल् *move*; लराइ or लरावट् *fighting*, of R. लर् or लड़् *fight*; चलाव् *dispatch*, of C. R. चलाव् *cause to go*. Very commonly the fem. expresses the *wages or price* paid for doing a thing, as रखवाई or रखाई *wages for keeping*, of R. रख् *keep*; कटवाई *wages for cutting*, of R. काट्; बनवाइ or बनाई or बनावट् *making* or *price for making* of C. R. बनाव् *make*; लिखवाई or लिखाई *wages for writing* or *dictation*, of R. लिख् *write* or C. R. लिखाव् *dictate*. The masc. strong form is very rarely used and, as a rule, has some special meaning; thus पहिरावा *dress* (lit., *what is to be put on*), of R. पहिर् *put on, wear*; बुलावा *a call*, of C. R. बुलाव् *call*, but बुलवाई, बुलावट् *calling*; मिलावा *mixture*, of R. मिल् *mix*; चढावा *sacrifice*, of C. R. चढाव् *sacrifice* (lit., *cause to ascend*).

312. The third, fourth, fifth and sixth sets are used to form *nouns of agency.* The fourth set is the one commonly employed. Thus खाबू or खब्बू *glutton* or खवइया or खवैया *eater*, of R. खा *eat*; डराबू or डरब्बू or डरालू or डरवाला or डरवइया *timid, coward*, of R. डर् *fear*; रखवारू or रखवारा or रखवइया or रखइया *guardian*, of R. रख् *keep*; कगडारू or कगडालू *quarrelsome*, of R. कगड़ *quarrel*; छवइया *thatcher*, of R. छा *thatch*; दिवइया *giver*, of R. दे *give*; चढवइया *rider*, of R. चढ् *mount*; देखवइया *observer*, of R. देख् *see*; सुनवइया *listener*, of R. सुन् *hear*; बनवइया *maker*, of C. R. बनाव् *make*, etc. The fem. makes nouns of act., as रखवारी *guarding*.

313. *Affinities.* The first and second sets occur in all Gḍs. as suff. of the part. fut. pass. or of nouns of act. (i. e., of the infinitive), exc. in P.[1]). Thus the first set in B. (wk. f.) इब् (in the fut. tense act., S. Ch. 146) and (st. f.) इबा or (by elision of ब्) contr. श्रा (as "gerund or verbal noun", S. Ch. 149, i. e., as part. fut. pass. and inf.); this same श्रा or (uncontracted) इये (= इवे = इए) is used also in an *active* sense as a suff. of nouns of agency; e. g., घासकाटा *a grass cutter* (S. Ch. 154. 149). Similarly in O. (wk. f.) इब् (in the fut. act. Sn. 27) and (st. f.) इबा or contr. श्रा (Sn. 30). Also in W. H. (as inf. and part. fut. pass.) (st. f.) Br. श्रबौँ or श्रवौ or इबौँ or इबौ or Mw. श्रबोँ or श्रबो or इबोँ or इबो (obl. f. श्रबे or इबे, as in E. H.). In G. it occurs as the suff. of a part. fut. pass., ending in (st. f.) m. श्रवो, f. श्रवी, n. श्रवुँ, and forms the so-called "potential" (Ed. 57); e. g., मारे छोडवो हतो lit., *by me he should be delivered*; also as suff. of the infinit., viz. (st. f.) श्रवुँ neut. (Ed. 50. 112); e. g., छोडवुँ *to deliver*. Also in S. it occurs; though never to form an inf., but only a part. fut. pass. in इबो (in the fut. tense pass. Tr. 336), and strangely also a part. present pass. (Tr. 54); e. g., छडिबो pres. *being given up* (Tr. 331) or fut. *he shall be given up* (Tr. 336). Perhaps it exists also in the M. inf. termin. ऊँ, a strong form, contr. for इऊँ = इबूँ (Man. 61, 5. 71);

---

1) The so-called P. „gerund" (Ld. 24. 45. 81) ending in इश्रा m., ई f., is identical with the past part. pass.; see the § on compound verbs.

e. g., सोटूँ *to loose* (for *सोडिऊं = Mw. छोडिबो॑, G. छोडवुं) 1). — The second set, which now forms in E. H. and similarly in W. H. verbal nouns only, is still used in M. to form the part. fut. pass., ending in (st. f.) आवें neut. (called "supine" in Man. 62. 61, 5), with an obl. f. आवया (= E. H. अबे) or (by eliding व्) contr. आया (= E. H. ऐ, B. इये). It also occurs in M. with the sense of a part. pres. pass. in the formation of the pres. conj. tense, ending in आवा m., आवी f., आवें n.; e. g., M. मी सुटावा *I may be loosed* (lit. *I am to be loosed*), or म्याँ सोडावा *I may loose him* (lit. *by me he may be loosed* or *by me he is to be loosed*); see § 509, 3. — The other sets occur also in W. H., except that there is no change of ल् to र् in the 5th and 6th sets; e. g., W. H. रखवाल् or °ला, f. °ली; कगड़ाल्. The 5th set occurs in M. as अवाट् or अवाटू (see Bs. II, 60; e. g., कन्हवाटू *pitiful*, of R. कन्हू *moan*); and in G. as अवानो (commonly used to form the fut. tense act.; e. g., छोडवानो *he shall deliver*, of R. छोड् Ed. 61), the original pass. sense of which may be seen from its use in the so-called "potential" (Ed. 57); e. g., मारे छोडवानो हतो lit., *by me he should be delivered*. The sixth set occurs in M. as आड् or आडू (see Man. 114. Bs. II, 60; e. g., खेळाडू *frolicsome*, of R. खेल् *play*; खाजाडू *itching*, of R. खाज् *itch*); in S. as आरो or आरू (Tr. 53; e. g., घारारो or घोरारू *pedlar*, of R. घोर् *seek*; पीजारो *cotton-carder*, of R. पिञ् *card*).

314. *Derivation.* The original of these suff. is the Skr. krit तव्य forming the part. fut. pass. It is often added with the connecting vowel इ; thus इतव्य. The addition of इ is general in Pr. (Vr. 7, 33. H. C. 3, 157) and universal in Gḍ. The suff. इतव्यम् (nom. sg. neut.) becomes in Pr. एअव्वं or इअव्वं (H. C. 3, 157) and in Ap. *एव्वं or एवं (H. C. 4, 438. K. I. 53 in Ls. 469, 5) or इव्वं (K. I. 50 in Ls. 468, 3); finally in E. H. इब् or अब्. Similarly,

1) If it were not the long vowel ऊ, it might be taken as a contr. of the Pr. एउं or इउं = Skr. इतुम् H. C. 3, 157; like the M. conj. part. in ऊण = Pr. एऊण or इऊण, Skr. *इत्वानम्.

with the pleon. अ added, Skr. इतव्यकम्, Pr. एअव्वअं or इअव्वअं, Ap. Sr. (a) एव्वउं (H. C. 4, 438. 4, 354) or Ap. Mg. (b) एवा (= *एव्वए or *एव्वअं, cf. § 54), W. Gd. (a) इबौँ or अबौँ or E. Gd. (b) इबा or अबा or S. Gd. (b) अबेँ (= *एव्वअं). Thus Skr. कर्त्तव्यम् (or *करितव्यम्), Pr. करेअव्वं or करिअव्वं, Ap. *करेव्वं or करिव्वं or करेवं, E. H. करिब् or करब्; again Skr. कर्त्तव्यकम्, Pr. करेअव्वअं or करिअव्वअं, Ap. (a) *करेवअं or (b) करेव्वउं or (c) करेवा; Gd. (a) M. करावेँ, (b) W. H. करिबौँ, (c) O. करिबा. It should be remarked, that H. C. expressly gives the neut. wk. f. एवं (H. C. 4, 441) as an inf. suffix, while the corresponding st. f. एव्वउं and एवा (H. C. 4, 438) are mentioned as suff. of the part. fut. pass. — The suff. अवाई is a comp. of the suff. अव् or आव् + suff. आई of § 220; and the suff. अवइया a comp. of suff. आव् + pleon. suff. ऐया (of the redundant form, § 202); and the suff. अवारू or अवारा a comp. of suff. आव + pleon. suff. अरू or अरा (§ 209); and the suff. आवट् a comp. of suff. आव + ट्. The nature of the latter element (ट्) is obscure. Perhaps it represents the Skr. suff. ता of abstract nouns (§ 220, also contained in the suff. अवाई) or त्वम् (or fem. *त्वा in Mg., see Wb. Bh. 437); thus Skr. इतव्यता or °त्वम् = Mg. इअव्वत्ता or Ap. *एव्वट्टा, E. H. आवट्; the change of त् to ट् (as in पट्टणं for पत्तन H. C. 2, 29) may be owing to a confusion with the suff. आवट् or आहट् (§ 284) derived from the Skr. वृत्ता = Pr. वट्टा. — Again the suff. आई, अइया and आरू (or आलू) are contr. respectively from the suff. अवाई, अवइया and अवारा (or अवाला), by the elision of व्; just as the E. H. obl. f. ए is contr. for B. इये (= इवे), and the M. obl. f. आया for आवया (§ 313). — The suff. तव्य, in course of time, lost its originally pass. sense and became active, as in B. आ and इये (see § 313); in the other Gds., this process was facilitated by the addition of the pleon. suff. ऐया and अरा = Ap. Pr. अअअ (= अकके) and अउअ, the उ of which latter suff. changed, as usual in Gd., to ड़् or ल् or र् or न्. E. g., Ap. रक्खेव्वअउउ (Skr. रक्षितव्यः), W. H. रखवाली or E. H. °रा; Ap. खेल्लेव्वअउउ, M. *खेलआडू or contr. खेलाडू. Similarly the originally pass. suff. अनीया (of the part. fut.) and इत (of the past. part.) have become active in Gḍ. (see §§ 316. 305). It is a remarkable fact, that the suff. तव्य has suffered a precisely analogous change in the Latin *tivus*. Its derivatives occur very rarely in classic Latin, and, as a rule, are used passively, as *captivus* "prisoner", *votivus* „dedicated"; but *stativus* "appointed" or "stationary" is both pass. and act., and *fugitivus* "fugitive" is active. But in the later (low) Latin they are very common, and, as a rule, used actively; as *effectivus* „effective", *operativus, contemplativus, negativus*, etc.

Fourth Group.

315.

Set.	Com. gen.	Masc.	Fem.
1)	अन्	अना	अनी
2)	आवन् or आन्	अउना or ओना	अउनी or ओनी
3)	अनिहार्	अनिहारा	अनिहारी
4)	—	अनेवारा or °ला	अनेवारी or °ली

The forms of com. gen. are weak, the others strong. The second set, on being added to caus. and den. roots in आव्, supersedes that termin. For the rest, see § 298, note.

316. *Meaning.* These suff. are used to derive 1) part. fut., both pass. and act., and 2) verbal nouns, both of act. and agency, from any root. The nouns of agency are, in fact, *part. fut. act.*, implying the habit of doing a thing. As to the change of the sense from pass. to act., see § 309. The verbal nouns of act., formed by these suff. and used as infinitives in W. H. and the other Gḍs., are seldom or never employed so in E. H.

317. All those suff. (exc. the strong femin. of the third set) are occasionally used to form the part. fut. pass., and generally have some particular meaning. Thus देन् or देना or देनी *what is to be given, a debt*, of R. दे *give*; लेन् or लेना or लेनी *what is to be taken, a receipt*, of R. ले *take*, as in the phrase लेन् देन् *intercourse, traffic*; बाजन् or बजना *what is to be played, a musical instrument*, of R. बज् *be played*; ओढ़ना or ओढ़नी *what is to be put on, a cloak or sheet*, of R. ओढ़् *put on, wear*; बिछावन् or बिछउना or बिछौना or f. °नी *what is to be spread, bed-clothes*, of R. बिछ् or बिछाव् *spread*; खेलउना or खेलौना, f. °नी *what is to be played*

with, a toy, of R. खेल् *play*; भरउना or भरौना *what is to be loaded, a load,* of R. भराव् *load*; कहौनी (H. H. कहानी) *what is to be said, a story,* of R. कह् *speak*; पहिरावन् or पहिरौनी *what is to be put on, garments,* of R. पहिर् *put on*; छउनी or छौनी *encampments, barracks* (lit., *what is to be thatched*), of R. छा *thatch*; पढ़न् or पढ़नी *what is to be read, spell, charm,* of R. पढ़ *read.* Again होना, f. होनी, or m. f. होनिहार् or m. °रा, or m. होनेवारा, f. °री *what is to be, possible, future,* and अनहोना *impossible,* of R. हो (but होनेहारी *possibility, futurity*).

318. The third and fourth sets (exc. the strong femin. of the former) are used to form part. fut. act. or nouns of agency. Thus m. f. करनिहार्, m. °रा *one who is going to do or a doer,* of R. कर् *do*; m. f. पढ़निहार् or m. पढनिहारा or पढ़नेवारा or °ला, f. °री or °ली *one who is going to read, a reader,* of R. पढ़ *read*; m. f. देनिहार् or m. °रा or m. देनेवाला or °रा, f. °ली or °री *one who is going to give, a giver,* of R. दे *give,* etc. Occasionally also the strong forms of the first and second sets form nouns of agency, as हँसना, f. °नी *jester,* of R. हँस् *laugh*; डरउना or डरौना, f. °नी *coward, timid,* of R. डर् *fear*; सुहउना or सुहौना, f. °नी *pleasing,* of R. सुहाव् *please*; घिनउना or घिनौना, f. °नी *disgusting,* of R. घिनाव् *nauseate*; पहिरउनी or पहिरौनी *a tire-woman,* of C. R. पहिराव् *attire.* The fem. in अनी often signifies an instrument, and the masc. in आन् a place; thus fem. खोदनी *a spade* (lit., *digger*), of R. खोद् *dig*; लेखनी *style, pen,* of R. लेख् *write, engrave*; कतरनी *scissors,* of R. कतर् *cut*; सुननी *sense of hearing,* of R. सुन् *hear,* etc.; and masc. उठान् *area, court,* of R. उठ् *rise*; बझान् *place for ensnaring,* of R. बझ् or बझाव् *ensnare*; टिकान् *halting-place,* of R. टिक् *halt.*

319. The weak forms of the first and second sets and the strong femin. of the first, second and third sets are commonly used to form nouns of act. Thus m. कहन् or f. कहनी *speaking, speech,* of R. कह् *speak*; सुनन् or सुननी *hearing,* of R. सुन् *hear*; लेन् or लेनी *taking,* of R. ले *take*; करन् or करनी [1]) *action,* of R. कर् *do*; रहन् or रहनी [1]) *existence, living,* of R. रह् *remain, live*; होनी [1]) *occur-*

1) Also करतब्, रहतब्, होतब् or होनिहार्, which are clearly part.

rence, accidence, of R. हो *be*; सुफावन् *direction, advice,* of R. सुफाव् *show*; मनावन् *agreement, respect,* of R. मान् *respect* or मनाव् *persuade*; वद्गनी *dispute,* of R. वद्ग् *fight*; लिखनी *writing,* of R. लिख् *write*; सिखावन् *instruction,* of R. सिखाव् *teach,* etc. Especially the suff. आन्; as उड़ान् *flying,* of R. उड़् *fly*; कुदान् *leaping,* of R. कूद् *leap*; चढ़ान् *ascent, riding,* of R. चढ़ *mount, ride*; डोलन् or डोलान् *movement,* of R. डोल् *move*; बइठान् *sitting, session,* of R. बइठ् *sit*; धरान् *holding,* of R. धर् *hold*; पकरान् *seizure,* of R. पकर् *seize*; सिचान् *irrigation,* of R. सीच् *irrigate*; उठान् *rising,* of R. उठ् *rise*; चलान् *clearance,* of R. चलाव् *dispatch*; लड़ान् *fighting,* of R. लड़् *fight,* etc.

Note: उड़ान् *flying,* etc. may be also उड़ाव्, उड़ाई, उड़ावट्, etc.; see § 308. — The derivatives of the 1st and 2nd sets must not be confounded with those of the Skr. suff. अन, which are not E. H. formations but received from the Skr. as tats. or tadbh. The suff. अन no longer exists as such in Gd., nor apparently did it do so in Pr. Its derivatives in E. H. can be often recognized by the fact of the non-existence of their roots in it. Thus E. H. पान् *beverage,* दान् *giving,* मान् *respect,* गवन् or गमन् *going,* बधावन् *presents,* etc., whose roots *पा, *दा, *मा, *गम्, *वर्धाप्, etc. do not exist in E. H., at least in this particular form. But sometimes it may remain doubtful, whether an E. H. word is an old tadbh. deriv. of the Skr. suff. अन or an E. H. formation of the present group.

320. *Affinities.* These suff. occur in all Gds.; but those of the 4th set are not properly E. H., nor generally E. or S. Gd. (cf. S. Ch. 154. Man. 113, 2), but introduced into them from the W. Gd., especially from W. H., P. (Ld. 24, 80) and S. (Tr. 76 अनवारो or अनेवारो). — The third set is that commonly used in E. H.; it occurs also in W. H., P. (Ld. 24, 80) and S. (Tr. 75); in G. it is contr. to अनार् (forming the fut. act. tense, Ed. 61), also in M. अणार् or अणारा (forming the fut. part. act. or nouns

---

fut. pass. and thus disclose the etymological character of the words in the text.

of agency, Man. 63, 3. 64, 4). — The first and second set is used in all Gds. in the same way as in E. H.; moreover, the masc. strong form commonly serves as the (so-called) infinitive in W. H. (अनौँ or अनो in Br. and अनोँ or अनो in Mw.), P. (अणा or अना Ld. 24, 80); also in M. (neuter) अणेँ (called "gerund" in Man. 61, 100. 62); and, in the weak form, in B. अन or अनि or आन् or आनि (S. Ch. 149. 186), O. अणा or आणा (Sn. 30, 38), W. H. (Br.) अनि, S. अणु or इणु (Tr. 54. 251), N. अनु. The strong form exists also as a suff. of the part. fut. pass. in W. H. m. अनो, f. अनी, and S. m. अणो or इणो, f. अणी or इणी (Tr. 279. 55).

321. *Derivation.* The original of these suff. is the Skr. krit अनीय, which in Pr. becomes अणीअ (Vr. 2, 17. H. C. 1, 248) or अणिअ (as in पाणीअ or पाणिअ *water* = Skr. पानीय Vr. 1, 18. H. C. 1, 101) or अणअ (or अणय Wb. Bh. 418. H. C. 4, 443. 441). The latter form has already dropped the passive signification and become a suff. of act. or agency. From the Ap. forms अणिअ or अणअ, by the addition of the pleon. suff. उ or उअ or अउ or अउअ, arise the forms अणअउ or अणअउअ, which become अणार् or अनार् or अणारा or अनारो in M. and G.; and the form अणअअउअ, which (inserting euph. व्) appears in S. as अनवारो, W. H. अनवालो; and the forms अणिअअउ or अणिअअउअ, which (inserting euph. ह्) appear in E. H. etc. as अनिहार् or अनिहारा. The simple Ap. form अणअ (H. C. 4, 443) appears in E. H. etc. as अना. The simple Ap. अणहुं, which forms the inf. (H. C. 4, 441) appears in the W. H. infinitive in अनौँ or अनो; and the Ap. inf. suff. अणहिं (H. C. 4, 441) in the W. H. inf. suff. अने or shortened अनि. — It is probable that in the popular usage the two krit suff. अन (pleon. अनक = Pr. अणअ) and अनीय have become confused, so as to make a correct allotment of their respective derivatives a matter of difficulty. But as there can be no doubt, that the passive suff. तव्य has become an active suff. of act. and agency (see § 314), it is extremely probable that the same change has occurred in the case of the similar suff. अनीय, the modern derivatives of which exhibit remarkably analogous forms and meanings to those of the

suff. तव्य. — The secondary suff. वाला or वारा (§ 293) have contributed a further cause of popular confusion.

Fifth Group.

322. Set. 1) Fem. अत् or अती. Set. 2) Fem. आवत् or औती. The forms in ई are strong, the others weak. As to the manner of adding them, see § 298, note.

323. These suff. are used to derive nouns of act. from a root; but they exist only in a limited number of words. Thus the first set in चुकत् or चुकती *settlement*, of R. चुक् *finish*; चुनत् *plaiting, plaits*, of R. चुन् *plait*; बसती *dwelling, village*, of R. बस् *dwell*; भरती *filling up, enlistment*, of R. भर् *fill*; चढ़ती *rising, gain*, of R. चढ़् *rise*; बढ़ती *increase*, of R. बढ़् *increase*; घटती *decrease*, of R. घट् *decrease*; लगती *belonging, assessment*, of R. लग् *belong*. Occasionally the root is not in use, as in अढ़त् *commission* (lit., *increase*), of R. *अढ़्; बिनती *information, petition*, of R. *बिन्. The second set in समुकावत् or समुकौती *explaining*, of R. समुकाव् *explain*; छुटौती *release*, of R. छुटाव् *release*; मनौती *security*, of R. मनाव् *cause to trust*.

324. *Affinities.* These suff. exist in all Gds. Those of the second set, however, appear to be extinct in B. and O., see Bs. II, 108. In M. they are ऊत् and अवती; in G. ओती or उती; in P. and W. H. आवत्, औती. Thus W. H. and P. समुकौती, G. समजुती, M. समजूत; W. H. and P. मनौती, G. मनोती; W. H. and P. चुकौती, M. चुकवती. S. seems to have only the first set in अति (Tr. 49).

325. *Derivation.* The original of these suff. is the Skr. krit ति (fem.), added to the caus. or denom. radical suff. आप् (§ 349); thus आप्ति or, with pleon. क added, आप्तिका; and in Pr. अत्ती or अत्तिआ, in E. H. अत् or अती. Thus Skr. विज्ञाप्तिका, Mg. विन्नत्तिआ, E. H. बिनती; or Skr. *वर्धाप्तिका (of R. वृध्), Mg. वड्डत्तिआ, E. H. बढ़ती; or Skr. *अर्धाप्तिः (of R. ऋध्), Mg. अड्डत्ती (cf. T. V. 3, 1. 13)[1]), E. H. अढ़त्, M. अडत्, O., B., G., S. आडत् (see Bs.

1) According to H. C. 4, 81 Pr. substitutes आअड्ड for the Skr. R.

II, 53). — By the dissolution of the conjunct त्त, the forms Pr. श्रावत्ती or श्रावत्तिश्रा, E. H. श्रावत् or श्रोती might arise; thus Skr. *मनाप्तिका, Mg. *मणावत्तिश्रा, E. H. मनौती (for मनवती or मनउती, §§ 25. 34. 78).

Sixth Group.

326. Com. gen. श्र. Masc. श्रा. Fem. ई.

The form श्र is weak; the others are strong. As to the manner of adding them, see § 298, note.

327. These suff. are used to derive nouns of act. from any root. As a rule they are fem. Thus सूझ् *sight*, of R. सूझ् *see*; लथेड़् f. *draggling* (W. H. लथेड़), of R. लथेड़् *draggle;* चपेट् f. or चपेटा m. *a slap*, of R. चपेट् *slap;* खेल् m. or f. *play*, of R. खेल् *play;* चाल् f. *walking, conduct, custom*, of R. चाल् or चल् *walk;* पकड़् f. *seizure* (W. H. पकड़), of R. पकड़् *seize;* हँस् m. f. or हँसा m., हँसी f. *laughter*, of R. हँस् *laugh;* दउड़् f. or दउड़ा m. or दउड़ी f. *running, race*, of R. दउड़् *run;* रगड़् f. or रगड़ा m. *rubbing*, of R. रगड़् *rub;* फेर् m. or फेरा m. or फेरी f. *turning, circumambulation*, of R. फेर् *turn;* दाब् m. *pressure, force, fear*, of R. दाब् *press;* बोल् m. or बोली f. *speech, dialect*, of R. बोल् *speak;* पछताव् m. or पछतावा m. *repentance*, of R. पछताव् *repent*, etc.

328. *Affinities.* These suff. exist in all Gḍs., with very slight differences: W. H. has m. f. श्र, and m. श्रौ or श्रो, f. ई; S. m, उ, f. श्र or इ, and m. श्रो, f. ई (Tr. 46, 47); G. m. f. श्र, and m. श्रो, f. ई; M., B. and O. have the same as E. H. Thus M. बोल्, बोली *speaking, language* (Man. 107); बाँध्, बाँधा *binding, embankment*, of R. बाँध् (Man. 107), etc.; S. भोल् f. *error*, E. H. भूल्, of R. भुल्; S. घाटि f. or घाटो m. *decrease*, of R. घट्; S. फेरु m. *turning* (Tr. 46. 47). Further examples see in Bs. II, 51. 52.

329. *Derivation.* The original of these suff. is the Skr. krit श्र, which (in the nom. sing.) forms m. श्रः, f. श्रा and, with pleon. क added, m. श्रकः, f. इका. These are in Mg. m. ए, f. श्रा,

---

व्याप्; T. V. 3, 1. 13 gives श्राश्रड्ड; thus H. C. श्राश्रड्डइ, T. V. श्राश्रड्डइ. The derivation is obscure; but it seems rather to be connected with the R. श्रध्.

and m. अए्, f. इआ; whence E. H. m. f. अ (cf. §§ 42. 45) and m. आ, f. ई (cf. §§ 47. 51). Thus Skr. क्रीडः or क्रीडा (or खेला), Mg. खेल्ले or खल्ला (cf. H. C. 4, 382), E. H. खेल्; again Skr. हसः or हसिका, A. Mg. हसे or हसिआ, E. H. हँस् or हँसी, etc.

Seventh Group.

330. . Com. gen. ऊ or आऊ.

Both forms are strong. Causal roots in आव् take the suff. आऊ which supersedes the caus. termination; that is, ऊ is added to आव्, the व् of which is elided.

331. These suff. are used to derive nouns of (habitual) agency from any root. Thus ऊ in खाऊ *eater, glutton,* of R. खा; उचाटू *vexatious,* of R. उचाट् *vex*; मारू *fighter, beater,* of R. मार् *beat;* मूँडू *ascetic* (lit., *one who shaves his head*), of R. मूँड् *shave;* काटू *cutter, biter,* of R. काट् *cut, bite;* कारू *sweeper, broom,* of R. कार् *sweep* (W. H. काड़्); जागू *vigilant,* of R. जाग् *wake;* बिगाड़ू *spoiler,* of R. बिगाड़् *spoil,* etc. Again आऊ; in कगड़ाऊ *quarrelsome,* of R. कगड़् *quarrel;* उड़ाऊ *spendthrift,* of R. उड़ाव् *squander* (lit., *cause to fly*); कमाऊ *laborer, bread-winner,* of R. कमाव् *labor, earn;* टिकाऊ *stationary,* of R. टिक् *stop;* बिकाऊ *saleable,* of R. बिक् *sell* (intrans.); फुसलाऊ *coaxer, tempter,* of R. फुसलाव् *coax.* Occasionally the root no more exists in E. H. as डाँकू or डाकू *robber,* of R. *डाँक् *bite* or *overpower.*

332. *Affinities.* These suff. are not properly E. H., nor E. Gd., but W. Gd., whence they have been introduced. W. H., P. and S., like the E. H. (Tr. 51), have ऊ and आऊ; G. appears to have a weak form in उ, as खाउ *eater,* काडु *broom,* etc.; see Bs. II, 37 where other examples will be found; it may, however, be strong; for G. has a tendency to shorten a strong final ऊ or ओ; e. g., Ap. Pr. सोखउं, Mw. सोनो is in G. सोनुँ or सोनु *gold* (Skr. सुवर्णकम्).

333. *Derivation.* The original of these suff. is the Skr. krit तृ or, with pleon. क added, तृक; the ऋ of which has a tendency to change to उ in Pr. (cf. H. C. 3, 44), also in Páli (see Ms. 40. Bs. II, 57). Whence (nom. sing.) Pr. ऊ or उओ (= *तुः or

*तुकः), W. Gḍ. उ or ऊ; e. g., Skr. भर्त्ता *husband* (base भर्तृ), Pr. भत्तू (H. C. 3, 44), Gḍ. *decst* (E. H. has भताड़, Pr. भत्तारा H. C. 3, 44); Skr. पिता *father* (base पितृ), Pr. पिऊ or पिउओ (H. C. 1, 131), P. पिउ or पिऊ; Skr. भ्राता *brother* (base भ्रातृ), Pr. भाऊ or भाउओ (H. C. 1, 131) or Ap. भ्राऊ or भ्राउउ (cf. H. C. 4, 398), P. भाउ or भाऊ or भराउ or भराऊ (cf. Ld. 10, 30), S. भाउ, M. भाऊ. Similarly Skr. दंष्टृकः (of R. दंश् or दंस्) *one who bites or overpowers*, Pr. डक्कुओ (cf. H. H. 2, 2 डक्को = Skr. दष्टः *bitten*), Ap. डक्कुउ, W. Gḍ. डाकू *robber*. — The suff. तृ was often added in Skr. with the connecting vowel इ; thus इतृ. This was, probably, generally done in Pr. (see the analogous cases of the suff. इत and इतव्य §§ 306. 314), and universally in Gḍ. Whence we have in Pr. इऊ or इउओ and (with absorption of इ) in W. Gḍ. उ (G.) or ऊ (W. H., P., S.). Thus Skr. खादिता *eater* (base खादितृ), Pr. खाइऊ or खाइउओ, G. खाउ or W. H. खाऊ; Skr. मारितृ *beater*, Pr. मारिऊ or मारिउओ, G. मारु or W. H. मारू, etc. — The suff. आऊ contains the caus. or denom. suff. आप्; thus Skr. कर्मापयितृ *worker*, Pr. कम्मावेउओ or कम्मावउओ, W. Gḍ. कमाऊ, where व् is elided and the hiatus-vowels contracted, as usual in caus. or denom. verbs (e. g., W. H. part. pres. कम्मातु *working* = Pr. कम्मावंतो or कम्मावेंतो).

Eighth Group.

334.	Set.	Com. gen.	Masc.	Fem.
	1)	अक्	अका	अकी
	2)	आक्	आका	आकी

The forms of com. gen. are weak; the others strong. As to the manner of adding them, see § 298, note.

335. The first set forms nouns of act. In many cases the original root is no longer in use; and the derivative itself, in its weak form, is employed as a root. The weak form is, as a rule, fem. Thus बइठक् f. or बइठका m. *sitting, seat*, of R. बइठ् *sit*; कसक् f. *pain*, of R. कस् *tighten*; तड़क् f. *cracking, cleft*, तड़का *daybreak*, of R. *तड़ or तड़क् (W. H. तड़क्) *crack*; चमक् f. or चमका m., °की f. *glittering*, of R. *चम् (*wave*) or चमक् *glitter*; झलक् f. *glitter*, झलकी f. *glance*, of R. *ज्वल् or झलक् *glitter*; झपक् f. or °का m. or

°की f. *snatch, wink,* of R. *कप् *be quick* (Skr. ग्रध्यर्प्?); कटक् f. or °का m. *twitch,* of R. *कट् *be quick* (Skr. ग्रध्यट्?); फड़क् f. *palpitation,* फड़की *partition, screen,* of R. फाड़् *split;* फाटक् m. *gate,* of R. फाट् *split;* सड़क् f. *road,* of R. सट् *join?*, etc.

336. The second set is used to derive nouns of agency from roots. Thus चराक् m. or f. *an animal that grazes,* of R. चर् *graze;* चलाक् m. or f. *active, clever,* चलाकी f. *cleverness* (see § 257), of R. चल् *walk, move;* दउड़ाक् m. or f. *runner, racer,* of R. दउड़् *run;* लराक् m. or f. or °का m., °की f. *quarrelsome,* of R. लर् (W. H. लड़्) *fight;* उड़ाक् m. or f. *capable of flying, fledged,* of R. उड़् *fly;* पइराक् *swimmer,* पैराकी *act or art of swimming,* of R. पइर् *swim,* etc.

337. *Affinities.* These suff. exist in all Gḍs.; but the W. Gḍs. have final ग्रो or ग्रो for E. Gḍ. ग्रा; and S. has ग्राकु or ग्राकू for E. H. ग्राक् or ग्राका (Tr. 52, 9). Examples, see in Bs. II, 31—33. 42. 43. They are exactly the same as in E. H.

338. *Derivation.* The original of these suff. is the Skr. krit ग्रक, which is really a compound of the krit suff. (or nominal termin.) ग्र and the nominal base क (probably = कृत् *doing,* of R. कृ *do*) meaning *doing, agent.* On this subject see § 353. The derivatives of the suff. ग्रक, therefore, are really compound words, made up of two nominal bases, one ending in ग्र, the other being क; e. g., Skr. कर्षक = कर्ष + क lit. *making a tightening,* E. H. कसक्. An initial क् of the second part of a compound has a tendency to be preserved or even doubled in Pr.; e. g., ग्रम्हक्केरं or ग्रम्हकेरं (H. C. 2, 99 = ग्रम्ह + केरं), पडिक्कूलं or पडिकूलं (H. C. 2, 93 = पति + कूलं), मुक्को or मुग्रो (H. C. 2, 99 = मू + क lit. *made fast,* i. e., *dumb*). Hence the preservation of it in the Gḍ. suffixes. — The second set, probably, contains the denom. suff. ग्राप्, and is equal to Skr. ग्रापक; thus Skr. उड्डापकः, Mg. उड्डावके or उड्डाग्रके, E. H. उड़ाक्, with elision of व् and contraction of the hiatus-vowels.

SECOND CHAPTER. ROOTS.

339. The usual rule in Hindí grammars for ascertaining the form of the root is, to reject the suff. of the infinitive. This rule holds good for the E. H. also. The root is obtained by detaching the suff. अब् or इब् (§ 308). Thus R. पढ़् from inf. पढ़ब् *to read;* R. बूझ् from inf. बूझब् *to know;* R. खा from inf. खाइब् or खाब् *to eat.* In some cases, however, a व् or य् must be either supplied or omitted; thus R. पाव् from inf. पाइब् *to obtain* (for *पाविब § 33); R. जी from inf. जीयब् *to live;* R. चू from inf. चूवब् or चूअब् *to drip;* R. रो from inf. रोवब् or रोअब् *to weep,* etc. It will be found that with a few exceptions (about 25) which have a final vowel, all E. H. roots terminate with a consonant.

340. The same result, however, is obtained by taking the 3d pers. sing. pres. conj. (see § 495) and detaching from it the termination ऐ (or य्); thus R. पढ़्, from पढ़ै *he reads;* R. बूझ्, from बूझै *he knows;* R. पाव्, from पावै *he obtains;* R. खा, from खाय् *he eats;* R. जी, from जीयै *he lives;* R. चू, from चूऐ *he drips;* R. रो, from रोए or रोवै *he weeps.* Moreover, this, unlike the ordinary method, presents the E. H. root in the most convenient form for comparing it with the original Skr. root which it represents. Thus while in such cases as that of the inf. पढ़ब् *to read* and 3. sg. pres. conj. पढ़ै *he reads,* both forms lead equally well to the original Skr. root पठ्, through their respective Skr. and Pr. equivalents (viz., inf. Ap. Pr. पढिब्बं, Skr. पठितव्यम् and pres. Pr. पढइ, Skr. पठति); on the other hand, in such cases as बूझब् *to know,* it is only the 3. sg. बूझै *he knows,* which leads through its equivalents, Pr. बुज्झइ, Skr. बुध्यते (i. e. बुध्-य-ते), to the original (Skr.) form of the root बुध्; for the inf. बूझब् can, by no possibility, be an equivalent of the Skr. बोधितव्यम्. Its Skr. equivalent would be, if it could exist at all, some such form as *बुध्यितव्यम्. Such inf. as बूझब्, in fact, are purely Gḍ. formations, made from a previously changed radical form बूझ्. For the explanation of this and similar radical changes, see §§ 344—349.

341. *Affinities.* On the whole, the Gds. show a very close agreement with one another, as regards roots; especially the E. and W. H. The differences are, in general, only phonetic. Thus E. H. uses ड़् and ल्, where W. H. has ड़् and ल् (see §§ 29. 30); e. g., E. H. पड़् *fall*, W. H. पड़्; E. H. चड़् *walk*, W. H. चल्. Or E. H. has छ where M. has त्स् (see § 11); e. g., E. H. छुट् *be loosed*, छोड़् *loose*, M. सुट्, सोड. Or E. H. has an aspirate, where M. has a tenuis (see § 145, note); e. g., E. H. सिख् or सीख् *learn*, M. शिक्, etc. Sometimes the difference is greater, and is either phonetic or due to different derivation; e. g., E. H. बैस् *sit*, N. बस्, P. बह्, S. विह (Skr. उपविश्, cf. § 173); or E. H. सूत् *sleep* (den. of the Skr. part सुप्त, § 352), W. H. सो (Skr. R. स्वप्). Sometimes the same root, though it may exist in both languages, is common in one, but uncommon in the other; e. g., E. H. गोहराव् *call*, W. H. पुकार्. There are, however, a few roots, especially in S. and M., which do not exist in E. H.; e. g., S. पस् *see*, M. पाह् *see*, but E. H. दिस् or देख्, which are also S. and M.

342. If the E. H. roots are examined, they will be found capable of division into two classes. Firstly, those which, though disguised more or less by phonetic modifications, are direct representatives of old Skr. roots (single or compound); secondly such as, though ultimately connected with Skr. roots, are not directly traceable to any of them. Examples of the first kind are: E. H. चल्, Skr. चल् *walk*; E. H. तप्, Skr. तप् *be hot*; E. H. जान्, Skr. ज्ञा *know*; E. H. कर्, Skr. कृ *do*; E. H. बो, Skr. वप् *sow*; E. H. खा, Skr. खाद् *eat*; E. H. चू, Skr. श्चुत् *leak*; E. H. कोप्, Skr. कुप् *be angry* (§ 148); E. H. बोल्, Skr. वद् *speak*; E. H. मल्, Skr. मृद् *rub*; E. H. तूट् or टूट्, Skr. त्रुट् *break* (§ 174); E. H. घस्, Skr. घर्ष् *rub*; E. H. परिस्, Skr. स्पर्श् *touch* (§ 58, note); E. H. परोस्, Skr. परिविष् *distribute* (§ 122, 5); E. H. देख्, Skr. दृश् *see*; E. H. उठ, Skr. उत्था *rise*; E. H. झाँड़्, Skr. अध्यर्द् *sweep* (§ 172), etc. Of the second kind are: E. H. भूल् *forget*, cf. Skr. भ्रमर्; E. H. छाह् *wish*, cf. Skr. उत्साह (§ 173); E. H. बइठ् *sit*, cf. Skr. उपविष्ट (§ 173); E. H. पइठ् *enter*, cf. Skr. प्रविष्ट; E. H. सूत् *sleep*, cf. Skr. सुप्त; E. H.

निकाल् or निकाड़् *eject*, cf. Skr. निष्कृष्ट (cf. §§ 113. 114); E. H. जताव् *make known*, cf. Skr. ज्ञाप्; E. H. पलट् or पलय् *turn over*, cf. Skr. पर्यस्त (§ 143); E. H. पक् *cook*, cf. Skr. पक्व; E. H. पहिचान् *recognize*, cf. Skr. परिचयनम् (§ 69); E. H. झाँक् *spy, peep*, cf. Skr. ध्यां कृ; E. H. ओँक् *vomit*, cf. Skr. वम् कृ; E. H. कड़क् *crack, rumble*, cf. Skr. कर्द कृ; E. H. धौँक् *blow*, cf. Skr. धुमं कृ, etc. The first class of roots I shall designate *primary*, the other *secondary*.

1. PRIMARY ROOTS.

343. The phonetic disguises which affect the primary roots and make them differ more or less from their Skr. originals, are generally owing to the following causes: 1) phonetic permutation of the radical consonant or vowel; 2) the incorporation of the Sanskritic „class-suffix" into the root; 3) the change of the Sanskritic „class" of the root; 4) the addition of the pleonastic radical suff. आपि. Not unfrequently several of these causes act together. On the other hand a few roots, favored by peculiar phonetic circumstances, remain altogether unchanged so as to be identical in E. H. and in Skr.

344. *Phonetic permutation.* 1) Final radical consonants are principally exposed to this cause of change, because through the accretion of the (so-called) „class-suffix", they generally become medial, and then, in their progress through Pr. and according to its laws, liable to permutation or elision. Thus E. H. खा *eat* for Pr. खा, Skr. खाद्; as 3[d] sing. pres. Skr. खादति, Pr. खाअइ or खाइ (Vr. 8, 27), E. H. खाय्. Sometimes, however, a root contains a final consonant which Pr. tolerates, and thus identical roots arise; e. g., E. H. चल् *walk* for Pr. चल्, Skr. चल्; as Skr. चलति, Pr. चलइ, E. H. चले. Hence, when the E. H. exhibits an (apparently) identical root with Skr. (as E. H. तप् *be hot*), containing a final consonant, which would ordinarily be liable to change in Pr., the identity is open to suspicion, and is, probably, to be accounted for in a different way, namely by the incorporation of „the class-suffix", see § 345: — 2) Initial radical consonants are rarely

liable to change, and, indeed, never change, unless they are compound consonants or a prefix is added, when the initial cons., being now medial, is either changed or elided in Pr.; but such roots are of unfrequent occurrence in E. H.; thus E. H. चू *leak* for Pr. चु (चो), Skr. श्च्युत् or च्युत्; as Skr. श्च्योतति, Pr. चुअइ (H. C. 2, 77) or चोअइ, E. H. चूऐ; or E. H. परोस् *offer food* for Pr. परिवेस्, Skr. परिवेष् (caus. of परि-विष्); as Skr. परिवेषयति, Pr. परिवेसेइ or परिवेसइ, E. H. परोसै (§ 122, 5). Very exceptionally a real single initial cons. is changed; e. g., E. H. हो *be* for Pr. हुव, Skr. भू (§ 176, note), as Skr. भवति, Pr. हुवइ or होइ (Vr. 8, 1), E. H. होय् *he is*; but the original भ् is preserved in the E. H. past part. भइल् *been*. — 3) Radical vowels occasionally suffer a change; sometimes through the vocalisation of an adjoining semivowel (य् or व्, §§ 121. 122); thus E. H. हो *be* for Pr. हुव or हव, Skr. भू; E. H. भीज् *moisten* for Skr. अभ्यार्द्र् (§ 172); sometimes by the ordinary phonetic laws; thus E. H. मल् *rub* for Pr. मल्, Skr. मृद्, as Skr. मर्दति, Pr. मलइ (H. C. 4, 126), E. H. मलै (§ 109); or E. H. तूट् or टूट् *break* for Pr. तुट्ट्, Skr. त्रुट्, see §§ 143. 147. 174; E. H. कोप् *be angry* for Pr. कुप्प्, Skr. कुप्, see §§ 143. 148. — 4) Exceptionally the initial vowel of the prefix of a compound root is elided; as E. H. छाह् *wish* for Pr. *उच्छाह्, see § 173; or E. H. काँढ़् *sweep* for Pr. अक्कड्ढ्, see § 172.

345. *Incorporation of the „class-suffix“.* Skr. roots are divided into *ten* classes, according to the suffix which they assume for the purpose of forming the conjugational base for the four principal tenses or moods (pres., imperf., potent., imper.). In all other tenses these „class-suffixes“ are rejected and the root used alone. Already in Pr., however, it had become the custom, sometimes to incorporate the class-suff. and to use the root, thus amended, as the conjug. base in all tenses (or moods) and derivative verbs (passive, causal, etc.). In Gḍ. this usage has been still more extended. Thus E. H. has R. जान् *know* for Pr. जाण् and जा, Skr. ज्ञा, through incorporating the suff. ना of the IXth class, as Skr. जानाति, Pr. जाणाइ (cf. H. C. 3, 154. Ls.

348 = ञा + णा + इ) or ञाणाइ (Vr. 8, 23 = ञाण् + अ + इ); E. H. ञानै; or E. H. चुन् *gather* for Pr. चुण् or चिण् or चि, Skr. चि, through incorporating the suff. नु of the Vth cl.; as Skr. चिनोति, Pr. चिणोइ (cf. Ls. 347 = चि-णो-इ) or चिणइ or चुणइ (Vr. 8, 29. H. C. 4, 238 = चिण् or चुण् + अ + इ), E. H. चुनै; or E. H. नाच् *dance* for Pr. णच्, Skr. नृत्, through incorporating the suff. य् of the IVth cl., as Skr. नृत्यति, Pr. णच्चइ (Vr. 8, 47 = णच्च् + अ + इ), E. H. नाचै, etc. It should be noticed, that the incorporation of the class-suff. is more or less optional in Pr. and, indeed, exceptional as regards the so-called „general" tenses and derivat. verbs (cf. Wb. Spt. 59); but in Gd. it is absolute. It may be surmised that, while this was the case in the literary Pr., in the more vulgar Ap. dialects, from which the Gd. took its immediate origin, incorporation was the usual, perhaps the general, practice. That it was a real incorporation of the suff. into the root, even in Pr., can be seen clearly from those forms in which according to Skr. usage the class-suff. could have no place; such as ञाणिअं (lit., Skr. *ञानितम्) *known*, but also regularly णायं (H. C. 4, 7), for Skr. ज्ञातम्; or Pr. ञाणिऊण (lit., Skr. *ञानित्वा) or regularly णाऊण (H. C. 4, 7), for Skr. ज्ञात्वा *having known*; or Pr. ञाणावेइ (H. C. 3, 149), for Skr. ज्ञापयति (lit. *ज्ञानापयति) *he caused to know*; or Pr. चिणिहिइ or चिव्विहिइ (H. C. 4, 243), for Skr. चेष्यति (lit. *चिनिष्यति or *चिन्विष्यति, i. e., चिन् or चिनु-इष्यति) *he will gather*; or Pr. चिव्वइ (H. C. 4, 242), for Skr. चीयते (lit., Skr. *चिन्व्यते or Pr. *चिणुईअइ) *it is gathered*; or Pr. सुणइ (Spt. 46) or सुणीअइ (cf. H. C. 4, 302. Dl. 24, lit. *सुन्यते), but also regularly सुव्वइ (H. C. 4, 242), for Skr. श्रूयते (lit. *श्रुव्यते) *it is heard*; or Pr. सुणिऊण (lit., Skr. *सुनित्वा) or regularly सोऊण (H. C. 4, 241), for Skr. श्रुत्वा *having heard*; or Pr. णचाविअइं (H. C. 1, 33), for Skr. नर्त्तितानि (lit. *नृत्यापितानि) *caused to dance*; or Pr. करिअ (lit. *कर्य) or regularly कदुअ (H. C. 4, 272), for Skr. कृत्वा *having done*, etc. In E. H. this incorporation is so thoroughly established, that the old radical forms have entirely disappeared, and their places have been taken by the new ones, even, e. g., as the base for the formation of the ver-

bal noun in अन्न् which is the source of the modern infinitive (§§ 308—314); thus E. H. जानन्न् *to know* for Skr. ज्ञातव्यम् (lit. *ज्ञानितव्यम्); E. H. नाचन्न् *to dance* for Skr. नर्त्तितव्यम् (lit. *नृत्यितव्यम्), etc. This process explains why many Skr. roots ending in a vowel terminate in E. H. with a consonant.

Note: In most of the above examples there is not only an incorporation of the class-suff., but simultaneously also a change of the „class"; see § 347.

346. An exactly analogous process is the *incorporation of the passive suff.* य, by which means a few intransitive roots are formed in E. H. from Skr. transitive (active) roots; e. g., the Skr. R. चप् is trans. *press,* but the E. H. R. चप् is intrans. *be put down, be abashed,* and equal to the Skr. pass. R. चप्य; as Skr. pass. चप्यते *he is pressed,* Pr. चप्पइ, E. H. चपे, etc. Sometimes both the Skr. and Gḍ. Rs. are intrans.; e. g., E. H. चार् (W. H. चाल्) and Skr. चल् *walk,* as Skr. pass. चल्यते (but act. चलति), Pr. चल्लइ (Vr. 8, 53, but act. चलइ H. C. 4, 231), W. H. चाले or E. H. चारे (but act. W. H. चले, E. H. चरे), etc. In rare cases both are trans.; e. g., E. H. सीच् and Skr. सिच् *irrigate*; as Skr. pass. सिच्यते (but act. सिञ्चति), Pr. सिचइ (H. C. 4, 230, but act. सिंचइ H. C. 4, 239), E. H. सीचे (but act. सीँचे), etc. Other examples, see § 348.

Note: In most cases of this kind also a change of „voice" from pass. to act. takes place; see § 348.

347. *Change of „class".* The Skr. distribution of roots into ten classes had already in Pr. become, to a considerable extent, obliterated. In Gḍ. it has disappeared altogether. While Skr. has ten classes, of which the I^st^ (incl. VIth) and the Xth (incl. denom. and causal) include by far the largest number of roots, Pr. has, in the main, only two, of which one corresponds to the Skr. VIth (or I^st^) and the other to the Skr. X^th^ cl. The remaining classes occur in Pr. only in extremely isolated and exceptional cases; but as a rule, roots belonging to them are transferred into the VIth [1]) (or occassionally X^th^) class, either 1) by

1) It is usual to say the I^st^ cl. (cf. Wb. Spt. 59. Ls. 334); but it seems

substituting the suff. अ of the VIth (or X[th]) for their proper class-suff. (नु of the Vth, न of the VIIth, उ of the VIIIth, ना of the IXth, य of the IVth), see H. C. 4, 239; or 2) by incorporating the latter with the root and, when necessary, eliding and changing the final vowel of such class-suff. (उ, आ) into अ, the characteristic of the VIth and X[th] classes (cf. Wb. Spt. 59 ff. Ls. 334); or 3) by interpolating the suff. अ of the VIth class. For example; R. चि *gather* is in Skr. of the Vth cl., base चिनु, hence 3. sg. pres. चिनोति, but in Pr. it becomes of the VIth cl., by incorporating नु and changing उ to अ, hence base चिण, 3. sg. pres. चिणइ (Vr. 8, 29); or again R. प्राप् *obtain* is in Skr. of the Vth cl., hence base प्राप्नु, 3. sg. pres. प्राप्नोति, but in Pr. of the VIth cl., by substituting the suff. अ of the VIth for नु, hence base पाव, 3. sg. pres. पावइ (H. C. 4, 239); or again R. भञ्ज् *break* is in Skr. of the VIIth cl., hence base भनज्, 3. sg. pres. भनक्ति, but in Pr. of the VIth cl., by incorporating न and eliding its अ, hence base भञ्ज, 3. sg. pres. भंजइ (H. C. 4, 106); similarly in Pr. पीसेदि or पिंसेदि (Ls. 347), for Skr. पिनष्टि, there is a transfer of the R. पिष् from the VIIth into the Xth cl.; or again R. कृ *do* is in Skr. of the VIIIth cl., hence base करु, 3. sg. pres. करोति, but in Pr. of the VIth or I[st] or X[th] cl., by changing the suff. उ of the VIIIth to अ, hence base °क्कु (i. e., क्र) or कर or करे (i. e., करय), 3. sg. pres. °क्कुइ (as in धुक्कुइ Spt. 173 = Skr. थूत्करोति) or करइ (Vr. 8, 13)

---

to me, on the whole, that the form which such Pr. roots take, is more accurately described as that of the VIth cl. The I[st] differs from the VIth cl. by *guṇating* and *accentuating* the radical vowel; the VIth does not guṇate the radicals and accentuates the suffixal vowel. Now in many cases Pr. does not guṇate the rad. vowel; e. g., in चिणाइ, सुणाइ, where if they were of the I[st] cl., it should be चेणाइ, सोणाइ; for the Rs. are, practically, चिण्, सुण्. Again in many other cases the final rad. sound is a comp. cons., which precludes the guṇation of the rad. vowel and thus renders it impossible to determine the class by this sign; e. g., in भंजइ, पावइ. Here the class could only be determined by the accent; but as Pr. (and Gd.) is devoid of the old Aryan accent, this aid to determine the class also fails. Thus circumstances are in favor of its being the VI class.

or करेइ (H. C. 4, 337); or again R. ज्ञा *know* is in Skr. of the IX cl., hence base ज्ञाना, 3. sg. pres. ज्ञानाति, but in Pr. of the VIth or Xth, by incorporating ना and changing आ to अ, hence base जाणा or जाणे (i. e., ज्ञानय), 3. sg. pres. जाणाइ (Vr. 8, 23) or जाणेइ (Dl. 15); or again R. ग्रह् *seize* is in Skr. of the IXth cl., hence base गृह्णा, 3. sg. pres. गृह्णाति, but in Pr. of the VIth or Xth, by substituting their suff. अ (अय) for ना, hence base गेंह or गेंहे (i. e., गेंहय), 3. sg. pres. गेंहइ (Vr. 8, 15) or गेंहेदि (Dl. 90); or again R. नृत् *dance* is in Skr. of the IVth cl., hence base नृत्य, 3. sg. pres. नृत्यति, but in Pr. of the VIth or Xth, by incorporating य, hence base णच्च or णच्चे, 3. sg. pres. णच्चइ (Vr. 8, 47) or णच्चेदि (Dl. 50); or again R. रुद् *weep* is in Skr. of the IInd cl., hence irregular base रोदि, 3. sg. pres. रोदिति, but in Pr. of the VIth or Ist cl., by substituting their suff. अ for the irreg. इ of the IInd cl., hence base रुद or रोद, 3. sg. pres. रुअइ or रुवइ (H. C. 4, 226. Spt. 311 or contr. रोइ H. C. 4, 368) or रोअइ or रोवइ (H. C. 4, 226); or again R. या *go* is in Skr. of the IInd cl., hence base या, 3. sg. pres. याति, but in Pr. of the VIth cl., by interpolating its suff. अ, hence base जाअ, 3. sg. pres. जाअइ (H. C. 4, 240 or contr. जाइ H. C. 4, 240. 350). Moreover, there was already in Pr. a tendency to run its two (remaining) classes, the VIth and Xth, into *one*, either by transferring the roots of the VIth into the Xth; or *far more commonly* by reducing the roots (whether primitive or denom. or caus.) of the Xth into the VIth, through changing the Xth class-suff. ए into the VIth class-suff. अ (see H. C. 3, 158. 149. Wb. Spt. 60. Ls. 341. 342. 344). Thus 1) change of the VIth cl. into the Xth; e. g., हसेइ (H. C. 3, 158), for हसइ (H. C. 3, 158. Skr. हसति) *he laughs*; करेइ (H. C. 4, 337), for करइ (Vr. 8, 13) *he does*; नच्चेइ (Dl. 50), for नच्चइ (Vr. 8, 47) *he dances*, etc.; 2) change of the Xth cl. into the VIth; e. g., कहइ (H. C. 4, 2), for कहेइ (Spt. 35. cf. H. C. 4, 267), Skr. कथयति, from R. कथ् *speak*; or चिंतइ (H. C. 4, 422), for चिंतेइ (Spt. 156. cf. H. C. 4, 265) *he thinks*; or साहइ (Spt. 260), for साहेइ (Spt. 188), Skr. साधयति, from R. साध् *accomplish*; again in causals: दरिसइ

(H. C. 3, 149), for दरिसेइ, Skr. दर्शयति, from R. दृश् *see*; or करावइ (H. C. 3, 149), for करावेइ (H. C. 3, 149), Skr. कारयति, from R. कृ *do*; or हसावइ (H. C. 3, 149), for हसावेइ (H. C. 3, 149), from R. हस् *laugh*; or भमावइ (H. C. 3, 151), for भमावेइ (H. C. 3, 151) *he causes to roam*, from R. भ्रम्, etc. In E. H. (and Gḍ. generally) this process reaches its natural conclusion by all roots whatsoever (whether primitive or derivative) having been transferred to a single class, which practically corresponds to the VIth of Skr. While, therefore, in Skr. roots belong to ten, and in Pr. (in the main) to two classes, they all belong in E. H. to one and the same. Thus (see the above examples) E. H. चुनै = Pr. चुणइ; E. H. पावै = Pr. पावइ; E. H. भंजै = Pr. भंजइ; E. H. पीसै = Pr. पीसइ or पिंसइ; E. H. करै = Pr. करइ; E. H. जानै = Pr. जाणइ; E. H. गहै = Pr. गेण्हइ; E. H. नाचै = Pr. नचइ; E. H. रोऐ = Pr. रोअइ; E. H. जाय् (W. H. जावै) = Pr. जाइ (or जाअइ); E. H. हसै = Pr. हसइ; E. H. कहै = Pr. कहइ; E. H. चिंतै = Pr. चिंतइ; E. H. करावै = Pr. करावइ; E. H. हसावै = Pr. हसावइ, etc. Some E. H. roots ending with an anomalous long vowel, as पी *drink*, चू *drip*, are probably to be explained on the principle of the interpolation of the VIth class-suff. अ; just as in the case of the above mentioned R. जा *go*. Thus E. H. पीयै *he drinks* presupposes a Pr. form *पिअअइ or *पिअयइ, instead of the common Pr. पिअइ (H. C. 4, 10) or पियइ (H. C. 1, 180), Skr. पिवति, which would be in E. H. either *पीइ or *पियै; similarly E. H. चूऐ *it drips* = Pr. *चुअअइ, for the ordinary Pr. चुअइ (H. C. 2, 77).

Note: Some Skr. roots are conjugated in several classes, one of which is the usual one, while the others are either rarely used or confined to the Vedas. It will be found, that some Gḍ. roots which have apparently changed their Skr. class, have really preserved such an unusual or vedic class. Thus R. तप् *be hot* is in Skr. both of the I[st] cl., तप, and also, but rarely, of the IVth cl., तप्य. The latter is the modern E. H. तप् (Pr. तप्प). The former would have become in E. H. तव or तो, through Pr. तव (cf. तवइ H. C. 1, 231). Again R. मृ *die* is in Skr. of the VIth cl., म्रिय,

but in the Vedas of the I[st] cl., मर. The latter is preserved in the E. H. मर्, Pr. मर (Vr. 8, 12 मरइ, E. H. मरै). It is possible that other modern Gḍ. roots, which have apparently changed their class, have really preserved an ancient traditional one of colloquial use, even though in many instances no evidence of it has survived either in Skr. or Pr. literature.

348. An exactly analogous process is the *change of „voice“*. In the case of some simple roots, their passive radical forms, made in Skr. with the suff. य्, are used in Pr. in an active sense and substituted in their place (cf. Wb. Spt. 64. S. Gdt. in J. G. O. S. XXIX, 492). By this process, practically, such roots are transferred in Pr. from their proper Skr. class into the VIth (or X[th]), and in E. H. into the VIth. Thus R. भज् *break* is in Skr. of the VIIth cl., hence base भनज्, 3. sg. pres. भनक्ति; its pass. root or base is भज्य, hence 3. sg. pres. भज्यते *he is broken*. Now Pr. treats this form, as if it were an active one of a R. भज् of the IVth cl., and, by incorporating the (really passive, but practically IVth cl.) suff. य, makes the root to be of the VIth; hence base भज्ज, 3. sg. pres. भज्जइ *he breaks* (cf. Spt. 168 भज्जंतस्स, Dl. 42 विभज्ज). Again R. रुध् *hinder* is in Skr. of the VIIth cl., hence base रुणध्, 3. sg. pres. रुणद्धि; but in Pr. it is of the VIth cl., by incorporating न and eliding its अ; hence base रुंध, 3. sg. pres. रुंधइ (Vr. 8, 49). The Skr. pass. base is रुध्य, hence 3. sg. pres. रुध्यते *he is hindered*; in Pr. this becomes रुज्झइ (or रुब्भइ) and is used both in its proper pass. sense (*he is hindered* H. C. 4, 245. 248) as well as in the act. sense (*he hinders* H. C. 4, 218); that is, Pr. transfers the R. रुध् into the VIth cl., by incorporating the pass. suff. य and employing it in an act. sense. Examples of this kind are not uncommon. Thus R. शक् *can* forms Pr. सक्कइ, for Skr. शक्नोति (Vr. 8, 52. H. C. 4, 230). Now clearly सक्कइ is the equivalent of the Skr. pass. शक्यते, used actively. The real equivalent for the Skr. (V[th] cl.) शक्नोति is the alternative Pr. form सक्कुणोइ (cf. Dl. 36 सक्कुणोमि). Again R. लग् *belong* forms Pr. लग्गइ (Vr. 8, 52), which cannot be = Skr. (I[st] cl.) लगति, but = Skr.

pass. लायते; again R. स्फुट् *burst* forms Pr. फुट्टइ or फुडइ (Vr. 8, 53). Of these, evidently, the former = Skr. pass. स्फुट्यते, the latter = Skr. act. (VIth cl.) स्फुटति. Again R. सिच् *sprinkle* forms both सिच्चइ (H. C. 4, 230) = Skr. pass. सिच्यते, and सिंचइ (H. C. 4, 239) = Skr. act. (VIth cl.) सिञ्चति. Again R. हन् *kill* forms either हम्मइ = Skr. pass. हन्यते and used both as an act. (Vr. 8, 45) and as a pass. (H. C. 4, 244), or हणइ (Dl. 72) = Skr. act. हन्ति. Again the R. विक्री *sell* (i. e. वि-क्री) forms both विक्केइ and विक्किणइ, of which the latter = Skr. act. विक्रीणीते; but that the former = Skr. pass. विक्रीयते is shown by the E. H. बिकै *it is sold* which is still used exclusively in a pass. or intrans. sense. This Pr. form विक्केइ, by showing that the termin. एइ may represent the Skr. pass. termin. ईयते, throws light on some strange Pr. forms, which thus are shown to be passives, used actively. Thus Pr. धेइ *he places,* of the R. धा, is the same as Skr. pass. धीयते; for from the usual Skr. act. (III[d] cl.) दधाति it cannot be phonetically derived. Thus also देइ (Cw. 99) *he gives,* of R. दा, is probably the Skr. pass. दीयते; and Pr. चेइ *he gathers* (T. V. 2, 4, 72), of R. चि, is the Skr. pass. चीयते rather than an assumed new I[st] cl. चयति (as Wb. Spt. 60); and Pr. °ठेइ or °थेइ (Ls. 345) *he stands,* of R. स्था, is the Skr. pass. स्थीयते rather than an assumed new I[st] cl. स्थायति, of R. स्थै (? as Ls. 135); and Pr. उड्डेइ *he flies* (Cw. 99), of R. उद्-डी, is the Skr. IVth cl. उड्डीयते (in reality a pass. form) rather than the Skr. I[st] cl. उड्डयते. All these last mentioned forms in एइ, as regards their termination, resemble the Pr. X[th] cl., which likewise ends in एइ, as Pr. कहेइ = Skr. कथयति; 'and thus they come to be treated as if they were really X[th] cl. formations, and may all be optionally transferred into the VIth cl. Just as कहेइ may change to कहइ, so देइ to दइ (Spt. 216), °ठेइ to °ठइ (H. C. 4, 17), and, no doubt, the others similarly, though in their case the Pr. evidence is wanting. But the fact is proved by the E. H., which here again makes the change absolute and transfers all pass.-act. roots to the VIth cl. Thus E. H. बिकै = Pr. विक्कइ or विक्केइ; E. H. °है (in पहिरै *he put son,* see § 133) = Pr.

°धइ or °धेइ; E. H. संचे = Pr. संचइ or संचेइ; E. H. उठे = Pr. उट्ठइ or उट्ठेइ; the only exception is E. H. दे (or देय) for Pr. देइ. Again E. H. सके = Pr. सक्कइ; E. H. लगे = Pr. लग्गइ; E. H. फुटे = Pr. फुट्टइ; E. H. चारै or W. H. चाले = Pr. चल्लइ; E. H. सोचे = Pr. सिचइ.

Note: The cause, no doubt, of this confusion in Pr. of the pass. and act. was the great likeness between the form of the (active) IVth cl. and that of the passive. Even in Skr. they can only be distinguished by the accent, which in the IVth cl. is thrown on the radical, but in the pass. on the suffixal vowel; thus act. नंह्यते *náhyate he binds*, but pass. नह्यते *nahyáte he is bound.* In Pr., where the accent is disused, the identity becomes complete. In this way some passives became associated in the popular mind with the IVth cl. and came to be used as actives. Most, if not all, the facts might be explained, by supposing a transfer in Pr. of certain roots into the VIth cl., but such a change of class is otherwise quite unsupported; and the explanation by means of a change of voice seems much simpler.

349. *Addition of the pleonastic suffix* आपि. In Skr. the causal roots are occasionally formed by adding the suff. आपि (Pr. आवि, E. H. आव) instead of the ordinary causal suff. इ; e. g., caus. R. अध्यापि (3. sg. अध्यापयति *he teaches*), of R. अधी (i. e., अधि-इ) *read*; see other examples in M. M. 217. 218. In Pr. any C. R. may be formed at pleasure with either of these suff. (Vr. 7, 26. 27. H. C. 3, 149. Wb. Spt. 64. 65. Wb. Bh. 436); e. g., Pr. कारेइ or करावेइ *he causes to do* = Skr. कारयति or *करापयति. In E. H. the C. R. is *always* formed with आपि; the original C. Rs. formed with इ, so for as they have survived, having become primitive transitive roots (see §§ 471—473). Thus E. H. करावै *he causes to do,* not *कारै, which does not exist; again E. H. मरावै *he causes to die* (i. e., causing death indirectly), but मारै *he beats* or *he kills.* Now it has been shown in § 347, that, in Pr., roots of the VIth cl. are occasionally transferred into the Xth cl. (H. C. 3, 158), i. e., practically are formed like causal roots with इ;

and hence they also occasionally assume the (caus.) suff. आवि, which in their case, of course, is practically pleonastic (cf. H. C. 3, 158 सुणाउ perhaps contr. for सुणावउ or सुणाविउ); e. g., Pr. has the pleon. R. सुहावि = Skr. सुख् or *सुखापि (3. sg. सुहावेइ Spt. 169), E. H. सुहाव्. In E. H. these pleon. roots are still more common; e. g., चुराव् *steal*, Pr. *चुरावि, Skr. चुर्; E. H. गरियाव् *abuse*, Pr. *गलिहावि, Skr. गल्ह्, etc. See the List of Roots. There can be little doubt, however, that such Gd. pleon. Rs. as well as their Skr. originals are in reality *denominative* roots (see § 352).

2. SECONDARY ROOTS.

350. Secondary roots may be divided into three classes, according to their origin. I shall distinguish them as 1) *derivative*, 2) *denominative*, and 3) *compound*.

351. *Derivative Roots.* In E. H. there sometimes exist pairs of roots, of which one member is intrans. and corresponds to the Skr. simple or (sometimes) passive root, and the other is trans. and represents the corresponding Skr. causal root. In these cases the intrans. has a short and the trans. a long vowel. Thus E. H. सर् *issue* intrans. = Skr. S. R. सृ, and E. H. सार् *accomplish* (lit. *cause to issue*) trans. = Skr. C. R. सारि; or E. H. मर् *die* intr. = Skr. S. R. मृ, and E. H. मार् *kill* trans. = Skr. C. R. मारि; E. H. बुड् *sink* intr. = Skr. S. R. ब्रुड् and E. H. बोड् *immerse* trans. = Skr. C. R. ब्रोडि, etc. In a similar manner, by shortening the radical vowel, E. H. sometimes derives new intrans. from trans. roots, when, on phonetic grounds, only the latter can be shown to have an equivalent in Skr. or Pr.; vice versa, in a few cases, by lengthening the radical vowel, E. H. derives trans. from intrans. roots, when only the latter exist in Skr. or Pr. The latter process is resorted to only very exceptionally, because E. H. has its own special means of forming causal (or trans.) roots with the suff. आव (see §§ 349. 474). Thus E. H. possesses a number of new pairs of roots, of which one member is original, while the other is derivative. Thus E. H. निबाह् *accomplish*

is trans. and equivalent to the Skr. C. R. निर्वाहि, of the trans. S. R. निर्वह्; from निव्वाह् E. H. derives an intrans. R. निव्वह् *be accomplished*, which cannot, phonetically, be derived from the Skr. pass. R. निर्वह्य or निर्वाह्य; for these forms would become in Pr. निव्वुज्झ, and thence E. H. *निव्वझ्. Again E. H. नहा *bathe* is equivalent to the Skr. S. R. स्ना (Pr. ण्हा). From it E. H. derives the intrans. R. नह् *flow*, for which Skr. offers no equivalent. It is, as if नहा were a trans. C. R., and नह् is to it, as कर् *do* is to करा (or कराव्) *cause to do*. On the other hand, E. H. संठ् or सठ् *combine* is intrans. and equivalent to the Skr. intrans. S. R. संस्था (Pr. संठा or संठ). From it E. H. derives a trans. (or caus.) R. साँठ् or साठ्, which cannot be derived, phonetically, from the Skr. C. R. संस्थापि, Pr. संठाव, etc.

352. *Denominative Roots.* Nouns which are used as roots for the purpose of forming new verbs, are called denominative roots. The practice of thus using nouns is very ancient. Even among the recognised Skr. simple roots, there are many which are really denominative. Pr. and Gd. have considerably added to their number. Theoretically the power of using nouns as roots is unlimited, and a great variety of nouns are actually thus employed upon occasion in Skr., Pr. and Gd.; see examples in M. M. 227—230. Wb. Spt. 60. 65. Wb. Bh. 429. 437. I speak here, however, only of such nouns, as are formally recognised and treated as roots and enumerated as such in *dhátupáthas* (or lists of roots). Such radical nouns or denominative roots 1) always end in अ; 2) may be either common nouns or participles (see also Wb. Bh. 429); and 3) belong, as regards Skr., generally to the Xth class, but occasionally also to the I[st]. In Pr., with its tendency to obliterate class-differences (see § 347), they are all made optionally to belong to the VIth cl., to which they belong without exception in E. H. Thus, e. g., the following roots are derived from common nouns in Skr.: R. मार्ज् *scour*, from मार्ज *scouring*, a krit-derivative of the S. R. मृज् *scour*; or R. मार्ग् *seek*, from मार्ग *seeking*, a krit-deriv. of the S. R. मृग् *seek*; both

preserved in E. H. as माँत् and माँग्. Again Skr. roots derived from participles are amongst others: R. वेड् *surround,* from वेट *enclosure,* perhaps a past part. pass. of S. R. विग् or विष् with suff. त; or R. कड् *pull* from कट *pulled,* a past part. pass. of S. R. कष् (or कृष्) *rub, pull* with suff. त; both preserved in E. H. as वेढ़् and काढ़् (cf. Cw. 99. Wb. Spt. 107). Examples from the E. H. and Pr. are: 1) roots derived from common nouns: R. जम् *germinate,* from Skr. जन्म *birth,* a krit-deriv. of the S. R. जन् *be born*; thus 3. sg. pres. Skr. *जन्मयति, Pr. जम्मेइ or जम्मइ (H. C. 4, 136), E. H. जमै; again R. धार् or ढार् or ढाल् *pour,* from Skr. धार *flowing,* probably connected with the S. R. धाव् *run*; Skr. *धारयति, Pr. धाडेइ or धाडइ (T. V. 3, 1. 14, where it is said to be a substitute of Skr. निःसरति), E. H. धारै or ढारै *he pours.* Again 2) roots derived from participles: R. पलट् or पलथ् *turn over,* from Skr. पर्यस्त *turned over,* the past part. pass. of the Skr. Cp. R. परि-अस् *turn over* with suff. त; Skr. *पर्यस्तयति, Pr. पल्लट्टइ or पल्हत्थइ (H. C. 4, 26. 200), E. H. पलटै or पलथै *he turns over*; again R. पीट् *beat,* from Skr. पिष्ट *beaten,* the past part. pass. of the Skr. S. R. पिष् *beat* with suff. त; Skr. *पिष्टयति or पिट्टयति (?, Spt. 173. Comm.), Pr. पिट्टेइ (Spt. 173 for *पिट्टेइ) or पिट्टइ, E. H. पीटै *he beats.* Examples, from the E. H. or Pr., of denominative roots, formed with the pleonastic suff. of the Xth cl. आपय (Pr. आवे, H. आव, see § 349), are the following. One root derived from a common noun is सुहाव् *be pleasant,* from Skr. सुख *pleasure* (said to be a compound of सु *good* and ख *a mine,* a krit-deriv. of the S. R. खन् *dig*), Skr. सुखयति or *सुखापयति, Pr. सुहावेइ (Spt. 169) or सुहावइ, E. H. सुहावै *it is pleasant.* A root derived from a participle is चिताव् *make known,* from Skr. चित्त *known,* the past part. pass. of the Skr. S. R. चित् *know* and suff. त; Skr. *चित्तापयति, Pr. *चित्तावेइ or *चित्तावइ, E. H. चितावै *he makes known.*

353. *Compound Roots.* The great diversity and intricacy of the old Skr. system of radical „classes" must always have formed a formidable obstacle to its being adopted in the language of the common people. An evidence of this fact has been already

noted in § 347, in the decided tendency of Pr. and still more of Gḍ. to reduce the ten Skr. classes to one. But they made use, besides, of an other remedy, viz., instead of inflecting the root itself, they took some very simple form of a noun derived from it and construed it with the inflected root कृ *do.* This is still a common practice in modern H., where numerous verbs are formed from (especially foreign) nouns by construing them with the verb करब् *to do*; thus जमा करब् *to collect,* बंद् करब् *to shut,* बेल् करब् *to boil,* पास् करब् *to pass an examination,* मेल् करब् *to mix,* ध्यान् करब् *to meditate,* बिचार् करब् *to think* (for बिचारब्, as in English *to make answer* for *to answer*), etc. Even in Skr., paraphrased roots of this kind are often found; thus न्यक् + कृ *make low, degrade,* चिरं कृ *make long, delay,* etc. (see more examples in M. W. Skr. Lex. under Art. कृ). In fact, any suitable noun might be thus turned into a verb. But it is not of these, that I speak here, but of a special and small class from among them, in which the construction of the noun with the R. कृ has become so firmly established by more or less obscure causes, as to produce, through constant usage, a coalescence of its two component parts (N. + R.) into one single simple form, and the recognition and treatment of this compound form as a simple root. Such roots I designate *compound* roots. Thus there is in Skr. a paraphrased verb फुत् + कृ or फुत् + कृ *blow,* whence फुत्करोति *he blows*; this appears in Pr. as फुक्कइ or फुक्कइ and in E. H. as फूँकै. In Skr. the two component parts, N. फुत् and R. कृ, are still separate and clearly recognisable, but they have already in Pr. and still more in E. H. coalesced into *one* form, Pr. फुक्क्, E. H. फूँक् which is now recognised in E. H. as a simple root; in reality it is compound. This process of amalgamation must have been already at work in old times, for among the recognised simple roots of Skr. are found several, which are clearly compound; as बुक्क् *bark* (cf. H. C. 4, 169) = वू or वद् + कृ; धक्क् *destroy* = धक् + कृ or ध्वत् + कृ (acc. sg. neut. of N. दह् or ध्वस्); फक्क् *swell* = स्फट् + कृ; चिक्क् *pain* = चृत् + कृ; टंक् *bind* = तन् + कृ, etc. There can hardly be a doubt as to the compound character (as above explained) of such roots; though the exact phonetic process, by which it was produced, may be obscure. The following may be found a probable explanation. It has been shown in § 348, that in Pr. passive roots are often employed in an active sense; and that sometimes they are recognisable by the termination एइ, which is occasionally reduced to अइ. It is probable, therefore, that the Pr. form केइ or कइ (as in वोक्केइ or वोक्कइ Spt. 173 = Skr. वुत्करोति) is a passive-active form, or identical with the Skr. pass. क्रियते, used actively. There are in E. H. a few forms which support this view. Thus it has the form ओढै which is both active (*he wears*) and passive or intrans. (*it is worn* or *it wears*); the corresponding Pr. forms would be उअड्डइ or उअड्डेइ; and in Skr. we find the form उपध्रियते which is both pass. and act. (VIth class). In fact, in this particular case, the properly passive form उपध्रियते has already in Skr. assumed an active sense; for the usual active form of the R. धृ is धरति, of the I[st] class. Similarly the R. मृ *die* is said to be in classic Skr. an active belonging to the VIth class (म्रियते). It is, however, really passive with an active sense[1]); for the proper active voice, which has been lost in the classic Skr., but preserved in the Vedic and also in Pr. and E. H., is (like that of R. धृ) of the I[st] cl. (मरति). It is precisely the same with the R. कृ *do*. Its Skr. pass. form क्रियते has come to be occasionally (i. e., in compound roots) used in Pr. as an active (of the VIth cl.). Its corresponding proper active form is (like that of the Rs. मृ and धृ) करति, of the I[st] class, and, though lost in classic Skr., still preserved in the Vedic and in Pr. (करइ) and E. H. (करै). But although the Pr. केइ or कइ and the E. H. कै have generally assumed an active meaning, their original passive signification is still apparent enough in some cases. Thus E. H. चहकै,

1) The change, in this case, was facilitated by the R. मृ being intrans. Besides, as both the VIth cl. and the pass. accentuate the suffixal vowel, there is absolutely no difference, externally, between the act. VIth cl. म्रियते *mriyâte* and the pass. म्रियते *mriyâte*.

from E. H. R. बहक् *stray* (i. e., lit. *be turned out,* scl., *of the right path*) represents the Pr. बहिक्कइ or बहिक्केइ and Skr. बहिष्क्रियते; or E. H. उचकै, of the E. H. root उचक् *be raised, rise*, representing the Pr. उच्चक्कइ or उच्चक्केइ and Skr. (Vedic) उच्चाक्रियते *he is carried on high,* etc. [1]). It has been stated already that in such compositions the R. कृ was usually constructed with some simple derivative noun. The simplest form of a noun, derived from the simple root, is the root itself; as Skr. R. रुध् *hinder,* N. रुध् *hindrance.* The next simplest is a noun, formed by one of the krit-suffixes त् or श्र; as Skr. R. च्यु *cease,* N. च्युत् *ceasing*; or R. कष् *pain,* N. कष *pain.* In constructing such a noun with the R. कृ, it is, if it has the form of the simple root or is formed with the krit-suff. त्, immediately joined with the R. कृ; as N. रुध् *hindrance,* acc. sg. neut. रुत्, whence Cp. R. रुत् + कृ = E. H. रोक् *hinder*; or N. च्युत् *ceasing,* acc. sg. neut. च्युत्, whence Cp. R. च्युत् + कृ = E. H. चुक् *cease.* Or if it is formed with the krit-suff. श्र, it is joined with R. कृ by means of a connecting vowel, generally ई; e. g., N. कष *pain,* when Cp. R. कषीकृ = E. H. कसक् *pain* [2]). It will be seen that in such compounds the initial क् *k* of the R. कृ or of its inflected form क्रियते is preceded either by a consonant or a long vowel; hence in Pr., according to its phonetic usages, the क् is always doubled, either by assimilating the consonant or shortening the vowel; thus Skr. रुत्-क्रियते = Pr. रुक्केइ or रुक्कइ *he hinders*;

---

1) In the Vedas the R. कृ is also of the IInd cl., thus 3. sg. pres. parasm. कर्त्ति, atm. कृते. The latter would be in Pr. क्कइ and by transfer into the Xth cl. (§ 347) क्केइ. This may serve as an alternative explanation, if the pass.-act. theory given in the text be not accepted.

2) This ई is, probably, the debris of an old case-ending. In Vedic Skr. occasionally आ is used, which is also without doubt an old case-ending, such as we see, e. g., in Skr. बलात्कृत: lit. *violently treated, forced* (बलात् abl. sg. of बल *violence*); thus Ved. उच्चाक्रियते *he is carried up* = Pr. उच्चक्केइ, E. H. उचकै *he rises.* As these C. Rs. were probably formed in very old times, it was possibly the connecting vowel आ rather than ई, which was used in them. However, it makes no practical difference, whether it was आ or ई; for in E. H. both are equally reduced to श्र.

Skr. च्युत्-क्रियते, Pr. चुक्केइ or चुक्कइ *he ceases*; Skr. कषीक्रियते = Pr. कसिक्केइ or कसिक्कइ *it pains*; indeed the doubling of क् is already insured by the following र् (in कृ). In E. H., finally, according to its phonetic laws, the double क्क् is reduced to single क् (§ 143). Thus Pr. रुक्कइ = E. H. रोकै (§ 148); Pr. चुक्कइ = E. H. चुकै (§ 146); Pr. कसिक्कइ = E. H. कसकै (§ 58). This explains the preservation in E. H. of the initial क् of the R. कृ, which, therefore, is an almost unerring indication of the presence of a compound root, in which it now forms the terminal sound; thus E. H. चुक् *cease*, रोक् *hinder*, कसक् *pain*. Similarly E. H. चमक् *glitter*, 3. sg. pres. चमकै, Pr. *चमक्कइ or *चमक्केइ, Skr. *चमत्क्रियते, comp. of N. चमत् (onomatop.) and R. कृ *do*, etc.

Note: Sometimes, though a C. R. does not exist in E. H., nominal derivatives of it do. Thus नक्कु *degraded, vile*, from the unused C. R. नक्, Pr. नक्क, Skr. न्यक्कृ *degrade* = नि-अंच्-कृ.

354. It remains briefly to notice a small number of E. H. roots, which probably belong to the one or the other of the above mentioned two principal classes, but which I am not able satisfactorily to trace to a Skr. origin. They must have been subject to extreme phonetic deterioration. They may be divided into:

1) such as are, probably, primary roots; e. g., टस् *burst*, टूग् *vex*, टेर् *shout*, टेल् *remove*, टेव् *sharpen*, टो *handle, grope*, ठाँस् *cram*, ढो *carry*, तग् *stich*, तच् *be parched*, थिज् *be congealed*, तिहुड़् or त्योढ़् or त्योड़् *bend*, पतूर् *drip*, पसा *skim*, पहुड़् or पौढ़् *repose*, पैना *sharpen*, पो or पोव् or पोह् *make bread* or *thread*, मूच् *shut*, गुर् *acquire a taste*, लच् *bend*, लट् *be laden*, लिड or लील् *swallow*, लेट् *recline*, लोट् *turn over, return*, सन् *be mixed, be soiled* and tr. सान् *mix, soil*, सोढ *review*, हट् *be perverse*, हिच् *loathe*, etc.

2) such as are, probably, secondary roots, and divisible into: a) *denominative*; as गोहराव् *call*, हलग् *be kindled*, etc.; — b) *compound*; as डाँक् *scold*, टोक् *prevent, challenge*, भटक् *go astray*, etc.; — c) to these may be added a class of roots which end in ल् or ड़

(or ड़्) or ड्; as टहल् or टहर् *walk to and fro* (cf. N. टहल् f. *service, drudgery*); ठहल् or ठहर् *stop, remain* (cf. ठहर् or ठाँव् *a place*); ढकेल् or धकेल् or धकोल् *shove* (cf. ढक्का or धक्का *a shove*); बहल् *pass agreeably, be amused* (cf. R. बह् *flow*); भिसल् *be dazzled* (cf. Pr. R. भिस् H. C. 4, 203 = Skr. भास्); झगड़् *quarrel*; लथड़् *be draggled* or लथेड़् *draggle*; लताड़् or लतेड़् (lit. *kick*) *insult, exhaust by labour* (cf. लात् or लत् *a kick* and लतर् *an old shoe*); झपट् *spring* or झपेट् *attack suddenly* (cf. झप् *quick*); चपट् *be flattened* or चपेट् *flatten* (cf. R. चाप् or चाँप् *press* and N. चाप् *a bow*); रपट् *slip* or रपेट् *chase* (cf. रापी or राँपी *an iron scraper* or *knife*); लपट् *adhere* or लपेट् *enclose, fold* (cf. N. लप् *palm of the hand hollowed so as to hold water*); घसट् or घसिट् or घसीट् *drag* (cf. R. घस् *rub*); बुकोट् *scratch* (cf. बुकट् or बुक्का *claw, a handful*). The forms with a penultimate long vowel are, as a rule, trans.; those with a short one, intrans. These roots, however, are not properly E. H. or E. Gḍ., but introduced from W. Gḍ. It will be shown (in § 476) that in W. Gḍ. there are causal roots in आल् or अला (W. H.), आड or अवाड (G.), आर् or अरा (S.); e. g., W. H. बिठला or बिठाल् *cause to sit*, G. खवाड् *cause to eat* (Ed. 114), S. डियार् *cause to give*, घारा *cause to wound* (Tr. 256. 257). It seems probable, that these W. Gḍ. causals and the above mentioned (W. Gḍ.) secondary roots have an identical origin. There is, moreover, a curious analogy in Pashtu (see Tr. in J. G. O. S. XXXIII, 7 ff.). It has a class of secondary roots in *ēd* (infinit. in *ēdal*), which are, as a rule, intrans.; e. g., *bahēd flow* (cf. E. H. बहल्), *matēd be broken* (cf. Skr. मृष्ट *rubbed*); *kēd be done*; but occasionally trans.; e. g., *āvrēd hear, blōsēd torment, puṣtēd ask* (cf. Skr. पृष्ट *asked*). Occasionally the primary root exists also, as *zang* or *zangēd swing*, *kṛ do* and *kēd be done*; just as in E. H. चाँप् and चपेट् *flatten*. And further, the causal roots may be made with *ēd* in Pashtu [1]).

---

1) Trumpp explains the Rs. in *ēd* as being compounds with *kēd be done*. This might suit the intrans., but not the trans. and caus. Rs. in *ēd*; moreover the R. *kēd* itself requires to be explained; for it is clearly a derivative of the R. *kṛ do*.

The origin of these roots is very obscure. Possibly they are denominative roots, derived from nouns which are themselves again derived from others by the secondary or pleonastic suff. अल्ल, इल्ल, अड, etc. (cf. §§ 209. 245) or वट्ट (cf. § 285). Or perhaps they may be compound roots, formed from the Skr. R. वृत् (Pr. वट्ट), of which the terminal ट् (or अट्, एट्, एड) is the sole remnant, as क् (of R. कृ, Pr. क्क) is in the other compound roots. Thus Skr. घर्षे वर्तते *he is occupied in rubbing, he drags* = *घर्षवर्तयति den. of *घर्षवर्त, Pr. *घस्सवट्टइ = *घस्सअट्टइ = *घस्सयट्टइ = E. H. घसेटै or घसीटै. At all events, in some cases, these roots have an alternative form, ending in क्: thus कपट् and कपक्; चपट् and चपक्; लपट् *cling* and लपक् *spring*; cf. also E. H. अोचट् and अोचक् *suddenly*.

355. There is also in E. H. a very small number of what may be called *tatsama* roots; viz., denom. roots formed from tats. nouns. Some are comparatively modern formations. Thus गर्ज् *thunder* (Skr. गर्ज); त्याग् *abandon* (Skr. त्याग); धूप् *perfume* (Skr. धूप); भोग् *enjoy* (Skr. भोग); लोभ् *be enamoured* (Skr. लोभ), etc.

THIRD SECTION. INFLEXION OF NOUNS.

FIRST CHAPTER. THE SUBSTANTIVE.

1. FORMS OF THE SUBSTANTIVE.

356. Every subst. admits of three forms: the short, long and redundant. The short is the primary form, which is given in dictionaries, and by which it is generally known. It is, as a rule, the only one admissible in good or literary language. The other two forms are more or less vulgar. They are made by adding to the short form the pleon. suff. of the fourth and sixth sets of the first group, as explained in §§ 199. 200 (q. v.). E. g., masc. sh. f. मीत् *friend*, lg. f. मितवा or °वाँ, red. f. मितौवा or °वाँ or मितौ; fem. sh. f. खाट् *bed*, lg. f. खटिया or °याँ, red. f. खटियवा or °वाँ;

masc. sh. f. बेटा *son*, lg. f. बेटवा or °वाँ, red. f. बेटौवा or °वाँ or बेटौ; fem. sh. f. सीता *Sítá*, lg. f. सितिया or °याँ, red. f. सितियवा or °वाँ; in इ; masc. sh. f. मुनि *sage*, lg. f. मुनिया or °याँ; red. f. मुनियवा or °वाँ; fem. sh. f. आँखि *eye*, lg. f. अँखिया or °याँ; red. f. अँखियवा or °वाँ; in ई; masc. sh. f. भाई *brother*, lg. f. भइया or भैया or °याँ; red. f. भइयवा or भैयवा or °वाँ; fem. sh. f. धूरी *axle*, lg. f. धुरिया or °याँ; red. f. धुरियवा or धुरीश्रा or °वाँ; in उ; masc. sh. f. तरु *tree*, lg. f. तरुवा or °वाँ; red. f. तरुअवा or तरूवा or °वाँ; fem. sh. f. पतोहु *daughter-in-law*, lg. f. पतोहुवा or °वाँ; red. f. पतोहुअवा or पतोहूवा or °वाँ; in ऊ; masc. sh. f. नाऊ *barber*, lg. f. नउवा or नौवा or °वाँ; red. f. नउअवा or नौअवा or नऊवा or °वाँ; fem. sh. f. बहू *daughter-in-law*, lg. f. बहुवा or °वाँ; red. f. बहुअवा or बहवा or °वाँ, etc.

Note: Sometimes the W. H. long and red. forms are used; as कन्हैया or कन्हइ *krishna*, रमै or रमैया *Rám*.

357. Many subst. (especially among those in अ) admit of two forms, a weak and a strong. Most of them, however, (especially those in इ and उ) exist in one of these forms only. The weak form is the original one; the other is made by adding to it the pleon. suff. of the first set of the first group, as explained in § 196 (q. v.). Thus 1) in अ or आ; masc. भेड़ or भेड़ा *ram*, माथ् or माथा *forehead*, बास् or बासा *dwelling*, बाल् or बाला *child*, etc.; fem. भेड़् or भेड़ी *ewe*, लाठ् or लाठी *staff*, मूठ् or मूठी *fist*, etc.; in इ or ई; masc. very rare, e. g., ज्ञान (ज्ञानि) or ज्ञानी *wise man*; fem. बाति or बाती *wick, light*, बहिनि or बहिनी *sister*, etc.; in उ or ऊ; masc. very rare, e. g., पीलु or पीलू *elephant*; fem. बहु or बहू *daughter-in-law*, पतोहु or पतोहू *daughter-in-law*. 2) Only in अ; masc. सोनार् *goldsmith*, कहार् *porter*, देव *god*, बाघ् *tiger*, बैल् *ox*, घर् *house*, नाम् *name*, फूल् *flower*, पेट् *stomach*, पेड़ *tree*, etc.; fem. बात् *word, event*, नाँक् *nose*, नीँद् *sleep*, etc. 3) Only in आ; masc. लरिका or छोकरा *boy*, बनिया *merchant*, घोरा *horse*, काँटा *thorn*, कुत्ता *dog*, मोढ़ा *footstool*, etc.; fem. only tats., as दुर्गा *Durgá*, सीता *Sítá*, or semitats., as किरपा *mercy*, etc. 4) Only in इ, rarely; masc. generally tats., as मुनि *a Muni*, or semitats., as रिखि *a Rishi*, etc.; fem. आगि *fire*, आँखि *eye*, etc. 5) Only in ई; masc. धोबी *washerman*,

माली *gardener,* तेली *oilman,* हाथी *elephant,* नाती *grandchild,* भाई *brother,* बहिनोई *brother-in-law,* कोढ़ी *leper,* पानी *water,* मोती *pearl,* घी *clarified butter*; fem. घोड़ी *mare,* बिल्ली *cat,* लड़िकी or छोकड़ी *girl,* माई *mother,* टोपी *hat,* मोड़ी *drain,* माखी *fly,* etc. 6) Only in उ; rarely, masc. tats. तरु *tree,* गुरु *teacher,* etc.; fem. *deest.* 7) Only in ऊ; masc. नाऊ *barber,* पहरू *watchman,* हिन्दू *a Hindú,* आलू *potato,* पेटू or खाऊ *glutton,* etc.; fem. मेहरारू *woman,* जोरू *wife,* जलू *leech,* बालू *sand,* etc.

Note: On the meaning of these various forms, see § 201.

2. GENDER.

358. There are only two genders, the masculine and the feminine. No practically workable rules can be given to recognise the gender of a subst. by its termination; excepting, that short forms in आ (exc. tats., like दुर्गा) are always masc.; e. g., घोड़ा *horse,* हाँडा *pot,* गोला *ball,* जूता *shoe,* etc., and that such short forms in ई, as have a synonymous masc. in आ, are always fem.; e. g., घोड़ी *mare,* हाँडी *pot,* गोली *bullet,* जूती *shoe,* etc. As a rule E. H. subst. retain the gender which they had in Skr.; but Skr. neuters become masc. in E. H. This affords, on the whole, a safe guide for those who can use it. Where there is a natural gender, that of course, determines the grammatical gender also. For the rest, the gender must be learned by practice.

359. The difficulty of determining the gender of E. H. words by their termin., is easily explained. Compare §§ 42 to 53. The termin. ई and ऊ must be uncertain, because they are contractions of the Mg. Pr. termin. masc. इए or उए, fem. इआ or उआ; thus Pr. fem. घोडिआ *mare* = E. H. घोड़ी; but Mg. Pr. masc. तेल्लिए *oilman* is likewise = E. H. तेली; again Mg. Pr. fem. बालुआ *sand* = E. H. बालू, but Mg. masc. बिच्छुए *scorpion* is also = E. H. बिछू. — The E. H. termin. इ and उ must be uncertain, because they were so even in Pr. and Skr., where their nom. sg. in ई and ऊ (Pr.) or इः, उः (Skr.) may be of either gender. — On the other hand, since the Pr. termin. आ, whether masc. or

fem., always becomes अ in E. H. (e. g., Pr. masc. राश्रा or राया *king*, E. H. राउ or रै; Pr. fem. वत्ता *word*, E. H. बात्), no E. H. short form in आ can be fem. (always excepting tats., which have not passed through Pr.); and since every final E. H. आ of a short form stands for a Mg. masc. अए, therefore all E. H. short forms in आ must be masc. Similarly, since every final E. H. इ of a short form, which corresponds to a synonymous masc. short form in आ, stands for a Pr. fem. इआ, all such E. H. short forms in इ must be fem. — Finally the termin. आ of E. H. long and redundant forms must be uncertain, because it is a contraction of the Mg. Pr. gen. termin. masc. आह्, fem. आअ (§§ 369, 2. 365, 1); e. g., E. H. नतिया *grandchild* = Mg. नत्तिश्राह् (Skr. नप्तृकः, H. C. 1, 137); but E. H. बुढ़िया *old woman* is also = Mg. वुड्ढिआअ. — The number of words, which are masc. or neut. in Skr., but fem. in E. H., is limited; and in the case of most of them the change had already taken place in Pr. Thus (see Vr. 4, 26. H. C. 1, 35. S. C. 1, 1. 53) Skr. n. अक्षि *eye*, Pr. n. अच्छिं or f. अच्छी or *अक्खी, E. H. f. आँखि; Skr. m. रश्मिः *cord*, Pr. m. or f. रस्सी, E. H. f. रस्सी[1]); Skr. m. अञ्जलिः *handful*, Pr. m. or f. अंजली, E. H. f. (also m.) अंजलि; Skr. बलिः *offering*, Pr. m. or f. बली, E. H. f. बली; Skr. m. विधि (*good*) *conduct*, Pr. m. or f. विही, E. H. f. बिही; Skr. n. पृष्ठम् *back*, Pr. n. पिट्ठं or f. पिट्ठी, E. H. f. पीठ; Skr. m. कुक्षिः *belly*, Pr. m. or f. कुच्छी, E. H. f. कोख् or कोख्; Skr. n. चौर्यम्, Pr. n. चोरिश्रं (Vr. 3, 20) or f. चोरिश्रा (Spt. 210), E. H. f. चोरी[1]). Again Skr. m. ग्रन्थिः *knot*, Pr. m. or f. गंठी (H. C. 1, 35), E. H. f. गाँठ् (also m.); Skr. m. बाहुः *arm*, Pr. m. बाहू or f. बाहा (H. C. 1, 36. S. C. 1, 1. 54), E. H. f. बाह् or बाँहि; Skr. n. अन्त्रम् *intestines*, Pr. f. अंती (in Ap. अंत्रडी H. C. 4, 445. T. V. 3, 4. 69), E. H. f. आँत्; Skr. n. अस्थि or अस्थिकम् *bone*, Pr. n. अट्ठिअं (cf. Spt. 100) or f. अट्ठी (H. C. 2, 32), E. H. f. आंठी. To these may

1) The Pr. fem. चोरिश्रा is really a different word, i. e., = Skr. चोरिका (cf. Wb. Spt. 45); so also the E. H. fem. रस्सी is really derived from the masc. रस्सा; see §§ 257. 262.

be added, as examples of what seem to be purely E. H. changes, E. H. f. आगि *fire*, Skr. m. अग्निः, Pr. m. अग्गी (Vr. 5, 18. S. R. fol. 9[b]); E. H. f. देह *body* (but S. m. डेहु), Skr. m. देहः, Pr. m. देहो (Spt. A, 63); E. H. f. सोँह् *oath*, Skr. m. शपथः or n. शपथम्, Pr. m. सवहो (Vr. 2, 15) or n. सवहं (Spt. 361); E. H. f. बिंदु or बिंदी or बूँदु or बूँदी *drop*, Skr. m. बिन्दुः, Pr. m. बिंदू or n. बिंदुं (H. C. 1, 34. S. C. 1, 1. 52); E. H. बाई *wind*, Skr. m. वायुः, Pr. m. वाऊ (Vr. 5, 18)[1]). The strong E. H. forms बिंदी (or बूँदी) and बाई seem to be diminutives (Pr. *बिंदिआ, *वाइआ) and to presuppose Pr. fem. forms *बिंदा, *वाया; just as Pr. fem. बाहा and masc. बाहू *arm*. Curious anomalies are, E. H. वस्तु *thing* (S. regularly tadbh. वथु fem. Tr. 105) and धातु *metal* (also वस्त् and धात्), which are masc., but are sometimes used as fem., though they are *tats.*, which always keep their original gender, in this case n. and m. respectively in Skr. Of words in which the gender has changed from fem. in Skr. to masc. in E. H., there is, I believe, only one; and the change took place in Pr.; viz., Skr. fem. प्रावृष् *rainy season*, Pr. m. पाउसो (Vr. 4, 18. H. C. 1, 31. S. C. 1, 1. 50), E. H. m. पाउस् or पावस्[2]). As regards the change of Skr. neut. to E. H. masc., it had already taken place in Pr., in the case of all neut. ending in the cons. न् and स् (Vr. 4, 18. H. C. 32. Wb. Bh. 404. 420); thus Skr. n. कर्म (base कर्मन्) *work*, A. Mg. m. कम्मे (Bh. 163. 167) or Mh. कम्मो, E. H. m. कम्; Skr. n. यशः *renown*, A. Mg. m. जसे (Bh. 420) or Mh. जसो, E. H. m. जस्; Skr. n. उरस् *breast*, A. Mg. m. उरे, E. H. उर्; Skr. n. पयस् *milk*, A. Mg. m. पये, E. H. m. पए or पै; Skr. n. चक्षुस् *eye*, Pr. m. चक्खू (H. C. 1, 33. S. C. 1, 1. 51, also n. चक्खुं), E. H. m. चख्, etc. Sometimes also the change took

1) E. H. f. ताँत् *string* is not = Skr. m. तन्तुः (as Bs. II, 174 after Tr. 89 says), but = Skr. f. तन्त्री. — The E. H. बाई *wind*, however, is more probably = Skr. f. वातिः.

2) The other word mentioned by the Pr. Gramm., m. सरओ = Skr. f. शरद्, occurs in E. H. only as a fem. semitats. सरद्. — There is, however, also a Skr. m. प्रावृषः.

place in the case of neut. in अ (Skr. nom. sing. अम्; see H. C. 1, 33. S. C. 1, 1. 51), especially in Mg. (Wb. Bh. 416. Ls. 399. 408. 429) and in Ap. (H. C. 4, 445. Ls. 461. 476); thus Skr. n. कुलम् *family,* Pr. n. कुलं or m. कुलो, Ap. m. कुलु (H. C. 4, 361), E. H. m. कुल्; Skr. n. दुःखम्, A. Mg. n. दुक्खं or m. दुक्खे (Bh. 190. 191), E. H. m. दुख्; Skr. n. नयनम् *eye,* Pr. n. णअणं or m. णअणो or णयणो, E. H. m. नयन् or नैन्; Skr. n. वचनम् *word,* Pr. n. वअणं or m. वअणो or वयणो, Ap. वयणु (H. C. 4, 387), E. H. बयन् or बैन्; Skr. n. लोचनम् *eye,* Pr. n. लोअणं or m. लोअणो or लोयणो, E. H. m. लोयन्; Skr. n. हृदयम् *heart,* Pr. n. हिअअं (Vr. 1, 28) or Mg. m. हिअए (Bh. 394, also हडक्के) or Mh. हिअओ (Urv. 23, 10 in Pl. Diss. 5), E. H. m. हिया; Skr. n. धनम् *wealth,* Mg. m. धणे (Vr. 11, 11) or Ap. धणु (H. C. 4, 358), E. H. m. धन्; Skr. n. शिरस् *head,* Mh. n. सिरं (H. C. 1, 32), but Ap. m. सिरु (H. C. 4, 445), E. H. m. सिर्. In Gḍ. (exc. M., G. and exceptionally W. H.) the Pr. tendency to change neut. into masc. is extended to all neut.; thus Skr. n. दाम (base दामन्) *string,* Pr. n. दामं (H. C. 1, 32), but E. H. m. दाम् (sometimes even fem.); Skr. n. गृहम् *house,* Pr. n. घर, M. n. घर्, but E. H. m. घर्; Skr. n. घृतम् *clarified butter,* Pr. n. घिअं, M. n. घीँ, but E. H. m. घी; Skr. n. दधिकम् *sour milk,* Pr. n. दहिअं, M. n. दहीँ, but E. H. m. दही; Skr. n. पानीयम् *water,* Pr. n. पाणिअं (Vr. 1, 18), M. n. पानीँ, but E. H. m. पानी; Skr. n. मौक्तिकम् *pearl,* Pr. n. मोत्तिअं (Spt. 314), M. n. मोतीँ, but E. H. m. मोती; Skr. n. मस्तकम् *head,* Pr. n. मत्थिअं, M. n. मातीँ, but E. H. m. माथी; Skr. n. सुवर्णकम् *gold,* Pr. n. सोण्णअं or सोण्णयं (cf. Spt. 194), O. H. सोनयं, M. n. सोनेँ, but E. H. m. सोना; Skr. n. अश्रुकम् *tear,* Pr. n. अंसुअं, M. n. अंसूँ, but E. H. m. आँसू (O. H. अंसुअ in Chand Devagiri 22); Skr. n. युगम् *yoke,* Pr. n. जुअं, M. n. जूँ, but E. H. m. जू or strong form जुआ; Skr. (st. f.) n. कर्त्तव्यकम् *doing,* Pr. n. करिअव्वअं, Ap. n. करेव्वउ (H. C. 4, 438) or करिव्वउं, W. H. n. करिबौँ or m. करिबो, O. m. करिबा, E. H. (wk. f.) m. करिब् or करब्.

360. *Affinities.* As regards the gender of nouns, E. H. occupies an intermediate position. The M. and G. have preserved the three genders of the Skr. and Pr. Again B. and O. distinguish

-no gender at all. But E. H. has at least two genders, masc. and fem. Generally speaking it agrees in that respect with W. H., P., S. and N.; though traces of the old neut. survive in W. H. in the infinitives in अनौँ and इबौँ or अबौँ, as indicated by the final anunásika. — All the above mentioned E. H. instances of change of gender are common to W. H. and, as a rule, to the other Gḍs. also.

3. NUMBER.

361. There are only two numbers, the singular and the plural. The plur. of nouns, which signify *rational beings,* is formed 1) generally by adding the noun लोग् *people*, without any change in the sing. noun; or 2) less commonly by using the same form of the noun as in the sing. Thus *disciples* may be either चेलालोग् or less frequently चेला, from sing. चेला; or *daughters* बेटीलोग् or बेटी, from sg. बेटी. The plur. of any other being or thing can, generally, be formed only in the second way. Thus *horses* is घोड़ा but not घोड़ालोग्; *words* is बात्, not बातलोग्, from the sing. घोड़ा and बात्. In such cases, if the noun be in the nom. case, the context must decide its number. The plural, formed with लोग्, I shall call the *compound*, the other the *simple*.

Exception. A few nouns optionally form anomalous plurals, as जन् *man*, pl. जने; मनुख् *man*, pl. मनइ.

362. The termination of the subst. suffers no change in the sing. nor in the nom. and acc. *proper* of the plur.; but in the oblique cases of the plur. the suff. अन्, इन्, उन् are added to subst. in अ or आ, इ or ई, उ or ऊ respectively. In the case of the comp. plur. they may be added either to the noun itself or, as is more common, to the plur. sign लोग्. The form thus made, I shall call the *oblique plural*; that of the obl. cases of the sing. and of the nom. and acc. *proper* of the (simple) plur., the *oblique sing.*; and that of the nom. sing., the *direct* form. See examples in § 379.

Exception. Subst. in ई, signifying *inanimate* objects, do not make the oblique plur. (with इन्) in the short, but only in the long and red. forms; see examples in § 379.

363. *Affinities.* 1) In E. H. the nom. and acc. *proper* of the simple plur. of all subst. are identical with the obl. form of the sing.; the reason of which will be explained in § 369. The same, in principle, is the case in all Gḍs., except in O. and, partially, M. In the latter the fem. and neut. subst. have a special dir. form of the plur., whilst in O. there is no simple plur. at all (exc. in the plur. sign माने, see below Nro. 2. 3). But the B. and N. are peculiar in adding to the obl. sg. a special case-affix to denote its nom.-plur.-application; viz., B. रा, N. ह्; and N. has the further peculiarity of using an archaic obl. sg. in हे or ह (see §§ 364, 3. 365, 6). Thus E. H. ob. sg. चेला, nom. pl. चेला *disciples,* W. H. obl. sg. चेले, nom. pl. चेले; B. obl. sg. चेला, nom. pl. चेला-रा, N. old obl. sg. चेलाहे or चेलाह, nom. pl. चेलाहे-ह or चेलाह-ह, etc.; for other examples see §§ 364, 3. 369, 1. — 2) The E. H. has both a simple and a comp. plur., the former for all subst., the latter (as a rule) for those only which denote *rational beings.* Formerly the O. also had, for subst. denoting rational beings, a simple plur. which, in the case of अ-bases, ended in ए (see Bs. II, 198; e. g., कुमारे pl. of कुमार *boy*); but now the comp. plur. (made with माने) only is used. For all other subst. the O. has no plur. at all (see Sn. 14). None of the other Gḍs. possess a comp. plur.; B. using the simple plur. for rational beings only (S. Ch. 44. 53); the rest of the Gḍs., for all subst. alike. The comp. plur. is made, in O. with माने, obl. f. मानन्, in E. H. with लोग्, obl. f. लोगन्. Thus nom. pl. E. H. चेला or चेला-लोग् *disciples,* O. चेला-माने; dat. pl. E. H. चेलन्-के or चेला-लोगन्-के, O. चेला-मानन्-कु. It should be observed, however, that, for the purpose of emphasizing the plur. meaning, a periphrastic plur. may be formed in all Gḍs. for any subst. whatsoever, by appending to the sing. some suitable collective noun, such as गण् *troop,* वर्ग् *class,* सकल् or सब् *all,* etc. — 3) All Gḍs. have an obl. f. of the simple plur. (see

table, below), exc. the N., B. and, apparently, G. which use the form of the nom. pl. in the obl. cases also. Thus E. H. nom. pl. चेला, obl. चेलन्; H. H. चेले, obl. चेलों, etc.; but G. nom. and obl. चेलाव्र् or (variously spelled) चेलाउ or चेलाओ. However, in G. the final anunásika (Pr. anusvára), which usually distinguishes the obl. plur. (see § 368, 6), may have been dropped. Where there is no simple plur., as in O., there can be, of course, no obl. plur. But the O. and E. H. comp. plur. signs माने and लोग् (see Nro. 2) form a regular obl. pl. मानन् and लोगन्. As to the N. and B., see § 364, 2. 3. — 4) As regards the sing., the general tendency of the Gds. is to assimilate the obl. to the dir. form. In the E. Gḍ. the assimilation is complete, no subst. (of whatever termin.) having its obl. differing from its dir. form. In W. Gḍ. (exc. S.) and N. Gḍ., it is almost complete, the only exceptions being strong nouns in आ. In S. the obl. form of masc. nouns in उ and ओ, and of com. gen. nouns in ई and ऊ is different from the direct. In S. Gḍ. the two forms differ in most nouns of whatever termination. It must, however, in all cases be understood, that the obl. f., though *now* it may outwardly be the same as the dir., is not really identical with it, but has a different origin, as will be shown in § 365. Thus nom. sg. A. Mg. सामिए or सामिश्र = dir. f. M. and E. H. सामी, or nom. sg. Mh. सामिश्रो, Ap. सामिउ = dir. f. S. सामी *lord*; and gen. sg. A. Mg. सामिश्राह् = obl. f. M. साम्या, E. H. (lg. f.) समिया; or gen. sg. Ap. सामिश्रहो or °ह = obl. f. O. H. सामिश्रह्, S. सामिश्र, W. H. and E. H. सामी. Again nom. sg. A. Mg. घोडए or घोडश्र = dir. f. M. and E. H. घोडा, or nom. sg. Mh. घोडश्रो, Ap. घोडउ = dir. f. S. घोडो; and gen. sg. A. Mg. घोडश्राह् = obl. f. M. घाड्या (for *घोडया), E. H. (lg. f.) घोड्वा; or gen. sg. Ap. घोडश्रहो or घोडश्रह् = obl. f. O. H. घोडश्रह् or O. P. घोडश्रहि, G., W. H., E. H. घोडा, P., H. H. घोड़े. — 5) The subjoined tables give a comparative view of the various terminations of the Gḍ. dir. and obl. forms. Observe, that where a form is not ascribed to any particular Gḍ., it belongs to all; and where no gender is mentioned, it is common.

Direct forms singular

of weak bases	in अ	अ; exc. S., O. H., O. P. उ m., अ f.
	in इ	इ; exc. M., H. H. ई m. n., इ or अ f.
	in उ	उ.
of strong bases	in आ	E. Gḍ., H. H., P. आ m., Br. आ or औ m., Mw., S., N. ओ m., G. ओ m., उँ n., M. आ or ऊ m., एँ or ऊँ n., O. H. ओ or अय m. अयं n.
	in ई	ई; exc. M. ई m. f., ईँ n., O. H. ई m., इय f.
	in ऊ	ऊ; exc. M. ऊ m. f., ऊँ n., G. उ c. g.

Direct forms plural in M.

of weak bases	in अ	आ f., एँ n.	of strong bases	in आ	ईँ or एँ n.
	in इ	ई f.		in ई	या f., येँ n.
	in उ	*deest*		in ऊ	वा f., वेँ n.

Oblique forms singular

of weak bases	in अ	अ; exc. B. अ or ए, M. आ m. n., ए f., O. H. अ or अह or अहि, O. P. अ or अहि.
	in इ	इ; exc. M. ई, O. H. इ or इह or इहि, O. P. इ or इहि.
	in उ	उ; exc. M. ऊ, O. H. उ or उह or उहि.
of strong bases	in आ	B., O., E. H., Mw. आ m., Br. आ or ए m., H. H., P., S. ए m., M. या or आ m. n., G. आ m., आँ n., O. H. अअह or अअहि m. n.
	in ई	ई; exc. S. इअ, M. या m. n., ये f. or ई c. g., O. H. इअह or इअहि.
	in ऊ	ऊ; exc. S. उअ, M. वा m. n., वें f. or ऊ c. g., O. H. उअह or उअहि.

Oblique forms plural

of weak bases	in अ	E. H. अन्, H. H. ओँ, Br. औँ or अन् or अनि, Mw., M. आँ, P. आँ m., ईआँ f., G. ओ, S. आँ or एँ or अनि c. g., उनि f., O. H. आन् or अन् or अन्ह or अन्हि.
	in इ	E. H. इन्, H. H. इयोँ, Br. इयौँ or इन् or इनि, Mw. याँ, P. इआँ, G. इआ, M. ईँ, S. इआँ or इएँ or इनि or इअनि or इउनि, O. H. इन् or इन्ह or इन्हि.
	in उ	E. H. उन्, H. H. उओँ, Br. उन or उनि, Mw., P. उआँ, G. उओ, S. उनि, M. ऊँ, O. H. उन् or उन्ह or उन्हि.

N. B., in B., O., N. *deest* throughout.

of strong bases (the rest as in the weak bases):

in आ | P. इयाँ m, S. आँ or एँ or अनि m., G. आत्र् (or आओ) m., आँ n., M. याँ or आँ m. n.

in ई | Br. इयौं or इयन् or इयनि or इन or इनि, P. ईआँ, G. ईओ, M. याँ or ईं.

in ऊ | Br. उओं or उअन् or उअनि or उन् or उनि, P. ऊआँ, S. उआँ or उएँ or उअनि or उनि, M. वाँ or ऊँ.

Obl. forms used as nom. plur.

of weak bases:

in अ | B. अ-रा or ए-रा, N. अहे-रु or अह-रु, E. H. अ, H. H. अ m., एँ f., Br., O. H. अ m., एं f., Mw. अ m., आँ f., P. अ m., इआँ f., S. अ m., आँ or ऊँ f., M. अ m., G. अ m., ओ c. g.

in इ | B. इ-रा, N. इहे-रु or इह-रु, E. H. इ, H. H., Br. इ m., इयाँ f., Mw. इ m., याँ f., P. इ m., इआँ f., S. इ m., इऊँ f., G. इ m., इओ c. g., M. इ c. g.

in उ | B. उ-रा, N. उहे-रु or उह-रु, E. H. उ, H. H., W. H., P. उ m. उआँ f., S. उ m., ऊँ f., G. उ m. or उओ c. g., M. उ.

N. B., in O. *deest* throughout.

of strong bases:

in आ | B. आ-रा, N. आहे-रु or आह-रु, E. H., Mw., S. आ m., H. H., P. ए m., Br. आ or ए m., G. आ or आव् m., आँ or ओँव् n., M. ए or ऊ m.

in ई | B. ई-रा, N. ईहे-रु or ईह-रु, E. H. ई, G. ईओ, H. H. ई m., इयाँ f., Br. ई m., ईं or इयाँ f., Mw. ई m., याँ f., P. ई m., ईआँ f., S. ई m., ईयूँ f., M. ई m.

in ऊ | B. ऊ-रा, N. ऊहे-रु or ऊह-रु, E. H., S. ऊ, H. H., W. H. ऊ m., उआँ f., P. ऊ m., ऊआँ f., G. ऊओ or ऊ c. g., M. ऊ m.

N. B., in O. *deest* throughout.

Note: It will be observed, that in W. Gḍ. the obl. plur. of weak nouns in इ and उ generally adopts the obl. termin. of strong nouns in ई and ऊ, and vice versa in E. H. the obl. plur. of strong nouns in आ, ई, ऊ the obl. termin. of the weak nouns in अ, इ, उ.

364. *Derivation of the plural signs.* 1) The O. माने or, shortened, मान is, probably, identical with the E. H. plur. मनइ *men* (§ 361, exc.; from Skr. मानव *man*; not मान *measure*, as Bs. II, 199), and is a plur. noun with the old termination ए, obl.

अन् (see § 363, 2). The E. H. लोग् *men* (Skr. लोक § 102) is also a plur. noun, as shown by its obl. f. लोगन् (§ 363, 2), and, like मान, is shortened for लोग. The shortened form मान is not used with rational beings (see Sn. 11). — 2) The B. is generally said to form a comp. plur. with the pl. sign दिग्, which is sometimes (see Bs. II, 200) believed to be none other than the Skr. दिक् *region, side.* But there can be little doubt, that this identification is a mistake. For a) the B. दिग ends in (quiescent) अ, while the Skr. दिक् does not; b) a final Skr. क् would not become ग् in either Pr. or Gḍ.; c) the Skr. दिक् is merely the nom. sg. of the base दिश्, while the B. दिग, if anything, is an obl. f., i. e., equal to the Skr. gen. sg. (see § 366) which is दिशः (Pr. दिसो or rather दिसाए, cf. H. C. 1, 19. 3, 30); d) the sg. दिश् (or nom. दिक्) is not a collective noun and, therefore, could not serve to form a plur.; on the other hand e) in the plur. (like माने, लोग) it would be Skr. दिशः, Pr. दिसाओ, which would not produce the B. दिग. I am inclined to believe, that दिग is not a real word, but merely a compound of two case-affixes. The ordinary B. gen. pl. ends in देर्. This I divide into दे (base) and र् (case-aff.), just as in the gen. sg.; thus देवदेर् *of gods* = देवदे-र्, just as देवेर् *of a god* = देवे-र् (see § 365, 6). Here देवदे, like देवे, is an obl. f.; its dir. f. would be देवदा (or देवद); and, in fact, the two forms, thus deduced, are the same as the P. gen. sg. देव-दा and its obl. f. देव-दे. It should be observed that the B. uses the gen. sg. to serve as a plur. base (see § 369); its nom. pl. देवे-रा *gods* is but the st. f. of its gen. sg. देवे-र् *of a god.* Similarly it uses an other (now obsolete) gen. sg. देव-दा, to serve as the pl. base of the obl. cases, which are made by adding certain case-affixes. Before the latter, as usual, the base is inflected, i. e., देव-दा becomes देव-दे, and with the gen. aff. र् it is देव-दे-र्. With the dat. aff. के it ought to be देव-दे-के; but के has a tendency to change to गे (just as in W. H. among the *Mairs* the gen. aff. are गो, गा, etc. for को, का; in N. गर् *to do* for कर्) and दे to become दि (just as the B. and E. H. dat. aff. के is in O. कि); hence it is देव-दि-गे

(or देवद्दिग्गे, as it is commonly spelled, see S. Ch. 58, with two ग्ग्, to compensate for the shortening of ए). Similarly with the loc.-aff. ते or के-ते, it is देव-द्दि-गे-ते (just as, e. g., in H. H. dat.-acc. उस-के-ताईं *to him*, lit. *up to him*). In course of time this origin was forgotten and an imaginary noun द्दिग formed, and henceforth treated like a real noun. Thus a dat. द्दिग्-के and a gen. द्दिगेरू was made. The form द्दिगेरू, however, is, according to S. Ch. 50 not commonly used in speaking, which points to a surviving consciousness on the part of the people of the unfitness of the formation. The occurrence of the ordinary P. gen.-aff. दा in B., at the two furthest extremities of the Gḍ. area, is no doubt remarcable; but it is by no means the only fact of its kind. Thus there is the same peculiar auxil. past tense in the O. थैला *he was* and in S. थिओ, P. था; and indeed the ordinary B. and O. gen.-aff. रू occurs also in the distant Mw. रो (see § 377, 1). In each case, these words are almost entirely absent in the intermediate Gḍs.; though occasionally थो and दा are met with in W. H. (see Kl. 70. 157), and था and थ्यो are the regular forms in H. H. and N. respectively, and रु occurs in the plur. of N. (see Nro. 3). It will be shown also in § 377, 3, that the B. instr.-aff. द्दिया is connected with the gen.-aff. दा. — 3) There is a close analogy between the N. and B. plur. The former is made by adding हेरु or हरु to the sing. But these plur. signs are not, as it has been supposed, nouns, but are compounded of the old gen. or obl. termin. हे or ह (see § 365, 6) and the gen.-aff. रु, which is identical with the B. gen.-aff. रू, but has preserved the old termin. उ. In fact, the N. plur. termin. हेरु is identical with the B. gen. termin. एरू and the B. plur. termin. एरा; the latter being the st. f., the other two wk. forms. Thus N. देवहे-रु or देवह-रु *gods* = B. देवे-रा (or gen. देवे-रू). The B. ए is but a contraction of the older form अहे or अहि. In the O. Gḍ. the gen. or obl. sg. in अहे or अहि or अह or (shortened) ए was used as a nom. plur. (see § 369); e. g., जने *men* = जनहि lit. *of man* scl. multitude; and in order to make it a plur. base capable of declension, the declinable gen.-aff. हृ or (st. f.) हृा (a curtailed nomin. base, § 377) was added. Thus the N. जनह्-हृ (originally a gen. sg., = Ap. Pr. जनहो केहृ) is now a plur. base, which can be regularly declined; e. g., gen. जनह्-हृ-को *of men*, dat. जनह्-हृ-लाई *to men*, etc. Similarly in B.; only instead of declining the plur. base जन-हृा, it substitutes in the obl. cases an other plur. base जन-द्रा or जन-द्र, which was also originally a gen. sg. Thus gen. जन-देृ-रृ *of men*, dat. जन-द्रि-गे *to men*, etc. But, as in the case of the B. द्रिग्, the true nature of the N. हेृ or हृ is now forgotten, and it is supposed to be a real noun; see also § 369, 1.

365. *Derivation of the obl. terminations.* It will be seen from the table of obl. termin. (§ 363), that they are divisible into two great types, of which those of the M. and S. are respectively most characteristic, and which can be best distinguished in the sing. In M. the sg. obl. forms end in a long, in S. in a short vowel. Thus M. obl. sg. (wk. f.) m. आ, f. ए, m. f. ई, m. f. ऊ, and (st. f.) m. या, वा, f. ये, वे; again obl. pl. (wk. f.) m. f. आँ, ईँ, ऊँ, and (st. f.) m. f. याँ, वाँ. But in S. obl. sg. (wk. f.) m. f. अ, इ, उ, and (st. f.) m. f. आ or ए (= अअ), इअ, उअ (or in the other Gds. contracted ई, ऊ); again obl. pl. (wk. f.) m. f. अँ or एँ (in W. H. ओँ, ओँ), and (st. f.) m. f. इआँ or इएँ, उआँ or उएँ (in W. H. इयोँ or इयोँ, उओँ or उओँ). To the S. type belong the W. and N. Gds.; to the M. type, of course, the S. Gḍ. (i. e. M.), though exceptionally, a few forms of the S. type have found admittance into M.; viz., the M. strong obl. forms in आ, ई, ऊ. The E. Gds. again are a mixture of both; for their short (incl. weak and strong) forms are of the S. type, and their long forms of the M. This double character can be best seen in E. H. — The original of the Gḍ. oblique form is the Pr. genitive (see § 366). The obl. f. of the M. type goes back to the M. gen.; that of the S. type to the Ap. gen. — 1) *Deriv. of the Mg. type.* The suff. of the gen. sg. are in Mg. Pr. स्स (or श्श = Skr. स्य) or ह (Vr. 11, 12. H. C. 4, 299), which are added indifferently to all three kinds of bases in अ, इ and उ of whatever gender (see § 367).

Before इ the final of the base is lengthened. Thus there are two sets of Mg. gen. termin.: 1) अस्स, इस्स, उस्स and 2) आह, ईह, ऊह or, with strong bases, 1) अअस्स, इअस्स, उअस्स and 2) अआह, इआह, उआह. In M. (representing the old Dk. Pr. of the Mg. Pr. type, see Introd.) the 1st set becomes (§§ 143. 147) आस, ईस्, उस् or (st. f.) यास् (for अयास् or इआस), वास् (for उआस्), and the 2nd set (dropping ह्[1])) आ, ई, ऊ or (st. f.) या (for अया or इआ), वा (for उआ). In the E. H. (= old A. Mg. Pr.) only the 2nd set occurs; viz., (lg. f.) अवा, इया, उवा (with euph. य् and व्). Both sets are preserved in the M. dat., which is identical with the old gen. (see Vr. 6, 64); thus M. देवास् or देवा *to a God* = Dk. Pr. देवस्स or देवाह, Skr. देवस्य. But, in M., the first set is also preserved in its proper gen. sense in the so-called post-position साठीं, which is really a compound of the gen. termin. स् and the post-position आठीं (= Ap. Pr. अट्ठहिं, Skr. अर्थे *for the sake of*); thus M. देवासाठीं lit. *for the sake of God*, i. e. देवास् आठीं = Dk. Pr. देवस्स अट्ठहिं, Skr. देवस्य अर्थे. The 2nd set is used as the termin. of the ordinary M. and E. H. obl. form, and as such retains its old gen. sense. Thus M. dat. देवा लाईं lit. *for the benefit of God* = Dk. देवाह लाहहिं, Skr. देवस्य लाभे; or (lg. f.) M. देव्या लाईं = Dk. देवयाह लाहहिं, Skr. देवकस्य लाभे; or E. H. dat. देववा के lit. *at the side of God*, A. Mg. देवआह कहि, Skr. देवकस्य कक्षे. — 2) The suff. of the gen. sg. of fem. nouns in आ, ई and ऊ is in Pr. ए (= Skr. यास्) or, shortened, इ or अ (Vr. 5, 22. 23. H. C. 3, 29. 30). The form अ is, evidently, the latest, whence it passed into Gd. Thus the latest Mg. Pr. gen. termin. are: आअ, ईअ, ऊअ or, with strong bases, इआअ, उआअ. In M., these become ए (for आय with euph. य्), ई and ऊ (dropping अ), and (st. f.) ये, वे (for याय, वाय); and in E. H., (lg. f.) इया, उआ or उवा (dropping अ and inserting euph.

---

1) As to the Gd. tendency to drop a final ह, see § 32. In the O. H. of Chand *shāh* king is often spelled सा, and *sīh* lion सी; e. g., करी आनि साहाब सा बन्धि गोरी, *Revataṭa* 43; or रा चावँड तेतसी *Devagiri* 51 for साहाब साह् and तेतसीह्.

यू and वू). These M. and E. H. termin. occur in their obl. forms. Thus M. obl. f. जीभे *of a tongue*, contr. for Dk. जीभाय or जिब्भाश्र or जिब्भाइ or जिब्भाए = Skr. जिह्वायाः, of M. जीभू, Dk. जिब्भा (H. C. 2, 57), Skr. जिह्वा. — 3) There are some M. strong masc. and fem. nouns in ई and ऊ, the obl. form of which ends also in ई and ऊ instead of in या m. (ये f.) and वा m. (वे f.). Thus m. विंचू *scorpion* has obl. f. विंचवा or विंचू; m. हत्ती *elephant* has obl. f. हत्ती (not हत्त्या); f. घोडी *mare* has obl. f. घोडी, (not घोड्ये), f. सासू *mother-in-law* has obl. f. सासवे and सासू. It is just possible, that here ई and ऊ may be contractions of या, ये and वा, वे respectively; but it is much more probable that they are Ap. Pr. forms which have been mixed up in M. with Dk. Pr. forms (see Nro 6)[1]). The same remarks apply to the E. Gd. obl. forms in श्रा, ई, ऊ of short-form nouns in श्रा, ई, ऊ. Thus E. H. obl. f. घोरा *of a horse* might be contracted from A. Mg. gen. घोडश्राह; but it is much more probably a contraction of the Ap. Pr. घोडश्रहो. — 4) The suff. of the gen. pl. are in Mg. Pr. णं or ण (Vr. 5, 4. 4, 16. H. C. 3, 6. 1, 29 = Skr. नाम्) and हँ (H. C. 4, 300), which are added indifferently to bases in श्र, इ and उ of whatever gender (see § 367), and before which the final of the base is lengthened. Thus there are two sets of Mg. Pr. termin.: 1) श्राणं, ईणं, ऊणं and 2) श्राहँ, ईहँ, ऊहँ, or, with strong bases, 1) श्रश्राणं, इश्राणं, उश्राणं and 2) श्रश्राहँ, इश्राहँ, उश्राहँ. In M. the 1st set becomes श्राँना, ईँना, ऊँना[2]) or (st. f.) याँना (for श्रयान or इश्रान), वाँना

---

1) That both the Mg. and Ap. gen. have contributed to the M. obl. forms, can be clearly seen from the following example: Skr. nom. घोटकः, gen. घोटकस्य becomes, in M., nom. घोडा, obl. घोड्या; analogously Skr. वर्त्मसरकः should be, in M., nom. वाटसरा, obl. वाटसर्या, but it becomes वाटसरू, obl. वाटसरा. The reason is, that the former represent Mg. forms: nom. घोडए, gen. घोडश्राह; the latter Ap. forms: nom. वट्टसरउ, gen. वट्टसरश्रह or °हो.

2) These forms are usually divided into श्राँ + ना, ईँ + ना, ऊँ + ना, and ना is considered to be an aff., and the rest to be the ordinary obl. f. This is possible, as ना might be a modification of the ordinary M. dat. aff. ला, analogous to the G. sg. and pl. dat. aff. ने. But in that case,

(for उश्रान), and the 2nd set becomes (by elision of ह् and contraction of the hiatus-vowels) श्राँ, ईँ, ऊँ or (st. f.) याँ (for श्रयाँ or इश्राँ), वाँ (for उश्राँ). In E. H. the first set becomes (by shortening the initial vowel) श्रन्, इन्, उन्, or (lg. f.) श्रवन्, इयन्, उश्रन्, and the 2nd set (lg. f.) श्रवाँ, इयाँ, उश्राँ (with euph. व् and य्). In O. H. (Chand and Kabir), however, examples of the 1st set with a long vowel still occur; e. g., महिलानं *of women*, द्रव्यान *of riches*, गुरून *to teachers* (Bs. II, 219. 207. 282). In M., the 1st set is, just as in the sing., preserved in the dat. (= old gen.); thus M. देवाँना *to Gods* = Dk. देवाणं, Skr. देवानाम्. In E. H. the 1st set forms the termin. of the ordinary obl. pl., with the sense of the gen.; e. g., loc. देवन् मे lit. *in the midst of Gods* = A. Mg. देवाण मज्झि, Skr. देवानां मध्ये. The 2nd set forms the termin. of the ordinary obl. pl. in M: and obl. sg. in E. H.[1]), also retaining the sense of the gen.; e. g., loc. M. देवाँ ठाईँ lit. *in the place of Gods* = Dk. देवाहँ ठाणाहिं, Skr. देवानां स्थाने, or (lg. f.) M. देव्याँ ठाँईं = Dk. देवयाहँ ठाणाहिं, Skr. देवकानां स्थ°; or (lg. f.) E. H. देववाँ मे *in a God* = A. Mg. देवश्राहँ मज्झि, Skr. देवकानां मध्ये. — 5) The masc. nouns in ई and ऊ, mentioned in Nro. 3 as having an obl. sg. in ई and ऊ for या, वा, similarly have an obl. pl. in ईँ and ऊँ, which might be contractions of याँ and वाँ, but more probably are Ap. forms (see Nro. 7). Thus हत्ती *elephant* has obl. pl. हत्तीँ (not हत्त्याँ), विंचू *scorpion* has obl. pl. विंचवाँ or विंचूँ. — 6) *Deriv. of the S. type.* The suff. of the gen. sg. are, in the Ap. Pr., हो and हे or, shortened, हु or हि (H. C. 4, 338. 336. 351 and 4, 350. 341. 352. K. I. 30. 34. 36. 35. 29 in Ls. 451. 462), which are added alike to bases in श्र, इ, उ of whatever gender (see § 367). Thus there are two sets of Ap. termin.; viz. 1) श्रहो, इहो, उहो or श्रहु, इहु, उहु

---

one would expect ना to be used also in the sg., which is not the case. On the whole, I think it more probable, that the whole is *one* suff., to which, however, a mistaken popular etymology has given an anomalous final श्रा; the forms ought to be श्राँन, ईँन, ऊँन.

1) This confusion of sg. and pl. forms may be also otherwise observed in Gḍ., see § 367, 5.

and 2) अहे, इहे, उहे or अहि, इहि, उहि or, with strong bases, 1) अअहो, इअहो, उअहो or अअहु, इअहु, उअहु and 2) अअहे, इअहे, उअहे or अअहि, इअहि, उअहि. In old Gd. (O. H., O. P.) the 1st set becomes अह, इह, उह or (dropping ह) अ, इ, उ, and the 2nd set अहि or ए (contr. for अहि = अइ), इहि, उहि, or in strong bases, 1) अअह, इअह, उअह or आ (for अअ), इअ, उअ, and 2) अअहि or आय (for अअइ) or ऍ or ए, इअहि, उअहि. The 1st set (in ह) is still found in the O. W. H. of Chand, the 2nd set (in हि) in the O. P. of the Granth (see Tr. A. Gr. CXXVI), in the O. H. of Kabir, Tulsí Dás, etc. and in the O. B. of Vidyápati, etc., in their proper sense of the gen. sg.; e. g., गोचार परह चारै सु गोइ । *a herdsman tends the cattle of an other* (Chand 28, 62), or बोल बोलहु अविचारह । *you speak a speech of inconsiderateness* (Ch. 28, 50), or चहुवानह पास । *by the side of the Chahuván* (Ch. 28, 33). Again राम नाम लै बेराधारा ऽ सो तै ले संसारहि पारा ॥ i. e., *so thou mayest reach the farther shore of the world* (Kabir Ram. 75, 3), or जीवहि मरन न होइ ॥ i. e., *of the soul there is no dying* (Kabir Ram. 22, 6). Again प्रपाऊँ पुर नर नारि बहोरी । ममता जिन पर प्रभुहि न थोरी ॥ i. e., *concerning which the pride of the Lord is not small* (Tulsí Dás, Bal. 10), or होइहि संतत पियहि पियारी ॥ *there will be offspring of the beloved one of the beloved* (T. Dás, Bal. 26), or को गुण दोषहि करै विचारा ॥ i. e., *who takes account of virtue and vice* (T. Dás, Bal. 30). In the sense of the dat. (= old gen.) हि is very common in O. H. [1]); thus रंगअवनि सत्र मुनिहि दिखाई ॥ i. e., *he showed all the decorations to the sage* (T. Dás. Bal.), or आपु जुवराजपद रामहि देउ ॥ i. e., *give the heir-apparentship to Rám* (T. Dás Ayodh. 5); also in O. B., e. g., आनहि *to another* (see Bs. II, 229). Both ह and हि also occur as the termin. of the obl. f.; e. g., कह्यौ सम पान ततारह । *he spoke with the Khán Tartár* (Chand 28, 58), or तत्तारह उप्परह । *upon the Tartár* (Ch. 29, 19); or आदिहि ते सत्र कथा सुनाई *he narrated the whole story from the beginning* (T. Dás

---

1) Also often in the sense of the acc. (= dat. = old gen.); e. g., बहु विधि राम शिवहि समुकावा । परवती कर जन्म सुनावा ॥ i. e., *in many ways Rám admonished Shiva and narrated the story of the birth of Parvati* (T. Dás, Bal. 26), etc. See also Kl. 65. 283. 286 and § 367, 3,

in Bs. II, 212). These examples contain also instances of the curtailed form of the gen.; thus राम नाम लै *taking the name of Ráma*, प्रणाऊँ पुर नर नारि *I salute the men and women of the town*, पियारी संतत (for पियारिश्र) *offspring of the beloved one*, etc. In modern Gḍ. both sets occur only in their curtailed forms (with one exception in N., see below): 1) श्र, इ, उ and 2) ए or, in strong bases, 1) श्रा, इश्र or ई, उश्र or ऊ and 2) श्राय् or ऐ or ए. The 2nd set is still preserved in the B. and O. dat. (= old gen.; especially in words denoting inanimate objects; but generally in poetry and *ṭheṭh bháshá*; see S. Ch. 46, 2. 59, 4. 62. 63. Sn. 14. 15); thus B. and O. घरे *to a house* = O. Gḍ. घरहि, Ap. Pr. घरहे, Skr. गृहस्य; B. दीने *to the poor*, O. Gḍ. दीनहि, Ap. दीणहे, Skr. दीनस्य; B. तामाय् *to copper*, O. Gḍ. तामाहि or तामश्रहि, Ap. तम्वश्रहे, Skr. ताम्रकस्य, etc. But both sets are used in all Gḍs. (with the exceptions in Nros 1—5) as the ordinary termin. of the obl. sg., and as such retain their old gen. sense. They are distributed among the various Gḍs. in the following manner. The contracted weak form ए is confined to the gen. and loc. sg. and nom. pl. of B.; thus B. gen. sg. देवे-र lit. *done of God*, O. Gḍ. देवहि कर, Ap. देवहे केरु, Skr. देवस्य कृतः (see § 377); loc. sg. देवेते *in God*; nom. pl. देवे-रा *Gods*, O. Gḍ. देवहि करा, Ap. देवहे केरउ, Skr. देवस्य कृतकः scl. सङ्घः (see § 364, 2). N. has preserved even the full old form (in हे or ह) in its nom. pl.; thus N. देवह-रु or देवहे-रु *Gods*, O. Gḍ. देवह करु, Ap. देवहे or °हो केरु, Skr. देवस्य कृतः (scl. सङ्घः). The contr. st. f. श्रा occurs in B., O., Mw. and G.; E. H. has श्रा and ए, Br. श्रा and ऐ (i. e. श्रा in subst., ए or ऐ in adj.); P. and S. have ए; thus gen. sg., B., O. घोडा-र, Mw. घोडा-रो, E. H. घोरा कै, Br. घोडा कौ, G. घोडा नो, P. घोडे दा, S. घोडे जो *of a horse*, O. Gḍ. घोडश्रह or °हि करौ or केरौ, Ap. घोडश्रहो or °ह केरउ, Skr. घोटकस्य कृतकः; again E. H. भले कै, Br. भलै कौ *of good*, O. H. भल्लश्रहि क°, Ap. भल्लश्रहे क°, Skr. भद्रकस्य क°. The uncontr. st. f. इश्र and उश्र are possessed by S. only; the contr. ई and ऊ by all other Gḍs.; thus loc. sg., E. H. etc. हाथी मे, but S. हथिश्र मे॑ lit. *in the midst of the elephant*, O. Gḍ. हथिश्रह माँहो॑, Ap. हत्थिश्रहो मज्झहिं, Skr. हस्तिकस्य मध्ये; or E. H. etc. बिछू मे, but

S. विछुअ में in the midst of the scorpion, O. Gḍ. बिछुअह म°, Ap. विच्छुअहो म°, Skr. वृश्चिकस्य म°, etc. The weak forms अ, इ, उ are common to all Gḍs; thus dat. sg., O. नर कु, B., E. H. नर के, Br. नर कौं, Mw. नर नै, G. नर ने, P. नर नूं, N. नर लाई, S. नर खे lit. *by the side of the man,* Skr. नरस्य कक्षे. — 7) The suff. of the gen. plur. are, in the Ap. Pr., हं, हुं and हिं (H. C. 4, 339. 340. 337. cf. 347. 351. K. I. 31. 32. 28 in Ls. 451), which are added indifferently to bases in अ, इ, उ of whatever gender (§ 367). Thus there are three sets of Ap. Pr. termin.: 1) अहं, इहं, उहं, 2) अहुं, इहुं, उहुं, 3) अहिं, इहिं, उहिं or, with strong bases, 1) अअहं, इअहं, उअहं, 2) अअहुं, इअहुं, उअहुं, 3) अअहिं, इअहिं, उअहिं. In O. H. the 3[d] set is still found in the sense of the dat. (= old. gen.); thus मातुपितहिं पुनि यह मत भावा *this counsel, again, pleased (her) parents* (T. Dás. in Kl. 286); or दीन्ह असीस सबहिं सुखमानी *he gave a blessing to all of happy import* (T. Dás, Bal.); or जो तुम्हहिं सुता पर नेहू। lit. *if to you there is love for your daughter* or *if there is love of you for your daughter*[1]). In modern Gḍ., ह is elided and the hiatus-vowels contracted; thus 1) आँ, ईं, ऊँ, 2) औं or ओं, (इहुं deest), ऊँ, 3) ऐं or एँ, ईं, (उहिं deest) or, in strong bases, 1) आँ, इयाँ or याँ, उआँ or वाँ, 2) औं or ओं, इयौं or इयों or इयूँ, उओं or उओं or ऊँ, 3) ऐं or एँ, इएँ or ईं, उएँ. Most of these forms serve as the termin. of the ordinary obl. plur., and, as such, retain their original gen. sense. They are distributed among the various Gḍs., as follows. The forms आँ (wk. or st.), इयाँ or याँ, उआँ or वाँ occur in S., P. and Mw.; the forms औं or ओं (wk. or st.), इयौं or इयों, उऔं or उओं in Br. and H. H.; the forms एँ (wk. or st.), इएँ, उएँ in S., and the st. forms ईं and ऊँ in M. Thus loc. pl.; S., P., Mw. नराँ में lit. *in the midst of men,* Ap. णरहं मज्झहिं, Skr. नराणां मध्ये; Br. नरौं में, H. H. नरों में, Ap.

---

1) Also often in the sense of the acc. (= dat. = old gen.); e. g., तब रामहिं बिलोकि बैदेही *then Vaidehí having beheld Ráma* (T. Dás, Bal.); रामहिं is here the plur. majestatis; but the pl. हिं is often used for the sg. हि, see § 367, 5.

नरहुं म°; S. नरें में, Ap. णरहिं म°; or in st. f., S., P., Mw. घोड़ाँ में *in the midst of horses*, Ap. घोडग्रहं मज्झहिं, Skr. घोटकानां मध्ये; Br. घोड़ों में, H. H. घोड़ों में, Ap. घोडग्रहुं म°; S. घोड़ें में, Ap. घोडग्रहिं म°, etc. Again M. dat. pl. हत्ती ला lit. *for the benefit of elephants*, Ap. हत्थिग्रहिं लाहि, Skr. हस्तिकानां लाभे, etc. The rest of the forms are used as termin. of the nom. pl.; see § 369[1]). — 8) I add a few more examples to illustrate the preceding remarks: *Weak bases in* अ: masc. or neut., जल *water*; gen. sg., Skr. जलस्य, 1) Mg. Pr. (a) जलस्स or (b) जलाह, M. (a) जलास् or (b) जला; 2) Ap. Pr. (c) जलहो or (d) जलहे, O. Gḍ. (c) जलह or (d) जलहि, M. Gḍ. (c) जल (in all) or (d) जले (in B. and O.). Fem. जिह्वा *tongue*, gen. sg. Skr. जिह्वायाः, 1) Mg. Pr. (a) जिब्भाए or जिब्भाइ or जिब्भाग्र or जिब्भाय (with euph. य्), M. (a) जिभे; 2) Ap. Pr. (b) जिब्भहो or (c) जिब्भहे, O. Gḍ. (b) जीभह or (c) जीभहि, M. Gḍ. (b) जोभ (in all) or (c) जीभे (in B., O.). *Gen. plur.*, Skr. जलानाम्, जिह्वानाम्, 1) Mg. Pr. (a) जलाणां, जिब्भाणां or (b) जलाहँ, जिब्भाहं, M. (a) जलाँना, जिभाँना or (b) जलाँ, जिभाँ, E. H. (a) जलन्, जीभन्, Br. (a) जलन् or जलनि, जीभन् or जोभनि, S. (a) जलनि, जीभुनि; 2) Ap. Pr. (c) जलहं, जिब्भहं or (d) जलहुं, जिब्भहुं or (e) जलहिं, जिब्भहिं, O. H. (e) जलहिं, जिब्भहिं, S., P., Mw. (c) जलाँ, जिभाँ, Br. (d) जलों, जीभों, H. H. (d) जलों, जोभों, S. (d) जलें, जिभें. — *Strong bases in* अ: masc. or neut., ताम्रक *copper*; gen. sg., Skr. ताम्रकस्य, 1) Mg. Pr. (a) तम्बयस्स or (b) तम्बयाह (with euph. य्); M. (a) ताँब्यास् or (b) ताँब्या, E. H. (lg. f.) (b) तामवा (with euph. व्); 2) Ap. Pr. (c) तम्बग्रहो or (d) तम्बग्रहे, O. Gḍ. (c) ताँबाह or (d) ताँबाहि, O., E. H. (c) तामा, W. H., N., G. (c) ताँबा, B. (c) तामा or (d) तामाय्, P., H. H. (d) ताँबे, S. (d) टामे. *Fem.*, see fem. strong bases in इ. *Gen. plur.*, Skr. ताम्रकानाम्, 1) Mg. Pr. (a) तम्बयाणां or (b) तम्बयाहँ, M. (a) ताँब्याँना or (b) ताँब्याँ, E. H. (lg. f.) (a) तामवन् (with euph. व्) or (b) तामवाँ (but used in the sg.); E. H. has also the anomalous short form तामन्, Br. ताँबन् or ताँबनि, S. टामनि; 2) Ap. Pr. (c) तम्बग्रहं or (d) तम्बग्रहुं or (e) तम्बग्रहिं, P., Mw. (c) ताँबाँ, S. (c) टामाँ, Br. (d) ताँबों, H. H. (d) ताँबों, S. (e) टामें. *Fem.*, see fem. strong

1) Some of them are also used to form the loc., instr. and abl. sg. or pl. in S., P. and M.; see §§ 367, 2. 376, 3. 378, 3.

bases in इ. — *Weak bases in* इ: masc. or neut., कवि *poet.*; gen. sg., Skr. कवेः (lit. कविस्य); 1) Mg. Pr. (a) कविश्श or (b) कवीह, M. (a) कवीस् or (b) कवी; 2) Ap. Pr. (c) कविहो or (d) कविहे, O. Gd. (c) कविह or (d) कविहि, M. Gd. (c) कवि (in all). *Fem.* भित्ति *wall*; gen. sg., Skr. भित्त्याः or भित्तेः (lit. भित्तिस्य); 1) Mg. Pr. (a) भित्तिश्श or (b) भित्तीह, M. (a) भीँतीस् or (b) भीँती; 2) Ap. Pr. (c) भित्तिहो or (d) भित्तिहे, O. Gd. (c) भीतिह or (d) भीतिहि. P., S. (c) भिति, B., O., E. H., W. H., G. भीत. *Gen. plur.*, Skr. कवीनाम्, भित्तीनाम्; 1) Mg. Pr. (a) कवीणं, भित्तीणं or (b) कवीहँ, भित्तीहँ, M. (a) कवीँना, भीँतीँना or (b) कवीँ, भीँतीँ, E. H. (a) कविन्, भीतिन्, Br. कविन् or कविनि, भीतिन् or भीतिनि, S. कविनि, भितिनि or (lg. f.) भितिअनि or भितिउनि; 2) Ap. Pr. (c) कविहं, भित्तिहं or (d) कविहुं, भित्तिहुं or (e) कविहिं, भित्तिहिं, O. H. (c) कविहिं, भीतिहिं, in M. Gd.; only the long forms occur; viz. Ap. Pr. (c) कविअहं, भित्तिअहं or (d) कविअहुं, भित्तिअहुं or (e) कविअहिं, भित्तिअहिं, Mw., P., S. (c) कवियाँ, Br. (d) कवियौँ, H. H. (d) कवियोँ, भीतियोँ, S. (c) कविएँ, भित्तिएँ. — *Strong bases in* इ: masc. or neut., मालिक *gardener*; gen. sg., Skr. मालिकस्य; 1) Mg. Pr. (a) मालिअश्श or (b) मालिआह, M. (a) माल्यास् or (b) माल्या, E. H. (lg. f.) (b) मलिया; 2) Ap. Pr. (c) मालिअहो or (d) मालिअहे, O. Gd. (c) मालिअह or (d) मालिअहि, S. (c) मालिअ, E. H. etc. (c) माली. *Fem.* घोटिका *mare*; gen. sg., Skr. घोटिकायाः, Ap. Pr. (a) घोडिअहो or (b) घोडिअहे, O. Gd. (a) घोडिअह or (b) घोडिअहि, S. (a) घोडिअ, E. H., M., etc. (a) घोडी. The Mg. forms exist only in M. monosyllabic words and E. H. long forms: as स्त्रिका *woman*; gen. sg., Skr. स्त्रिकायाः, Mg. *स्त्रियाए or *स्त्रियाइ or *स्त्रियाय, M. स्त्रिये, E. H. स्त्रिया (tats.); similarly E. H. (lg. f.) घोरिया. *Gen. plur.*, Skr. मालिकानाम्, घोटिकानाम्; 1) Mg. Pr. (a) मालिआणं, घोडिआणं or (b) मालिआहँ, घोडिआहँ, M. (a) माल्याँना, घोड्याँना or (b) माल्याँ, घोड्याँ, E. H. (lg. f.) (a) मलियन्, घोरियन् or (b) मलियाँ, घोरियाँ (but used in the sing.); Br. (a) मालियनि, घोड़ियनि, S. (a) मालिअनि or माल्यनि or मलिउनि or माल्युनि, घोडिअनि or घोडिउनि, etc.; E. H. has also the anomalous short forms मालिन्, घोरिन्, Br. and S. मालिनि, घोड़िनि; 2) Ap. Pr. (c) मालिअहं, घोडिअहं or (d) मालिअहुं, घोडिअहुं or (e) मालिअहिं, घोडिअहिं, S. (a) मालिआँ or माल्याँ, घोड़िआँ or घोड़्याँ, Mw. (a) माल्याँ, घोड्याँ, P. (a) मालीआँ, घोड़ीआँ

(with anomalous ई), Br. (d) मालियौँ, घोड़ियौँ, H. H. (d) मालियोँ, घोड़ियोँ, S. (e) मालिएँ, घोडिएँ. — *Weak bases in* उ: masc. or neut., गुरु *teacher*; gen. sg., Skr. गुरोः (lit. गुरुस्य); 1) Mg. Pr. (a) गुलुअश्श or (b) गुलूह, M. (a) गुरूस्य or (b) गुरू; 2) Ap. Pr. (c) गुरुहो or (d) गुरुहे, O. Gḍ. (c) गुरुह or (d) गुरुहि, M. Gḍ. (c) गुरु (in all). *Fem.* like masc. *Gen. plur.*, Skr. गुरूणाम्; 1) Mg. Pr. (a) गुलूणं or (b) गुलूहँ, M. (a) गुरूँना or (b) गुरूँ, E. H. (a) गुरुन्, Br. (a) गुरुन् or गुरुनि, S. (a) गुरुनि; 2) short forms *desunt* in Gḍ.; in their place the long forms are used: Ap. Pr. (c) गुरुअहं or (d) गुरुअहुं or (e) गुरुअहिं, P. (c) गुरुआँ, Mw. (c) गुर्वाँ, Br. (d) गुरुऔँ, H. H. (d) गुरुओँ, O. H. (e) गुरुहिं or गुरुअहिं. *Fem.* like masc. — *Strong bases in* उ: masc. or neut., वृश्चिक *scorpion*; gen. sg., Skr. वृश्चिकस्य; 1) Mg. Pr. (a) विच्छुअश्श or (b) विच्छुआह, M. (a) विंचूास् or (b) विंचूा, E. H. (lg. f.) (b) बिछुआ or बिछुवा; 2) Ap. Pr. (c) विच्छुअहो or (d) विच्छुअहे, O. Gḍ. (c) बिछुअह or (d) बिछुअहि, S. (c) बिछुअ, E. H. (c) बिछू, M. (c) विंचू. *Fem.* वालुका *sand*; gen. sg., Skr. वालुकायाः; 1) Mg. Pr. (a) वालुआए or वालुआइ or वालुआय, M. (a) वालूे, E. H. (lg. f.) (a) बलुआ or बलुवा; 2) Ap. Pr. (b) वालुअहो or (c) वालुअहे, O. Gḍ. (b) बालुअह or (c) बालुअहि, S. (b) वालुअ, E. H., etc. बालू. *Gen. plur.*, Skr. वृश्चिकानाम्; 1) Mg. Pr. (a) विच्छुआणं or (b) विच्छुआहँ, M. (a) विचूाँना or (b) विंचूाँ, E. H. (lg. f.) (a) बिछुअन् or (b) बिछुआँ (but used in the sing.), Br. बिछुअन् or बिछुअनि, S. बिछुअनि; E. H. has also the anomalous short form बिछुन्, Br. and S. बिछुनि; 2) Ap. Pr. (c) विच्छुअहं or (d) विच्छुअहुं or (e) विच्छुअहिं, P. and S. (c) बिछुआँ, Mw. (c) बिछूाँ, Br. (d) बिछुऔँ, H. H. (d) बिछुओँ, S. (e) बिछुएँ. *Fem.* like masc. — G. is peculiar in dropping the final anunásika in the obl. plur. of masc. and fem. nouns; e. g., G. obl. pl. देवो *Gods* for *देवोँ, Ap. देवहुं; fem. जीभो *tongues* for *जीभोँ, Ap. जिब्भहु; again in strong bases: G. masc. obl. pl. घोडाव or घोडाउ [1])

---

1) These forms are sometimes spelled with final ओ, as घोडाओ (so in Ed. 36. Bs. II, 189); the really correct spelling is with उ or व्, as written for me by a Paṇḍit. But it is quite customary now in Gḍ., to spell the same final sound as उ or व् or ओ; thus in W. H. देउ or देव् or देओ *god*, चढाउ or चढाव् or चढाओ *attack*.

horses for *घोडाउँ, Ap. घोडग्रहुं; fem. पोथीउ *books*, Ap. पोत्थिग्रहु. According to H. C. 4, 351, even in the Ap. Pr., fem. nouns have no final anuswára. But G. retains it in neut. nouns; e. g., G. obl. pl. सोनाँवू or सोनाँउ, Ap. सोणग्रहुं. On the other hand, it adds it anomalously in the sg. neut.; as G. obl. sg. सोनाँ *gold* for *सोना, Ap. सोणग्रहो.

366. *Origin of the obl. form.* 1) The Gḍ. obl. f. is identical with the Skr. and Pr. gen. case. For a) it has been already shown (§ 365) that the suff. of the former can be phonetically traced back to those of the latter. b) It will be shown in §§ 375—378, that the Gḍ. case-affixes are, in reality, nouns (generally in the loc. case); as such they must be constructed with the gen. of the noun, which they govern; hence it follows that the obl. f., in which the latter is always put, when it takes a case-aff., must be the old gen.; e. g., E. H. नरन् मे वाटै *he is in the midst of men*, O. H. नरन्ह महि वाटै, Pr. नराणं मज्झि वट्टइ, Skr. नराणां मध्ये वर्त्तते. c) Pr. Gramm. state expressly (H. C. 4, 422. T. V. 3, 3. 56) that the word केर, which is the same as the E. H. gen. aff. कै or कर or O. H. केर, is constructed with the gen., whence it follows that the obl. form, with which those gen. aff. are constructed, is the old gen. d) It can be shown, that Pr. has a tendency to substitute the gen. in the place of all other obl. cases and to make it the *one, universal inflexion.* This proves that the obl. form, which is the one, universal inflexion in Gḍ., must be the old gen. In Pr. this is but an other instance of its general tendency to produce uniformity of grammatical forms. Two instances of this have been already noticed; the one in regard to roots (§ 347), the other referring to bases (§ 205). Here we have a third instance, affecting the *cases.* In Skr. there are, generally, seven cases or inflexions: the nom., acc., instr., dat., abl., gen., loc. In Pr. the dat. has (almost) entirely disappeared, and its place been taken by the gen. (Vr. 6, 64. H. C. 3, 131); but there is a tendency to substitute the gen. for the other obl. cases also, so as to leave only two inflexions, the nom. and gen. This is

expressly stated by Pr. Gramm. (H. C. 3, 134. T. V. 2, 3. 39). In the Ap. Pr. that process of substitution is especially marked. Its gen. suff. are expressly stated to form the abl. (compare H. C. 4, 336. 337. 341. 351 with 4, 338. 340) and the loc. (H. C. 4, 340) also [1]). In Gḍ. there are only two inflexions left, the direct form or nomin., and the obl. form or gen. But in order to obviate the necessary ambiguity of this uniformity, Gḍ. adds different affixes to the obl. form, to indicate the particular *case*, in the sense of which the obl. form is to be understood. Thus the obl. form with कै means the gen., with से the instr., with मे the loc., etc. In this way the original seven cases are re-established in Gḍ. — 2) It should be observed, however, that since there are in the Ap. Pr. several gen. suff. for the sing. (हो and हे) and the plur. (हं, हुं, हिं), several obl. forms are possible in the Gḍs. and do actually exist in most of them. In the latter case, one of them is used as the *general* obl. form and always constructed with case-aff.; but the other constitutes a *special* obl. form for one or, at most, two cases, and, as a rule, takes no affix. Thus there is in G. and Mw. the *general* obl. f. sg. in आ = Ap. gen. in अहो, and the *special* obl. f. sg. in ऐ or ए = Ap. gen. in अहे; e. g., G. instr. घोडा पो or घोडे *by a horse*; Mw. loc. घोडा माँ or घोडै *in a horse*. — 3) It is curious to observe that the levelling process noted just now, has a tendency, both in the Ap. and in Gḍ., to reduce the whole declension to *one inflexion*, by substituting (§ 369) the obl. form even for the dir. form or nom. case. The cause, possibly, was their similarity; thus in the Ap. the nom. sg. would be देवओ or देवउ *god* (Skr. देवकः), the gen. sg. देवहो or देवहु; whence, by inserting an euph. ह in the nom., the two forms would be easily assimilated.

---

1) Exceptionally all these cases are preserved in Pr.; thus the dat. sg. in the sense of „for the sake of" (H. C. 3, 132. 133), as देवाय *for the sake of god*; in the Ap. Pr., the abl. sg. in आहु or आउ (Ls. 461), and the loc. sg. in इ (H. C. 4, 334 = Skr. ए). The abl. sg. in आउ survives even in S. poetry (Tr. 118).

367. *Distribution of the Pr. gen. suff.* The ordinary Pr. suff. of the gen. sg. is स्स and of the pl. णं. There are also the suff., sg. ह, pl. हँ which are peculiar to Mg., and sg. हो or हे, pl. हं, हुं or हिं which are peculiar to Ap. 1) The ordinary Pr. suff. are derived from the Skr. sg. स्य, pl. नाम् (i. e. न् + आम्). In Skr., नाम् is added to all three kinds of bases in अ, इ and उ; but स्य is added only to अ-bases. In Pr. both णं and स्स, and similarly the special suff. ह, हं, etc., are added to all three kinds. In Vr. 5, 8. H. C. 3, 10 स्स and णं are apparently limited to *a*-bases, but the succeeding rules Vr. 6, 60. H. C. 3, 124 extend them to *i*- and *u*-bases also; and this is born out by Pr. literature. Hence there can be no doubt, that the Mg. ह and हँ and the Ap. हो, though apparently limited by H. C. 4, 299. 300. 338 to *a*-bases, in reality belong to *i*- and *u*-bases also. This is born out by the evidence of modern Gd.; and, moreover, it is expressly affirmed by K. I. and Md. Thus H. C. 4, 336. 338 gives हो to the gen. and abl. of masc. (always incl. neut.) *a*-bases; and हे to the abl. of masc. *i*- and *u*-bases (4, 341)[1]). Again K. I. (30. 34 in Ls. 451. 462) gives हो to the gen. of all masc. bases and to the abl. of masc. *i*- and *u*-bases; and हे (29. 36) to the abl. of all masc. bases and to the gen. of masc. *a*-bases. Again both H. C. (4, 350) and K. I. (35) give हे to the gen. and abl. of all fem. bases. Lastly Md. gives both हो and हे to the abl. of all masc. and fem. bases[2]). These conflicting statements really supplement each other, as shown by modern Gd. It should be remembered, 1) that the abl. and gen. are identical in Ap. Pr. (as, indeed, they ge-

1) H. C. 4, 336 gives हु as the abl. suff. of *a*-bases, but this is merely a shortening of हो, which is given by Md. (see next footnote). As to the gen. of *i*- and *u*-bases, H. C. is silent; which seems to indicate, that it may be हो by the analogy of *a*-bases, and हे by the usual identity of the gen. and abl. of cases.

2) Md. says: ङसेस्तु हे हो च ॥ ङसेः स्थाने हेहौ च स्यातां ॥ रुक्खहे पडिदु । रुक्खहो ॥ (अग्गिहे) । अग्गिहो ॥ बालाहे । बालाहो ॥ i. e., *the abl. sg. has* हे *or* हो, *as „he is fallen from a tree, from fire, from a girl"*. On the gen., I cannot find any rule; which would seem to show that it is identical with the abl.

nerally are even in Skr.), and 2) that the Ap., no doubt, varied slightly in the localities of the different grammarians. The general result is, that in the Ap. Pr. both हो and है were used to form both the gen. and abl. of all bases in *a*, *i*, *u*, whether masc., fem., or neut. — The case of the Ap. plur. suff. हं and हुं is similar. In H. C. 4, 339. 340 हं is ascribed to the gen. and हुं to the abl. (4, 337. 341) of all masc. bases, and हुं (4, 340) also to the gen. of masc. bases in *i* and *u*. Again K. I. (31. 32) gives हं to the gen. of all masc. bases and to the abl. (33) of masc. bases in *i* and *u*, and हुं to the abl. (28) of masc. bases in *a*. Lastly Mḍ. allows both हं and हुं to all masc., both in the gen. and abl. [1]). As regards the fem. bases, both K. I. and Mḍ. are silent, which really means, that their gen. and abl. do not differ from those of the masc. (and neut.). This is confirmed by H. C. 4, 351, who gives to the fem. gen. and abl. the suff. हु, which is either the same as the sg. gen. and abl. suff. हु or हो (H. C. 4, 336. 338), or identical with the pl. gen. and abl. suff. हुं dropping the anuswára. The general result again is, that in the Ap. Pr. both हं and हुं are used to form both the gen. and abl. pl. of all bases in *a*, *i*, *u*, whether masc., fem., or neut. And this is born out by the state of the modern Gḍs. — 2) As to the Ap. pl. suff. हिं, both H. C. (4, 347) and Mḍ. [2]) ascribe it to the loc. and instr. plur. K. I., by his silence (Ls. 463), probably implies the same thing; since हिं was already the instr. pl. suff. in the Mh. Pr. (Vr. 5, 18). But it appears to have been used also for the gen. plur. This is, perhaps, the true reading

1) Mḍ. says: हंहुं भ्यसः ॥ भ्यसो हंहुमो स्यातां ॥ रुक्खहं पडिदु ॥ परहुं चलिदु ॥ वाहुल्यात् । रुक्खाहिंतो । परेसुंतो ॥ सुपो वा । आमो वा । हंहुमो स्यातां ॥ वम्भणाहं । वम्भणाहुं । ब्राह्मणानामित्यर्थे । वम्भणाणं ॥ i. e., the abl. pl. takes हं or हुं; as „it fell from the trees“, „he came from foreign (countries)“; also the loc. and gen. pl. take हं and हुं, as „of Bráhmans“.

2) Mḍ. says: हिंभिस्त्रिसुपां ॥ त्रिष्वेषां हिं स्यात् । पुरिसहिं । वणहिं । वहुहिं ॥ i. e., all bases in *a*, *i*, *u* take हिं in the loc. and instr. plur., as „in or by men, in or by forests, in or by wifes“.

in K. I. 32 (Ls. 451. 464), where हे॑ is given for the gen. plur. Again both H. C. (4, 340) and Mḍ. (see footnote 1, p. 205) allow the gen. suff. हं and हुं to the loc. plur. also; vice versa, the loc. suff. हिं may have been allowed to the gen. At all events, in O. Gḍ., हिं is found as a suff. of the dat. (= old gen.); and in M. Gḍ. (S.) it appears as the obl. pl. suff. एँ (contr. for अहिं); see examples in § 365, 7. Indeed the term. अहिं seems to occur in the contracted form एं even in the Ap. Pr.; though as a term. of the instr. *sing.* (see H. C. 4, 343. K. I. 23. 24). The examples in Mḍ. are: वणाएं *by a forest,* वालाएं *by a girl,* अग्गिएं *by fire,* वाउएं *by wind*; they would be equal to *वणाअहिं, *वालाअहिं, *अग्गिअहिं, *वाउअहिं. Here एं can hardly be = Skr. term. एन (as Ls. 461); for the latter would not be added to fem. bases in आ. Moreover, as will be shown in Nro. 3, the sing. term. अहि is similarly contracted to ए. It may, also, be added that the pl. term. अहिं is similarly used as a term. of the loc. *sing.* (see K. I. 26. 27. Ls. 451. 463), as घरहिं or घरे or घरि *in a house.* In Gḍ., this practise of using the pl. suff. for the sing. is sometimes extended to all plur. suff. हं, हुं, हिं; see Nro. 5. — 3) The Ap. sing. suff. हो is sometimes shortened to हु (H. C. 4, 336. 351); thus H. C. has रुक्खहु, but Mḍ. (see footnote 2, p. 204) रुक्खहो *from a tree* or *of a tree*; sometimes even to ह, according to Ls'. conjecture of K. I. 34 (Ls. 462); e. g., अग्गिहो or अग्गिह *of fire*; sometimes even ह is dropped (H. C. 4, 345). In the form हु it still occurs in the O. P. of the Granth (Tr. A. Gr. CXXVI) and expresses the abl. In the form ह it is often found in the O. W. H. of Chand, and expresses the gen., abl., loc., act., acc.-dat.; thus *gen.* in गोचारु परह चारै सु गोइ। i. e., *the herdsman tends the cows of an other* (28, 62), or सेन भोमह करि किन्निय। i. e., *he dispersed the Army of Bhima* (38, 41), or चल्यो उदै क्रूरह बलिय। i. e., *he marched at the rise of mighty Saturn* (27, 47), or वन तृष मृग्ग सिंघह रु गज्ज। i. e., *in the forest is plenty of deer, lions and elephants* (27, 13); *abl.* iu फूलह सुधारु धरु। *having adorned the body with flowers* (38, 37) or तत्र सुमंत परधांनह पुछिय। i. e., *then he asked good counsel of the Premier* (28, 88);

loc. जांने कि अकासह मान दिन । *just as in the sky the measure of day,* i. e., *the sun* (26, 25), or न्याय तौ कलह न किज्जै । i. e., *justice is not done in the Kali age* (28, 41); *act.* बीसलह राज कथि पुब्ब कथ्य । i. e., *Visala rája told the whole story* (1, 82) or तप सु छंडि तुअरह । i. e., *the Tuar has abandoned asceticism* (28, 55); *acc.* अनंगपालह बुल्लाइय । i. e., *he has called Anangpála* (28, 9), or अनंगेसह लेआउ । i. e., *bring ye Anangesa* (28, 77). The form without ह is the common one in M. Gd.; see § 365, 6. — 4) The Ap. sg. suff. हे of the gen. and abl. is sometimes also used as a loc. suff., e. g., एत्ताहे *now,* lit., *in that,* scl. *time* (H. C. 2, 134; the same एत्ताहे is an abl. *from that,* H. C. 3, 82. 83), or एत्तहे *in this,* तेत्तहे *in that,* scl. *place* (H. C. 4, 436). But, as a rule, it is shortened to हि, when it expresses the loc. (H. C. 4, 341. 352), e. g., कलिहि *in the Kali age*; and after *a*-bases ह may be elided, as पच्छइ *behind, after* (H. C. 4, 420 for *पच्छहि), अग्गइ *before* (H. C. 4, 391), एम्वइ *thus* (H. C. 4, 420), but commonly the term. अहि (or अइ) is contracted to ए (H. C. 4, 334), e. g., तले *below* for *तलइ or *तलहि[1]). In this contracted form ए, it is also used in the Ap. Pr. to express the instr. sg. (of fem. nouns)[2]); see H. C. 4, 349. 333. K. I. 38 and Md. स्त्रियां च ए च स्यात् ॥ वुड्डिए । धेनुए । णइए । वहुए । वालाए ॥ i. e., fem. bases also take ए (viz. besides एं, as वालाएं), as *by intelligence, by a cow, by a river, by a wife, by a girl*; contr. for *वुड्डिअहि, *णइअहि (Skr. नदिकायाम्). In the form हि it still occurs in the O. P. of the Granth, to express the gen., abl., dat. and acc. (see Tr. A. Gr. CXXV); also in O. H., to express the gen., abl., loc., dat. and acc.; thus *gen.* in राजहि तुम पर प्रीति विशेषी *there is a special love of*

1) This ए is usually considered to be the Skr. and (Mh. Pr.) loc. suff. ए; but that old suff. is hardly likely to have survived so long; and has been, indeed, worn down to इ in Ap. (H. C. 4, 334); e. g., Ap. तले or तलि *below*; the former = Ap. तलहि, the latter = Skr. तले.

2) This cannot be the Mh. Pr. instr. suff. ए; for that suff. had already in the Mh. Pr. been (optionally) worn down to इ or अ, and, moreover, requires the lengthening of the final vowel of the base (Vr. 5, 22); thus the instr. sg. of नदी *river* is in Mh. Pr. णाईए or णाईइ or णाईअ, but in the Ap. णइए.

the king for you (T. Dás in Kl. 286); *abl.* को किहि वंसहि उपन्यो (Chand I, 167 in Bs. II, 211), or गुरुहि पूछ करि कुलिविधि राजा *the king having enquired from the Guru performed the family rites* (T. Dás in Kl. 65); *loc.* in किहि काज रिषि आयो घरहि *for what cause, Rishi, hast thou come into the house* (Chand I, 45 in Bs. II, 211); *dat.* बहु विधि चेरिहि आदर देइ *in many ways he shows honor to the bond-maid* (T. Dás in Kl. 286); *acc.* मुनि रघुबरहि प्रसंस *the sage extolled Raghubar* (T. Dás in Kl. 283); see other examples in § 365, 6. The contr. form ए is used in B. and O., to express the dat.-acc., loc. and instr.; as घरे *to or in or by a house* (see S. Ch. 59, 4. 62. Su. 15); and in B. even for the nom. (S. Ch. 56, see § 369). In G. and Mw. it is used to express the instr. (or act.) and loc.; thus G. घरे, Mw. घरै *by or in a house* (Kl. 66, a. Ed. 31, 87. 34, d); in H., P., S. it is used for the loc.; thus घरे *in the house* (Ld. 12, 37. 77, 133. Tr. 120, 7). — 5) The Ap. Pr. gen. *plur.* suff. are sometimes used in the *sing.* Thus in the Ap., the suff. हिं (or the term. अहिं), which commonly expresses the loc. or instr. pl. (H. C. 4, 347) is often used for the loc. sg.; see K. I. 26. 27 (in Ls. 451. 462); e. g., सुरहिं or सुरे or सुरि *in a god*; and, in the contracted form एं, for the instr. sg. (H. C. 4, 343, see Nro. 2); e. g., अग्गिएं *by fire* for *अग्गिअहिं (Skr. अग्निकेन). In O. H. the suff. हिं is as often used for the dat., acc. and loc. in the sing. as in the plur.; thus *dat.* in कहु केहि रंकहिं करौं नरेसु, i. e., *say, what pauper shall I make a king* (T. Dás in Kl. 283); *loc.* in निज लोकहिं बिरंच गये देवन्ह इहै सिखाइ। i. e., *Brahmá, having taught this the gods, went to his own world* (T. Dás in Kl. 122); *acc.* in रामहिं प्रेम समेत लखि सखिन समीप बुलाइ i. e. *beholding Ráma with affection she called near her friends* (T. Dás in Bál.), etc. Similarly it occurs in M., in the contracted form ईं, both in the loc. sg. and plur. (Man. 17, 45. 27, 66. 28, 2); as घरीं *in a house* or *in houses* for *घरहिं; and, in the contracted form एँ, in the instr. sg. (Man. 17, 45. 28, 66); e. g., घरें *by a house* for *घरहिं [1]). Also E. H.

1) This explains why the M. instr. in एँ is seldom used except with the postpositions करून or कडून (Man. 28, note 1); for it is really a gen.

and W. H. occasionally have it, in the contr. form ऐँ or ए, in the loc. sing.; as पाइँ or पाछेँ *behind, after* for *पच्छहिँ (see § 77, exc.). Again the suff. हुं (or term. अहुं) which in Ap. Pr. expresses the abl. and loc. *plur.* (H. C. 4, 340), is used in S. for the abl. sg. in the forms अउँ or ओँ or ऊँ (Tr. 118), in P. for the abl. or, occasionally, loc. sg. in the form ओँ (Ld. 12, 37), and in W. H. for the loc. sg. in the form ऊ; thus S. घरउँ or घरोँ or घरूँ, P. घरोँ *from a house*, or P. पाछोँ, W. H. पाछू *behind, after*, for *घरहुं, *पच्छहुं. Again the suff. हं (or termin. अहं), which in the Ap. expresses the abl. and loc. *plur.* (see Nro. 2), is used in M. for the loc. both of the sing. and plur. in the contr. form आं (Man. 17, 45. 27, 66. 28, 2); e. g., घरां *in a house* or *in houses*, for *घरहं; also occasionally in E. H. and W. H.; e. g., E. H. इहाँ, W. H. यहाँ *here*, lit. *in this*, scl. *place*, for *एहहं (Skr. इदृशे); in S. it forms the abl. sing. (Tr. 117, 5); e. g., घराँ *from a house*, मंझाँ *from within*, for *मज्झहिं. Lastly the Mg. Pr. gen. plur. suff. आहँ (H. C. 4, 300) is used in E. H. for the obl. sing.; thus घोड़वाँ (कै *of*) *a horse*, for Mg. घोडआहँ; see § 365, 4. — 6) The gen. sg. suff. हो and हे are also used in Ap. Pr. and Gḍ. to express the nom. and voc. sg. or pl.; see § 369.

368. *Origin of the gen. or obl. suffixes.* 1) The Skr. gen. sg. suff. स्य becomes in Pr. स्स (Vr. 5, 8) according to the usual phonetic laws (Ls. 274. 275; see §§ 150. 137). But though स्स is the common form, yet in the pronouns Pr. already shows a tendency to reduce it to स and to lengthen the preceding vowel (see § 150, 2); e. g., gen. masc. कास = कस्स *of whom* (Vr. 6, 5. H. C. 3, 64); neut. कीस *why* = *किस्स (Ls. 326); fem. कीसे = *किस्से (Vr. 6, 6. H. C. 3, 64). In Gḍ. this process is extended to all gen., including those of nouns, as may be seen in M. (see § 365, 1); in Br. the two pronom. gen. जास *of which*, तास *of him* (Kl. 122. 133) are its only relics. Besides स्स (K. I. 30 in Ls. 451)

---

or obl. form, and as such naturally takes a postposition; see § 366, 1; if it were, as commonly supposed, identical with the old Skr. instr. in एन, the addition of the postpos. would be very superfluous and anomalous.

the Ap. Pr. has स्सु or सु; in the latter case with or without the lengthening of the preceding vowel (H. C. 4, 338. 358. K. I. 30); though it is not clear, how the final उ arose. Traces of this Ap. form have survived in the O. H. and Br. pronom. gen. तासु, जासु; e. g., तासु किज्ञो चंद कहिय *of him the glory Chand has told* (Chand 1, 46 in Bs. II, 316, see Kl. 122. 133). The O. W. H. of Chand has occasionally nominal gen. in अस (perhaps = Ap. असु); e. g., पुत्री वरी उज्ञेन दिसि। पहिल्लै पंगस पुत्र॥ i. e., *a daughter has married in Ujainland, first the son of Paṇga* (25, 22). The O. P. of the Granth appears to have a gen. in असि (Tr. A. Gr. CXXVI). — 2) The Skr. स्य, however, also changes in Pr. to ह or हि, with the lengthening of the preceding vowel (cf. Ls. 398); the conj. स्य् becoming ह्, as in the fut. suff. हामि, हिइ for स्यामि, स्यति (Vr. 7, 12. 13), and the vowel being lengthened by way of compensation. The form ह is limited to the Mg. Pr. (Vr. 11, 12), and हि to the abl. case (Vr. 5, 6), which is identical with the gen.[1]). Thus Pr. abl. वच्छाहि *from a calf* (lit. gen. *of a calf*), Mg. Pr. gen. वच्छाह *of a calf*, Pr. गिरीहि *from a mountain*, गुरूहि *from a teacher* (H. C. 3, 124). The Ap. Pr. gen. suff. हे is, probably, an other modification of the Skr. स्य (cf. Ls. 462), which, because of its final ए being heavy, does not lengthen the preceding vowel; as वच्छहे, गिरिहे, गुरुहे[2]). In O. Gd. it is shortened to हि (as वच्छहि, गिरिहि, गुरुहि), the gen. character of which is shown by its being especially used for the dat. (= old gen., see examples in §§ 365, 6. 267, 4) or generally for the obl. in connexion with case-aff. which require the gen. (see § 366, 1. b). In that particular kind of Apabhraṃṣa (probably Gujaráti or Marwáṛí) which is treated by H. C. 4, 350, this shortened obl. or gen. suff. हि was, in the case of masc. and neut. nouns, confined to the loc. sing., probably because the alternative gen. suff. हो or हु (see Nro. 3) were used in the gen.

1) It may be observed that even in Skr. the abl. takes the gen. suff. अस् in the case of all bases, exc. those in अ.

2) Exceptionally the vowel is lengthened in Mh. Pr., e. g., एत्ताहे *from that* (H. C. 3, 82), but Ap. Pr. एत्तहे (H. C. 4, 420) = Skr. इतः or एततः.

(incl. dat. and abl.). — 3) There is an other Ap. Pr. gen. suff. हो or shortened हु (H. C. 4, 336. 338)[1]), which, however, has no connection with the Skr. स्य. Its origin is obscure. Ls. 462 identifies it with an assumed Skr. suff. स्व. It seems more probably to be identical with the Skr. abl. plur. suff. भ्यस्, which in Pr. would regularly change to ब्भो or हो (cf. Pr. जीहा or जिब्भा *tongue* in H. C. 2, 57 and § 120) and easily serve as a gen. suff. also. In the Ap. of H. C. 4, 351 हु actually occurs as an abl. and gen. *plur.* suff. The change of „number" would be analogous to that in the case of the Pr. abl. pl. suff. हिंतो which is used in the sing. also (see H. C. 3, 8. 9, see also § 367, 5). — 4) The Skr. gen. plur. suff. नाम् becomes in Pr. णं or ण (Vr. 5, 4) with the lengthening of the preceding vowel; as Skr. वत्सानाम्, Pr. वच्छाणं *of calfs.* This form has survived in M., E. H., Br. and S., see § 365, 4. — 5) The Skr. gen. pl. suff. नाम्, however, also changes in Pr. to ण्हं or ण्ह, हं and हँ, the last with, the former two without the lengthening of the preceding vowel. The process is quite regular; a) Skr. न् is doubled, and the preceding long vowel shortened, as in Pr. खण्णू = Skr. स्थाणुः, Pr. तुण्हिक्को = Skr. तूष्णीकः, Pr. थुल्लो = Skr. स्थूलः, etc. (H. C. 2, 99, see Ls. 143. 276); b) the Pr. ण्ण् is changed to ण्ह (see § 161 and Ls. 271); c) Pr. ण्ह *ṇha* is changed to हं *haṃ* (projecting the *anusvára*, for *ṃha*), or to हँ, prolonging, in the latter case, the preceding vowel, to compensate for the loss of the *anusvára* (see §§ 143. 149). Thus, e. g., Skr. °आनाम् is in Pr. *अणं = अण्हं = अहं = आहँ. The form ण्हं is added in Pr. to numerals only, as पंचण्हं *of five* = Skr. पञ्चानाम् (H. C. 3, 123), and exceptionally to pronouns, as कइण्हं *of how many* = Skr. कतीनाम् (H. C. 3, 123). The form हँ is added also to nouns, especially in Mg. Pr. (H. C. 4, 300). The form हं is used only in the Ap. Pr. (H. C. 4, 339). In Gḍ. all three forms are used

---

1) Observe that in the Ap. of H. C. the gen. suff. हो (H. C. 4, 338) becomes हु when used for the abl. (H. C. 4, 336); just as the gen. suff. हे (H. C. 4, 350) becomes हि when used for the loc. (H. C. 4, 352).

with nouns (see § 365, 4. 7); though न्ह or न is limited to E. H., Br. and S. — 6) There is also an Ap. Pr. gen. pl. suff. हुं (H. C. 4, 340), the origin of which is obscure. Ls. 463, 11 derives it from the Pr. abl. pl. suff. सुन्तो (Vr. 5, 7). It may possibly be identical with the Ap. Pr. gen. and abl. suff. हु (see Nro. 3), to which, being both plur. and sing., perhaps an inorganic *anusvára* was added, to distinguish better its plur. character by making a pair हु, हुं analogous to the other two pairs of Ap. suff., sg. इ, pl. इं, and sg. हि, pl. हिं. — 7) There is, lastly, an Ap. plur. suff. हिं (H. C. 4, 347) or हें (K. I. 32 in Ls. 451). Ls. 310, 3 identifies it with the Skr. pl. instr. suff. भिस्. It is more probably identical with the Skr. abl. suff. भ्याम्[1]), which would regularly change in Pr. to हें or हिं (for ओं or भिं), and easily come to be used in the Ap. Pr. for the gen. (K. I. 32) and instr. or loc. (H. C. 4, 347) of the plur. Its gen. character is shown by its being still used in O. Gḍ. for the dat. (= old gen., see examples in §§ 365, 7. 367, 2. 5), and in S. for the act. (= old instr.) and obl. generally; thus O. H. dat. नरहिं *to men*, S. act. नरें *by men* or obl. नरें खे *to men*.

369. *Derivation of the direct terminations.* 1) A comparison of the various Gḍ. terminations of the obl. sing. and plur. with those of the dir. or nom. plur. will show at once that the latter are always identical with the former. Sometimes it is some obl. form of the sg., sometimes (apparently) of the pl.; again sometimes it is an obl. form of the same Gḍ., sometimes of an other, which is thus used for the nom. plur.; but in every case it is *some one* obl. form. To this rule the M. fem. and neut. nouns form the only exception. For example compare the following weak forms: a) *masc.*, the S. nom. pl. ज्ञन *men* with the S. obl. sg. ज्ञन *man* (nom. sg. ज्ञनु), and the E. H. nom. pl. ज्ञने (§ 361, exc.)

1) Even in Skr. the suff. भ्याम् is used for the instr. and dat. also, similarly the pl. abl. suff. भ्यस् for the dat. and, in the modified form भिस्, for the instr.; there is also a dat. sg. suff. भ्यम् in Skr., as तुभ्यम् *to thee*. — If हुं be rightly identified with सुंतो, हिं might be derived from the Pr. abl. pl. suff. हिंतो (Vr. 5, 7).

with the B. obl. sg. ज़्ने; b) *fem.*, the Br. nom. pl. जीभैं or जीभें *tongues* with the S. obl. pl. जिभें; the Mw., P. and S. nom. pl. जीभाँ or जिभाँ with the S. obl. pl. जिभाँ; the S. nom. pl. जिभूँ with the abl. sg. (really obl. pl., § 367, 5) जिभूँ; the W. H., P. nom. pl. भित्तियाँ *walls* with the S. obl. pl. भितियाँ; the S. nom. pl. भितिऊँ with the S. abl. sg. (really obl. pl.) भितिऊँ (or भितूँ), etc. Again strong forms: a) *masc.*, P., H. H., M. nom. pl. घोडे *horses* with the P., H. H. and S. obl. sg. घोडे; the B., O., E. H., W. H., S., G. nom. pl. घोडा *horses* with the B., O., E. H., W. H., G. obl. sg. घोडा; b) *neut.*, the G. nom. pl. सोनाँ *goldpieces* with the G. obl. sg. सोनाँ; c) *fem.*, the W. H. and P. nom. pl. घोडियाँ *mares* with the S. obl. pl. घोडियाँ; the S. nom. pl. घोडिऊँ with the S. abl. sg. (really obl. pl.) घोडिऊँ; the W. H. nom. pl. पोथीं *books* (Kl. 64, 130) with the P. loc. pl. पोथीं *in books*[1]); the W. H. and P. nom. pl. सासुआँ *mothers-in-law* with the S. obl. pl. सासुआँ, etc. It will be observed, that in the case of fem. nouns the dir. pl. is identical with the obl. pl., but in the case of masc. and neut. it is the same as the obl. sg. The difference, however, is probably in appearance only. For, no doubt, the pl. obl. forms when employed as dir. pl. are used as sing., just as in the S. abl. and M. loc. (see § 367, 5). There can be no doubt, that these so-called nom. plur. forms are *elliptic* phrases, which must be filled up by supplying some collective noun, as लोग *people*, गन *troup*, etc. The E. H. practice of forming the plur. by the addition of such a collective noun, illustrates this theory (§ 361). Such nouns would require the principal word to be in the *gen.* case; and this explains the use of the obl. form, which is the same as the old gen. (§ 366). In B. it is actually the gen. sg. (not merely the obl. f.), which is used to form the plur.; e. g., B. obl. f. देवे, gen. sg. देवे-र् *of a god*, nom. pl. देवे-रा *gods*; here रा is merely the strong form of र्; see § 364, 2. Similarly in N. the plur. is an archaic form of the gen. sg., composed of the

1) The form पोथीं, both in the nom. and loc. pl., is a contraction for पोथिएँ = Ap. पोथिअहिं.

gen.-affix ह (for कह or केह, § 377) and the O. Gḍ. gen. sg. in हे or ए (§ 365, 6). Thus O. Gḍ. gen. or obl. sg. देवहे or देवह, N. nom. pl. देवहे-ह or देवह-ह *gods*; see also § 364, 3. Thus the H. H., P. or S. nom. pl. घोड़े *horses* is really as much as Ap. Pr. घोडग्रहे scl. गणु = Skr. घोटकस्य गणः, lit. *a troop of horse.* The nom. pl. of nouns in इ, उ, ई, ऊ is, of course, of the same character; though it does not come out so strikingly. — 2) The obl. sg. is sometimes even used to form the nom. sing. Thus always in the long forms: e. g., E. H. nom. sg. रमवा or रमवाँ, M. राम्या (for *रामया) *Ráma* = obl. form E. H. रमवा or रमवाँ, M. राम्या = A. Mg. or Dk. Pr. gen. sg. रामग्राह or pl. रामग्राहँ (see § 365, 1. 4)[1]). But sometimes also in masc. short forms; viz. in B. weak forms in ए, and B., P., Br. and H. H. strong forms in ग्रा. Thus in B. the nom. sg. may be देवे *a god,* घोड़ाए *a horse* (for the usual देव, घोड़ा), both obl. forms = O. Gḍ. gen. sg. देवहि, घोड़ाहि (§ 365, 6); see S. Ch. 56, where these nom. are described as loc. Again P. or Br. or H. H. nom. sg. घोड़ा *a horse* = O. Gḍ. gen. or obl. sg. घोड़ाह or घोडग्रह, Ap. Pr. घोडग्रहो. With these exceptions, the nom. sg. of short forms in all Gḍs. is simply a modified form of the Pr. nom. sg., as explained in §§ 40—54. Thus S., G., Mw. घोड़ो, Br. घोड़ौ = Ap. Pr. nom. sg. घोडउ, Pr. घोडग्रो; E. H., B., O., M. घोड़ा = Mg. Pr. nom. sg. घोडग्र or घोडइ or घोडए (Vr. 11, 10) = Skr. घोटकः; again E. H., B., O., M. देव *a god* = Mg. Pr. nom. sg. देव or देवि or देवे; W. H., P., G., N. देव or S., O. W. H., O. P. देवु = Ap. Pr. nom. sg. देवु, Pr. देवो, Skr. देवः. — 3) The nom. pl. of fem. and neut. nouns in M. is identical with the old Pr. nom. pl. The suff. of the nom. pl. neut. is in Pr. इं (Vr. 5, 26 = Skr. नि), before which the final vowel of the base is lengthened; in the Ap. Pr. it is also इं, but without lengthening the preceding vowel (H. C. 4, 353). Hence the termin. are in Mh. Pr. ग्राइं, ईइं, ऊइं, in Ap. Pr. ग्रइं, इइं, उइं, or with strong bases ग्रग्रइं, इग्रइं, उग्रइं. These be-

---

1) Not = Mg. Pr. nom. sg. रामए; for ए could not well become ग्रा; and it would not account for the final *anunásika* in E. H.

come in M. एँ (इइं and उइं *desunt*) or, with strong bases, एँ or ईं, येँ, वेँ. Thus M. घरें *houses*, Ap. घरइं, Pr. घराइं, Skr. गृहाणि; M. वाँसरें *calves*, Ap. वच्छडअइं, Skr. वत्स°; M. केलीं *plantains*, Ap. केलअइं, Pr. कयलआइं (H. C. 1, 167), Skr. कदरकाणि; M. मोत्यें *pearls*, Ap. मोत्तिअइं, Pr. मोत्तिआइं, Skr. मौक्तिकानि; M. अंसूं (or अंसवें), Ap. अंसुअइं, Pr. अंसुआइं, Skr. अश्रुकाणि. — 4) The suff. of the nom. plur. fem. is in Pr. ओ or उ or may be dropped altogether (Vr. 5, 19. 20); so also in the Ap. Pr. (H. C. 4, 344. 348). Thus M. जीभा *tongues* (nom. pl. of जीभ), Pr. जिब्भा or जिब्भाउ or जिब्भाओ, Skr. जिह्वाः; or M. घोड्या *mares*, Pr. घोडिआ or घोडिआउ or घोडिआओ, Skr. घोटिकाः; or M. सासा (or सासवा) *mothers-in-law*, Pr. सासुआ or सासुआउ or सासुआओ, Skr. श्वश्रुकाः. — 5) The use of the gen. sg. (or obl. form) for the nom. sg. or pl. is expressly taught by Mḍ. for the Ap. Pr. As this is a point of some importance, I will quote his rules on the subject. They are: a) उत्सुमोः ॥ सुमोरुत् स्यात् ॥ चन्दु । राउ । अग्गिउ । महुउ, etc. (cf. H. C. 4, 331), i. e., *a*-bases have *u* in the nom. and acc. sg., as *moon, king, fire, honey*; b) होच ॥ सुमोर् हो च स्यात् ॥ रुक्खहो ॥ i. e., they have also *ho* (gen. suff., see H. C. 4, 338) in the nom. and acc. sg., as *tree*; c) सो पुंस्य् अत ओ क्वचित् ॥ सप्पो ॥ i. e., masc. *a*-bases have sometimes *o* (cf. H. C. 4, 332), as *serpent*; d) जसो हे च ॥ रुक्खहे । बालाहे ॥ *a*-bases have also हे (gen. suff., see H. C. 4, 350) in the nom. plur., as *trees, girls*; e) स्त्रियाम् उच् च जश्शसोः ॥ बालाउ ॥ चकाराद् बालाहे ॥ i. e., fem. *a*-bases have *u* (cf. H. C. 4, 348) or हे in the nom. and acc. plur., as *girls*; f) इं नपुंसके दीर्घो वा ॥ नपुंसके जश्शसोर् इं स्यात् ॥ प्राग् दीर्घो वा ॥ वणाइं । वणइं ॥ महूइं । महुइं ॥ i. e., neut. bases have *iṃ* in the nom. acc. pl., and the preceding vowel may be long, as *woods, honeys*. — 6) It may be further observed, that the voc. sg. and pl. throughout the Gḍs. is identical with some one Gḍ. form of the obl. sg. or nom. pl. Thus in *masc.*; E. H. obl. sg., voc. sg., nom. pl. alike घोड़ा *(of a) horse, oh horse*, or *horses*; H. H. and P. obl. sg., voc. sg. and nom. pl. alike घोड़े; voc. pl. H. H. घोड़ो, P. घोड़िउ (= *घोड़यु or *घोड़उ); S. nom. pl. and voc. sg. घोड़ा, voc. pl. घोड़ा or घोड़उ or घोड़ो; G. obl. sg. and voc. sg. घोड़ा, nom. pl. and voc. pl. घोड़ाउ or घोड़ाव् (or घोड़ाओ); M. obl. sg. घोड्या,

nom. pl. घोड़े, voc. sg. घोड़या or घोड़े. So also in fem. nouns [1]). The identity of the voc. sg. and pl. with the obl. sg. and nom. pl. is expressly taught by Pr. Gramm., who ascribe the two suff. of the gen. sg. हो and हे to the voc. Thus Mḍ. states: सम्बुद्धौ सौ हे च ॥ स्त्रियाम् इत्य् एव ॥ वालाहे । पाइहे ॥ चकारान् महाराष्ट्रीवच् च ॥ i. e., the voc. sg. of fem. only takes *he*. The Mh. Pr. forms would be वाले, पाइ. The latter forms alone are enjoined by K. I. 17, 18 (in Ls. 450), who does not identify them with the Mh. Pr. forms. In this he is correct; for वाले is a mere contraction for वालहे or वालहि; and पाइ has dropped the suff. हे or ह, just as in the obl. or gen. sg. (cf. H. C. 4, 345). The form ए is preserved in P. fem. nouns; as जिभे *oh tongue*, मावें *oh mother*, धीए *oh daughter*; but also extended to masc. sg.; as घोड़े *oh horse*, and to masc. pl., as देवे *oh gods*. Again Mḍ. continues: त्रिषु हो जसः ॥ त्रिषु जसो हो स्यात् ॥ रुक्खहो । वणाहो । पाइहो ॥ i. e., the voc. pl. of all bases in *a*, *i*, *u* takes *ho*. So also H. C. 4, 346 and K. I. 29 (in Ls. 450). In M. Gḍ. the suff. हो becomes उ (for हु) or अ (for ह), which are contracted with a preceding अ to ओ or आ respectively; e. g., P. voc. pl. घोड़ीउ *oh mares* = घोड़िअहु (with ई for इअ) = Ap. घोड़िअहो; or S. नरो or नराँ *oh men* for *नरउ or *नरअ = *नरहु or *नरह, Ap. णरहो. Gḍ. extends the contr. form आ even to the sing.; e. g., P. voc. sg. देवा *oh god*, but voc. pl. देवे *oh gods*; the former being derived from Ap. देवहो, the latter from Ap. देवहे. Indeed, as such it is noticed by K. I. 26 (in Ls. 450) as already occurring in the Ap. Pr. The general result seems to be, that in the Ap. Pr. both हे and हो or its modifications are used to form both the voc. sing. and the voc. pl. of all bases in *a*, *i*, *u* whether masc., fem. or neut.

4. CASE.

370. There are seven cases, viz. nominative (incl. vocative), accusative, instrumental, dative, ablative, genitive and locative.

---

1) Exceptionally, the voc. pl. is the same as the obl. pl.; e. g., Mw. nom. pl. and voc. pl. घोड़ाँ *oh horses* or *(of) horses*.

The nom. serves also as the voc., and in that case some interjection, as हे, रे or अरे, is generally prefixed; e. g., nom. राम् *Ráma*, voc. हे राम् *oh! Ráma*; nom. बेटा, voc. अरे बेटा *oh! son*; nom. दुर्गा, voc. रे दुर्गा *oh! Durgá*, etc. The E. H. has no (eighth) case of the „agent", or (as I shall call it) *active case*.

371. *The active case.* The absence of the act. case in E. H. is a point of great importance, as it helps to determine its affiliation or position with regard to the other Gḍ. languages. This case is one of the main features that distinguish the W. and S. Gḍs. from the E. Gḍs. The latter are without it; the former possess it. E. H., therefore, as not having the act. case, belongs to the E. Gḍ. group, and is more nearly allied to B. and O., than to W. H. — The rationale of the act. case is as follows. The old organic past tenses active of the Skr., mostly very complicated forms, were in Pr. already disused (cf. Wb. Spt. 63) with a few fragmentary and rare exceptions (cf. Vr. 7, 23. 24. H. C. 3, 162. 163). The inconvenience of this want was obviated by the simple expedient of giving to the sentence the passive construction; thereby turning the subject or nom. case into the instr. case and the past tense act. into the past part. pass. This method of expressing the past act. was already much used in Skr.; and in Pr. it has become the common one; thus „they have not devoured that" may be in Skr. ते एतद् न आचेरुः or in pass. constr. तैर् एतद् अनाचीर्णम्; but in Pr. only the latter तेहिं एअं अणाइस्सं (cf. H. C. 3, 134). But there is yet a simpler way of using the pass. constr.; viz., by employing the past part. pass. in an *act. sense*, whereby the change of the nom. case into the instr. in the subj. becomes unnecessary. This practise may have originated from the use of the past part. pass. of intrans. verbs in an act. sense, which is very common in Skr.; as अहं गतः *I went* for अहं जगाम. In Pr. it is already found occasionally extended to trans. verbs (cf. Gl. in J. G. O. S. XXVII, 492), as *Setub.* 6, 51 आढत्ता दीसिउं णिसिअरच्छाआ *the shadows of the night-walkers began to be seen* (Skr. निशिचरच्छाया द्रष्टुम् आरब्धाः), and intrans., ibid. 8, 30 दीसिउं पउत्तं

सेउत्तंधस्स मुहुं *the head of the bridge began to be seen*, or ibid. 7, 71 घेप्पिउं पउत्ता पवंगा *the monkeys began to be taken*, etc. Now of these two methods of using the past part. pass. to supply the past tense act., the former, i. e., *the real pass. constr. with the subj. in the instr. case*, was adopted by the W. and S. Gḍs., while the other, i. e., (what I may call) *the pass.-act. constr. with the subj. in the nom. case*, was chosen by the E. and N. Gḍs., and, of course, these latter make the past part. pass. to agree in number and gender with the subj. Thus „*they have not eaten that*" is in E. H. ईलोग् ऊ न खैलेन्, in W. H. इन्हों ने वह् न खायौ. Here खैलेन् is the 3^d plur. masc. 2nd pret. (formed from the past part. pass. खैल् or खायल्, see § 307), agreeing with the nom. ईलोग् and governing the acc. ऊ; while खायौ is the nom. sg. masc. (of the past part. pass. खायौ) agreeing with वह् and governed by the instr. or rather act. इन्हों ने. — It has been stated already (§ 366, 1. d) that the tendency of the later Pr. was to substitute the gen. for every other case. Thus the example of the gen. in the place of the instr., given by H. C. 3, 134, is तेसिं एअं अणाइण्णं, where तेसिं is the gen. plur. (= Skr. तेषाम्) for the instr. तेहिं (= Skr. तैः) [1]. It has also been stated (ibid.) that this Pr. tendency has become in Gḍ. an absolute law, and also, that the Gḍ. so-called obl. form is identical with the old Pr. gen. Hence, as regards the W. Gḍ. and S. Gḍ., their method of expressing the past tense act. by means of the *real pass. constr. with the subj. in the instr. case*, may now be stated thus, that they express it by means of the *past part. pass. with the subj. in the obl. form* (= old gen.-instr.). Now there is every reason to believe, that this was once the universal usage in the whole of the W. and S. Gḍ.; that is, that in the pass. constr. the mere obl. form was used without the addition of any affix (ने or

---

1) His other examples are: धणस्स लद्धो for धणेण लद्धो *acquired with money*, or चिरस्स मुक्का for चिरेण मुक्का *long delivered*; here the gen.-instr. has not the sense of the act.

ने"). Thus in the O. H. (of Chand, Kabir, Behári Lál, etc.) the aff. never or very rarely occurs [1]). In O. S. it cannot have been used; for it does not exist even in the M. S. Nor was it used in O. P. (see Tr. A. Gr. CXXVI); nor, as far as I can ascertain, in O. M. (see Man. 138) and O. G. Even in the modern S. (Tr. 113, 3) and Mw. (Kl. 66, 132. a) it is always omitted; also, as a rule, in G. (Ed. 87) and not, unfrequently, in Br. (Kl. 287, 543) and P. (Ld. 7, 22. 73, 119). Indeed, it may be said to be really confined to the literary forms of the Gd. languages and, therefore, to be comparatively modern. Such, at all events, is the case with Hindí, where it is confined to the H. H. (or Urdu) and originated at the same time with the literary cultivation of the language. The latter took place in the sixteenth century around the centre of the Moghul empire in Western Hindústán. In the low dialects of those parts the following dat. aff. are in use, G. ने", Mw. नै", P. नूं; and it so happens that in G. the same aff. ने" is also used as an aff. of the act. case in the pass. constr. It may be concluded, therefore, that the founders of the H. H. adopted what they found current as a dat. aff. in their regions for the act. case also. It should be remembered, that the mere obl. f. which originally was the act. case was often outwardly not to be distinguished from the nom. This was too inconvenient for a literary language which necessarily aims at grammatical precision. Seeing, then, two dat. aff. current in different parts of their neighbourhood (viz., कौ" or को in Br., नै" or ने in Mw.) they assumed one (ने) for the act., while they reserved the other (को) for the dat.; and thus, as will be seen, any confusion between the act. and the dat. in H. H. was avoided. Possibly, the dat. aff. ने was already employed, in some cases, by the common people (as in G.) to signify the act., and thus a precedent was

---

1) It must be remembered, that in many cases the obl. f. happens not to differ from the dir. or nom.; thus in Pr. R. 1, 49 (in Bs. II, 267) दुस and रास are not nom., but obl. f., just as तिन and तिहि in the other cited verses.

afforded. The choice of the dat. aff. to supply an affix of the act. must have been felt to be natural; for it has merely the general sense of „referring to“. An affix, having such a vague and general meaning, might well be employed to express any relation in which a noun may stand in a sentence. — This theory of the identity of the act. aff. with that of the dat., with which I entirely agree, was, I believe, first propounded by Beames (II, 270). The common theory of its identity with the Skr. instr. termin. एन or ना can hardly be seriously maintained, and has been well refuted by the same writer (ibid. 266). — It should be mentioned, that G. and Mw. employ a special obl. f. in ए or ऐ for the act. case sing., their general obl. f. ending in ञा, see § 366, 2; while S. uses its general obl. f. for the act. case also. — The various act. case-aff. are: H. H. ने, Br. नेँ, M. sg. नेँ or pl. नीँ, P. नै, G. ने or पो, N. ले. The aff. थोँ in G. and होँ, सोँ or थ्रोँ in M. do not belong to the act., but to the instr. or abl., just as से in E. H. (see §§ 372. 376). — N. alone has the curious anomaly of using the act. case with ले together with the act.-pass. constr.; i. e., of constructing the subj. like the W. Gds., but the verb like the E. Gds. (see § 487).

Note: On the derivation of the act.-dat. affixes see § 375.

372. All cases, exc. the nom. and acc. (*proper*) are formed by adding to the obl. form of the noun certain affixes which are the same for both numbers. These are the following: instr. or abl. से *by, with* or *from*; dat. के *to*, gen. कै, के or कर्, करे *of*, loc. मे *in*. The acc. proper is identical with the nom.; but commonly, as in all Gds., the dat. is substituted for the acc. See paradigms in § 379.

Note: The following aff. are also sometimes used: dat. कहं, abl. सोँ or सेन or ते or थोँ, loc. मेँ or म or माँ or मांक or माँहोँ.

373. For the gen., there are two sets of aff.: 1) कै and के, 2) कर् and करे. Of these two sets, nouns (i. e., subst., adj., and numer.) may affix only the former (कै, के), while pron. may

take either pair at pleasure. Of the two members of each pair the former (कै, करू) are used when the governing word is in the nom. or acc. proper; the latter (के, करे) when it is in any obl. case. The number and gender of the governing word make no difference in this respect. Thus घरू कै सामी आवत् बा *the master of the house is coming*; घरू के सामी से कहहू *tell ye the master of the house*; घरू कै लोग् आवत् बाटै॑ *the people of the house are coming*; घरू के तिरियालोगन् के बुलावहू *call ye the women of the house.* Again ई ओकरू or ओकै घरू बाटै *this is his house*; ऊ एकरे or एके घरू मे॑ बाटै *he is in his house*; ऊ एकरू or एकै पोथी बाटै॑ *those are his books*; ऊ एकरे or एके पोथी मे पढैला *he reads in his book.*

374. *Affinities.* Besides the want of the act. case (§ 370), E. H. shows its affinity to E. Gd., as against W. Gd., also in the government of the gen. aff. In the W. Gd. the form of the aff. changes not only with the case, but also with the number and gender of the governing word; it is for the *nom. sg. masc.* Br. कौ, H. H. का, Kn. को, Mw. रो, G. नो, P. दा, S. जो; *obl. sg. masc.* Br., H. H., Kn. के, Mw. रा or रै, G. ना, P. दे, S. जे; *nom. sg. neut.* G. नुँ; *obl. sg. neut.* G. नाँ; *nom. sg. fem.* Br., H. H., Kn. की, Mw. री, G. नी, P. दी, S. जी; *obl. sg. fem.* Br., H. H., Kn. की, Mw. री, G. नी, P. दी, S. जे or जिअ; *nom. pl. masc.* Br., H. H., Kn. के, Mw. रा, G. ना or नाव्, P. दे, S. जा; *obl. pl. masc.* Br., H. H., Kn. के, Mw. रा, G. ना or नाव्, P. दे or दिआँ, S. जे or जनि; *nom. pl. neut.* G. नाँ or नाँव्, *obl. dto.*; *nom. pl. fem.* Br., H. H., Kn. की, Mw. री, G. नीउ, P. दीआँ, S. जूँ or जिउँ; *obl. pl. fem.* Br., H. H., Kn. की, Mw. री, G. नीउ, P. दीआँ, S. जे or जिनि or जुनि or जिअनि or जिउनि (see Ld. 7. Tr. 129). The S. Gd. and N. Gd. follow the W. Gd. practice; thus *nom. sg. masc.* M. चा, N. को, *obl.* M. चे or च्या, N. का; *nom. sg. neut.* M. चे॑, *obl.* चे or च्या; *nom. sg. fem.* M. ची, N. की, *obl.* M. चे or च्या, N. की; *nom. pl. masc.* M. चे, N. का, *obl.* M. चे or च्या, N. का; *nom. pl. neut.* M. ची॑, *obl.* चे or च्या; *nom. pl. fem.* M. च्या, N. की, *obl.* M. चे or च्या, N. की (see M. 27. 41). On the other hand, in B. and O. the form of the gen. aff. never changes; not even, as in E. H., with

the case. — The case-aff. have a great variety of forms in the different Gḍs.; they are exhibited in the subjoined table.

	B.	O.	E. H.	H. H.	Br.	Mw.
dat. acc.	के	कु or कि	के	को	कोँ	नै
abl. instr.	हइते	ह, कह	से	से	सोँ	सूँ
gen.	र्	र्, कर्	कै, कर्	का	को	रो
loc.	ते	रे, करे	मे	मेँ	मेँ	माँ
act.	—	—	—	ने	ने	obl.

	G.	P.	S.	M.	N.
dat. acc.	ने	नूँ	खे	ला	लाई
abl. instr.	थी	ते	खोँ, खाँ	सीँ, हीँ, हून्, ऊन्	सँग
gen.	नो	दा	जो	चा	को
loc.	माँ	मै	मेँ	त्	मा
act.	obl. or ने	नै	obl.	नेँ	ले

Besides these affixes which are allotted to particular *cases,* there is a large number of others, which are used to modify the noun in various senses which may, in a general way, be referred to the dat., abl. or loc. These may be divided into two classes, according as they are or are not added to the obl. form of the noun by means of the gen. aff. In the former case, I shall call them *postpositions,* in the latter, *affixes.* Many of them, however, belong to both classes, sometimes in the same, sometimes in different languages; e. g., E. H. बदे is a postpos. in के कर् बदे *what for,* but an aff. in केह् बदे *what for*; again लये or लिये is a postpos. in E. H., W. H. घर् के लये or लिये *for the sake of the house,* but an aff. in S. घर् लइ (Tr. 404). The following list contains most of these aff. or postpos.; their meanings (indicated by numbers) generally are; *for* or *to* 1, *till* or *up to* 2, *with* 3, *by* 4, *from* 5, *in* or *at* 6. Thus a) (Skr. लग्न), B. लागात् or O. B. लागि, E. H. लग्, लगि 2, W. H. लागि 1, S. लगे or लगि 1, G. लगी 1, M. लागीँ or लागुनि 1, N. लागी 1; b) (Skr. लब्ध), E. H. लिये 1, W. H.

लये or लए or लयें or लौं or लों 2, P. लई 1, S. लाइ or लइ 1, G. लोधे 1, M. ला 1, N. लाई 1; c) (Skr. स्थान), B. ठाईं 1, थेके 5, O. ठा-रे 1, ठा-रु or हुँ or ठाउँ 5, E. H. थों 5, W. H. थों 5, G. थी 5, P. थीं or थों or O. P. थावहु or थो or थों 5, ठाइ or थानि 1, N. थाजि 5 or 6, M. ठाईं 6; d) (Skr. कर्ण), W. H. कने or कनै or काँनी or कणि 1, P. कन्नी 1, G. काने 1, S. काणे or काणि or कने or कनि 1, कनाँ or कनों 5; e) (Skr. पक्ष), B. पक्ष or पाके, E. H. पाहीं, W. H. पै, P. पाहों 5; f) (Skr. कक्ष), B. काछे or के 1, O. कु or कि 1, E. H. के or कँहँ 1, Br. कौं 1, H. H. को 1, O. H. कहं or कहुं or कहूं or काहुं 1, O. P. कह or कहु or कउ or को or कू or कूँ 1, S. खे 1 or खाँ or खों 5; g) (Skr. तरित ?), B. तक् 2, ते 6, E. H. तक् 2, ते 5, W. H. तक् or तलक् or ताईं or तईं 2, ते or तें 5, P. ताईं or तीकु or तीकुर or तेडी 2, तें or उतों or उताँ 5, S. ताईं or तोईं or तोडी or तोणी 2, ताँ or तों 5, ते 6; h) (Skr. वार्त), E. H. बाट 1, S. वटे 1, बाटाँ 5, G. वते 1, N. बाट 5; i) (Skr. वरे), E. H. वरे 1, M. वरून 5; k) (Skr. कार्य), E. H. काज् 1, O. H. काज 1; l) (Skr. कृत), S. करे or करि 1, M. करून 5, करिताँ 1; m) (Skr. अग्र), M. आठीं; n) (Skr. सङ्ग), B. सने 3, E. H. सन् or सने or सेन् or सेनी 3, W. H. सणि 1, P. सणे 1, S. साँगि or साँगाँ 1, सणु or साणु 5, N. सँगँ 5; o) (Skr. सदृश), Mw. सारू or सारू 1, S. सारू 1, G. सारू 1; p) (Skr. समाधा ?), W. H. सूधी 2, S. सूधाँ 5; q) (Skr. भवन्त°), B. हइते 5, O. H. हुंतो or हूँतो 5, N. भन्दा 5; r) (Skr. कृत्वा), B. करिया 4, E. H. कर् or करि 4, W. H. करि or करके 4, P. करके 4; s) (Skr. दृष्ट्वा), B. दिया 4; t) (Skr. पार्श्व), E. H., W. H. पास 6, P. पास 6, पासों 5, S. and G. पासे 6, M. पासों 6, पसून् 5; u) (Skr. पर), B. पर् or परे 6, E. H. पर् or परि 6, W. H. पर् or परि or पै 6, P. पर् 6, परों 5, S. परे 6, पराँ or परों 5; v) (Skr. मध्य), B. मध्य or मध्ये or माके 6, E. H. माँक् or माँहीं or में or मे or मा or म 6, W. H. में or मों or माँ or माँय् or मई or माहैं 6, O. H. मधि or मझि or मझि or माँक or मज्कं or माहैं or माँहीं or माही or महि or मैं 6, O. P. मै or माहि 6, S. मंके or में 6, माँ or मों 5, G. माँ 6, O. M. माझी 6, M. मध्ये 6; w) (Skr. अभ्यन्तर), B. भितर् or भितरे 6, E. H. and W. H. भीतर् 6; x) (Skr. कड), M. कड 6, कडून् 5; y) (Skr. मस्त), S. मथे 6, G. माटे 1, N. माथि 6; z) (Skr. सिरस्), P. सिर् 6, S. सिरे 6; aa) (Skr. वृत्य), W. H. बीच् 6, P. विच् 6, O. P. विचि 6, S. विचे 6; and others.

375. *Derivation of the dat. affixes.* 1) In B. there is a dat. postpos. काछे (Ş. Ch. 62, 215) meaning lit. *near*; and the O. H. has a dat. aff. कहँ or कहुँ or कहूँ or काहूँ, which often also means *near, by the side of*; e. g., ऋधि सिधि संपति नदी सुहाईं । उमगि अवध अंबुधि कहं आईं ॥ i. e., *fair rivers of prosperity, success, wealth, overflowing came near to the sea of Avadh* (see Bs. II, 253 where some more examples will be found). This points to the Skr. loc. कक्षे *at the side of* as their source. In the Ap. Pr. it would be कच्छे (as in B.), or *कक्खे or *कक्खहुं (see § 378) or probably *कहे or *कहि or *कहहुं (or *काहहुं, see § 116). The latter would contract in O. H. to कहूँ (or काहूँ), and in M. W. H. to कौं or (with the loss of anunásika) in H. H. को. The former, कहि, contracts in E. H. and B. to के (see S. Ch. 49) and is shortened in O. to कि (Sn. 13). Similarly the O. कु (Sn. 13) is a shortened form of the H. H. को (= कहुँ). The S. खे has arisen from कहे or कहि by the metathesis of ह्, just as in भेंस् *buffalo* for वहिस or महिस, गधा *donkey* for गद्हा (Pr. गड्डह H. C. 2, 37). — 2) Again the G. has the dat. postpos. लीधे *for* (Ed. 115) and W. H. लये or लयें or लए (Kl. 273, 508), H. H. लिये, S. लाइ or लइ (Tr. 404), P. लई. These are identical with the past part. G. लीधो, W. H. लयौ, H. H. लिया (see § 307) = Skr. लब्धः *obtained, benefited*. This points to the Skr. loc. लब्धे lit. *for the benefit of* (lat. *commodo*) as their source. In the Ap. Pr. it would be *लहिए or *लहिअहिं or (eliding ह) लइए or लइअहिं, whence contr. W. H. लये or लयें or P. लई, and still more contr. ले or *लैं. The form ले exists in N. as an act. aff. (§ 371); but लैं and ले further change to Mw. नैं and G. ने, which latter is used in W. H. as an act. aff. (§ 371). The change of ल् to न् occurs also in the B. नेउन् (S. Ch. 189) and O. नेबा (Sn. 36) *to obtain* = H. H. लेना, E. H. लेब्. The contraction of लये to ले is like that of the Br. भये or हये to भे or हे *they were* (Kl. 225, 438. 201). Another Ap. loc. would be *लहिअहुं or *लइअहुं (see §§ 307. 378, 3) which would contract to *लयूँ or लौं or लों. The last two forms exist in W. H. in the sense of *up to, until*. From लों arises the P. dat. aff. नूँ. Those forms of this dat. aff.

which have आ, as N. लाई, S. लाइ, M. ला, are probably to be referred to the Ap. Pr. loc. लाहि or लाहे, Skr. लाभे lit. *for the benefit of.* — 3) There is another set of dat. postpos. which has been much confused with the preceding one, though it is of an entirely different origin; viz. E. H. लग् or लगि, W. H. लागि, S. लगे or लगि, G. लगी, N. लागी, M. लागीँ, H. H. लग्. It means *up to, until,* or *on account of, for,* and is derived from the Skr. loc. लग्ने lit. *in contact with.* In the Ap. Pr. it is लग्गे or लग्गि, whence the Gd. लगे or लगि or लग् or लागि; or Ap. Pr. लग्गहिं, whence the Gd. लागीँ or लागी or लगी[1]). P. has also the abl. postpos. लागोँ and S. लाकूँ (Tr. 401, ?लागूँ ?) *from up* = Ap. Pr. abl. लग्गहुं. — 4) The dat. postpos., B. ठाईँ and O. ठा-रे, are clearly the same as the Ap. Pr. loc. ठाणि or ठाणे, Skr. स्थाने *in the place of*; B. also uses the tats. स्थाने itself. — 5) The M. आठीँ (in the so-called postpos. साठीँ, see § 365, 1) is = Ap. Pr. loc. अट्ठहिं, Skr. अर्थे lit. *in the interest of.* — 5) The B. पाके (for पाखे, see § 145, note), E. H. and W. H. पाहीँ or पै, P. पाह् (Ld. 74) are = Ap. loc. *पक्खे or *पाहे or *पाहहिं, Skr. पक्षे lit. *at the side of* (see § 116); B. also uses the tats. पक्षे; and P. has also an abl. postpos. पाहोँ (Ld. 74) = Ap. *पाहहुं. — 6) The set, W. H. कणि (Km., see Kl. 69) or कने (Br.) or कनै or कानीँ (Mw.), P. कन्नी, S. कने or कनि or काने or कानि (Tr. 401. 407), G. काने, which is also used in the lit. sense of *at the side of,* is = Ap. loc. कण्णे or कण्णहिं and probably (as Tr. 401) = Skr. कर्णे or कार्णे (lit. *at the ear* or *belonging to the ear,* i. e., *side*). — 7) The forms, B., E. H., W. H. तक् or तलक्, W. H. तईँ or ताईँ, P. ताईँ or तोकु or तोकुर् or तेडो (Ld. 76. 126), S. ताईँ or तोईँ or तोडो or तोणी (Tr. 399) meaning *up to, till, to,* I believe, form one set, together with the abl. aff., W. H. ते, तेँ, P. ते, उतोँ, उताँ (Ld. 77), S. ताँ, तोँ (Tr. 400), meaning *from up to,* and the loc. aff., B., P., S. ते

1) The O. M. लगुनि or लगोनि is the conj. part. of the same verb, = Pr. लग्गिऊण; so also might be the G. लगी = Pr. लग्गिअ; but not (as Bs. II, 260. 261) the M. लागीँ, on account of the final *anunásika.*

on, upon (S. Ch. 49. Ld. 77. Tr. 400). I am inclined to connect them with the, Skr. past. part. तरित (or उत्तरित, of the R. तॄ) *passed to*, hence *up-to, upon, from-upon.* The loc. तरिते would become Ap. तरिए or *तइए (see § 124) and contract to Gḍ. ते, just as Gḍ. ले arises from लहिए, etc. (see above Nro. 2). The elements कू, कु I take to be the dat. aff. कि, कु (as in O.), and the elements डी, णी to be pleon. suff. (see § 209). — 8) The set, Mw. सरू or सारू, S. सारू, G. सारु, which mean lit. *conformable to* (Tr. 400) and thence *for the sake of*, I connect with the Skr. सदृश *like*, Ap. obl. (or loc.) सरिहहु or सरिसहु (cf. § 292). — 9) The dat. aff., W. H. सणि (Km., see Kl. 69), S. सँगि (Tr. 407), meaning *on account of, for*, together with the abl. aff., E. H. सन् or सने or सेन् or सेनी *with, from*, P. सणो *with* (Ld. 74), S. साणु or सेणु *with* (Tr. 401), N. सँगँ *from*, S. साँगाँ *on account of* (Tr. 407), I connect with the Skr. सङ्गे, which may mean *in company with* (from R. सम् + गम्) or *in attachment to* (from R. सञ्ज्). The conj. ङ्ग् would readily pass into ण् or न्, cf. पण for पक्ष (H. C. 2, 43. Wb. Bh. 403, see also p. 21). — 10) The W. H. सूधी (Kl. 69) *up-to, till* and S. सूधाँ *along with* (Tr. 401), the former a loc., the latter an abl., I would connect with some derivative of the R. समाधा (Ap. *सवँड or *सउँड), meaning *collected, adjusted*, whence *with* or *up-to.* — 11) The dat. aff., E. H. बाटे, S. वटे (Tr. 402), G. वते (Ed. 115), meaning *for* or *instead*, and the abl. aff., N. बाट्, S. वटाँ *from* (Tr. 402), I connect with the Skr. वार्त्त (or वर्त्त or वृत्त) *welfare*, Pr. वट्ट or वत्त (cf. H. C. 2, 29. 30), loc. वार्त्ते lit. *in favor of, for*, whence *in place of, instead.* — 12) The dat. aff. E. H. वरे and the abl. aff. M. वरून् are derived from the Skr. वर *boon, advantage.* — 13) The E. H. काज् is the Pr. loc. कज्जे, Skr. कार्ये *for the work* or *sake of.* — 14) The S. करे or करि is contracted for *करिए = Skr. कृते *for the sake of*, and the corresponding abl. aff. is the M. करून्; similar is the M. dat. aff. करिताँ which is apparently a loc. sg. of the pres. part. (see §§ 300. 307). — 15) As to the relics, in M., of the organic dat. in आस्, ईस्, उस् sg. and आँना, ईँना, उँना plur., see § 365, 1. 4.

Note: I think the identification of the S. खे with *कहे more consonant with Gḍ. analogy (see § 132, note) than Trumpp's theory that खे = Skr. कृते, by the loss of र् and consequent aspiration of क् (i. e., कृते = क्रिते = खिए = खे Tr. 115). For this process there is, I believe, no analogy in Gḍ. The examples, to which Tr. refers (मिर्धंगु *tabor*, हिर्धो *heart*, for Skr. मृदङ्ग *a drum*, हृदय *heart* Tr. V.), are not analogous. For 1) र् has *not* disappeared, and 2) it has aspirated the *following*, not the preceding cons.; whereas, in the case of खे, it is the preceding cons., and र् has disappeared. According to the adduced analogy, Skr. कृते would become किर्थे, not खे. There is *one* really analogous case in Pr. in the adverbial suff. त्र, for which Pr. has त्थ (e. g., Pr. एत्थ or एत्थु *here* = Skr. अत्र), but the case is unique, and the identification of त्थ with त्र (Ls. 251) is, to my mind, doubtful, see § 469. — Beames' remarks on my theory (II, 258) are founded on a misunderstanding. I hold that both the W. H. को and the B. काहे are the same words, in as much as both are various modifications of the same Skr. words; and that the H. form represents a later phase of phonetic development than the B. form, in as much as B. has preserved the aspirate cons. of the Pr., while H. has worn it down to the simple aspirate ह् (in कहुँ) and even dropped it altogether (in कोँ, को); but not, that the one is actually derived from the other. The H. form comes after the B. *phonetically*, though not *historically*; only in this sense can one be said to be *derived from* the other.

376. *Derivation of the abl. and instr. affixes.* 1) Pr. has the instr. suff. हिंतो and सुंतो (Vr. 5, 7), both in the plur. (H. C. 3, 7), but हिंतो also in the sing. (H. C. 3, 8). Of these the former contracts to M. होँ, the latter to E. H., W. H. सोँ, Mw. सूँ, G. शूँ; similarly as the 3. pl. pres. termin. Skr. अन्ति, Pr. अंति contracts in Gḍ. ऐँ or एँ or इँ (see § 497, 2 f.). In the Ap. Pr., there is an abl. aff. होंतओ or होंतउ (H. C. 4, 355), which appears in O. H. (Chand) as हुंतो or हूँत [1]). These forms

1) हूँत् is a wk. f. = Ap. Pr. होंतु or हुंतु.

are really part. pres. of the verb भू *to be* (cf. H. C. 3, 180). The modern B. has still an abl. aff. हइते, and N. भंदा, which are part. pres. (cf. S. Ch. 148, and see § 300), representing the Pr. forms हवंत° and भवंत or भंत (cf. H. C. 4, 60 हवंति and H. C. 4, 365 भंति = Skr. भवंति *they are*). The rationale of this usage may be explained (as Bs. II, 237) „by supposing the idea to be that of having previously been at a place, but not being there now, which involves the idea of having come away from it"; thus Ap. तहाँ होंतउ आगदो (H. C. 4, 355), O. H. तहाँ हुंतो आयो, N. ताँहाँ भंदा आयो, B. ओथा हइते आइल् *from there* (lit. *being there*) *he has come*. The Ap. and O. H. forms are *direct*, i. e., *he who is there* (lit. *the there being*) *has come*; the B. and N. forms are *oblique* and may be taken as loc., i. e., *in being there he has come*. Possibly the ordinary Pr. suff. हिंतो and सुंतो may be also pres. part. of the Rs. भू *be* and अस् *be* respectively, slightly modified for हंतो (cf. H. C. 4, 406 हंति)[1]) and संतो (cf. H. C. 1, 37). Just as हंतो or हुंतो (H. C. 4, 61) have become हिंतो, so संतो or सुंतो may become सिंतो; and this form appears to exist in the N. सित्[2]), and in the S. सें (Tr. 401), E. H. and H. H. से, G. थे and M. सीं or शीं[3]). The S. साँ (Tr. 401) I would similarly derive from संतो which is still used by S., in the form संदो, as a gen. aff. (Tr. 129), or from संते which is still used in E. H. as an adv. part. *on being* (see § 488, note). — The Pr. suff. हिंतो and सुंतो are used for the

---

1) Pr. has a tendency to change अ to इ in the suff. अंति of the 3. pl. and अंत° of the part. pres., see Wb. Bh. 404. 428, and B. has इते in the pres. part. for E. H. अते (§ 300).

2) With त् for न्त्, as in the M. 3. pl. pres. अत् for Pr. अंति, and in the E. H. pres. part. in अत्, B. इत् for Pr. अंतो (§ 300).

3) The M. सीं or शीं cannot be divided (as Bs. II, 272) into स् + ईं, the former being the termin. of the (Pr.) gen. sg., the latter the Pr. instr. plur. suff. हिं; thus M. देवासीं = देवास् or देवस्स + हिं. No doubt, modern M. case aff. (like नें in त्याच्या नें *by him*) may be added to a gen.; for they are relics of what were formerly full nouns. But ईं is not an aff., but the relic of an old suff.; see at the end of this paragraph.

instr. only, but the Ap. aff. होंतउ for the abl. also; similarly ह्रीँ and हीँ are confined, in M., to the instr., but in the other Gds. the corresponding aff. express both the instr. and abl. Thus instr. in E. H. ओह् से कइलू गइलू *done by him* or *with it*, but abl. in तहाँ से आइलू *come from there.* They never have in E. H. strictly the sense of „in company with"; thus *gone with him* is not ओह् से गइलू but ओह् के संग् गइलू; but they appear to be used so occasionally in S. (Tr. 403), e. g., वह पुनहू सेँ पलकु *return with Punahú a moment*; and, of course, the instr. easily admits of this sense. — The Pr. हिंतो (H. C. 3, 7. 8) and the Ap. होंतउ (H. C. 4, 372. 373) are used both in the sing. and plur.; but हिंतो was in Pr. originally confined to the plur. (Vr. 5, 6. 7), and the M. हीँ is so still; on the other hand, both M. and all other Gds. extend सीँ, सोँ, से, etc. to the sing. also, while the corresponding Pr. सुंतो is limited to the plur. — The M. abl. aff. हून् or, curtailed, ऊन् can not well be derived from the Pr. हिंतो (as Ls. 311. Bs. II, 234. 236); though it may be (like the O. H. हूँतू) traced to the Ap. होंतउ (or rather the wk. f. होंतु) by the change of न्त् to न्, as in the S. suff. अनि of the 3. plur. pres. for Pr. अंति. Indeed this derivation would hardly admit of a doubt, but for the fact, that in O. M. the aff. is हूनि or हूनियाँ, which points to its being a conj. part., the suff. of which is in O. M. उनियाँ or उनि and in M. M. ऊन् (see § 491). Accordingly it would be equal to होऊन *having been.* Similarly N. uses the conj. part. देखि *having seen* as an abl. aff.; e. g., ताँहाँ देखि निस्क्यो *he came out from there,* माँझ् देखि *from the midst.* But very possibly (as Bs. II, 236 suggests) some confusion may have taken place between the abl. aff. हून् and the conj. part. होऊन; and, on the whole, the identification of हून् with हुंतो seems most to commend itself[1]). — 2) As regards the other groups of abl. and instr. aff. or postpos., the B. ठाँइ

---

1) With Bs.' identification (II, 272) of the M. हीँ with Pr. हिं and of the H. सोँ or से with Skr. समं (II, 274) and with Ls.' derivation (310) of हिंतो from हिं + तस् I cannot agree.

(S. Ch. 229) and O. ठा-ह or ठाउँ or ठुँ (Sn. 13) are derivatives of Skr. स्थान, ठाँइ or ठा (ह is the abl. aff.) being = Ap. loc. ठाणि, and ठाउँ or ठुँ = Ap. abl. ठाणाहु. Identical with these, only substituting थ् for ठ् (cf. H. C. 4, 16) is the other set: N. थाञि, P., E. H., W. H. थो॑ (Ld. 77), G. थी (Ed. 115), all = Ap. loc. थाणि; and O. P. थाव्हु or थों or थो, M. P. थो॑ = Ap. abl. थाणाहु; in the B. थेके (S. Ch. 62. 230) and G. थकी the aff. के and की are superadded. — 3) The explanation of the set of instr. aff., E. H. सन्, सने, सेन्, सेनी, S. साणु or सेणु *with*, and of the abl. aff., E. H. ते, ते॑, P. उतो॑, S. ताँ or तो॑, has been given in § 375. So also that of the M. abl. aff. करून् and वरून्, and of the N. बाट, S. बटाँ. Others, as M. पासून्, P. पासो॑, and P. परो॑, S. पराँ or परो॑, and S. माँ or मो॑ or मंफाँ and S. मयाँ, will be explained in § 378. — 4) There are also some relics of the old organic instr. or abl. Thus M. has an instr. sing. suff. एँ (Man. 17), which is the Ap. instr. sg. suff. एं (H. C. 4, 342), probably contracted for अहिं (see § 367, 5); e. g., M. देवेँ *by a god*, Ap. देवें, for *देवहिं. Again M. has an instr. pl. suff. ईँ, which is contracted from the Ap. instr. pl. suff. अहिं (H. C. 4, 347); e. g., M. देवीँ *by gods* = Ap. देवहिं. Again there are the abl. sg. suff. आँ and अउँ or ओ॑ or उँ in S. (Tr. 117, 5) or ओ॑ in P. (Ld. 12) which are the same as the Ap. abl. plur. suff. अहं and अहुं (H. C. 4, 337. 339, see § 367, 5); e. g., S. घराँ *from a house* = Ap. Pr. घरहं, or S. घराउं or घरो॑ or घरूँ, P. घरो॑ = Ap. घरहुं.

377. *Derivation of the gen. affixes.* The O. H. possesses a gen. aff., which in the weak form, dir. and obl., sing. and pl., is केर् m., केरि f., and in the strong form, *masc.*, dir. sg. केरा (E. H.) or केरो, केरौ (W. H.), obl. sg. and dir. pl. केरे (E. H. and Br.) or केरा (Mw.); *fem.*, dir. and obl., sg. and pl. केरी. The same forms exist also in O. P. (Tr. A. Gr. CXXVI) and in O. G., which latter adds the st. form neut. sg. केरुँ, pl. केराँ (see Bs. II, 283). Thus masc. sg. केर् in सो सुग्रीव केर लघु धावन, i. e., *it is Sugriva's little messenger* (T. Dás, Lanká) or मिटै न जीवन्ह केर कलेसा *the pain of the creatures is not removed* (T. Dás in Kl. 72); fem. sg. केरि in सीता केरि करहु

रखवारी, i. e., *keep a watch of Sitá* (T. Dás in Kl. 72); masc. sg. dir. केरा in एक नारि व्रत रघुपति केरा, i. e., *to have one wife is the rule of Raghupati* (T. Dás, *Lanka*), or केरो in को तेरा पुत्र पिता तूँ काको मिथ्या भ्रम जग केरो, i. e., *who is thy son, whose father art thou, (such questioning) is a delusion and error of the world* (Kabír, Suravalí 12), or केरौ in दौरै गज अंधं चाहुवान केरौ *blindly ran the elephant of the Cháhuván* (Chand 20, 141); masc. sg. obl. केरे in आखर केरे वखत मे॑ बंदे किस का करोगे दीदार *at the time of the end, oh friend, to whom will you look up?* (in Kabir's Rekhtás); masc. pl. dir. केरे in ये किरीट दशकंधर केरे *these are the diadems of Ravana* (T. Dás, Lanká), or केरा in जान्हवी केरा तरंग तजी ने तट मा॑ जाइ कूप खादे रे *having left the waves of Ganges he goes on to the bank and drinks from a well* (Narsingh, Kávyad. 2, 4 in Bs. II, 283); fem. sg. dir. केरी in सुनि कठोर वाणी कपि केरी *having heard the stern voice of the monkey* (T. Dás, Lanká), etc. Some more examples will be found in my Essay I. in J. B. A. S. XLI, 127. 128. Bs. II, 281—284. Kl. 72. On referring to the rules for the treatment of adj. (§§ 381. 384. 386) it will be seen, that these gen. aff. केर etc., are treated exactly like adj. This remark applies also to the other sets of gen. affixes. The O. H., namely, possesses also another set, which is merely a slightly modified form of the former. It consists of the weak forms, dir. and obl., sg. and plur., कर m., करी f. Thus masc. dir. sg. कर in कौन रंग है जीव को ता कर करहु विवेक *what is the pleasure of life, of that make investigation* (Kabír, Ramaini 24), or चत्रि जाति कर रोष *the wrath of the warrior-caste* (T. Dás, Lanká); or plur. सब कर आजु सुकृत फल बीता *to day the fruit of the good deeds of all has passed away* (T. Dás Ayodhyá 343 in Bs. II, 279); fem. sg. dir. करि in सु भट सोसन विन किन्निय । हय किन्निय विन नरनि । सेन भीमह करि किन्निय ॥ lit. *the warriors without heads he made, the horses he made without men, the army of Bhima he dispersed* (Chand, Somabadha 41). For some more examples, see again my Ess. I, Bs. and Kl. *ibidem*. This set is preserved in E. H., which adds the corresponding strong forms, masc. dir. sg. करा, obl. sg. and nom. pl. करे, fem. sg. and pl., dir. and obl. करी. They are confined, however, to the pronouns (see § 439). They occur also in O., but are limited to the plur., in connection with the plur. sign मानन् (obl. f. of माने § 363, 2); thus gen. देव-मानन्-कर् *of gods,* where कर् is both masc. and fem., sing. and plur.; again loc. or dat. देव-मानन्-करे *to gods* and abl. देव-मानन्-कह *from gods,* where करे and कह are the regular O. dat. and abl. of कर् (cf. O. हाते *to* or *in a hand,* हातु *from a hand* of हात् *hand,* see Sn. 15). In the sing., O. curtails कर्, करे, कह into र्, रे, ह respectively, e. g., जन-र् *of a man,* but जन-मानन्-कर् *of men*; जन-रे *to a man,* जन-ह *from a man.* Again B., N. and Mw. possess only these curtailed forms; viz., B. the wk. f. र् in the gen. (e. g., sg. जने-र् *of a man,* pl. जन-दे-र् *of men*; sg. चेला-र् *of a disciple,* pl. चेला-दे-र् *of disciples,* see § 364, 2), and the st. f. रा in the nom. pl. (e. g., जने-रा *men,* lit. *(multitude) of man*; चेला-रा *disciples,* see § 369); N. the weak f. ह in the nom. pl. (e. g., जनहे-ह or जनह-ह *men,* चेलाहे-ह or चेलह-ह *disciples,* see § 364, 3); Mw. the st. f. रो m., री f. (e. g., जन-रो घर् *the house of a man,* जन-रै घरै *in the house of a man,* जन-रा घर्-नै *to the house of a man,* जन-रा घर् *the houses of a man,* जन-री बात् or बाताँ *the word* or *words of a man*). Similarly in Mw. and E. R., the conj. part. कर् is curtailed to र् (e. g., मर-र् *having died* = H. H. मर् कर्, see § 491)[1]. On the other hand, र् may be elided and the hiatus-vowels contracted; whence arise the st. forms का or को or कौ m., की f., के or का obl., for करा or करो, etc., and the weak forms कै or के or shortened कि or क comm. gen. for करि or कर्. Thus masc. dir. sg. in प्रान इन-कै दुष मुक्कै *his life departs from pain* (Chand 26, 2); fem. dir. sg. in सुनहु बिभीषण प्रभु-कै रीती। *hear, o Vibhúshan, the lord's custom* (T. Dás, Sundara 298 in Bs. II, 278); masc. dir. sg. क in प्रेम-क गुण कहब सब कोइ *every one will say (it is) the quality of love* (Vidyapati, Pad. in Bs. II, 281); fem. dir. sg. in पितु आयसु सब धरम-क टीका *(to obey) a father's command is the crown of all virtue* (T. Dás, Ayodhya 334 in Bs. II, 283); masc.

---

1) Similarly और् *and* is shortened in E. H. to अर् and curtailed in N. to र्; e. g., थिया र् *and they were.*

obl. sg. क in हरि सु उडरै छिन-क महि *Hari can save in an instant* (Chand 1, 60 in Bs. II, 283) or फुटल बाँधुलि कमल-क संग *the bándhuli has flowered with the lotus* (Vidyapati in Bs. Ind. Antiq. Febr. 1873). In the E. H., as a rule, the weak forms कै and के only are used. The former, however, is now constructed only with dir., the latter with obl. forms (e. g., जन कै घर *the house of a man*, but जन के घर मे *in the house of a man*); perhaps by way of assimilation to the W. H. obl. के, if the E. H. obl. के is not actually identical with it. The st. forms का or को sometimes occur already in O. Gd.; thus को in कंठसोभ बर इंद को । नाम कह्यो परवान ॥ *the name of this verse is truly called Kanṭasobha* (Chand 27, 31); fem. की in कथा मंड चहुआंन की कहि *they well told the story of Chahuán* (Chand 27, 22); obl. के in सूकर स्वान के जन्मै धरई । जो गुरु केरी निंदा करई, i. e., *he will take the births of a swine and dog who causes the disgrace of his teacher* (in Kabir's Rekhtás). They are the ordinary gen. aff. in W. H. (exc. Mw.) and H. H. Lastly there is an example of a fem. st. f. किय in कथा जंपि ससीवृत्त किय । अब कहत कथा विस्तार किय । जो राजन दूतन करिय ॥ *narrating the story of Sasivritta, he now tells the story in detail, which the messengers of the kings had told* (Chand 25, 41); and the corresponding masc. occurs, e. g., in the O. P. abl. aff. किअहु (Tr. A. Gr. CXXV) which is a regular Ap. Pr. abl. of किओ [1]). There can hardly be a doubt, *prima facie,* that all these various sets of gen. aff. are merely different modifications of the same original form. Turning to Pr., we find the 1st set not unfrequently occurring in the following forms: 1) in the wk. f. sg. केरो or केरु m., केरी f., केरं or केरु n.; st. f. sg. केरओ m., केरिआ f., केरअं or केरउं n., or (specially in Mg. Pr.) केरको etc. or केलके etc. They are treated in every way like adj., i. e., they are fully declined in conformity with the governing subst. Thus masc. केरो in H. C. 2, 147. 148; n. केरं in H. C. 2, 99. 148; *masc.* केरओ in एसो क्खु अलंकारओ अज्जआ केरओ *this surely*

---

1) It is quite analogous to the above mentioned O. abl. aff. कहु, which is a curtailed form of the Ap. abl. करहु or करो.

is the ornament of the lady (Mrchh. act. 4. Skr. आर्यायाः अलङ्कारः); *fem.* in मम केलिका वड्ढवालिआ *my turn of slaughter* (Mrchh. act. 10. Skr. मम वधपारी); *neut.* in कस्स केरकं एदं पवहणं *whose is this conveyance* (Mrchh. act. 6. Skr. कस्य प्रवहणम्) or तुम्हहं केरउं धणु *your wealth* (H. C. 4, 373. Skr. युष्माकं धनं); masc. instr. sg. in जसु केरें हुंकारडएं मुहहु पडंति तणाइं *on account of whose (the lion's) roaring the grass falls from the mouths (of the deer)* (H. C. 4, 422. Skr. यस्य हुंकारेण) [1]). It will be observed, that केर is here used in Pr. as a gen. aff. precisely as in Gḍ. For 1) it takes its dependent noun in the gen. (= Gḍ. obl. form) and agrees with its governing noun as an adj.; thus compare T. Dás' जीवन्ह केर कलेसा *the pain of the creatures* or Chand's भीमह करि सेन *the army of Bhima* with H. C.'s तुम्हहं केरउं धणु *the wealth of you*; 2) it is *pleonastic*, i. e., it has no meaning of its own and might be omitted from the passage without affecting the sense; thus तम्हहं धणु and तुम्हहं केरउं धणु [2]) or कस्स पवहणं and कस्स केरकं पवहणं are absolutely identical in meaning, just as जीवन्ह कलेसा or भीमह सेन would be in Gḍ.; 3) it is added merely to distinguish or emphasise the gen. or, in other words, simply as a gen. aff.; just as in Gḍ., where it is added only to distinguish the obl. f. in its gen. sense from its other senses; this, indeed, is expressly affirmed by H. C. 4, 422 संबन्धिनः केरतणौ i. e. सम्ब° परे केर° भवतः *after (or in addition to) the gen. kera and taṇa are used*; and then follows the example जसु केरें etc. (see above). It cannot be doubted, then, but that the Pr. केरो, etc. are identical with the Gḍ. केर, etc. and therefore, *prima facie,* with the other Gḍ. sets of gen. aff. Now, according to old Indian tradition, the Pr. केर is the same as the Skr. past part. कृत *done, made,* of the R. कृ *do.* I believe, this tradition can be shown to be correct both on *intrinsic* and *phonetic* grounds. In the first place, the phrase *done by* most easily lends itself to express the gen. sense „*of*"; thus in H. C.'s example

1) More exam. will be found in my Essay I. in J. B. A. S. XLI. 129. 130, and in an article by Pischel in the Ind. Antiq. April 1873. p. 121. 122.

2) H. C. 4, 373. 380 expressly states that तुम्हहं by itself is the gen. plur.

the phrase जसु केरें हुंकारउएं lit. *through the roaring made by whom* is equivalent to *through whose roaring*. It may be remarked here, that in the literary Pr. the word केर is usually not added to the gen., but compounded with its dependent noun; the gen. construction being confined, as a rule, to the Ap. and the lower Mg. dialects; thus Mh. Pr. रायकेरं *royal*, पारकेरं *foreign* (H. C. 2, 146) or अम्हकेरो *ours*, तुम्हकेरो *yours* (H. C. 2, 147. 1, 246. 2, 99), but Ap. Pr. अम्हहं केरउ *ours*, तुम्हहं केरउ *yours* (H. C. 4, 373. 359) or Mg. Pr. कश्श केलके *whose* (Mrchchh. 96, 22), तविश्शणोए केलका *of an ascetic* (Mrchh. 152, 6), etc. Originally केर cannot have been pleonastic, but must have had a meaning of its own, and supposing the latter to have been the past part. „done", केर would naturally be first used in the compounding construction; thus Mh. रायकेरं = Skr. राजकृतं lit. *done by a king*, Mh. अम्हकेरं or अम्हक्केरं (H. C. 2, 99) = Skr. अस्मत्कृतं *done by us*[1]). But the original meaning was soon lost sight of, and केर looked upon as a mere possessive (gen.) suff. and used in the compound constr., or even as a gen. aff. and, in this case, appended pleonastically to the gen. The former usage is expressly taught by H. C. in his rules on the Mh. Pr. इदमर्थस्य केरः i. e., *kera is used as a possessive suff.* (H. C. 2, 147) and परराजभ्यां क्कडिक्कौ च i. e., *kka, ikka and kera are used as possessive suff. after para and rája* (H. C. 2, 148), i. e., like the Skr. possessive suff. ईय and कीय. The latter usage is taught by him in his rule on the Ap. Pr. (quoted above) संबन्धिनः केरतणौ (H. C. 4, 422)[2]). — The identification (by Psch. in the

1) E. g., Pr. रायकेरं वयनं = Skr. राजकृतं वचनं lit. *speech made by a king*, i. e., *a king's speech*.

2) The comp. usage probably preceded the pleon. one; accordingly we find the comp. form Mh. Pr. तुम्हकेरो *yours* contracted in the later Ap. Pr. to तुम्हारा (H. C. 4, 434) which occurs in the Ap. beside the pleon. form तुम्हहं केरउ (H. C. 4, 357). Probably the Ap. तुम्हारा is really = *तम्हकरिश्रो, see § 73. — The curtailment of कर, करो to र, रो in B., O. and Mw. may perhaps be traced back to the original compounding usage. — The Skr. suff. कीय itself may well be derived from the past part. कृत.

Ind. Ant. Dec. 1873, p. 368 and Ls. 118. Wb. Spt. 38. 66) of केर with the Skr. part. fut. pass. कार्य is untenable. For 1) the meaning of कार्य *what is to be done* would not produce a gen. without a violent wrench (so rightly Bs. II, 286), and 2) phonetically, all Pr. analogies are (not, as Ls. thinks *for*, but) *against* it. In all the examples mentioned by the Pr. gramm., it is a *short* अ which absorbs a following इ; thus Pr. सेज्जा, वेल्ली, पेरंतो or पेरंतो, सुंदेरो, अच्छेरो, वम्हचेरो are = Skr. शय्या, वल्लिः, पर्यन्तः, सौन्दर्यः, आश्चर्यः, ब्रम्हचर्यः (Vr. 1, 5. H. C. 1, 57. 58. 59) [1]). On the other hand Skr. °आर्य° becomes in Pr. °अज्ज° or °आरिअ° (Vr. 3, 17. 10, 8. H. C. 2, 24. 4, 314); e. g., Pr. भज्जा or भारिआ = Skr. भार्या *wife*; Pr. कज्जं or कारिअं = Skr. कार्यम् *to be done* [2]). — *Secondly*, the identification of केर with कृत is supported by Pr. and Gḍ. phonetic analogies. Skr. roots in ऋ, as कृ, धृ, मृ, सृ, etc., become in Pr. कर, धर, मर, सर, etc. (Vr. 8, 12. H. C. 4, 234) and form their past part. by means of the connecting vowel इ (Ls. 363), as करिओ, धरिओ (H. C. 1, 36), मरिओ, सरिओ (H. C. 4, 355 पसरिअउं = Skr. प्रसृतकम्), etc. By the transfer of इ into the preceding syllable, करिओ and the

---

1) H. C. 1, 78 gives Pr. गेज्झं for Skr. ग्राह्यं; but even this single case is no real exception; for Skr. has both गृह्यं and ग्राह्यं; and the Pr. गेज्झं is clearly the former; just as Skr. गृह्णाति is in Pr. गेण्हइ (H. C. 4, 209); that is, Skr. गृह्यं = *ग्रह्यं = Pr. गेज्झं. — The Pr. मेत्त or मेत्थ for Skr. मात्र is not an exception; for no इ has been absorbed; besides the derivation from मात्र is doubtful; Ls. 128 suggests an original मित्र.

2) Mḍ. 19, 4 allows to the Ps. Pr. °अरिअ° also, but not °एर°; viz. र्यस्य रिअः प्राग्घ्रस्वो वा। र्यस्य रिअः स्यात्। प्राक् ह्रस्वश्च वा स्यात्॥ भारिआ। भरिआ॥ कार्ये कच्च् च दृश्यते। कच्चं। चकारात् कारिअं। करिअं च॥ i. e., „*ry* becomes *ria* and the preceding vowel may be short or long". — Skr. कार्य never becomes कार in Pr. (as Psch. ibidem); the Skr. कार is a different word, with an active sense, *doing*, while कार्य is passive, *what is to be done*. The B. gen. आपनकार्, आजिकार्, कालकार् do not contain a gen. aff. कार्; there is no such B. aff.; but the forms are regular gen. of आपना *own*, आजिका *of to-day*, कलका *of yesterday* (gen. आपनका-र्, etc.), which words exist in H. also and may be declined through all cases, both in H. and B.; see S. Ch. 115.

st. f. करिश्रश्रो become केरो and केरश्रो, just as Skr. आश्चर्यम् *wonderful* becomes in Pr. अच्छरिश्रं or अच्छेरं (Vr. 1, 5. H. C. 1, 58). Similarly Pr. उक्केरो *a heap* and देरं *a door* are, in all probability, modified from the past part. pass. Pr. उक्करिश्रो *heaped up* and दरिश्रं *split*, of the Rs. उत्कृ and दृ resp.[1]). The modified part. forms केरो and केरश्रो are never used in Pr. or Gḍ. but as gen. aff., while the unmodified forms करिश्रो and करिश्रश्रो serve both as proper part. and as gen. aff. No examples, indeed, I believe, of the latter two forms in either usage have been found as yet in Pr. literature. But notwithstanding this, their existence would be but in accordance with the general rule of the Pr. gramm. (Vr. 8, 12. H. C. 4, 234) that the conjugational base is कर् (not कृ). And what is more, they do actually exist in Gḍ. as the *ordinary past part.* of the verb कर् *to do*; see § 307; which §, moreover, will show, that in Gḍ. the part. forms of कर् are the same as the gen. aff. Thus the gen. aff. करा or कर् m., करी or करि f. occur identically as part. in O. H. (T. Dás) and Bs. and, in the slightly modified form करो m., in Kn., कर्यो m. in Mw. and कर्यौ m. in Br., करी f. in all (see Kl. 205, 3. 207, 390. 213, 405. 216, 414. 223, 431). The O. H. gen. aff. किय or O. P. abl. aff. किश्रहु occur as the ordinary H. H. part. किया m., किई f. *done*. The contr. gen. aff. का or क do not, I believe, occur as part., but quite analogous contractions are the part. गा or ग for गया or गिया *gone*, भा or भ for भया *been*, पा for पाया *found* in Bs. (see Kl. 225, 438. 230, 449) and O. H.; e. g., तमसि तमसि सामंत सब्ब। रोस भरि ग प्रथिराज ॥ i. e., *in great passion were all the chiefs, with wrath was filled Prathiráj* (= H. H. भर् गया). The E. H. part. कइल्, M. केला, B.

1) Pr. gramm. (H. C. 1, 58. 79) identify them with the Skr. उत्कर् and द्वारं, which, of course, can be true as to the meaning only. Ls. 118 derives उक्केरो from a supposed vulgar form उत्कर्य, which shows that he himself felt, that Pr. analogy requires a *short* अ before य् to produce ए; for according to rule (Pan. 3, 1. 120. 124) the part. fut. pass. ought to be उत्कार्य. — The common Skr. past part. is उत्कीर्ण; but Pr. would form, as usual, उत्करित.

करिल° presuppose an original form करिद् or करित (§§ 109.307). The st. form कर्यौं m. (= Ap. करिश्रउ) is found frequently in the O. H. of Chand; thus ब्रिंद् ललाट प्रसेद् । कर्यौं संकर् गजराजं ॥ *of the drops of perspiration made a chain the elephant* (Revaṭaṭa 3); or तिहि उप्पर् चामंड । कर्यौं हुस्सैन षांन सत्ति ॥ *upon this Chámaṇḍ made Hussain Khán ready* (Revaṭaṭa 58); and the st. form करिय f. (= Ap. करिइआ) in करिय अरज्ज उमराउ *the nobles made petition* (Revaṭaṭa 96), or सब्ब मिलि सु ताहि पुज्जा करिय *all assembling made adoration of him* (Adiparv. 96); again the wk. form करि f. in करि सलाह संमेल करि *they (made) took counsel having made an assembly* (Revaṭaṭa 96), etc. — Thus the gen. aff. of W. H., E. H., N., B. and O. form a group by themselves, all being derivatives of the past part. कृत. — 2) To this group I would also affiliate the M. aff. चा m., चो f., चें n. In the O. M. the forms चिया m., चियें n. (Man. 138) occur, from which the modern forms are contracted, just as M. H. का from O. H. किय. In M. the initial क् has been palatalised by the influence of the succeeding palatal इ; just as in Pr. चिलादो for Skr. किरातः (Vr. 2, 33) and in Pr. अम्हेच्चयं *ours*, तुम्हेच्चयं *yours* (H. C. 2, 149) beside Pr. अम्हक्केरं and तुम्हक्केरं (H. C. 2, 99. 2, 147). In fact, in the two last examples we have, in a slightly modified form, the O. M. gen. aff. चिया (cf. E. H. गया, but B. गिया *gone*). According to Pr. gramm. (H. C. 2, 147. 149) अम्हेच्चयं is but an other form of अम्हक्केरं, which shows that it is = *अम्हक्कयं = *अम्हक्कइअं = *अम्हक्करिअं, the इ having been transferred into the preceding syllable अक्क् and having palatalised it into एच्च्. — The M. चा is sometimes identified with the Skr. suff. त्य (as Bs. II, 289. Man. 132, 3). This theory assumes, that an old suff. has in comparatively modern times changed into an aff.; for the M. चा is not added to the base (as the Skr. suff.) but to the obl. form, i. e., to the old gen. Such a change would be, as far as I know, altogether unique, without any analogy or evidence to support it. The word केर (unlike त्य) was never a real suff., though sometimes it is practically used like one in Pr.; but it is a real noun with a meaning of its own, viz. *made* or *done*; and this accounts for its peculiar use as an aff. constructed with the obl. f. On the other hand, the change of क् to च् through a following इ is supported by the examples above quoted, to which may be added the S. neut. interrog. pron. छा *what* (i. e., *chhá* = *khiá* = *kihá*) corresponding to the P. किश्रा and W. H. क्या for *किहा (cf. P. obl. किह् दा *of whom*); also the G. शो m., शी f., शुं n. *who* for *छो, *छी, *छुं (see § 438, 5)[1]. — 3) The P., S. and possibly G. and Konkaní gen. aff., I believe, form a distinct group. The P. gen. aff. are: दा m., दी f. The same aff. occurs in B. as a component part of the plur. sign, viz. दे or दि in देर्, दिगे (see § 364, 2), and as the instr. aff. दिया with which may be compared the P. obl. plur. masc. दिश्रां, see § 374. I believe them to be identical with the past part. दिया *given* of the verb दे *to give* (see § 307), and their origin to be precisely analogous to that of the preceding groups. The past part. *given*, just like the part. *made*, would easily produce the gen. sense „*of*"; e. g., the P. तंत्र दी वाणी lit. *the sound given by an instrument* is the same as *the sound of an instrument*. — The S. gen. aff. are जो m., जी f. Here the original initial द् has been palatalised by the following palatal इ. Other examples of the same change are the P. श्रजिहा or श्रजेहा *of such sort* (Ld. 19) and the S. इजो *this* (Tr. 198, for *idhio* = *idiho*, see § 132, note) for Skr. ईदृशः; the S. उजो *that* (Tr. 202) = Skr. *एवदृशः; the Ap. Pr. एज्जाहो (Ls. 455, for *एदिश्राहो = *एदाइहो) = Skr. एतादृशः; the S. कुजाडो *what* (cf. H. कुजा *where*) for Skr. *केवदृशः (see § 438, 4). — The O. P. has a gen. aff. डा (Tr. A. Gr. CXXVI), where the initial द् has been cerebralised, as in the M. S. डिश्रनु *to give* (Tr. 276. H. H. देना). The modern G. gen. aff. नो m., नी f., नुं n. I am inclined to count with this set by the not uncommon change of द् or ड् to ण् or न् (§ 106). They might be, however, as Bs. II, 287 suggests, curtailed forms of the gen. aff. तणो, तणी, तणुं, which occur in

---

1) In the Romance languages the change of the guttural into the palatal is very common, even before the vowel *a*; e. g., lat. *camera*, french *chambre*, engl. *chamber*; lat. *caminus*, fr. *cheminée*, engl. *chimney*, etc.

O. G. and still earlier in the Ap. Pr. (H. C. 4, 422, e. g., अइ भग्गा अम्हाहं तणा *that is the fortune of us*). They still occur occasionally in Br. (तनौ) and Mw. तणो or तणूं m., तणी f., तणां plur. (see Kl. 68, 73). — The Mewárí gen. aff. ड़ो m., ड़ी f., ड़ा or ड़े obl. (Kl. 68) and Konkaní लो, etc. (Bs. II, 287) I am also inclined to refer to this group, on account of the cerebral ड़, which appears to be a modification of the ड् in the O. P. डा. They might be, however, identified with the Mw. रो, etc. (as Bs. II, 287), which occur also in O. P. (see Tr. A. Gr. CXXVI). And I may add here, that the aff. का, केरा, चा of the other groups and the S. जा occur in O. P. also (see Tr. ibidem). — 4) There is one more peculiar group of gen. aff.; viz. in Mw. (poetry) हंदो m., हंदी f. (Kl. 68. 73); in S. sg. dir. संदो m., संदी f., obl. संदे m., संदिअ f., plur. dir. संदा m., संदिऊँ f., obl. संदे॑ or संदनि m., संदिनि or संदिअनि or संदिउनि f.; in Ksh., with a sg. noun, sg. संदु m., संज़ f., pl. संदि m., संज f., with a plur. noun, sg. हिंदु m., हिंज़ f., pl. हिंदि m., हिंज f. (see Bs. II, 290)[1]). Bs. (II, 291) identifies them with the Pr. pres. part. हंतो and संतो *being* of the Rs. भू and अस् *to be*. This is quite possible. But perhaps an other derivation may be suggested. They may be divided into सं-दो, हं-दो or हिं-दो; the first parts स and हं or हिं being the Pr. gen. termin. of the sing. and plur. resp. (§ 365, 1. 7), and दो the gen. aff. as in P. Thus Mw. जनहंदो or Ksh. जनहिंदु *of men* being really जनहं or जनहिं + दो or दु; S. जनसंदो and Ksh. जनसंदु *of a man* being जनस-दो for the Pr. gen. sg. जणास्स. This would explain the singular difference in Ksh. between the sing. and plur. aff. On the other hand, one would have to assume that S. has lost the plur. and Mw. the sing. forms. But these curious gen. aff. are at present too little known, to allow of any satisfactory theory being propounded.

---

1) Bs. transliterates سنزه by संज़ह्, which is hardly correct. The final ه is merely a mater lectionis, to indicate that the word in which it is used ends in a short or, sometimes, long *a*; e. g., نه = न *not*, به = व *with*, بنده = वंदा *servant*, etc. Hence either संज *sañja* or संजा *sañjá*; probably the former.

378. *Derivation of the locative affixes.* 1) The original of the aff. में etc. is the Skr. loc. मध्ये *in the midst of*, which in Ap. Pr. becomes मज्झे or मज्झि or मज्झहिं. From these Ap. forms arise two Gḍ. sets, one retaining झ्, the other changing it to ह् (see § 117). To the first set belong the B. माझे, S. मंझे for Ap. मज्झे; the O. H. मझि or माँझ, E. H. माँझ् for Ap. मज्झि, and the O. M. माझीं (or माझीं) for Ap. मज्झहिं; also the S. abl. aff. मंझों or मंझाँ *from-within* for Ap. मज्झहुं or मज्झहु. To the second set belong the O. H. महि for Ap. मझि, and the O. H. माँहैं or माँहीं or माँही, E. H. and Br. माँहों, Mw. माहे or माईं or मईं (for *महीं) for Ap. मज्झहिं; also the E. H. मे contracted from महि, W. H. में contr. from *महों, E. H., W. H., G. माँ, N. मा similarly contr. from *महाँ = मझाँ (cf. S. abl. aff.) = Ap. मज्झहं; and W. H. मों for *महों = मझों (cf. S. abl. aff.) = Ap. मज्झहुं. Both, माँ and मों, occur in S. also as abl. aff. — 2) Other groups of loc. aff. or postpositions are: a) the M. ठाईं = Ap. ठाणहिं, and the N. थाञि = Ap. थाणि, for Skr. स्थाने *in the place of*; b) the N. माथि and S. मथे *upon* = Ap. Pr. मत्थि or मत्थे for Skr. मस्ते *on the head* or *top of*, and the corresponding S. abl. aff. मथाँ *from-upon*; similar to these are: S. सिरे, P. सिरू *upon* = Ap. सिरे for Skr. सिरसि *on the head of*; c) the B. भितर् or भितरे, E. H., W. H. भीतर् *within* (see § 172); d) in all Gḍs. पर् or परि or पर *upon*, Ap. Pr. परि (H. C. 4, 438), Skr. परे *beyond*; and the corresponding abl. aff. S. पराँ and S. or P. परों *from-upon*; e) the S. and G. पासे, P. and W. H. पास् = Ap. पासि or पासे, and M. पासीं = Ap. पासहिं, for Skr. पार्श्वे *by the side of*; f) the S. विचे, P. विच्, O. P. विचि, W. H. बीच् *within* = Ap. विच्चे or विच्चि, perhaps for Skr. वृत्ये lit. *surrounded by*; cf. H. C. 4, 421, where the Ap. विच्च is said to be a substitute for Skr. वर्त्तमान; g) the M. ंत् *ṃt*, as in घरांत् *in a house*, कवींत् *in a poet*, मधूंत् *in honey* (Man. 30. 31), is probably a curtailment of the Pr. अंतो or अंत (H. C. 1, 14. 60) for Skr. अन्तर् *within*; and related to it, in all Gḍs., अंतर् = Ap. अंतरु (H. C. 4, 350), for Skr. अन्तरम् *within*. — 3) There are also some relics of the old organic loc.: a) loc. sg. in इ in most Gḍs.,

for Ap. इ, Skr. ए; b) loc. sg. in ऐं or ए in most Gds., or ई in N., P., G., for Ap. ए or अइ or अहि; c) loc. sg. in ऐं or एँ in E. H., ईं in P., or loc. sg. and pl. in ईं in M., for Ap. sg. and pl. अहिं; d) loc. sg. in आँ in E. H., W. H., or loc. sg. and pl. in आँ in M., for Ap. pl. अहं; e) loc. sg. in ओं or ऊ in W. H., for Ap. pl. अहुं. Examples see §§ 367, 5. 375, 1. 2. 77. 78.

5. DECLENSION.

379. There is only *one* declension. All subst. are declined exactly alike; and the base never changes, exc. in the obl. cases of the plur., where अन्, इन्, उन् are added (see § 362). One example, therefore, of a subst. fully declined will be sufficient. But as a matter of convenience, I shall add a list of nom. and gen. of a subst. of every form, gender and termin., leaving it to the student to supply the remainder.

1. Masculines in अ.

a) Short form: राम् *Rám.*

	Sing.	Simple plur.	Comp. plur.	
nom.	राम्	राम्	राम-लोग्	or रामन्लोग्
acc.	राम् or रा°के	राम् or रामन् के	राम-लोग् or °गन् के	or रामन्लोग् or °के
instr.	राम् से	रामन् से	राम-लोगन् से	or रामन्लोग् से
dat.	राम् के	रामन् के	राम-लोगन् के	or रामन्लोग् के
abl.	राम् से	रामन् से	राम-लोगन् से	or रामन्लोग् से
gen.	राम् कै, °के	रामन् कै, °के	राम-लोगन् कै, °के	or रामन्लोग् कै, °के
loc.	राम् मे	रामन् मे	राम-लोगन् मे	or रामन्लोगन् मे
voc.	हे राम्	हे राम्	हे राम-लोग्	or हे रामन्लोग्

b) Long form: रम-वा or रम-वाँ.

	Sing.	Simple plur.	Comp. plur.	
nom.	रम-वा	रम-वा	रम-वालोग्	or रम-वन्लोग्
acc.	रम-वा or र° के	रम-वा or रम-वन् के	रम-वालोग् or °गन् के	or रम-वन्लोग् or र°के
instr.	रम-वा से	रम-वन् से	रम-वालोगन् से	or रम-वन्लोग् से
dat.	रम-वा के	रम-वन् के	रम-वालोगन् के	or रम-वन्लोग् के
abl.	रम-वा से	रम-वन् से	रम-वालोगन् से	or रम-वन्लोग् से
gen.	रम-वा कै, °के	रम-वन् कै, °के	रम-वालोगन् कै, °के	or रम-वन्लोग् कै, °के

	Sing.	Simple plur.	Comp. plur.	
loc.	रमन्वा मे	रमन्वन् मे	रमन्वालोगन् मे	or रमन्वन्लोग् मे
voc.	हे रमन्वा	हे रमन्वा	हे रमन्वालोग्	or हे रमन्वन्लोग्

c) Redundant form: रमौवा or रमौआ or रमौवाँ or रमौआँ.

nom.	रमौवा	रमौवा	रमौवालोग्	or रमौवन्लोग्
acc.	रमौवा or र° के	रमौवा or °वन् के	रमौवालोग् or °गन् के	or रमौवन्लोग् or र° के
instr.	रमौवा से	रमौवन् से	रमौवालोगन् से	or रमौवन्लोग् से
dat.	रमौवा के	रमौवन् के	रमौवालोगन् के	or रमौवन्लोग् के
abl.	रमौवा से	रमौवन् से	रमौवालोगन् से	or रमौवन्लोग् से
gen.	रमौवा कै, °के	रमौवन् कै, °के	रमौवालोगन् कै, °के	or रमौवन्लोग् कै, °के
loc.	रमौवा मे	रमौवन् मे	रमौवालोगन् मे	or रमौवन्लोग् मे
voc.	हे रमौवा	हे रमौवा	हे रमौवालोग्	or हे रमौवन्लोग्

Note: The long and redundant forms in आ may be pronounced with a final *anunásika* (see §§ 195. 365, 4); thus gen. रमन्वाँ कै or रमौवाँ कै, etc. — Subst. which do not denote *rational* beings, can not form the comp. pl. (see § 361); thus gen. घरन् कै *of houses*, बाघन् कै *of tigers*, not घरलोगन् कै, बाघलोगन् कै.

2. Masculines in आ.

a) Short form: बेटा *son*.

	Sing.	Simple plur.	Comp. plur.	
nom.	बेटा	बेटा	बेटालोग्	or बेटन्लोग्
gen.	बेटा कै, °के, etc.	बेटन् कै, °के, etc.	बेटालोगन् कै, °के	or बेटन्लोग् कै, °के, etc.

b) Long form: बेटन्वा or बेटन्वाँ.

nom.	बेटन्वा	बेटन्वा	बेटन्वालोग्	or बेटन्वन्लोग्
gen.	बेटन्वा कै, °के, etc.	बेटन्वन् कै, °के, etc.	बेटन्वालोगन् कै, °के	or बेटन्वन्लोग् कै, °के, etc.

c) Redundant form: बेटौवा or बेटौवाँ, etc.

nom.	बेटौवा	बेटौवा	बेटौवालोग्	or बेटौवन्लोग्
gen.	बेटौवा कै, °के, etc.	बेटौवन् कै, °के, etc.	बेटौवालोगन् कै, °के	or बेटौवन्लोग् कै, °के, etc.

3. Masculines in इ.

a) Short form: रिषि *rikhi patriarch*.

nom.	रिषि	रिषि	रिषिलोग्	or रिषिन्लोग्
gen.	रिषि कै, °के, etc.	रिषिन् कै, °के, etc.	रिषिलोगन् कै, °के, etc.	or रिषिन्लोग् कै, °के, etc.

b) Long form: रिसिया or रिसियाँ.

	Sing.	Simple plur.	Comp. plur.
nom.	रिसिया	रिसिया	रिसियालोग् or रिसियन्लोग्
gen.	रिसिया कै, °के, etc.	रिसियन् कै, °के, etc.	रिसियालोगन् कै, °के or रिसियन्लोग् कै, °के, etc.

c) Redundant form: रिसियवा or रिसियवाँ.

nom.	रिसियवा	रिसियआ	रिसियवालोग् or रिसियअन्लोग्
gen.	रिसियवा कै, °के, etc.	रिसियअन् कै, °के, etc.	रिसियवालोगन् कै, °के or रिसियअन्लोग् कै, °के, etc.

4. Masculines in ई.

a) Short form: भाई *brother*.

nom.	भाई	भाई	भाईलोग or भाइन्लोग्
gen.	भाई कै, °के, etc.	भाइन् कै, °के, etc.	भाईलोगन् कै, °के or भाइन्लोग् कै, °के, etc.

b) Long form: भइया or भैया or भइयाँ or भैयाँ.

nom.	भैया	भैया	भैयालोग् or भैयन्लोग्
gen.	भैया कै, °के, etc.	भैयन् कै, °के, etc.	भैयालोगन् कै, °के or भैयन्लोग् कै, °के, etc.

c) Redundant form: भैयवा or भैयवाँ.

nom.	भैयवा	भैयवा	भैयवालोग् or भैयवन्लोग्
gen.	भैयवा कै, °के, etc.	भैयवन् कै, °के, etc.	भैयवालोगन् कै, °के or भैयवन्लोग् कै, °के, etc.

5. Masculines in उ.

a) Short form: तरु *tree*.

nom.	तरु	तरु	*deest.*
gen.	तरु कै, °के, etc.	तरुन् कै, °के, etc.	

b) Long form: तरुवा or तरुआ or तरुवाँ or तरुआँ.

nom.	तरुआ	तरुआ	*deest.*
gen.	तरुआ कै, °के, etc.	तरुअन् कै, °के, etc.	

c) Redundant form: तरुअवा or तरुअवाँ.

nom.	तरुअवा	तरुअवा	*deest.*
gen.	तरुअवा कै, °के, etc.	तरुअवन् कै, °के, etc.	

6. Masculines in ऊ.

a) Short form: नाऊ *barber*.

nom.	नाऊ	नाऊ	नाऊलोग् or नाउन्लोग्
gen.	नाऊ कै, °के, etc.	नाउन् कै, °के, etc.	नाऊलोगन् कै, °के or नाउन्लोग् कै, °के, etc.

b) Long form: नउआ or नौआ or नौवा or नउआँ etc.

	Sing.	Simple plur.	Comp. plur.
nom.	नौवा	नौवा	नौवालोग् or नौवन्लोग्
gen.	नौवा कै, °के, etc.	नौवन् कै, °के, etc.	नौवालोगन् कै, °के or नौवन्लोग् कै, °के, etc.

c) Redundant form: नउअवा or नौअवा or नौअवाँ, etc.

nom.	नौअवा	नौअवा	नौअवालोग् or नौअवन्लोग्
gen.	नौअवा कै, °के, etc.	नौअवन् कै, °के, etc.	नौअवालोगन् कै, °के or नौअवन्लोग् कै, °के, etc.

7. Feminines in अ.

a) Short form: बात् *word, thing, event.*

nom.	बात्	बात्	*deest.*
gen.	बात् कै, °के, etc.	बातन् कै, °के, etc.	

b) Long form: बतिया or बतियाँ.

nom.	बतिया	बतिया	*deest.*
gen.	बतिया कै, °के, etc.	बतियन् कै, °के, etc.	

c) Redundant form: बतियवा or बतियवाँ.

nom.	बतियवा	बतियवा	*deest.*
gen.	बतियवा कै, °के, etc.	बतियवन् कै, °के, etc.	

8. Feminines in आ.

a) Short form: दुर्गा *Durgá.*

nom.	दुर्गा	दुर्गा	दुर्गालोग or दुर्गन्लोग्
gen.	दुर्गा कै, °के, etc.	दुर्गन् कै, °के, etc.	दुर्गालोगन् कै, °के or दुर्गन्लोग् कै, °के, etc.

b) Long form: दुर्गिया or दुर्गियाँ.

nom.	दुर्गिया	दुर्गिया	दुर्गियालोग् or दुर्गियन्लोग्
gen.	दुर्गिया कै, °के, etc.	दुर्गियन् कै, °के, etc.	दुर्गियालोगन् कै, °के or दुर्गियन्लोग् कै, °के, etc.

c) Redundant form: दुर्गियवा or दुर्गियवाँ.

nom.	दुर्गियवा	दुर्गियवा	दुर्गियवालोग् or दुर्गियवन्लोग्
gen.	दुर्गियवा कै, °के, etc.	दुर्गियवन् कै, °के, etc.	दुर्गियवालोगन् कै, °के or दुर्गियवन्लोग् कै, °के, etc.

9. Feminines in इ.

a) Short form: आगि *fire.*

nom.	आगि	आगि	*deest.*
gen.	आगि कै, °के, etc.	आगिन् कै, °के, etc.	

b) Long form: अगिया or अगियाँ.

	Sing.	Simple plur.	Comp. plur.
nom.	अगिया	अगिया	*deest.*
gen.	अगिया कै, °के, etc.	अगियन् कै, °के, etc.	

c) Redundant form: अगियवा or अगियवाँ.

nom.	अगियवा	अगियवा	*deest.*
gen.	अगियवा कै, °के, etc.	अगियवन् कै, °के, etc.	

10. Feminines in ई.

a) Short Form: लाठी *staff.*

nom.	लाठी	लाठी	*deest.*
gen.	लाठी कै, °के, etc.	*deest* (§ 362, exc.)	

b) Long form: लठिया or लठियाँ.

nom.	लठिया	लठिया	*deest.*
gen.	लठिया कै, °के, etc.	लठियन् कै, के, etc.	

c) Redundant form: लठियवा or लठियवाँ.

nom.	लठियवा	लठियवा	*deest.*
gen.	लठियवा कँ, °के, etc.	लठियवन् कै, °के, etc.	

11. Feminines in ऊ.

a) Short form: बहू *daughter-in-law.*

nom.	बहू	बहू	बहूलोग् or बहुन्लोग्
gen.	बहू कै, °फे, etc.	बहुन् कै, °के, etc.	बहूलोगन् कै, °के or बहुन्लोग् कै, °के, etc.

b) Long form: बहुवा or बहुआ or बहुआँ, etc.

nom.	बहुआ	बहुआ	बहुआलोग् or बहुअन्लोग्
gen.	बहुआ कै, °के, etc.	बहुअन् कै, °के, etc.	बहुआलोगन् कै, °के or बहुअन्लोग् कै, °के, etc.

c) Redundant form: बहुअवा or बहुअवाँ.

nom.	बहुअवा	बहुअवा	बहुअवालोग् or बहुअवन्लोग्
gen.	बहुअवा कँ, °के, etc.	बहुअवन् कै, °के, etc.	बहुअवालोगन् कै, °के or बहुअवन्लोग् कै, °के, etc.

SECOND CHAPTER. THE ADJECTIVE.

1. FORMS OF THE ADJECTIVE.

380. Every adj. admits of three forms: the short, long and redundant. The short is the primary form, which is given in the dictionaries and by which it is generally known. The other two are more or less vulgar. The latter are made by adding to the weak form (see § 381) the pleon. suff. of the second, third and fifth sets of the first group, as explained in §§ 198. 199. Thus, *masc.*, sh. f. मोट् *thick*, lg. f. मोटक्का or मोटका, red. f. मोटक्कवा or मोटकवा; *fem.*, sh. f. मोट्, lg. f. मोटक्की or मोटकी, red. f. मोटक्किया or मोटकिया; *masc.*, sh. f. बड़ा *great*, lg. f. बड़क्का or बड़का, red. f. बड़क्कवा or बड़कवा; *fem.*, sh. f. बड़ी, lg. f. बड़क्की or बड़की, red. f. बड़क्किया or बड़किया; *com. gen.*, sh. f. भारी *heavy*, lg. f. *masc.* भरिक्का or भरिका, *fem.* भरिक्की or भरिकी, red. f. *masc.* भरिक्कवा or भरिकवा, *fem.* भरिक्किया or भरिकिया; *com. gen.*, sh. f. गरु *heavy*, lg. f. *masc.* गरुक्का or गरुका, *fem.* गरुक्की or गरुकी, red. f. *masc.* गरुक्कवा or गरुकवा, *fem.* गरुक्किया or गरुकिया, etc.

381. All adj. of the short form in अ admit of two forms, a weak and a strong. The weak form ends in अ and is the original one; the strong form is made by adding to this the pleon. suff., आ m., ई f., of the first set of the first group, as explained in § 196. Thus, *masc.*, wk. f. लाम् *long*, st. f. लामा; *fem.*, wk. f. लाम्, st. f. लामी; or wk. f., *com. gen.*, ऊच् *high*, st. f. *masc.* ऊचा, *fem.* ऊची, etc. Adj. in ई and ऊ exist only in the strong form; their weak forms in इ and उ are obsolete. Thus st. f., *com. gen.*, भारी *heavy*, हलू *light*; the wk. f. भारि, हरु or हलु occur in O. H. (Tulsí Dás).

382. The adj. of the strong form in ई admit of two forms, the contracted and uncontracted. The latter is made by adding the pleon. suff. इउँ to the former, see § 197. Thus भारी or भरिउँ *heavy*. Of the uncontracted a long form भरिउँका m., भरिउँकी f., may be made, but no redundant form.

383. When adj. are used as subst. or parts of proper names, their long and redundant forms are made exactly like those of real subst. Thus सेठन्वा (not सेठन्का), lg. f. of सेठ् a name of a caste (lit. *best*, Skr. श्रेष्ठ); or मिठवा ग्राम् the name of a species of mangoe, but मिठका ग्राम् any sweet mangoe.

2. GENDER.

384. Adj., like subst., have only two genders, masc. and fem. Strong and long adj. change, in the fem., the final आ to ई, and redundant adj. अवा to इया (see §§ 258 ff.). In other adj. the two genders are identical in form. Thus the wk. f. मीठ् *sweet*, छोट् *small*, etc., and the st. f. भारी *heavy*, हलू *light*, etc. are *gen. com.*; but st. f. *masc.* मोठा, छोटा, *fem.* मोठो, छोटो, etc., and lg. f. *masc.* मिठका or मिठक्का, *fem.* मिठकी or मिठक्की, etc., and red. f. *masc.* मिठकवा, *fem.* मिठकिया, etc.

385. *Affinities and Derivation.* All other Gḍs. have, like the E. H., a fem. in ई for their strong forms in आ (E. and S. Gḍ. and P.) or ओ or औ (W. and N. Gḍ.). Thus *masc.* B., O., W. H. काला, E. H. कारा *black*, M., P. काळा, G. काळो, S. कारो; *fem.* B., O., W. H. काली, M., P., G. काळी, E. H., S. कारी, etc. But the B. and O., as a rule, and even the E. H. not unfrequently, dispense with the use of strong adj. in आ. In S. the weak forms in उ (corresp. to अ in the other Gḍs.) have a fem. in इ or अ (Tr. 99. 152); in all other Gḍs. the fem. ends in अ; thus S. अधु *half*, *fem.* अध or अधि, but E. H., B., O., G. *masc.* or *fem.* श्राध्. In E. H., however, the fem. wk. f. in इ is preserved in the part., when the latter are used to form participial tenses (see §§ 502 ff.); thus *fem.* करति, of *masc.* करत् *doing*, in the 2. sg. pret. conj. करतिस् *if thou didst* (*fem.*); or कइलि fem., of कइल्, in the 2. sg. pret. ind. कइलिस् *thou didst*; करबि fem., of करब्, in the 2. sg. fut. ind. करबिस् *thou wilt do*, etc. In H. H. the weak fem. in अ and इ cannot properly be used. In Skr., adj. in अ generally form their fem. in आ; but in Pr. they may optionally have a fem. in आ or ई (Vr. 5, 24. H. C. 3, 32), which become अ or इ in Gḍ.

(see §§ 42. 43). As to the derivation of the fem. term. इ and इया see § 262.

3. DECLENSION.

386. Adj. are declined precisely like subst., with the following exceptions: 1) strong adj. in आ change it to ए in the obl. form sg. and pl. — 2) long adj. in का or क्का change आ to ऊ in the voc. sg., and also throughout the plur., if the adj. is used in a derisive sense (i. e. परिहस्ये). Thus, *dir. form,* nom. sg. ई मीठा आम् आटै *this is a sweet mangoe*; *obl. form,* acc. sg. ऊ मीटे आम् के खैलेस् *he ate a sweet mangoe*: dir. f., nom. sg. ऊ मिठका आम् आटै *that is a sweet mangoe*; obl. f., acc. sg. ऊ मिठके आम् के खैलेस् *he ate a sweet mangoe*; dir. f., nom. sg. ओकर् अच्छा घोरा आटै *his is a good horse*; obl. f., loc. sg. ऊ अच्छे घोरा पर् चढल् आटै *he is mounted on a good horse.* Again, dir. f., nom. pl. ई मीठा आम् आटैं *these are sweet mangoes*; obl. f., acc. pl. ऊ मीटे आमन् के खैलेस् *he ate sweet mangoes*; dir. f., nom. pl. ऊ मिठका आम् आटैं *those are sweet mangoes*; obl. f., acc. pl. ऊ मिठके आमन् के खैलेन् *he ate sweet mangoes*: dir. f., nom. pl. ओकर् अच्छा घोरा आटैं *his are good horses*; obl. f., loc. pl. ऊ अच्छे घोरे पर् चढल आटैं *they are mounted on good horses.*

387. *Affinities.* The M. and Br. agree with the E. H. in inflecting, in the sing., their strong adj. in आ differently from their strong subst. in आ. While the termination of the obl. sing. of subst. is आ in E. H. and Br. and या in M., that of the obl. form of adj. is ए in all three. In the other Gds. the adj. does not differ from the subst. in the obl. sg. Thus, gen. sg., E. H. बडे घोरा कै *of a big horse,* Br. बडे घोडा को, M. बडे घोड्या चा; but Mw. बडा घोडा रो, G. वडा घोडा नो, P. बडे घोडे दा, S. बडे घोडे जो, B. बडा घोडा-र्, etc. In all Gds. the obl. form of adj. is the same in both plur. and sing., except in S., where their obl. f. pl. may be optionally like that of the subst. (Tr. 145); thus, gen. pl., E. H. बडे घोरन् कै *of big horses,* Br. बडे घोडों को, M. बड घोड्यां चा, Mw. बडा घोडां रो, G. वडा घोडाव् नो, P. बडे घोडिआं दा, S. बडे घोडें जो

or घोड़े॰ घोड़े॰ ज़ो, etc. It must, of course, be understood, that if an adj. is used substantively, and not attributively, it is declined in every respect like a real subst.; and that in all Gḍs.

4. COMPARISON.

388. The degrees of comparison cannot be indicated by any change in the (positive) form. The comparative is expressed by putting the object with which another is compared in the abl. (made with the aff. से), and the superlative by prefixing to the adj. either the adj. itself or the pron. सब् *all* in the abl. case; e. g., ओकरे मोट् बर्दा से मोर् बर्दा अच्छा बाटै *my bullock is better than his fat bullock*; ओह् से बड़ा *greater than he*; ई सब् से मिठका आम् बाटै *this is the sweetest mangoe*, lit., this is a mangoe sweet (compared) with all (others); अच्छी स अच्छी तरकारी *the best vegetable*; अच्छे से अच्छे चाउर् कै भात् *the best (cooked) rice*. Sometimes, however, the comp. is expressed by the long form of the adj. (see § 198), as it emphasizes its meaning. Thus के बड़का बाटै *which is the elder one*; ऊ छोटका बाटै *that is the younger one*.

389. *Affinities*. In all Gḍs. the comp. and superlat. degrees are formed precisely as in E. H.; see S. Ch. 83. Sn. 21. Man. 40, 78. note 1. Ld. 15. Ed. 45, 97. 98. Tr. 156. Thus, comparative, E. H. ओह् से बड़ा *greater than he*, B. ताहा हइते बड़, O. ताहा-ठु बड़, M. त्याहून् बड़ा, Br. वा सो॰ बड़ो, Mw. उण् सूँ बड़ो, G. आ थी बडो, P. उह् ते बड़ा, S. हुन खाँ बड़ो; and superlat., E. H. सब् से बड़ा *greatest*, B. सकल् हइते ब°, O. सकल-ठु ब°, M. सर्वाहून् ब°, Br. सब् सो॰ ब°, Mw. सब् सूँ ब°, G. सभ थी ब°, P. सब् ते ब°, S. सभ खाँ ब°.

THIRD CHAPTER. THE NUMERAL.

390. There are various kinds of numerals in E. H., as cardinals, ordinals, multiplicatives, collectives, reduplicatives, fractionals, beside which there are some others, as proportionals, subtractives, distributives, indefinitives, which are expressed by various modes of paraphrase.

1. CARDINALS.

391. Their forms from *one* to *hundred* are the following:

1. एक्	21. ऐकइस्	41. ऐकतालिस्	61. ऐकसठि	81. ऐक्यासी
2. दुइ	22. बाइस्	42. बयालिस्	62. बासठि	82. बयासी
3. तीनि	23. तेइस्	43. तैँतालिस्	63. तिरसठि	83. तिरासी
4. चारि	24. चौबिस्	44. चौवालिस्	64. चौँसठि	84. चौरासी
5. पाँच्	25. पचीस्	45. पैँतालिस्	65. पैँसठि	85. पचासी
6. छ	26. छब्बिस्	46. छियालिस्	66. छाछठि	86. छियासी
7. सात्	27. सताइस्	47. सैँतालिस्	67. सरसठि	87. सत्तासी
8. आठ्	28. अठाइस्	48. अडतालिस्	68. अडसठि	88. अट्ठासी
9. नौ	29. ओनतिस्	49. ओनचास्	69. ओनहत्तर	89. नवासी
10. दस्	30. तीस्	50. पचास्	70. सत्तर्	90. नब्बे
11. ऐग्यारह्	31. ऐकतिस्	51. ऐक्यावन्	71. ऐखत्तर्	91. ऐक्यानबे
12. बारह्	32. बतिस्	52. बावन्	72. बहत्तर्	92. बानबे
13. तेरह्	33. तैँतिस्	53. तिरपन्	73. तिहत्तर्	93. तिरानबे
14. चौदह्	34. चौँतिस्	54. चौवन्	74. चौहत्तर्	94. चौरानबे
15. पन्दरह्	35. पैँतिस्	55. पंचावन्	75. पछत्तर्	95. पंचानबे
16. सोरह्	36. छत्तिस्	56. छप्पन्	76. छिहत्तर्	96. छानबे
17. सतरह्	37. सैँतिस्	57. सत्तावन्	77. सयत्तर्	97. सत्तानबे
18. अठारह्	38. अडतिस्	58. अट्ठावन्	78. अठत्तर्	98. अट्ठानबे
19. ओनइस्	39. ओनतालिस्	59. ओनसठि	79. ओनसी	99. निनानबे
20. बीस्	40. चालिस्	60. साठि	80. अस्सी	100. सौ

392. Some of the cardinal numbers admit one or more slightly different forms; but those marked with an asterisk are used only in the multiplication table, and those marked with two asterisks, only in the formation of cardinals above *a hundred*; thus:

1. यक्	5. पच्* or	11. इग्यारह् or	38. अरतिस् or	54. चौअन् or
2. दो*	पाच्	ग्यारह्	अठतिस्	चउअन्
3. तिन्* or	6. छह्* or	15. पनरह्	44. चवालिस् or	55. पचपन्
तीन्	छव्	24. चवबिस् or	चउआलिस्	67. सड़सठि or
4. चर्* or	7. सत्*	चउबिस्	48. अरतालिस् or	सतसठि
चार्	8. अठ्	30. तिस्*	अठतालिस्	68. अरसठि

71. ऐकहत्तर्	78. अठहत्तर् or	95. पनचानवे	100. सै ** or
75. पचहत्तर्	अठन्नत्तर् *	99. निन्नानवे or	सो ** or
77. सतहत्तर्	84. चवरासी	निन्यानवे	शल्

The final syllables °बिस्, °तिस्, °लिस् may, optionally, be spelled °बीस्, °तीस्, °लीस्; thus 24 चौबिस् or चौबीस्, 33 तैंतिस् or तैंतीस्, 40 चालिस् or चालीस्; but 21 ऐकइस्, not ऐकईस्; 23 only तेइस्, not तेईस्. Again all numbers of the seventh decade may drop the final इ; thus 60 साठि or साठ्, 66 छाइठि or छाइठ्, etc. Again the initial syllable ओन्° may also be spelled वन्°; thus 19 ओनइस् or वनइस्, 79 ओनासी or वनासी.

393. All cardinals above *a hundred* are formed by subjoining the lower number to the higher without any intervening conjunction; thus:

101. एक सै एक	103. एक् सै तीन्	105. एक् सै पाँच्	210. दुइ सै दस्
102. एक् सै दुइ	104. एक् सै चार्	200. दुइ सै	220. दुइ सै बीस्
	300. तीन सै	1000. सहसर्	
	400. चार् सै	100,000. लाख्	
		10,000,000. कोँरा	

1874. एक् सहसर् आठ् सै चौहत्तर्

2,154,210. ऐकइस् लाख् चौवन् सहसर् दुइ सै दस्, etc.

394. The cardinals between *one hundred* and *two hundred* are differently formed, when employed in the multiplication table (पहाड़ा). Namely up to 120 the higher number is subjoined to the lower one with which it is compounded by means of उतर् *above*, the initial उ of the latter combining with the final अ of the preceding word to ओ (ओतर्); thus 108 is अठोतर्सा, i. e., अठ + उतर् + सो *eight-above-hundred*. From 120 and optionally from 110 up to 160 and optionally up to 170, the connecting vowel आ is interposed, instead of उतर्, except in the fifth decade where चालिस् *forty* is curtailed to चाल्. In the rest the original form remains unchanged. Moreover, in the second, third and fourth decade the penultimate short vowel is lengthened. The accent is always on the antepenultimate of the whole compound;

e. g., 161 *eksāṭṭháso*, 152 *bavānnáso*, 112 *barāhdso*, etc. Thus the forms of these cardinals are the following:

101. ऐकोतरूसो	117. सतराहासो	140. चालसो	170. सत्तरसो
102. द्विलोतरूसो	118. अठराहासो	141. ऐकतालसो, etc.	171. एकत्तरसो
103. तिलोतरूसो	119. ओनैसासो	149. ओनचासासो	179. ओनासीसो
104. चलोतरूसो	120. बीसासो	150. डेढ़सौ	180. अस्सीसो
105. पिचोतरूसो	121. ऐकैसासो	151. ऐक्यवन्नासो	181. ऐक्यासीसो
106. छिलोतरूसो	122. बड़सासो	152. बवन्नासो	189. नवासीसो
107. सतलोतरूसो	123. तेइसासो	153. तिरपन्नासो	190. नब्बेसो
108. अठोतरूसो	124. चाव्वीसासो	154. चोवन्नासो	191. ऐक्यानब्बेसो
109. निनरोतरूसो	125. पचोसासो	155. पनचौनासो	192. बानब्बेसो
110. दहोतरूसो	126. छब्बीसासो	156. छपन्नासो	193. तिरानब्बेसो
111. ऐनरोतरूसो	127. सतैसासो	157. सतवन्नासो	194. चोरानब्बेसो
112. बरहोतरूसो	128. अठैसासो	158. अठवन्नासो	195. पनचानब्बेसो
113. तेरहोतरूसो	129. ओनतीसासो	159. ओनसट्ठासो	196. छानब्बेसो, etc.
114. चौदहोतरूसो	130. तीसासो	160. साठसो	199. निनानबेसो
115. पनराहासो	131. ऐकतीसासा, etc.	161. ऐकसट्ठासो, etc.	200. दुइ सौ
116. सोराहासो	139. ओनतालसो	169. ओनहत्तरसो	

395. The following are alternative forms of some of the preceding cardinals:

101. इकोतरसो	113. तेराहासो	119. ओनइसासो	163. तिरसठसो
102. द्वियोतरसो	114. चौदाहासो	121. ऐकइसासो	164. चौसठसो
106. छियोतरसो	115. पन्दरहोतरसो	155. पचपन्नासो	165. पैंसठसो
108. अठोतरसो	116. सोरहोतरसो	159. ओनसाठसो	166. छाछठसो
111. इगरोतरसो	117. सतरहोतरसो	161. ऐकसठसो	170. सत्तरिसो
112. बराहासो	118. अठरहोतरसो	162. बासठसो	

396. *Affinities.* On the whole the numeral forms are very much alike in all Gḍs. There are, however, three main points of difference. In the first two the E. Gḍ. differs from the W. and S. Gḍ., in the third the W. Gḍ. from the E. and S. Gḍ. — Firstly; in E. Gḍ. the final syllable of the second, third, fourth and fifth decades is short (viz. अह्, इस् or विस्, तिस्, लिस्) but in W. Gḍ. it is long (viz. आँ or अहँ, ईस् or वीस्, तीस्, लीस्), G. only being a partial exception; thus:

	O.	B.	E. H.	W. H.	P.
13.	तेर	तेर	तेरह्	तेरा	तेराँ
14.	चोद्	चौद्द	चौदह्	चौदा	चौदाँ
23.	तेइश्	तेइश्	तेइस्	तेईस्	तेई
24.	चविश्	चव्विश्	चौव्विस्	चौबीस्	चौबी
32.	त्रत्रिश्	बत्रिश्	बत्तिस्	बतीस्	बती
46.	पइँचाल्लिश्	पयँताल्लिश्	पैँताल्लिस्	पैँतालीस्	पैँताली

	S.	M.	G.	H. H.
13.	तेरहँ	तेरा	तेर	तेरह्
14.	चोउहँ	चौदा	चउद्	चोदह्
23.	ट्रेवीह	तेवीस	त्रेवीश्	तेईस्
24.	चोवीह	चौवीस्	चोवीश्	चौबीस्
32.	बट्रीह	बत्तीस्	बत्रिश्	बतीस्
46.	पंञताल्लीह	पंचेचालीस्	पञताल्लीश्	पैँतालीस्

Secondly; in E. Gḍ. a final short इ is retained, while in W. Gḍ. it is dropped, S. only being a partial exception; thus:

	O.	B.	E. H.	W. H.	P.	M.	G.	S.	H. H.
2.	दुइ	दुइ	दुइ	दो	दो	दोन्	बे	ब	दो
3.	तिनि	तिनि	तीनि	तीन्	तिंन	तीन्	त्रण्	ट्रे	तीन्
4.	चारि	चारि	चारि	चार्	चार्	चार्	चार्	चारि	चार्
60.	षाठिए	षाठि	साठि	साठ्	संठ	साठ्	सठि	साठ्	साठ्

With regard to सत्तर् *seventy* alone, all Gḍ. languages agree in dropping the final इ, excepting O. and S. which have सत्तोरि and सत्तरि respectively; and E. H. optionally in सत्तरि सै *seven hundred.* — Thirdly; in W. Gḍ. the syllable च, but in the E. and S. Gḍ. either the conjunct त्र् or the whole increment चत्र् of the Pr. चत्तालीसा *forty* is always elided in the fifth decade. In this case E. H. occupies an intermediate position; thus:

	M.	O.	B.	E. H.	P.	S.	G.
41.	एकेचालीस्	एकचालिश्	एकचल्लिश्	एकताल्लिस्	एकताली	एकेताल्लीह	एकतलीश्
42.	बेचालीस्	बयालिश्	बेयाल्लिश्	बयालिस्	बैताली	बाएताल्लीह	बेंतालीश्
43.	त्रेचालीस्	तेयालिश्	तेताल्लिश्	तेँतालिस्	तैताली	ट्रेताल्लीह	तेँतालीश्
44.	चव्वेंचालीस्	चौचालिश्	चोयाल्लिश्	चौवालिस्	चौताली	चोएताल्लीह	चुमालीश्

	M.	O.	B.	E. H.	P.	S.	G.
45.	पंचेचालीस्	पइँचालिश्	पयँताल्लिश्	पैँतालिस्	पैँताली	पंजतालीह	पञतालीश्
46.	छेचालीस्	छयालिश्	छचल्लिश्	छियालिस्	छिताली	छाएतालीह	छँतालीश्
47.	सत्तेचालीस्	सतचालिश्	सतचल्लिश्	सैँतालिस्	सैँताली	सतेतालीह	सुडतालीश्
48.	अट्ठेचालीस्	अठचालिश्	आठचल्लिश्	अड़तालिस्	अठताली	अठेतालीस	अडतालीश्

Some minor differences are the following: 1) S. and P. change the final स् of ओस्, तीस्, लीस्, तास् into ह्, which is generally afterwards dropped by P.; thus S., P. वीह् 20, P. तीह् or त्रीह, S. ट्रीह 30, S. ट्रेवीह 23, वट्रीह 32, P. तेई or त्रेई, वती or वत्री, S. चालीह, P. चाली 40, S., P. पंजाह 50, S. बावंजाह, P. ववंजा 52, etc. Similarly these two languages alone change the initial स् of साठ् 60 into ह्; e. g., 61 P. इकाहट्, S. एकहठि, while P. also changes ठ् to ट् (see § 145, exc. 2). With regard to सत्तर् 70, again, all Gds. agree in changing the initial स् to ह्, except O.; thus 71 B. एकातर् (= *एकअतर् = एकहत्तर्), E. H. एखत्तर् or एकहत्तर्, W. H. एकहत्तर्, P. इकहत्तर्, S. एकहतरि, M. एकाहत्तर्, but O. एकस्तुरि (= *एकसतुरि). — 2) M., G. and S. alone retain the initial व् of वीस् or वीह 20 in compounds; see § 123, note. — 3) G., S., B. and optionally P. retain र् in त्रिश् or त्रीह 30 and its compounds; as 31 B., G. एकत्रिश्, P. इकत्ती or इकत्री, S. एकट्रीह, 30 B., G. त्रिश्, P. तीह् or त्रीह्, S. ट्रीह, etc. — 4) B. alone doubles ल् in चल्लिश् 40 and its compounds, as एकचल्लिश् 41, etc. — 5) M. alone preserves the semitats. सट 60 in compounds, as एकसट 61, बासट् 62, etc.; but साठ् 60 (see Man. 43). — 6) P. alone forms optionally नभे॑ for नवे॑ 90 in compounds, as इकानवे॑ or इकानभे॑ 91, etc.; but नव्वे or नब्बे 90 (see Ld. 85). — 7) S. alone preserves the full termination अहँ, while the others contract it to आँ or आ or shorten it to अह् or अ; thus 12 S. बारहँ, but P. बाराँ (= *बारअँ = *बारहँ), M. बारा, W. H. बारा, or E. H. बारह्, B., O., G. बार्.

397. *Derivation.* 1. एक् regularly for Pr. एक्को (Vr. 3, 58. § 143); as to the forms गक्, ऐक् and इक् see §§ 170. 171. Pr. has also the forms एगो (H. C. 1, 176) and एओ (H. C. 2, 99); the latter does not occur in E. H., but the former in compounds; e. g., ऐगरोतरसो 111 or shortened इग्, e. g., इगरोतरसो 111. —

2. दुइ regularly for Pr. दुए (Ls. 318, see § 45) or दुवे (Vr. 6, 57); the Mg. Pr. has दुवे or दो or दोण्णि (Wb. Bh. 424. see H. C. 3, 130); the first is preserved in E. H., B., O. दुइ, the second in E. H. दो (§ 392), the third in M. दोन् and S. ड्ठ (Tr. 158); Pr. has also the form बे (H. C. 3, 120) which is preserved in the G. बे and S. ब; the P. and W. H. have दो. — 3. तीनि regularly for Pr. तिण्णि (Vr. 6, 56. cf. §§ 143. 147). — 4. चारि see § 153. — Pr. दुवे or दोण्णि, तिण्णि, चत्तारि are gen. comm. (Vr. 3, 56. 57. 58); but they appear to have arisen from the Skr. neut. द्वे or *द्वानि, त्रीणि, चत्वारि respectively (see Ls. 318. 319). The Skr. masc. द्वौ is perhaps represented by the Pr. and Gḍ. दो. Mg. Pr. has a masc. तओ (Wb. Bh. 475) = Skr. त्रयः *three*, but it has not survived in Gḍ. Pr. has also the masc. चत्तारो (Skr. चत्वारः nom.) and चउरो (= Skr. चतुरः acc., see M. M. 124) H. C. 3, 122. Wb. Bh. 425, but they do not occur in Gḍ.; the latter, however, survives in the Ksh. चोर् *tsor* (Bs. II, 132). — 5. पाँच् or पाच्, 7 सात्, 8 आठ् regularly for Pr. पंच, सत्त, अट्ठ = Skr. पञ्च, सप्त, अष्ट (see §§ 143. 147); S. and P. have पंज, P. सत्त, अट्ठ, S. सत, अठ, B. आट. — 6. छ, also Pr. छ (Wb. Bh. 425. Ls. 319) for Skr. षट्, eliding final ट् (Vr. 4, 6) and changing ष to छ् (Vr. 2, 41); also W. H., S. and G. छ; E. H. has a form छह which occurs also in S. छह, M. सहा and Ksh. शिह् (Bs. II, 132) and which represents perhaps the Skr. form षष्, Pr. *छस or *छह with final श (cf. Ls. 220. H. C. 1, 19. cf. M. दहा 10). E. H. has also a form छव् corresponding to B. छय्, O. छअ, W. H. and P. छे, with euphonic व् or य् for elided ह्; Pr. has also छअ see Ls. 320. — 9. नौ or नउ regularly for Pr. नव, Pr. has also नअ (Ls. 320) which does not occur in E. H., but in O. नअ and B. नय; P. नो॰ and S. नँवँ add an anunásika. — 10. दस् regularly for Mg. Pr. दस (Wb. Bh. 426. H. C. 1, 262), Skr. दश; Pr. has also दह (Vr. 2, 44) which is only preserved in P. दह् (also दस्), S. डह, M. दहा, Ksh. दह् (Bs. II, 133). — As the latter part of the compound numerals of the second decade, Skr. दश becomes in Pr. दह or डह or रह (H. C. 1, 219), in Gḍ. दह or लह or रह. Thus 11 Skr. एकादश, Pr. *एगारह,

E. H. ऐग्यारह or इग्यारह or ग्यारह. As to its euphonic ग्, see § 135; it is more properly W. Gḍ.; for B. एगार, O. एगार, M. अकरा have it not; while W. H. ग्यारह, P. गिआरां, G. अगिआर have it. The other P. form एआरह (Vr. 2, 44) occurs only in S. यारहँ. The Pr. has also दस, रस (Wb. Bh. 426. H. C. 3, 123), which have not survived in Gḍ. — 12. Skr. द्वादश, Pr. बारह (Vr. 2, 44), E. H. बारह, B., O., G. बार, M., W. H. बारा, P. बारां, S. बारहँ. — 13. Skr. त्रयोदश, Pr. तेरह (i. e. त्रयदश for त्रयः + दश cf. H. C. 1, 165)[1]), E. H. तेरह; other Gḍs. see § 396. — 14. Skr. चतुर्दश, Pr. चउद्दह (Vr. 2, 14. H. C. 1, 171), E. H. चौदह; other Gḍs. see § 396. — 15. Skr. पञ्चदश, Pr. पण्णरह (H. C. 2, 43, but पण्णरहो Vr. 3, 44), E. H. पनरह (§ 392 and in पनराहासो 115, see § 394); so also B. पनेर (perhaps rather for the Pr. form पण्णारह, see Ls. 320. Cw. 24, note); the usual Gḍ. form, however, inserts an euphonic द् (§ 135), as E. H. पंद्रह, O. पंद्र, W. H. पंद्रा, P. पंद्रां, S. पंद्रहँ or पंधँ, M. पंधरा, G. पंद्र. — 16, see § 105, note, E. H. सोरह, B. सोल, O. सोह्ल (with a strange metathesis), W. H. सोला, M. सोळा, P. सोलां, S. सोरहँ, G. सोळ. — 17. Skr. सप्तदश, Pr. सत्तरह (T. V. 1, 3. 42), E. H. सतरह; other Gḍs. see § 396. — 18. Skr. अष्टादश, Pr. अट्ठारह (T. V. 1, 3. 42. cf. H. C. 3, 123), E. H. अठारह, G. अढार, S. अउहँ (cf. 38. 48 below); other Gḍs., as in § 396. — 19. Skr. ऊनविंशतिः, Mg. ऊनवीसा (Wb. Bh. 426), E. H. ओनइस्, W. H. उनीस्, B. ऊनिश्, O. उणाइश्; Skr. has also एकोनविंशतिः, Mg. एकूनवीसा (Wb. Bh. 426), only preserved in M. एकुणीस्, O. H. अगुनीस् and गुनीस्, G. ओगणीस्; the P. has उन्नीह and S. उणीह or उणिवीह with ह् for स् (see § 396). — As to 21 एकइस्, etc. see §§ 123. 129. The (apparently anomalous) आ in सत्ताइस् is probably (as Bs. I, 291) caused by the ancient accent of the oxytone *saptá*. Of all dissyl-

1) The Pr. form तेरह is explained in H. C. 1, 165 as containing a change of the first अ together with the following cons. and vowel to ए; that is, in Skr. त्रयोदश the first अ together with the following syllable यो (i. e. cons. य् + vow. ओ) becomes ए; hence तेरह. Cowell's view, therefore, (Cw. 121, note) as to the Pr. Gramm. theory is more correct than Beames' (II, 135).

labic numerals only sapt*á* and asht*á* are oxytone, all others are barytone, *éka, pâñcha, nâva, dâṣa,* etc.; now Gḍ. has आ in सत्ताइस्, अठाइस्, but अ or ई (for अइ) in एकइस् (W. H. एकीस्) and पचीस् (for पचइस्, M. पंचवीस्). In Skr. the influence of the accent is seen in अष्टादश, अष्टाविंशति, अष्टात्रिंशत्, etc.; but not in सप्तदश, सप्तविं°, सप्तत्रिंशत्; in Pr. and Gḍ. both sets show it in the third decade, but neither set in all other decades; e. g., 37 सैँतिस्, 38 अठतिस्, 47 सैँतालिस्, 48 अठतालिस्, and in Skr., too, the accent of अष्ट only optionally influences the form after the first four decades; e. g., 48 अष्टचत्वारिंशत् or अष्टाचत्वारिंशत्, etc. — 20 बीस् regularly for Pr. वीसा (H. C. 1, 28) or वीसई (Mḍ. 4, 3. Ls. 320), Skr. विंशतिः. — 30 तीस् regularly for Pr. तीसा (H. C. 1, 28) or तीसआ (Mḍ. 4, 3. Ls. 320), Skr. त्रिंशत्. — 32 बतिस् regularly for Pr. बत्तीसा (T. V. 1, 4. 79), with ब on account of the following double त्, Skr. द्वात्रिंशत्. — 33 तैँतिस् regularly for Pr. तेत्तीसा (H. C. 1, 165, see § 149), Skr. त्रयस्त्रिंशत्; M. has तेहतीस् (Man. 43) beside the regular तेतीस्. — 35 पैँतिस् see § 156, W. H. पैँतीस्, P. पैँती, G. पैँत्रिश्; but M. पस्तीस् (Man. 43, for पसतीस् with स् for च्, cf. § 11) and S. पंत्रट्रीह. — 37 सैँतिस् see § 153, also W. H. सैँतीस्, P. सैँती, B. साँइत्रिश्; but M. सद्तीस् or सततीस्, G. साडत्रिश्, S. सतट्रीह. — 38. Skr. अष्टात्रिंशत्, Pr. अट्ठतीसा (Wb. Bh. 426), O. अठतिश्, B. आठत्रिश्, S. अठट्रीह, P. अठती, M. अठतीस् or अडतीस्, E. H. अठतिस् (§ 113) or अडतिस् or अरतिस् (§ 145, exc. 2), G. आडत्रिश्. — 40. E. H. चालिस् see § 153. — 41. Skr. एकचत्वारिंशत्, Pr. एक्कचत्तालीसा or (eliding च) *एकअत्तालीसा and (contracted according to Vr. 4, 1), E. H. एकतालिस्; this derivation is proved by the S. एकेतालीह, which is contracted from एकयतालीह with euph. य्. The usual explanation, identifying °तालिस् with °चालिस्, assumes a changes of च् to त्; thus Pr. एकचत्तालीसा = एकचआलीसा = एकचालीस् = एकतालिस्; but such a change of च् to त् is not only intrinsically improbable, but also lacks all evidence. Similarly are formed 43 तेँतालिस् (see § 152), 49 ओनतालिस्, 45 पैँतालिस् (see § 156), 47 सैँतालिस्, 48 अठतालिस् (see § 145, exc. 2). The latter is in Pr. also अडयाले (Wb. Bh. 412); here both the syllable च *cha* and the conjunct त्त् *tt* are elided; so also in the Gḍ. forms: 42 ब्रयालिस्, 44 चौवालिस्, 46 छियालिस् (see §§ 152. 153); as to the other Gḍs. see § 396, 3; Pr. has 42 बायालीसं (Wb. Bh. 412). — 50. Skr. पञ्चाशत्, Pr. *पंचासा, E. H. पचास् (see §§ 143. 146), also W. H. पचास्, G., O. पचाश्, but the nasal is preserved in B. पंचास्, P. पंजाह् and S. पंजाह्. The common Pr. form is पण्णासा (Vr. 3, 44. H. C. 2, 43); it is preserved in the M. पन्नास् 50 and in the curtailed form पन् or वन् of the compound numerals of the 6th decade of all Gḍs., exc. P. and S.; thus वन् in 52 E. H. बावन्, W. H., G. dto., O. बाश्रन्, B. बाउन्न, M. बावन्न, Pr. बावण्णं (Wb. Bh. 426), Skr. द्वापञ्चाशत्; 57. E. H., O., W. H., G. सतावन्, M. सत्तावन्न, Pr. *सत्तावण्णा or °ण्णं, Skr. सप्तपञ्चाशत्; 58. E. H., O., W. H., G. अठावन्, M. अट्ठावन्न, Pr. *अट्ठवण्णं, Skr. अष्टापञ्चाशत्; 55. E. H., O., G. पंचावन्, M. पंचावन्न, Pr. पंचावण्णा (H. C. 2, 174), Skr. पञ्चपञ्चाशत्; B. contracts सातान्न 57, आठान्न 58, पंचान्न 55. The other E. H. form पचपन्, which is also H. H., presupposes a Pr. form *पंचप्पण्णा. There is another Pr. form पणावण्णा (H. C. 2, 174) or पणावन्नं (Wb. Bh. 426), but it has left no trace in Gḍ. Again पन् in 56 E. H., W. H. छप्पन्, O., G. छपन्, B. छापान्न, M. छपन्न, Pr. *छप्पण्णा, Skr. षट्पञ्चाशत्; 53. E. H. तिरपन्, W. H. तिरपन् or त्रेपन्, G. त्रेपन, M. त्रेपन्न, O. तेपन्, B. तिप्पान्न presuppose a Ap. Pr. form *त्रिप्पण्णा (cf. H. C. 4, 398), Skr. त्रिपञ्चाशत्; the common Pr. form तेवण्णा (H. C. 2, 174) does not occur in Gḍ.; 54. W. H., G. चोपन्, M. चोपन् or चौपन्न, regularly for Pr. *चउप्पण्णा, Skr. चतुःपञ्चाशत्; but in E. H. चौअन् or चउअन् or (with euph. व्) चौवन्, O. चउवन्, B. चोयान्न the conjunct प्प् has been elided (see § 154). The unusual Pr. form पंचासा 50 is preserved in E. H. 49 ओनचास्, with the syllable प *pa* elided, precisely as च *cha* in ओनतालिस् 39 (see above); thus Skr. ऊनपञ्चाशत्, Pr. ऊणावंचासा or ऊणपंचासा, whence B. ऊनपंचास्, G. ओगणपचाश्, S. उणिवंजाह्, P. उणवंजा or उणंजा, O. उनंचाश्, E. H. ओनचास्; but M. regularly एकुणपन्नास्. Moreover it is used throughout in P. and S., thus S. ट्रेवंजाह्, P. तिवंजा or तिरवंजा 53; S. चोवंजाह्, P. चोवंजा or चुवंजा 54; S. पंजवंजाह्, P. पंचवंजा 55; S. छवंजाह्, P. छिपंजा or छिवंजा 56, etc. — 60. Skr. षष्टिः, Pr. सट्ठी (Wb. Bh. 426), E. H. साठि, B. साठि, M., G., W. H. साठ्, P. सट्ठ, S. सठि; the O. साठिए adds a pleonastic ए.

In the compounds, M. has सट, S. हठि and P. हट, see § 396. Otherwise they differ little. But 61 is in P. इकाहट, 62 in O. बाश्रासठि with श्रा; 63. O., B. तेसठि, G. तेसाठ, W. H. त्रेसठ् or तिरसठ्, M. त्रेसट्ट, P. तेहट्ट or त्रेहट्ट, S. ट्रेहठि; 65. B. पयँसठि, M. पाँसट्ट, W. H. पैँसठ्, P. पैँहट्ट, but O. पंचसठि, G. पंचसाठ्, S. पंजहठि; 66. O. छश्रसठि, M. सासट्ट, S. छाहठि, W. H. छियासठ्, P. छिश्राहट्ट, B. छसठि; 67. E. H. सतसठि or सउसठि or सरसठि, M. सतसट्ट or सट्सट्ट, W. H. सरसठ्, see § 107; the others retain त्, O. सतसठि, B. सातसठि, P. सताहट्; 68. E. H. श्रउसठि or श्ररसठि, see § 145, exc. 2, M. श्रउसट्ट or श्रड्सट्ट, W. H. श्रउसठ् or श्ररसठ्, see § 145, exc. 2; but O. श्रठसठि, S. श्रठहठि, P. श्रठाहट्ट, B. श्राठसठि; 69. B. ऊनसत्तर्, all others regularly °हत्तर्, see § 396. — In the Bh. the following curtailed forms occur, 62 वावट्ठि, 64 चोयट्ठी (but also चउसट्ठी), 66 छावट्ठि, and even 61 एगट्ठि, 67 सत्तट्ठि (Wb. Bh. 426), which (if trustworthy) may be explained by the intermediate change of स् to ह् (as in P. and S.) and subsequent elision of ह्. — 70. E. H. सत्तर् see § 108; so also in the other Gḍs. see § 396. In the compounds there is little difference, but 72 is in O. बाश्रस्तुरि, B. बाहात्तर्, S. बाहत्तरि, M. बाहत्तर्; 73. M. त्रेहत्तर् or त्र्याहत्तर्, B. तेहात्तर्, O. तेस्तुरि; 74. M. चौर्याहत्तर्; 75. M. पंचेहत्तर्; 76. O. छश्रस्तुरि, B. छेयात्तर्, S. छाहत्तरि, M. शाहत्तर् or शेहत्तर् (see § 55); 77. B. सातात्तर्, M. सत्याहत्तर् or सत्तेहत्तर्, P. सतत्तर्; 78. B. श्राठात्तर्, P. श्रठत्तर्, M. श्रठ्याहत्तर् or श्रठ्ठेहत्तर्. — 80. Skr. श्रशीतिः, but Pr. श्रसीइ with श्रा (Wb. Bh. 426), and so in B. श्राशी; but E. H., W. H., P. श्रस्सी with double स्, which explains the श्रा of B.; in S. श्रसी and O. श्रशी one स् has been elided; as to M. ऐँशी and G. एँसी, see § 148. In the compounds, which differ very little has all Gḍs. have श्रासी, exc. M., which श्रायँशी; thus 81. E. H. एक्यासी, M. एक्यायँशी; on the euph. य् see § 135. — 82. B. बियाशी, M. ब्यायँशी, P., S. बिश्रासी, O. बयाशी, B., E. H., W. H. बयासी. — 86. O. छयाशी, M. शायँशी, S. छहासी; 83. M. त्र्यायँशी, G. तेश्रासी or त्यासी; 84. Pr. चउरासी (Wb. Bh. 426), M. चौर्यांशी; 87. M. सत्यांयशी; 88. M. श्रठ्ठ्यांयशी; 89. M. नव्यायँशी, E. H., W. H. नवासी are Skr. नवाशीतिः; but M. has also एकुणनवुद्द, B. ऊननवुइ, O. ऊणानउ, P. उणानवे", S. उणानवे = Skr. एकोननवतिः. — 90. Skr. नवतिः, Pr. नउए (Wb. Bh.

426), E. H. नव्वे, O. नब्बे, B. नब्बइ, M. नव्वद, W. H. नव्वे, S. नवे, P. नव्वे or नब्बे; these Gd. forms seem to presuppose a Pr. form *नव्वए; the origin of the final ए is obscure; so also is that of the connecting vowel आ which occurs in all the compounds of नवे, and is especially marked in S. and M.; e. g., 92. S. बिआनवे, M. ब्याण्णव; 93. S. ट्रिआनवे, M. त्र्याण्णव; 94. E. H. चौरानवे, S. चोरानवे, M. चौर्याण्णव, etc.; it occurs already in Pr. सत्ताणउए 97 (Wb. Bh. 426), E. H. सतानवे, S. सतानवे, M. सत्याण्णव. — 99 is in S. नवानवे, B. निवानव्बइ, M. नव्याण्णव (with euph. य् see § 135) for Skr. नवनवतिः; the E. H. and W. H. निनानवे or नियानवे apparently exchange न् for व्, though it might be also a modification of उ in the P. नडिन्नवे॑ or नडिन्नभे॑ (see § 396, 6) which are probably connected with the other S. forms नधानवे or वधानवे; for these as well as for the P. forms I know no satisfactory explanation. O. alone has अनेशत्, perhaps for Skr. ऊनशतम्. — 100. E. H., W. H., S., G., P. सौ or सो is the Ap. Pr. सउ (cf. H. C. 4, 331), Skr. शतम्, and E. H., P. सै, B. श, O. शये, M. शे॑ is the Mg. Pr. सअं or सयं (Wb. Bh. 426); as to E. H. सल् see § 109. — The compounds above 100, formed with उत्तर, occur also in M. (Man. 44) and S. (Tr. 165); in the latter they may be formed up to 200; they are also found in Pr. (see Wb. Bh. 427); in the Bh. the original ओ is reduced to उ, but Gd. preserves it; e. g., 107 सत्तुत्तरं सयं (Bh. 15[a]), S. सतोतरसौ; or Ap. Pr. पंचोत्तरसउ, S. पंत्रोतरसौ, E. H. पिचोतरसो (§ 55); 106. S. छहोतरसौ, E. H. छियोतरसो or छिलोतरसौ (see § 55); the latter as well as 104 E. H. चलोतरसौ (for चुलो°, cf. Pr. चुलसीत 84 in Wb. Bh. 425), S. चोरोतरसौ, 103 E. H. तिलोतरसो or तियो°, S. ट्रिरोतरसो, 102 E. H. दिलोतरसौ or दियो° (see § 69), S. बिरोतरसौ, M. दुवोत्तरशे॑ are formed anomalously; the Skr. would be षडुत्तरशतं, चतुरुत्तर°, त्र्युत्तर°, द्व्युत्तर°. Very anomalous are the E. H. सतलोतरसो 107 (for *सतोतरसो) and निगरोतरसो 119; there seems to be here some confusion with the forms of 111 and 117. — The other compounds formed with the connecting vowel आ occur also in S., which has ओ; e. g., 112. E. H. बराहासो, S. बारहो सौ; 115. E. H. पनराहासो, S. पन्द्राहो सौ, etc. E. H. shortens the first आ by § 25, and lengthens the second झ, probably, for the sake of euphony. The first part of these compounds is probably a collective or aggregate numeral; see §§ 404. 405; e. g., E. H. तीसा, S. द्रीहो *a sum of thirty,* whence E. H. तीसा सो, S. द्रीहो सौ 130, i. e., *100 plus the sum of 30,* or E. H. तेरहाँ, S. तेरहो *sum of thirteen,* whence E. H. तेराहासो, S. तेरहो सौ 113, etc.

398. *Declension.* All cardinals can be declined, when used as subst., in which case they are inflected like them; thus gen. pl. पाँचन् कै *of five,* etc. But दुइ *two* and तीनि *three* have a special form in these circumstances; viz. दूनो or दुन्हुन् or दुनहुन् *two* and तीनो *three*; thus gen. pl. दूनो कै or दुन्हुन् कै or दुनहुन् कै *of two,* तीनो कै *of three.* When they are used as adj., they are not inflected; thus पाँच् जनन् कै *of five men,* दुइ जनन् कै *of two men,* तीनि जनन् कै *of three men.*

399. *Affinities and Derivation.* M. has special obl. forms दोँहो॑, तिहो॑, चोहो॑ for दोन् *two,* तीन् *three* and चार् *four* (Man. 46). When used adjectively with *persons,* they are changed to दोघे m., दोघी f., दोघे॑ n. *two*; similarly तिघे, तिघी, तिघे॑ *three,* चौघे, चौघी, चौघे॑ *four* (Man. 46). Otherwise the declension is regular; thus gen. एका चा *of one,* दोँहो॑ चा or दोघाँ चा *of two.* — S. has the obl. forms बिनि or बी॑, ट्रिनि or ट्री॑, चइनि or चई॑ for ब *two,* ट्रे *three,* चारि *four*; otherwise the declension is regular; thus gen. ब्रिनि जो *of two,* पंजनि जो *of five,* etc. (Tr. 169. 171). S. inflects the cardinals, when they are used adjectively (Tr. 171); as दहनि बैरिनि खे or दहे॑ बैरिएँ खे *to ten enemies*; बिनि or बी॑ बैरिनि खे बी॑ बैरिएँ खे *to two enemies.* — In the E. H. form दुनहुन् the conjunct न्ह has been dissolved (see § 138). The second उ of दुन्हुन् is probably euphonic, for *दुन्हन्. In this and the other E. H. and M. special obl. forms the plur. suff. has been apparently reduplicated. The Pr. gen. pl. is दोण्हं or बेण्हं *of two* (H. C. 3, 119), तिण्हं *of three* (H. C. 3, 118), which are contr. in S. to बी॑, ट्री॑ or slightly modified ब्रिनि, ट्रिनि; but E. H. दूनो or दुन्हुन्, M. दोँहो॑ would presuppose the Pr. form *दोण्हहुं or *दोण्हण्ह, etc.

2. ORDINALS.

400. The formation of the ordinals from the cardinals has been explained in §§ 263—266. They are treated in every respect like adj., i. e., they admit of a weak and strong form (§ 381), and the latter has a fem. in ई or ईँ (§ 384) and an obl. masc. ए or एँ (§ 386). The following are the first seven ordinals of which some are formed peculiarly: *First*, wk. f. पहिल् or पहेल् c. g., or st. f. पहिला or पहेला or °लका m., °ली or °लकी f.; *second*, wk. f. दूसर् or दुसरब् c. g., or st. f. दुसरा or दुसरवाँ or दुसरका m., °री or °रईँ or °रकी f.; *third*, wk. f. तीसर् or तिसरब् c. g., or st. f. तिसरा or तिसरवाँ or तिसरका m., °री or °रईँ or °रकी f.; *fourth*, wk. f. चउथ् or चौथब् c. g., or st. f. चौथा or चौथवाँ or चौथरका m., °थी or °थईँ or °रकी f.; *sixth*, wk. f. छट्ठब् c. g., or st. f. छट्ठा or छट्ठवाँ m., छट्ठी or छट्ठईँ f.; *fifth*, wk. f. पंचब् c. g., or st. f. पचा or पंचवाँ m., पची or पंचईँ f.; *seventh*, wk. f. सातब् c. g., or st. f. सत्ता or सतवाँ m., सत्ती or सतईँ f. The rest are formed exactly like the forms of the *fifth* and *seventh*. Their obl. forms are, e. g., gen. sg. or pl., masc. पहिले कै *of the first*, दसवेँ कै *of the tenth*; fem. पहिली कै, दसईँ कै, etc. When they are used as subst., they are inflected like them; thus gen. sg. पहिला कै *of the first one*, pl. पहिलन् कै *of the first ones*; but पहिले जन् कै *of the first man*, पहिले जनन् कै *of the first men*, etc.

401. *Affinities and Derivation.* For the derivation of पहिल् see §§ 118. 213. B. and O. पहेला or पहिला (Ṣ. Ch. 105. Bs. II, 142), M. पहिला, W. H. पहलौ or पहिलौ or °लो, P. पहिला, G. पेहेलो, S. पेहेरो॑ or पेहेर्यो॑ or पहर्यो॑. The first ए of the G. and S. forms is merely euphonic (see § 57). — The deriv. and affin. of दूसर् and तीसर् see in §§ 270. 271, and for the deriv. of चौथ्, see § 78. B. and O. have चौथ (*chauthō*) or चौथा (Ṣ. Ch. 105), M. चवथा, W. H. चौथौ (Br.) or चौथो (Mw.), P. चौथा, G. चोथो, S. चोथो॑. — The E. H. छट्ठा, B. and O. *deest*, W. H. छट्ठौ or छट्ठो, G. छट्ठो are derived from Pr. छट्ठओ, st. f. of Pr. छट्ठो (H. C. 1, 265), Skr. षष्ठः, the M. सहावा, P. छेवाँ, S. छहो॑ are formed anomalously (as if Skr. *षषमः) from the Gḍ. cardinals M. सहा, P. छे, S. छह. The E. H.

forms इठवाँ, दुसरव् or दुसरवाँ anomalously contain the suff. अव् or अवाँ, see § 264. The forms पहिलका, दुसरका, तिसरका contain the pleon. suff. अका (see § 198). The form चौथरका is formed anomalously after the analogy of दुसरका, तिसरका. As to the deriv. and affin. of the rest, see §§ 265. 266.

3. MULTIPLICATIVES.

402. The multiplicatives denote how many times a number is multiplied. They are formed from the cardinals by adding the suff. आ or आँ or आँई॰, excepting the first six which are made in a peculiar way. They are used only in the multiplication table.

1. ऐकं or ऐकै or के or कं	6. इक् or इक्का or इक्के or छाक्
2. दूनी	7. सते
3. तियाँ or त्रिका or तिरिका	8. अठे or आठ्
or त्रिके or तिरिके or ति	9. नवाँ or नवाँई॰
4. चोक् or चौका	10. दहाँ or दहाँई॰, etc.
5. पचा or पचे or पुरे	

403. The forms ऐकं and ऐकै are only used in the phrase ऐकं एक् or ऐकै एक् *once one is one*; and पचा only in पचा पचीस् *five times five are twenty five*. The form पुरे is used only when the product contains the words पच् or पै॰ *five*, i. e., when it is fifty or an odd multiple of five (excepting, however, पाँच् *five*, पंदरह् *fifteen* and पचीस् *twenty five*). As to the other alternative forms, no strict rule can be given; the practice varies according to local or individual fancy. In general it may be said, that the shorter forms, as ति, आठ्, इक् or छाक्, are used when the product is polysyllabic. The multiplicative always takes the middle place in the sentence. The following tables are given as examples:

10 × 1 is 10, etc.		3 × 1 is 3, etc.	
दस् के दस्	दस् इक्के साठि	तीन् के तीन्	तीन् छाक् अठारह्
दस् दूनी बीस्	दस् सते सत्तर्	तीन् दूनी छ	तीन् सते एकइस्
दस् तियाँ तीस्	दस् अठे अस्सी	तीन् त्रिका नौ	तीन् अठे चौबिस्
दस् चोक् चालिस्	दस् नवाँ नब्बे	तीन् चोक् बारह्	तीन् नवाँ सताइस्
दस् पुरे पचास्	दस् दहाँ सौ	तीन् पचे पंदरह्	तीन् दहाँई॰ तीस्

13 × 1 is 13, etc.

तेरह् के तेरह्	तेरह् शाक् अठनुनर्
तेरह् दूनो इब्बिस्	तेरह् सते ऐक्यानब्ये
तेरह् ति वनतालिस्	तेरह् आठ् चलोतरसो
तेरह् चौका बावन्	तेरह् नवाँ सतराहाँसो
तेरह् पुरे पैँसठि	तेरह् दहाँइँ तोसासो

The table of one is formed in a peculiar manner; thus:

ऐकै एक्	चर् के चार्	सत् के सात्	दहाँइँ दस्
दु के दुइ	पच् के पाँच्	अठ् के आठ्	
तिन् के तीन्	छ के छह्	नवाँइँ नौ	

The multiples of five are formed thus:

पच् के पाँच्	चार् पचे बोस्	सात् पुरे पैँतिस्	दस् पुरे पचास्
दो पचे दस्	पचा पचीस्	आठ् पचे चालिस्	इग्यारह् पुरे पंचावन्
तीन् पचे पंदरह्	छ पचे तोस्	नौ पुरे पैँतालिस्	बारह् पचे साठि, etc.

404. *Affinities and Derivation.* The forms in ए are probably obl. forms or nom. plur. of the resp. nom. sing. in आ, as सते of सता, अठे of अठा, etc. For the rest see § 407. The multiplicatives are identical with the collectives or aggregates; thus तीन् अठे चौब्बिस् means lit. *three sums-of-eight are twenty-four.*

4. COLLECTIVES.

405. The following words are used to express some aggregate sums: जोरा or जोरी *a pair*, चौकरा or °री or गंडा *a four*, गाहो *a five*, कोडी *a score*, सैकरा *a hundred*, सहसर् *a thousand*, लाख् *a hundred thousand*, कोँरा or करोर् *ten millions*. Collectives may also be formed by adding आ or आँ to the cardinals, so especially बोसा *a score*, तोसा *a thirty*, चलोसा *a forty*, also एका *a one*, पंचा *a five*, सता *a seven*, अठा *a eight*, नवाँ *a nine*, दहाँ *a ten*, etc. The multiplicatives दूनी, तियाँ or त्रिका, चोक् or चौका, छाक् or छक्का may be used as collectives.

406. All collectives are subst.; those in अ (*quiescent*) or आ are masc.; those in ई fem.; they are declined precisely like all other subst.

407. *Affinities.* These numerals probably occur in all Gḍs., though they are not noticed by all Gḍ. grammarians. As to S. see Tr. 178—181 (§§ 26. 27); thus एको or हिको 1, ब्रिको 2, ट्रिको 3, चउँको or चउँकु or चउँकड़ो 4, पंज़ो 5, इको 6, सतो 7, अठो 8, नाँओ॑ 9, ड्हो॑ or ड्हाको 10, वीहो or वीहारो or विहारो or कोड़ो 20, ट्रीहो or ट्रीहारो or ट्रिहारो 30, चालीहो or चाल्हारो (for *चालीहारो) 40, पंजाहो or पञाहो 50, साठीको 60, सविये or सौकिड़ो 100, सहासु or हज़ारु 1000 (Tr. 168), लाखु 100000, कोड़ु or किरोड़ि 10000000. As to P., see Ld. 85. 86, thus काउ or काऊँ 1, टूणी 2, तिआउँ or तिआऊँ 3, चौका 4, पाँजा 5, इका 6, साता 7, आठा 8, नाइआँ 9, दाहा or दहाका 10, कोड़ी or बीहड़ो or बीहा 20, पंजाहा 50, सेकड़ा 100, सहसर् or हज़ार् 1000, लक्ख 100000, करोड़ 10000000, etc. As to W. H., see Kl. 105—107; they do not much differ from E. H.; एकाई 1, टूना or टूनो or ज़ोड़ा or ज़ोड़ो 2, ती or तीन् 3, पंज़ा 5, नम् or नम्मा 9, दहाम् or दहाई 10, कोड़ी or बीसा 20, सैकड़ा 100, सहस or हज़ार् 1000, करोड़ 10000000; some collectives are formed by adding the fem. suff. ई (for masc. आ), as बतीसी *a thirty two,* पचीसी *a fifty,* etc. In M. सहस or हज़ार् 1000, लाख् 10000, कोट or क्रोड़् 10000000.

408. *Derivation.* Collectives are derived in Skr. by means of the suff. क, whence the Gḍ. forms arise regularly. Thus *unit,* Skr. एककम्, Pr. एक्कअं, E. H. एका; *triad,* Skr. त्रिकम्, Pr. तिअं, W. H. ती, E. H. ति; *score,* Skr. विंशकम्, Pr. वीसअं, E. H. बीसा; *hexad,* Skr. षट्कम्, Pr. छक्कं, E. H. छाक्; *quaternion,* Skr. चतुष्कम्, Pr. चउक्कं, E. H. चौक्; *pentad,* Skr. पञ्चकम्, Pr. पंचअं, E. H. पंचा, etc. Sometimes the pleon. suff. क (see § 195) is added; thus *triad,* E. H. तियाँ or त्रिका, Pr. तिअअं, Ap. Pr. त्रिक्कअं, Skr. त्रिककम्; *quaternion,* E. H. चौका, Pr. चउक्कअं, Skr. चतुष्ककम्; *hexad,* E. H. छक्का, Pr. छक्कअं, Skr. षट्कम्; *ten millions,* E. H. कोँरा or कोँड़ा, Pr. कोडिअं, Skr. कोटिकम् (or *कोटकम्); sometimes the pleon. suff. रा (or ड़ा, see § 209) is superadded; as *four,* E. H. चौकरा, W. H. चौकड़ो, Ap. Pr. चउक्कडउ, Skr. चतुष्क°; *hundred,* E. H. सैकरा, W. H. सैकड़ो, Ap. Pr. सयक्कडउ, Skr. शतक°, etc.; perhaps also E. H. ज़ोरा, W. H. ज़ोड़ो, Ap. Pr. *जुअडउ (cf. H. C. 2, 15 विज्जं = Skr. विद्वान्),

Skr. द्विक°, though this might be a noun derived from the R. जुड़् or जुड़् *join*. Sometimes the „collective" sense is emphasised by making the numeral an abstract noun by means of the suff. ग्राई (see § 220); thus W. H. एकाई *unit*, E. H. नवाई *nine*, दहाई *decade*, etc. — Differently derived is दूगा m. and दूनी f. *duad*, viz. from Pr. दुउणग्रं (cf. H. C. 1, 94), Skr. द्विगुणकम्. — As to the E. H. सहसर् and करोर् see §§ 138. 135. — The E. H. गंडा is properly a noun, the Skr. गण्डकः, lit. *aggregate of four sides* (?); so is also the E. H. गाहो, lit. *the aggregate of the five (ancient) planets* (Skr. ग्रह). — For the E. H. कोरी or कोडी *score* I know no satisfactory explanation; possibly it may be connected with कोडी, (Skr. कपर्दक) *aggregate of twenty shells* (?).

5. REDUPLICATIVES.

409. The reduplicative numbers are defective. Only the following occur in E. H.; यकेहरा *onefold, single*, दुहरा or दोहरा *twofold, double*, तेहरा *threefold, triple*, चौहरा *fourfold, quadruple*. The rest are made by adding the word बार् or बेर् *time* to the cardinal numbers; as पाँच् बार् or पाँच् बेर् *five times, quintuple*, etc.

410. The reduplicatives are adj. and treated precisely like those of the strong form (§ 381); that is, they make a fem. in ई (§ 384), as दोहरी, तेहरी, etc., and an obl. form in ए (§ 386), as दोहरे, etc.

411. *Affinities*. The reduplicatives exist in all Gḍs. As to W. H. see Kl. 105. In P. there are 1 इकहरा or कहिरा, 2 दोहरा, 3 तिहरा, 4 चौहरा or चउहरा, 5 पंज़ौहरा or पंजउहरा, 6 छेग्रौरा, 7 सतौरा; and even the „ordinal" suff. भ may be added pleonastically; thus पंज़ौहरभ *quintuple*, just as पंजभाँ or पंजवाँ *fifth* (Ld. 88). In S. there are, 1 हेकर् or हेकार्, 2 ब्रिहर् or ब्रिहार्, 3 ट्रिहर् or ट्रिहार्, 4 चोहर् or चोहार् (Tr. 184). M. adds पट *strip* instead of हरा; thus 1 एकपट्, 2 दुप्पट्, 3 तिप्पट्, 4 चौपट्, 10 दसपट, etc. (Man. 42). Similarly W. H. adds लड़ा *string*, e. g., 3 तिलड़ा, 4 चोलड़ा (see Kl. 105). — B. and O. seem to use tats. forms; as एकधा, द्विधा, etc. (see Ṣ. Ch. 109. Sn. 24).

412. *Derivation.* Reduplicatives are formed in Skr. by the addition of the *quasi*-suff. विध (from विधा *form, manner*), which in Pr. becomes विह् or, curtailed, ह्, whence, probably by the addition of the pleon. suff. रा (see § 209, or in S. आर्), arises the E. H. हरा. Thus in the Bh. (Wb. Bh. 425. 426) the following occur: 2 दुविह, 4 चउव्विह, 5 पंचविह, 6 छव्विह, or contracted 1 एगाहिय, 2 वेहिय, 3 तेहिय (perhaps from Skr. विहित past part. of R. वि-धा). Accordingly Skr. द्विविध° *twofold,* Pr. दुविह° (H. C. 1, 94) or वेविह°, whence contracted Ap. Pr. दोहउउ or वेहउ, and W. H. दोहरौ or E. H. दोहरा, S. त्रिहर्. The S. form त्रिहार् presupposes an Ap. Pr. वेहअडु, containing the pleon. suff. क and उ. Compare the names of the E. H. metre दोहा masc. (Skr. द्विविधकः) and Pr. दोहडिया fem. However, the Pr. ह and Gḍ. हर् might be also derived from the Skr. *quasi*-suff. ध or धा, as in द्विधः (from द्विधा *in two parts*).

6. FRACTIONALS.

413. The following fractional numbers occur in E. H. Those marked with an asterisk are used both as subst. and adj.

$^1/_2$	*आधु or *आधा	$^1/_{16}$	सोरहो or सोरहिया
$^1/_3$	तिहाई or तिहइया or तिहैया	$1^1/_4$	*सवा or सवाई or सवइया or सवैया
$^1/_4$	*पाउ or *पाव or चौथाई or चौथइया or चौथैया	$1^1/_2$	*डेऊ़ or डेऊा or डेऊे or देऊ़ or देऊा or देऊे
		$2^1/_2$	*आढ़ा or अढ़ाई or अढ़इया or अढ़ैया
$^1/_{10}$	दहाई or दहइया or दहैया	$^3/_4$	पाउन् or पौना

It is to be noted, that पउने or पौने deducts *one fourth,* but सवा adds *one fourth* and साढ़े *one half* to the numeral to which they are prefixed. Thus एकु पाउ सेर् *one fourth of a ser*; आधु सेर् or आधा सेर् *half a ser*; पउन् or पौना सेर् *three quarters of a ser*; सवा सेर् *one ser and a quarter*; डेऊ़ सेर् *one ser and a half*; पौने दुइ सेर् *one ser and three quarters* (lit., one quarter less than two sers); सवा दुइ सेर् *two sers and one quarter*; आढ़ा सेर् or अढ़ाई सेर् *two sers and one half*; साढ़े तीनि सेर् *three sers and one half,* etc.

414. None of the adjectival fractionals change their form in construction with a subst., except आधा *half* which makes re-

gularly fem. आधी (§ 384), and obl. form आधे (§ 386). Thus आधी राति *midnight*, आधे माग् मे *at half-way*.

415. *Affinities.* These fractionals occur in all Gds., though there are additional forms in some of them. Thus 1/4, W. H. पाओ or चौथाई, P. पाउ or चुथाई, S. पाउ or चोथे or चोथाई or चोथा, G. पा, M. पाव्, B. चोरि or सिकि, O. पा or पाए; 1/3, W. H., P. तिहाई, S. ट्रिहाई, B. तिहाइ; 1/2, W. H. आध् or आधौ, P. अद्ध or अद्धा, S. अधु or आधो, G. अरधो, M. अर्धा, B. आध् or अर्ध or अर्धक्, O. अध or अर्ध or अर्धक्; 3/4, W. H., P. पौन्, G. पोणो, M. पाऊण; 1/4, W. H. सवा or समा or सम, P. सवा or सवाई or सवाइआ, S. सवाई, G. सवा, M. सव्वा, B. सउया; 1 1/2, W. H. डेढ़ or डौढ़ा or डेओढ़ा, P. डेढ़ or डूढ़ or डूढ़ा or डेउढ़ा, S. डेढु or डेढे, G. डोढ, M. दीड्, B. देढ़, O. देढ़; 2 1/2, W. H. अढ़ाई or ढामा or ढाम्, P. ढाई or ढाइआ or ढाया, S. अढ़ाई, G. अढी or हडी, B. अढ़ाई, O. अढ़ाइ; 3 1/2, W. H. हूँठा or होटा, P. ऊठा or ऊँटा or ऊटा; 4 1/2, W. H. ढौँचा, P. ढौँचा (or पोचा ?); 5 1/2, W. H. पौँचा, (P. पौँचा ?); 6 1/2, W. H. खोँचा; 7 1/2, W. H. सतोँचा. Again *minus* 1/4, W. H., B., O., P. पौने, S. पोणो or मुणो, G. पोणा, M. पाउणे or पावणे; *plus* 1/4, W. H., P., S., G. सवा, M. सव्वा, B. सउया, O. सउआइ; *plus* 1/2, W. H., P., O. साढ़े, S. साढ़ा (or साढु), G. साडा, M., B. साडे. See Kl. 103. 105. Ld. 85. 86. 87. Tr. 184. 185. Ed. 48. Man. 45. Ṣ. Ch. 109. Sn. 24.

416. *Derivation.* आध् or आधा regularly for Pr. अद्धो or अद्धओ, Skr. अर्द्धः or अर्धकः. — तिहाई, चौथाई, दहाई, सोरही are abstract nouns derived with the suff. ई or आई from the ordinal or cardinal forms (see § 220). The ह् in तिहाई is probably merely euphonic, for तिआई = तीआई = Pr. तइअ° (H. C. 1, 101) = Skr. तृतीय°. — पाउ or पाव् (or H. H. पाओ) regularly for Ap. Pr. पाउ, Pr. पाओ, Skr. पादः; O. पा or पाय् or पाए = Mg. पाए or पाये. — सवा curtailed from Ap. Pr. सवाउ, Pr. सवाओ, Skr. सपादः; O. सवाइ, Mg. सवाए or सवाये. — साढ़े is the obl. form of साढ़ा (which, however, is never used), regularly for Pr. सड्ढओ, Skr. सार्धकः from स + अर्ध (lit. *with a half*). — पउने or पौने is the obl. form of पौना or wk. form पाउन् or पौन्, regularly for Pr. पाओणो, Skr. पादोनः, from पाद् + ऊन, lit. *one quarter less.* — The forms देढ़ा or डेढ़ा, आढ़ा,

उठा, etc. are made by compounding अर्ध half with the next highest ordinal; thus $3^1/_2$ is in Mg. Pr. अद्धुट्ठ° (see Wb. Bh. 425), which is evidently shortened for अड्ढोट्ठ° = अढ + अउट्ठ° = अढ + चउट्ठ° (cf. H. C. 2, 33) = अर्ध + चतुर्थ° lit. *half-fourth*. The same shortening of ओ to उ occurs in Mg. सत्तुत्तरं for सत्तोत्तरं = Skr. सप्तोत्तरम् (Wb. Bh. 427). Next Pr. अढोट्ठ° is changed to अहोट्ठ° (see § 119) and the initial अ is dropped (see § 172), whence arises the W. H. हूटा or हूँटा or (dropping ह्) the P. ऊठा or ऊँटा (cf. § 145, exc. 2). Again $2^1/_2$ is in Mg. Pr. अड्डाइज्जा (Wb. Bh. 425), which is contr. for अड्ढअइज्जा or अड्ढ + अइज्जा = अड्ढ + तइज्जा (cf. H. C. 4, 339 तइज्जी) = Skr. अर्ध + तृतीया lit. *half-third*. An alternative Pr. form of तइज्जा is तइआ (cf. H. C. 1, 101), whence arises Pr. अड्ढअइआ or contracted अड्ढाइआ or E. H. अढाई or अढइया or (dropping initial अ, § 172) P. ढाइआ or ढाई. Similarly $4^1/_2$ must be Skr. अर्धपञ्चमः *half-fifth*, Ap. Pr. अड्ढवंचउ or contracted अड्ढौंचउ, whence (dropping initial अ, § 172) P. ढौंचा, W. H. ढोंचा. Similarly $1^1/_2$ would be in Skr. अर्धद्वितीयः, Mg. अड्ढदुइए (or *अड्ढुद्विइए), and transposing अड्ढ° and °दुइ° (or *द्विव), द्विवड्ढ, which form occurs in the Bh. (see Wb. Bh. 190. 411) and whence is contracted E. H. देड्ढ or डेढ़, M. दीड़ or G. डोढ़ or P. डेउढा and डूढा or W. H. डोढ़ा. — The forms पौंचा, खोंचा, सतोंचा are anomalous and fanciful forms, made after the analogy of ढोंचा under a mistaken idea of its true derivation. They have, certainly, no connection with ऊँचा *high* (as Kl. 108). The ख् of खोंचा is merely the modern pronunciation of ष् in the Skr. षष्, and shows that the word is of modern origin, without any foundation in Pr. — In the W. H. समा or सम the व् of सवा has been changed to म् (see § 134), as W. H. नम्मा or नम *nine* for नवा. In the W. H. ढामा or ढाम corresponding to P. ढाया or ढाई the म् appears to be merely euphonic.

7. PROPORTIONALS.

417. Proportional numbers are made by adding the word गुना *time* to the cardinal numbers; thus दुइ गुना *two times*, तीनि गुना *three times*; चारि गुना *four times*; पाँच् गुना *five times*, etc.

There are also the contracted forms दुगुना *twice*, तिगुना *thrice*, चौगुना *four times*.

418. *Affinities and Derivation.* The proportionals exist in all Gḍs. Thus B. दुइगुण् 2, etc. (Ṣ. Ch. 109), O. तिनि गुण् 3, etc. (Sn. 24), W. H. दुगुना 2, तिगुना 3, चौगुना 4, सतगुना 7, etc. (Kl. 105); P. uses either the full or the contracted forms throughout; e. g., दूणा or दूणो 2, तीउणा or तिगुणा 3, चौणा or चौगुणा 4, पचौणा or पंज़ौणा 5, छिग्रोणा or छिगुणा 6, सतौणा or सतगुणा 7, अठौणा or अठगुणा 8, नौणा or नौगुणा 9, दसौणा or दसगुणा 10, etc. (Ld. 87). S. has only the contracted forms: thus हेकूणो 1, बोणो 2, ट्रीणो 3, चऊणो or चौणो 4, पंज़ूणो 5, छहूणो 6, सतूणो 7, अठूणो 8, नऊणो 9, उहूणो 10, etc. (Tr. 182). S. has also हेकूटो *once*, बीटो *twice*, which, perhaps, are contractions of हेक-पटो, त्रिपटो, as in M. which uses पट् instead of गुण्; thus एकपट् 1, दुप्पट् 2, तिप्पट् 3, चौपट् 4, etc. (see § 411). — E. H. दुगुना regularly for Pr. दुगुणाअं, Skr. द्विगुणाकम्; E. H. तिगुना for Pr. तिगुणाअं, Skr. त्रिगुणाकम्; and E. H. चौगुना for Pr. चउग्गुणाअं, Skr. चतुर्गुणाकम्.

8. SUBTRACTIVES.

419. Subtractive numerals are made by adding कम् *less*; thus 99 is एक् कम् सै *one hundred less one*; 48 is दुइ कम् पचास् *fifty less two.*

420. *Affinities and Derivation.* कम् is thus used also in B. (Ṣ. Ch. 110), and in W. H., H. H., and probably in all W. Gḍs., as it is a persian word. B. uses also the Gḍ. word घाइट् (Ṣ. Ch. 110).

9. DISTRIBUTIVES.

421. Distributive numbers are made by repeating the numeral; thus दुइ दुइ *by twos, two each*; दस् दस् *by tens, ten each.* Sometimes distribution is idiomatically expressed by the word पाछे *after*; e. g., बाह्मनन् के दुइ दुइ पैसा दिहलेस् or बाह्मनन् पाछे दुइ प० दि० *he gave the Bráhmans two paisás each.* Sometimes करि *having made* is added to the reduplicated num.; e. g., दुइ दुइ करि दि० *he gave two to each.*

422. *Affinities.* This practice of reduplication is common to all Gds.; thus B. दश् दश् or दश् दश् करिया *by tens* (S. Ch. 108. 245), O. दुइ दुइ *by twos* (Sn. 24), and so in all. B. also expresses distribution by adding the particle टा or टी to a single numeral, as दश् टा करिया देउ *give ten to each* (S. Ch. 245).

10. DEFINITIVES.

423. Definiteness or emphasis is given to a number by adding the suff. ओ or ओँ; thus दोनो बरिस् *the two years*; तीनोँ दिन् *the three days*; चारोँ बाह्मन् *the four Bráhmans,* etc. A final इ is dropped before the suff., e. g., चारोँ of चारि *four,* साठोँ of साठि *sixty,* etc.

424. *Affinities and Derivation.* This suff. is used also in W. H. (see Kl. 101), to which it more properly belongs. It is the same as the suff. of the obl. plur. (see §§ 362. 363. 365, 7), which is occasionally transferred to the nom. plur. also (see § 369).

11. INDEFINITIVES.

425. Indefiniteness in a number is expressed either by prefixing or suffixing एक् *one* to the numeral, as एक् दस् *about ten,* सो एक् *about one hundred,* etc.; to एक् itself आध् *half* is added, एक् आध् *about one.* Or it may be expressed by joining another number according to the following rules: 1, every number is used with the one immediately following, as तीनि चारि *about three,* दस् इग्यारह् *about ten,* etc.; or 2, ten or any multiple of ten is used with the next following multiple of five or ten; as दस् पंद्रह् or दस् बीस् *about ten* or *any number between ten and fifteen* or *between ten and twenty*; बीस् पचीस् or बीस् तीस् *about twenty*; or 3, exceptionally 2 is used with 4, दुइ चारि *about two,* 5 with 7, पाँच् सात् *about five,* 8 with 10, आठ् दस् *about eight,* 10 with 12, दस् बारह्, 12 with 14, बारह् चौदह् *about twelve,* 20 with 50, बीस् पचास् *about twenly.*

426. *Affinities.* These usages are probably common to all Gds. As to B. see S. Ch. 106. 107, and as to W. H. see

Kl. 101. B. also expresses indefiniteness by prefixing one of the particles गोटा, गोटो, खान्‌ or थान्‌, गाछ्‌ to a numeral (Ṣ. Ch. 106); O. uses गोटा (Sn. 24); S. suffixes खनु (Tr. 180). Thus B. or O. गोटा त्रिश्‌ or B. खान्‌ त्रिश्‌ or S. द्विहारो खनु *about thirty.* — The B. खान्‌ or थान्‌, S. खनु is, probably, the Skr. स्थाणुः *stake* or *post,* which becomes in Pr. थाणू or खाणू (H. C. 2, 7) or खणू (H. C. 2, 99). — The B. गोटा or गाटो is probably the Skr. गोष्टकः or गोष्ठिकः *assembly, heap,* and गाछ्‌ probably the Skr. गच्छ *a progression.*

FOURTH CHAPTER. THE PRONOUN.

427. There are six kinds of pronouns, 1) the personal, 2) the correlative, 3) the reflexive, 4) the honorific, 5) pronominal adjectives and 6) pron. adverbs. The genitives of the personal and reflexive pron. serve to express the corresponding possessive pron.

1. PERSONAL PRONOUNS.

428. E. H. possesses pron. for the first and second person only. For the third pers. the remote demonstr. pron. is used. The pers. pron. are alike for both genders. The forms of the 1st pers. are, dir. sg. मैं *I,* obl. sg. मो or मों, dir. and obl. pl. हम्‌ *we*; those of the 2nd pers. are, dir. sg. तैं *thou,* obl. sg. तो or तों, dir. pl. तूँ *you,* obl. pl. तोहू.

429. There is a long form of the pers. pron., which, however, now occurs only in the fem. plur. and is made by adding the suff. अनी (see §§ 209. 214) to the obl. plur., thus हमनी *we,* तोहनी *you.*

Note: The weak form हमन्‌ *we* occurs in the O. H. (Kl. 127); the corresponding form of the 2nd pers. would be *तोहन्‌ *you.* From these are derived the strong fem. forms हमनी and तोहनी, to which would correspond the strong masc. *हमना and *तोहना, obl. *हमने and *तोहने. Some of these masc. forms may be in actual use. All alike are very vulgar and almost exclusively used by women, even in a sing. sense [1]). A plur. तुमन् and even a sing. तुइन् actually exists in Gw. (see Kl. 129). See similar long forms of the correlative pron. in § 436.

430. *Affinities and Derivation.* 1) *The first pers. pron. sing.* The dir. form is essentially the same in the E., S. and N. Gḍs.; thus B. मुइ, O. मु or मुइ or मुहि, E. H. मैं (Bh.) or मईं or मयँ (Bs.), M. मी, N. मैं or मो; also H. H. मैं. It is quite different in the W. Gḍs., viz. W. H. हौं (Br.) or हाँ (Kn.) or हूँ (Mw.), P. हउँ, G. हुँ, S. आँऊँ or आँ (dropping ह्). The other forms, however, also occur dialectically in the W. Gḍs., viz. W. H. and P. मैं, S. मूँ or माँ, but, as a rule, they are only used as the obl. form; e. g., abl. sg. Mw. मैं सूँ *from me*, P. मैं थों, S. मूँ खाँ or माँ खाँ; act. sg., W. H. and P. मैं, G. मैं, S. मूँ or माँ. On the other hand, the proper dir. form आँ is occasionally used as an obl. in S. (Tr. 190), and so also हउँ in P. (Ld. 16). This shows that the forms with initial म् are properly obl., and have been anomalously transferred to the nom. sg., as has occasionally happened in the case of subst. (see § 369). — *The obl. form* is essentially the same in all Gḍs.; viz. B. and O. मो, E. H. मो (Bh.) or म्वा or म्वहि (Bs.), O. H. मोहि or मुहि, W. H. मोहि or मुहि or मो or मैं or मे (Br.) or मैं or म्हैं or (shortened) म or म्ह or म्हो or म्हा or मा (Mw.)[2]), P. मे or मै, S. मूँ or माँ or मुहुँ [3]), G. म or मा or मैं [4]), M. म or मी or म्याँ [5]), N. म or मैं or मो or मे [6]). — There are, then, in Gḍ. two principal types: 1) that of the proper dir. forms हौं, etc.; 2) that of the various obl. form मैं, मो, etc., some of which are also occasionally used as direct forms.

1) I may state here as a general fact, that among the vulgar in India the plur. forms of the pron. and verb are almost universally used in the place of the sing. Inattention to this fact has led to many errors in the statements of Kl. and Bs. as to E. H.

2) मे and मा or म्हा only in the gen. मेरो (Br.), मारो or म्हारो (Mw.).

3) मुहुँ only in the gen. मुहुँ जो.

4) मा only in gen. मारो, and मैं in the act.; but acc. म ने.

5) मी and म्याँ only in the act., but acc. म ला, etc.

6) मे only in gen. मेरो, मैं only in the act. मैं ले.

The dir. forms are modifications of the Ap. Pr. nom. sg. हउँ (H. C. 4, 375) or हमुं (K. I. 39 in Ls. 451) or हगु (Md. अस्मदो हगु सुना साऊं । अस्मदु इत्यधिकारः । हमु भणामि ॥, i. e., *asmad* has *hamu* in the nom. sg.; here the rules on *asmad* commence; hamu bhaṇami *I speak*). The Skr. nom. sg. is अहम्, which becomes in Pr. अहं or हं (Vr. 6, 40) or str. form अहअं (Vr. 6, 40) or *हअं. The latter regularly H. C. 4, 354 changes to हउं in Ap. Pr.[1]), and this becomes in P. हउँ, in Br. हौं, in Kn. हों, in Mw. हूँ, in G. हुँ. — The Gḍ. obl. forms are modifications of the Pr. gen. sg. forms मइ or मह (H. C. 3, 113) or महु (H. C. 4, 379). The form मइ is used in Mh. Pr. for the gen., abl., instr. and loc. sg. (H. C. 3, 113. 111. 109. 115), and in the Ap. Pr. for the instr. loc. and acc. sg. (H. C. 4, 377); that is, it has evidently become a general obl. form. There can be little doubt, that मइ is a curtailment of *महि (see § 126) and the three forms *महि, महु and मह are evidently made by means of the Ap. gen. or obl. suff. हि, हु, ह (shortened for हे and हो, see §§ 365, 6. 367, 3). In the Ap. Pr. the corresponding pl. suff. हिं, हुं, हं are sometimes transferred to the sg. (see § 367, 5); accordingly we find in the Ap. Pr. also the alternative forms मइं (for *महिं, cf. § 126), महुं and महं (see K. I. 44 in Ls. 451, and H. C. 4, 377. 3, 113)[2]). Now the Ap. मइ or *महि is modified in O. to मुहि

1) Ls. 330 explains the form अहअं as = अहमं, analogous to Pr. तुमं and तुं or तं (H. C. 3, 90); this seems to be supported by the Ap. from हगु; that form, however, is somewhat doubtful; it might well be a false reading for हउं. It appears to me more probable that अहअं is the regular strong form of अहं, and equal to *अहकं, as shown by the corresponding Mg. अहके (Vr. 11, 9) which according to Mg. usage retains the क्; there is also a Mg. form हके or हगे (Vr. 11, 9), which represents a Mh. form *हअं and the Ap. हउं; H. C. 4, 354 expressly states that the Pr. strong form termin. अअं (अकं) changes to अउं in the Ap. Pr.

2) The Ap. Pr. has मइं according to H. C. 4, 377, but मइ according to Md. मइ ङिटाम्भिः । मइ । मयि मया मां वार्थः ॥ again it has महु according to H. C. 4, 379, but महुं according to K. I. and Md. ङसिङस्भ्यां मज्झमहुंमहा । अयः

or मुइ, in B. मुइ, in Bs. म्वहि (for *मुहि, i. e. व for उ, § 71), Br. मुहि (in assimilation to तुइ), and contracted in P. to मे or मै, M. मी. The Ap. मइं is in Bs. मइँ or मयँ, in E. H., W. H., P., N. मैँ, in M. मोँ or म्याँ (for मेँ, i. e. या for ए, cf. § 71). The Ap. मइ is in O. H., B., O., E. H. मो[1]) (for *मउ, § 126, cf. तउ in Nro. 2) or Bs. म्वा, and the Ap. महुं in E. H., N. मोँ and in S. मुहुँ (in assimilation to तुहुँ) or मूँ. The Ap. Pr. मइ occurs in O. H. (e. g., मइ सम *like me*, cf. Kl. 121 [2])), and is shortened in M., G., N. to म, in O. मु, in W. H. म or म्ह; and the Pr. मइं is in S. माँ. Lastly in the O. H. and in Br. the obl. suff. हि is pleonastically superadded to the obl. form मो, making it मोहि. — 2) *The second pers. pron. sing.* The circumstances here are precisely analogous to those of the 1st pers. pron., with the exception, that of the old Skr. nom. sg. त्वम्, Pr. तं or तुं or तुवं or तुमं (H. C. 3, 90) no trace has survived in Gḍ. In all Gḍs. alike, and even in the Ap. Pr., the old gen. sg. or obl. form has taken the place of the dir. form (cf. § 369). Thus as dir. forms are used in B. तुइ, in O. तु or तुइ or तुहि, E. H. तइँ or तयँ (Bs.) or तैँ (Bh.), N. त, W. H. तै or तैँ or तूँ (Br.) or तूँ or थूँ (Mw.), P. तूँ, S. तूँ, M. तूँ, G. तुँ; as obl. forms in B. and O. तो, E. H. तो or तोँ (Bh.) or त्वा or त्वाँ or त्वहि (Bs.), N. तैँ or तँ[3]), W. H. तोहि or तो or तू or तेँ or ते (Br.) or थो or थेँ or था or थ (Mw.) or तोई or त्वो or त्वे (Gw., Km.)[4]), P. तै or त, S. तो or तुहुँ[5]), G. त or तु or तेँ or

ख्युः ॥ and in the *Nágara Ap.* मनेत्यर्थे महुं च स्यात् । महुं घरु सुन्दरु । चकारान् मम च ॥ lastly the Ap. has मइ according to Mḍ. in the above quotations, and the Mh. Pr. has both मइ and मइं according to H. C. 3, 113.

1) In the O. H. of Chand मो occurs as a gen., e. g., नाथ मो नाम चंद *Lord! my name is Chand* (Kl. 121).

2) Or, Chand 25, 28 मइ सगपन सा करिहि सु केमं ॥ *how will she make my kinship*, etc.

3) तैँ only in the act. तैँ ले *by thee*.

4) ते and था only in the gen. तेरो (Br.), थारो (Mw.), तू and तैँ only in the act. in Br. तूने or तैँने, but in Mw. generally, e. g., abl. तैँसूँ or थेँसूँ, see Kl. 128.

5) तुहुँ only in the gen. तुहुँजो.

तुँ or ता [1]), M. तूँ or त्वाँ or तु [2]). All these obl. forms are various modifications of the Pr. gen. sg. forms तइ or तइं, तउ (modified for *तहि or *तहिं, *तहु, cf. महु in Nro. 1), तुह or तुहं, तुहुं [3]), which are derived by means of the gen. or obl. suff. हि, हु, ह or हिं, हुं, हं from the bases त or तु (for Skr. त्व). To complete the series, the form तुहि must be added, which is preserved in the O. H. and Br. तुहि, Bs. त्वहि, O. तुहि or तुइ, B. तुइ, Gw. (lg. f.) तुइन्; and also the form तह [4]) which is preserved in the Br. gen. तेरो, Mw. थारो *thine* for Ap. *तहारउ, just as Br. मेरो, Mw. मारो or म्हारो *mine* = Ap. महारउ (H. C. 4, 358) from Ap. gen. मह. The Pr. तइ or *तहि appears in P. तै or ते or (shortened) G. त, Mw. त or थ; and the Ap. Pr. तइं or *तहिं in Bs. तइँ or तयँ, Bh., Br., N. तैं, Mw. थैं, G. तें, N. तँ. The Ap. Pr. तउ or *तहु becomes

---

1) ता only in the gen. तारो, तें and तूँ only in the act. तें or तुँए, त or तु in the acc. त ने or तु ने.

2) M. तूँ or त्वाँ only in the act.

3) The form तइ is used as an obl. form in the Mh. Pr. for the gen., abl., instr., loc. sing. (H. C. 3, 99. 96. 94. 101) and in the form तइं in the Ap. Pr. for the instr., loc. and acc. sg. (H. C. 4, 370) and Mḍ. तइं ङिटाम्भि: । एभि: सह युष्मदस् तइं स्यात् । तइं । त्वया त्वयि त्वां वा ॥ The form तउ is used in the Ap. Pr. for the gen. and abl. sg. (H. C. 4, 372), and तुह for the gen., abl. and loc. (Mḍ. ङिङसिङसां तुहतुज्झतम्भतुब्भाः स्युः ॥ see also K. I. 44 in Ls. 451) and तुहं for the gen. and abl. (K. I. 44 in Ls. 451); the same form तुह and तुहं are also used for the nom. sg. both in the Mh. (H. C. 3, 90) and Ap. Pr. (K. I. 39 in Ls. 451); the form तुहुं is used in the Ap. Pr. for the nom. sg. (H. C. 4, 368. Mḍ. युष्मदस् तुहं । युष्मद इत्यधिकारः । सुनेत्येव । तुहुं सोअसि ॥ i. e., *thou sleepest.* The identity of the nom. forms तुह or तुहं with the gen. forms तुह or तुहं has been already pointed out by Ls. 465, and that the nom. form तुहं is really a gen. is shown by the fact of its still being used in S. for the gen. तुहुं जो (Tr. 191. 193). In तइ, तइं, तउ a medial ह has been dropped, as is shown by the Mw. obl. थैं or थ (contr. for *तहिं, *तह); and the forms in इं (= *हिं), हं, हुं are gen. pl., used in a sing. sense, precisely as in the case of मइं, महं, महुं (see Nro. 1).

4) तह is given as an obl. form by De Tassy in his Hindi Gramm. (Kl. 121).

in O. H., B., O., E. H., S. तो[1]), and in W. H. ता or थो, Bs. त्या, and a corresponding Ap. form *तउं is preserved in the E. H. तो॑ or त्वाँ, M. त्वाँ (cf. § 71). The Ap. तुह becomes in O., M., G. तु and is preserved also in the E. Gd. तोरा *thine* for Ap. तुहारा (cf. H. C. 4, 434). The Ap. तुहं or तुहुं becomes in P., S., G. तूँ, Mw. तूँ or तूँ, Br. तू. Lastly, O. H. and Br. form तोहि by pleonastically supperadding the obl. suff. हि to the obl. form तो; and similarly S. forms the gen. तुहें (तो), abl. तोहाँ by pleonastically adding the obl. suff. एँ and आँ (or हें, हाँ). — 3) *The first pers. pron. plur.* The circumstances here are the same as with the 2nd pers. pron. sing. No trace of the old Skr. nom. pl. वयम् has survived in Gd.; Pr., however, has वअं or वयं (H. C. 3, 106). But Gd. and, generally also Pr., use one of the many obl. forms of the Skr. base अस्म as their direct form. Thus the various dir. forms in Gd. are: B. आमि or आम (to the latter, as usual, the pl.-aff. रा is added, आम-रा), O. आम्भे, E. H. हम्, N. हामी (to which, as usual the pl.-aff. हरु or हेरु is added, हामीहरु or हामीहेरु), M. आम्ही, W. H. हम् (Br.) or म्हे or म्हैं (Mw.), G. अमे or हमे; and S. and P. असीं. The various Gd. obl. forms are: B. आमा, O. आम्भ or अम्भान (the latter only in the dat. अम्भाकु), E. H. हम् (Bh.) or हम्ह (Bs. see Kl. 127), N. हामी, M. आम्हा or आम्हीं (only act.) or आम् (only in the gen. आम्चा), W. H. हम् or हमन् or हमनि or हमों or हमैं (Br.) or माँ or म्हाँ (Mw.) or हमुं (Gw.)[2]), G. अम् or अमे or हमे (only act.) or अमा (in the gen. अमारो); P. असा or सा or हमा or (only act.) असीं, S. असां or असाँहे or असाँहूँ. All these forms are modifications respectively of the following Pr. gen. or obl. forms: a) अम्ह or अम्हि or अम्हे, b) अम्हाणं, c) अम्हहं, d) अम्हहिं or अम्हइं, which may be spelled also अम्भा° (H. C. 4, 412). Of these the first set अम्ह, अम्हि, अम्हे are modifications of the vedic

1) In the O. H. of Chand तो occurs as a gen. sg., e. g., सुनिय बात तो तात। *having heard the word, thy father*, etc.

2) हमैं only in the dat. and acc. हमैं कों; हमा only in the gen. हमारा *our*.

obl. form अस्मे; and अम्ह, अम्हे are used in Pr. for the gen., instr., acc., nom. (H. C. 3, 114. 110. 108. 106) and अम्हे in the Ap. for the acc. and nom. (H. C. 4, 376)[1]. The Pr. अम्हो or अम्हे becomes आम्भे in O., अमे or हमे in G., and म्हे in Mw.; and the Pr. अम्ह becomes अम् in G., हम् in W. H. and E. H., and आम् in M. — The Pr. form अम्हि or अम्मि, though clearly a mere modification of the plur. obl. form अम्हे (or अम्मे), has assumed the sense of the sing. and is used for the nom. and acc. sing. (H. C. 3, 105. 107). It is so employed also in one of the Ap. Pr. (Md. अहन् अयें अम्मिहुंममा: । अम्मि पणिदु (?) । एवं हुंमम (?)). It has only survived in the B. आमि *I*. As to the second Pr. set अम्हाणं or अम्भाणं, it is the regular gen. plur. of the base अम्ह or अम्भ (H. C. 3, 114, see § 365, 4) and has survived in the O. अम्भान् and W. H. हमन् or हमनि. As to the third and fourth Pr. set अम्हहं, अम्हइं, to which must be added a form *अम्हहुं, they are regularly derived with the Ap. gen. or obl. suff. हं, हुं, हिं (see § 365, 7) from the base अम्ह. The form अम्हहिं or (dropping ह्) अम्हइं is limited in the Ap. to the nom., acc. and instr. (H. C. 4, 376)[2], but in Gd. it occurs also in the dat. (= old gen.); thus in O. H. हमहिँ and contracted in Br. हमैँ, H. H. हमेँ, Mw. म्हैँ, M. अम्हाँ or अम्हा, N. हामी. The form *अम्हहुं is not noticed by the Pr. Gramm., but it appears in Br. as हमौँ, H. H. हमोँ, Gw. हमुँ. The Ap. form अम्हहं, especially mentioned by H. C. 4, 380 as the gen. plur., survives in Mw. म्हाँ or माँ or (dropping the *anunásika*) in B. अमा, M. अम्हा, W. H., P. हमा, G. अमा. — The anomalous P. and S. forms with स्

1) H. C. allows both अम्हे and अम्हइं to the nom. and acc.; K. I. gives अम्हे to the nom. and अम्हइं to the acc. (K. I. 40 in Ls. 451); again Md. allows both अम्भे and अम्भाइं to the nom., but only अम्भाइं to the acc., thus अम्भाइ इति जश्शसभ्यां । अम्भाइ अक्कमु पेक्ख वा । अम्भे च जसा । अम्भे भणामु । चकाराद् अम्भाइं च ॥.

2) H. C. has only अम्हइं and allows it only to the nom. and acc., but Md. has both अम्भहिं and अम्भाइं and allows them also to the instr., thus अम्भाइं अम्भहि अम्भो अम्भाहिं अम्भेहिम् इति च भिसा । पञ्च स्युः । अम्भइ भणिदु । एवमन्यानि ॥.

cannot have arisen from the ordinary Pr. or Ap. forms, but must be referred to some peculiar Pr., which changed the conjunct स्म् of the Skr. base अस्म to स्स् instead of to म्ह् or म्म्[1]). Otherwise, however, their formation is exactly analogous to those of the other Gḍ. forms; thus P. and S. असीँ is analogous to M. अम्ही and would presuppose a Pr. form *अस्सहिं or *अस्सइं; and the P. असा, S. असाँ to P. हमा, Mw. म्हाँ, presupposing Pr. *अस्सहं. In the S. असाँहे and असाँहूँ the obl. suff. हेँ, हूँ (for एँ, ऊँ) are pleonastically supperadded. — 4) *The second pers. pron. plur.* The circumstances here are exactly analogous to those of the first pers. pron. plur., substituting only the base तुम्ह or तुम्भ (= Skr. युष्म) for अम्ह or अम्भ. A simple enumeration therefore of the various Pr. and Gḍ. forms will suffice. Pr. and Ap. have: a) तुम्ह or तुम्हे (H. C. 3, 91. 93. 4, 369); b) तुम्हाणं (H. C. 3, 100); c) तुम्हहिं or तुम्हइं (H. C. 4, 369), d) तुम्हहं (H. C. 4, 373) or e) *तुम्हइं, all plur., and f) तुमे (H. C. 3, 92. 94. 101) in the sing. (like अम्मि). In Gḍ. there are, 1) the following dir. forms: B. तुमि (f), O. तुम्भे (a), E. H. (a) तूँ (Bh., for तूहूँ) or तोह् or तोँह् or (a) तुम्ह् (Bs.), W. H. (a) तुम् (Br.) or (a) थे or (c) थैँ (Mw., for *तहे or *तहैँ, with अ for उ as in G., S. and P.); G. तमे (a), M. तुम्ही (c), N. (f) तिमि (like B. तुमि) or (c) तिमी (with इ for अ or उ, as in Br. तिहारौ *yours*), S. (c) तव्हीँ or तवीँ or तहीँ or तईँ or (c) अव्हीँ or अवीँ or अहीँ or आँईँ or अँईँ, P. (c) तुसीँ (for Pr. *तुस्सइं). And 2) the following obl. forms: B. (d) तोमा or (a) तोम (only in the nom. pl. तोम-रा), O. (a) तुम्भ or (b) तुम्भान् (only in the dat. तुम्भकु), E. H. (a) तोह् or तोँह् (Bh.) or (a) तुम्ह (Bs.), W. H. (a) तुम् or (e) तुम्हौँ or (c) तुम्हैँ

---

1) The loc. suff. स्मिन् admits both changes in the pron. of the ordinary or Mh. Pr. (H. C. 4, 59. 60, e. g., सव्वस्सिं or सव्वम्मि or सव्वहिं for *सव्वम्हिं *in all*), but only म्मि in subst. (H. C. 3, 11, e. g., देवम्मि *in god*); on the other hand the Mg. Pr. admits a form ंसि *ṃsi* or सि *si* even in subst. (Wb. Bh. 417, as देवंसि or देवस्सि). This is noteworthy; for the P. and S. phonetic system shows also in other points (see §§ 16. 18. 14) an affinity to that of the Mg. class of Prs. and Gḍs. The Páli admits both स्मिन् and म्हि in subst. (St. G. 62).

(only in the dat.) or (d) तुम्हा or तिहा (only in the gen. तुम्हारौ or तिहारौ), all these in Br., or (e) तुमँ (Gw.) or (b) तुमन् (Km.) or (d) थाँ (Mw., for *तहाँ, see S.), G. (d) तमा (in the gen. तमारो) or (a) तम् or (a) तमे (only act.), M. (d) तुम्हा or (c) तुम्ही˘ (only in the act.) or (a) तुम् (only in the gen. तुम् चा), N. (f) तिमि or (c) तिमी, S. (d) तव्हाँ or तवाँ or तहाँ or ताँ or (d) अव्हाँ or अवाँ or अहाँ or आँ, P. (d) तुसा (for Pr. *तुस्साहं) or (d) तुहा or तुआ or (d) तुमा or (c) तुमी˘ (only in the act.). As to the origin of the S. forms; the उ of the Pr. तुम्हइं is changed to अव् (similarly as in Bs. त्वहि *to thee* for तुहि) and म् is elided, whence S. तव्ही˘; next either ह् or व् is dropped, making तवी˘ or तही˘; finally व् or ह् is elided, making तई˘; the other S. set अव्ही˘, etc. arises in a precisely similar way from the Pr. forms derived from the Pr. base उम्ह (H. C. 3, 99. 95). — 5) *There remain a few peculiar obl. forms*: viz., of the first pers. pron., M. मज् or माझे or माझ्या (Man. 47. 85), G. मज, W. H. मुज, H. H. मुझ् or मुझे, and of the second pers. pron., M. तुज् or तुझे or तुझ्या, G. तज्, H. H. तुझ् or तुझे, P. तुध्. These obl. forms are modifications of the Pr. gen. मज्झ (H. C. 3, 113) or Ap. मज्झु (H. C. 4, 379), Pr. तुज्झ (H. C. 3, 99) or Ap. तुज्झु (H. C. 4, 372) or तुध्र (H. C. 4, 372). The origin of these forms is obscure. In Pr., the forms मज्झ and तुज्झ are treated as regular bases, just like Pr. अम्ह and तुम्ह, Skr. अस्म and युष्म, and declined as *nouns*. Thus in the gen. sing. the pure base मज्झ or अम्ह (H. C. 3, 113) is used after the Ap. Pr. fashion, i. e., dropping the gen. suff. (H. C. 4, 345); loc. sg. मज्झम्मि or अम्हम्मि (H. C. 3, 116), gen. pl. मज्झाणं or अम्हाणं (H. C. 3, 114), loc. pl. मज्झसु or अम्हसु (H. C. 4, 117), etc. In Gḍ. the gen. sg. (or pure base) मज्झ, तुज्झ become H. H. मुझ्, तुझ्, M. मज्, तुज् (with ज् for झ्, § 145, note). And Gḍ. derives from them even regular obl. st. forms, H. H. मुझे, तुझे, M. माझे or माझ्या, तुझे or तुझ्या (just as H. H. घोड़े, M. घोड्या of घोड़ा *horse*). The corresponding direct st. forms exist only in M. माझा m., माझी f., *माझे˘ n., and तुझा, तुझी, तुझे˘. They serve both as the gen. sing. of the personal pron., and as possessive pron. In E. H., also, the possess. pron. are often used in the place of the pers. pron.; thus abl., E. H. हमरे सों˜ or हमरा सों˜, just as M. माझ्या हून्, loc. E. H. मोरे मे, M. माझ्यांत्. It appears, probable, therefore, that the bases मक and तुक are really those of possessive pron. and perhaps connected with Skr. मदीय *mine* and त्वदीय *thine* by substituting the Pr. bases मह, तुह for म, त्व (or मद्, त्वद्); thus महइय = मक्षा = मक्क or तुहइय = तुक्षा or तुहक (cf. H. C. 3, 91. nom. pl. तुझे) = तुक. Or they might be referred to the Skr. bases मादृश *like me*, त्वादृश *like thee*, which would easily assume a possessive meaning (see §§ 218. 251), and which might change in Pr. to मह्रिह = मक्ख, तुह्रिह = तुक्ख. It may be remarked that a somewhat analogous process has taken place in the case of the demonstrative pron.; thus Pr. एहो is both *that* and *such-like* = Skr. ईदृश, and S. has इको = इक्खो = ईदृशः (see § 438, 4). This would explain also the P. form तुध, which would be = तुदह = त्वादृश, and the ऱ् in the Ap. Pr. form तुध्र might be a reminiscence of the Skr. ऋ of दृश[1]). Ls. connects मक and तुक with the gen. sing. of the pers. pron. *मस्य and *त्वस्य, but these change regularly to मह or महि, तुह or तुहि (see Nros 1. 2); I believe, there is no example of the Skr. conjunct स्य् ever changing to क्क् in Pr.

431. Personal pron. are declined precisely like nouns, with the exception that in the gen. they use their corresponding possessive pron. (§ 449). The weak form of the latter is preferred in the nom., and the st. form in the obl. cases: thus मोर् बाप् or rarely मोरा बाप् *my father*, but मोरे बाप कै *of my father*; हमार् माई or rarely हमरी माई *our mother*, but हमरी माई कै *of our mother*, etc.

432. A sort of pleonastic declension may be made by adding the case-aff. to the obl. form of the gen. in ए; but in

1) Or again, मक might be = मह-क्र, and तुक = तुह-क्र and तुध = तुह-द; क्र and द being the gen. postpositions which occur in O. H. and O. P., and are still used in M., P. and M. S. They may have existed in Pr. already, just as the modern gen. postpositions चा, का, केरा lit. *done* (see § 377).

the *khaṛī bhāshā* this is restricted to the loc., as मो मे or मोरे मे *in me*, हम मे or हमरे मे *in us*, etc.

432a. 1. First personal pron.

a) Simple form: मैं *I*, हम् *we*.

	Sing.	Simple plur.	Comp. plur.
nom.	मैं	हम्	हमलोग्
a., d.	मो के or मों के	हम् के	हमलोग् के or हमलोगन् के
i., abl.	मो से or मों से	हम् से	हमलोग् से or हमलोगन् से
gen.	मोर् or मोरा, मोरी, मोरे	हमार् or हमरा, °री, °रे	हमलोग् कै, के or हमलोगन् कै, के
loc.	मो मे or मों मे or मोरे मे	हम् मे or हमरे मे	हमलोग् मे or हमलोगन् मे

b) Emphatic form: मैं हीं or मैं हूँ *even I*.

	Singular.		Plural.	
nom.	मैं हीं	मैं हूँ	हम हीं	हम हूँ
a., d.	मोही के	मोहू के	हम हीं के	हम हूँ के
i., abl.	मोही से	मोहू से	हम हीं से	हम हूँ से
gen.	मोरै or मोरे ही	मोरौ or मोरे हूँ	हमरै or हमरे ही	हमरौ or हमरे हूँ
loc.	मोही मे or मोरै मे or मोरे ही मे	मोहू मे or मोरौ मे or मोरे हू मे	हम हीं मे or हमरै मे or हमरे ही मे	हम हूँ मे or हमरौ मे or हमरे हूँ मे

432b. 2. Second pers. pron.

a) Simple form: तैं *thou*, तूँ *you*.

	Sing.	Simple plur.	Comp. plur.
nom.	तैं	तूँ	तूँलोग्
a., d.	तो के or तों के	तोह् के	तूँलोग् के or तूँलोगन् के
i., abl.	तो से or तों से	तोह् से	तूँलोग् से or तूँलोगन् से
gen.	तोर् or तोरा, तोरी, तोरे	तोहार् or तोहरा, °री, °रे	तूँलोग् कै, के or तूँलोगन् कै, के
loc.	तो मे or तों मे or तोरे मे	तोह् मे or तोहरे मे	तूँलोग् मे or तूँलोगन् मे

b) Emphatic form: तैं हीं or तैं हूँ *even thou*.

	Singular.		Plural.	
nom.	तैं हीं	तैं हूँ	तूँ हीं or तुँहईं	तूँ हूँ or तुँहऊँ
a., d.	तोही के	तोहू के	तुँहईं के	तोहऊ के
i., abl.	तोही से	तोहू से	तुँहईं से	तोहऊ से
gen.	तोरै or तोरे ही	तोरौ or तोरे हू	तोहरै or तोहरे ही	तोहरौ or तोहरे हू
loc.	तोही मे or तोरै मे or तोरे ही मे	तोहू मे or तोरौ मे or तोरे हू मे	तुँहईं मे or तोहरै मे or तोहरे ही मे	तोहऊ मे or तोहरौ मे or तोहरे हू मे

Note: हो and हू may or may not be spelled हों, हूँ; also हम and तुँह may be spelled हमँ and तुँहँ before हों and ईं (see § 67); e. g., हमँ हों के *to us*, तुँहँ ईं के *to you*. — The gen. pl. may also be तोहारे, हमारे, etc.

2. THE CORRELATIVE PRONOUNS.

433. By the term „correlative pronoun" I here designate the demonstrative, the relative, the interrogative and the indefinite. The demonstrative pron. include the near, the far and the general. The forms of the *near dem.* are: dir. sg. or pl. ई (also यह or emphatic एहै or इहै or इहई), obl. sg. ए or एह (or emph. एही), pl. एन्ह (or emph. एन्हहीं); of the *far dem.*: dir. sg. or pl. उ (also वह or emph. ओहै or उहै or उहई), obl. sg. ओ or ओह (or emph. ओही), pl. ओन्ह (or emph. ओन्हहीं); of the *general dem.*: dir. sg. or pl. ते (or emph. तेहै or तिहई), obl. sg. ते or तेह (or emph. तेही), pl. तेन्ह (or emph. तेन्हहीं); of the *relative*: dir. sg. or pl. जे (or emph. जेहै or जिहई), obl. sg. जे or जेह (or emph. जेही), pl. जेन्ह (or emph. जेन्हहीं); of the *interrog.*: dir. sg. or pl. के (or emph. केहै or किहई), obl. sg. के or केह (or emph. केही), pl. केन्ह (or emph. केन्हहीं); of the *indef.*: dir. sg. or pl. कं or केहू, obl. sg. or pl. के or केहू. These forms are alike for the masc. and fem.

434. The interrog. pron. has a peculiar form in the sing.: dir. का, obl. का or काहे, when inanimate objects are spoken of. It is, in fact, practically a *neuter*. The obl. काहे is used only, when no subst. is expressed. Thus का करैलह *what do you do*, का घरू मे *in what house*, काहे से खइबे *with what wilt thou eat it?* In the plur., the ordinary forms are used.

435. The general dem. pron. has an alternative dir. form से *he, that* for both, sing. and plur. It is generally used instead of ते, but has no emph. forms to express which तेहै, तिहई are used.

436. All correlative pron., exc. the near and far. dem., have long forms, made by adding the pleonastic suff. अन् (see §§ 209. 214). They are treated like adj., i. e., they may be

either weak or strong (§ 381), they are alike in the sing. and plur. (§ 386), and they form a strong fem. in ई (§ 384) and a strong masc. obl. in ए (§ 386). Thus *weak forms*: dir. and obl., sg. and pl., com. gen., तवन् or तउन् or तौन् *he*, ज़वन् or ज़उन् or ज़ौन् *which*, कवन् or कउन् or कौन् *who*, कौनो *any one*; *strong forms*: sg. and pl., masc. obl. तउने or तौने, ज़उने or ज़ौने, कउने or कौने; fem. dir. and obl. तउनी or तौनी, ज़उनी or ज़ौनी, कउनी or कौनी. The existence of the strong masc. dir. forms *तउना or तौना, etc. is doubtful.

437. *Affinities.* In the following list, forms of the same origin are designated by the same letter. Thus *a*, *a* denote forms of the same group, *a*, *a* or *α*, *α* forms of the same variety of the same group, etc. It will be noticed, that the various groups have been much intermixed, the dir. form of a declension sometimes belonging to one group or variety, and its obl. form to another.

1) *The near dem. pron.*; *dir. sg.*, B. (a) ए or (c) इनि; O. (a) ए or एहि or (*α*) इहा; (E. H.) Bh. (a) ई or ऐह् or इह or यह् or Bs. या; (W. H.) Br. (a) यह् or यहु or इहु or Mw. (*α*) यो or ओ (masc.) and या or आ (fem.); P. (a) इह or एह् or अह or (f) इत्; S. (a) ही or हे (com. gen.) or (a) हीउ or हिउ (masc.) and हीअ or हिअ (fem.) or (*α*) इहो or ईहो or इओ or ईओ (masc.) and इहा or ईहा or इआ or ईआ (fem.) or (e) इको (masc.) and इका (fem.); G. (a) आ or ए; M. (a) हा (masc.), ही (fem.), हें (neut.); N. (*α*) यो. *Obl. sg.*, B. (a) ए or (*α*) इहा or (c) ईहाँ, O. (*α*) इहा or एहा or एहाँ; (E. H.) Bh. (a) ए or ऐह् or Bs. (a) या or यहि; (W. H.) Br. (a) इहि or या or यहि or Mw. (c) इणा or ईं or (*γ*) इणी or अणी or H. H. (b) इस् or (*β*) इसे (in the dat. and acc. only); P. (a) इह or अह or (b) इस् or एस् or ऐस् or (c) इन् or एन् or ऐन् (only act.); S. (c) हिन् or इन् (or इनाँ only abl.); G. (a) आ or ए; M. (a) ह्या or या (masc.) and हि or इ (fem.) or ह्यास्, हीस् (only dat.); N. (a) ए or (b) यस् or Km. (*α*) ये or ए. *Dir. plur.*, B. and O. *deest*; (E. H.) Bh. (a) ई or ऐह् or यह् or इह or Bs. (a) ए or एन्ह or इन्; W. H. (a) यह् or (*α*) ये or यै or ऐ; P. (a) इह or एह् or अह; S. (a) ही or हे or (*α*) इहे or (e) इके; G. (a) आ or एओ; M. (a) हे (masc.), ह्या

(fem.), हों (neut.); N. (a) इन् or एन्ह्. *Obl. plur.*, B. and O. *deest*; (E. H.) Bh. (a) ऐन्ह् or Bs. यन्ह् or इन्ह् or यन् or इन्; (W. H.) Br. (a) इन् or (c) इन्हों (or इन्हें dat. acc. only), or Mw. (a) याँ or आँ or (c) इयाँ or अयाँ; P. (c) इनाँ or इन्हां or एनाँ or (a) अहाँ or (c) इनीं or इन्हीं or एन्हीं or एनीं (act. only); S. (a) इनि or हिनि or (c) इननि or हिननि or इन्हनि or इन्हिनि or इन्हें; G. (a) एओ or (c) एवन्; N. (a) इन्ह् or इन् or Km. (a) यूँ or (c) इनूँ or इनो.

2) *The far dem. pron.*; *dir. sing.*, B. (a) ओ or (c) उनि; O. *deest*; E. H. (a) ऊ or ओह् or वह् or उह्; (W. H.) Br. (a) वह् or वुह् or वुहि or उहि or (α) वो or Mw. (α) ऊ or वू (masc.) and वा (fem.); P. (a) उह् or ओह्; S. (a) हू or ऊ (com. gen.) or हो or ओ (masc.) and हुअ or उअ (fem.); G. (d) ओलो or पेलो (masc.), ओली or पेली (fem.), ओलुँ or पेलुँ (neut.); M. *deest*; N. (a) ऊ. *Obl. sing.*, B. (a) ओ or (α) उहा or (c) उँहा; O. *deest*; (E. H.) Bh. (a) ओ or ओह् or Bs. (a) वहि; (W. H.) Br. (a) उहि or वा or वाहि or (b) उस् or विस् or (β) उसे or विसे (dat. acc. only) or Mw. (c) उण or वीं or (γ) उणीं or वणी; P. (a) उह् or (b) उस् or (c) उन् or ओन् (only act.) or (f) उत्; S. (c) हुन् or उन् or उनिह or उन्हिअ or उन्हे (or हुनाँ or उनाँ abl. only); G. (d) ओला or पेला (masc.), etc.; M. *deest*; N. (b) उस् or Gw. (α) वे. *Dir. plur.*, B. and O. *deest*; (E. H.) Bh. (a) ऊ or ओह् or वह् or उह् or Bs. (a) ओ or उन्ह्; W. H. (a) वह् or (α) वे or वै; P. (a) उह् or ओह्; S. (a) हू or हो or (α) हूए or ऊए or होए or उहे; G. (d) ओला or पेला (masc.), etc.; M. *deest*; N. (c) उन्ह् or उन्. *Obl. plur.*, B. and O. *deest*; (E. H.) Bh. (a) ओन्ह or Bs. (a) उन्ह or उन्; (W. H.) Br. (a) उन् or उनि or (c) उन्हों or (a) विन् or विनि or (c) विन्हों (or उन्हें or विन्हें dat. acc. only) or Mw. (a) वाँ or व्याँ or (c) उणाँ or वणाँ; P. उनाँ or उन्हाँ (or उनीं or उन्हीं act. only); S. (a) हुनि or उनि or (c) हुननि or उननि or उन्हनि or उन्हिनि; G. (d) ओलाओ or पेलाओ; M. *deest*; N. (a) उन् or उन्ह् or Km. (a) ऊँ or (c) उनू or उनो.

3) *The general dem. pron.*; *dir. sing.*, B. (a) से or (α) ताहा or (c) तिनि or तेहूँ; O. (a) से or सेहि; E. H. (a) ते or से or तेऊ or तिहि or (c) तवन् or तउन् or तौन्; W. H. (a) सो; P. (a) सो; S. (a) सो (masc.) and सा (fem.); G. (a) ते; M. (a) तो (masc.), ती (fem.), तें (neut.);

N. (a) त्यो or (c) तुन्. *Obl. sing.*, B. (*a*) ताहा or (c) ताँहा; O. (a) ता or (*a*) ताहा or ताहाँ or ताहिं; (E. H.) Bh. (a) ते or तेह् or Bs. (a) त्या or त्यहि or (c) तवन् or (*γ*) तउने or तौने; (W. H.) Br. (a) ता or ताहि or तिहि or तिहु or (b) तासु (gen. only) or H. H. (b) तिस् or (*β*) तिसे (dat. acc. only) or Mw. (c) तिण or तिणी or तणी; P. (a) तिह् or (b) तिस् or (c) तिन् (act. only) or (f) तित्; S. (a) ताँहिँ (or तहाँ abl. only); G. (a) ते; M. (a) त्या (masc.) and ति (fem.); N. (a) त or तो or (b) तस् or (c) तुन् or Km. (a) तइ or तै. *Dir. plur.*, B. and O. *deest*; E. H. (a) ते or तेह् or तिह् or (c) तवन् or तउन् or तौन्; W. H. (a) सो; P. (a) स; S. (a) से; G. (a) ते or तेओ; M. (*a*) ते (masc.), त्या (fem.), तीं (neut.); N. (c) तुन्. *Obl. plur.*, B. and O. *deest*; (E. H.) Bh. (a) तन्ह् or (c) तौन् or (*γ*) तौने or Bs. (a) त्यन्ह् or त्यन् or तेन्; (W. H.) Br. (a) तिन् or तिनि or (c) तिन्हों (or तिन्हें dat. acc. only), or Mw. (a) त्याँ or ताँ or (c) तिणाँ; P. (c) तिनाँ or तिन्हाँ (or तिन्हीं or तिनीं act. only); S. (a) तिनि or तनि or (c) तिननि or तिनिनि or तिन्हनि or तिन्हिनि; G. (a) तेओ or (c) तेम्; M. (a) त्याँ; N. (a) तिन्ह or तिनह् or Km. (a) त्यूँ or (c) तनू or तनन्.

4) *The relat. pron.*; *dir. sing.*, B. (a) ये or (*a*) याहा or (c) यिनि; O. (a) ये or येहु or (c) येउ or येउँ or यों; E. H. (a) जे or जेह् or जिह् or (c) जवन् or जउन् or जौन्; (W. H.) Br. (a) जौ or जो or (c) जौन or Mw. (a) ज्यो; P. (a) जो; S. जो (masc.) and जा (fem.); G. (a) जे; M. (a) जो (masc.), जी (fem.), जें (neut.); N. (a) जो or (c) जुन्. *Obl. sing.*, B. (*a*) याहा or (c) याँहा; O. (a) या or याहिँ or याहा; (E. H.) Bh. (a) जे or जेह् or (c) जौन् or (*γ*) जौने or Bs. (a) ज्या or ज्यहि; (W. H.) Br. (a) जा or जाहि or जेहि or H. H. (b) जिस् or (*β*) जिसे (dat. acc. only), or Mw. (c) जिण or जीं or जण or जणी; P. (a) जिह् or (b) जिस् or (c) जिन् (act. only) or (f) जित्; S. (a) जाँहिँ; G. (a) जे or (c) जेवन्; M. (a) ज्या or जा or जे (masc.), जि (fem.); N. (a) ज or जो or (b) जस् or (c) जुन् or Gw. (a) जइ or जै. *Dir. plur.*, B. and O. *deest*; (E. H.) Bh. (a) जे or जेह् or जिह् or (c) जवन् or जउन् or जौन् or Bs. (a) जेन्ह्; (W. H.) Br. (a) जौ or जो or (c) जौन् or Mw. (a) ज्यो; P. (a) जो; S. (a) जे; G. (a) जे or जेओ; M. (a) जे (masc.), ज्या (fem.), जीं (neut.); N. (c) जुन् or (a) जिन्ह्. *Obl. plur.*, B. and O. *deest*; (E. H.) Bh. (a) जन्ह or Bs. (a) ज्यन्ह् or ज्यन् or जेन्; (W. H.) Br. (a) जिन् or जिनि

or (c) तिन्हों (or तिन्हैं dat. acc. only), or Mw. (a) त्याँ or ताँ or (c) तिणाँ or तणाँ; P. (c) तिनाँ or तिन्हाँ (or तिनो or तिन्हो act. only); S. (a) तिनि or तनि or (c) तिन्हनि or तिन्हिनि or तिननि or तिनिनि; G. (a) तेओ; M. (a) त्यां; N. (a) तिन्ह् or तुन्ह् or Km. (a) त्यूँ or (c) तनू or तनन्.

5) *The interrog. pron.*; *dir. sing.*, B. (a) के (com. gen.) or कि or कोन् (both neut.); O. (a) के or केहु or (c) केउ or केउँ or कौं (all com. gen.) or (a) कि or (b) किस or (c) कण (all neut.); E. H. (a) के or केह् or किह् or (c) कवन् or कउन् or कोन् (com. gen.) or (a) का or काह् (neut.); (W. H.) Br. (a) को or कौ or (c) कौन् or कौनु or Mw. (c) कोण् or कुण् or कण् (all com. gen.), or Br. (a) का or कहा or क्या or Mw. (a) काँइँ or कँइँ (all neut.); P. (a) किहड़ा or (c) कौण् (com. gen.) or (a) की or किआ (neut.); S. (a) केहो or केओ or (d) केरहो or केहरो or केह् or (e) कुड़ाड़ो (all com. gen.) or (a) छा or कोहु or कुहु (neut.); G. (a) शो (masc.), शी (fem.), शुँ (neut.) or कओ (masc.), कई (fem.), कयुँ (neut.) or (c) कोण् (com. gen.); M. (c) कोण् (com. gen.) or (a) काय् (neut.); N. (a) को or (c) कुन्. *Obl. sing.*, B. (*α*) काहा (com. gen.) or (a) कि or (b) किसे (both neut.); O. (a) का or (*α*) काहा or काहिँ (all com. gen.); (E. H.) Bh. (a) के or केह् (com. gen.) or (a) का or काहे (neut.) or Bs. (a) क्वा or क्वहि (com. gen.); (W. H.) Br. (a) का or काहि or किहि or Mw. (c) कुण् or कण् or कौ or कुणी or कणी or H. H. (b) किस् or (*β*) किसे (dat. acc. only) com. gen., or काहे (neut.); P. (a) किहड़े or किह or (b) किस् or (f) कित् or (c) किन् (act. only) com. gen., or कास् or काह् (neut.); S. (a) केहे or (d) केरहे or कँहिँ or (e) कुड़ाड़े (com. gen.); G. (a) के or (c) कोण् (com. gen.); M. (c) कोणा or कोण्या or कोणे (or काणी instr. only) com. gen., or (b) कसा or कस्या or कशा or कश्या (all neut.); N. (a) क or को or (b) कस् or (c) कुन् or Gw. (a) कइ or कै. *Dir. plur.*, B. and O. *deest*; E. H. and W. H. like sing.; P. (a) किहड़े or (c) कौण्; S. (a) केहा or (d) केरहा or केरे or (e) कुड़ाड़ा (com. gen.); G. (a) कआ (masc.), कई (fem.), कआँ (neut.); M. and N. like sing. *Obl. plur.*, B. and O. *deest*; (E. H.) Bh. (a) केन्ह् or Bs. (a) क्वन्ह् or क्वन् or केन् or किन्; (W. H.) Br. (a) किन् or किनि or (c) किन्हों (or किन्हैं dat. acc. only); Mw. (c) कुणाँ or कणाँ; P. (c) किनाँ or

किन्हाँ (or किनी॑ or किन्ही॑ act. only); S. (a) केहनि or (d) केर्हनि or (a) किनि or कनि or (c) किन्हनि or किन्हिनि or किननि or किनिनि; M. (c) कोणाँ (com. gen.) or (b) कसाँ or कशाँ (neut.); N. (a) कुन्ह or Gw. (a) क्यूँ or कनू or कनन्.

6) *The indefinite pron.*; *dir. sing.*, B. (a) केह्; O. (a) केहि or (c) कौणासि or कउणासि; (E. H.) Bh. (a) केहू or (c) कौनो or Bs. (a) केऊ or कोऊ; W. H. (a) कोई or कोउ or (c) कौनौ; P. (a) कोई; S. (a) को or कोई (masc.), का or काई (fem.), को (neut.); G. (a) कोइ; M. (c) कोणी or कोणही; N. (a) कोहि. *Obl. sing.*, B. (a) काहा; O. (a) काहा; E. H. like dir.; (W. H.) Br. (a) काहू or (b) किसू or किसी or (c) कौनो or Mw. (a) को॑ or (c) कुणी or कणी; P. (b) किसे or किसी; S. (a) कँहिँ or कँही॑; G. (a) कोइ; M. (c) कोणा or कोणहा; N. (a) कोहि or (b) कसै. *Dir. plur.*, B. and O. *deest*; E. H., W. H., P. like sing.; S. (a) के or केई or कई or कँईं; G. (a) कई; M. (c) कोणी. *Obl. plur.*, B. and O. *deest*; E. H. and W. H. like sing.; P. (b) किसे or किसी or (c) किन्हाँ; S. (c) किने or कने or कनी or कन्ही॑; M. (c) कोणहाँ.

438. *Derivation.* It will be observed that in the preceding list there are *six* principal types of forms, which I have severally marked with a, b, c, d, e, f, and the characteristic features of which are the letters ह् (occasionally elided), स्, न् (or ण्), ल् (or र्), क् (or ज्), त् respectively. The derivation of these forms is involved in many difficulties, the explanation of which, however, in most cases (I think) will be found to be the fact, that the forms which are now used as simple pron. were originally those of pron. adj. of quality or quantity.

1) The pron. of quant. are in Skr. इयत् (or Ved. ईवत्), तावत्, यावत्, कियत् (Ved. कीवत्) *so large* or *so much*, etc. In Pr. these become एव, तेव, जेव, केव (cf. H. C. 4, 407. 408) or एम, तेम, जेम, केम (K. I. 10. 11. 12 in Ls. 450. 451), or slightly modified इव, तिव, जिव, किव or इम, तिम, जिम, किम (K. I. 10. 11. 12); sometimes they are variously spelled एँव or इँव, etc. (H. C. 3, 397. 401) or एम्व or इम्व, etc. (cf. H. C. 4, 418); again they may be shortened to ए, ते, जे, के (see Wb. Bh. 422). Thus the Ap. Pr. uses the first set एव, etc., with the addition of the pleon. suff. उ,

as quant. pron., एवडु, तेवडु, etc. (H. C. 4, 407. 408 and see § 218), and S. and P. similarly use the shortened forms ए, ते, etc. with the pleon. suff. डो or डा; viz. S. एडो, तडो, etc., P. एडा, तेडा, etc. Again G. uses the set एव, तेव, etc., itself without adding any pleon. suff., as qual. pron., एवो, तेवो, etc. But already in the Ap. Pr. these quant. (or qual.) pron. had come to be commonly used as *simple pron.*; so especially the bases इम *he* or *this* (H. C. 4, 361. 3, 72; it is also so used in Skr. in the obl. cases of इदम्) and किम *what* (K. I. 13 in Ls. 450); again as *pron. adv.*, viz. एँव, तेँव *thus*, etc. (H. C. 4, 401; एव or एवम्, an acc. sg., occur even in Skr.), or एम्वइ *so, thus* (H. C. 4, 420, a loc. sg. cf. H. C. 4, 334) and एम्वहिं *now* (H. C. 4, 420, also a loc. sg., cf. H. C. 4, 357). Again the shortened bases (कि etc.) occur in the Ap. Pr. abl. sg. किहे (H. C. 4, 356, with the abl. suff. हे of nouns in इ, cf. H. C. 4, 341), and perhaps in the pron. adv. तिह, जिह, किह (H. C. 4, 401, lit. abl. sing. with suff. ह, shortened for हे). Again the shortened forms ते (ते?), से are mentioned by Mḍ. as nom. sg. (ते से एस सुना यत्तदेतदां । एषां सुना सह ते से एस इत्यू एते स्युः । ते (?) पुरिसो महिला वणं वा । एवं से एस ॥). The latter are used in all E. Gḍs. and in G. as nom. sg.; thus E. H. ए, ते or से, जे, के. By adding the regular obl. sing. suff. ह (shortened for Ap. हो or हु, see § 365, 6) the E. H. obl. forms ऐह्, तेह्, जेह्, केह् are derived and by adding the regular obl. plur. suff. न्ह (see §§ 365, 4. 368, 5) the plur. obl. forms ऐन्ह्, तेन्ह्, etc. The older form in हु is occasionally met with, as तिहु (Kl. 137, c). The corresponding obl. form made with the gen. or obl. suff. हि (shortened for Ap. हे, see §§ 365, 6. 368, 2) is found in Bs. and Br.; thus Br. याहि (for *एहि) or इहि, तेहि or तिहि, etc., Bs. यहि (for *इहि), त्यहि (for *तिहि), etc. Again (just as with nouns, see § 365, 6) the obl. suff. ह or हि may be dropped in E. H.; thus Bh. ए, ते, etc., Bs. या, त्या (= ए, ते), etc., Br. या, ता, etc. In the obl. pl. of Bs. the suff. न्ह usually drops the ह (as in E. H. and Br. nouns, see § 368, 5); thus Bs. इन्ह or यन्ह or इन् or यन्, etc. In Br. it optionally ends in इ; e. g., Br. इन् or इनि, तिन् or तिनि, etc. (cf. O. H. कविन्ह or कविन्हि, Br.

कविन् or कविनि, obl. pl. of कवि *poet*). In P., also, the short obl. sg. forms in इ occur; e. g., इह्, तिह्, etc.; and, on the other hand, in S. the short obl. pl. forms in नि; as इनि or हिनि (transposed for *इन्हि), तिनि or तनि (with अ for इ, see § 26). As regards the S. obl. sg. इन् or हिन्, etc. and the Br. obl. pl. इन्हों, etc., P. इनाँ or इन्हाँ, etc., see below Nro. 2. — Just as the forms of the near demonstr. pron. have arisen from the shortened form ए of the old quant. pron., so those of the far dem. pron. have originated from the long form of the quant. pron. Thus the E. H. obl. sg. ओह् is a contraction of *अवह्, shortened (see § 26) from the Ap. Pr. gen. *एवहु or *एवहो. The other E. H. obl. form ओ has dropped the final ह्. The dir. sing. ओ or ऊ is a contraction of the Ap. Pr. nom. sg. *एव or *एवु. In G. the latter contracts to आ *that* (abl. आ थी *from that*). There is, also, in H. a fuller obl. form वाहु (Kl. 137, d) for *ओहु = *एवहु; and in Br. there is the obl. form वाहि for *ओहि = Ap. *एवहि or *एवहे. And so forth as to the rest of the forms of the far dem. pron. and their derivatives; they are exactly analogous to those of the near dem. pron., as explained above. Here, also, must be mentioned the S. neut. interrog. pron. कोहु or कुहु *what, why* (Tr. 208); it is an obl. form and contracted form *कवहु for Ap. *केवहु or *केवहो.

2) Among the Ap. Pr. quant. pron. एवडु, तेवडु, जेवडु, केवडु (H. C. 4, 407. 408, see Nro 1) the last one is already used in the Ap. as a simple pron. But it shortens एव to अव (cf. § 26 and Nro 1, p. 291) and changes उ to ण (cf. § 106), and thus becomes कवणु (H. C. 4, 367). In E. H. it appears as कवन or कउन् or कोन्, in W. H. कौन् or कोन्, P. कौण्, G. and M. कोण्, Mw. कुण् or कण्, N. कुन्. Similarly Ap. जेवडु becomes in G. जेवन्, in E. H. जवन् or जउन् or जौन्, W. H. जौन्, N. जुन्; and Ap. तेवडु becomes in E. H. तवन् or तउन् or तौन्, N. तुन्. E. H. makes a regular obl. form कौन् or कौनि, representing the Ap. gen. sg. कवणा or कवणाहे (H. C. 4, 425) with or without the gen. suff. हे. The Ap. एवडु gives rise to the B. उनि *that*; the intermediate forms G. एवन्, P. ओन् or उन्, Mw. उण् occur only as obl. forms sing.;

Mw. has also the alternative obl. sg. उणी or वणी beside उण्, just like E. H. कोन्ह् and कोने. Mw. possesses also the corresponding plur. obl. forms उणाँ or वणाँ; and similarly in the other pron., as obl. sg. कुण् or कण् or कुणी or कणी, obl. pl. कुणाँ or कणाँ. The latter are regularly contracted from the Ap. Pr. gen. pl. कवणाहं, etc. These obl. pl. occur, also, in P. उनाँ or उन्हाँ, Br. उन्हौं (= Ap. gen. *अत्रणाहं = एवउहुं), S. उननि or उन्हनि or (with ह् transposed) हुननि. The Br. possesses also as plur. obl. forms उन्हैं (used only in the sense of the dat. and acc.), in O. H. उनहिँ which are made by the Ap. obl. pl. suff. हिं (see § 367, 2). Corresponding to the Ap. quant. pron. एवडु, etc., S. has the shorter forms एडो, तेडो, जेडो, केडो. Just as the Ap. एवडु becomes in B. a simple pron. उनि, so एडो, तेडो, जेडो by changing ड् to ण् give rise to the B. simple pron. इनि, तिनि, यिनि (read जिनि)[1]. This set exists also in P. एन् or इन्, Mw. इण्, S. इन, etc., which, however, occur only as obl. forms sing. There are, also, the fuller obl. sg. forms, Mw. इणी or अणी, S. इनिह (also spelled इन्हिअ or इन्हो) or इन्हे (for *इनहे), N. इनह or इनहे (in the plur. इनह-रू or इनहे-रू, also spelled इन्ह-रू, इन्हे-रू, retaining the obl. suff. हे or ह, see § 364, 3)[2]. There are, also, the corresponding obl. pl. forms Mw. इणाँ or अणाँ, Km. इनू or इनो, P. एनाँ or एन्हाँ or इनाँ or इन्हाँ, Br. इन्हौं, S. इन्हे or इननि or इन्हनि or हिननि (probably with an anomalously transposed ह्, for इनन्हि, cf. § 368, 5). Moreover, Br. has a dat. इन्है, O. H. इनहिं, and P. an act. एन्हीं or इन्हों. The obl. forms in न्हाँ, न्हौं, न्हे contain the Ap. Pr. gen. pl. or obl. suff. हं, हुं, हिं respectively (see § 365, 7, being contractions of *नहं, *नहुं, *नहिं). These remarks apply, *mutatis mutandis,* also to the analogous forms of the relat., interrog., and gen. dem. pron. in Mw., P. and S. — Even the original forms एडो, तेडो, etc. occur in S. as simple pronom. adv.; viz. in

---

1) It should be noticed that here, again, the far dem. उनि is founded on the longer form एवड, but the near dem. on the shorter एड.

2) S., also, has an obl. sg. हिन् which stands for *इन्ह = इनह.

the obl. form एडे or एडहँ or एडहुँ *hither*, तेडे or तेडहँ or तेडहुँ *thither*, केडे or केडहँ or केडहुँ *whither*[1]). Some of these exist, also, in E. H. (with the usual change of ड् to न्), एने *hither*, तेने *thither*, जेने *whither-soever*, केने *whither*.

3) The Ap. Pr. quantit. pron. एव, तेव or तिव or तेम, जेव or जिव or जेम, etc. (see Nro 1) seem to have also produced the following Gḍ. simple pron.; viz. O. येउँ, केउँ, G. जेव, तेव (also spelled जेउ, तेउ or जेओ, तेओ) or जेम, तेम which, however, appear to be used only as obl. plur. forms (see Ed. 41. 43); also G. कओ m. (कई f., कउँ n.), probably for *कवो, shortened from the strong form केवो, which occurs in G. as a qualit. pron.; S. has केओ m. (केई f., Tr. 209); the corresponding weak form *कउ occurs in Br. कौ or को, N. क्यो, and is used alike for masc. and fem., sing. and plur. (just like Ap. एहु, see Nro 6). Similarly N. has त्यो (for *तिवो) and ज्यो, Mw. ज्यो or जो, Br. जौ, P. जो; M. also has masc. जो, but makes a regular fem. जी and neut. जें, and obl. sg. ज्या or जे, obl. pl. ज्याँ, dir. pl. जे, ज्या, जीं; a fact which points to their origin from the strong forms *जओ, *जई, *जयं. To the M. obl. pl. ज्याँ corresponds the Mw. obl. pl. ज्याँ, Gw. ज्यूँ. The S. has m. जो, but a rather anomalous f. जा, pl. जे c. g. Exactly analogous are M. sg. तो, ती, तें, pl. ते, त्या, तीं; obl. sg. त्या, ति, pl. त्याँ, Mw. त्याँ, Gw. त्यूँ. The G. neut. कउँ was used already in the Ap. Pr. as pronom. adv. कउं *why* (H. C. 4, 416). Also तउ, जउ are mentioned as Ap. Pr. acc. (= nom.) and gen. sg. forms by Mḍ. in the following two sútras: यत्तदोर् अमा जउ तउ। अमा सह यत्तदोर् जउ तउ स्यात्। जउ मग्गसि तउ देमि॥ i. e., *yat tad* become *jaü taü* in the acc. sg.; e. g., what thou askest, that I give; and ङसिङस्भ्याँ जउ तउ च। यत्तदोर् इत्य् एव। चकारात् पक्षे प्राकृतवत्॥ i. e., *yat tad* become *jaü taü* in the abl. and gen. sg. or they have the regular Pr. forms[2]). I believe, N. is the only Gḍ., which

1) The forms in हँ, हुँ are, properly, obl. plur., but used as sing.

2) My MS. reads यत्तदो मा जउ पतिउ। अमा सह यत्तदोर्जउ तउ स्यात्। जउ म° तउ द°; there can be little doubt, that जउ, तउ (or perhaps जउं, तउं) is the true reading as shown by the succeeding sútra, where the MS. reads जउ,

admits जो, तो as obl. forms; viz. in the abl. sg. जो बाट or जो सँगँ *from which*, तो बाट or तो सँगँ *from him*. — In G., एम, तेम *thus*, etc. occur also as pron. adv. (Bs. II, 336, 337); so also in O. H. केम or केमं *how*, etc. [1]). B. adds the pleon. suff. अन् (§§ 209. 214); thus एमन् or एमनि or एमने, तेमन् or तेमनि or तेमने *thus*, etc. (see S. Ch. 216).

4) From the Ap. Pr. quantit. pron. एवडु, तेवडु, etc. are also derived the G. far dem. pron. ओलो or पेलो *he, that* and the pronom. adv. अइले or ऐल्हे *now*, तइले or तैल्हे *there*, etc. by the change of ड् to ल्. Thus Ap. एवडो becomes *अवडो, *अवलो or contr. ओलो or पेलो (for वेलो with an anomalous hardening of व् to प्). The N. अइले or ऐल्हे (for *एलहे) is a loc. (or obl. form) sing. made with the obl. suff. हे and is = Ap. Pr. एवडहे (see § 469). The Pr. loc. sg. ताला *there*, जाला *where*, काला *where* (H. C. 3, 65) are probably to be explained in a similar manner. Possibly the S. interrog. केह् *who* may be identified with the short quant. pron. केडु by the change of ड् to र्; but it may be also (as Tr. 206) the curtailment of the Ap. qual. pron. *केरिहु, a slight modification of the ordinary Pr. केरिसो, Skr. कीदृशः. The Ap. strong form *केरिहो becomes in S. the simple pron. केहों *what* (usually spelled केह्रो with transposed ह्). Substituting in केरिहो the long Ap. form केव° for के°, and the original द् for र्, we obtain केवदिहो (cf. Pr. कीदिसो Ls. 116); and similarly एवदिहो or एदिहो for the ordinary Pr. एरिसो or *एदिसो, Skr. ईदृशः. Here the palatal vowel इ changes द् to ज़्, and thus in S. the Ap. *एदिहो and *एवदिहो become the simple pron. इहो *this* (for *इज़िहो, just as S. केहों for केरिहो) and उहो *that* respectively; the one being the near, the other the far dem. pron., corresponding to the short and long

तउ. In the original MS., which was in the Oṛiya characters उ (or उं) would be hardly distinguishable from ड्.

1) E. g., Chand Pr. Ráj 25, 28 कहै ँ नट्ट सों ँ राजन वर प्रेमं । मह सगपन सा करिहि सु केमं ॥ i. e., says the king to the actor, full of affection: how will she make kinship with me? or 1, 82 जरों ँ ताप उधरों ँ केम नथ्थ । i. e., I am hot with fever; how can I remove it, oh Lord?

qual. pronominal forms. Similarly the S. कुत्ताउो *what* stands for the Ap. *केवदिहअउउ (with the pleon. suff. अउउ, see § 217, H. C. 4, 429). In H. there is a pron. adv. कुत्ता *where*. In the Ap. there is a qualit. pron. एत्ताहु *such-like* (K. I. 5, see Ls. 449, 455) = Skr. एतादृशः. In P. there is the qual. pron. अजिहा or अजेहा *of this sort* (Ld. 19, 56).

5) The pron. of qual. are in Skr. ईदृशः, तादृशः *such-like*, etc. They become in the Ap. Pr. एहु, तेहु, जेहु, केहु (H. C. 4, 402) or (in the st. form) एहो, केहो etc. The first of these एहो or एहु or एह was already used in Pr. as a simple pron. *he* or *this* (H. C. 4, 362)[1]), and it occurs in most Gds. as the dir. form of the near dem.; thus P. एह् or इह्, Br. इहु or यहु or यह्, E. H. इह or ई (for *इअ dropping ह्) or ऐह्. O. has एहि which appears to be founded on the form *एहे mentioned by K. I. 8 in Ls. 449, and is Ap. Mg. (see § 46). The S. हो or हे or हिउ (for इह, एह्, इहु) transposes the ह्; and the S. इओ (for इहो) elides it; so does also the N. यो (for इओ) and Mw. यो; and the Mw. ओ drops the initial य् of यो. In M. the initial इ or ए is dropped; thus हा m., ही f., हे॑ n. (for Ap. *इहउ, *इहिआ, इहुं, all st. forms) with a regular obl. sg. ह्या, pl. ह्याँ, and dir. pl. हे m., ह्या f., ही॑ n. The Ap. Pr. qual. pron. केहो occurs in S. as the adjectival simple pron. केहो (fem. केही) or (eliding ह्) केओ *which* (Tr. 209); so also in G., where, however, ए is shortened to अ, thus G. कओ (fem. कई, n. कउँ). But perhaps these S. and G. forms are rather to

1) H. C. limits all three forms to the nom. and acc. sg., but Mḍ. only एहो and एहु, while he appears to allow एह for all cases; thus तदश्चेह सुपा। सुपा सह तदो (दश्चा ते सेश्च?) एहः स्यात्। एह ज्ञपो वाला वपां वा। चकारात् पूर्वोक्तरूपम्॥ i. e., *tad* in declension becomes *eha* or (*ima*) as before mentioned. The reading in brackets is doubtful; perhaps it is to include the pron. अदस्; as in the succeeding rule: एहो एहु च स्वम्भ्यां। स्वम्भ्यां सह तदद्सोर् एहो एहु च स्यातां। एहो सोहेइ देक्ख वा। एष शोभते। एतं पश्येति। एवं एहु। चकारात् पूर्वोक्तं च॥ i. e., in the nom. and acc. sg., *tad* and *adas* become *eho* or *ehu* or as before mentioned (*eha*). Mḍ. is correct; for *eha*, being a pure base, may serve as an obl. form, while एहो and एहु are proper nominatives.

be connected with the base केव (see Nro 3). In P. the pleon. suff. ड़ा is added, thus केहड़ा *which*, ज़ेहड़ा *whichsoever* (fem. °ड़ी). — Connected with the Ap. Pr. केहो is also the W. H. (so-called) neut. interrog. pron. कहा or P. किश्रा *what*, with ए shortened to इ and अ. They are really obl. forms. The P. किश्रा stands for *किहा and is contracted in H. H. to क्या. S. transposes ह् (i. e., क्हिश्रा *khiá*, § 132, note) and changes क्हि *khi* to छ *chh* by the influence of the palatal इ, thus making छा (Tr. 208). Similarly G. changes *किहो, *किहो, *किहुं into शो, शो, शुं (for छो, छो, छुँ, see § 11, for *क्हिश्रो, *क्हिई, *क्हिउं). — Here is also to be mentioned the peculiar E. and W. Gḍ. (exc. G.) general dem. pron. से or सो, O. also सेहि *that*, which I am inclined to derive from the Skr. सदृशः *like*. It would become in the Ap. Pr. *सेहो or *सेहु or *सेह, just as Ap. एहो, एहु, एह for ईदृशः; and it would easily acquire the meaning of *such-like* in correlation with the relat. pron. ज़े or ज़ो. It is commonly (Bs. II, 314) identified with the Pr. nom. sg. सो (H. C. 3, 3) or the Pr. gen. sg. से (H. C. 3, 81). But the Gḍ. से is *never* an obl. form; and both the Gḍ. से and सो are used indifferently in the nom. sg. and plur. Besides the S. सो forms a fem. सा and plur. से; and the O. सेहि seems to be an analogous form to O. एहि. Possibly the E. H. nom. sg. and pl. ते, ज़े, के may be identified with the Ap. qual. pron. तेहु, ज़ेहु, केहु (H. C. 4, 402) or तेह, ज़ेह, केह, by dropping the final ह्; for a form तेह, etc. appears in the emphatic forms तैहे, etc.

6) The same Skr. qual. pron. इदृशः, etc. also become अइसो, तइसो, ज़इसो, कइसो (H. C. 4, 403) or अइसु, तइसु, etc. (cf. H. C. 4, 331. 332) in the Ap. Pr. In Gḍ. अइ is changed to ऐ or ए or इ or अ; thus strong forms: W. H. ऐसौ, तैसो, P. and H. H. ऐसा, तैसा, N. यसो (for *ऐसो or *इसो, see §§ 71. 171), तसो, M. असा, तसा, etc. But the weak forms ज़सु or ज़स्, तसु or तस्, etc. also occur in Br. (see Bates' Hindi Dict.) and O. H. Thus Chand in Pr. Raj 24, 52 थांन थांन नर् उडै। चंद तस उप्पम पाइय ॥ i. e., *from place to place men fly up* (i. e., *like birds*), *such a simile has Chand devised*. In modern Gḍ., however, the weak forms have become

simple pron. Thus P. ऐस् or एस् or इस्, तिस्, N. यस्, तस् *he* or *this*, etc. They are found only as obl. forms. The corresponding fuller obl. forms in ए also occur; thus H. H. has इसे, तिसे (as dat. acc. *to him* or *him*) besides इस्, तिस्, etc., (just as E. H. कौन् and कौने, see Nro. 2; contr. for Ap. अइसहि or अइसहे, see § 365, 6). B. has the gen. sg. किसे-र् *of what*, dat. loc. किसे *to or in what* (S. Ch. 122; just as B. देवे-र् *of god*, देवे *to or in god* of देव्). M. has not only the sing. obl. कसा or कस्या (= Ap. Mg. gen. कइसाह or कइसयाह, Skr. कीदृशस्य or कीदृशकस्य, see § 365, 1), but also the pl. obl. कसाँ or कस्याँ (= Ap. Mg. gen. कइसाहँ, etc., § 365, 4) *of whomsoever* (see Man. 54; just like M. obl. sg. देवा, pl. देवाँ of देव् *god*). The existence of these fuller obl. forms shows that the shorter ones (तिस्, जिस्, etc.) cannot, probably, be identified with the Pr. gen. तस्स, जस्स, Skr. तस्य, यस्य, etc. (as Bs. II, 315).

7) Again the before mentioned (see Nro. 1) Skr. quant. pron. इयत्, तावत्, etc. are changed in the Ap. Pr. to एत्तिउ (H. C. 4, 341), तेत्तिउ, जेत्तिउ, केत्तिउ (cf. H. C. 4, 383) or, in the strong form, to एत्तिओ, तेत्तिओ, etc. (H. C. 4, 395, cf. 2, 157, for *एत्तिअउ, etc.). The latter become in W. H. इत्तौ, तित्तौ, etc., H. H. इत्ता, तित्ता, O. एते, तेते, etc. (Bs. II, 332); the former in S. एति°, तेति°, etc., G. एट°, तेट°, etc., W. H. and P. इत°, तित°, etc., E. H. ऐत°, तेत°, etc., B. एत्, तेत्, etc. (S. Ch. 85). As a rule, these weak forms add some pleon. suff. (ना or रो or लो); thus P. इतना, तितना, etc., S. एतिरो, तेतिरो, etc., G. एटलो, etc. (see §§ 452. 453). But the plain weak form is used in P. as a simple pron.; thus इत्, तित् *he* or *that*, जित् *which*, कित् *who* (Ld. 22, 66); it occurs, however, only in the obl. sing. (e. g., gen. तित् दा *of this*). Both these shorter obl. sg. and the corresponding fuller obl. sg. forms are used as pron. adv.; thus Br. इत् or इतै *here*, तित् or तितै *there*, etc., P. इत्थे, तित्थे, etc., S. इति or इते or इत्थि or इत्थे, तिति or तिते or तित्थि or तित्थे, etc. The forms इत्थि, इत्थे, etc. are contracted from इत्तहि or इत्तहे, तित्तहि or तित्तहे, etc. These are loc. sg., made with the Ap. Pr. obl. suff. हे (see § 365, 6), and occur even in the Ap. Pr.

itself, as एत्तहे *here*, तेत्तहे *there*, etc. (H. C. 4, 436)[1]). By the side of the shorter forms एत्तिअ, केत्तिअ, etc., Pr. uses also the longer forms एवत्तिअ, केवत्तिअ, etc. (see Wb. Bh. 422); and as Pr. एत्तिओ originates the W. H. near quant. pron. इत्तो, so Pr. *एवत्तिओ (shortened *अवत्तिओ, *ओत्तिओ) becomes the far quant. W. H. उत्तो *that much*, H. H. उत्ता. The corresponding weak forms are S. ओत्ति°, G. आट°, W. H. and P. उत°, E. H. ओत°, B. अत् (S. Ch. 85, see §§ 452. 453); and the pron. adv. are, Br. उत् or उतै, P. उत्थे, S. उत्ति or उते or उत्थि or उत्थे; and P. uses उत् as a simple pron. in the obl. cases; e. g., उत् दा *of him, of that.*

8) The following Gḍ. pron. forms appear to be remnants of the old simple pron. The Skr. gen. sg. तस्य, यस्य, etc. become in the Ap. Pr. तस्स, जस्स or तास, जास or तासु (also तस्सु H. C. 4, 419), जासु (H. C. 4, 358. 3, 63). In O. H. the following instances of the latter two kinds of forms occur, तास or तासु and जास or जासु[2]), in Br. only तासु and जासु (Kl. 122, a); and P. has कास् as the obl. form of the neut. interrog. pron. (*of what*, Ld. 20, b). But in the Ap. Pr. the gen. or obl. form is also made by adding the ordinary obl. suff. हो or हे, before which the vowel may be either long or short; thus तहे, कहे (H. C. 4, 359) or ताहे, काहे (H. C. 3, 65), एत्तहे (H. C. 4, 436) or एत्ताहे (H. C. 3, 82. 2, 134); again ताहो, काहो or ताह, काह, etc.[3]). Some of the forms with आ

1) Perhaps the Ap. Pr. forms एत्थु *here*, तेत्थु *there*, etc. (H. C. 4, 404) may be similarly explained as contr. from एत्तहु, तेत्तहु, etc., made with the abl. or obl. suff. हु (H. C. 4, 336, see § 365, 6); and the Ap. Pr. forms जत्तु *where*, तत्तु *there*, etc. (H. C. 4, 404) as acc. neut. in उ (H. C. 4, 331) or as containing the abl. suff. तो or तु (= Skr. तस्). Some of these Ap. forms have been received into the literary Pr.; viz. एत्थ (for एत्तह = एत्तहु) or एत्ताहे or एत्तो, see H. C. 3, 82. 83. Vr. 6, 20. 21, where they are expressly described as being abl. sing.; and जत्थ, तत्थ, कत्थ, see H. C. 2, 161 and Wb. Bh. 422 (कत्थ and एत्थं = *एत्तहं abl. pl., § 365, 7).

2) Thus Chand, Pr. R. 25, 16 तास राज समीपं। रहो नट विधा उचारं॥ i. e., *near that* king I remain to practise the art of the actor.

3) Mḍ. says: दीर्घो ऽस्से वा ङसादेशे। स्सावर्जिते ङसादेशे एषां (i. e. किंयत्तदां) दीर्घो वा स्यात्। काहो। काह। कासु। काहं। काहुं। एवं यत्तदोः॥ स्से। कस्स। जस्स॥

are preserved in Gḍ.; thus ताहि, जाहि, काहि (for *ताहे, etc.) and ताहु, जाहु, काहु (for ताहो, etc.) in Br. (Kl. 122. 226) and, as the obl. form of the so-called neut. interrog., काहे in E. H. and Br., and काह् in P.; in O. H. also ताह् or ता [1]). The Ap. Pr. loc. sg. is तहिं, जहिं, कहिं (H. C. 4, 357); apparently these have become general obl. forms in S. तँहिँ, जँहिँ, कँहिँ, and with आ in O. ताहिँ, जाहिँ, काहिँ, and perhaps serve as neut. interrog. pron. in Mw. काँईं or कँईं (dropping ह्) and also in the Ap. Pr. काइं (H. C. 4, 367) and कइं (H. C. 4, 426).

9) The indefinite pron. are made by adding the emphatic particles उ or ई (see § 550) to the interrog. pron. Thus E. H. केहू *any one* = केहु + उ *kehu* + *u* and कोनो = कोन + उ *kauna* + *u*, M. कोणी = कोण् + ई *kon* + *i*, H. H. कोई = को + ई *ko* + *i*.

439. *Declension.* Correlative pron. are declined regularly like nouns, with the following two exceptions: 1) those of the short form (ई, ऊ, ते, जे, के, § 433) may optionally use in the gen. the aff. कर् or करा. This affix is treated precisely like an adj.; i. e., it follows the gender, number and case of the governing noun. Thus कर् is the weak form, of com. gen. and incapable of inflexion, but करा is the masc. st. form (§ 381), making a fem. करी (§ 384) and obl. masc. करे (§ 386), fem. करी, both in the

---

i. e., *ka, ya, ta* may become *ká, yá, tá* before the gen. suff., exc. when the latter is *ssa*. — It will be observed, that हे is a general obl. suff.; for in H. C. 4, 359 (तहे) it is a gen. suff., in H. C. 3, 65 (ताहे) and H. C. 4, 436 (एत्तहे) and H. C. 2, 134 (एत्ताहे) it is a loc. suff.; in H. C. 3, 82 (एत्ताहे) it is an abl. suff. Moreover, हे may be shortened to हि and ह, see H. C. 2, 161 (तहि, तह); and ह or त्थ is an abl. suff. in H. C. 3, 82 (एत्थ = *एत्तह), but a loc. suff. in H. C. 2, 161 (तत्थ = *तेत्तह).

1) Thus Chand Pr. Ráj 25, 36 न न हंस धीर् न न सुष्य ताह ॥ i. e., *neither his soul nor his felicity was firm*; again 25, 16 ता ग्रह सु पात्र अनेक गुन ॥ i. e., *in his house is a daughter of many virtues.* — It may be observed, that the so-called neut. interrog. pron. is, in reality, merely some obl. form of the common interrog. pron.; thus M. has काय् (for *काहि = *काइ); Bs. has काह् and Bh. का (for काह्) *what.*

sing. and plur. (§ 386); but करे may be used, though anomalously, as a fem. obl. The strong forms are not commonly used in the nom., nor the weak forms in the obl. cases. Practically, therefore, the aff. are; dir. form कर् c. g., obl. करे m. or करी f.; just like कै and के. It should be observed also that the latter aff. only (but not कर्, करे) can be used with the full pron. obl. forms in ह् (viz. एह्, ओह्, तेह्, जेह्, केह्) and with the emph. obl. forms in ही (as एही, ओही, etc. § 433). Thus dir. form sg. or pl. के कर् घर् or केह् कै घर् or rarely के करा घर् *whose house* or *houses*; के कर् मेहर् or केह् कै म° or rarely के करी म° *whose wife* or *wives*; obl. sg. के करे घर् मे or केह् के घर् मे or rarely के कर् घर् मे *in whose house*; के करी मेहर् से or केह् के मेहर् से or rarely के कर् or के करे म° से *from whose wife*; obl. pl. के करे घरन् मे or केह् के घरन् मे *in whose houses*; के करी मेहरन् से or केह् के म° से or rarely के करे म° से *from whose wives*; etc. — 2) There is no acc. proper, identical with the nom., but only the (improper) acc. formed with the dat. aff. के. Thus *whom* is के के or केह् के or कवन् के or कौने के, but not simply के or कवन्.

440. Optionally a sort of pleon. declension may be made, by adding the case-aff. to the ordinary obl. form of the gen. in ए. In the *khaṛí bhásháí*, however, this is not commonly done, exc. in the loc.; e. g., sg. ओ करे मे *in him*, pl. ओन्ह् करे मे *in them*, etc.

441. 1. Short form.

a) Simple form: ई *he, this.*

	Sing.	Simple plur.	Comp. plur.
nom.	ई	ई	ईलोग्
acc., dat.	ए के or एह् के	एन्ह् के	एन्ह् लोगन् के
instr., abl.	ए से or एह् से	एन्ह् से	एन्ह् लोगन् से
gen.	ए कै, के or एह् कै, के or ए कर्, करी, करे	एन्ह् कै, के or एन्ह् कर्, करी, करे	एन्ह् लोगन् कै, के
loc.	ए मे or एह् मे or ए करे मे	एन्ह् मे or एन्ह् करे मे	एन्ह् लोगन् मे

b) Emphatic form: इहे or इहौ *even he, even this.*

Singular.

nom.	इहै or इहई	इहो or इहऊ
acc., dat.	एही के	एहू के
instr., abl.	एही से	एहू से
gen.	एही कै or एही कर् or ए करै or ए करे हो	एहू कै or एहू कर् or ए करो or ए करे हू
loc.	एही मे or ए करै मे or ए करे ही मे	एहू मे or ए करो मे or ए करे हू मे

Plural.

nom.	इहै or इहई	ऐन्ह हूँ
acc., dat.	ऐन्ह हीँ के	ऐन्ह हूँ के
instr., abl.	ऐन्ह ही से	ऐन्ह हूँ से
gen.	ऐन्ह हीँ कै or ऐन्ह हीँ कर् or ऐन्ह करै or ऐन्ह करे हीँ	ऐन्ह हूँ कै or ऐन्ह हूँ कर् or ऐन्ह करो or ऐन्ह करे हूँ
loc.	ऐन्ह हीँ मे or ऐन्ह करै मे or ऐन्ह करे हीँ मे	ऐन्ह हूँ मे or एन्ह करो मे or ऐन्ह करे हूँ मे

Note: Like ई are declined ऊ *that,* ते *he,* जे *which,* के *who;* only substituting ऊ, ओ, उ, ओ and ते, ति, ते, etc. for ई, ए, इ, ऐ respectively. — All forms with ऐ or ओ may, optionally, be spelled with इ or उ; e. g., ऐन्ह के or इन्ह के *to these,* and ओन्ह के or उन्ह के *to those,* etc.

442. 2. Long form: तवन् or तउन् or तौन् *he, this.*

Sing. and simple plur.

	Com. gen.	Fem.
nom.	तवन्	तउनी
acc., dat.	तौने के	तौनी के
instr., abl.	तौने से	तौनी से
gen.	तौने कै, के	तौनी कै, के
loc.	तौने मे	तौनी मे

Compound plural.

	Com. gen.	Fem.
nom.	तौनेलोग्	तौनीलोग्
acc., dat.	तौनेलोग् के or तौनेलोगन् के	तौनीलोग् के or तौनीलोगन् के

	Com. gen.		Fem.	
instr., abl.	तौनेल्लोग् से	or तौनेल्लोगन् से	तौनील्लोग् से	or तौनील्लोगन् से
gen.	तौनेल्लोग् कै, के	or तौनेल्लोगन् कै, के	तौनील्लोग् कै, के	or तौनील्लोगन् कै, के
loc.	तौनेल्लोग् मे	or तौनेल्लोगन् मे	तौनील्लोग् मे	or तौनील्लोगन् मे

Note: Like तवन् are declined जवन् *which* and कवन् *who*; also अापन् *own* (§ 449). — Their forms may, optionally, be spelled with अव or अउ or अो according to § 34; e. g., तउने के or तौने के *to this.*

442a. Short form: के or केहू. Long form: कौनो *any one.*

	Sing. and simple plur.			Compound plural.		
nom.	के	केहू	कौनो	केल्लोग्	केहू लोग्	कौनो लोग्
a., d.	के के	केहू के	कौनो के	के लोग् के	केहूलोग् के	कौनोलोग् के
i., abl.	के से	केहू से	कौनो से	or के लोगन् के	केहूलोगन् के	कौनोलोगन् के
gen.	के कै, के	केहू कै, के	कौनो कै, के	etc.	etc.	etc.
loc.	के मे	केहू मे	कौनो मे			

Note: Like केहू is declined जेकेहू *whosoever.*

3. THE REFLEXIVE PRONOUN.

443. The reflexive pron. *self* is अाप्. It is alike for both genders, and is declined regularly like a subst., but has no plur.; the sing. form being used for both numbers; dat. sg. and pl. अाप् के *to himself* and *to themselves.*

444. *Affinities.* W. H. and P. use the same refl. pron. अाप्; O. has अापे or अापणा, B. अापनि (with obl. अापना), M. अापण्; while in S. it is पाण; H. H. has in the dir. form अाप्, but in the obl. अाप् or अपने. The M., B. and O. forms अापणा and H. H. obl. अपने are properly the corresponding possess. pron. (*own*), see § 449; it is in fact a sort of pleonastic declension, see §§ 440. 432.

445. *Derivation.* The original of the refl. pron. is the Skr. subst. अात्मा (nom. sg. of अात्मन्) *soul* or *self.* In Pr. it becomes अप्पा or अत्ता (H. C. 2, 51. Vr. 3, 48) or अप्पो (H. C. 3, 56) or Ap. Pr. अप्पु (or st. f. अप्पउ H. C. 4, 422). In Gḍ. it is अाप्; in O. H. and Br., also, अापु. The Pr. form अत्ता, I believe, has left no trace in Gḍ. In Pr. the pron. also assumes a long form

अप्पाणो (H. C. 2, 51. 3, 56), Ap. Pr. अप्पाणु (H. C. 4, 396), which survives in the S. पाणा with the loss of the initial अ; O. H., also, has it as m. अपानु, f. अपानि (Kl. 124, 231). Cw. 46 mentions also a Pr. form अत्राणो, which, however, has left no trace in Gḍ., and is, probably, a false reading.

4. THE HONORIFIC PRONOUN.

446. The hon. pron. is substituted for the pron. of the 2nd pers. sg. तैँ and pl. तूँ, in respectful address. It is, in the wk. f. रावरु or राउरु c. g., in the st. f. रउरा or रौरा m., रउरी or रौरी f. It is declined regularly like a subst. (§ 379). But the refl. pron. आपु may also be used as a honorific; and in that case it always forms the comp. plur. आपु लोगु when applied to more than one person.

447. *Affinities and Derivation.* The use of राउरु as a hon. pron. seems to be confined to E. H.; but आपु and its cognate forms are used so in all Gḍs.; thus B. uses आपनि (S. Ch. 114. 115. note, with obl. f. आपना or आपनका), O. आपणा (Sn. 18), W. H. आपु, P. आपु (Ld. 20, 58), etc. — The original of राउरु I believe to be the Skr. noun राजकुल° (or राजकुल्य) *royal,* Pr. राअउल° or राउल° (Vr. 4, 1. H. C. 1, 267), see § 78.

5. PRONOMINAL ADJECTIVES.

448. By the term. *pron. adjectives.* I designate the possessive pron. (as *mine, thine, own*), the correl. adj. of quantity and quality, and the indefinite pron. *all, whosoever, some.*

a) Possessive pronouns.

449. Possess. pron. may be derived from the first and second pers. and from the refl. pron. Those of the first pers. pron. are: wk. form मोरु c. g. *mine,* or st. f. मोरा m., मोरी f.; and wk. f. हमारु c. g. *our,* or st. f. हमरा m., हमरी f. Those of the second pers. are: wk. f. तोरु c. g. *thine,* or st. f. तोरा m., तोरी f.; and wk. f. तोहारु c. g. *your,* or st. f. तोहरा m., तोहरी f. Those of the refl. pron. are: wk. f. आपनु c. g. *own,* or st. f.

अपना m., अपनी f. They are declined regularly like adj. of the corresponding form (see § 386). The possess. pron. of the third pers. is identical with the gen. of the near or far dem. pron.; viz., wk. f. एकर् or ओकर् c. g. *his* or *her*, or st. f. एकरा or ओकरा m., °री f.; and wk. f. ऐन्हकर् or ओन्हकर् c. g. *their*, or st. f. ऐन्हकरा or ओन्हकरा m., °री f.

Note: The following bye-forms also occur: हमारा *our*, तोहारा *your*, fem. °री. — The adj. निज् *own* is also frequently used as a refl. pron.

450. *Affinities.* The forms of these pron. do not differ materially in the Gds., exc. in M., S. and, partially, P. They are: of the first pers., B. मोर्, आमार्; O. मोर् or मोहोर्, अम्भर्; W. H. मेरौ, हमारौ (Br.) and मारो or म्हारो, माँरो or म्हाँरो (Mw.); G. मारो, अमारो; N. मेरो, हाम्रो; but P. मेरा, असाडा or साडा; M. माका, आम्-चा; S. मूँ-जो or मुहुँ-जो, असाँ-जो. Of the second pers., B. तोर्, तोमार्; O. तोर्, तुम्भर्; W. H. तेरो, तुम्हारौ or तिहारौ (Br.) and थारो (or थाऊ), थाँरो (Mw.); G. तारो, तमारो; N. तेरो, तिम्रो; but P. तेरा, तुसाडा or तुहाडा; M. तुका or तुम्-चा; S. तो-जो or तुहुँ-जो, तव्हाँ-जो or अव्हाँ-जो. It should be observed, that B. and O. use आमार्, अम्भर् and तोमार्, तुम्भर् as sing. *mine, thine,* and form new plur., B. आमा-देर् and even मो-देर् *our*, तोमा-देर्, तो-देर् *your*, O. अम्भमानङ्कर्, तुम्भमानंकर्. Similarly also N. हामीहेरु-को, तिमिहेरु-को or तिमीहेरु-को. B. forms also आमादिगेर् or आमार्-देर् or आमार्-दिगेर् and similarly तोमादिगेर्, etc. — Of the refl. pron.: E. H. आपन् or अपना, O. H. आपुन् or अपुना, Br. अपनो or आपनो, M. आपला, P. आपणा, N. आफना, G. आपणो, but also आपन्-नो, O. आपणा, but also आपणा-र् (Sn. 18), S. पाँ-जो or पाँहँ-जो. — The possess. pron. of the third pers. are made in all Gds. in the same way as in E. H.

451. *Derivation.* It will be observed that these adj. pron. are made by simply adding the gen. aff. (see the list in §§ 374. 377 also §§ 272—280) to their corresponding subst. pron. In some cases the aff. still remains a separate word; thus in S. मूँ-जो *mine*, M. आम्-चा *our*, P. तुसा-डा *your*, S. पाँ-जो *own*, Mw. आप-रो *own*, O. आपणा-र् *own*. In others it has coalesced with the base into one

word; as E. H. मोर् *mine*, हमार् *our*, etc. The latter contain two of the ancient gen. aff. केर् and कर्, on the derivation of which see § 377. The former appears in the ordinary Pr. possess. pron. of the plur. अम्हकेरो *our*, तुम्हकेरो *your* (H. C. 2, 147); in the sing., however, the ordinary Skr. forms seem to have been used, thus Pr. मईअ *mine* = Skr. मदीय (H. C. 2, 147). The aff. कर always elides क्, and coalesces with the base; thus in the Ap. Pr. महारउ (H. C. 4, 358) or महारा (H. C. 4, 434) *mine* (for *महकरउ or *महकरा, मह being the gen. of हउं *I*, cf. H. C. 3, 113), or contracted in the Nágara Ap. मेरो (Md. त्वदीये तेर । मदीये मेर ॥); so also in Br. मेरौ or in Mw. मारो or म्हारो. The E. H. मोर् is founded on a form *महुकरो (from gen. महु, H. C. 4, 379) or has been assimilated to तोर् *thine*. Again Ap. Pr. तुहारु (cf. H. C. 4, 434) *thine* stands for *तुहकरु (from gen. तुह, H. C. 3, 99) and is contracted in E. H. to तोर्. The Br. तेरौ and Mw. थारो presuppose an original form *तहकरा (from gen. तह, see § 430, 2) or have been assimilated to मेरौ, म्हारो. Again Ap. Pr. अम्हारा (H. C. 4, 434) *our* (= *अम्हकरा, from gen. or base अम्ह H. C. 3, 113. 114) becomes, by transposition of ह्, H. H. हमारा, W. H. हमारौ; or, by elision of ह्, B. आमार्, G. अमारो; or, by elision of अ, Mw. म्हांरो; or, by shortening आ, O. अम्भर्, E. H. हमरा. Similarly Ap. Pr. तुम्हारा for तुम्हकरा, whence H. H. तुम्हारा, E. H. तोहरा, etc. — The P. form असा-डा (or सा-डा with loss of अ, just as in Mw. म्हांरो), तुसा-डा or तुहा-डा are made with the old gen. aff. डा (= M. P. दा, see § 377, 3); as to the स् of असा, तुसा see § 430, 3. 4. It will be observed that in P. and M. the plur. only, but in S. both the plur. and sing. are made by a separate gen. aff. As regards the M. forms माका, तुका see § 430, 5. — As to आपन् or अपना, see §§ 60. 111. The Mw. आपरो contains either the gen. aff. रो, or the र् is a modification of the Pr. ल् of अप्पुल्लो (H. C. 2, 163). — The S. पाँहिं-जो appears to contain the old gen. *पानह (Ap. अप्पाणाहो), contracted to पान्ह = पाँहिं (see § 132, note).

b) Correl. pron. of quantity and quality.

452. The pron. of quant. are: एता or ऐतना *this much*,

तेता or तेतना *that much*, ज़ेता or ज़ेतना *as much*, केता or केतना *how much*. They are strong forms, and consequently are treated precisely as adj. of a like form; that is, they have a fem. in ई (§ 384, as एती or ऐतनी, etc.), and an obl. form in ए (§ 386, as gen. एते के or ऐतने कै *of so much*, etc.). Sometimes also the forms ऐतेक् or ऐतिक् or ऐतक् or इतेक् इतिक् or इतक् or अतेक्, etc.; उतेक् or उतिक्, केतेक् or कितेक् or कतेक् or केतिक् or कितिक् or कितक्, and so forth of ज़ेत°, तेत°, are met with (see Bs. in J. R. A. S. vol. III, 490 and Kl. 141), see § 26. I have also met with the forms ज़ैठा or ज़ोंया *as much*, कोंया *how much*.

453. *Affinities*. Nearly the same forms are used in all Gds.; thus B. एत, अत, तत, यत, कत or एतक्, अतक्, etc. (S. Ch. 84); एत, etc. are sounded *etŭ*, etc., but एतक् *etak*; hence gen. एत-र्, but एतके-र्. O. एते, तेते, येते, केते, W. H. (Br.) इत्तो or इतनो, उत्तो or उतनो, तित्तो or तितनौ, etc. or (Mw.) इतरो, उतरो, तितरो, etc., P. इतना, उतना, तितना, etc., G. एटलो, आटलो, तेटलो, etc. (Ed. 44), S. एतिरो or हेतिरो, ओतिरो or होतिरो, तेतिरो, etc. (Tr. 224), M. इतका or इतकाला, तितका or तितकाला, etc. (Man. 52; also किती or कितीक? as Tr. 223), N. यति, उति, तति, ज़ति, कति.

454. *Derivation*. The quant. pron. in Pr. are एत्तिओ, तेत्तिओ, ज़ेत्तिओ, केत्तिओ (H. C. 2, 157) or Ap. Pr. एत्तिउ (H. C. 4, 341), केत्तिउ (H. C. 4, 383), etc.; and in the strong form: Pr. एत्तिअओ, etc., Ap. एत्तिअउ, etc. The Mg. Pr. would have wk. f. एत्तिए or एत्तिइ or एत्तिअ (Vr. 11, 11) or st. f. एत्तिअए or एत्तिअके or एत्तिअकए (see § 202), etc. Now Mg. एत्तिअ contracts to O. एते, N. यति, etc.; Mg. एत्तिअए to E. H. एता; Mg. एत्तिअकं to E. H. ऐतेक् or ऐतिक् or ऐतक्, B. एतक्; Mg. एत्तिअकए to M. इतका. In Pr. the pleon. suff. लो may be added: एत्तिलो (for एत्तिअलो, see § 58, note) or Ap. Pr. एत्तुलो, etc., whence G. एटलो, etc. (with ट or ड for त or त्त, as in Pr. पट्टण for Skr. पत्तन H. C. 2, 29), S. एतिरो, etc., E. H. ऐतना (see §§ 58. 111. 214). In M., the pleon. suff. ला may be superadded to the pleon. suff. का, thus इतकाला, etc. (lit. Ap. *एत्तिअकअलउ). The Gd. forms उति, उतेक् or उतिक्, आतिरो, etc. are similarly derived from the Pr. एवत्तिआ (see Wb. Bh. 422), as explained in

§ 438, 1. 7. — The Pr. forms एत्तिओ, तेत्तिओ, etc. are in Skr. इयत्तिकः, तावत्तिकः, etc. — The E. H. forms कोथा, जोथा or जैठा are perhaps derived from केवत्तिअ, जवत्तिअ with an anomalous aspiration, as in M. कवढा, and cerebralisation, as in G. जटलो.

455. *Cognate quant. forms.* By the side of the forms एत्तुलो, तेत्तुलो, etc. The Ap. Pr. has the forms एवडु, तेवडु, जेवडु, केवडु (H. C. 4, 407. 408), made by adding the pleon. suff. डु to the quant. pron. एव, तेव, जेव, केव, in Ved. Skr. ईवत्, कीवत्. M. has them in the strong form एवढा or (with pleon. ला) एवढाला, तेवढा or तेवढाला, etc. (Man. 52); so also G. एवडो, आवडो, तेवडो, etc.; S. also has them, but in the shorter form एडो or हेडो, ओडो or होडो, तेडो, etc. (Tr. 224), made by adding the pleon. suff. डो to the short quant. pron. ए, ते, जे, के (see § 438, 1), so also P. wk. f. एडू or ऐडू, तेडू or तैडू, etc., and st. f. एडा, तेडा, etc.; also O. एडे, तेडे, जेडे, केडे (Bs. II, 336). In this form the quant. pron. usually expresses *size*, i. e., *so large, how large,* etc. In S. the diminutive suff. ड़ो may be added, as एडिड़ो or हेडिड़ो, ओडिड़ो or होडिड़ो, तेडिड़ो, etc. (Tr. 224), meaning *so small*, etc. — The W. H. has also तै, जै, कै which are derived from the Skr. quant. pron. ततिः, यतिः, कतिः, Pr. तई, जई (H. C. 1, 177), कई (H. C. 1, 180?), Ap. Pr. तइ, जइ, कइ (H. C. 4, 376).

456. The pron. of qual. are: अइसन् or ऐसन् *of this kind*, तइसन् or तैसन् *of that kind*, जइसन् or जैसन् *of which kind*, कइसन् or कैसन् *of what kind*. They are the same in the masc. and fem., and are declined regularly, like any adj. (see § 386). But they may also take the strong obl. forms; viz. in the sing., m. ऐसने, f. ऐसनी, etc., in the plur. m. ऐसनन्हू (or ऐसनेन्हू), f. ऐसनिन्हू, etc.

457. *Affinities.* There is much difference among the various Gḍs. as regards these pron. There are four main types, the characteristics of which are: 1) स, 2) ह, 3) व or म and 4) ड or र or ल. To the first or स-type belong: E. H. ऐसन्, तैसन् and in Bs. also ऐस् or अस् or यस्, तैस् or तस्, etc.; W. H. ऐसौ, वैसौ, तैसौ (Br.) or इस्यो, उस्यो, तिस्यो (Mw.), etc.; M. असा or असला or असलाला, तसा or तसला or तसलाला, etc. (Man. 52); and

N. यसो, उसो, तसो, etc. Of the second or ह-type are: P. एहा or इहा or अजिहा or अजेहा, तेहा or तिहा, etc., S. इहड़ो or हिअड़ो, तिहड़ो, etc. Of the third or व-type are: G. एवो, आवो, तेवो, etc., B. एमत् or एमन्, तेमत् or तेमन, etc., O. एमन्त्, तेमन्त्, etc. Of the fourth or ड-type are: Mw. ऐड़ो or ऐरो, वैड़ो or वैरो, तैड़ो or तैरो, etc., Gw. ऐनो or ऐनू or अनू, वनो or वनू, तनो or तनू, etc. (Kl. 141).

458. *Derivation.* The qual. pron. in the Ap. Pr. are either अइसो, तइसो, जइसो, कइसो (H. C. 4, 403) or एहु, तेहु, जेहु, केहु (H. C. 4, 402) or in the strong form, एहड or (contr.) एहो, etc., (K. I. 9, in Ls. 449). The former set produces the स-type, the latter the ह-type. M. असला, etc. and E. H. ऐसन्, etc. add the pleon. suff. ल or न, see §§ 111. 214. M. even reduplicates the suff. ल in असलाला, etc. The S. इहड़ो, etc. add the pleon. suff. ड. The P. अजिहा preserves the ह-type in a more complete form; for it stands for a Pr. form एदिहओ = Skr. ईदृशः (see § 438, 4). — The Skr. qual. pron. are ईदृशः, तादृशः, यादृशः, कीदृशः, which become in Pr. एरिसो, तारिसो, जारिसो, केरिसो (H. C. 1, 142) or एदिसो, तादिसो, etc. (see Ls. 115). As a rule र् (or द्) is elided (see § 124), whence the Ap. Pr. अइसो, etc. (see § 25, note); and स् (or श्) is changed to ह्, whence Ap. एहो, तेहो contracted for *अइहो, *तइहो, etc. (see Ls. 455). It may be observed, that the P. and S., which alone have the ह्-type, similarly change the स् (or श्) of Pr. वीसा 20, तीसा 30 (Skr. विंशति, त्रिंशत्) into ह्, P. वीह्, तीह्, S. वीह, ट्रीह. — The forms of the व- and ड-types were originally quant. pron. The Skr. इयत् (Ved. ईवत्), तावत्, etc. become in Pr. एव, तेव, etc. or एम, तेम, etc. (cf. Wb. Bh. 422. Ls. 458), whence G. एवो, तेवो, etc. and B. एमन्, तेमन्, etc. (with pleon. suff. अन, see §§ 209. 214); and the O. एमन्त्, B. एमत्, etc., perhaps, are based on the Skr. इयतकः, etc., Pr. *एवन्तओ, and probably contain the suff. Skr. वत्, मत्, Pr. वन्त, मन्त (see §§ 232. 236). — The Mw. ऐड़ो or ऐरो, etc. are identical with the S. quant. pron. एड़ो, P. एडा, etc.; and so also the Gw. एनो, where ड़् has been changed to न् (see §§ 106. 438, 2) — The forms, Br. वैसो and Gw. वनो

are founded on the Ap. Pr. forms *एवड्डगो (= Skr. *एवादृशः) and एवडो respectively.

c) Indefinite pronouns.

459. The indef. pron. *all, every one* is सब्र् or सभ or emph. सबै or सभै. It is the same in both genders, and is declined regularly like any other adj. of the weak form. But when plurality is to be emphasised, it has an obl. form सभन् or सब्रहन्; thus gen. सब्र् or सभ कै *of all* taken as *a whole,* but सभन् or सब्रहन् कै *of all* taken *severally.*

460. *Affinities.* The forms of this indef. pron. are nearly alike in all Gḍs. Thus B. सब्र्, O. सबु, W. H. सब्र् or सब्रर्, P. सभ, G. सभ or सर्व (Ed. 44, 1), S. सभु m., सभ f., or सभुको m., °की f., M. सर्व, N. सब्. S. has the emph. forms सभोई and मिड्योई or मिडोई. — E. H. also uses सकर् or सगर् and सारा *all, whole.*

461. *Derivation.* The original is the Skr. सर्वः, which becomes in Pr. सव्वो, in the Ap. Pr. सव्वु (H. C. 4, 366) or *सव्रु (cf. H. C. 4, 399, see § 135, note). The former becomes O. सबु, E. H., N., Br. सब्र्, the latter Br. सब्रर् (emph. सब्रै). The form सभ has an anomalous aspirate (see § 131), perhaps analogous to N. आफु *self* for आपु, अघि *before* for आगि, etc. — The S. सभुको adds the pleon. suff. को. — The G. and M. सर्व is a semitats. — The strange S. मिड्योई or मिडोई, I believe, to be merely a curtailment of the emph. सभोई or सब्रोई. The final ई is the emph. particle; the initial म् of the remainder मिडो stands for व (see § 134); the final इड्यो or इडो is a pleon. suff., the same as in S. पेहेयों or पेहेरो *first* (see §§ 118. 213), थोरिडो *very little* (Tr. 79), एडिडो *so small* (§ 455). In S., स् often changes to ह् (see Tr. XXX); hence सब्र° may have become हब्र° or हम°, next म्ह° (by suppressing अ), next म° (cf. Mw. म्हाँरो or मांरो *our* for Br. हमारो). — The E. H. सगर् is the Skr. सकल° (see § 102); and सारा is, perhaps, really the past part. of सारब् *to complete,* the causal of the R. सृ (= Skr. part. सारितः), or it may be the Skr. सार्वः.

462. The indef. pron. *whoever* is जेकेहू which is both masc. and fem.; and जेकिछु *whatever,* which is used with *things* only.

They are compound forms, made of जे and कहू or किछु, and are declined regularly like their component parts; thus gen. sing. जेकेहू कै *of whomsoever.*

463. *Affinities and Derivation.* This pron. is formed in the same way in all Gds. by compounding the relat. with the indef. pron. Thus S. जेको m., जेका f., जेको n. (Tr. 213); B. जेकिछु or जेकोन् n. (S. Ch. 127), etc. As to its derivation, see § 438.

464. The indef. pron. *some* is केतना or कई which is masc. and fem., and किछु or कुछ् or कछु which refers to *things* only. They are declined regularly like adj. Thus gen. केतने लोगन् कै *of some men,* कई घोरन् के *of some horses,* किछु बात् के *of some thing.* When केतना is used independantly, it forms the obl. केतनन्, and to कई the pleon. aff. एक् (§ 289) is added; thus gen. केतनन् कै or कईएक् के *of some.*

465. *Affinities and Derivation.* The impersonal indef. pron. is in B. किछु, O. किछि, Br. कछु, H. H. कुछ्, M. काँहीं, Mw. काँईं or कँईं, S. को, P. कुछ्. I know no satisfactory derivation for किछु, perhaps it is Pr. *किंचि हु = Skr. किंचित् खलु.

466. Here may be added the E. H. आन् or दूसर् or अउर् or पराई *another,* and एक् दूसर् *one another.*

Note: आन् is the Mg. अन्ने (cf. H. C. 3, 58), Skr. अन्यः; — अउर् is the Mg. अवले, Skr. अपरः; — पराई seems to be connected with the Skr. परकीयः; it also occurs in the Ap. Pr. पराई (H. C. 4, 350) or पराया (H. C. 4, 376). — On दूसर् see § 271.

6. PRONOMINAL ADVERBS.

467. The E. H. pron. adv. are the following: a) *of place,* इहँ or इहाँ or इहवाँ or एठें or एठाँ or ऐठेन् or एठान् or ऐठाईं *here;* ताँ or तहँ or तहाँ or तहवाँ or तेठाँ or तेठेन् *there;* जाँ or जहँ or जहाँ or जहवाँ or जेठेन् *where;* काँ or कहँ or कहाँ or कहवाँ or केठेन् *where?* The same in emph. form are: इहवैं or ऐहीठें or ऐहीठाँ *even here;* तहवैं or तेहीठें or तेहीठाँ *even there;* जहवैं or जेहीठें or जेहीठाँ *even where;* कहवैं or केहीठें or केहीठाँ *even where?*

b) *of direction,* ऐहर् or ऐहवर् *hither*; श्रोहर् or श्रोहवर् *thither*; तेहर् or तेहवर् *thither*; जेहर् or जेहवर् *wither*; केहर् or केहवर् *wither?*

c) *of time,* अब्र् *now,* तब्र् *then,* जब्र् *when,* कब्र् *when?* In emph. form: अब्रही॑ or अबहियै॑ *even now*; तब्रही॑ or तबहियै॑ *even then*; जब्रही॑ or जबहियै॑ *even when*; कब्रही॑ or कबहियै॑ *even when?*

d) *of manner or cause*: यूँ or एउँ or एश्रो॑ or अइसे or ऐसे *in this manner* or *for this cause*; त्यूँ or तेउँ or तेश्रो॑ or तइसे or तैसे *thus* or *therefore,* also *then*; ज्यूँ or जेउँ or जेश्रो॑ or जइसे or जैसे *in which manner* or *for which cause,* also *when*; क्यूँ or केउँ or केश्रो॑ or कइसे or कैसे *how* or *why* or काहे *why,* केह् कात् or काहे ब्रदे· *what fore,* काहे॑ *why not?*

468. · *Affinities.* Forms of the same origin are designated by the same letter. — a) *Adv. of place*; B. (a) एथा or हेथा, श्रोथा or होथा, तथा or सेथा, यथा (i. e. जथा), कोथा or (h) ए खाने, श्रो ख°, से ख°, ये ख°, कोन् ख°, or (d) हेदे *here,* or (*γ*) हेरो *here.* O. (*α*) एठा, सेठा, येठा, कोठा, or (h) ए-ठा-रे, येउँ ठारे, केउँ or को॑ ठारे, etc. Bs. (*a*) ऐठ्याँ or ऐठ्यन्, श्रोठ्याँ or श्रोठ्यन्, तेठ्याँ or तेठ्यन्, etc., or (b) उहँ or उहाँ or उहवाँ, इहँ, etc. (as in E. H.); (W. H.) Br. (a) इत् or इतै, उत् or उतै, तित् or तितै, जित् or जितै, कित् or कितै or कत्, or (b) यहाँ or याँ, वहाँ or वाँ, तहाँ or ताँ, जहाँ or जाँ, कहाँ or काँ; Mw. (*α*) श्रठे or श्रठी or ईँठै, उठे or उठी or ऊँठै, जठै or जठी (or जैँठै?), कठै or कठी or कैँठै or कोठै (also श्रडे, जडै, etc., Kl. 265); P. (a) इत्थे, उत्थे, तित्थे, जित्थे, कित्थे; S. (a) इति or हिति or इते or हिते or इत्थे, उति or हुति or उते or हुते or उत्थे, तिति or तति or तित्थि or तिते or तित्थे or तते, जिति or जित्थि or जति or जिते or जित्थे or जते (also जाते or जात्थे), किति or कित्थि or कति or किते or कित्थे (Tr. 392. 393); G. (b) हियाँ, श्राँही॑, त्याँ or तही॑ or ताँहाँ, ज्याँ or जही॑ or जाँहाँ, क्याँ or कही॑ or काँहाँ (Ed. 115. Bs. II, 336. 337); M. (a) येथे॑, तथे॑, जेथे॑ or जिथ, केथे॑ or (*u*) कोठे॑ (Man. 100); N. (b) ह्याँ or यहाँ or याँहाँ or आहाँ, वहाँ or वाँहाँ, तहाँ or ताँहाँ, जहाँ or जाँहाँ, कहाँ or काँहाँ.

b) *Adv. of direction*; B. (c) एमने, अनने, कमने; O. (*γ*) एने, केने; E. H. (c) ऐह-र् or ऐहव-र्, etc.; in some parts also (*γ*) एने or (c) एमह-र् or (*γ*) एनह-र्, etc. (cf. Kl. 266); W. H. इधर्, उधर्, तिधर्,

ज़िधर्, किधर्; P. unknown; S. (γ) एडे or हेडे or एडहँ or ऐडहैँ or एडहुँ or हेडहुँ, ओडे or होडे or ओडहँ etc., तेडे or तेडहँ or तेडहुँ, ज़ेडे etc., केडे etc.; G. (γ) आपणी-गम्, तेपणी-गम् (cf. Bs. 336. 337); M. (c) इकडे or हिकडे (Man. 127), तिकडे, ज़िकडे, किकडे; N. (b) याँहिँ, वाँहिँ, ताँहिँ, ज़ाँहिँ, काँहिँ. The adv. of place may also be used in all Gds.; generally with the dat. aff. added; e. g., E. H. तहाँ के, O. सेठा कु *thither*, etc.

c) *Adv. of time*; B. (c) एबे, तबे, यबे, कबे (S. Ch. 207) or (h) ए-खन्, त-खन्, य-खन्, क-खन्; O. (c) एबे, तेबे, येबे, केबे; E. H. (c) अब्, तब्, ज़ब्, कब्; W. H. (c) अबै or अबे, तबै or तौ (= तब्), ज़बै or ज़ौ, कबै, or (d) ज़दू or ज़दै or ज़दा or तदू, तदू or तदै, कदू or कदै or कदा or कदू, or (e) ज़रे, तरे; O. H. (c) ताम, ज़ाम; P. (d) तदू, ज़दू, कदू; S. (c) ताँ, ज़ाँ, or (γ) तडिहो॑, ज़डिहो॑, कडिहो॑; M. (c) एव्हाँ, तँव or तेव्हाँ, ज़ँव or ज़ेव्हाँ, कव्हाँ (Man. 100. 125), or (a) आताँ *then* (Man. 100); N. (c) अब्, तब्, ज़ब्, कब्, or (c) अइले or ऐल्हे, तइले or तैल्हे, ज़इले or ज़ैल्हे, कइले or कैल्हे, or (e) अरू, तरू.

d) *Adv. of manner*; B. (γ) हेन्, केन्, or (c) एमन् or एमत् or एमनि or एमने or एमते, अमनि, तेमन् or तेमत् etc., येमन् or यमत् etc., कमन् or कमत् or किमत् etc. (S. Ch. 216. 217. 218); O. (c) (एमन्त, सेमन्त, येमन्त?), केमन्त or कियाँ or काहिँ-क or काहा-र; O. H. एम or एमि, तेम or तिमि, ज़ेम or ज़िमि, केम or किमि; P. (c) एउँ, तउँ, ज़उँ, कीउँ; S. (c) ई॑अ or हो॑अ or ईंअ or हिंअ or इएँ, ऊंअ or हूंअ or ऊँअ or हुँअ or उएँ or हुएँ, तो॑अ or तिँअ or तिएँ, ज़ो॑अ or ज़िँअ or ज़िएँ, को॑अ or किँअ or किँए; G. एम्, आम्, तेम्, ज़ेम्, केम्; M. (f) असे॑, तसे॑, ज़से॑, कसे॑ (Man. 101. 126); N. (f) यसै, तसै, ज़सै, कसै, or यस्तै, तस्तै, ज़स्तै, कस्तै, or (h) यसो-गरि, तसो-गरि, etc., क्यान् *why*.

I may add here, that pron. adv. implying *from* or *up-to* are made in all Gds. by adding abl. or loc. aff. to the above mentioned pron. adv. Thus O. के-हु *whence*, E. H. कहाँ-से or केहरू-से *whence*, कब्-से *since when*, कब्-तक् or कहाँ-तक् *how long*, S. के-सी॑ or का-सी॑ or के-सींअ or के-ताई॑ *how long* (Tr. 394); N. काँहाँ-बाट् or काँहाँ-देखि *whence*, etc. But in P., M., Mw., S. and occasionally in the other Gds. they may be made by giving to the adv. of place or direction a different (abl.) inflection; thus P. (a) इत्यो॑

hence, उत्थो॑ *thence,* etc. (Ld. 70. 103); M. (a) एथून् (Man. 126) or इकडून् *hence,* तिकडून् *thence,* etc. (Man. 100, 2. d); Mw. (*a*) श्रठा सूँ *hence,* कठा सूँ *whence,* etc.; S. (a) इताँ or इताऊँ or इतहूँ or इताहूँ or (*γ*) एडाँ or एडाऊँ or एडहूँ or एडाहूँ *hence,* etc. (Tr. 394. 391); O. काहुँ *whence.*

469. *Derivation.* The case of the pron. adv. is similar to that of the pron. themselves (see § 438). Here also, there are six different types, marked *a* (or *α*), *b*, *c* (or *γ*), *d*, *e*, *f* respectively; and the adverbs are in reality obl. forms of what were originally qual. or quant. pron. adj. Thus: 1) the Ap. Pr. uses the obl. form (or loc. sg.) in हे of the quant. pron. एत्तिग्र, etc. as pron. adv. of place (as explained in § 438, 7), एत्तहे, तेत्तहे, etc. (H. C. 4, 436); in P. and S. they are contracted to इत्थे (for *इत्तहे), तित्थे or (eliding हू) W. H. इतै, तितै or S. इते, तिते or (shortening the final ए) इति, तिति, etc. The M. येथे॑, तेथे॑, etc. are similarly contracted from Ap. Pr. एत्तहिं, तेत्तहिं (with the obl. or loc. suff. हिं H. C. 4, 357, see also § 378, 3); and the B. एथा, तथा (also एथाय्, तथाय्, see S. Ch. 214. 222), etc. from the Pr. एत्ताहे (H. C. 3, 82. 2, 134), etc. There is also a series of by-forms of this *a*-type (marked *α*) which substitute ठ् for थ्; e. g., Mw. श्रठै, तठै (like S. इत्थे), E. H. ऐठे॑, तेठे॑ (like M. येथे॑), O. एठा, सेठा (like B. एथा), etc.; analogously to the change in the pron. adj., G. एटलो *so many* for E. H. ऐतना, S. एतिरो, etc. It appears, that some confusion originated at an early period between the terminations था and ठा, थे॑ and ठे॑, थे and ठे and the nouns (loc.) थान् or ठान्, थाइँ॑ or ठाइँ॑ *in a place.* The E. H. emph. forms एही-ठाइँ॑ or एही-ठे॑, etc., and the O. येउँ-ठारु, केउँ-ठारु can hardly be explained on any other theory. Indeed, the real phrases, E. H. ए थान् *in this place,* ते थान् *in that place,* etc., B. ए खान्, त खान् (with ख् for स्थ् as in Pr. खाणू for Skr. स्थाणुः, H. C. 2, 7) are not unfrequently used. — Again 2) Ap. Pr. uses the loc. sg. in हिं or इं of the quant. pron. एम्व as a pron. adv. of time and manner: एम्वहिं *now* (H. C. 4, 420) and एम्वइं or एम्वइ *thus* (H. C. 4, 421. 420). In B. and O. they are contracted to एवे or एत्रे, and in W. H. shortened to श्रबै *now,*

O. H. इनि *thus* (for *एमि), S. इएँ *thus* (for *इने' or *इवे"). Similarly the W. H. तत्रे, O. H. तिनि, S. तिएं, etc. postulate an Ap. Pr. तेम्त्रहिं or तेम्वइ, etc. The Ap. Pr. also uses the plain obl. form (without suff., H. C. 4, 345) एम्त्र *thus* (H. C. 4, 420), तेम or तेवँ or तिम or तिवँ *thus*, etc. (H. C. 4, 401. 397). They become in O. H. and G. एम, तेम, etc., in S. एउँ, तउँ (changing व *va* to उ) or इयँ, तियँ (eliding म् or व्) or ईअ, तीअ, etc. (with ई, perhaps, to compensate for the elision of the conj. म्व्), in W. H. contracted यौं, त्यौं, etc. or E. H. यूँ, त्यूँ (for *एउँ, *तेउँ) *thus*, etc.; but also as adv. of time M. तंव *then*, E. H. and H. H. अब् *now*, तब् *then*, N. अब्, तब्, etc. B. adds the pleon. suff. अन्, thus एमने or एमनि or एमन् *thus*, etc. (= Ap. Pr. *एम्वउइ); so also W. H. एवन् *thus*, etc. B. also uses these forms as adv. of place or direction, thus एमने *here* or *hither*. N. adds to them the pleon. suff. ल and uses them as adv. of time; thus एल्हे (= Ap. Pr. *एविल्लहे) or अइले (= Ap. *एविल्लइ), etc. The O. H. and E. H. use the shorter form ए, etc. for एव or एम्व, etc., and add the pleon. suff. न (= Ap. उ); thus एने *here* or *hither*, etc. (for B. एमने, Ap. Pr. *एम्वउइ); so also S., which preserves the original उ; thus एउे *hither*, etc. S. also uses the obl. or loc. suff. हँ and हुँ (H. C. 4, 340, see also § 378, 3) instead of ए; thus एउहँ or एउहुँ *hither*, etc. These last forms are purely Ap. Pr., exc. that in that language they would be loc. *plur*. Similarly the obl. suff. हँ is used in the M. एव्हाँ *now*, etc. (for *एव्हअँ with transposed ह् for *एवहँ). In the M. forms इकडे *hither*, etc. (shortened for *एकडे) both the pleon. suff. क and ड have been added. The simpler forms ठिको, तिको (without ड) occur in Mw. (see Kl. 132). This seems to me more probable, than the assumption of a compound इ + कडे *on this side* from the subst. कड *side* (as Man. 127). S. also uses the obl. or loc. suff. हिँ (H. C. 4, 347. 357), probaby confused with the emph. aff. ई or ही, in तडिहोँ *then*, etc. — The Ap. also uses the forms ताम, जाम (for तेम, जेम = Skr. तावत्, यावत्, H. C. 4, 406) as adv. of time. They are in O. H. (Chand) ताम, जाम and in S. ताँ, जाँ. — The E. H. एहर् *hither*, etc. (lit. एह-र्) contain the loc. suff. र (shortened for रे,

as in O. हत-रे *in the hand*) and the obl. form एेह् (on which see § 438, 1); similarly E. H. ऐह्वर् (transposed for एेवह्र्), ऐगह्र् or ऐम्ह्र्, ऐनह्र् or ऐन्ह्र् *hither*, etc. contain the obl. forms ऐवह् or ऐमह् or ऐनह् of the bases एव or एग or एन. — Again 3) the Ap. Pr. has the pron. adv. तहाँ, जहाँ, कहाँ (H. C. 4, 355). They are stated by H. C. to be abl. forms in the phrases तहाँ होंतश्रो श्रागदो *he came thence*, etc. That phrase means lit. *he came being there*, i. e., *from there*. In fact, होंतश्रो is the abl. aff. added to the adv. of place तहाँ, just as in O. H. तहाँ हुंतो, E. H. तहाँ से (see §§ 376, 1. 468, p. 312). Those Ap. Pr. forms are still used as adv. of place in E. H. and W. H. तहाँ *there*, etc. or, slightly modified, in G. and N. ताँहाँ, etc. They are, I think, derived by means of the obl. suff. हं (forming gen., abl. and loc. in Ap. Pr., see § 376, 4) from the qual. bases Ap. Pr. एह, तेह, etc., but shortening ए to इ or श्र; thus Ap. Pr. एहहं, E. H. इहाँ (for *इहश्रं), W. H. यहाँ; Ap. Pr. तेहहं or तहाँ, E. H. तहाँ (compare Ap. Pr. तुम्हहं होंतश्रो श्रागदो *he came from you*, H. C. 4, 373). Similarly the Ap. Pr. obl. or loc. suff. हिं is contained in the G. तहीं *there*, etc. (for Ap. *तेहहिं) and perhaps in the N. ताँहिँ *thither*, etc. — Again 4) the forms M. श्रसें, N. यसे, E. H. ऐसे *thus*, etc. are obl. forms of the Ap. Pr. qual. pron. श्रइसो, etc. (H. C. 4, 403, the Ap. instr. would be श्रइसें, loc. श्रइसइ or श्रइसे H. C. 4, 342. 334, but see § 367, 2. 4 on such obl. forms). — Again 5) the W. H. forms इधर् *hither*, etc. are perhaps contracted for इदह-र् and connected with the Pr. qual. pron. एद्दह, etc. (H. C. 2, 157); the medial श्र being suppressed and the loc. aff. र् (for रे) added. To this type belong the B. हेदे *here* (S. Ch. 215) for *एथे or *एदहे = Pr. loc. sg. एद्दहे, and the W. H. adv. of time जदै or जदा or जद्द or जद् *when*, तदै *then*, etc. for *जदहे (eliding ह्) or Pr. जेद्दहे, etc. Similarly W. H. has इदरं *hither*, etc. by the side of इधर्, etc. — Again 6) the Mw. तरै, जरै, N. तर्, जर् *then*, *when* are, perhaps, connected with the Skr. तर्हि, जर्हि; or they may be of the same origin as the P. जेडे *whither*, तेडे *thither* (see Nro. 2 changing ड् or ड़ to र्); and the B. हेरो *here* (S. Ch. 215) also belongs to this type. — Lastly, the B. ए खन् *now*, etc. are compounds of ए *this* and खन् *moment* (Skr. क्षण, Pr. खण H. C. 2, 20), and the N. यसो गरि *thus*, etc. of यसो *such* and गरि *having done* (conj. part. of the R. कर् *to do*, for करि); just like B. एखान् *here* (see Nro. 1).

FOURTH SECTION. INFLECTION OF VERBS.

FIRST CHAPTER. FORMS OF THE VERB.

470. There are two *kinds* of verbs, the transitive and the intransitive; two *degrees*, the simple and the causal, of which the causal is always transitive; two *voices*, the active and the passive, of which the intransitive verb possesses only the active, but the trans. has both; four *moods*, the indicative, conjunctive, imperative, infinitive, to which may be added as a fifth mood the participles.

1. KINDS.

471. A trans. verb is formed from an intrans. by lengthening the radical vowel, viz. अ to आ, इ to ई or ए, उ to ऊ or ओ; and *vice versa* an intrans. from a trans. by shortening the same vowel. Thus from the intr. कट्ब् *to be cut* comes the trans. काट्ब् *to cut*; similarly गड्ब् *to be buried*, गाड्ब् *to bury*; मर्ब् *to die*, मार्ब् *to kill*; लद्ब् *to be laden*, लाद्ब् *to load*; मिलब् *to be mixid*, मेलब् *to mix*; दिखब् *to be seen*, देखब् *to see*; दिसब् *to be seen*, दीसब् *to see*; लिपब् *to be smeared*, लीपब् *to smear*; खुलब् *to be opened*, खोलब् *to open*; छुटब् *to be loosed*, छाड्ब् *to loose*; गुथब् *to be plaited*, गूथब् *to plait*. Again from the trans. उखाड्ब् *to pluck up* comes the intr. उखड्ब् *to be plucked up*; likewise नहायब् *to bathe*, नहब् *to flow*, etc., see also § 351. Trans. and intr. verbs are conjugated alike, except in the 3. sg. 2nd pret. ind., where they have different forms (see § 504); e. g., tr. कइलेस् *he did*, but intr. गइल् *he went*.

472. *Affinities.* In all Gḍs. these sets of trans. and intr. verbs occur; but in M. and S. the trans. root may optionally end in इ; thus M. सुट् *to get loose,* but सोडि *to loose*; S. मर् *to die,* but मारि *to kill* (see Tr. 48); e. g., M. सुटतों *I get loose,* but सोडितों *I loose* or (in Konkaní, see Man. 68, uote) सोडतों; again सुटला *it got loose,* but सोडिला *he loosed*; again सुटत् *getting loose,* but सोडीत् *loosing,* etc.; again S. मरणु *to die,* but मारिणु (or in Láṛí) मारणु *to kill*; again मरु *die thou,* but मारि *kill thou*; again मरंदो *dying,* but मारिंदो *killing*; again S. सुनि or सुनु *hear thou,* सुनंदो or सुनींदो *hearing,* etc. But E. H. छुटतों, छुटलों, छुटत्; मरब्, मर्, मरत्; and so also छोड़तों, छोड़लों, छोड़त्; मारब्, मार्, मारत्; सुन्, सुनत्.

473. *Derivation.* As a rule, the E. H. intrans. and its respective trans. verb correspond to the simple verb and its resp. causal in Skr., where the causal is made by lengthening the radical vowel of the simple verb with *guṇa* or *vṛddhi.* In some cases, however, the E. H. trans. and intr. verbs correspond to the Skr. act. and pass. verbs; see § 351. The originally causal character of such Gḍ. trans. verbs is shown by their possessing the Skr. causal suff. इ in M. and S.

2. DEGREES.

474. The causal is formed from the simple verb by adding the suff. आव् to the root (see §§ 339. 349). To the causal root, thus formed, the infin. suff. अब् or इब् is reattached. If the simple root contains a long vowel it is shortened; viz. आ to अ, ई and ए to इ (or ऐ), ऊ and ओ to उ (or ओ). Thus S. V. करब् or करिब् *to do,* S. R. कर्, whence C. R. कराव्, inf. कराइब् (eliding व् by § 33) *to cause to do*; or S. V. मिलब् *to mix,* S. R. मिल्, whence C. R. मिलाव्, inf. मिलाइब् *to cause to mix*; similarly S. Vs. पीयब् *to drink,* लेब् *to take,* घूमब् *to turn,* बोलब् *to speak,* whence C. Vs. पियाइब् *to cause to drink,* लियाइब् or लेयाइब् *to cause to take,* घुमाइब् *to cause to turn,* बुलाइब् or बोलाइब् *to call,* etc.

Exception. खाब् or खाइब् *to eat,* R. खा, forms its causal खियाइब् *to cause to eat* for *खयाइब् (cf. § 55).

Note: Observe that, according to §§ 25. 33. 34, the suff. आव् may, in certain positions, undergo various changes, viz. व is elided before इ or ई; आ, when antepenultimate, is shortened to अ, and व् vocalised to उ, while अ + इ may change to ऐ and अ + उ to औ. Thus चलाई *he will cause to walk* (for *चलावी); चलइबों or चलैबों *I shall cause to walk* (for *चलाविबों); चलउतों or चलौतों *I cause to walk* (for *चलावतों); but चलावत् *he causes to walk* (not चलउत्).

475. *Affinities.* The causal is formed nearly in the same way in all Gḍs.; but B., O., H. H. and S. use the caus. suff. आ, as C. R. पढ़ा *teach* of S. R. पढ़् *read*; E. H. and G. have आव्, as पढ़ाव्; W. H. has आव् or आउ, as पढ़ाव् or पढ़ाउ; P. and N. have आउ, as पढ़ाउ; M. has अवि, as पढ़वि. The shortening of आव् to अव् (as in M.) also occurs occasionally in Hindí (poëtry), as पुरव् for पुराव् *fill* (see Kl. 207) and पुरव् for पुराव् *fill* (Kl. 228); so also the contraction of आव् to ओ, as रिसो for रिसाव् *be angry* (Kl. 228); and H. H. optionally contracts आव् to ओ in डुबो or डुबा *immerse* of R. डूब्, and भिगो or भिगा (for भिगाव्) *moisten* of R. भीग; also in P. भिगो (Ld. 67); M. accasionally changes अवि to इव in trans. verbs, as सोडिव or सोडवि *loose* (Man. 78, note. 110), and sometimes retains आव्, as बोलावि or बोलवि *call* (Man. 109). — Monosyllabic roots, ending in a vowel, form in most Gḍs. irregular caus.; thus the C. Rs. of R. खा *eat* are in B. खाओया (S. Ch. 129), O. खुआ (Sn. 37), E. H. खियाव्, W. H. खवाव् (or खवा Kl. 207. 217), P. खुआउ (Ld. 67), M. खाववि (Man. 77), G. खवाड् (Ed. 114), S. खाराइ (Tr. 257), H. H. खिला. Again of R. दे *give* they are in B. देओया (S. Ch. 129), O. दिया (Sn. 37), E. H. दियाव् (also Bs. दिवाव्), W. H. दवाव् or दिराव् (Kl. 214), M. देववि or देविच् (Man. 118), G. दवाड्, S. डिआर (Tr. 256), H. H. दिला. Exactly analogous are the C. Rs. of the Rs. जा *go* and ले *take*; but H. H. has लिवा *cause to take*, not *लिला. Similarly formed are the C. Rs. of पी *drink*, सी *sew*, जी *live*; thus S. पिआर्, जिआर् (Tr. 256), G. सीवाड् (Ed. 114), H. H. पिला, सिला, जिला; but E. H. regularly पियाव्, सियाव्, जिलाव्. Also of the Rs. चू *leak*, सो *sleep*, रो *weep*,

धो *wash*, ढो *carry*, बो *sow*; thus H. H. धुला, ढुला, बुला, धुला, ढुला, G. ववाड् (but H. H. बोआ), S. बुआर् (Tr. 256). Some roots which end in consonants, form irregular causals in the same manner; thus R. सिख् or सीख् *learn* has in H. H. सिखला, S. सेखार् (Tr. 257) *teach*, but regularly in E. H. and W. H. सिखाव्, N. सिखाउ, M. सिकवि (Man. 78), B. and O. (also optionally H. H.) सिखा; again R. देख् *see* in H. H. optionally दिखला or दिखा, P. दिखाल् or दिखलाउ (Ld. 67), S. डेखार् (Bs. I, 242) *show*, but regularly E. H. and W. H. दिखाव्, N. देखाउ, etc. Again R. कह् *speak* in H. H. optionally कहला or कहा (*be called*, in pass. sense, see § 354, 2), G. कहेवडा (Bs. I, 243), but regularly in E. H. कहाव्. Again R. बह् or बिह् *sit* (Skr. उपविश्) in H. H. बहला (in the sense of *amuse*, lit. *cause to sit*), P. बहाल् (Ld. 87), S. विहार् (Tr. 256). Again R. बैठ् *sit* (Skr. उपविष्ट) in H. H. optionally बिठला or बैठाल् or बैठा; and R. पैठ् *enter* (Skr. प्रविष्ट) in H. H. पैठाल् (Kl. 186). Again R. पाह् *see* in M. पाहवि (cf. Man. 75); R. लिह् *write* in M. लिहवि (Man. 77); R. जोह् *regard* in H. जुहार् *salute* (lit. *cause to be regarded*); R. ऊभ् *be excited* (cf. H. C. 2, 57) in H. उभार् *excite*; R. उथ् *rise* in S. उथार् (Tr. 257); R. सुम्ह् *sleep* in S. सुम्हार्; R. ड्रिज् *be afraid* in S. ड्रिजार्; R. विंहिज् *bathe* in S. विंहिजार् (Tr. 257); R. जम् *eat* in G. जमाड् (Ed. 50); R. घट् *diminish* in G. घटाड् (Bs. I, 243), and others.

476. *Derivation.* Caus. verbs are formed in Skr., as a rule, by adding the suff. अय (or इ) to the S. R., but exceptionally also by means of the suff. आपय (or आपि), as कम्पापयति *he causes to tremble* from S. R. कम्प्; चापयति *he causes to collect* from S. R. चि, etc. In Pr. these two suff. become ए and आवे resp. (Vr. 7, 26. 27); in later Pr. (by a change of class, see § 347) अ and आव, and finally in Gḍ. अ-*quiescent* and आव् (see § 349). Besides, while in Skr. the formation with आपय is exceptional, in Pr. the two modes of formation with ए and आवे are equally common; and finally in Gḍ. the formation with आव् (or आउ or आ) is the exclusive one, while the other is only preserved in the trans. verbs (see §§ 471—473). Thus Skr. S. R. मृ *die*, C. R. मारय (or

मारि) *kill*, Pr. मारे or मार, E. H. मार्; again Skr. कृ *do*, C. R. कारय (or *करापय), Pr. कारे or कार or करावे or कराव, E. H. कराव्; or in the 3. sg. pres. ind. Skr. मारयति, Pr. मारेइ or मारइ, E. H. मारे; Skr. कारयति, Pr. कारेइ or कारइ or करावेइ or करावइ, E. H. करावै. — The Gḍ. suff. आव् changes व् to उ in N. and P. (cf. § 34) and drops it in B., O., H. H. and S.; it also shortens आ to अ in M. The Pr. suff. आवे becomes in M. अवि or अव (cf. § 472); the former is trans. and forms causals, the latter is intr. and forms potent. pass. (see § 483). — The irregular monosyll. verbs appear to use the double causal (see §§ 477. 478) in the place of the ordinary one; compare e. g., M. खाववि *cause to eat* (for *खावावि), B. खाओया (for *खावा with आओ for आव्), W. H. खवाव्, O. खुआ (with उ for अव्) with M. निजववि or निजविव *cause to cause to sleep* (Man. 109); again S. खारा *cause to eat* (contr. for *खआरा) with S. फेरारा *cause to cause to turn* (Tr. 258). The G. खवाड् *cause to eat* is transposed for *खवडा; the original form is preserved in G. केहेवडा *cause to speek* from R. कह्, and the suff. अवडा or अवाड् belong to the double causal, as may be seen from the M., where roots in ह्, as a rule, take the double caus. suff. अववि (Man. 77); e. g., लिहववि *cause to write* from R. लिह्. Similarly the S. suff. आर or आरा (for *अवार or *अवराव्), H. H. आल् or आला are double causal suff. The origin of these strange forms °डा, °रा, °ला which are confined to the W. Gḍs. (espec. G. and S.) is very obscure. The identification of ल् with the प् of the Skr. caus. suff. अय (as Bs. I, 241) is hardly correct; for the H. ल् as well as the S. र् are modifications of the G. ड् (or ड़्)[1], but the Skr. प् could not possibly change into ड्. It should be observed, that there is a remarkable similarity between the Gḍ. caus. formation and that of Psh. The latter language forms causals by means of the suff. अव or एड्; the former corresponding to the M. अवि, G. आव्, S. आ; the latter to the G. आड, S. आर,

---

1) Not *vice versa*; ड् sometimes changes to ल्, see § 105; but never ल् to ड्.

H. H. आल्. See also the remarks in § 354, 2. A few instances of caus. in आउ occur in the Pr.; e. g., भमाडेइ or भमाडइ (besides the regular भामेइ or भमावेइ or भमावइ) of R. भ्रम् *roam* (H. C. 3, 151); also तमाडइ (H. C. 4, 30. see also H. C. 4, 161); धंसाडइ *he looses* (H. C. 4, 91).

477. From the caus. verb an other causal may be formed, precisely in the same way, by adding the suff. आव् to the caus. root, the long आ of which is shortened to अ. Thus S. V. पढ्ब् *to read*, S. R. पढ्, C. R. पढाव् *cause to read* (i. e. *teach*), whence other C. R. पढ्वाव्, inf. पढ्वाइब् *to cause to cause to read* (i. e. *to cause to teach*). This I shall designate the *double causal*. It may, obviously, be formed from the simple verb immediately, by adding to the S. R. the compound or reduplicated suff. अवाव्. These double causals are conjugated in every respect like the ordinary causals.

Note: The double caus. of a trans. verb implies that something is done by the intervention of a *third* person; as करब् means *to do*, कराइब् *to cause an other person to do it*, but करवाइब् *to order an other person to cause a third person to do it*. In the case of an intr. verb, the double caus. has the sense of an ordinary caus., and the ordinary caus. the sense of a trans.; as बनब् *to be made*, बनाइब् *to make*, बनवाइब् *to cause an other person to make it*.

478. *Affinities and Derivation*. The double caus. probably exists in all Gds., and it is formed in the same way by reduplicating the ordinary caus. suff. Thus E. H. has अवाव्, W. H. अवाव् or अवाउ, P. अवाउ, M. अवि or अविव (Man. 109), G. अवाव् (or अवडा), S. आरा (Tr. 257), H. H. (and probably B. and O.) अवा. Thus of R. पढ् *read*, double caus. R. in E. H. पढ्वाव्, W. H. पढ्वाव् or पढ्वाउ, P. पढ्वाउ, M. पढ्वविं or पढविव, G. पढ्वाव्, S. पढारा, H. H. पढ्वा *to cause to cause to read*. The principle of the formation of the double caus. seems to be analogous to that of the redundant forms of subst. (see § 203). As there the pleon. suff. क, so here the caus. suff. आपि is reduplicated (i. e. *अपापि or *अपापय).

3. VOICES.

479. The passive voice is formed by adding to the past part. of the act. verb the auxiliary जाइब्, which is the same as the intrans. verb जाइब् *to go* and is conjugated in the same manner. The past part. undergoes no change whatever may be the gender or number of the subj. Thus act. खाइब् *to eat,* pass. खायल् जाइब् *to be eaten*; or पढैला *he reads,* pass. पढल् जाला *it is read.* This I shall call the *compound passive.*

Exception. The pass. of the verbs जाइब् *to go* and होइब् *to become* is not formed with their ordinary past part. गयल् and भयल् but with the special past part. forms जायल् and होअल् (see § 304).

Note: Observe that the comp. pass. is very rarely used in E. H. or, indeed, in any of the Gds. It is commonly paraphrased by means of compound verbs; e. g., *to be beaten* is मार् खाइब्, lit. *to eat a beating,* not मारा जाइब्.

480. *Affinities.* All Gds. form this pass. by composition with the verb जाइब्, except S. and optionally Mw., N. and P. In the latter it is made by adding some suffix to the root; viz. S. इज, Mw. ईज (see Kl. 214), N. इय, P. ई. But P., Mw. and, probably, N. also use the comp. pass. The B. and O. do not use their past part. in इल् but that in आ in the formation of the pass. base, after the manner of the W. Gds. The E. H. and M. alone use the part. in अल (or इल) for the pass. (see § 303). Thus E. H. पढल् or पढिल् जाय् *it may be said,* M. पढिला (or पढला) जाए *it was wont to be read* (Man. 99); but B. पढा जाय् (S. Ch. 142), O. पढा जाये (Sn. 39), H. H. पढा जाए (or जावे), W. H. पढि जाए or पढ्यौ or पढ्यो जाए, P. पढिआ जावे (Ld. 60), G. पढ्यो जाय्; but S. पढिजे (Tr. 259. 331), Mw. पढीजै, N. पढिये, P. पढीए[1]). The latter kind of pass. is occasionally preserved in H. and M.; thus

---

1) Thus in the 3. sg. fut. pass. Mw. पढीजेलो *it will be read,* N. पढियेला, P. पढीएगा.

in the H. H. respectful imperatives: कीजे (cf. S. किजगु *to bé done* Tr. 260), दीजे, पीजे, लीजे, सीजे, मूझे, हूजे lit. *let it be done, given, drunk, taken, sewn, died, been* (cf. Kl. 164, d); also H. H. करिये, पढ़िये, etc. *let it be done, read,* etc., W. H. करीजे or करजे, पढ़ीजे or पढ़जे, etc. (Kl. 212, a); again in the M. पाहिजे *it is wanted* (Man. 90). In O. E. H., O. W. H., O. P. and O. M. they are also often met with; in O. M. sometimes even in an active sense (Man. 139). Thus in O. E. H. (Tulsí Dás) करिय or करिये or करीजे *let it be done* (Kl. 220. 422), करियत *being done* (part. pres., cf. Kl. 220, a), O. P. करीश्रतु or करीश्रत; in O. M. करिजे *let it be done,* करिजेतो *it is being done,* करिजेला *it has been done,* करिजेल *it will be done* (Man. 139). Similarly in S. छडिजे *it may be given up,* छडिजेयो *it is being given up* (Tr. 301. 333).

481. *Derivation.* The origin of the modern comp. pass. can be distinctly traced. In Skr. the pass. is made by the suff. य. In Pr. this becomes ईश्र or इज्ज (Vr. 7, 8. H. C. 3, 160), and in Gd. इय or ई or ईज or अज or इज. Thus Skr. पठ्यते *it is read,* Pr. पढीश्रइ or पढिज्जइ, whence P. पढीए or N. पढ़िये or Mw. पढ़ीजै or पढ़जै or S. पढिजे. Again Skr. क्रियते *it is done,* P. किज्जइ (H. C. 1, 97) or करिज्जइ (H. C. 4, 250) or करीश्रइ, whence H. H. कीजे, S. किजे, Mw. करीजै or करजे, O. M. करिजे, P. करीए, N. करिये. In O. H. and M. H. (Bs. or Br.) the pass. forms पढ़ि जाय्, करि जाय् are used. This shows that the old forms पढिजे, करिजे began to be looked upon as compounds of the past part. पढ़ि, करि (= Pr. पढ़िश्र, करिश्र, Skr. पठित, कृत, see § 302) and the verb जै (contracted for जाय्, Pr. जाइ, Skr. याति) *it goes.* This misunderstanding, being once established, naturally led to the further step of using the ordinary past part. (in अल and यो or आ) in conjunction with the verb जा *to go* to form the pass.; thus पढ़िजै became पढ़ि जाय्, पढ़ा or पढ़्यो or पढ़ल् जाय्. It is probable, however, that the old Skr. suff. य itself is a curtailment of the R. या (= Gd. जा) *to go*; so that the language has merely reverted to the point whence it started. It may also be observed, that there is a tendency in Pr. to shorten a final radical आ, which would facilitate the con-

fusion of the R. जा (= जा) with the suff. जा. Thus Pr. has जंति *they go* (H. C. 4, 388) for Skr. यान्ति; Pr. उत्थइ *he rises* (H. C. 4, 17) from R. उत्था (= *उत्याति); Pr. थवइ *he raises* (H. C. 4, 357) = Skr. स्थापयति; Pr. दइ *he gives* (Wb. Spt. 59) from R. दा; etc.

482. Besides the comp. pass., made with जाइब् (§ 479), E. H. possesses an other pass., the root of which is made by adding the suff. आ to the root of the act. verb. If the latter contains a long vowel, it is shortened, precisely as in the formation of the causal (see § 474). These pass. roots in आ are conjugated precisely as any other intrans. roots in आ. Thus act. R. पढ़् *read*, pass. R. पढ़ा *be read*, inf. पढ़ाइब् *to be read*, just like inf. जाइब् *to go* of the intr. R. जा *go*; again act. R. घूम् *turn*, pass. R. घुमा *be turned*, inf. घुमाइब् *to be turned*, etc. Though this pass. may be used in the same sense as the comp. pass., yet properly and generally it has a peculiar, viz. a potential, signification. Hence I shall call it the *potential passive*. Thus पढ़ाला means *it can be read*, while पढ़ल् जाला means *it is read*.

Exception. The R. खा *eat* makes its pot. pass. R. खिया *be eaten*.

Note: As the pot. pass. may have the sense of the ordinary pass., so the comp. pass. may have that of the pot. pass. Thus पढ़ल् जाला may mean *it can be read*, and पढ़ाला *it is read*.

483. *Affinities*. The pot. pass. also exists in M. and G. I think it probable that other Gḍs. also possess it, but it does not seem to have attracted the attention of grammarians. In M. it is formed by means of the suff. अव or अवव, and in G. by the suff. आ or अवा. The longer suff. अवव and अवा are used with monosyllabic roots and roots ending in ह्. Thus E. H. छोड़ाय् *it can be loosed*, G. छोडाय्, M. सोडवे; again E. H. कहाय् *it can be said*, G. केहेवाय्, M. कहवे. This pass. is called in the Man. 75 „the potential verb" and in Ed. 54 „the first potential mood", in Ed. 107 „the passive verb" and in Ed. 51, d apparently „the deponent". It is constructed in E. H. and G. with the instr. case of the agent, but in M. either with the act. (classically) or

the acc. (colloquially), see Man. 75, 128. note, where, however, the case is erroneously called the dative.

484. *Derivation.* A comparison of the suff. of the pot. pass. with those of the causals (§§ 474. 477) will at once show their identity. Thus the E. H. and G. pot. pass. suff. आ is identical with the B., O., H. H. and S. caus. suff. आ, and the G. pot. pass. suff. अवा with the H. H. double caus. suff. अवा; again the M. pass. pot. suff. अव and अवव are the same as the M. caus. suff. अवि and double caus. अववि, even as regards the shortening of the original आ of the suff. आव or अवाव. Again the pot. pass. suff. and the caus. suff. have precisely the same influence on the root; thus in E. H. the R. खा *cat* becomes खिया in the pass. and खियाव् in the caus. (see §§ 474, exc. 482, exc.). Lastly the longer pass. suff. अवा and अवव and the double caus. suff. अवाव् and अववि are used precisely in the same way; viz. they are added principally to monosyllabic roots. So far, then, there can be no question as to the identity of the forms of the pot. pass. and the two causals. But the sense and mode of construction of the pot. pass., also, prove that identity. In fact, it is merely a caus. with a peculiar reflexive sense. Thus E. H. caus. मैँ पोथी पढ़उलोँ might be translated: *I caused* (some one) *to read the book*, or briefly, *I caused the book to be read*. Similarly the E. H. पोथी पढायल् is either *the book caused* (some one) *to read itself* or *the book caused itself to be read* (by some one). It will be seen at once that, practically, this is the same as the pass. *the book was read.* It will also be noticed, that the agent who reads (*some one* or *by some one*) may be expressed either by the acc. or the act. case. Accordingly both cases may be used in M., मला (acc.) or माझ्यानेँ (act.) पोथी पढ़वली *by me the book was read*, lit. *the book caused me to read itself* or *the book caused itself to be read by me.* In E. H. and G. the instr. only is employed; thus E. H. मो से पोथी पढ़ायल् or G. मारा थीँ पोथी पढ़ायी. This pass. is now commonly used in a potential sense, *by me the book could be read*; but that sense is not really inherent in the peculiar form of the verb,

but only attached to it conventionally. For even the ordinary comp. pass. may take that meaning; thus मो से पोथी पढ़ल् गयल् *by me the book could be read.* On the other hand, the pot. pass. may have the ordinary pass. sense; see § 482, note.

4. MOODS.

485. *Infinitive.* The infinitive is made by adding the suff. अब् or इब्, obl. अबे or इबे or ऐ to the root of the verb, as explained in §§ 308—310. Thus पढ़ब् *to read* of R. पढ़; पढ़बे से or पढ़ै से *by reading*; again खाइब् or खाब् *to eat* of R. खा; खइबे or खैबे or खाबे or खाये से *by eating,* etc.

Note: For affinities and derivation, see §§ 313. 314.

486. *Adjective participles.* The pres. part. is made by adding the suff. अत् c. g., and the past part. by adding the suff. अल् or इल् c. g. to the root of the verb, as explained in §§ 298. 299. 302. 303. Thus पढ़त् c. g. *reading,* पढ़ल् c. g. *read*; खात् c. g. *eating,* खाइल् or खायल् c. g. *eaten,* etc. The fut. part. is identical with the infinitive, see §§ 310. 485.

Note: For exceptions see § 304; and for affinities and derivation see §§ 300. 301. 305—307.

487. *Prayogas.* The past and fut. part. are used with a pass. sense in the pass. and the infin. respectively, but with an act. sense in the past and fut. tenses act. Thus E. H. मै छोड़ल् जालो॑ *I am loosed,* मै छोड़ब् बाटो॑ *I am to be loosed,* but घोरा के (or घोरा) मै॑ छोड़लो॑ *I did loose the horse,* घोरा के मै॑ छोड़बो॑ *I shall loose the horse,* or पोथी के (or पोथी) मै॑ पढ़लो॑ *I did read the book,* प॰ के मै॑ पढ़बो॑ *I shall read the book.* The latter usage (with the part. in the act. voice and the subj. in the nom. case and the obj. in the acc.) is what I have called (§ 371) the *pass.-act. construction,* or the कर्तरि प्रयोग् of the native grammarians. It is peculiar to all E. Gḍs. Thus the above sentences are in B.: आमि (or मुइ) छोड़ा जाइ, but घोड़ा के (or घोड़ा) आमि छोड़िलाम् and घ॰ के आ॰ छोड़िब; पोथी के आमि पढ़िलाम and घ॰ के आ॰ पढ़िब; in O. मुहि छोड़ा जाइँ, but घोड़ा कु मुहि छोड़िलि (or अम्भे छोड़िलुँ) and घ॰ कु म॰ छोड़िबि

(or अ° छोड़िआ); पोथी कु मुद्दि पढ़िलि and प° कु म° पढ़िबि. On the other hand, the W. and S. Gḍs. always use these participles in the pass. sense, and, in consequence, where they are employed to express the pret. ind. and pres. conj. (see § 509, 3) tenses act., they take the subj. in the act. case and the obj. in the nom., and agree with the latter in number and gender. This usage I call the *pass. constr.*; and it is the कर्मनि प्रयोग् of the nat. gramm. Thus M. मी सोडिला जातों I *am loosed*, but घोडा मीं सडिला *I did loose the horse* (lit. *the horse was loosed by me*) or पोथी मीं वाचिली *I did read the book* (lit. *the book was read by me*), घोडा मीं सोडावा *I may loose the horse* (lit. *the horse may be loosed by me*), or प° मीं वाचावी *I may read the book* (lit. *the book may be read by me*). The same in W. H. हौं छोड़्यो जावों, but घोड़ा मैं ने छोड़्यो, पोथी मैं ने बाँचो; or in S. आँऊँ छडिबो आँहियाँ [1]), but घोड़ो मूँ छडिओ, पोथी मूँ पढ़ी; or in H. H. मैं छोड़ा जाता हूँ, but घोड़ा मैं ने छोड़ा, पोथी मैं ने पढ़ी. There are, however, a few verbs in M., which take the E. Gḍ. *pass.-act. constr.*; as पढ़णें *to read*, पावणें *to obtain*, पिणें *to drink*, बोलणें *to speak*, लेणें *to take* and others (see Man. 32); thus मी पोथी पढ़लों *I did read the book*, not मीं पोथी पढ़ली. — There is a third kind of constr. which is also confined to the W. and S. Gḍs. It is likewise a pass. constr., but differs from the ordinary one, by having the obj. in the acc. case, and the part. in the nom. sing. masc. or neut. It is, in fact, a sort of impersonal pass. constr., and is called by nat. gramm. the भावी प्रयोग्. Thus in this constr. the above sentences would be: M. घोड्या ला मीं सोडिलें lit. *as to the horse, it was loosed by me*, पोथी ला मीं वाचिलें lit. *as to the book, it was read by me*; W. H. (Br.) घोड़ा कौं मैं ने छोड़्यौ, पोथी कौं मैं ने बाँच्यौ; S. घोड़े खे मूँ छडिओ, पोथिअ खे मूँ पढ़िओ. — Lastly there is a fourth constr., which, I believe to be confined to the N. Gḍ. (N.). It is *pass.-act.*, but differs from

1) Here, the part. छडिबो is in the pass. voice, but in the pres., instead of the fut. tense, see § 313; but S. has also the old pass. आँऊँ छडिजाँ थो, see § 480.

that common in E. Gḍ. by having the subj. in the act. case, with which, however, the verb (i. e. past part.) agrees in number and gender. Thus the same sentences in N. are: घोडो मैं ले छोड्यो lit. *as to me, I loosed the horse,* पोथी मैं ले पढ्यो lit. *as to me, I read the book*; or with a fem. subj. घोडो स्त्री ले छोडी lit. *as to the woman, she loosed the horse.*

488. *Adverbial participle.* This part. is the same as the obl. of the strong form of the adj. part., and ends, according to the tense (see § 486), in अते, अले (or इले), अब्रे (or इब्रे). The pres. adv. part. commonly takes the emphatic particle ई, which coalesces with its termination to अतै. In order to distinguish more clearly the resp. time, some noun or case-affix is often added; thus समै *time* after अते, से *from* after अले, के *to* or बदे *for* after अब्रे. Thus पढते or पढतै or पढते समै *on reading* or *during the time of reading*; पढले or पढले से *after reading* or *on condition of reading*; पढब्रे or पढब्रे के or पढब्रे बदे *for reading* or *for the purpose of reading* or *on the point of reading.*

Note: The pres. adv. part., as a rule, expresses *coincidence*; the past, *precedence* or *condition*; the fut., *imminence* or *object.* The distinction between the pres. and past, however, is not very strictly observed. — The past adv. part. and the conj. part. may be interchanged, as पोथी पढि आयल् or पोथी पढले से आयल् *he came, having read* or *from reading the book.* — Instead of होते *on being* संते is sometimes used.

489. *Affinities.* These adv. part., as a rule, exist in all Gḍs., and are used in the same manner, as in E. H. Their termin. are: in B. इते, इले (S. Ch. 148. 184. 185), O. अंते, इले (Sn. 28), M. अताँ (or emph. अताँना, Man. 63. 64), H. H. अते (emph. अते ही), ए, अने (Kl. 311, 2. 3. 309, d. e), P. अदे, ए (Ld. 79, 146. 78. 139), S. अंदे, ए (Tr. 485. 487). See S. Ch., Kl. and Tr. for syntactical observations and examples. They apply equally to E. H.

490. *Conjunctive participle.* This part. is made by adding the suff. ऍ or इ to the root of the verb. It is, however, usually changed to य्, after a vowel, and dropped after a con-

sonant. In order to emphasise the part. the aff. के is commonly superadded. Thus पढ़े or पढ़ि or पढ़् or पढ़े के or पढ़ि के or पढ़् के *having read* from R. पढ़्; खाइ or खाय् or खाइ के or खाय् के *having eaten*; होय् के etc. *having been* from Rs. खा, हो. The simple conj. part. without के is especially used in the formation of compound verbs (see § 537), as कहे देब् or कह् देब् *to inform*, खाय् लेब् *to eat up*, श्राय् जाइब् *to come on*, etc.

491. *Affinities and Derivation.* The suff. of the conj. part. in Skr. are य or त्वा. The former is used for comp., the latter for simple roots; but in the Ved. Skr. य may be used for either kind. In Pr. (both in Sr. and Mg., H. C. 4, 271. 302) they become इश्र and ऊण respectively. Both are preserved in Gḍ.; so, however, that इश्र is common to the E., W. and N. Gḍ., while ऊण is confined to S. Gḍ. and, optionally, E. R. Thus B. has इया (S. Ch. 148), O. इ (Sn. 28), E. H. ए or इ or *quiescent*, W. H. इ or *quiescent* (Kl. 202, 378. 209, 394), P. इ or *quiescent* (Ld. 79), G. ई (Ed. 113), S. ई or ए (Tr. 280. 281), N. ई; but M. ऊन्, E. R. ऊने (Kl. 209, 394). Thus Skr. कृत्वा (or कार्य) *having done*, Pr. Sr. करिश्र (H. C. 4, 272), E. H. करे or करि or कर्, N. गरी, etc., or Pr. करिऊण, M. करून्, E. R. करूने. Or Skr. प्राप्य *having obtained*, Pr. पाविश्र, E. H. पाइ or पाय्, N. पाई, etc., or Pr. पाविऊण, M. पावून्, E. R. पावूने. I know no satisfactory explanation of the final ए of the E. R. form ऊने. Similar are the O. M. forms श्रोनि or श्रोनियाँ (also उनि or उनियाँ, see Man. 138. 139, as करोनियाँ or करोनि *having done*), and the Mg. Pr. form दाणि (Vr. 11, 16, as करिदाणि; also Mḍ. 12, 17)[1]. Analogous to the latter, there might have been a Pr. form *दूणि, from which rather than from the Mg. दाणि the modern M. and E. R. forms appear to be derived. Both Pr. forms दाणि and दूण (or ऊण) are modifications of the Ved. Skr. and Páli त्वानं, a by-form of the ordinary Skr. त्वा (see Wb. Bh. 435), which occurs in the

---

1) Mḍ's sútra seems to be, क्त्वो दाणिश्च स्यात्। पुच्छिदाणि। पक्षे पुच्छिश्र॥ i. e., *having asked*; but both H. C. 4, 272. 302 and T. V. 3, 2. 10. 27 omit दाणि and replace it by दूण.

Pr. of the Bh. as त्ताणं, just as Skr. त्वा becomes in Pr. त्ता (Wb. Bh. 435) or दुअ (H. C. 4, 272). If त्वानम् be (with Ls. 289) the acc. sg. of a base त्वान (or त्वन्), the Pr. दाणि or Gḍ. ओनि, ऊने might be a loc. sg. for *त्ताणे or *तूणे (cf. H. C. 3, 56); and the Gḍ. ओनियाँ might be an emphatic form of the same[1]). — Of the Pr. form दुअ (as in कदुअ *having done*, गदुअ *having gone*, H. C. 4, 271) no traces, I believe, have survived in Gḍ. — The aff. के is itself a contraction of the E. H. conj. part. कय् *having done* of R. कर्. It also occurs in P. के (Ld. 24, 79), in Br. के or कै or कर् or करि (Kl. 202); in E. R. it is curtailed to र् (for कर्); e. g., मार-र् *having beaten* for मार्-कर्; खा-र् *having eaten* for खा-कर् (Kl. 209, 394). Mw. has the aff. ने for के; e. g., कर्-ने *having done* = Br. कर्-के (Kl. 209, 394). The two aff. are related to each other precisely as the G. gen. aff. नो is to the W. H. को or कौ (see § 377). In H. H. the aff. is reduplicated, कर्-के; e. g., मार्-कर्-के *having beaten*; similarly E. R. reduplicates कने (Kl. 209, 394) and N. कन् (shortened for के-ने); e. g., N. गरीकन् *having done*, खाइ-कन् *having eaten*, बसी-कन् *having sat*, etc.

492. *Nouns of agency.* This is made by adding the suff. अनिहार् e. g. to the root of the verb, as explained in §§ 315. 316. 318. Thus पढनिहार् *a reader* from R. पढ्; खानिहार् *eater* from R. खा, etc. According to circumstances, these nouns may have the sense of a pres. part. or a fut. part.; thus पढनिहार् may mean *one who is reading* or *one who is going to read.*

Note 1: The masc. strong form in अनिहारा is also used occasionally; likewise the W. H. suff. अनेवारा (for अनेवाला), fem. °री; but the fem. strong form in अनिहारी only forms nouns, expressing an act; thus पढनेहारा *a (male) reader*, but पढनेहारी the act. of *reading* (not *female reader*), see § 319.

Note 2: For affinities and derivation see §§ 320. 321.

---

1) Ls. 400 supposes दाणि to have lost a final anuswára (for *दाणिं) and to have changed the अ of *दाणं = त्ताणं to इ.

SECOND CHAPTER. TENSES.

493. There are three tenses, the present, past and future, each of which may be either simple or periphrastic (see § 510). The indicative mood possesses all three; the conjunctive has only two, the pres. and past; the imperative has only one, the present. Every tense possesses two numbers, sing. and plur.; and three persons, first, second and third; and also, though with the exception of the pres. conj. and imper., two genders, masc. and fem.

494. Some of the tenses are formed from the root of the verb, others from the participles. From the root are formed the three pres. tenses of the ind., conj. and imp.; from the part., the past and future tenses, viz. the first and second preterite ind., the past conj. and the fut. ind. Tenses made from the root will be called *radical*; those made from the part., *participial*. A third class, made by adding an auxiliary verb to a participle, I shall call *periphrastic*.

1. RADICAL TENSES.

495. ***Present conjunctive and imperative.*** These are identical in every respect, and are made by adding to the root the subjoined suff., according to the number and person (but not gender) of the subj. In the 2. sing. the suff. may optionally be omitted. After roots in आ the forms of the suff. are slightly modified by coalescence with that letter.

	Sing.	Plur.	after Rs. in आ	Sing.	Plur.
1. pers.	ओँ	ईँ		आवँ्	आईँ
2. pers.	उ or quiesc. अ	अह् or अ		ओ or आ	आह् or आ
3. pers.	ऐ	ऐँ		आय्	आँयँ्

Note 1: The pres. conj. is occasionally used in the sense of the fut. indic.

Note 2: The 2. pl. ends throughout the conjugation either in अह् *ah* or अ *a*. The latter (अ), being the resultant of the dropping of the final ह् of गह्, is always *sounded* (see § 24, exc.). It is important to observe this circumstance, as, in the future tense, it forms the only difference between the 1. pl. and the 2. pl., and affects the vowel combination. Thus पढ़ब् *parhab we shall read*, but पढ़ब *parhaba you will read*; खाब् *kháb we shall eat*, but खाब *khába you will eat*, or खाइब् *kháïb we shall eat*, but खइब *khaïba* or खैब *khaiba you will eat* (see § 508). So पढ़ *parha read you*, but पढ़् *parh read thou*. Again पढ़ैल *parhaila you read*, not पढ़ैल् *parhail* (see § 500). — In Kellogg's Hindi Grammar (p. 201. 233—241) the forms of the 2. pl. are given, by mistake, as forms of the 2. sg. Colloquially the plur. is commonly used in the place of the sing. This practice, probably, has been the cause of the misapprehension.

496. *Affinities.* The E. H., I believe, is the only Gḍ. language, in which the pres. of the conj. and of the imper. are completely identical. In W. Gḍ. the two tenses are also alike, with the exception of the 2. sg. But in S. Gḍ., N. Gḍ. and E. Gḍ. (exc. E. H.) the differences are more numerous; viz. 2. and 3. sg. differ in B., 2. and 3. sg. and pl. in N., and 1., 2. and 3. sg. and 2. and 3. pl. in M. — The tense, which is *now* the pres. conj. in E. H., exists in all Gḍs., but in some of them it has slightly modified its original meaning. It was originally the same as the Skr. and Pr. pres. indic.; and this sense it has preserved in M., though it is now used only in a special case, viz. as a *historical present* or what practically amounts to a *habitual past* (see Man. 59, 3, e. g., तो बहेर् निघे *he sallies forth* = *he used to sally forth*); but in O. M. it is employed for the ordinary pres. indic. (Man. 138). Again in B., O. and G. it is both a pres. indic. and a pres. conj. (see S. Ch. 136. 142. Sn. 27. 32. Ed. 54). On the other hand, in E. H., W. H., P., S. and N. it is only a pres. conj. (see Tr. 284—287. Ld. 23, 74. 53)[1]). As a natural

1) Even in these languages it may still be heard occasionally as a pres. ind., e. g., E. H. गुरु तोह् के बोलावै *the teacher calls you*; see also Tr. 287, note and Kl. 206. 212, 402. a; and in O. H. it is still the ordinary

consequence the W. and N. Gḍ. and E. H. form a new pres. indic. by adding to the old pres. some auxiliary verb (see §§ 500. 501). On the other hand, M. employs, for the purpose of expressing the pres. conj., the part. fut. (called *supine* in Man. 62, see §§ 313. 509, 3), ending in the sing. in आवा m., आवी f., आवेँ n., in the pl. आवे m., आव्या f., आवीँ n. G. may do the same; there the termin. are अवो m., अवी f., अवुँ n. (called *second pres. of the second pot.* in Ed. 54, see § 509, 3)[1]). — In all W. Gḍs. the pres. conj. (i. e., the old pres. ind.) may be used as a future. Such was the case in O. M. also (Man. 59, 3. note); but it is not so in modern M. In O. M. it was also used in the sense of the *habitual past* (Man. 59, 3. note), as it is in modern M. (see above); but of this usage there are traces even in Pr.; see Wb. Spt. 63; e. g., तइआ ण रमसि *thou wast not wont to enjoy* (Spt. 91), or तइआ ण णेसि *thou wast not wont to direct* (Spt. A, 38). — The following table shows the various Gḍ. termin. of this tense:

Present conjunctive or old pres. indic.

	M.	N.	B.	O.	E. H.	H. H.	Br.	Mw.	P.	G.	S.
1.	एँ[3]	उ, ए	इ	इ, अइँ	ओँ	ऊँ	औँ	ऊँ, उँ	आँ	उँ	आँ
2.	अस, एस्[1]	इस्, ए[1]	इस्[1]	उ[1]	उ, अ q.	ए[1]	ऐ[1]	ए[1]	एँ[1]	ए[1]	एँ, इँ[2]
3.	ए[4]	ए[10]	ए[7]	अइ, ए[7]	ऐ	ए	ऐ	ए	ए	ए	ए
4.	ऊँ	औँ, ए	इ	उँ, इ	इँ	एँ	ऐँ	आँ	ये	ये	ऊँ
5.	आँ[5]	औ, ए	अ	अ	अहु, अ	ओ	औ	ओ	ओ	ओ	ओ
6.	अत्[6]	अन्, ए[8]	एन्[8]	अंति[9]	एँ	एँ	ऐँ	ऐ	अपा	ए	अनि

In the pres. imper.: 1) अ quiesc.; 2) इ or उ; 3) ऊँ; 4) ओ or ऊ; 5) आ; 6) ओंत् or ऊत्; 7) उ (or B. उक); 8) उन्; 9) अंतु or उंत; 10) ओस्.

pres. ind. (Kl. 221, 224). — In the various Gḍ. grammars this tense is called by a great variety of names; thus *second potential* or *optative* by Ed. 54, *potential* by Tr. 284, *indefinite future* of the pot. mood by Ld. 53, *contingent future* by Kl. 158. 163, *prospective conditional* by Eth. 73; but *pres. subjunctive* by S. Ch. 136. Sn. 32.

1) With trans. verbs the karmaṇi prayoga must be used (see § 487), because this part. is properly pass.; but with intrans. verbs the kartari prayoga; in the latter case, M. adds in the 2. pers. the suff. स् sg. and त् pl., but the first and third pers. are alike. Thus M. तूँ सुटावास् *thou*

497. *Derivation.* 1) The Gḍ. pres. conj. and pres. imp. are the same as the Skr. pres. indic. and pres. imp. respectively. But in the same measure as the Skr. pres. indic. assumed a conj. sense in Gḍ., it also became capable of doing duty for the pres. imp. and was, consequently, confounded with it; but so, that, as a rule, the pres. conj. superseded the pres. imper., while in the 2. pers. the imp. took the place of the conj. It will be observed that M., in which the pres. indic. has fully preserved its original indic. sense, possesses both tenses (pres. ind. and pres. imp.) in a complete form, and in B. and O., where its indic. sense is predominant, the greater part of the two senses is preserved; while in W. Gḍ. and E. H., where its sense is almost exclusively conj., the amalgamation of the two tenses is more or less complete. This amalgamation had already begun in Pr. [1]). Thus in the Ap. Pr. the suff. of the 1. sg. उं, 2. sg. हि and, possibly, 2. pl. हु of the imper. are optionally, though commonly, substituted for the suff. मि of the 1. sg., सि 2. sg. and ह 2. pl. pres. indic. (H. C. 4, 383. 384. 385; e. g., Ap. कड्डउं or कड्डमि *I cut* = Skr. कर्तयामि, E. H. काटों or कटों; Ap. रुअहि or रुअसि *thou weapest* = ved. Skr. रुदसि; Ap. इच्छहु or इच्छह *you wish* = Skr. इच्छथ). On the other hand, even in the Mh. Pr. the suff. मो and ह of the 1st and 2nd pl. pres. ind. are also used for the imper. and conj. (H. C. 3, 176; e. g., M. हसह *you laugh* or *you may laugh* = Skr. हसथ or हसत or हसेत; Mh. हसामो *we laugh* or *we may laugh* = Skr. हसामः or हसाम or हसेम). — 2) *Pres. conj.* (= old pres. ind.): a) The termin. of the 1. sg. is in Skr. आमि, Pr. आमि or अमि (H. C. 3, 141. 154. Vr. 7, 3. 30), Ap. Pr. अमि or अउं (H. C. 4, 385).

---

mayest get loose, but त्वाँ घोडा सोडावा *thou mayest loose the horse* (lit. *by thee the horse may be loosed*); again मी or तो सुटावा *I or he may get loose.*

1) Analogous is the occasional use in Pr. of the pres. ind. as a (pret.) conj., of which Wb. Spt. 62. 82 gives a few examples; thus Spt. 326 जइ ण होंति *if they were not* (= Skr. यदि न भवंति). The Gḍs. do not use the old pres. ind. in this manner, but express the pret. conj. by means of the part. pres. (see §§ 506. 507); thus E. H. जौ न होतैं.

The former is preserved in the O. अइँ, M. एँ, B. इ; e. g., Skr. पठामि *I read,* Pr. पढामि or पढमि, O. पढइँ, M. पढेँ, B. and O. पढि. The latter becomes in O. H. अउँ, Br. औँ, E. H. ओँ, H. H. ऊँ, Mw. ऊँ or उँ, G. उँ, N. उ; thus Ap. Pr. पढउं *I read,* O. H. पढउँ, Br. पढौँ, E. H. पढोँ, H. H. and Mw. पढूँ, G. पढुँ, N. पढु. The S. and P. आँ, as पढाँ, must be a modification either of अउँ = ओँ or अइँ = एँ. The Psh. and Pers. have अम्. — b) The term. of the 2. sg. is in Skr. असि, Pr. असि (H. C. 3, 140. Vr. 7, 2), Ap. Pr. असि or अहि (H. C. 4, 384). The former is preserved in the O. H. असि or (by transfer of इ into the preceding syllable, see § 148, note) ऐस, M. अस् or एस्, B. and N. (by shortening of ए) इस्; thus Skr. पठसि *thou readest,* Pr. पढसि, O. H. पढसि or पढैस्, M. पढस् or पढेस्, B. and N. पढिस्. The latter becomes in O. H. अहि (still used in Br., see Kl. 202, 380) or अइ, W. H. ऐ, H. H. and G. ए; also P. एँ and S. एँ or ईँ, but with an anomalous anunásika; thus Ap. Pr. पढहि, O. H. पढहि or पढइ, W. H. पढै, H. H. and G. पढे, P. पढेँ, S. पढेँ or पढोँ. The Psh. has ए and Pers. ई. As to the E. H. and O. उ, O. H. उ or सु (Kl. 218, e. f), see Nro. 3, h. — c) The term. of the 3. sg. is in Skr. अति, Pr. अइ (H. C. 3, 139. Vr. 7, 1), which is preserved in the O. H. अइ (also अहि with anomalous ह्), O. अइ, but generally contracted to ऐ in E. H. and W. H. or ए in the rest; thus Skr. पठति *he reads,* Pr. पढइ, O. H. पढइ, O. पढइ or पढे, E. H. and W. H. पढै, B., M., N., H. H., G., P., S. पढे. The Psh. has ई and the Pers. अद्. — d) The term. of the 1. pl. is in Skr. आमः, in Pr. आमो or आमु or आम or अमो or अमु or अम (H. C. 3, 144. 155. Vr. 7, 4. 31) or इमो or इमु or इम (H. C. 3, 155. Vr. 7, 31), Ap. Pr. इमु etc. or अहुं (H. C. 4, 386). The form अहुं, probably, contains an euph. ह् for अउं for Pr. अमु (see § 127, note), perhaps to distinguish it from the 1. sg. अउं (for Pr. 1. sg. imper. अमु, see Nro. 3, g) and to assimilate it to the 1. pl. अहिं [1]). It becomes in N. औँ, M. and

1) Compare also the O. H. 3. sg. अहि beside अइ (Nro. 2, c). — Cw. XXIX and Ls. 335 give optional 1. pl. termin. अम्हो, अम्ह (e. g., हसम्हो, हसम्ह *we laugh*). These, if correct, would account for the ह् in the Ap. अहुं; but I know no authority for them; H. C. 3, 147. Vr. 7, 7 give only म्हो,

S. उँ, O. उँ or उ; thus Skr. पठामः *we read,* Pr. पढामो or पढामु or पढमु, Ap. Pr. पढहुं, N. पढौं, M. and S. पढूं, O. पढुँ or पढु. The Pr. form इमु or इम contracts in E. H. to ईं (see § 127), B. and O. (shortened) इ; thus Pr. पढिमु or पढिम, E. H. पढीं. The intermediate form would be *इअँ, which may either contract to ईं (like M. पाणीं *water,* for Pr. पाणिअं, § 83, exc.) or drop final अ (like E. H. करि *having done,* for Pr. करिअ, § 491); hence E. H. पढीं, O. पढि. But apparently at an early period, it also became transposed to अइँ and modified to अहिँ, in assimilation, probably, to the 3. pl. अहिं. Both अइँ and अहिँ occur in O. H. and are contracted to ऐं in Br. and एँ in H. H.; thus O. H. पढइँ or पढहिँ, Br. पढैं, H. H. पढें. In the strange G. and S. form ये, there seems to be a reminiscence of the original intermediate form *इअँ; thus G. and S. पढ्ये, perhaps for *पढिअँ or *पढिअइँ. The Mw. आँ is a modification of the N. औं or the Br. ऐं, similarly as in the case of the P. and S. 1. sg. आँ (see Nro. 3, a). The Psh. has उ, the Pers. ईम्. — e) The term. of the 2. pl. is in Skr. अथ, in Pr. अह (H. C. 3, 143. Vr. 7, 4) or अहं (with euph. anusvára, see H. C. 1, 27. Ls. 336), in Ap. Pr. अह or अहु (H. C. 4, 384). The former is only preserved in E. H. अह or अ, B. and O. अ, and M. आँ (for अहं); thus Skr. पठथ *you read,* Pr. पढह or पढहं, E. H. पढह, B. and O. पढ, M. पढाँ. The latter, I am inclined to explain as identical with the Skr. अथः of the 2. dual; it would regularly become in Pr. *अहो or अहु [1]). In O. H. it becomes अहु or अउ, in Br. and N. औ, in the rest ओ; thus Ap. Pr. पढहु, O. H. पढहु or पढउ, Br. and N. पढौ, E. H., H. H., Mw., P., G., S. पढो. The Psh. has अई, the Pers. ईद्; the latter is represented by the Pr. इत्थ (H. C. 3, 143 as हसित्थ *you laugh*) which, however, has left no trace in Gḍ. — f) The term. of the 3. pl. is in Skr. अन्ति, in Pr. अंति (H. C. 3, 142. Vr. 7, 4), in Ap. Pr. अंति or अहिं (H. C.

म्ह for the Skr. स्मः *we are,* where म्ह is perfectly regular for स्म् by H. C. 2, 74. Vr. 3, 32.

1) Just as 1. pl. Pr. आमो or आमु for Skr. आमः; see also Nro. 3, 1; Ls. 468 identifies it with the Skr. ध्वम् of the átman. 2. pl. imper., but this would have changed to Pr. ह्वं, as felt by himself, p. 336.

4, 382). The former is only preserved in O. अंति and M. अत् (see § 146, note); thus Skr. पठन्ति *they read*, Pr. पढंति, O. पढंति, M. पढत्. The latter becomes in O. H. अहिँ or अइँ, E. H. and Br. ऐँ, H. H. एँ, also Mw. ऐ and G. ए with loss of anunásika; thus Ap. Pr. पढहिं, O. H. पढहिँ or पढइँ, E. H. and Br. पढैँ, H. H. पढेँ, Mw. पढै, G. पढे. The origin of the Ap. form अहिं is disclosed by the O. H. termin. अन्हि or एन्हि (for *इअन्हि) of the pret. tense (see § 503). It appears that अंति was changed to अंदि, then to अन्नि and finally to अन्हि (see § 161). The O. H. अन्हि is preserved in the S. अनि, B. एन् (with transfer of इ into the preceding syllable, § 148, note), P. अण्, N. अन्. Thus S. पढनि, B. पढेन्, P. पढण्, N. पढन्. The Psh. has ई and the Pers. अन्द् (softened for अन्त्). — 3) *Pres. imper.*: g) The term. of the 1. sg. is in Skr. आनि, which, however, is a peculiar suff. and does not exist in Pr. The latter has the regular suff. आमु or अमु (H. C. 3, 173. Vr. 7, 18); in the Ap. Pr. it becomes अउं (see § 127)[1]) and becomes a suff. of the pres. conj. (or indic., H. C. 4, 385, see § 497, 2, a). In M. it contracts to ऊं, but remains a suff. of the 1. sg. imper.; while in E. H. it contracts to ओँ and passes to the pres. conj., and so in all W. Gḍs. and in N. Gḍ. On the other hand, B. and O. have lost it, and use the suff. इ of the pres. conj. instead. Thus (Skr. पठानि), Pr. पढामु or पढमु *let me read*, Ap. Pr. पढउं *I may read* or *I read*, M. पढूं *let me read*, E. H. पढोँ *I may read* or *I read*, etc. — h) The term. of the 2. sg. is in Skr. अहि (suff. हि) or अ; Pr. has preserved the regular termin. असु besides अहि and अ (H. C. 3, 173. 174. 175. Vr. 7, 18), and the Ap. Pr. has, besides अहि, also ए or इ or उ (H. C. 4, 387. K. I. 62 in Ls. 453). The term. असु must have existed in the Ap. Pr.; for it is still found occasionally in O. H., both in the sense of the imper. and the pres. conj. (see Kl. 218, f. 220, 1). Similarly the term. अहि is used also for the pres. indic. in the Ap. Pr. (H. C. 4, 383) and for the pres. conj. in W. Gḍ. (see

1) I prefer this explanation of the origin of the Ap. term. अउं to that previously given in § 122, note.

§ 497, 2, b), but in the O. H. is still occurs both for the imper. and the pres. conj. (Kl. 204). The Ap. termin. ए is a contraction of अय (of the Xth class or causal imper.) and represents the Skr. and Pr. term. अ, while the Ap. term. इ is a curtailment of ए, and the term. उ perhaps a corruption of the अ. This is clearly shown by the S., which has preserved both इ and उ, and uses the former for trans. verbs (which correspond to the old caus. and Xth class verbs, see §§ 472. 473), while it adds the latter to intrans. verbs (Tr. 251). The term. उ is preserved also in O. H. (see Kl. 218, e. 220, 1), E. H. and O., but has assumed also the sense of the pres. conj.; while throughout Gḍ. (exc. S. and optionally O. H. and E. H.) it becomes *quiescent* (i. e. अ qu.) when used in its proper sense of the imper. Thus Pr. पढसु *read thou*, but O. H. पढ़सु *read thou* or *thou mayest read*; or Pr. पढहि *read thou*, Ap. Pr. पढहि *read thou* or *thou readest*, O. H. पढ़हि *read thou* or *thou mayest read* or *thou readest*; or Skr. पठ *read thou*, Pr. पढ, Ap. पढु, O. H. and E. H. पढ़ु *read thou* and *thou mayest read*, O. पढ़ु *thou mayest read*, E. H. पढ़् *read thou* or *thou mayest read*, all other Gḍs. (exc. S.) पढ़् *read thou*. Again Pr. पढे (cf. H. C. 3, 158) *read thou*, Ap. पढे or पढि, S. पढ़ि. — i) The term. of the 3. sg. is in Skr. अतु, in Pr. अउ (H. C. 3, 173. Vr. 7, 18) and becomes in M. ओ or ऊ, O. उ, B. उ-क्, N. ओ-स् (or after vowels व-स्). The additions, क् in B. and स् in N., are pleon. suff. of obscure meaning and origin; perhaps they are enclitic pronouns, viz. indef. के or 3. pers. से (see § 503). Thus पठतु *let him read*, Pr. पढउ, M. पढ़ो or पढ़ू, O. पढ़ु, B. पढ़ुक्, N. पढ़ोस् (or जावस् *let him go*). — k) The termin. of the 1. pl. is in Skr. आम; but Pr. substitutes the termin. आमो or अमो (H. C. 3, 176. Vr. 7, 20) or अमु and Ap. Pr. अहुं (K. I. 64, in Ls. 453) of the pres. indic. The same is also done in all Gḍs.; thus (Skr. पठाम), Pr. पढमो or पढमु *let us read*, Ap. पढहुं, N. पढ़ौं, M. पढ़ूं, etc., see § 497, 2, d. — l) The termin. of the 2. pl. is in Skr. अत; but Pr. substitutes the termin. अह (H. C. 3, 176. Vr. 7, 20) of the pres. indic. The Ap. Pr. has अउ (K. I. 63, in Ls. 453) which is the same as अह of the pres. indic. (see § 497, 2, e), but has dropped इ[1]). It occurs also in all W. Gds., and after vowels in N.; while the Pr. ह is preserved in the E. Gds. and M., and also, after consonants, in N. Thus (Skr. पठत), Pr. पठह *read you,* E. H. पढ़ह् or पढ़ (*parha*), B., O. and N. पढ़, M. पढ़ा (for *पढ़अ = पढ़ह); but Ap. पढ़उ, Br. पढ़ौ, Mw., G., P., S. पढ़ो, in fact identical with the 2. pl. pres. conj. (see § 497, 2, e). — m) The term. of the 3. pl. is in Skr. अन्तु, Pr. अंतु (H. C. 3, 176. Vr. 7, 20), it is preserved in the O. अंतु or उत् (by transfer of उ into the preceding syllable, § 148, note), M. ओत् or ऊत्, B. and N. उन्. Thus Skr. पठन्तु *let them read,* Pr. पढंतु, O. पढ़ंतु or पढ़ुत, M. पढोत् or पढ़ूत्, B. and N. पढ़ुन्. The change of उत् to उन् is analogous to that of अत् to अन् (see § 497, 2, f). The other Gds. substitute the 3. pl. of the pres. conj. — 4) As regards the contracted E. H. terminations, they will be understood from the following examples: Skr. खादति *he eats,* Pr. खाअइ or खाइ (H. C. 4, 228), E. H. खाय्; Skr. खादामि *I eat,* Pr. खाअमि or खामि, Ap. Pr. खाउं, E. H. खावँ, etc.

Note: It may be observed, that B. uses the termin. of the 3. pl. for the 2. pl. in respectful address: thus pres. B. पढ़ेन् *you read* (lit. *they read*), pret. पढ़िलेन् *you read* or पढ़ियाछेन् *you have read,* पढ़ियाछिलेन् *you had read,* fut. पढ़िबेन् *you will read,* etc. In M. this is always done in the 2. pl. of the pres. conj. (see § 509, 3), the termin. of which आवेत् m., आव्यात् f., आवीं त n. really belong to the 3. pl. See also § 501, footnote on p. 342.

498. The pres. imper. may optionally add the following suff. in the 2. person.; viz., sing. इहे and plur. इह; e. g., पढ़िहे *read thou,* पढ़िह *read you.* This is a respectful form of the imper., implying request or prayer rather than command, and may be called a *precative.* Sometimes it is used in the sense of a simple future.

499. *Affinities and Derivation.* These suff. are identical with the corresponding suff. of the old Skr. and Pr. future. The use of the fut. to express the imper. is easily intelligible.

---

1) Ls. reads ऊ, which is probably a false reading for उ or हु.

The corresponding Skr. termin. are: sg. इष्यसि, pl. इष्यथ, in the Ap. Pr. sg. इहहि and pl. इहह or इहहु, in E. H. sg. इहे (for *इहइ = इहह), pl. इह (for *इहह्); in O. S., and occasionally M. S., pl. इहो (for *इहउ); e. g., गन्हिहो *seize ye* (Tr. 266). — The corresponding suff. in W. H. are: sg. इये and pl. इयो; that is, the medial ह् is elided, and the hiatus filled up by the connecting semivowel य्. P. has sg. ई, pl. ईओ (Ld. 44); B. has pl. इओ (S. Ch. 147); and S. has sg. इजि or एजि or इजा or इजाइ, pl. इजो or एजो or इजाउ or इजाह (Tr. 266. 267); G. sg. अजे, pl. अजो; Mw. sg. अजै or ईजै or अज्ये, pl. अजो or ईजो or अज्यो (Kl. 211. 212); Br. sg. इजे or इज्ये or ईये or इजै or ईजै, pl. इयौ or इज्यौ or ईयौ or इजो or ईजो (Kl. 204). I am inclined to think, that the W. Gḍ. forms are really passive, but used actively. Thus (Skr. पठ्यसे), Ap. Pr. पढीअहि or पढिज्जहि or पढेज्जहि (H. C. 3, 175), Br. पढीयै or पढिज्ये, P. पढी, or Mw. पढीजे, S. पढिजे or पढेजे, G. पढजे; plur. (Skr. पठ्यध्वे), A. Pr. पढीअहु or पढिज्जहु, Br. पढीयौ, P. पढीओ, Mw. पढीजो, S. पढिजो or पढेजो. The increment इज्ज or इज्जा or एज्ज or एज्जा is found also in Pr. All verbs in Pr. may use it in the 2. pers. of the imper. (H. C. 3, 175), while the verb हो (Skr. भू) *to be* and others ending in a vowel (H. C. 3, 178. K. I. 315, in Ls. 357) may adopt it in any tense. This shows, I think, that these forms cannot well be identified with the single Skr. precative (or benedictive) tense (as Ls. 357)[1]), but constitute a regularly conjugated passive verb which, however, has assumed an active sense (see § 348). Thus *pres. tense*, Pr. होइ or होज्जइ *he is* (H. C. 3, 178) = Skr. भवति or (pass.) भूयते. There is also a longer form होज्जाइ, where the tendency of the pass. suff. य to revert to its original radical state या (which is fully developped in the Gḍ. pass., see § 481) already shows itself; for Pr. होज्जाइ is, as it were, a compound of भू + याति lit. *he is going to be*; compare the real H. H. compound हो जाए *he becomes*, E. H. होय् जाय्. Again in the *imper.*, Pr. होउ or होज्जउ *let him be* = Skr. भवतु or

1) It is probable, however, that the Skr. pass. and prec. are formed on the same principle, by compounding the auxil. verb या *to go* with the root; e. g., 3. sg. भूयात् *may he be* = R. भू and 2nd aorist यात्.

(pass.) भूयन्तां (lit. *भूयतु, for the Pr. prefers the parasm. suff., see Ls. 333); also Pr. होज्जाउ (H. C. 3, 178) = *भू + यातु. Again in the *fut.*, Pr. होहिसि or होज्जहिसि *thou wilt be* = Skr. भविष्यसि or (pass.) भविष्यसे (lit. *भूयस्यसे, for Pr. incorporates the pass. suff. य, see § 346); also Pr. होज्जाहिसि (H. C. 3, 178) = *भू + यास्यसि. Again in the *imper.*, Pr. हससु or हसेज्जसु *laugh thou* (H. C. 3, 175) = Skr. हस or (pass.) हस्यस्व; also Pr. हसेज्जहि or contr. हसेज्जे (H. C. 3, 175), whence S. हसेज्ञि or हसिज्ञि. S. has also a longer form हसेज्ञाइ or हसिज्ञाइ lit. = *हस् + याहि. Similarly S. pl. हसेज्ञो or हसिज्ञो *laugh ye* presuppose a Ap. Pr. (not mentioned by H. C.) हसेज्जहु. In Pr. all the personal suff. may be dropped, and that, in all tenses alike; thus leaving the mere increment इज्ज or एज्ज as a universal termination; and this curtailed form may be used with all roots, whether ending in a vowel or consonant; thus Pr. होज्ज or होज्जा may mean: *he is* or *he may be* or *let him be* or *he was* or *he has been* or *he will be*, etc.; similarly पढेज्ज or पढेज्जा may mean: *he reads, he will read*, or *let him read*, etc. (H. C. 3, 177). Of this usage, however, I believe, there is no trace in Gḍ.

500. *Present indicative.* This tense is made by adding the following suff. to the root of the verb according to the gender, number and person of the subj.

	Sing. Masc.	Fem.	Plur. Masc.	Fem.
1.	एँलों (or एँल्यों)	एँल्यूँ	इँला	इँला
2.	एँले or एँलेस्	एँलो or एलिस्	एँल or एँलह (or एँल्यह्)	एँल्यू
3.	एँला	एँले	एँलैं or एँलेन्	एँलीं or एँलिन्

Optionally the initial एँ may be changed to अ (§ 26); thus masc. अलों, fem. अल्यूं, etc.; but 1. pl. only इँला. After roots in आ or ए and the R. हो, the initial एँ or अ (but not इँ) is dropped. Thus 1. sg. masc. लों, fem. ल्यूँ, etc.; but 1. pl. always इँला.

501. *Affinities and Derivation.* 1) It has been stated in §§ 496. 497 that the old pres. indic. has been changed into the pres. conj. in E. H., N. and the W. Gḍs. Accordingly these languages (exc. P. see Nro. 2, p. 343) form a new pres. indic. by adding to the old tense some auxil. verb, viz. in Bh. लों, Mth.

छौ, N. छुँ, Br. हौँ or हूँ (Kl. 206, a), Mw. हूँ or छूँ (Kl. 212, 402), G. छुं (Ed. 54), S. थो (Tr. 293). The Mth., N., Br., Mw. and G. forms छौ, छुँ or छूँ, हूँ or हौँ are those of the pres. tense of the auxil. verb *to be* (see § 514, 4. 5); but while Br., Mw. and G. simply add them to the unchanged termin. of the pres. conj., Mth. and N. first reduce the latter to the uniform type ऐ and अ respectively. Thus Br. करौँ हौँ or करूँ हूँ, Mw. करूँ हूँ or करूँ छूँ, G. करूँ छुं, but Mth. करै छौ, N. गर छुँ or गर छूँ *I do*; Br. करै है, Mw. करै है or करै छै, G. करे छे, Mth. करै छै, N. गर छस *thou doest*, etc. The S. form थो is the past part. of the auxil. verb थिअणु *to be* (contr. for थिओ, Tr. 305, see § 514, 6), and is simply added to the pers. termin. of the pres. conj., but agrees in gender and number with the subj.; thus S. masc. करिआँ थो *I do*, fem. करिआँ थी, pl. masc. करिऊँ था *we do*, fem. करिऊँ थिऊँ, etc. The E. H. form लौँ is the 2nd pret. of the auxil. verb आव् *to come*, curtailed from ऐलौँ (see § 509, 4). It is conjugated regularly (see § 504), with the exception of the 3. sg. and 1. pl., where it has ला for *लू and *लो (i. e., 3. sg. ऐल् or आयल्, 1. pl. ऐलो); and the pers. termin. of the pres. conj., to which it is added, are not the ordinary ones but a uniform type in ऐ (as in Mth.) or in अ (as in N.), with the exception of the 1. pl. which preserves its regular term. ई [1]). It may be observed, that in Gw. the forms, sg. लो, pl. ला, are used as an auxil. verb, in the sense of *he is*, *they are*, etc., by the side of the ordinary W. H. है, छ, छ, etc. (Kl. 198, 200); e. g., Gw. कोई लो or कोई छ or कोई है or कोइ छे

1) The uniform ऐ-type can easily be explained. In Br. the 2. and 3. sg. pres. conj. ends in ऐ, the 1. pl. in ऐँ. In O., the 1. sg. ends in अइँ which would easily contract to ऐ. Lastly in Br. the 3. pl. एन् is also used in the 2. pl. (see S. Ch. 142 and § 497, note; e. g., करेन् *they do* and *you do*); this is sometimes also done in Bs. (e. g., अहेँ or अहेन् *they are* or *you are*; but the proper 2. pl. अहहु or अहु or अहौ is also used); similarly the E. H. 3. pl. ऐँ would intrude into the 2. pl. Final anunásika is dropped. According to these analogies every person of the E. H. pres. conj. might end in ऐ. The अ-type of the N. is but a shorter form of the ऐ-type (see § 26).

is there any one? In E. H. the forms of the pres. indic. are sometimes used in the sense of a future indic.; e. g., E. H. माई आवँले तव् खाईला i. e. *when mother comes, then we shall eat.* Now it will be shown in § 509, 4, that the fut. indic. is made precisely in the same way (by adding the auxil. part. ल *come* to the pres. conj.) in Mw., M. and N.; and it may be observed, that in the Br. and P. their fut. indic., which is made in an analogous way by adding the auxil. part. ग *gone* to the pres. conj. (§ 509, 5), is also used as a pres. indic. in the case of the substant. verb *to be*; thus compare Br. and P. है or हैगा (हैगो) masc. *he is*, fem. है or हैगी with Br. होयगो, H. H. होगा, P. होवेगा masc., °गी fem. *he or she will be*; again Br. हैं or हैंगे masc. *we are*, fem. हैं or हैंगी, P. masc. हाँ or हाँगे, fem. हाँ or हाँगीआँ with Br. होयँगे, H. H. होंगे, P. होवाँगे masc. *we shall be*, fem. Br. °गी. H. H. °गी, P. °गीआँ, etc. Again the presence of a long vowel in the antepenultimate, as E. H. सूतैलों *I sleep* (of R. सूत्), proves the composite character of the forms of the pres. indic. (viz. सूतै + लों); for otherwise, if they were single words, such a vowel would be shortened by the rule of § 25. Lastly these composite forms naturally yield the sense of a pres. indic. Thus सूतैलों which means lit. *I have come (that) I may sleep* or *I have come to sleep*, may easily pass into *I am sleeping* or *I sleep.* Literally these forms express, that the action is the *present result* of preceding events; e. g., „I have come to be happy" is equal to „I am happy" now. — 2) The H. H. and P. and, optionally, the Bs., Br. are peculiar in adding the auxil. verb हूँ, हाँ, अहेउँ, हों resp., not to the old pres. tense, but to the pres. part. in ता, दा, त्, तु resp. Thus sing. Bs. करत् अहेउँ masc., °ती अ° fem. (Kl. 241), Br. करतु हूँ or °तो हों m., °ति or °ती हूँ or हों f. (Kl. 202, a. 204, 283), P. करदा हाँ m., °दी हाँ f. (Ld. 29. 37. 46), H. H. करता हूँ m., °ती हूँ f. *I do*; plur. Bs. करत् अहो m., °ति अहो f., Br. करत् हैं or °त हैं m., °ति or °ती हैं f., P. करदे हाँ m., °दीआँ हाँ f., H. H. करते हैं m., °ती हैं f. *we do*, etc. Sometimes the auxil. verb is omitted; but in that case, the forms are properly those of the pret. conj. — 3) In M. the old pres. indic. has assumed the sense of a *habitual past* (§ 496). Hence it forms a new pres. indic. by suffixing the ordinary personal termin. to the pres. part. in अत् (Man. 69. 72), in the same way as in the E. H. pret. conj. (§ 506). Thus M. करितों m., करित्यें f., करितें n. *I do*; करितोस् m., करितीस f., करितेंस् n. *thou doest*, etc. — 4) In B., O. and optionally in G., the old pres. indic. having retained its original indic. sense (§ 496), is still used as such (S. Ch. 142. Sn. 27. Ed. 54). Thus B. करि, O. करइँ, G. करुँ *I do*; B. करिस्, O. करु, G. करे *thou doest*, etc. — 5) I add a comparative table of the terminations:

Singular.

	B.	O.	E. H.	Mth.	Br.	Mw.	G.
1.	इ	अइँ	एँ लों	ऐ छौ	औ हौं	ऊँ हूँ, ऊँ छूँ	उँ, उँ छुँ
2.	इस्	उ	एँ लेस्	ऐ छें	ऐ है	ऐ है, ऐ छै	ए, ए छे
3.	ए	अइ	एँ ला	ऐ अछि	ऐ है	ऐ है, ऐ छै	ए, ए छे
	N.	**S.**	**M.**	**Bs.**	**Br.**	**H. H.**	**P.**
1.	अछुं, अछूं	आँ थो	अतों	अत् अहेउँ	अतु हौं 1)	अता हूँ	अदा हाँ
2.	अ छस्	एँ थो	अतोस्	अत् अहेस्	अतु है	अता है	अदा हैं
3.	अ छ	ए थो	अतो	अत् अहै	अतु है	अता है	अदा है

Plural.

	B.	O.	E. H.	Mth.	Br.	Mw.	G.
1.	इ	उँ	ई ला	ऐ छी	ऐं हैं	आँ हाँ, आँ छाँ	ये, ये छैये
2.	अ	अ	एँ लह्	ऐ छौ	ओ हौ	ओ हो, ओ छो	ओ, ओ छो
3.	एन्	अंति	एँ लेन्	ऐ अथि	ऐं हैं	ऐ है, ऐ छै	ए, ए छे
	N.	**S.**	**M.**	**Bs.**	**Br.**	**H. H.**	**P.**
1.	अ छूं 2)	ऊँ था	अतों	अत् अहौ	अत् हैं	अते हैं	अदे हाँ
2.	अ छौ	ओ था	अताँ	अत् अहह् 3)	अत् हौ	अते हो	अदे हो
3.	अ छन्	अनि था	अतात्	अत् अहेन् 3)	अत् हैं	अते हैं	अदे हन्

In the fem., S. changes थो and था to थी and थिऊँ, Br. अतु to अति, H. H. अता and अते to अती, P. अदा and अदे to अदी and अदीआँ; M. sg. 1. अत्ये ँ or अतें, 2. अत्येस् or अतेस् or अतीस्, 3. अती

1) Or, masc. अतौ हौं, fem. अती हौं, etc.

2) Or, अ छुँ.

3) Or, 2. अत् अहौ, 3. अत् अहैं.

or अत्यो or अते; pl. fem. like masc. — *In the neut.*, M. has sg. 1. अतें, 2. अतेंस्, 3. अतें; pl. neut. like masc.

2. PARTICIPIAL TENSES.

502. *First preterite indicative.* A past tense indic., which I shall call the *first preterite* to distinguish it from the other form of the past indic. (§ 504), is made by modifying the termination of the past part. in इअ or इ (see § 302) in the following manner according to the number and person (but not the gender) of the subj.

Sing. 1. यों, 2. इस्, 3. इस्. Plur. 1. आ, 2. यों, 3. इन्.

There is no difference in meaning between the first and second preterites; they only differ in usage; the first pret. is said to be confined to the language of towns (*nágari bhāshá*).

Exception. As to some verbs which use an irregular past part. see § 304. E. g., कर्ब् *to do* uses the forms किय (for किइअ) in the 1. sg. and 1. 2. pl., and किह् in the 2. 3. sg. and 3. pl.; thus sing. 1. कियों, 2. किह्स्, 3. किह्स्; plur. 1. किया, 2. कियों, 3. किह्न्. Like कर्ब् are conjugated धर्ब् *to place*, देब् *to give*, लेब् *to take*.

503. *Affinities and Derivation.* This tense exists in all Gḍs., exc. M.; but it is formed in a variety of ways. — 1) In O. H., E. H. and N. it is made by adding the suff. of the pres. conj. to the weak past participial form in इअ or इ (§ 302). These suff. (after subtracting the initial अ of the terminations, see § 497) are: 1. sg. उँ or इँ (as in O. H. करउँ, O. करइँ *I do*); 2. sg. सि or हि or उ (as in O. H. करसि or करहि or E. H. करु *thou doest*); 3. sg. इ or (with anomalous ह्) हि (as in O. H. करइ or करहि *he does*); 1. pl. उँ (as in N. करौं *we do* for *करउँ or N. जाउँ *we go*); 2. pl. हु (as in O. H. करहु *you do*); 3. pl. न्हि or नि (as in S. कनि or करीनि *they do*, Tr. 287). The part. termin. इअ is generally contracted to ए and, sometimes, to अ in O. H. — a) The 1. sg. suff. उँ occurs in O. H. and E. H.; thus पढ़िअ + उँ = O. H. and Bs. पढेउँ or पढउँ, Bh. पढ्यों *I read*; the 1. sg. इँ in N.; e. g., पढ़िअ + इँ = N. पढें *I read* or थिअ + इँ = N. थें or थियें *I was*. —

Again b) the 2. sg. हि or उ occur in O. H.; thus पढिअ + हि = O. H. पढेहि or पढिअ + उ = O. H. पढेउ or पढउ *thou readst*; the 2. sg. सि in O. H. and Bs., thus पढिअ + सि = O. H. पढेसि, Bs. पढिसि; in E. H., N. and, optionally, in Bs. it is shortened to स्, Bs. पढेस्, Bh. and N. पढिस्, or थिअ + सि = N. थ्येस् or थियेस् *thou wast.* — Again c) the 3. sg. suff. हि occurs in O. H.; thus पढिअ + हि = O. H. पढेहि *he read.* The 3. sg. इ does not exist in this tense. The E. H. adds the aff. स्, which in the longer form सि, occurs also in O. H. and Bs.; thus पढिअ + aff. सि = O. H. पढेसि, Bs. पढिसि or पढेस्, Bh, पढिस् *he read.* Though these 3. sg. forms outwardly resemble those of the 2. pers., they can scarcely have the same origin[1]). The same 3. sg. aff. स् exists also in P.; e. g., पढिओस् *he read,* कीतोस् *he did* (Ld. 69); and also in N., though not in the pret. but the imper. (see § 497, 3. i, p. 338); e. g., पढोस् *let him read.* It is possibly a shortened form of the 3. pers. pron. सॆ, enclitically attached in a manner similar to the more general S. practice of affixing curtailed pron. forms to the verb (see Tr. 345 ff.); thus S. पढिउ-सि *he read,* फिरिउ-सि *he turned round* (Tr. 368). The N. adds in the 3. sg. no suff. at all, but uses the strong instead of the weak part. form; thus N. masc. पढ्यो or पढियो *he read,* fem. पढी *she read,* or masc. थ्यो or थियो *he was,* fem. थिई *she was.* — Again d) the 1. pl. उँ occurs in N.; thus पढिअ + उँ = N. पढ्यूँ or पढ्युँ *we read,* or थिअ + उँ = N. थिउँ or थ्यूँ or थ्युँ *we were.* The O. H. and Bs. use (just as in the pres. conj.) the suff. of the 3. pl. न्हि or नि, thus पढिअ + न्हि (for न्ति) = O. H. पढेन्हि, Bs. पढिनि or पढेन्. The E. H. (Bh.) 1. pl. termin. आ is, perhaps, a modification for *आँ, containing the same 1. pl. termin. अँ as the 1. pl. of the Mw. pres. conj. (see § 497, 2. d, p. 336); thus E. H. पढा *we read* for *पढ्याँ = पढिअ + अँ. — Again e) the 2. pl. हु occurs in O. H., E. H. and N.; thus पढिअ + हु =

1) O. H. has, in the 3. sg., forms in अउ or एउ resembling those of the 2. pers., e. g., पढेउ or पढउ *he read,* but here उ is, probably, not a conjugational, but a pleon. suff. = Ap. Pr. पढिअउ, Pr. पढिअओ, Skr. पठितकः, corresponding to the S. 3. sg. पढिओ, N. पढ्यो.

O. H. पढेहु, N. पढिउ or पढ्यौ, Bh. पढ्यौ, Bs. पढिउ *you read,* or N. गिअ + उ = गियउ or थ्यौ *you were.* — Again f) the 3. pl. न्हि occurs in O. H., as पढेन्हि *they read,* and नि in Bs. पढिनि and न् in E. H. and N. पढेन्, Bh. पढिन्. The N., however, has more usually a suff. ए, which is perhaps a modification of *ये or *यँ, containing the same 3. pl. suff. ए or एँ as the 3. pl. of the G. and H. H. pres. conj. (see § 497, 2. f, p. 337); e. g., N. पढे *they read* for *पढ्ये or *पढ्यें = पढिअ + एँ, or N. थ्ये or थे *they were.* Sometimes N. omits the suff. altogether, and uses only the strong form of the past part.; thus N. पढ्या *they read,* गिया or थ्या *they were.* — It will be observed, that this mode of forming the pret. indic. practically amounts to treating the past part. as a denominative verbal root. The treatment, generally, of past part. as denominative roots is not uncommon in E. H. (see § 352), and existed even in Pr. (see Wb. Bh. 429). In this particular case, no doubt, the practice originated from the similarity, in Pr., of participles, used denominatively, to participles accompanied by the auxil. verb अस् *to be.* Thus compare the denom. form, 1. sg. Pr. पढिअमि, Ap. Pr. पढिअउं (= Skr. *पठितामि) *I read* with the common compound form, Pr. पढिअ म्हि (H. C. 3, 147) = Skr. पठितोऽस्मि. — 2) In B. and O. this tense is made by adding the pres. tense of the auxil. verb आछि or अछि *I am* to the past part. in इअ or इ resp.; thus 1. sg. B. पड़िलाछि *I read* for पड़िअ or पड़ि + आछि, O. पड़िअछि = पड़ि + अछि; 2. sg. B. पड़िलाछे, O. पड़िअछु *thou readst,* etc. — 3) S. combines these two methods in the formation of this tense; viz., in the 1. sg. and pl. it adds (like the B. and O.) the auxil. verb सि *I am* and सों *we are* (for हि and हों, § 11); e. g., 1. sg. S. हलिउ-सि masc., हलिअ-सि fem., or (in poëtry) हलिओ-सि m., हलिआ-सि f. *I went* (= O. चलिअछि), pl. masc. हलिआ-सों, fem. हलिउँ-सों *we went* (हलिउ being the masc. and हलिअ the fem. nom. sing. of the weak and हलिओ, हलिआ of the strong form of the past part.). In the 2. sg. and pl. it adds (like the E. H.) the person. term. of the pres. conj., sg. एँ and pl. उ; thus 2. sg. हलिएँ masc. (i. e., base हलिअ + suff. हि), हलिएँ or हलिआँ

fem. *thou wentest*; pl. masc. हल्यउ (= E. H. चल्यौ), fem. हलिउँ *you went.* In the 3. sg. and pl. it adds (like the N.) no suff. at all, but uses the strong instead of the weak participial form; thus 3. sg. हलिओ masc., हली fem. *he* or *she went* (= N. चलियो, चली); pl. masc. हलिआ, fem. हलिउँ *they went* (= N. चल्या, चली). These remarks, however, apply only to intrans. verbs. In the case of trans. verbs, S. never adds any suff. or auxil. verbs, but uses only the strong past part. form; that is, in effect, trans. verbs have in S. only a 3. pers. sg. and pl. (but no 1st and 2nd persons)[1]. It is a circumstance in which all W. Gḍs. agree with S., and which explains the peculiarity, that for the 1. and 2. pers. they can only employ the *Bhávi prayoga* or impers. pass. construction (see § 487); e. g., *the disciple left me* is in Br. चेला ने मो कौं छोड़्यौ, S. चेले मूँ खे छड़िओ lit. *by the disciple in regard to me it was left*, „me" being either masc. or fem.; but not the *Karmani prayoga* or personal pass. contr. चेला ने हौं छोड़्यौ masc. or हौं छोड़ी fem., S. चेले आँउँ छड़िओ masc. or आँउँ छड़ी fem., lit. *by the disciple I was left.* On the other hand, for the 3. pers., both the Bhávi and Karmani prayoga may be used; thus *the disciple left that book* may be in Br. चेला ने ओह् पोथी कौं छोड़्यौ, S. चेले हुन् पोथी खे छड़िओ lit. *by the disciple, in regard to the book, it was left (Bhávi)* or Br. चेला ने उ पोथी छोड़ी, S. चेले हू पोथी छड़ी lit. *by the disciple that book was left (Karmani).* — 4) With regard to intrans. verbs, the W. H., P. and G. use (like S.) the past part. in the Kartari prayoga, but (unlike S.) they do not add any suff. or auxil. verb; thus *I walked* is in W. H. हौं चल्यौ m., हौं चली f., G. हुँ चल्यो m. or चली f., but S. आँउँ हलिउसि m. or हलिअसी f. — 5) I add a comparative table of the terminations:

---

1) It should be recollected that, in W. Gḍ., trans. verbs admit only of the pass. constr., which converts what, with us, is subj. into the obj. Thus our 1. pers. sing. „I left him" becomes, in W. Gḍ., 3. pers. sg. „by me he was left". Accordingly, in W. Gḍ., there could be a first person only we should have the accus. of the 1. pers. pron. as obj.; e. g., our 3. pers. „he left me" ought to become, in W. Gḍ., 1. pers. „by him I was left". But even here W. Gḍ. has no first pers., but employs the impersonal constr. „by him in regard to me it was left".

Singular.

	B.	O.	O. H.	E. H.	N.	S.	
	intr. & tr.	intr. & tr.	intr. & tr.	intr. & tr.	intr. & tr.	intr.	tr.
1.	इयाछि [1])	इअछि	ऐउँ	यों	एँ	इउसि [2])	
2.	इयाछे	इअछु	ऐसि	इस्	इस्	इएँ	
3.	इयाछे	इअछइ	ऐ-सि	इ-स्	यो	इओ	इओ

	P.		G.		W. H.		H. H.	
	intr.	tr.	intr.	tr.	intr.	tr.	intr.	tr.
1.	इआ		यो		यौ		आ	
2.	इआ		यो		यौ		आ	
3.	इआ	इआ	यो	यो	यौ	यौ	आ	आ

Plural.

	B.	O.	O. H.	E. H.	N.	S.	
	intr. & tr.	intr. & tr.	intr. & tr.	intr. & tr.	intr. & tr.	intr.	tr.
1.	इयाछि	इअछुँ	ऐन्हि	आ	यूँ	इआसौं	
2.	इयाछ	इअछ	ऐहु	यौ	यौ	यउ	
3.	इयाछेन्	इअछंति	ऐन्हि	इन्	या [3])	इआ	इआ

	P.		G.		W. H.		H. H.	
	intr.	tr.	intr.	tr.	intr.	tr.	intr.	tr.
1.	ए		या		ए		ए	
2.	ए		या		ए		ए	
3.	ए	ए	या	या	ए	ए	ए	ए

1) These B. term. are, ordinarily, pronounced एछि, एछे, etc.; thus करियाछि is pronounced करेछि *karechhi*, not *kariyáchhi*. In fact, the old way of spelling has been retained, though the pronunciation has changed; just as in English we still write „night", but pronounce „nite". The old past part. करिअ is contracted to करे (just as in E. H. the conj. past करिअ becomes करे, see § 491); and अछि curtailed into छि. The older forms इयाछि, etc. may occasionally be heard in solemn addresses (sermons, etc.). The cons. छ *chh* is always pronounced *ts*, or even *s* (as in M. and Mw., see § 11); e. g., करियाछि (or rather करेछि) is pronounced *karetsi* or even *karesi*. — Similarly the B. term. of the conj. part. इया is ordinarily contracted into ए; e. g., करिया *having done* is pronounced करे.

2) Or इओसि m., इआसि f.

3) Or ऐन् or ए com. gen.

In the fem. sg., N. यो, S. इओ, P. इआ, G. यो, W. H. यौ and H. H. आ are changed to ई; and S. has 1. इअसि, 2. इएँ or इआँ; fem. pl., N. या, P. ए, G. या, W. H. and H. H. ए are changed to ईँ, and S. has 1. इऊँसोँ, 2. and 3. इऊँ.

Note: The plusperf. is a periphrastic tense in E. H. (see § 510, 7), exc. in Mth. which, like the B. and O., forms it by adding the past tense of the auxil. verb, Mth. छलोँ, B. आछिलाम्, O. थेलि *I was*, etc. (see § 514, 6) to the past part. in इअ or इ. The part. termin. इअ is contracted in Mth. to ऐ. Thus 1. sg. Mth. पढ़ैछलोँ, B. पड़ियाछिलाम्, O. पढ़िथेलि *I had read*, etc. The resp. termin. are: 2. sg. Mth. ऐछलेँ, B. आछिलि, O. इथेलु; 3. sg. Mth. ऐछल्, B. आछिलि, O. इथेल; 1. pl. Mth. ऐछलोँ, B. आछिलाम्, O. इथेलुँ; 2. pl. Mth. ऐछलोँ, B. आछिले, O. इथेल; 3. pl. Mth. ऐछलाह्, B. आछिलेन्, O. इथेले.

504. *Second preterite indicative.* This tense is made by modifying the termination of the past part. in अल् or इल् (§ 302) in the following manner according to the gender, number and person of the subj.

	Sing. Masc.	Sing. Fem.
1.	अलोँ (or अल्योँ)	अल्यूँ
2.	अलेस् (intr.) or अले	अलिस् or अली
3.	अल् (intr.) or अलेस् (tr.)	अल् (intr.) or अलेस् (tr.)
	Plur. Masc.	**Plur. Fem.**
1.	अली	अली
2.	अलह् or अल (or अल्यह्)	अल्यू
3.	अलेन् or अलैँ	अलिन् or अलीँ

In the 3. sg., trans. verbs take the suff. अलेन्, while the intrans. take अल्. Again in the 2. sg. masc. the suff. अलेस् is confined to intrans. verbs. The other suff. are common to both.

Note: In the eastern parts of the E. H. area the termin. are pronounced with इ, as इलोँ, इल्यूँ, etc. — The forms enclosed in brackets are less usual.

505. *Affinities and Derivation.* 1) This tense exists only in E. and S. Gḍ. It is made, like the first pret. indic., by

adding the personal suff. of the old pres. indic. (see § 503) to the weak form of the past part. in अल् or इल्, except in M., which adds them to the strong form in अला. It should be remarked, however, that B. and O. omit the suff. in the 3. sg. of all verbs, and E. H. in the 3. sg. of intrans. verbs. Again M. omits the suff. in the 3. sg. and pl. of intrans. verbs and in all persons, sg. and pl., of trans. verbs[1]). E. g., *he read the book* is in E. H. ऊ पोथी पढ़लेस्, B. ओ पोथी पढ़िल्, O. से पोथी पढ़िला, M. त्या नें पोथी वाचिली (Man. 65, 2, or exceptionally तो पोथी पढ़ला Man. 81, 133). On the whole the pers. suff. are added quite regularly. Thus a) 1. sg. उँ in E. H. and M.; e. g., wk. form, masc. पढ़ल + उँ = E. H. पढ़लों *I read*, fem. पढ़लि + उँ = E. H. पढ़ल्यूँ; here the final ऊँ is anomalous; it is possibly founded on the strong form पढ़ली = पढ़लिअ + उँ. Again strong form, masc. पढ़ला + उँ = M. पढ़लों; but in the fem. M. adds the 1. sg. suff. इँ; this may be clearly seen in the pres. indic.; e. g., पढ़ती = पढ़तिअ (Skr. पठन्तिका) + इँ = M. पढ़त्यें or पढ़तें *I read*; similarly पढ़ली = पढ़लिअ + इँ = पढ़लें *I read*. In the neut., M. uses either उँ or इँ; thus पढ़लों or पढ़लें. O. shows the same 1. sg. termin. इ (a shortened form of अइँ), as in its pres. indic.; thus पढ़िलि *I read*, just as अछइँ or अछि *I am*. The B. has the 1. sg. termin. आम्, which appears to have preserved the original pres. indic. termin. आमि (see § 497, 2); thus पढ़िलाम् (= Mg. *पढिदामि denom.). — Again b) the 2. sg. suff. सि or, shortened, स् occurs in E. H. and M.; thus wk. f. masc. रहल + सि = E. H. रहलेस् with transfer of इ into the preceding syllable; fem. रहलि + स् = E. H. रहलिस् *thou remainedst*; or st. f. masc. पढ़ला + स् = M. पढ़लास्, fem. पढ़ली + स् = M. पढ़लीस्, neut. पढ़लें + स् = M. पढ़लेंस् with an anomalous anunásika; for the suff. स् is anomalously added to the nom. sg. neut. पढ़लें instead of to the neut. base पढ़ले

1) M. which constructs transitive verbs passively, like the W. Gḍs. (see § 487), not actively, like the E. Gḍs., follows the usage of the former languages (see § 503, 3, p. 348) in adding no suff. to the past part. of such verbs.

(= *पऋलय = Mg. पढिदय = Skr. पठितक). The 2. sg. हि is found in E. H. and B.; thus wk. f. masc. पऋल + हि = E. H. पऋले or (shortened) B. पढिलि; fem. पऋलि + हि = E. H. पऋली *thou readst.* The 2. sg. उ is peculiar to O.; thus पढिलु, just as in the O. pres. indic. पऋु (see § 497, pp. 335. 336). — Again c) the 3. sg. सि occurs in the E. H. पऋलेसू. But there is no suff. in M., B., O. or in intrans. verbs of E. H.; thus M. पऋला m., पऋली f., पऋलें n. *he read,* गेला m., गेली f., गेलें n. *he went,* O. पढिला, गला c. g., B. पढिल्, गेल् c. g., E. H. गवल् c. g., but पऋलेस्. — Again d) the 1. pl. उँ is found in M. and O.; thus M. पऋलों c. g. or (shortened) O. पऋलुँ c. g. *we read.* The E. H. shows the same 1. pl. termin. इ (but without anunásika) as in its pres. conj. (§ 497, 2, d, p. 336); thus E. H. पऋली c. g. *we read* just as पऋीं *we read.* And the B. has preserved the original pres. indic. termin. श्राम्; thus पढिलाम् (= Mg. *पढिदाम denom., or *पढिदाम्ह). — Again e) the 2. pl. हु is preserved in the E. H. fem., thus पऋलि + हु or, perhaps, st. f. पढलिश्र + हु = E. H. पऋल्यू *you read.* Otherwise the 2. pl. ह or हं is used; thus wk. f. masc. पऋल + ह = E. H. पऋलह् or (dropping ह्, § 32) पऋल *parhala,* O. पढिल c. g.; the B. पढिले c. g. apparently contracts final श्रह *aha* to ए or stands for पऋलें, properly a 3. pl. form (see § 497, footnote and O. 3. pl. पढिले). Or st. f. पऋला + हं = M. पऋलाँ c. g. — Again f) the 3. pl. नि or, shortened, न् is preserved in E. H. and B.; thus wk. f. masc. पऋल + नि = E. H. पऋलेन्, B. पढिलेन् with transfer of final इ into the preceding syllable; fem. पऋलि + न् = E. H. पढलिन्. The E. H. also shows the other 3. pl. termin. ऐं in the masc. पऋलैं *they read* and, slightly modified, in the fem. पऋलीं, just as in the E. H. pres. conj. पऋैं *they read.* O. omits the anunásika, पढिले for *पढिलें. M. uses the strong form, but without any suff., पऋले. — 2) As regards the E. H. optional forms, 1. sg. श्रल्यों and 2. pl. श्रल्यह्, they contain probably the strong part. termin. श्रलय, with euph. य् for श्रलश्र; thus Skr. denom. *पठितकामि (= पठितकोऽस्मि), Mg. *पढिदश्रमि or *पढिदयमि, Ap. *पढिदयउं, E. H. पढिल्यों or पऋल्यों. — 3) I subjoin a comparative table of terminations:

Singular.

	B.	O.	E. H.	M.
1.	इलाम्	इलि	अलों m., अल्यूँ f.	अलों m., अलें f., अलों or अलें n.
2.	इलि	इलु	अलेस् m., अलिस् f.	अलास् m., अलीस् f., अलेंस् n.
3.	इल्	इला	अलेस् c. g., अल् c. g.	अला m., अली f., अलें n.

Plural.

	B.	O.	E. H.	M.
1.	इलाम्	इलुँ	अली c. g.	अलों c. g.
2.	इले	इल	अलह् m., अल्यू f.	अलाँ c. g.
3.	इलेन्	इले	अलेन् m., अलिन् f.	अले m., अल्या f., अलीं n.

Note: The B. and O. forms are of common gender.

506. *Preterite conjunctive.* This tense is made by modifying the termination of the pres. part. in अत् (§§ 298. 486) in the following manner, according to the gender, number and person of the subject.

	Singular. Masc.	Singular. Fem.	Plural. Masc.	Plural. Fem.
1.	अतों (or अत्यों)	अत्यूँ	अती or इत्	अती or इत्
2.	अतेस् or अते	अतिस् or अती	अतह् or अत (or अत्यह्)	अत्यू
3.	अत् or अतै	अत् or अतै	अतेन् or अतैं	अतिन् or अतैं

Note: The forms enclosed in brackets are more usual in Bs., than in Bh. — Occasionally this tense is used as a pres. indic.

507. *Affinities and Derivation.* 1) This tense exists in all Gḍs., with the exception, apparently, of S. But while W. Gḍ. uses the strong form of the pres. part. without addition, to express the pret. conj., the E. and S. Gḍs. make it by joining to the same part. the personal suff. of the old pres. indic. These composite forms are made exactly on the same model as those of the second pret. indic., see § 505, where the matter has been fully explained. The E. Gḍs. use the weak, but M. the strong form of the part. Thus 1. sg. masc. O. H. पढ़तेउँ or पढ़ताउं, E. H. पढ़त्यों or पढ़तों *(if) I read,* B. पढ़िताम् (S. Ch. 147), O. पढंन्ति (Sn. 32), M. पढ़तों (Man. 60, 4. 73); but W. H. पढ़तौ or पढ़तो, H. H. पढ़ता (Kl. 167, a), P. पढ़दा (Ld. 37. 46, etc.), G. पढ़तो (Ed. 54); fem. O. H. पढ़तिउँ or पढ़तेउँ, E. H. पढ़त्यूँ, B. and O. like masc.,

M. पढ़ते", but W. H., H. H., G. पढ़तो, P. पढ़दी; neut. M. पढ़तों", but G. पढ़तुँ, etc.; see the table of termin. below. The optional E. H. termin. इत् of the 1. pl. is, evidently, an intrusion from the B., where the pres. part. ends in इत, instead of in अत (see § 300). — It will be observed, that the M. termin. of the pret. conj. are nearly identical with those of its pres. indic.; the only difference being in the 3. sg. and plur. (e. g., 3. sg. masc. conj. अता, but indic. अतो; 3. pl. masc. conj. अते, but indic. अतात्) and in the 2. sg. masc. (viz. conj. अतास्, but indic. अतोस्). The indic. has more nearly preserved the old Pr. forms; and moreover, probably, uses the weak form of the part. Thus the M. 2. sg. indic. पढ़तोस् *thou readest* is the same as the Pr. पढंतो सि; while the M. 2. sg. conj. पढ़तास् *(if) thou readst* is rather a denom. formation पढ़ता + सि = Pr. *पढंतग्र-सि; see the remarks in § 503, 1, p. 347. — In the other Gḍs. the pret. conj. itself may be occasionally used as a sort of indefinite pres. indic. [1]). Examples of this usage, of expressing the pret. conj. by means of the part. pres. with or without the auxil. verb अस् *to be,* are already found in Pr. (see Wb. Spt. 62. 63). Thus Spt. 26 जइ जाणंतोऽसि ण कुणंतो *if thou knewest, thou wouldst not do.* This would be in M. जर जानतास् न करतास्, E. H. जो जानतेस् न करतेस्. Of the two Pr. methods, that which dispenses with the auxil. verb appears to have given rise to the W. Gḍ. form of the pret. conj., while the other which uses that verb apparently led to the S. and E. Gḍ. denom. forms of the same tense. The fact that the Gḍ. pret. conj., and the analogously-formed tenses of the 1st and 2nd pret. and fut. indic., have different forms for the several genders, is thus explained by the Pr. For the part. with or without the auxil. verb, must, of course, agree with the subj. in regard to gender. — 2) S., apparently possesses no special pret. conj., but uses instead of it the ordinary pres. indic. (see Tr. 501). — 3) I subjoin a comparative table of terminations:

---

1) Called *indefinite imperfect* by Kl. 167, 323, *frequentative* by S. Ch. 147, *first present subjunctive* by Ed. 54.

Singular.

	B.	O.	E. H.	M.
1.	इताम्	अंति	अतोँ m., अत्यूँ f.	अतोँ m., अतेँ f., अतोँ n.
2.	इतिम्	अंतु	अतेस् m., अतिस् f.	अतास् m., अतीस् f., अतेँस् n,
3.	इत्	अंता	अत् c. g.	अता m., अती f., अतेँ n.

	G.	W. H.	H. H.	P.
1.	अतो m., अती f., अतुँ n.	अतौ m., अती f.	अता m., अती f.	अदा m., अदी f.
2.	dto	dto	dto	dto
3.	dto	dto	dto	dto

Plural.

	B.	O.	E. H.	M.
1.	इताम्	अंतुँ	अती or इत् c. g.	अतोँ c. g.
2.	इत	अंत	अतह् m., अत्यू f.	अताँ c. g.
3.	इतेन्	अंते	अतेन् m., अतिन् f.	अते m., अत्या f., अतीँ n.

	G.	W. H.	H. H.	P.
1.	अता m., अती f., अताँ n.	अते m., अतीँ f.	अते m., अती f.	अदे m., अदीआँ f.
2.	dto	dto	dto	dto
3.	dto	dto	dto	dto

508. *Future indicative.* This tense is made by modifying the termination of the fut. part. in अब् or इब् (§§ 308. 486) in the following manner, according to the gender, number and person of the subject.

	Singular. Masc.	Singular. Fem.	Plural. Masc.	Plural. Fem.
1.	अबोँ	अब्यूँ	अबै or अब्	अबै or अब्
2.	अबेस् or अबे	अबिस् or अबी	अबह् or अब	अब्यू or अब्
3.	ई	ई	इहैँ	इहैँ

With the part. termin. इब् precisely similar suff. are formed; thus इबोँ m., इब्यूँ f., etc. As to the manner of adding them to the root, see § 308.

Note: Optionally the masc. termin. may be used with a fem. subj. — Occasionally this tense is used in the sense of the imperative.

509. *Affinities and Derivation.* The fut. is formed in six different ways in Gḍ., the distinguishing marks of which are the following consonants: 1) ह्, 2) स् or श्, 3) ब् or व् or म्, 4) ल् or न्, 5) ग्, 6) द्. — 1) The first two types are derived from the old Skr. and Pr. fut. In Skr. the fut. is formed by the suff. इष्य (i. e., स्य with the connecting vowel इ), which changes in Pr. either to इस्स (Mg. इश्श) or to इहि or इह (Vr. 7, 12—15. H. C. 3, 166—169, see also Wb. Bh. 431. Ls. 349—353). The Pr. इहि or इह becomes in Gḍ. इहि or इह or अह, and the fut. of this ह-*type* is preserved in O. H., W. H., and the 3. sg. and pl. of the E. H. Thus 3. sg. Skr. पठिष्यति *he will read,* Pr. (a) पढिहिइ or (b) *पढिहइ, whence O. H. (b) पढ़िहइ or पढ़िहहि (with euph. ह् §§ 69. 503, 1, p. 345), Br. पढ़िहै, Mw. (a) पढ़ही, E. H. पढ़ी (contracted for *पढ़िई for *पढ़िही); 3. pl. Skr. पठिष्यन्ति *they will read,* Pr. (a) पढिहिंति or (b) *पढिहंति, whence O. H. (b) पढ़िहहिं, Br. and E. H. पढ़िहैं, Mw. (a) पढही (for *पढहीँ). The forms of the 2. sg. and pl. of this type also occur in E. H., but only in the sense of the precative (§ 498). — 2) The Pr. इस्स becomes in Gḍ. ईस् or अस् (or ईश् or अश्), and the fut. of this स-*type* is preserved in O. P. (see Tr. A. Gth. CXXVI), Mw. and G. Thus 1. sg. Skr. पठिष्यामि, Pr. (a) पढिस्सामि (H. C. 3, 167) or (b) पढिस्सं (H. C. 3, 169) *I shall read,* O. P. (a) पढ़सा, Mw. पढ़िसूँ (= Ap. Pr. *पढिस्सउं), G. (b) पढ़ीश्; again 3. sg. Skr. पठिष्यति *he will read,* Pr. पढिस्सइ, O. P. पढ़सी, Mw. पढ़सी, G. पढ़शे. — The remaining four types of the fut. are purely Gḍ. formations; thus 3) the fut. of the ब-*type* is confined to the E. Gḍs. and is made by adding to the fut. part. the personal suff. of the old pres. ind. (§ 503), exactly on the same model as in the case of the second preterite (see § 505). In O. the ब् or व् may be changed to म् (see § 134, note). Thus 1. sg. masc. E. H. पढ़बों *I shall read,* B. पढ़िब (S. Ch. 146), O. पढ़िबि or पढ़िमि (Sn. 28); fem. E. H. पढ़ब्यूँ, B. and O. like masc. In B. and O. the 3. sg. and pl. also are of the ब्-type, while in E. H. they are of the ह-type (see Nro. 1); thus 3. pl. B. पढ़िबेग्, O. पढ़िबे or पढ़िमे, but E. H.

पढ़िहैं. A tense of the ब्-type also exists in M. and G.; but it is used as a pres. conj., not as a fut. indic. Moreover it is constructed passively (see § 496, p. 333). Thus M. म्यॉं छोड़वा (Man. 73), G. मारे छोड़वो (Ed. 54) *I may loose* (lit. *by me he may be loosed*) = E. H. मैं छोड़ब्यो *I shall loose.* There is apparently in Pr. an instance of a fut. (or imper.) of this type, mentioned by Ls. 422, देव्वु *you will give* or *give ye*; the same in E. H. would be देब *deba.* — 4) The fut. of the ल्-*type* exists only in M., Mw. and N. (incl. Gw. and Km.) and 5) that of the ग्-*type* only in Br. (incl. Kn.), H. H. and P. Both types are formed on the same principle, viz. by respectively adding the past part. ऐल (wk. f.) or ऐलो (st. f.) *come* and गयो (or गया) *gone* to the old pres. indic. (= habit. past in M., and pres. conj. in the others, see § 496) and, for this purpose, curtailing ऐल् and ऐलो to इल् or ल् and लो respectively and contracting गयो to गो (or गया to गा). M. uses the weak form इल् or ल्, Mw. the strong form लो, and N. either of the two. Moreover, N. sometimes adds the personal suff. of the old pres. (§ 503) or the auxil. verb हुँ *I am* (e. g., पढूँनेहूँ *we shall read*); on the other hand M. omits the part. ल in the 1. pl. (e. g., पढूँ *we shall read*). Lastly in both M. and N. the characteristic ल् is sometimes changed to न्. A tense of the ल्-type exists also in E. H., but it expresses the pres. indic. (see § 500). Similarly the auxil. verb हूँ *I am* forms in Br., Kn. and P. a tense of the ग्-type with the sense of the pres. indic. (Kl. 200. 197, 367). Thus 3. sg. masc. पढ़े-ल् or -लो = M. पढ़ेल्, Mw. पढ़ैलो, N. पढ़ला (with पढ़ for पढ़े, cf. § 501, 1, footnote, p. 342) *he will read,* but E. H. पढ़ैला *he reads*; fem. M. पढ़ेल्, Mw. पढ़ैली, N. पढ़ली *she will read,* but E. H. पढ़ैले *she reads*; or 3. pl. masc. M. पढ़ति + इल् = पढ़तील्, Mw. पढैला, N. पढला‍न् (st. f.) or पढ़लन् (wk. f.) or पढ़नन् (= पढ़ + ल or ला + न्) *they will read*; fem. M. पढ़तील्, Mw. पढ़ैली, N. पढ़लीन् (st. f.) or पढ़लन् or पढ़नन् (wk. f.). Again 3. sg. masc. पढ़ै + गो = Br. पढ़ैगो, H. H. and P. पढ़ेगा *he will read*; fem. Br. पढ़ैगी, H. H. and P. पढ़ेगी; or 3. pl. masc. Br. पढ़ैंगे, H. H. पढ़ेंगे, P. पढ़णगे *they will read*; fem. Br. पढ़ैंगी, H. H. पढ़ेंगी, P. पढ़णगीआँ, etc. But 3. sg. Kn. हैगो, P.

हैगा *he is,* 3. pl. Kn. हैँगे, P. हनगे *they are*; fem. sg. Kn. and P. हैगी, pl. Kn. हैँगी, P. हनगीआँ; P. has optionally है *he is,* हन् *they are*; H. H. has है, हैँ, etc.; but fut. H. H. होगा m., होगी f. *he (she) will be,* pl. होँगे m., होँगी f. *they will be,* Kn. होएगा, होएँगे m., °गी f.; P. होवेगा, होणगे m., °गी, °गीआँ f., etc. Literally, these futures mean: पढ़ैगो *he is gone (that) he may read,* पढ़ैल् or पढ़ैलो *he is come (that) he may read,* etc., compare the English: *he is going* (or *coming*) *to read.* — 6) The fut. of the द्-*type* is confined to S., and is formed by adding to the pres. part. in अंदु or इंदु the same termin., as are used for the first pret. indic. (see § 503, 3. 5). Thus 1. sg. masc. हलंदु + सि = S. हलंदुसि, fem. हलंदिअसि *I shall go*; 2. sg. masc. हलंदेँ, fem. हलंदिएँ or हलंदिआँ; 3. sg. masc. हलंदो, fem. हलंदी. This fut. lit. means: *I may be reading,* etc. — 7) I subjoin a comparative table of terminations:

Singular.

	G.	Mw.	Br.	E. H.	B.	O.
1.	ईश्	असूँ or अहूँ	इहौँ	अबोँ or इबोँ	इब	इबि
2.	अशे	असो or अही	इहै	अबेस् or इबेस्	इबि	इबु
3.	अशे	असी or अही	इहै	ई	इबे	इब्

	Br.	H. H.	P.	M.	N.	S.
1.	औँगो	ऊँगा	आँगा	एन्	ऊँला or अनेछु	अंदुसि
2.	ऐगो	एगा	एँगा	असील्	अलास् or अनस्	अंदेँ
3.	ऐगो	एगा	एगा	एल्	अला or अनेछ	अंदो

Plural.

	G.	Mw.	Br.	E. H.	B.	O.
1.	ईशूँ	असाँ or अहाँ	इहैँ	अबै or इबै	इब	इबा
2.	अशो	असो or अहो	इहौ	अबह् or इबह्	इबा	इब
3.	अशे	असी or अही	इहैँ	इहैँ	इबेन्	इबे

	Br.	H. H.	P.	M.	N.	S.
1.	ऐँगे	एँगे	आँगे	ऊँ	ऊँला or ऊँनेछूँ	अंदासीँ
2.	औगे	ओगे	ओगे	आल्	अलउ or उनेछौ	अंदउ
3.	ऐँगे	ऐँगे	अणगे	अतील्	अलान or अनन्	अंदा

In the fem. sing., Br., H. H., P., N. final ओ or आ changes to ई, as Br. औँगी, P. आँगी, etc.; plur. Br., H. H., N. ए or आ

changes to ई, and P. ए to ईआँ, as Br. ऐंगो, N. ऊँलो, P. अँगोआँ, etc. For the E. H. fem. form see § 508. S. has fem. sg. 1. अंदिअमि, 2. अंदिएँ or अंदिआँ, 3. अंदी; pl. 1. अंदिऊसीं, 2. and 3. अंदिऊँ. In the rest, the forms are com. gen.

3. PERIPHRASTIC TENSES.

510. Ten additional tenses are made in E. H., by adding the pres. indic. or conj., or the pret. indic. or conj., or the fut. indic. of an auxil. verb to the pres. part. in अत् (§ 298) or to the past part. in अल् (§ 302). These tenses are the following:

1) The *definite* or *durative present indicative*, made by adding the auxil. pres. indic. to the pres. part.; as पढ़त् आटै or पढ़त् हौवै *he is reading.*

2) The *future conditional*, made by adding the auxil. pres. conj. to the pres. part.; as पढ़त् होय् *(if) he be reading.*

3) The *definite preterite* or the *perfect indicative*, made by adding the auxil. pres. indic. to the past part.; as पढ़ले आटै or पढ़ले हौवै *he has read.*

4) The *future exact conditional*, made by adding the auxil. pres. conj. to the past part.; as पढ़ले होय *(if) he have read.*

5) The *durative* or *habitual preterite* or the *imperfect indicative*, made by adding the auxil. pret. indic. to the pres. part.; as पढ़त् रहल् *he was reading.*

6) The *durative present conditional*, made by adding the auxil. pret. conj. to the pres. part.; as पढ़त् होतै *(if) he were reading.*

7) The *pluperfect indicative*, made by adding the auxil. pret. indic. to the past part.; as पढ़ले रहल् *he had read.*

8) The *preterite conditional*, made by adding the auxil. pret. conj. to the past part.; as पढ़ले होतै *(if) he had read.*

9) The *durative future indicative* or *present dubitative*, made by adding the auxil. fut. indic. to the pres. part.; as पढ़त् होई *he will be reading.*

10) The *future exact indicative* or *preterite dubitative,* made by adding the auxil. fut. indic. to the past part.; as पढ़ले होई *he will have read.*

Note: For the purpose of expressing the *present conditional* the pret. conj. (§ 506) is used. Thus पढ़तै *(if) he read.* This completes the series of tenses of the condit. mood, which is merely a special application of the conj.

511. If the verb is a trans. one, the termin. of the past part. assumes the form अले, instead of अल्, in the formation of the additional tenses; but if the verb is intrans. the termin. is अल्, as usual; e. g., trans. पढ़ले बाटों *I have read,* but intr. रहल् बाटों *I have remained.* The termin. of the part. never suffers any change; but that of the auxil. verb changes in agreement with the number, person and (where possible) gender of the subj.; thus 1. sg. masc. पढ़त् बाटों, fem. पढ़त् बायूँ *I am reading*; 3. pl. masc. पढ़ले होवैं, fem. पढ़ले हईं *they have read.*

Note: The form in अले is really the adv. part. (see § 488), i. e., the loc. or obl. form of the past part. Thus पढ़ले बाटों means lit., *on having read I am.* Similarly B. uses the adv. pres. part.; e. g., B. पढ़िते छि lit. *on reading I am,* i. e., *I am reading*; B. पढ़िते छिलाम् lit. *on reading I was,* i. e., *I was reading.*

512. *Affinities.* Periphrastic tenses exist in all Gḍs. and are made in the same way as in E. H. But while B., O. and, in the case of the past part. of trans. verbs, E. H. add the auxil. verb to the adv. part. (S. Ch. 135. 194. Sn. 30. 31, see § 511, note), N. and, generally, E. H. add it to the weak, H. H., P., G., S. to the strong, and W. H. to either form of the adj. part. (see Ld. 37 etc. Ed. 54 etc. Tr. 316 etc. Kl. 167 etc.). Again M. adds it to the weak or strong form of the adj. part. or to one of the ordinary tenses (Man. 92—96), somewhat analogous to the formation of the pres. indic. in E. H. and the W. Gḍs. (see § 501, 1). They also vary as to the particular auxil. verb which they employ (see §§ 513. 514). Thus 3. sg. masc. pres. definite: O. पढ़ु अछइ *he is reading,* B. पढ़िते छे or प° आछे; but E. H.

पऱ्हत् ब्राटै or होवै, N. पढ्दू छ, Gw. पढ्दू or पढ्दो छ, Br. पढ्तु or पढ्तो है, Mw. पढ्तो है, H. H. पढ्ता है, P. पढ्दा है, S. पढंदो ग्राहे, G. पढ्तो होयछे; again M. पढ्त् ग्राहे or पढ्तो ग्राहे or पढ्त् ग्रसतो (Man. 93, 1. 2. 3); fem. O., B., E. H., N. like masc.; Gw. पढ्दू or पढ दी छ, Br. पढ्ति or पढ्ती है, H. H. पढ्ती है, P. पढ दी है, S. पढंदी ग्राहे, G. पढ्ती होयछे, M. पढ्त् ग्राहे or पढ्ती ग्राहे or पढ्त् ग्रसती.

513. The auxil. verbs which are employed to form the periphrastic tenses are the following: 1) ग्राटै or बाटै *he is*, 2) रहल् *he was* and 3) हौवै *he is*. The verb ग्राटै is defective; there exists only the pres. indic. The verb रहल् is the ordinary second pret. indic. of the regular verb रहब् *to remain*; but it is used as the past tense of the defective ग्राटै. The verb हौवै is a regular verb with a complete conjugation, from which the remainder of the defective tenses of the verb ग्राटै are supplied. Examples see in § 510.

Note 1: When the past tense रहल् is used as an auxil. verb, it expresses past action generally, „he was", precisely like था in H. H. But according to circumstances, it may retain its ordinary meaning „he remained", as the past tense of रहब् *to remain*, and express past action as enduring, precisely like रहा in H. H. Thus E. H. कहल् रहल् *he had said* = H. H. कहा था, or *he remained saying, he kept saying* = H. H. कहा रहा.

Note 2: The past tense भइल् or भयल् of the verb होब् *to be* is never used as a mere auxil. verb, but always has its full meaning „he became", and expresses the commencement and continuation of an action (§ 538, g). Thus E. H. कहत भयल् *he began saying*, but कहत् रहल् *he was saying*. The corresponding Gd. forms are: W. H. भयौ (auxil. थौ), M. झाला (aux. होता or ग्रसे), G. हवो (aux. हतो).

514. *Affinities and Derivation.* The various verbs which are used as auxiliaries in Gḍ. are the following: 1) The verb ग्राटै. It occurs as a defective auxil. in E. H. and B.; in both only in the pres. indic.; but in M. and S. it is a *principal* verb with a complete conjugation, and is used to form compound verbs; viz.,

M. वाटणें to appear (Man. 92; in W. H. in the denom. form वताणें), S. वतणु to continue (Tr. 344). It is derived from the Skr. R. वृत्, Pr. वत् or वट्. The B. pres. indic. (sg. 1. वटि, 2. वटिस्, 3. वटे; pl. 1. वटि, 2. वट, 3. वटेन्) is, as usual, identical with the old Pr. pres. indic. (see § 501, 4). Thus 3. sg. Skr. वर्त्तते, Pr. वट्टइ, B. वटे. From the other Pr. form वत्तइ comes the E. H. बाए् (for बाइ) or बा by the elision of त (§ 153). As regards the other E. H. forms बाटे, बाटा, etc. which are different for the two genders, it is more probable that they are denominatives, made by adding the personal suff. of the old pres. indic. (§ 503, 1, p. 345) to the part. Skr. वृत्त, P. वट्ट (H. C. 2, 29) *existing* (of R. वृत्). Thus 1. sg. masc. Skr. वृत्तोऽस्मि, Pr. वट्ट म्हि, Ap. Pr. *वट्टउं, E. H. बाटों *I am*; fem. Skr. (st. f.) वृत्तिकास्मि, Pr. वट्टिआम्हि, Ap. Pr. *वट्टिअम्हि or *वट्टिअउं, E. H. बाधूँ, etc. — 2) The verb रहब् is used only in E. H. as an auxil., and only in the 2nd pret. indic. Otherwise it is in E. H. as well as in all other Gds. a regular principal verb, „to remain". It is commonly (in E. H., W. H., P., S.) used to make a kind of (continuative) compound verb (see § 538, b). — 3) The verb होइब् *to be* occurs in E. H. as well as in all other Gds., both as an auxiliary and as a principal, with a complete conjugation. It is derived from the Skr. R. भू; thus 3. sg. pres. conj. E. H. होए्, Pr. होइ or हवइ (H. C. 4, 60), Skr. भवति. As an auxil., however, it has in E. H. a special pres. indic., which is made by adding the personal suff. of the old pres. indic. (§ 503, 1) to the part. Skr. भूत, Pr. हविअ (§ 307, 7) *being* or *been*. Thus 1. sg. masc. Skr. भूतोऽस्मि, Pr. हविअम्हि, Ap. Pr. *हविअउं, E. H. हउओं or होओं or हौवों (§§ 122. 69. 28); fem. Skr. भूतास्मि, Pr. हविआम्हि, Ap. Pr. *हविअउं, E. H. हउउँ or हयूँ (§ 123) *I am*, etc. On the other hand, as a principal verb, it has a regular pres. indic. होलों *I am*, etc. (see § 500). There is in E. H. a peculiar pleonastic form of this verb, which may be used optionally for its simple form, both when it is an auxil. and when it is a principal. It is made by adding the increment ख to the root हो; and the pleon. R. होख, thus made, is conjugated regularly.

Thus infin. होखब् *to be*; pres. indic. 2. sg. masc. होखेलेग् or °ले, fem. होखैलिस् or °ली; 2. pl. masc. होखैलह् or °ल, fem. °ल्यू, etc. (see § 517). There is also a peculiar negative form of this verb, which exists, however, only in the pres. tense and is the same for all three moods. It also shows the peculiar increment ख; thus 3. sg. masc. नैखै *he is not*, fem. नैखे or नैखो *she is not*, etc. (see § 518)[1]. The origin of these forms is obscure. Perhaps they are derived from the Skr. R. भू by means of the inchoative suff. च्छ or स्क. Just as the R. अस् *to be* forms in Pr. an inchoative अच्छ (= अच्छ = अस्क), so the R. भू or Pr. हुव or हव or हो (cf. H. C. 4, 60) might form in Pr. an inchoative *हुवक्ख or *हवक्ख or *होक्ख (= भुच्छ or भुस्क), in E. H. होख. The negative form नैख appears to have arisen by incorporating the negative particle न *not*. There are similar negative verbal forms in M., see Nro. 4. — 4) The verb अहै or आहे or है *he is*. It occurs in the S. Gḍ., N. Gḍ. and W. Gḍ. (exc. G.), but not in the E. Gḍ. (exc. Bs.); and it exists only in the pres. indic. (see Man. 88. Tr. 300. Kl. 201. Ld. 25), as shown in the following table:

Singular.

	O. H.	Bs.	M.	S.	Br.	Mw.	P.	N.	H. H.
1.	अहउँ or हौँ	अहेउँ or हौँ	आहेँ	आहियाँ	हौँ	हूँ	हाँ	हुँ	हूँ
2.	अहसि or अहहि or है	अहेस् or अहे	आहेस्	आहेँ or आहीँ	है	है	हैँ	हस्?	है
3.	अहइ or अहै or आहि	अहै	आहे	आहे	है	है	है	ह?	है

Plural.

	O. H.	Bs.	M.	S.	Br.	Mw.	P.	N.	H. H.
1.	अहहिँ or हहिँ	अही	आहीँ	आहियूँ	हैँ	हाँ	हाँ	हूँ?	हैँ
2.	अहहु or हहु	अहहू or अहो or अहेँ	आहाँ	आहियो	हो	हो	हो	हौ	हो
3.	अहहिँ or हहिँ or आहैँ	अहेन् or अहैँ	आहेन्	आहिनि or आहीनि	हैँ	है	हन् or हैन्	हुन्	हैँ

---

1) Beames in J. R. A. S. III, 495 mentions a negative form नाखे *he is not* and an affirmative खे *he is*, and Kl. 199, 373 follows him. But my authorities deny the existence of either form.

The origin of this auxil. verb is uncertain. It is commonly identified with the Skr. R. अस् *to be* (e. g., Tr. 300. 304). This view must assume a change of स् to ह्, and also a change of class; for the Skr. R. अस् is of the II. cl., while the Gḍ. verb is of the VI. cl.; e. g., 1. sg. O. H. अहउँ represents a Skr. form *असामि, Pr. *अहमि, Ap. *अहउं (see H. C. 4, 385); or Gḍ. अहै = Skr. *असति, Pr. *अहइ. None of the Pr. gramm., however, as for as I am aware, notice any such change in the R. अस्. There would be also a difficulty in accounting for the initial आ in M. and S. On the whole, therefore, I am inclined to identify this Gḍ. auxil. verb with the pres. indic. of the R. भू *to be*. This root may become in Pr. हुव (H. C. 4, 60) and in Gḍ. हु; thus 3. sg. Skr. भवति, Pr. हुवइ, Mw. हुै (Kl. 232). The form हुै would easily become है. On the other hand, instead of suppressing अ, it (or rather हू, see § 132) may be transposed; thus the Pr. R. हुव might become in Gḍ. अहु and thence आह, with आ as compensation for the elided व्; e. g., 3. sg. Pr. हुवइ = *अहुइ = Bs. अहै or M. आहे, etc. It may be observed, that the Skr. 3. pl. भवंति is even in Ap. Pr. contracted to भंति or हुंति (H. C. 4, 406. 416), which would regularly become हैं in W. H. (see § 497, 2. f, p. 337). The M. possesses a negative form of this verb. It is defective, occuring only in the pres. ind.; viz., sing. 1. नाहीँ, 2. नाहीँस्, 3. नाहीँ; plur. 1. नाहीँ, 2. नाहीँ, 3. नाहीँत्. There is an other defective negative verb in M., which occurs only in the pres. and pret. indic.; viz., *pres.* sing. 1. नव्हेँ, 2. नव्हेस् or नव्हस्, 3. नव्हे; plur. 1. नव्होँ or नव्हे, 2. नव्हाँ or नव्हेत्, 3. नव्हेत् or नव्हत्; *pret.* sing. masc. 1. नव्हतोँ, 2. नव्हतास्, 3. नव्हता; plur. 1. नव्हतोँ, 2. नव्हताँ, 3. नव्हते. See Man. 88. 89. This negative form, however, really belongs to the verb होइबा (M. होणेँ), see Nro. 3. Besides M. has a complete negative form of the verb असणेँ (see Nro. 5), which is made by changing the initial अ to न; e. g., inf. नसणेँ; 1. sg. pres. ind. नसतोँ *I am not*, from असतोँ *I am*, etc. See Man. 89. — 5) The verb अछइ or अछे or छे *he is*. It occurs in the S. Gḍ. and N. Gḍ., in all W. Gḍs. (exc. Br.), and in all E. Gḍs. (exc. Bh.

and Bs.). In M. it has a complete conjugation (Man. 84—86), even in a negative form, see Nro. 4; in B., Mth., Mw., P., Km. it exists in the pres. and pret. tenses; and the rest have it only in the pres. tense. In S. even the pres. is fragmentary. In M., P. and S., छ is changed to स् (see § 11). In B., though छ is written, स् is commonly pronounced, see footnote on p. 349. The following comparative table shows the various forms of this auxil. verb:

	O.		B.		Mth.	N.	Km.	Mw.	G.	P.	S.	M.
	Present. **Singular.**											
1.	अछि	or छि	आछि	or छि	छी	छुँ	छूँ	छूँ	छुँ	साँ	सि	असें
2.	अछु	छु	आछिस्	छिस्	छें	छस्	छै	छै	छे	सो	—	असस्
3.	अछइ	छइ	आछे	छे	अछि	छ	छ	छै	छे	सो	—	असे
	Plural.											
1.	अछुँ	छुँ	आछि	छि	छी	छूँ	छों	छाँ	छैये	साँ	सों or सूँ	असूँ
2.	अछ	छ	आछ	छ	छी	छौ	छा	छो	छो	सो?	—	असाँ
3.	अछंति	छंति	आछेन्	छेन्	छथि	छन्	छन्	छै	छे	सण्	—	असत्
	Preterite. **Singular.**											
1.	desunt		आछिलाम्	छिलाम्	छलों	desunt	छियो	छो	desunt	सा	desunt	असलों m., °लें f., °लों n.
2.			आछिले	छिले	छलें		छियो	छो		सा		असलास् m., °लीस् f., °लेंस् n.
3.			आछिल्	छिल्	छल्		छियो	छो		सा		असला m., °ली f., °लें n.
	Plural.											
1.	desunt		आछिलाम्	छिलाम्	छलों	desunt	छिया	छा	desunt	से	desunt	असलों c. g.
2.			आछिलेन्	छिलेन्	छलों		छिया	छा		से		असलाँ c. g.
3.			आछिलेन्	छिलेन्	छलाह्		छिया	छा		से		असले m., °ल्या f., °लीं n.

The forms of the pres. have assumed in M. and P. the sense of the (habit.) past (see § 496); thus M. असें, P. साँ *I was* (Man. 84. Ld. 25). The forms of the pret. sg. Km. छिया, Mw. छो, P. सा are masc. and change in the fem. to छी and सी; they are really past part.; those of B. and Mth. are of com. gen. and made according to the 2nd pret. ind. (see § 505). In M. the pres. ind. (also used as pres. conj.) is असतों, etc. (conjug. regularly, see § 501, 3. 5); the pres. conj. असावा, etc. (see § 496); the imper. असूँ, etc. (see § 496); the fut. असेन्, etc. (see § 509, 4. 7). I have observed in N. the 2. sg. fut. छेनस् = M. असशोल् (see § 509, 4. 7). The infin. is in M. असूँ or असणें (see § 313. 314); the pres. part. असत् (see § 486); the adv. part. असताँ, which I have also found in N. as छंदा *on being* (see § 489). — This verb also exists in Pr. (H. C. 4, 215. Ls. 346); e. g., 3. sg. अच्छइ *he is*, etc. The R. अच्छ (= अत्त or अस्क) is probably an inchoative form of the R. अस् *to be* or (according to some MSS. of H. C.) आस् *to dwell, exist.* — The only remnant of the original R. अस् which has survived in Gḍ. is the S. 3. sg. and pl. अथ = Pr. अत्थि, Skr. अस्ति. It is, however, used only in conjunction with pronom. suff. (Tr. 349), as अथमि *it is* or *they are to me.* Even in Pr., अत्थि is used for both numbers and all three persons (H. C. 3, 148); e. g., अत्थि अहं *I am*, अत्थि अम्हे *we are*, etc. — 6) The verb थाए or थिए *he is.* It occurs only in the W. Gḍ. and O. In G. and S. it has a complete conj. (see Ed. 72—81. Tr. 305—312). In the others it exists only in the pret. indic. tense (or past part., see Su. 26. Ld. 25. Kl. 200), as shown in the following comparative table:

Preterite. Singular.

	O.	Naip.	S.	Kn.
1.	थेलि c. g.	थियें or थें c. g.	थिउसे m., थिअसे f.	थो m., थी f.
2.	थेलु c. g.	थियेस् or थिस् c. g.	थिएँ m., थिअाँ f.	थो m., थी f.
3.	थेला c. g.	थियो or थ्यो m., थिई f.	थिओ m., थी f.	थो m., थी f.

	H. H.	P.	G.
1.	था m., थी f.	था m., थी f.	थयो m., थयी f., थयुँ n.
2.	था m., थी f.	था m., थी f.	थयो m., थयी f., थयुँ n.
3.	था m., थी f.	था m., थी f.	थयो m., थयी f., थयुँ n.

Preterite. Plural.

	O.	Naip.	S.	Kn.
1.	थेलुँ c. g.	थिऊँ or थ्यूँ c. g.	थिआसो m., थिऊँसो f.	थे m., थो f.
2.	थेल c. g.	थियौ or थ्यौ c. g.	थिअउ m., थिऊँ f.	थे m., थो f.
3.	थेले c. g.	थिये or थे c. g.	थिआ m., थिऊँ f.	थे m., थो f.

	H. H.	P.	G.
1.	थे m., थी f.	थे m., थीआँ f.	थया m., थयी f., थयाँ n.
2.	थे m., थी f.	थे m., थीआँ f.	थया m., थयी f., थयाँ n.
3.	थे m., थो f.	थे m., थीआँ f.	थया m., थयी f., थयाँ n.

The pres. conj. is: 1. sg. G. थाउँ, S. थिआँ; 2. sg. G. थाय्, S. थिएँ or थोँ; 3. sg. G. थाय्, S. थिए; 1. pl. G. थये or थैये, S. थिऊँ; 2. pl. G. थाओ, S. थिओ; 3. pl. G. थाय, S. थिअन् or थोन्. The pres. indic. is in G. थाउँ छुँ, etc., S. थिआँ थो, etc. (see § 501, 1. 5); the fut. indic. in G. थैश्, etc., S. थींदुसे, etc. (see § 509, 2. 6. 7); the imper. G. था or थाजे, etc., S. थीउ or थोजे, etc. (see §§ 497. 499); the infin. in G. थवुँ, S. थिअणु; the part. pres. in G. थतो, S. थींदो; the adv. part. in G. थते or थताँ, S. थींदे. — The original of this verb appears to be the Skr. R. स्था *stand, exist,* which in Pr. becomes ठा or था (H. C. 4, 16); e. g., 3. sg. Pr. ठाइ (H. C. 4, 436) or थाइ, G. थाय्; 3. pl. Pr. थंति (H. C. 4, 395) or *थाहिं (cf. H. C. 4, 382), G. थाय्. The S. थिअणु *to be* is derived from the R. स्था, just as S. पिअणु *to drink,* from R. पा, S. डिअणु *to give,* from R. दा; i. e., it is founded on a reduplicated radical form *स्थित (for the ordinary Skr. तिष्ठ), analogous to पिव, दद.

THIRTH CHAPTER. CONJUGATION.

1. THE DEFECTIVE AUXILIATY VERB.

515. There is only a pres. tense; the pret. is supplied from the verb रह्व् *to remain* and the rest from the complete auxil. verb होव् *to be* (see §§ 513. 516).

a) Present tense: *I am*, etc.

	Sing. Masc.	Fem.	Plur. Masc.	Fem.
1.	आटोँ[1])	आयूँ	आटी	आटी
2.	आटेस् or आटे	आटिस् or आटी	आटह् or आट	आयू
3.	आटै or आय् or आ	आटै or आय् or आ	आटैँ	आटीँ

b) Preterite tense: *I was*, etc.

	Sing. Masc.	Fem.	Plur. Masc.	Fem.
1.	रहलोँ	रहल्यूँ	रहलो	रहली
2.	रहलेस् or रहले	रहलिस् or रहली	रहलह् or रहल	रहल्यू
3.	रहल्	रहल्	रहलेन् or रहलैँ	रहलिन् or रहलीँ

2. THE WEAK COMPLETE AUXILIARY VERB.

516. This verb is complete with the exception of the pret., which is supplied from the verb रहब् *to remain, to dwell*; see § 513, note 2.

Indicative mood.

a) Present tense: *I am*, etc.

	Sing. Masc.	Fem.	Plur. Masc.	Fem.
1.	होवों[2])	हयूँ	हई	हई
2.	होवे	होवी	होवह् or होव	हयू
3.	होवै or हो	होवै or हो	होवैँ	हईँ

b) Preterite tense: *I was*, etc.

This is the same as the pret. of the def. auxil. verb; see § 515, b.

c) Future tense: *I shall be*, etc.

	Sing. Masc. and Fem.	Plur. Masc. and Fem.
1.	होबोँ or होइबोँ	होबै or होइबै or होब् or होइब्
2.	होबेस् or होइबेस् or होबे or होइबे[3])	होबह or होइबह् or होब or होइब
3.	होई	होइहैँ

---

1) Throughout, the initial consonant may optionally be व् *v* or ब् *b*, and in the low forms of E. H. the medial cons. may be ड़् or ड़् (§ 145).

2) The masc. form may throughout be used also as fem.

3) Fem. also: होबिस् or होबी or होइबिस् or होइबी.

Conjunctive mood.

d) Present tense: *I be*, etc.

	Sing. Masc. and Fem.	Plur. Masc. and Fem.
1.	होँहुँ	होँइँ
2.	हो	होह् or हो
3.	होय	होँय्

e) Preterite tense: *I were*, etc.

	Sing. Masc.	Fem.	Plur. Masc.	Fem.
1.	होतोँ or होत्योँ	होत्यूँ	होइत्	होइत्
2.	होतेस् or होते	होतिस् or होतो	होतह् or होत	होत्यू
3.	होत् or होतै	होत् or होतै	होतेन् or हेतैँ	होतिन् or होतोँ

Imperative mood.

f) Present tense: *let me be*, etc.; the same as pres. conj.

3. THE STRONG COMPLETE AUXILIARY VERB.

517. This verb is conjugated regularly throughout; see § 514, 3.

Indicative mood.

a) Present tense: *I am*, etc.

	Sing. Masc.	Fem.	Plur. Masc.	Fem.
1.	होखँलोँ	होखँल्यूँ	होखोला	होखोला
2.	होखँलेस् or °ले	होखँलिस or °लो	होखँलह् or °ल	होखँल्यू
3.	होखँला	होखँले	होखँलैँ	होखँलोँ

b) First preterite: *I was*, etc.

	Sing. Masc. and Fem.	Plur. Masc. and Fem.
1.	होख्योँ	होखा
2.	होखिस्	होख्यू
3.	होखिस्	होखिन्

Or: Second preterite.

	Sing. Masc.	Fem.	Plur. Masc.	Fem.
1.	होखलोँ	होखल्यूँ	होखलो	होखलो
2.	होखलेस् or °ले	होखलिस् or °लो	होखलह् or °ल	होखल्यू
3.	होखल्	होखल्	होखलैँ	होखलोँ

c) Future tense: *I shall be*, etc.

	Sing. Masc.	Fem.	Plur. Masc.	Fem.
1.	होखब्योँ [1])	होखब्यूँ	होखब् or °ब्यै	होखब् or °ब्यै
2.	होखब्येस् or °ब्ये	होखब्यिस् or ब्यी	होखबह् or °ब	होखब्यू
3.	होखी	होखी	होखिहैं	होखिहैं

Conjunctive mood.

d) Present tense: *I be*, etc.

	Sing. Masc. and Fem.	Plur. Masc. and Fem.
1.	होखों	होखीं
2.	होखु	होखह् or होख
3.	होखें	होखैं

e) Preterite tense: *I were*, etc.

	Sing. Masc.	Fem.	Plur. Masc.	Fem.
1.	होखतों or °त्यों	होखत्यूँ	होखती or °खित्	होखती or °खित्
2.	होखतेस् or °ते	होखतिस् or °ती	होखतह् or °त	होखत्यू
3.	होखतै or °त्	होखतै or °त्	होखतैं	होखतीं

Imperative mood.

f) Present: *let me be*, etc. Like the pres. conj.

Precative forms: 2. sg. होखिहे, 2. pl. होखिह or होखी.

g) Periphrastic tenses.

These are formed like those of the regular active verb पढ़ब *to read*, see § 521; e. g., मैं होखत् बाटों *I am being*, etc.

Participles.

Adjectival: pres. होखत् *being*, past होखल् *been*.

Conjunctive: होखे के *having been*.

Adverbial: pres. होखते or होखतै *on being*, past होखले *on having been*.

Infinitives.

Nom. होखब् *to be*, acc. होखे के or होखवे के, etc.

4. THE DEFECTIVE NEGATIVE AUXILIARY VERB.

518. This verb exists only in the present tense of the three moods; see § 514, 3.

1) Or: होखिबों, होखिब्येस्, etc.

a) Present indicative: *I am not*, etc.

	Sing. Masc.	Fem.	Plur. Masc.	Fem.
1.	नैखोँ or नैखूँ	नैख्यूँ [1])	नैखो	नैखी
2.	नैखेस् or नैखे	नैखिस् or नैखो	नैखह् or नैख	नैख्यू [1])
3.	नैखै	नैखी [1])	नैखैँ	नैखीँ [1])

b) Pres. conj. and imp. like the pres. indic.

5. THE REGULAR ACTIVE VERB.

519. There is only one conjugation. With the exception of a very few irregular verbs (see §§ 525—527), all verbs, whether ending in a consonant or a vowel, are conjugated precisely alike. One example, therefore, of an active verb, fully conjugated, is sufficient. For the sake of convenience, however, a list of the first persons sing. and plur. of a few typical verbs will be added; the remainder to be supplied by the student. It may be noted, as a practical rule, that an euphonic semicons. may be added to any verb which ends with a vowel; viz. य् to verbs in ई, and व् to verbs in ऊ or ओ. Thus every verb may be made to have a consonantal termination; and after the required verbal form has been made, the euph. cons. may be again omitted; and the resultant form will be that of the verb as ending in a vowel.

520. The elements.

पढ्न् *to read*; root पढ्; bases पढत्, पढल्.

The radical and participial tenses.

Indicative mood.

a) Present tense: *I read*, etc.

	Sing. Masc.	Fem.	Plur. Masc.	Fem.
1.	पढैलोँ or °ल्योँ	पढैल्यूँ	पढोला	पढोला
2.	पढैलेस् or °ले	पढैलिस् or °लो	पढैलह् or °ल or °ल्यह्	पढैल्यू
3.	पढैला [2])	पढैले	पढैलेन् or पढैलैँ	पढैलिन् or °लोँ

1) Or like masc.

2) Or पढलोँ, पढलेस्, पढला, and so on throughout.

b) First preterite: *I read*, etc.

	Sing. Masc. and Fem.	Plur. Masc. and Fem.
1.	पढ्योॅ	पढा
2.	पढिस्	पढ्यौ
3.	पढिस्	पढिन्

Or second preterite: *I read*, etc.

	Sing. Masc.	Fem.	Plur. Masc.	Fem.
1.	पढलोॅ or °ल्योॅ	पढल्यूँ	पढलो	पढली
2.	पढले	पढलिस् or °ली	पढलह् or °ल or °ल्यह्	पढल्यू
3.	पढलेन्	पढलेस्	पढलेन् or °लैॅ	पढलिन् or °लीॅ

c) Future: *I shall read*, etc.

	Sing. Masc.	Fem.[1])	Plur. Masc.	Fem.
1.	पढ्बोॅ [2])	पढ्ब्यूँ	पढ्ब् or °बै	पढ्ब् or °बै
2.	पढ्बेस् or °बे	पढ्बिस् or °बी	पढ्बह् or °ब	पढ्ब्यू or °बू
3.	पढी	पढी	पढिहैॅ	पढिहैॅ

Conjunctive mood.

d) Present: *I read*, etc.

	Sing. Masc. and Fem.	Plur. Masc. and Fem.
1.	पढोॅ	पढोॅ
2.	पढु or पढ्	पढह् or पढ
3.	पढे	पढैॅ

e) Preterite: *I read*, etc.

	Sing. Masc.	Fem.	Plur. Masc.	Fem.
1.	पढतोॅ or °त्योॅ	पढत्यूँ	पढती or पढित्	पढती or पढित्
2.	पढतेस् or °ते	पढतिस् or °ती	पढतह् or °त or °त्यह्	पढत्यू
3.	पढत् or °तै	पढत् or °तै	पढतेन् or °तैॅ	पढतिन् or °तीॅ

Imperative mood.

f) Present: *let me read*, etc. Like pres. conj.

Precative forms: 2. sing. पढिहे, 2. plur. पढिह.

---

1) Throughout the masc. forms may be used for the fem.

2) Or पढिबोॅ, पढिबेस्, and so on throughout.

521. The periphrastic tenses.

Indicative mood.

g) Durative or definitive present: *I am reading*, etc.

	Sing. Masc.	Sing. Fem.[1]
1.	पढ़त् बाटोँ or प° होवोँ	पढ़त् बाटूँ or प° हयूँ
2.	पढ़त् बाटेस् or बाटे or होवे	पढ़त् बाटिस् or बाटी or होवी
3.	पढ़त् बाटै or बाय् or बा or होवै or हौ	पढ़त् बाटै or होवै etc.
	Plur. Masc.	**Plur. Fem.**
1.	पढ़त् बाटी or प° हई	पढ़त् बाटी or प° हई
2.	पढ़त् बाटह् or बाट or होवह् or होव	पढ़त् बाटू or हयू
3.	पढ़त् बाटैँ or होवैँ	पढ़त् बाटीँ or हईँ

h) Durative pret. or imperfect: *I was reading*, etc.

	Sing. Masc.	Sing. Fem.
1.	पढ़त् रहलोँ	पढ़त् रहलूँ
2.	पढ़त् रहलेस् or °ले	पढ़त् रहलिस् or °ली
3.	पढ़त् रहल्	पढ़त् रहल्
	Plur. Masc.	**Plur. Fem.**
1.	पढ़त् रहली	पढ़त् रहली
2.	पढ़त् रहलह् or °ल	पढ़त् रहल्यू
3.	पढ़त् रहलेन् or °लैँ	पढ़त् रहलिन् or °लीँ

i) Durative future: *I shall be reading*, etc.

	Sing. Masc. and Fem.	Plur. Masc. and Fem.
1.	पढ़त् होब्योँ or प° होखब्योँ[2]	पढ़त् होब्यै or प° होखब्यै
2.	पढ़त होब्येस् or प° होखब्येस्	पढ़त् होबह् or प° होखब्यह्
3.	पढ़त् होई or प° होखी	पढ़त् होइहैँ or प° होखिहैँ

k) Definite pret. or perfect: *I have read*, etc.

	Sing. Masc.	Sing. Fem.[1]
1.	पढ़ले बाटोँ or प° होवोँ	पढ़ले बाटूँ or हयूँ
2.	पढ़ले बाटेस् or बाटे or होवे	पढ़ले बाटिस् or बाटी or होवी
3.	पढ़ले बाटै or बाय् or बा or होवै or हौ	पढ़ले बाटै or होवै etc.

---

1) Optionally the masc. forms may be used for the fem.

2) Or प° होइब्योँ or प° होखिब्योँ, etc.; in fact any of the forms given in §§ 516, c. 517, c may be used.

	Plur. Masc.	Plur. Fem.
1.	पढ़ले बाटी or प° हई	पढ़ले बाटी or प° हई
2.	पढ़ले बाटह् or बाट or हौवह् or हौव	पढ़ले बाट्यू or ह्यू
3.	पढ़ले बाटैँ or हौवैँ	पढ़ले बाटीँ or हईं

l) Pluperfect: *I had read*, etc.

	Sing. Masc.	Sing. Fem.
1.	पढ़ले रहलोँ	पढ़ले रहल्यू
2.	पढ़ले रहलेस् or °ले	पढ़ले रहलिस् or °ली
3.	पढ़ले रहल्	पढ़ले रहल्

	Plur. Masc.	Plur. Fem.
1.	पढ़ले रहली	पढ़ले रहली
2.	पढ़ले रहलह् or °ल	पढ़ले रहल्यू
3.	पढ़ले रहलेन् or °लैँ	पढ़ले रहलिन् or °लीँ

m) Future exact: *I shall have read*, etc.

	Sing. Masc. and Fem.	Plur. Masc. and Fem.
1.	पढ़ले होब्योँ or प° होखब्योँ	पढ़ले होब्बै or प° होखबै
2.	पढ़ले होब्येस् or प° होखब्येस्	पढ़ले होब्बह् or प° होखबह्
3.	पढ़ले होई or प° होब्बी	पढ़ले होइहैँ or प° होखिहैँ

Conjunctive mood.

n) Future conditional: *(if) I be reading*, etc.

	Sing. Masc. and Fem.	Plur. Masc. and Fem.
1.	पढ़त् होँहुँ or प° होखुँ	पढ़त् होईँ or प° होखोँ
2.	पढ़त् हो or प° होखु	पढ़त् होह् or हो or प° होखह् or होख
3.	पढ़त् होय् or प° होखै	पढ़त् होयँ or प° होखैँ

o) Durative pres. condit.: *(if) I were reading*, etc.

	Sing. Masc.	Sing. Fem.
1.	पढ़त् होतोँ	पढ़त् होत्यूँ
2.	पढ़त् होतेस् or प° होते	पढ़त् होतिस् or प° होती
3.	पढ़त् होत् or प° होतै	पढ़त् होत् or प° होतै

	Plur. Masc.	Plur. Fem.
1.	पढ़त् होइत्	पढ़त् होइत्
2.	पढ़त् होतह् or प° होत	पढ़त् होत्यू
3.	पढ़त् होतेन् or प° होतैँ	पढ़त् होतिन् or प° होतीँ

p) Fut. exact condit.: *(if) I have read,* etc.

Sing. Masc. and Fem.	Plur. Masc. and Fem.
1. पढ़ले होउँ or प° होओं	पढ़ले होईं or प° होओं
2. पढ़ले हो or प° होउ	पढ़ले होहू or प° होअहू etc.
3. पढ़ले होयू or प° होवै	पढ़ले होयँ or प° होवैं

q) Preterite condit.: *(if) I had read,* etc.

Sing. Masc.	Sing. Fem.
1. पढ़ले होतों	पढ़ले होत्यूँ
2. पढ़ले होतेस् or प° होते	पढ़ले होतिसू or होती
3. पढ़ले होत् or प° होतै	पढ़ले होत् or होते

Plur. Masc.	Plur. Fem.
1. पढ़ले होइतू	पढ़ले होइत्
2. पढ़ले होतहू or प° होत	पढ़ले होत्यू
3. पढ़ले होतेन् or प° होतैं	पढ़ले होतिन् or प° होतीं

522. Participles.

a) Adjectival: pres. पढ़त् *reading,* past पढ़ल् *having read* or *read.*

b) Conjunctive: पढ़् के or पढ़े के *having read.*

c) Adverbial: pres. पढ़ते or पढ़तै *on reading,* past पढ़ले *on having read.*

Infinitives.

Nom. पढ़ब् *to read,* acc. पढ़बे के or पढ़ै के *for to read* or *for reading,* instr. पढ़बे से or पढ़ै से, etc.

Noun of agency.

Masc. or fem. पढ़निहारू *reader,* or fem. पढ़निहारी.

6. LIST OF TYPICAL REGULAR ACTIVE VERBS.

523. Elements.

a) रहब् *dwell,*	root रह्,	bases	रहत्, रहल्
b) पीयब् *drink,*	„ पी or पीयू,	„	पीयत्, पीयल्
c) चूअब् *drip,*	„ चू,	„	चूअत्, चूअल्
or चूवब्,	„ (चूव्),	„	चूवत्, चूवल्
d) रोअब् *weep,*	„ रो,	„	रोअत्, रोअल्
or रोवब्,	„ (रोव्)	„	रोवत्, रोवल्.

a) Present indicative.

		Masc.	Fem.		Masc.	Fem.
3. pers. sing.	a)	रहैला	रहैले	plur.	रहैलेन्	रहैलिन्
	b)	पोयैला	पोयैले		पोयैलेन्	पोयैलिन्
	c)	चूऐला	चूऐले		चूऐलेन्	चूऐलिन्
	d)	रोऐला	रोऐले		रोऐलेन्	रोऐलिन्

b) First preterite.

		Masc. and Fem.		Masc. and Fem.
3. pers. sing.	a)	रहिस्	plur.	रहिन्
	b)	पोविस्		पोयिन्
	c)	चूइस्		चूइन्
	d)	रोइस्		रोइन्

Second preterite.

		Masc.	Fem.		Masc.	Fem.
3. pers. sing.	a)	रहल्	रहल्	plur.	रहलेन्	रहलिन्
	b)	पियलेस्	पियलेस्		पोयलेन्	पोयलिन्
	c)	चूम्रल्	चूम्रल्		चूम्रलेन्	चूम्रलिन्
	d)	रोम्रल्	रोम्रल्		रोम्रलेन्	रोम्रलिन्

c) Future indicative [1]).

		Masc. and Fem.		Masc. and Fem.
3. pers. sing.	a)	रही	plur.	रहिहैँ
	b)	पी or पोई		पोहैँ
	c)	चूई		चूइहैँ
	d)	रोई		रोइहैँ

d) Pres. conj. or f) Pres. imper.

		Masc. and Fem.		Masc. and Fem.
3. pers. sing.	a)	रहै	plur.	रहैँ
	b)	पोयै		पोयैँ
	c)	चूऐ		चूऐँ
	d)	रोऐ		रोऐँ

---

1) 1. pers. sing. masc. रहबोँ or रहिबोँ; पियव्रोँ or पोव्रोँ; चुम्रबोँ or चुइबोँ; रोम्रबोँ or रोइबोँ.

e) Preterite conjunctive.

		Masc. and Fem.		Masc.	Fem.
3. pers. sing.	a)	रहत् or रहतै	plur.	रहतेन्	रहतिन्
	b)	पीयत् or पीयतै		पीयतेन्	पीयतिन्
	c)	चूअत् or चूअतै		चूअतेन्	चूअतिन्
	d)	रोअत् or रोअतै		रोअतेन्	रोअतिन्

f) Precative forms.

		Masc. and Fem.		Masc. and Fem.
2. pers. sing.	a)	रहिहे	plur.	रहिह
	b)	पीहे		पीह
	c)	चूइहे		चूइह
	d)	रोइहे		रोइह

g) Durative or definite present.

		Masc. and Fem.		Masc.	Fem.
3. pers. sing.	a)	रहत् बाटै or र° हौवै	plur.	रहत् बाटैँ or हौवैँ	र° बाटीँ or हईँ
	b)	पीयत् बाटै or प° हौवै		पीयत् बाटैँ or हौवैँ	पी° बाटीँ or हईँ
	c)	चूअत् बाटै or चू° हौवै		चूअत् बाटैँ or हौवैँ	चू° बाटीँ or हईँ
	d)	रोअत् बाटै or रो° हौवै		रोअत् बाटैँ or हौवैँ	रो° बाटीँ or हईँ

l) Pluperfect indicative.

		Masc. and Fem.		Masc.	Fem.
3. pers. sing.	a)	रहल् रहल्	plur.	रहल् रहलेन्	रहल् रहलिन्
	b)	पीयले रहल्		पीयले रहलेन्	पीयले रहलिन्
	c)	चूअल् रहल्		चूअल् रहलेन्	चूअल् रहलिन्
	d)	रोअल् रहल्		रोअल् रहलेन्	रोअल् रहलिन्

The remaining periphrastic tenses are made after the analogy of Nro. g and l.

524. Participles.

	Adjectival.		Conjunctive.	Adverbial.	
a)	रहत्	रहल्	रह् के[1]	रहते	रहले
b)	पीयत्	पीयल्	पी के	पीयते	पीयले
c)	चूअत्	चूअल्	चूय् के	चूअते	चूअले
d)	रोअत्	रोअल्	रोय् के	रोअते	रोअले

1) Or: रहे के, पीए के, etc.

Infinitives.

a) रहब् Acc. रहैं कं or रहबे के
b) पोयब् „ पोयँ कं or पोबे के
c) चूअब् „ चूएँ के or चूअबे के
d) रोअब् „ रोएँ कं or रोअबे के

Noun of agency.

a) रहनिहारू, b) पोयनिहारू, c) चूअनिहारू, d) रोअनिहारू; fem. °री.

7. IRREGULAR ACTIVE VERBS.

525. There are three kinds of irregularities. *Firstly*; some verbs add the suffixes ल्, त् and ब् instead of ऐल् or अल् (of the pres. indic.), अत् (of the pres. part.) and अब् or इब् (of the future). This is done by all verbal roots in आ and ए and by the root हो *be*. But the roots in आ and the R. हो may optionally take इब्.

Secondly; some verbs have a special form of the past participle (and of all tenses derived from it), of the conjunctive part., and of the first preterite tense. These are the verbal roots: कर् *do*, धर् *put*, आव् *come*, पाव् *find*, जा *go*, दे *give*, ले *take*, हो *be*.

Thirdly; the two verbal roots दे *give* and ले *take* add no suffix in the 2. and 3. pers. sing. pres. conj. and imper.

Note also, that आव or अव, आय or अय, आइ or अइ are often contracted into ओ or ए respectively (see § 34).

The following verbs will serve as types: खाब् *to eat*, जाब् *to go*, देब् *to give*, होब् *to be*, करब् *to do*, आवब् *to come*. All other verbs in आ are conjugated like खाब्; लेब् *to take* is conjugated like देब्, धरब् *to put* like करब्, पावब् *to find* like आवब्.

526. a) Present indicative.

	1. sing.	3. sing.	1. plur.	3. plur.
a)	जालों	जाला	जाईला	जालेन्
b)	देलों	देला	देईला	देलेन्
c)	होलों	होला	होईला	होलेन्

b) First preterite.

	1. sing.	3. sing.	1. plur.	3. plur.
a)	गयो˘	गयिस्	गया	गयिन्
b)	दियो˘	दिहिस्	दिया	दिहिन्
c)	भयो˘	भयिस्	भया	भयिन्
d)	कियो˘	किहिस्	किया	किहिन्
e)	आयो˘	आइस्	आया	आइन्
f)	खायो˘	खाइस्	खाया	खाइन्

Second preterite.

	1. sing.	3. sing.	1. plur.	3. plur.
a)	गइलो˘ 1)	गयल् 1)	गइली 1)	गइलेन् 1)
b)	दिहलो˘	दिहलेस्	दिहली	दिहलेन् 1)
c)	भइलो˘ 1)	भयल् 1)	भइली 1)	भइलेन् 1)
d)	कइलो˘ 1)	कइलेस् 1)	कइली 1)	कइलेन् 1)
e)	अइलो˘ 1)	आयल् 1)	अइली 1)	अइलेन् 1)
f)	खइलो˘ 1)	खइलेस् 1)	खइली 1)	खइलेन् 1)

c) Future.

	1. sing.	3. sing.	1. plur.	3. plur.
a)	जाबो˘ 2)	जाई	जांब् or जाबै 2)	जइहै˘ 2)
b)	देबो˘	देई	देब् or देबै	देइहै˘
c)	होबो˘ 3)	होई	होब् or होबै	होइहै˘

d) Pres. conj. and f) Pres. imper.

	1. sg.	2. sg. 4)	3. sg.	1. pl.	2. pl. 5)	3. pl.
a)	जाँवँ्	जा	जाय	जाँई˘	जाह्	जाँयँ्
b)	दो˘	दे	दे	देई˘	देह्	दे˘
c)	हो˘ 6)	हो	होय्	होँई˘	होह्	होयँ्

1) Or: गैलो˘, गइल्, गैली, गैलेन्, ऐलो˘, आइल्, etc.

2) Or: जइबो˘ or जैबो˘, जाइब् or जइबै or जैबै, जैहै˘.

3) Or: होइबो˘ or होखबो˘ or होखिबो˘, etc. The verb आव् *come* formes regularly अइबो˘ or ऐबो˘ or अउबो˘ or औबो˘, आई, आइब् or आवब् or आउब्, अइहै˘ or ऐहै˘, etc.

4) Or: जो; but not देउ.

5) Or: जा; दह् or द; हो.

6) Or: होहुँ or होखो˘, as in §§ 516, d. 517, d.

e) Preterite conjunctive.

	1. sg.	3. sg. masc.	1. pl.	3. pl. masc.
a)	जातों	जात्[1])	जाइत्[2])	जातेन्[3])
b)	देतों	देत्	देइत्	देतेन्
c)	होतों	होत्	होइत्	होतेन्

f) Precative forms.

	2. sing.	2. plur.
a)	जइहे or जैंह	जइह or जैह
b)	देइहे	देइह
c)	होइहे	होइह

g) Periphrastic tenses.

These are made regularly by means of the pres. and past part. and the auxiliary verb; provided only, that trans. verbs use the past part. in ले, and intrans. verbs that in ल्. Thus, 3. sg. pluperf. गयल् रहल् *he had gone*, but दिहले रहल् *he had given*.

527. Participles.

	Adjectival.		Conjunctive.	Adverbial.	
a)	जात्,	गयल्[4])	जाय् के[5])	जातै,	गैले[4])
b)	देत्,	दिहल्	दे के	देतै,	दिहले
c)	होत्,	भयल्[4])	होतै के	होतै,	भैले[4])
d)	करत्,	कयल्[4])	कय् के	करतै,	कैले[4])
e)	आवत्,	आयल्[4])	आय् के	औतै,	एले[4])
f)	खात्,	खायल्[4])	खाय् के	खातै,	खैले[4])

	Infinitives.	Nouns of agency.
a)	जाब्[6]), जाए के or जाबे के	जानिहार्, fem. °री
b)	देब्, देए के or देबे के	देनिहार्, " °री
c)	होब्, होए के or होब् के	होनिहार्, " °री

1) Or: जातै, देतै, होतै.

2) Or: जाती, देती, होती.

3) Or: जातैं, देतैं, होतैं.

4) Or: गइल्, गइले; भइल्, भइले, etc.

5) Or contr. जै के, दै के, कै के, etc.

6) Or: जाइब्, जइबे or जैबे के; होइब्, होइबे के; आइब्, अइबे or ऐबे के, etc.

8. THE REGULAR COMPOUND PASSIVE VERB.

528. The forms of the pass. verb are composed of the past part. in अल् of the principal (i. e. active) verb and the tenses of the verb जाब् *to go* (§ 479). The formation of the past part. is explained in §§ 302—307; and the conjugation of the verb जाब् is given in §§ 525—527. The form of the past part. never changes, but the forms of the verb जाब् vary, as usual, according to the person, number and gender of the subject.

Present indicative.

	Sing. Masc.	Sing. Fem.
1.	पढल् जालों	पढल् जाल्यूँ
2.	पढल् जालेस् or प° जाले	पढल् जालिस् or प° जाली
3.	पढल् जाला	पढल् जाले
	Plur. Masc.	**Plur. Fem.**
1.	पढल् जाइला	पढल् जाइला
2.	पढल् जालहू or प° जाल	पढल् जाल्यू
3.	पढल् जालेन् or प° जालें	पढल् जालिन् or प° जालीं

The rest of the tenses may be formed after the above manner.

Participles.

Adjectival.	Conjunctive.	Adverbial.
पढल् जात्, प° गयल्	पढल् जाय् के	पढल् जाते प° गेले

Infinitives.	Nouns of agency.
पढल् जाब्, प° जाये के or प° जाबे के	पढल् जानिहार्; fem. °री

9. IRREGULAR COMPOUND PASSIVE VERBS.

529. There are only two irregular verbs; viz. जाब् *to go* and होब् *to be* (§ 479, exc.). The former uses the participial form जायल्, instead of गयल् in the formation of the compound pass., the latter the part. form होअल् or, optionally, भयल्. All other active verbs, which form an irregular past part. (see §§ 527. 304), use the same also in the compound pass. Thus, कयल् जाला *it is done*; दिहल् जाला *it is given*; but जायल् जाला *it can go* (lit. *it is gone*); होअल् जाला *it can be*, see § 530.

530. The pass. voice of intrans. verbs is only used in an impersonal and potential sense. Thus, मो से बइठल् नाहीँ जात्ता lit. *by me it cannot be sat*, i. e., *I cannot sit*; or मो से खरा नाहीँ होअल् (or भयल्) जात् बाटै *I cannot stand up*.

Note: The compound pass. verbs should be carefully distinguished from the compound intensive verbs; see § 538, a.

10. THE POTENTIAL PASSIVE VERB.

531. The potent. pass. verb, as to the formation of which see § 482, is conjugated precisely like any other (active) verb in अा, e. g., like खाब् *to eat*, the conjugation of which is given in §§ 525—527.

a) Present: *I can be read*, etc.

	Sg. Masc.	Fem.	Pl. Masc.	Fem.
1.	पढ़ाल्लोँ	पढ़ाल्यू	पढ़ाईला	पढ़ाईला
2.	पढ़ाल्लेस् 1)	पढ़ालिस् 1)	पढ़ालहू 1)	पढ़ाल्यू
3.	पढ़ाल्ला	पढ़ाले	पढ़ाल्लेन् 1)	पढ़ाल्लिन् 1)

b) Preterite: *I could be read*, etc.

1. sg. masc. पढ़इल्लोँ or पढ़ैल्लोँ; 3. sg. पढ़ायल् or पढ़ाइल्, etc. There is no first preterite form of the potent. pass.

c) Future: *I shall be able to be read*, etc.

1. sg. masc. पढ़इब्योँ or पढ़ैब्योँ or पढ़ाब्योँ, 3. sg. पढ़ाई; pl. पढ़इहैँ or पढ़ैहैँ, etc.

d) Pres. conj. or imper.: *I may be able to be read*, etc.

Sing. 1. पढ़ाँवँ 2. पढ़ा or पढ़ो 3. पढ़ांय्

Plur. 1. पढ़ाँईँ 2. पढ़ाहू or पढ़ा 3. पढ़ाँयँ

e) Pret. conj.: *I would be able to be read*, etc.

1. sing. masc. पढ़ातोँ; plur. पढ़ाती or पढ़ाइत्, etc.

Periphrastic tenses.

g) Dur. pres. 1. sg. masc. पढ़ात् बाटोँ or प॰ होवोँ, etc.

h) Dur. pret. „ „ पढ़ात् रहल्लोँ, etc.

i) Dur. fut. „ „ पढ़ात् होबोँ or प॰ होखब्योँ, etc.

---

1) Or: 2. sg. m. पढ़ाल्ले, f. पढ़ाल्ली; pl. m. पढ़ाल; 3. pl. m. पढ़ाल्लैँ, f. पढ़ाल्लोँ.

k) Perfect 1. sg. masc. पढायल् आटो or प० होवो or पढाइल् त्र° or प° हू°, etc.
l) Pluperfect „ „ पढायल् रहलो or पढाइल् र°, etc.

Participles.

Adjectival.	Conjunctive.	Adverbial.
पढात्, पढायल् or पढाइल्	पढाय् के	पढाते, पढइले or पढैले

Infinitives.	Nouns of agency.
पढाब् or पढाइब्, पढाये के or पढैबे के	पढानिहार्, fem. °री

11. IRREGULAR POTENTIAL PASSIVE VERBS.

532. There is only one anomalous case; viz. the verb खाब् *to eat.* It forms its potent. pass. root irregularly, viz. खिया; but the root, thus formed, is conjugated quite regularly. Observe also, that the verbs देब् *to give* and लेब् *to take* make their potent. pass. roots दिया and लिया (§ 482). The verbs आब् *to come,* जाब् *to go* and होब् *to be* possess no potent. passive.

12. THE SIMPLE CAUSAL VERB.

533. The simple causal verb, as to the formation of which see § 474, is conjugated regularly like any other (active) verb in ब्; provided that °आवो° becomes आई (§ 33) and antepenultimate °आव°, °आय° become अउ or औ, अइ or ऐ (§ 34).

a) Present: *I cause to read* or *I teach,* etc.

1. sg. masc. पढावैलो or पढाबलो; pl. पढाईला, etc.

b) First pret.: *I caused to read* or *I taught,* etc.

Sg. 1. पढायो, 2. and 3. पढाइस्; pl. 1. पढाया, 2. पढायौ, 3. पढाइन्.

Second preterite.

1. sg. पढउलो or पढौलो; pl. पढउली or पढौली, etc.

c) Future: *I shall cause to read* or *I shall teach,* etc.

Sg. 1. पढइबो or पढैबो or पढउबो or पढौबो, 3. पढाई, etc.
Pl. 1. पढाइब् or पढाउब्, 3. पढइहै or पढैहै, etc.

d) Pres. conj. or imper.: *I may cause to read,* etc.

Sg. 1. पढावों, 2. पढाव् or पढावु or पढाउ, 3. पढावे.
Pl. 1. पढाई„ 2. पढावह् or पढाव, 3. पढावैं.

e) Pret. conj.: *I would cause to read*, etc.

1. sg. masc. पढ़उतों or पढ़ौतों, 3. पढ़ावत् or पढ़ौते; pl. 1. पढ़ाइत्, etc.

g) Periphrastic tenses.

These are made regularly by means of the pres. and past part.; provided only, that causal verbs, being trans., use the past part. in ले. Thus 3. sg. masc. imperf. पढ़ावत् रहल् *he was causing to read* or *he was teaching*; again 3. sg. masc. perf. पढ़ौले बाटे *he has caused to read* or *he has taught*, etc.

Participles.

Adjectival.	Conjunctive.	Adverbial.
पढ़ावत् पढ़ावल्	पढ़ाय् के	पढ़ौते पढ़ौले

Infinitives.	Nouns of agency.
पढ़ाइब् or पढ़ावब्, पढ़ावे के or पढ़ैवे के	पढ़ौनिहार्; fem. °री

13. THE DOUBLE CAUSAL VERB.

534. The double caus. verb, as to the formation of which see § 477, is conjugated precisely like the simple causal verb (§ 533).

a) Present: *I cause to teach*, etc.

1. sg. masc. पढ़वावेलों or पढ़वावलों; pl. पढ़वाईला, etc.

b) First. pret.: *I caused to teach*, etc.

1. sg. पढ़वायों, 2. and 3. पढ़वाइस्; pl. 1. पढ़वाया, 3. पढ़वाइन्, etc.

Second preterite.

1. sg. masc. पढ़वउलों or पढ़वौलों, 3. पढ़वउलेस् or पढ़वौलेस्, etc.

c) Future: *I shall cause to teach*, etc.

1. sg. masc. पढ़वइबों or पढ़वैबों or पढ़वउबों or पढ़वौबों, 3. पढ़वाई, etc.

d) Pres. conj. or imper.: *I may cause to teach*, etc.

1. sg. पढ़वावों, 2. पढ़वाव् or पढ़वावु or पढ़वाउ; 1. pl. पढ़वाईं, etc.

e) Pret. conj.: *I would cause to teach*, etc.

1. sg. m. पढ़वउतो or पढ़वौतों, 3. पढ़वावत् or पढ़वौते; 1. pl. पढ़वाइत्, etc.

Participles.	Infinitive.
पढ़वावत् पढ़वावल्	पढ़वाइब् or पढ़वावब्

14. THE PASSIVE OF THE SIMPLE AND DOUBLE CAUSAL VERBS.

535. Causal verbs cannot form the potent., but only the compound passive! The latter is formed and conjugated precisely like that of any other (active) verb. Thus, simple caus. pass. infinit. पज़ावल् ज़ाब्‌ *to be caused to read* or *to be taught*; and double caus. pass. inf. परुवावल् ज़ाब्‌ *to be caused to teach*, and so forth.

15. IRREGULAR CAUSAL VERBS.

536. 1) The verb ख्याब्‌ *to eat* forms its simple causal खियावब्‌ *to cause to eat* or *to feed*, and its double causal खियवावब्‌ *to cause to feed*. Similarly the verbs लेव्‌ *to take* and देव्‌ *to give* form लियावब्‌, लियवावब्‌ and दियावब्‌, दियवावब्‌ respectively (§ 474, exc.).

2) The verbs ग्रावब्‌ *to come* and ज़ाब्‌ *to go* possess no causals. Instead of them, the intensitive compound verbs लेग्रावब्‌ *to bring* (= *to cause to come*) and लेज़ावब्‌ *to remove* (= *to cause to go*) are used (see § 538, a). These two compound verbs are conjugated precisely like the two simple verbs ग्रावब्‌ and ज़ाब्‌. Thus their infin. pass. are लेग्रायल् ज़ाब्‌ *to be brought* and लेज़ायल् ज़ाब्‌ *to be removed*.

3) Of the verb होब्‌ *to be* there is no causal in use, whether simple or double, active or passive.

FOURTH CHAPTER. COMPOUND VERBS.

537. Compound verbs are made by adding to the principal verb, which takes the form of the conj. part. (§ 490) or the oblique infin. (§ 485) or the adj. part. (§ 486), certain auxiliary verbs. In conjugating, the latter only are inflected, while the former remains unchanged.

538. The verbs most commonly used as auxiliaries to form such comp. verbs are:

a) For making *intensitives*; देब् *to give* (implying intensity), डालब् *to throw* (violence); आइब् *to come* and जाइब् *to go* (completion); परब् (or W. H. पड़°) *to fall* (chance); उठब् *to rise* (suddenness); लेब् *to take* (reflexiveness). In such intensitive comp. verbs the auxil. verb has no significance of its own, but merely serves to modify the meaning of the principal verb. The latter takes the form of the conj. part. Thus, फेँकब् *to throw*, but फेँक् देब् *to throw away*; तोर् डालब् *to break into pieces*, from तोरब् *to break*; बन् आइब् or बन् जाइब् *to be made up, completed*, from बनब् *to be made*; खाय् जाइब् *to eat up*, from खाइब् *to eat*; आय् परब् *to come accidentally, to turn up*, from आइब् *to come*; बोल् उठब् *to speak suddenly*, from बोलब् *to speak*; काट् लेब् *to cut for oneself*, from काटब् *to cut*; रख् लेब् *to place for oneself, to lay by*, from रखब् *to place*.

b) For making *continuatives*; रहब् *to remain* and जाइब् *to go*. In composition with रहब्, the principal verb may take the form either of the conj. or the adj. pres. part.; in conjunction with जाइब्, it may have only the form of the latter participle. Thus, बइठ् रहब् or बइठत् रहब् *to continue sitting*; again पढ़त् जाइब् *to continue reading*.

c) For making *frequentatives*; करब् *to do*. The principal verb takes the form of the obl. infin. Thus, पढ़ै करब् or पढ़बे क° *to read often*; आवै करब् or अइबे क° or ऐबे क° *to be in the habit of coming*.

d) For making *potentials*; सकब् *to be able*, जानब् *to know*. The principal verb takes the form of the conj. part. or, less usually, of the obl. infin. Thus, पढ़् सकब् or पढ़ै स° or पढ़बे स° *to be able to read*; खइबे जानब् or खैबे ज° *to be able to eat*.

e) For making *completives*; चुकब् *to finish*. The principal verb takes the form of the conj. part. Thus पढ़् चुकब् *to finish reading*, खाय् चुकब् *to finish eating*.

f) For making *desideratives*; छाहब् (or चाहब्) *to wish*. The principal verb takes the form of the adj. past part. or the obl. infin. Thus, पढ़ल् छाहब् or पढ़ै छ° or पढ़बे छ° *to wish to read*.

Very often these derivatives are idiomatically used to express merely *immediate futurity*, as घड़ी बजल् चाहत् बारे *the clock is about to strike*; बेरू बिसत्रे चाहेला *the time is about to pass.*

g) For making *inchoatives*; लागब् *to be applied* and होइब् *to become*. The latter occurs only in the past tense भयल् *he became*, and, in composition with it, the principal verb takes the form of the adj. pres. part., as पढ़त् भयल् *he began to read*. With लागब् it takes the form of the obl. inf., as पढ़ै लागब् or पढ़बे ल° *to begin to read.*

h) For making *permissives*; देब् *to give*. The principal verb takes the form of the obl. inf. Thus, पढ़ै देब् or पढ़बे देब् *to allow to read*; आवँ देब् or अइबे द° or ऐबे द° *to allow to come.*

i) For making *acquisitives*; पाइब् *to obtain*. The principal verb takes the form of the obl. inf. Thus, पढ़ै पाइब् or पढ़बे प° *to be allowed to read.*

539. *Affinities and Derivation.* 1) The form of the principal verb in intens., contin., potent. and complet. compound verbs is not, as sometimes said (see Kl. 188—191. Eth. 102. 103. Ld. 70), the root of the verb, but the conj. part. This can be clearly seen in E. H., especially in the case of verbs with vocal roots, where the root and the conj. part. have different forms; e. g., *to eat up* is खाय् (conj. part.) जाइब्, not खा (root) जाइब्; but also in others; e. g., फेँके देब् or फेँक् द° *to throw away*. In fact, these compounds literally mean *to come after having eaten*; *to give after having thrown*. Thus, लेआवे lit. means *to come after having taken*, i. e., *to bring*; पढ़े चुकब् or पढ़् च° *to give up after having read*, i. e., *to have done with reading*. The H. H., too, has preserved the full conj. part. form in its causals, where it optionally adds य् to roots in आ (see Kl. 188. 192); e. g., बताय् देना or बता द° *to show*. Again O. H. always uses the conj. part. in its original form in इ; as पढ़ि चुकनू *to have done reading*. Finally M. uses in these compounds the conj. part. in ऊन्; e. g., टाकून् देणे॑ *to cast away*, घेऊन् येणे॑ *to bring*, lit. *having taken* (from घेणे॑ *to take*) *to come* (see Man. 92); and likewise B. uses the conj.

part. in इया, G. in ई, S. in ई or ए, O. in इ; e. g., B. खाइया चूकन् *to have done eating* (S. C. 193); G. नाखी देवुं *to throw away* (Ed. 113); S. वठी वञणु *to take off,* करे चुकणु *to have done doing* (Tr. 339. 342), O. करि थाउँ *I am in the habit of doing* (Sn. 42). In the ordinary P., as in H. H., the form of the conj. part. does not differ from that of the root; e. g., वाच् सकणा *to be able to read,* खा हटणा *to finish eating* (Ld. 70, d). — 2) As regards those compounds in which the principal verb takes the form of the obl. infin., the latter is the acc. case of the infin. governed by the auxil. verb. Thus पड़े करब् *to read often* is lit. *to do reading,* मरबे काहब् *to be about to die* is lit. *to desire dying.* This is clearly seen from the O., which actually adds the acc. affix कु to the obl. inf. मरिबा कु चाहि *I desire to die,* करिबा कु लगि *I begin to do* (Sn. 41. 12). The termination of the obl. inf. is वा in G., इआ in P., ण in S.; e. g., G. जोवा लाग्यो *he began to see* (Ed. 51), P. पढ़िआ करदा *he is in the habit of reading* (Ld. 70, e), S. रुअण लगणु *to begin to cry* (Tr. 344, 4). The B. alone forms an exception, in using the obl. form of the pres. part. in इते (or the adverbial part.) in the place of the obl. inf.; e. g., B. मरिते चाहि *I desire to die,* करिते पारि *I am able to do* (S. Ch. 192, 4. 5). Kellogg's conjecture (p. 192), that the H. H. form in आ (as पढ़ा करना *to be in the habit of reading*) is not the masc. sing. of the past part. but a „gerund" (i. e., obl. infin.) and identical with the B. obl. inf. in आ (S. C. 149), is quite true. — 3) In those compounds, where the principal verb is in the form of an adj. part., the latter really stands in the position of a *predicate* to the subject or object of the (auxil.) verb. Thus ऊ पढ़त् जात् बाटे *he continues reading* is lit. *he is going as a reader,* or ऊ मरल् चाहत् बाटे *he wishes to die* is lit. *he wishes (himself) as dead.* It appears, therefore, that, strictly speaking, none of these so-called compound verbs are really compounds, but in every case the part. or infin. of the principal verb is in ordinary grammatical construction of some sort with the (so-called) auxil. verb. — 4) These various comp. verbs occur in all Gḍ. languages, and are generally formed in the same way, though sometimes a different auxil. verb is used. Thus B. and O. use पार् *cross* for सक् in potent. (S. Ch. 192, 4. Sn. 41, 2), B. थाक्, O. था *stand* for रह् in contin. and for कर् in frequent. (S. Ch. 191, 1. 192, 3. Sn. 42); P. has हट् *with draw*. S. वह् *take*, beside चुक्, in complet. (Tr. 342, c. Ld. 70, d); S. वञ् *go* for जा in intens. (Tr. 339, a). One exception has been already mentioned in Nro. 2. — 5) Traces of these comp. verbs already occur in Prákrit. Thus there are desideratives in the *Bhagavati*, made by constructing the R. इच्छ् *wish* with the past part. pass. in इय; e. g., इच्छामि सयम् एव मुंडावियं सयम् एव सिक्खावियं सयम् एव धम्मम् आइक्खियं, i. e., *I wish myself to shave, myself to instruct, myself to teach the law*, E. H. छाहो॑ आपही मूँडल् आपही सिखावल् आपही धाम् कै आयसु दिहल्. See Wb. Bh. 275. 433 [1]).

FIFTH SECTION. INDECLINABLES.

540. There are four kinds of indeclinables or words incapable of inflexion: 1) adverbs, 2) postpositions, 3) conjunctions, 4) interjections.

1. ADVERBS.

541. Adverbs may be either nominal, pronominal, numeral, verbal or original, according as they are derived from nouns, pronouns, numbers, verbs or from none of these. Again each of these classes may be divided into adv. of time, place and manner. Most adv. are native Hindí, but there are a very few of foreign

1) आइक्खियं may be derived from R. आ-दीच् (or आ-दिच्, for Skr. आ-दिश्, cf. Pr. देक्ख = दृक्ष्, for Skr. दृश्) „to instruct, to initiate". — The E. H. root छाह् or चाह् may be better derived from the noun इच्छा, by the loss of initial इ and the transfer of the aspiration of छ् (§ 132). Thus Skr. *इच्छायति, Pr. इच्छाअइ, Gd. छाहे or चाहै or छाहे. Accordingly § 173 should be corrected.

origin, whose native equivalents are obsolete. Again most adv. consist of only *one* word; but there are some that consist of a phrase or of a repetition of the original word. The following list of adv. lays no claim to completeness. The Sanskrit or foreign source of each is added in brackets.

542. *Nominal adverbs of time.* 1) नरसोँ *four days ago* or *four days hence* (for चरसोँ? Skr. चतुर्-श्वस्); तरसोँ *three days ago* or *three days hence* (Skr. त्रि-श्वस्); परसोँ *the day before yesterday* or *the day after to-morrow* (Skr. पर्-श्वस्); काल् or काल्ह् or काल्हि *yesterday* or *to-morrow* (Skr. कल्य); विहान् *to-morrow, at daybreak* (Skr. विभात); आज् or अजवा *to-day* (Skr. अद्य); अजौँ *hitherto* (Skr. अद्यापि); परयार् *the past year* (Skr. पर्-काल or पर्-वार्, cf. §§ 69. 30); तरके or भिनुसार् *at daybreak, at down* (W. H. तड़के, Skr. तटक, भिन्न-वासर्); नित्त *always* (Skr. नित्य); आग् or आगे *before* (§§ 77, exc. 78, exc.); पाछ् or पाछे or पाछैँ *afterwards* (§§ 77, exc. 78, exc.); पुन् or फुन् or फिन् (§§ 61. 131) or बहुरि *again* (Skr. पुनर्, बहु); निदान् *lastly* (Skr. dto). — 2) Adverbial phrases; ओ दिन् or पर् के दिन् *yesterday* (lit. *that day* or *day of before*); लोहिया लागत् (lit. *becoming red*) or अँधसुधारे (lit. *on clearing off of darkness*) *at down, early*; दिन् चढ़् के (lit. *the day having risen*) *late in the morning*; सब् दिन् *always* (lit. *every day*); बहुत् बेर् *frequently*; एक् बेर् *once* (etc., see § 409); आज् काल् or एन्हन् दिन् *now-a-days.* — 3) Repetitions; दिन् दिन् *every day*; कबहीँ कबहीँ or कब्बोँ कब्बोँ *sometimes*; बार् बार् *frequently.* — 4) Foreign; आखिर् *lastly* (arabic آخر).

543. *Nominal adverbs of place.* 1) अगारी or अगार॰ *before* (§§ 210. 77, exc. 78, exc.); पछारी or पछार॰ or पछवारे or पिछ॰ *behind* (§§ 210. 77, exc. 78. exc.); उपरिया *above* (Skr. उपरि); नीचू or निचइया *below* (Skr. नीच, of नि-अंच्); संमुह् or सामुह् *in front* (Skr. सम्मुख); बहिरि or बहिर॰ *without* (see § 217, p. 110); बीचे or बीचू *amidst* (Skr. वृत्य, of वृ *surround*, cf. § 374, p. 223, or from वि-अंच् *surround*); नगीच् or नगीचे (see § 545) or नियरे or नेरे or नियर *near* (Skr. निकट, cf. § 104); दूर् or लामे *far* (see §§ 172. 144): सबत्तर् *every where* (Ap. Pr. सव्वत्र, Skr. सर्वत्र). — 2) Phrases; काले कोस् *far* (lit. *some*

miles = W. H. किते कोस्, Skr. कियत्-क्रोश, Pr. काला, H. C. 3, 65, cf. §§ 438, 4. 464).

544. *Nominal adverbs of manner.* 1) अचानक् (Skr. अचेतनक?) or संजोग (Skr. संयोग) *accidentally, suddenly*; अलग् *separately* (Skr. अलग्न); बहुत् *much* (Skr. वहुत्र); हालो or हलदे or तुरंत् *quickly* (see § 545); तावरतोर् *very quickly*; साँचे *truly* (Skr. सत्य); अकारथ् (§ 545) or त्रिथो (Skr. वृथा) *in vain*; नीमन् (Skr. नियमन?) or नीके (persian نیکی) *well*; निर्फुल् or केवल् *merely* (Skr. dto); बड़् *very* (§ 145, exc. 2); सभिहे॑ or सम्मै॑ *altogether* (Skr. सर्व). — 2) Phrases; करम् से *accidentally* (lit. *by fate*); आपुस् से *mutually*; similarly, by adding रीति से or भाँति से or तरह् (arab. طرح) *in ... manner*, adverbs may be formed from any adj., as भली रीति से *in a good manner, well.* — 3) Repetitions; अलग् अलग् *severally*; रसे रसे or गवै॑ गवै॑ or धीरे धीरे or कले कले *slowly, by and by*; साचो साचा *truly*; लग् भग् *almost*; झूँठ् मूँठ् *falsely*; सचे मुच् *surely*. — 4) Foreign; ज़रूर् *necessarily* (arab. ضرور); जलदी *quickly* (pers. جلدی); कम् *a little* (pers. کم); खाली *only* (pers. خالی); अदब् दै के *especially* (lit. *giving respect*; arab. ادب); आस्ते आस्ते or अस्ते अस्ते *slowly* (pers. آهسته).

545. *Derivation.* Adverbs in ए or ऐ or ई are modifications of the Ap. Pr. loc. sing. in अहिं, as explained in §§ 77, exc. 378. — Adverbs in ऊ are modifications of the Ap. Pr. abl. or loc. sing. in अहुं, see §§ 78, exc. 376. 378. — Adv. in इ are modifications of the Ap. Pr. loc. sing. in ए or इ, see §§ 45. 378; e. g., Skr. कल्ये, Pr. कल्ले, Ap. कल्ले or कल्लि, E. H. कालि or कालिह. — Adv. in *a* quiescent are modif. of the Ap. Pr. acc. sg. or loc. sg.; see §§ 41. 45; e. g., Skr. कल्यं, Pr. कल्लं, E. H. काल्; the latter, however, might have arisen by the quiescence of the final इ in the Ap. Pr. कल्लि or E. H. कालि. — The element °सौ॑ (in परसौ॑, etc.) appears to be the contraction of an Ap. Pr. abl. or loc. सहुं (see § 376), of सो (Skr. श्वः), formed irregularly after the analogy of nouns (e. g., abl. दिवसहुं, of दिवसो *day*). — E. H. अजवा is derived with the pleon. suff. अवा from आज्, and अजवा is contr. to आजू, see § 199. — E. H. भिनुसार् contains an anomalous meta-

thesis of था, if it is correctly derived from Skr. भिन्नवासर् „broken day", „day-break"; whence Pr. *भिण्णवसार् or *भिण्णोसार्, E. H. भिनुसार्. — In फिन् and फुन् the फ् and इ are, perhaps, assimilations to फिर् (§ 547); S. has regularly पिणि or पुणि or पुणु (Tr. 410). — E. H. बहुरि is formed by the addition of the pleon. suff. र् to Skr. बहु, just as in E. H. बाहिरि, see §§ 543. 217. — E. H. अगारू, पछारू, etc. contain the pleon. suff. अड्अ (i. e., क + उ + क), as explained in §§ 210. 217. — E. H. उपरिया and निचइया contain the pleon. suff. इया, see § 199. — E. H. नगीच् is, probably, a corruption of the persian نزدیک, which may be heard in Hindí as नज़ीक् (see § 21, 2), and whence by transposition (see § 133) would arise नगीज़्; the क् being now medial, is regularly softened to ग्, see § 102. — E. H. हाली and हलदे are really W. Gḍ. adverbs; the former is the conj. part., the latter the obl. form of the pres. part. of the verbal root हाल् (M.), हल्ल् (P.), हल् (S.), हिल् or हल् (H.) *move, go.* Thus conj. part. S. हली (Tr. 313), pres. part. हलन्दू (Tr. 313), P. हल्लदे. — E. H. तुरंत् is the pres. part. of the verbal root त्वर् or तुर् *be quick.* — E. H. अकारथ् is regularly derived from the Skr. अकृतार्थ *having one's object not done, unsuccessful,* Pr. अकअत्थ or Ap. Pr. अकअर्थ, whence contr. E. H. अकार्थ् or अकारथ् (see §§ 137. 138).

546. The *pronominal* and *numeral adverbs* have been already enumerated in §§ 467—469 and in §§ 402. 417. 419 respectively.

547. *Verbal adverbs.* Many conjunctive participles may be used as adverbs; e. g., फिर् or फिर् के *again* (Skr. परि-इ *go round*), मिलि or मिल् के *together,* जान् के *knowingly,* हाली *quickly* (§ 545), etc. By the addition of the conj. part. कय् के or कै के *having done* to nouns, adjectives and numerals adverbial phrases may be formed; e. g., खुसी कय् के *gladly* (lit. *having made joy*); एक् एक् कै के *singly* (lit. *having made one by one*), etc.

548. *Particles of affirmation and negation.* The former are तो or तो तो or जो or हों or हां *yes,* काहू or काहे lit. *why not.* The latter are न or नाँहू or नाँहि or नाँहीं or नाहिन् *no, not.*

The prohibitive particle is जिन् *do not*, used with the imper. only. Thus ऐसन् जिन् करहु *do not act thus*, but ऐ° न or नाँहो˘ क° *you do not act thus.*

549. *Affinities and Derivation.* तो is a contr. of the Pr. ताव (Vr. 4, 6), Skr. तावत्. — E. H. जी, S. जीउ (Tr. 419) is the Skr. जीव, used (like Skr. आत्मा, E. H. आप्) as a term. of respect and, hence, of assent; cf. the English „sir". — The other affirm. and negat. particles were originally various forms of the auxiliary verb „to be". Thus E. H. हाँ and हो˘, S. हउ or हाँ (Tr. 418), B. हाँ or हुँ (S. Ch. 218) are the 1. sing. pres.; see § 514, 4. The 3. sing. pres. occurs in S. आँहे (Tr. 418) and M. होय् (Man. 101). B. also uses the 3. sing. pres. बटे of the other auxil. verb, see § 514, 1. The particles नाँह or नाँहि are compounds of the negative particle न and the 3. sing. pres. आहि *he is* (§ 514, 4); similarly नाँहो˘ and नाहिन् are compounds of न and the 3. plur. pres. आहो˘ and अहिन्; नाहिँ occurs in Pr. (H. C. 4, 419). As to the anunásika preceding ह्, see § 67. All these particles, however, are now used without respect to the person and number originally expressed by their form. — Instead of the E. H. जिन्, W. H. uses मत् or मति, S. म (Tr. 415), G. मा (Ed. 115); in Pr. मा or मं or म (H. C. 4, 418), Skr. मा.

550. *Particles of emphasis.* These are ई or ही *only, very* and उ or हूँ *also.* They are always used enclitically and often coalesce with the final अ of the principal word to ऐ or औ. E. g., क बाबू एहू पारी खात्ती रावै अनवैब की गूरौ। i. e., *what, father! shall you, this time, make only syrup or also molasses*; here रावै = राव ई, and गूरौ (or गूड़ो) = गूर उ.

551. *Affinities and Derivation.* ई is, perhaps, connected with the Skr. एव, Pr. वेअ or विअ (Vr. 9, 3); but as the true Pr. form is चेअ, चिअ (H. C. 2, 184), the derivation is doubtful. O. has इ or हिँ or हे˘ (Sn. 48), M. ही (Man. 101), H. H. ही. — E. H. उ, B. ओ (S. Ch. 237) are modifications of the Pr. वि, Skr. अपि (or ऽपि); Pr. has also पि (H. C. 2, 218); S. preserves both बि and पि (Tr. 410), and even aspirates भि or भी (Tr. 410); so also H. H. भी.

552. *Particles of interrogation.* क *what*; e. g., क धाग्रू! का करैल। i. e., *what, father! what are you doing?*

553. *Affinities and Derivation.* S. uses कि or की (Tr. 418), B. कि (S. Ch. 218), W. H. कि, क्यूँ. They are all connected with the interrogative pronom. base, see §§ 437, 5. 467, d.

2. POSTPOSITIONS AND AFFIXES.

554. Postpositions supply in E. H. (and Gḍ. generally) the place of what, in other languages, are prepositions. They are placed after the noun or pronoun which they govern; and the noun or pronoun takes the oblique form with or without the genitive affix कै or के. Postpositions constructed without a gen. aff. are *affixes* (§ 374, p. 222).

555. The following postpositions are commonly constructed without a gen. aff.; तरे *beneath* (Skr. तल *bottom*); पाहीँ (§§ 77, exc. 116. 375) or कने (§ 375) *at, near*; माँ or माँहीँ or माँझ् *in, within* (§ 378); ले (conj. part. of R. लग् *take*) or तक् (dto of R. तक् *see*) *till*; संगे or संग् *with* (Skr. सङ्ग); काहीँ *towards* (§§ 375. 116).

556. The following postpositions are commonly constructed with a gen. aff.; लगि *near, at* (§ 374); साथे *with* (Skr. संस्थ); सनती (often spelled सन्ती, cf. § 6, note) or पलटे *instead of* (§ 557); बाटे or बारे or बरे or बदे *for, by reason of* (§ 374); धोर् (Skr. ध्रवर्) or मुहेँ (Skr. मुख) *towards*; नाँईँ *like* (§ 557); besides many of the adverbs, enumerated in §§ 541—544. Also खातिर् *for, by reason of* (arab. خاطر).

557. *Affinities and Derivation.* Most of these have mentioned in §§ 374 ff. — The origin of बाटे is obscure; it is probably derived from the Skr. वर्त्त *being*; cf. the Pashtu *vatah*; or perhaps it may be a corruption of the Urdú वास्ते (arab. واسطی), see § 143; it is peculiar to E. H.; the W. H. has लिये. — E. H. बदे is sometimes used like the arabic بدل *in exchance for.* — E. H. सनती lit. *sacrifice, substitute.* see § 18, p. 23. — E. H. पलटे is Skr. पर्यस्ते *in return for,* see § 143. — नाईँ is probably connected with the root ज्ञा *know*; the Pr. has णाइ or णावइ (H. C. 4, 444).

3. CONJUNCTIONS.

558. *Copulative conjunctions*; अउरु or ओरु or अरु (§§ 5, b. 26) or औ *and*; पुनु or पुनि or फुनि or फिनु *moreover*; का — का *as well — as*.

559. *Affinities and Derivation.* E. H. ओरु, अरु, Bs. ओरु or वोरु is the Pr. अवरं or Ap. अवरु, Skr. अपरं; B. has आर (S. Ch. 237), Br. अरु, H. H. ओरु, P. अरु (Ld. 71), N. र. The latter rejects the initial अ (of अरु) and is used enclitically; e. g., उनु ले जाने — र भन्या *he knew and said*, or उठ — र माँक मा उभि *get up and stand in the middle!* — E. H. अउ or ओ, B. ओ, also compounded आरओ or आरो (S. Ch. 237), O. आउ or ओ (Sn. 46), M. व (Man. 103), Br. वो, S. अउँ (Tr. 410), are, probably, the Pr. अवि (H. C. 1, 41), Skr. अपि or अपिच. — S. has also अइँ or एँ (Tr. 410), P. अति or ति, O. H. (Chand) ति = Pr. अइ or ति, Skr. अति. — M. has also आणि or अणखी (Man. 103), G. अने or ने (Ed. 117); they are probably the Pr. अण° or अन्न°, Skr. अन्यत् or अन्यच्च lit. *another*. — E. H. पुनि, etc. (§§ 61. 131), O. पुणि (Sn. 46), S. पुणि or पिणि or पुणु (Tr. 410), are the Pr. पुणो or पुणु (Spt. 276. H. C. 4, 426), Skr. पुनर्. — W. H. has क्या — क्या *as well — as*. S. तिअँ — तिअँ (Tr. 410).

560. *Adversative conjunctions*; बरकि or बाकि or बरुकु (§ 561), लेकिनु (arab. لیکن), परु वै, बरनु *but*.

561. *Affinities and Derivation.* बरकि etc. are corruptions of the Persian بلکه, see § 143; W. H. बलकि, बाकि, बलुकु (Kl. 276), P. बल्कु (Ld. 71). — E. H. परु is the Skr. परम्, Pr. परं; also W. H., P., S. परु; on E. H., W. H. वै see § 124; P. has also अपर or एपर (Ld. 71) = Skr. अपरम्. — E. H. बरनु, W. H. बरण, P. बरं is Skr. वरम् or वरणाम्. — W. H. has also मगरु, P. मगवाँ or मगो (Ld. 71), S. मगरि (Tr. 412) = Pers. مگر. — O. has पुणि (Sn. 46), M. पण (Man. 103), G. पण (Ed. 117), S. पण (Tr. 412) = Pr. पुणु, Skr. पुनर्. — N. has तर, also M. तर (Man. II, 26), probably a corruption of Skr. तर्हि (or of तरम् *beyond, across*). — S. has also बिगिरि (Tr. 412), a corruption of the arab. بغير; also हर्याँ or हगो (Tr. 413), apparently connected with Skr. हस्त. — H. H., H. B., etc. use the Skr. परन्तु, किन्तु, etc.

562. *Disjunctive conjunctions*; ओ or की *or, either-or*; e. g., का! ई लेबह् की ऊ *will you take this or that*; बछेरा ओ बछेरी *a colt or a filly*; न — न or न तो — न *neither-nor*; e. g., न तो ई लेब्रो॑ न ऊ *I shall take neither this nor that*; चाहै — चाहै or की — की *whether-or*; e. g., चाहै ई ले चाहै ऊ *take either this or that* (2. sg. imp.) or *whether he take this or that* (3. sg. pres. conj.).

563. *Affinities and Derivation*. E. H. ओ is the Pr. व or वा (H. C. 1, 67), Skr. वा; H. H., H. B., H. O., etc. have वा, also अथवा; the latter is preserved in O. अवा, contr. form Pr. अहवा (H. C. 1, 67), Skr. अथवा. — E. H. की, B. कि (S. Ch. 240), O. कि or कि अवा (Sn. 46), M. की॑ (Man. 103), W. H. कि, P. के or अके (Ld. 71), S. कि or की (Tr. 412), N. कि are probably the Pr. किं, Skr. किम् *what*. — E. H. चाहै is the 3. sg. pres. conj. of the verb चाहब् *to desire*. — B. also uses हय्-नय् *either-or* (S. Ch. 240), S. तोडे-न त or तोपो-न त or जाँ-जाँ (Tr. 412); B. ना-ना or नय्-नय् *neither-nor* (S. Ch. 240), P. ना-ना (Ld. 81). — S. has जाँ *or* (Tr. 412). — W. H. and P. also use या, arabic يا (Kl. 275. Ld. 71).

564. *Conditional and concessive conjunctions*; जौ or जै *if*, तौ *then*; जौ *although*, तब्बो *yet, nevertheless*.

565. *Affinities*. 1) Condit.; B. जदि — तबे or तो (S. Ch. 238), O. जेबे — तेबे (Sn. 46), M. जर् — तर् (Man. II, 17), W. H. जौ or जो — तौ or तो, P. जे or जे कर् — ताँ (Ld. 71), G. जे or जो — तो (Ed. 117), S. जे or जे कर — त or ताँ (Tr. 417), N. अन्या — ता. — 2) Concess.; B. जदिओ — तबेओ or तबुओ or तर्॰ (S. Ch. 240), O. जेबे — तेबे or तेबेहे॑ (Sn. 46), M. जरी॑ or जरी — तरी॑ or तरी (Man. II, 17), W. H. (Br.) जौ हूँ — तौ हूँ (Kl. 275), P. भावे॑ — ताँ भी (Ld. 71), S. तोड or तोपा or जे or जे तोडे or जे तोपा — त or ताँ or त बि or तडही॑ बि (Tr. 411), N. ता — तर्.

566. *Derivation*. 1) Condit.; a) Skr. यदि (or यद्या), Pr. जइ (Vr. 1, 11), E. H. जै, P., S. जे. — b) Skr. यर्हि (Pr. जरि?), M. जर्; similarly Skr. तर्हि (Pr. तरि?), M. and N. तर्. — c) Skr. यावत्, Pr. जाव (H. C. 1, 11) or जाम्व (H. C. 4, 395) or जेम्व (H. C. 4, 401), E. H. and W. H. जौ, G. जो or S. जाँ (see § 563) or O. जेव (§ 468, c); similarly Skr. तावत्, Pr. ताव or ताम्व or तेम्व, E. H., W. H. तौ, B., W. H., G. तो or P. ताँ, S. ताँ or (shortened) त,

N. ता or O. तेबे, B. (shortening ए) तबे. — d) The N. भन्या is the conj. part. of the verb भन्नु *to say* (Skr. भणित्वा), and is always placed at the end of the conditional sentence; thus, वाँहाँ कल्याण् को पुत्र छ भन्या, ता तिमिहेरु को कल्याण् उस् माथि रहला है; न भन्या, ता फरू कि याउला, i. e., *if* (lit. *having said that*) *a son of peace be there, then your peace will remain upon him; if not, then it will again come.* — 2) The concessive conj. are made by adding to the condit. conj. some emphatic particle (see § 550); thus a) ओ or उ in B. यद्दिओ, Ap. Pr. यद्दिवि, Skr. यद्यपि; B. तबेओ = Pr. तेम्वइ वि, Skr. तावत्यपि (loc. sg.); B. तबु, E. H. तब्बो for तब्ब + उ. — b) हूँ in W. H. जौ हूँ, तौ हूँ. — c) ईं or हीं in M. जरी or जरी for जरि-ईं, तरी or तरी for तरि-ईं. — d) बि or भी in S. त ब्रि, P. ताँ भी, H. H. तो भी. — e) The emph. particle is reduplicated in O. तेबेहें for ते-बे-हें, S. तडेहीं ब्रि for तडे-हीं-त्रि. — f) The P. भावें is the Skr. भावेन *indeed, truly*; similarly N. uses ता, E. H., W. H. etc. तौ or तो; e. g., N. म ता परमेश्वर् देखि डराउँदि न, तरू म दिउँला, i. e., *I indeed am not afraid of god, yet I shall give.*

567. *Causal and final conjunctions*; a) जौ or जहू से *since*, तौ *therefore*. — b) जेहू से or तेहू से *therefore*. — c) काहे को *because, for*. — d) जेहू से *in order that, so that*. — e) का जाने *lest*. — f) नाहीं तौ *else*, otherwise (lit., *if not, then*).

568. *Affinities and Derivation*. a) B. जाइ — ताइ or ताइ ते (S. Ch. 239), O. जेणु — तेणु (Sn. 46), W. H. जिस् ते — तौ, P. जाँ — ताँ, S. जो — सो or जेलाँ — तेलाँ, etc. (see Tr. 414. 415); not uncommonly paraphrased, e. g., B. and O. जे हेतु — ते हेतु, M. ज्यापत्ती — त्यापत्ती, N. जस् कारण् — तस् कारण्, etc. — b) B. एमत् से or एमन् से, O. एणु, एनिमन्ते, M. त्यास् or म्हणुन्, W. H. जिस् ते or तिस् ते, P. ताँ, S. सो (Tr. 415); or paraphrased, e. g., B. ए जन्ये, ए निमित्त (S. Ch. 239), O. जे हेतु (Sn. 46), N. यस् कारण्, etc. — c) B. केनना, M. काँकी, W. H. क्यों कि or क्योंकि, H. H. क्यूँकि, N. क्यान्; or paraphrased, e. g., B. कारण् कि, M. कारण् की, etc. — d) B. एमत् से, एमन् से (S. Ch. 238), W. H. जिस् ते, P. ताँ. — e) B. कि जानि, O. कि जाणि, H. H. क्या जाने, lit. *what do I* or *does he know*; or B. पाछे, lit. *afterwards* (S. Ch. 240); H. H. न हो कि, S. म हुणे or न हुणु, lit. *may*

it not be that (Tr. 415). — f) B. नय् तो or न तु वा or नहि ले or नेले (S. Ch. 240), O. न तु, न तु वा, नोहि ला (Sn. 46. 125), M. नाहीं तर् (Man. 103), W. H. नाहीं तो, S. न तरि (Tr. 415). — Most of these conj. have a pronom. origin which has been explained in §§ 437. 469.

4. INTERJECTIONS.

569. The following are some of the most usual interjections; हे or हो or ओ or अरे or रे in addressing; राम् राम् in greeting; छी छी *fie! for shame*, in remonstrance; थुरी थुरी (or थुडी थु°) or थू थू *fit to be spitted on*, धिक्कार् *fit to be cursed* or *abused*, in disgust or abhorrence; हा हा or अह ह or बापरे *ah! alas!*, in surprise or grief; वाह् वाह् in admiration; हाँय् हाँय् in sorrow; भला or अच्छा *well!* in consent; दुत् or दुर् हो *be off!*; ले *lo!*

570. *Affinities and Derivation.* These interj. are common to all Gḍs. — Some occur in Pr.; e. g., छि छि and धिग् धिक् (H. C. 2, 174); थू थू (H. C. 2, 200), which, by adding the pleon. suff. री or डी, becomes थुरी थुरी; हा हा, अहह (H. C. 2, 217); अरे, रे (H. C. 2, 201); हं, हो (H. C. 2, 217?); हाँय् हाँय् is probably the Pr. and Skr. हा (H. C. 2, 192). — बापरे is probably बाप् रे *oh father!*

SIXTH SECTION. SPECIMENS OF EAST HINDÍ.

1. VOCABLES AND PHRASES.

571. The following nouns, current in E. H., are, I believe, not mentioned in any Hindí dictionary.

अददहा *weak*	इन्हन्[1]) *fuel (of grass, etc.)*	उजर्[1]) *white*
अहिवाती *wife*		ओअद् *wet*
इनारा *a well*	उजड्[1]) or उजबक् *rude*	ओद् *soft*

1) Bate in his Hindí dictionary gives: इन्धन्, उज्जल, उजड.

कचलोह् *unripe*
कर्वात् *sweepings*
करिया *black*
कुनह्[1]) *enemy*
कोँहडौ *sweet pumpkin*
खनहन् *good*
खबोर् or खब्बू *glutton*
खरखुद् *sweepings*
खरपात् *dried leaves*
गउदा or गबदा *fool*
गड्ही *cavity*
गदहाबसंत्[2]) *fool*
गरू *heavy*
गाँवँई *village*
गोईँठा *fuel of cowdung*
गोहार् *calling*
घटिहा *worthless*
घमोच् *fool*
चउआ[1]) *quadruped*
चिपरा or °री *fuel of cowdung*
चिरई *bird*
चोमर् *hard*
चोक् *excellent*
झाईपोई *family, race*
जावत् *all*
जावत् जगत् *every body*
जूडास् or जूडो *coldness*

जेँवाय् *husband*
झूर् *dry*
ठउर्[1]) *place*
ठंढई *coldness*
डरपोँक[3]) *cowardly*
डहर् or डाँडो *footpath*
धूमील् *dirty*
निउरा or नेओरा *finished*
निचाट् *solitary*
नेबर् *bad*
पगडंडी[1]) *footpath*
पताई *dried leaves*
परसिया *neighbouring*
पाकर् *clever*
पराय् की बात्[4]) *nonsense*
पालो *tree (branch?)*
पीयल् *yellow*
पूरा *village*
पेटास् *glutton*
पोँका *wet*
पोँच् *bad*
फोर् *hard*
बतोलिया *buffoon*
बरधा *ox, bullock*
बाबू or बापू *father*
बिगत् *individual*
बिपत् मह्आ[5]) *miserable*
बिरई or बीरो *small plant*

बोघू *wolf (tiger?)*
भइन् *sister*
भकुआ *simpleton*
भयो *younger brother's wife*
भयने *sister's son or husband's sister's son*
भिक्षा *alms*
भीखार् *beggar*
भुखर् *hungry*
भुलकर् *negligent*
मंडवी *company*
मटमइल् *dirty*
मनई *man*
मनसेट् *man*
मिरकुटहा *weak*
रचिक् *little*
लउर् *long, heavy stick*
ललतहा *weak*
लेजुर् or °री *cord, string*
संघत् *friendship*
संघती *friend*
सधुअई *honesty*
सुकाव् *sight*
सुबोता or °गोता *convenient*
सूखल् *dry*
सेवर् *unripe*
हरीयर्[1]) *green*

---

1) Bate in his H. dict.: कुन्ह, चौवा, ठौर, पगडंडी, हरियर्.
2) Lit., *sitting on an ass.*
3) Lit., *wet with fear.*
4) Lit., *word of irrelevancy.*
5) Lit., *stricken with misfortune.*

2. DIALOGUES[1]).

a) Between two friends.

1. Q. कह भाई! कहाँ से आवत् बाट? A. परसिया गाँव् से आईला. — 2. Q. उँहाँ से कब् चलल? A. भिनुसारे कै चलल् हई. — 3. Q. काह बदे उहाँ गयल् रहल? A. उहाँ एक् हमार् खेत् बाय्, ओके देखै के. — 4. Q. ओमे का बोवले बाट? A. खाली[1] रहर् बोवल् बाय्. — 5. Q. कह, भैया, येह् पारी के खेती कै हाल्! A. येह् पारी के खेती कै हाल् का पूछत् बाट? दैव् के बरसले[2] बिना बड़ा हरज्[3] भयल्. — 6. Q. आज् काल् तोहरे भाई नाही देखैलैं हैं[4]. A. हमरे भाई आज् काल् किला[5] मे नोकर्[6] बाटैं; एहर् बहुत् कम्[7] आवैलैं. — 7. Q. तोहरे बड़की गैया कं का खबर्[8] बाय्? A. बड़की गैया आज् काल् गाभिन् बाय्; कोयर् न मिलले[2] से टूट् गइल् बाय्. — 8. Q. गाभिन् भैले[2] कै महीना[9] भयल्? A. भयल् तो आठ् महीना, बाकि पेट् कुछ् उभरल् नाहीं देख् परत्. — 9. Q. कोरावत् बाय् की नाही? A. हाँ कुछ् कुछ् जान् परैला. — 10. Q. ई कौथा बियान् हौ औ केतना दूध् देले? A. ई अठवाँ बियान् होई; दूध् एकबेर् दुइ अढाई सेर् देले. — 11. Q. हम् के एक् बकरी खरीदै[11] कं बाय्, से तोहरे गावं पर् मिल् सकी? A. हमरे गाँवँ पर् तो बकरी बाटीं, लेकिन्[10] दाम् बड् तेज्[12] बाय्. — 12. Q. तोहार् बकरिया काँ भइल्? A. हम् चरै के बदे ओके गाँवैं पर् छोड़ले रहीला. — 13. Q. कुछ् दूध् देले? A. लड़िकन् के पीयै भर् के मिल् जाला. — 14. Q. अबकी ऊख् बोवले बाट की नाही? A. ऊख् तो बोवले बाटी, बाकि ओ मे कुछ् फाइदा[13] नैखै. — 15. Q. तोहरे इहाँ से नार् मोट् मँगनी मिल् सकी? A. काहें? भराई होय् जाय्, तब् ले ल[14]. — 16. Q. तोहरे इहाँ कै पुरवट् चलैला? A. तीन् पुरवट् नधले बाटी. — 17. Q. तोहरे आम् के बरिया मे कुछ् फर् होला की नाही? A. अबकी तो बदरी से पेड़न् मे लाही लग् गइल्; नाही तो बहुत् होत् रहल्. — 18. Q. थोड् आम् हमहूँ के अँचार् नावै के देत? A. जब् तोहार् मन् होय्, तब् आय् के तोड़वाय्[15] लय. — 19. Q. तोहार् लड़िकवा कुछ् पढैला की नाही? A. हाँ, गुरू किहाँ[16] जाला; अच्छर्[17] तो चीन्ह् गयल् बाय्; आज् काल् पहाड़ा पढत् बाय्. — 20. Q. पाठसाले मे नाही बैठाय् देत? A. कुछ् पढ़्

1) The following specimens of village-conversations were given to me by Paṇḍit Gopâl Bhaṭṭa of Benares. The spelling is his, excepting the *virâmas* and interpunctuations which I have added.

लें, तब् अठैय् देईं[18]. — 21. Q. हमहूँ अपने बेटौवा[19] के पाठसाले मे बैठावल् चाहीला. A. अच्छा! हमरे लड़िका के संगे ओहू के बैठाय् दीहा.

Notes: 1) pers. خاكى. 2) adverb. past part. 3) arab. حرج. 4) 3. pl. pres. ind. of the potent. pass. 5) arab. قلعه. 6) pers. نوكر. 7) pers. كم. 8) arab. خبر. 9) pers. صهينا. 10) arab. ليكن. 11) pers. خريد, treated as a denom. root. 12) pers. تيز. 13) arab. فايده. 14) 2. pl. imperative; or ले लहू or ले ल्यहू. 15) conj. part. of the double caus. 16) contr. for के इहाँ. 17) anomalous plur. of अच्छर, apparently made after Urdu (arabic) analogy, as हुकाम् *orders,* pl. of हुकम्. 18) 1. pl. pres. conj., used as future. 19) redundant form of बेटा.

b) Between master and servant.

1. Q. काल् लोहिया लागत् खेत् पर् जाये के होई. A. काहे के बदे? का, खेत् निरावे के? — 2. Q. हाँ, खेतो निरावै के अउर् बड़के खेतवा मे हरौ चलावै के. A. कै मजूरा[1] कै काम् बाय्? — 3. Q. जैठे से सपरै, तैठे लगाय् दीहे. A. धान् कै खेतवा भरहू के न होई. — 4. Q. कै दिन् मे भरल् जाई? A. दुइ दिन् कै काम् बाय्. — 5. Q. लवहू कै दिन् तो आय् गयल्. A. अच्छा, तब् ले चार् पाँच् मेहरारुन् के ठहराय् रक्खोला. — 6. Q. गैवन् के कोयर् दिहले, की नाहीं? A. घास् तो नाय् दिहले रहली. — 7. Q. भूसौ लेआय् के सानी चलाय् दे; साँझ् भइल्. A. अेर् बिसवले, हम् घरे[2] रोटी खाये जाव्. — 8. Q. अच्छा, जब खाय् के ऐहे, तब् गोरुन् के ओसारी मे बाँध् दीहे. A. तोहरे बदे ई बेरा का खाये के होई? — 9. Q. माई से कहे[3] दीहे की रोटी पोय् रखिहैं. A. खाली[1] रोटियै खैब? — 10. Q. अउर् का? दूध् के संगे खाय् लेब्. A. दाल् न होखो? — 11. Q. राति के हम् के दाल् नाही पचत्. A. जलदी खाये जैह! नाही तो रोटी जुड़ाय्[4] जाई. — 12. Q. जा लेजा, तैं तो जलदी[5] खाय् आव्; बिना तोरे ऐले हम् न जाबै. A. हम् तो जातै आटी; खाय् के हालियै आइब्. — 13. Q. भला, बोया के बदे कोठिला मे कुछ् जव् बाय् की नाहीं? A. न होई, तो बोऐ भर् के मोल् घाय् जाई. — 14. Q. केतना चाही बोवै के? A. एक् छ पसेरी मे होय् जाई. — 15. Q. काँको न चाही बोवै के? A. काँकू तो चाहे तोहरे बखार् मे होय्. — 16. Q. ई घरी देव् जो चार् बुन्दी कर् देतें, तो बड़ अच्छा होत्. A. देख! गोसैंयाँ कै मरजी[6] होई, तो बरसू जैहैं. — 17. Q. अरे! हाँ, काल् फार् के बदे थोरा लोहा खरीदै के बाय्. A. केतना लोहा चाही?

तोहरे घर् मे नैखे? — 18. Q. मतारी से पुछिहे तो. A. घाम् तो पियरायल् आतै मे; साँझ् भइल् चाहैले. — 19. Q. हो! देख्! गाई आवत् बाय्. A. एह् बेरा आवै के कौन् काम् रहल्? — 20. Q. ले! बेर् बिसवै चाहैला; तें जलदी[5] जो! A. अच्छा, ले! तुहऊँ जा! दिसा जंगल् से निपट् आव.

Notes: 1) pers. مزدور. 2) old loc. 3) conj. part. 4) conj. part. of potent. pass. 5) pers. جلدی. 6) arab. مرضی.

c) Between two sisters.

1. Q. कह, बहिनी! एहवर् कहाँ गइल् रहल्यू? A. रहिला के साग् खोंटै. — 2. Q. एह् पारी तोहरे खेतवा मे खाली रहिलै बोवल् बाय्? A. नाही, मटर् रहिला अउर् अरहर, तौन् चीज्[1], बोवल् बाय्. — 3. Q. तोहार् दुलहा आज् काल् कहीं बाहर् गयल् बाटैं? A. नाही, घरही तो बाटैं, लेकिन् खेत् पर् बहुत् रहैलैं. — 4. Q. तूँ रसोइयाँ कब् करैल्यू? A. दुपहर् के करीला; अब् जाय् के, तब् करब्. — 5. Q. तोहार् बिटियवा तो नीके बाय्? A. हँ, बाय् अच्छीतरह्[2]. — 6. Q. तोहार् गैयवा[3] कुछ् दूध् देले की नाही? A. का कहीं बहिनी? पहिले बियान् मे तो कुछ् नाही दिहलेस्; अबकी बियान् मे देखीं कुछ् देले की नाही. — 7. Q. केतना दिन् बियैले[4] भयल्? A. अबहीं तो आज् पँचवाँ दिन् हो; अबहीं ओकर् बछरुआ अच्छी तरह्[2] चल् नाही सकत्. — 8. Q. खरी कराई पखेव अच्छी तरह्[2] पाई, तो दूध् देई. A. देवै के तो बिचार् बाय्. — 9. Q. ओहे घरवा मे तुँहईं अकेल् रहल्यू[5] की औरो केहू रहैला? A. नाही, हमहीं अकेल् रहीला, लेकिन् चाहीला की और् केहू रह जात्, तो मनसायन् होत्. — 10. Q. एको कोठरी हमरे रहे लाइक्[6] होय्, तो हम् के द. A. बाय्, लेकिन् छोट बाय्, तोहार् निबाह् ओ मे न होई. — 11. Q. भला! कब्बहू तोहरे परोस् मे होई, तो हम् के बतैह. A. काहे? जौने घरवा मे तूँ रहैल्यू, तौने मे कौनो दिकदारी[7] बाय्? — 12. Q. दिकदारी कवन् बाय? भारा बहुत् लगैला. A. अच्छा! तो आव, हमरे ही घर् मे रह; कौनो तरह्[2] से निबाह् होय् जाई. — 13. Q. भला बहिन्! बड़् किरपा कैल्यू; हम् बहुत् दिकदार्[7] रहलीं ओहे घर् से. A. अच्छा! तो कब् से रहै के अइब? — 14. Q. अब् तो खरवाँस् बितले बाद्[8] अच्छी साइत् देखवाय् के आइब्. A. जरूर्[9] आवै के विचार् रखिह; हम् अपने मनसेधू से कहि के घर् सफा[10] करवाय् रक्खब्. — 15. Q. न जानी, खरवाँस् केतने दिन् रही! A. रह! हमरे परोस् मे एक् पंडित् रहैलैं; ओन्ह् से पूछ् के, तब् तोहू से कहब.

Notes: 1) pers. چیز. 2) arab. طرح. 3) redundant form of

गाई. 4) adverb. past part. of potent. pass. 5) shorter form of 2. pl. pres. ind. fem., for रहैल्यू. 6) arab. لايق. 7) arab. دق داریو. 8) arab. بعد. 9) arab. ضرور. 10) arab. صفا.

d) Between parents and son.

1. Q. (Father speaks): बेटा! सबेर् हो" उठ् के ऊख् के खेत् देखै के जैह! A. अब् तो तोरहू कै दिन् आयल्. — 2. Q. हाँ, लेकिन् कोल्हू कै काठ् टूट् गइल् बाय्; से खरीदै के होई. A. केतने दाम् पर् मिली? — 3. Q. ओ कर् जैसन् काठ् होय्, तैसन् दाम् लगै. A. कतरी बाय्, की उहो खरीदल् जाई? — 4. Q. कतरियो तो नाही बाय्, लेकिन् ओ कर् भर् के काठ् घर् मे होई; बढई बलवाय् के बनवाय् लिहल् जाई. A. क बाबू? येहू पारी खाली राबै बनवैब की गुरो? — 5. Q. नाही, दूनौ बनवाइब्. A. अब् हम् खाये जात् बाटी. — 6. Q. (Mother speaks): आव, बेटा, जलदी खाये के! A. आज् का रसोँई" कैले बाटिस्? — 7. Q. आज रसोँई" मे दाल् रोटी अउर् कोँहडउरी भइल् बाय्. A. दूध् बाय् की नाही? — 8. Q. थोर् एक् होई बाय्; पूत् बाँट् के खाय् लीहा! A. अच्छा! गोड़् धोवै के पानी भेजवाय् दे! — 9. Q. हे! इहाँ लोटा मे पानी रक्खल् बाय्; गोड़् धोव! A. बडकी थरिया मे हम् के परोसिहे! — 10. Q. अपने बापो के बलाय् ल्य! A. अच्छा! बलाय् लेआइला; आव बाबू खाये! — 11. Q. (Father speaks): बेटा! तूं खाय् ल्य, तब् हम पीछे से खाब्. A. काँहे"? — 12. Q. अबही" अच्छी तरह् से हम् के भूख् नैखे. A. नाही"! माई बलावत् बाय्. — 13. Q. अच्छा ल! आवत् बाटी. A. हे! गोड़् धोवै के पानी धयल् बाय्. — 14. Q. अच्छा! परोसवाव! A. माई! रसोइयाँ आज् कौन् करत् हौ? — 15. Q. (Mother speaks): तोहार् मेहर्. A. ओ के रोटी फुलावै नाही आवत्. — 16. Q. नाही" आवत्; तब्बो कच्ची नाही रहत्. A. पीढ़ा धै दे! — 17. Q. तूँ आव, तो सही! पीढ़ा तो इँहँई" रक्खल् बाय्. A. ले! बाबुओ ऐलैं", हमहूँ ऐली; जलदी परोसै के कह्. — 18. Q. परोस् दे रे! A. दुइ थरिया, छोटी बडी परोस्!

e) Between mother and boy.

1. Q. माई! खाये के दे! A. का खइबे? — 2. Q. का बाय् खाये के? A. रोटी बाय्; काहे से खइबे? — 3. Q. दूध् बाय् की नाही? A. दूध् तो कच्चा बाय्, लेकिन् नैनू बाय्; कहु, तो देई"; ओही से खाय् ले! — 4. Q. नैनू दूध् के हौ की दही कै? A. नाही"! आज् सबेरे दही मह के निकलले

रहली. — 5. Q. लेश्राव्. A. खाली नैनुवें, की श्रो मे कोनो मीठा मिलबे? — 6. Q. कौन् मीठा बाटे? A. राब् लेश्राई को गुर्? — 7. Q. नाही! राबै लेश्राव्! गुर् हम् के नाही भावत्. A. श्रच्छा! ले! तै वैठु! हम् लेश्राईला. — 8. Q. जल्दी लेश्राव्; नाही तो ऊ लरिकवा श्राय् जाई. A. तै गोड़् तो धोउ! हम् लेश्राईला. — 9. Q. दुइवे रोटी ले ऐहे! A. ई काहे? पेट् भर् खाय् ले! रसोइयाँ के श्रबही श्रबेर् होई. — 10. Q. श्रच्छा! तीन् दे! A. ले! खो!

f) Between two boys.

1. Q. का भाई! चलब खेलै के? A. श्रबही हम् खेली नाही; खाय् लेई, तब् चली. — 2. Q. कब् खैब? A. माई श्रावैले, तब् खाईला[1]. — 3. Q. तोहार् माई कहाँ गइल् बाय्? A. गोहन् के कोयर् देवै के. — 4. Q. तब् ले चल; खेल् श्राई. A. कौन् खेल् खेलब्? — 5. Q. लट्टू तोहरे पास् बाय् की नाही? A. लट्टू तो बाय्; लत्ती नैखै. — 6. Q. श्राव! लत्ती बनाई. A. कपडा कहाँ बाय्? — 7. Q. कपडा बहुत् मिली. A. लब! माइयो श्राइल्; श्रब् खाय् लेई; तब् सुचित् से खेली. — 8. Q. तब् से हमहूँ घर् से होय् श्राईला[1]. A. तूं काहे वदे घर् जात् बाट? — 9. Q. घोर् एक् दूध् धयल् बाय्; से हमहूँ पी श्राई. A. तोहरे[2] दूध् होला? — 10. Q. हाँ, बाकेन्[3] गैया कै दूध् हौ. A. श्रच्छा! जा! जलदी ऐह! — 11. Q. हम् तो गैली की ऐलो. A. जा जलदी!

Notes: 1) 1. pl. pres. ind., for fut. ind. 2) old loc.; elliptic, for तोहरे पास्. 3) pers. بالكه.

3. FOLKLORE.

a) The treasure in the field.

एक् बडा श्रादिमो[1] श्रंगूर्[2] कै बारी श्रो खेत् बोवलेस्; श्रोके चार् बेटवा रहलै; जब् ऊ मरै लगल्, तब् बेटवन् से कहलेस्; ए बेटा मोरे पास् जवन् धन् रहल्, तौन् क मै श्रंगूर् के खेतवा मे गाड् दिहले बाटो; से तूंलोग् खनब, तो पइबह्; जब् ऊ श्रादिमी मरि गयल्, तब् श्रोकर् सब् बेटौवा मिल् के खेत् के चारो श्रोर् से खनै लगलैं[3]; लेकिन् धन् कै खोज् न मिलल्; बाकी[4] खेत् श्रच्छी तरह् से खोदल् गयल्; श्रो से श्रंगूर् कै पेड् खूब्[5] पनकलैं; श्रोर् खूब् श्रँगूर् कै फल् उपजलैं; तब् तो सब् बेटा मिल् के श्रोके बेचलैं, श्रोर् बहुत् एक् धन् पौलें; बडा खुस्[6] भइलैं; एसे हमलोगन् के ई बात् सीखै के चाही, की बडा लोग् जौन् बात् कहें तौने के जरूर् मानै के चाही, टारै के न चाही; एही मे हमरे लोगन् कै कल्यान् होई; ई लडिकन् के सीखै के बदे कहनी हौवे.

Notes: 1) arab. آدمی. 2) pers. انگور. 3) shorter form for लगलैं, 3. pl. 2nd pret. ind.; see § 26. 4) pers. بلکه. 5) pers. خوب. 6) pers. خوش.

b) The two wise Bráhmans.

कौनो एक् बाम्हन् रहल्: ओके दुइ बेटा रहलैं; ऊ बाम्हन् कौनो जग्य करै लगल्; ओ मे एक् मछरी कै काम् परल्; तब् ऊ दूनो बेटौवन् से कहलेस्, की बेटा! तूँ दूनो जने समुद्र् के तीर् पर् जाय् के एक् मछरी लेआवह्; तब् पिता के आग्या पाय् के दूनो समुद्र् के तीर् पर् गैलेन्; और् उहाँ के मल्लाह् से कहलेन्, की हम् के एक् मछरी कै काम् बाय्, से तै पकड् दे; तब् मल्लाह् एक् मछरी बझाय् के दुनहुन् के आगे लेआय् के धै दिहलेस्; तब् ओन्ह् मे से एक् दुसरे के कहलेस् की तैं काहे नाँही उठाय् ले चलतेस्; तब् ऊ बोलल् की मै भोजनचतुर् बाटौं; मो के ए कर् गंध् आवेले; तब् ऊ बोलल् की मैहूँ। सयनचतुर् हौओं; ऐसे न उठैबों; ऐसहीं[1] उन्ह् दुनहुन् मे झगरा होवै लगल्; आखिर्[2] के दूनो लरत् लरत् राजा के पास् गैलैं और् राजा के आपन् समाचार् कहलैं; तब् राजा कहलेस्, की तू दूनो जने हम् के परिच्छा दह्; तब् हम् तोहर् बिद्या जानी; ऊ दूनो खजा[3] भइलैं परिच्छा देवै के; तब् पहिले राजा भोजनचतुर् कै परिच्छा लेवै बदे अच्छो रसोईयाँ बनवालैं; ओ मे अच्छी से अच्छी तरकारी, अच्छे से अच्छे चाउर् कै भात्, अच्छा से अच्छा पकवान् रिँधवालेन्; और् भोजनचतुर् के बलवाय्[4] के खाये के बैठोलेन्; तब् ऊ जैसे हीं भात् कै कवर् उठौलेस्, तैसेहीं ओ के ओ मे मुरदा[5] कै गंध् आयल्; से ऊ थरिया छोड् के उठ् गयल्; तब् राजा ओ के पुछलैं, की तैं काहे नाहीं खैले और् उठ् गैले? ऊ कहलेस् की भात् मे मुरदा के गंध् आवैले; तब् राजा किसान् के बलाय्[4] के पुछलेस् की चाउर् कैसन् रहल् और् कहा से लेआय् के तै मो के दिहल? किसान् बोलल् की आपन् खेत् से; तब् राजा पुछलेस् की ऊ खेत् केकर् हो? तब् किसान् कहलेस् की जिमीदार्[6] से हम् मोल् लिहले रहली; तब् राजा जिमीदार् के बलाय् के पुछलेस्, की ई भूँईं कैसन् रहल्? तब् जिमीदार् बोलल्, की ई भूँईं मुर्दघट्टा पहिले रहल्; तब् राजा भोजनचतुर् के कहलेस्, की तैं ठीक् भोजनचतुर् हौवे; फेर् सयनचतुर् के बोलाय् के राजा एक् अच्छी बिछवनादार् खटिया बिछवाय् दिहलेस्, और् ओ के सूतै के कहलेस्; ऊ सूतल्; लेकिन् ओ के राति भर् नीँद् नाँहीं आइल्; एह् कर् वट् से ओह् कर् वट्, ओकर् वट् से एह् कर् वट् करत् रहल्; सवेरे राजा ओ के बलौलेस्[4], और् कहलेस् की तैं राति भर सुख से सुतले? ऊ बोलल् की महराज समस्त राति मोके नीदँ नाहीं परल; राजा पुछलैं काहे? ऊ बोलल् कि बिछवना के परत

मे एक थार् थाटै से मोरे देँहू[7] मे गउत् रहल्; तब् राजा अपने नोकर् से बिछावन् उठवाय् के देखलेस तो ओ मे एक थार् दखायल्[8]; तब् राजा खुसो[9] होय्के ओके कहलेस् कि तैं ठीक् सयनचतुर् हौवे; ए करे बाद् राजा उन् दुनहुन् कै बहुतो तरह् से खातिरदारी कै कं बिदा कैलैं॥

Notes: 1) हूँ and हों are emphatic. 2) arab. آخر. 3) lit. *standing,* here *ready.* 4) shorter form for ओलवाय्; see § 26. 5) pers. مرده. 6) pers. زميندار. 7) for देह्, see § 67. 8) 3. sg. 2nd pret. ind. of potent. pass. 9) pers. خوشی *joy*; here used adjectively, through confusion with adj., formed like सुखो; see § 253.

c) The unfortunate Bráhman.

कौनो एक् ब्राह्मन् सोमशर्म्मा कुसुमपुर् गाँव मे रहत् रहल्; ऊ आपन् बियाह् देवस्वामी केहू अपने परोसिया ब्राह्मन् को बिटिया से कैलेस्; से एक् दिन् को बात् हो कि दूनो परानो अटारी पर् सूतल् रहलैं; एतने मे एक् कौनो बिद्याधर् ओही ओर् से अकास् मे विमान् पर् चढल् चल् जात् रहल्; से ओकर डीठ् ओहे मेहरारू पर् पर् गइल्; ऊ, ओकरे सुन्दरताई से मोहित् होय्, नीचे उतर्, ओके उठाय् लेगयल्; सवेरा भयल्, तब् सोमशर्म्मा अपने बिछौना के सून् देख् अपन स्त्री के चारो ओर् हेरै लगलैं, लेकिन् पता न पौलैं; तब् तो बौरहा के तरह् एहर् ओहर् घूमै लगलैं और भुखैलैं[1]; तब् केहू गिरस्थ[2] के घर् जाय् कहलैं कि हम् के कुछ् खाये के वदे थ; ऊ अपने स्त्री से कहलेस् कि ब्राह्मन् भुखायल् आय्, एके कुछ् दे; ऊ रसोँईं मे जाय्, एक् दोना भर् खीर् लं आय् के, ब्राह्मन् के दिहलेस्; ब्राह्मन् ऊ खीर ले के एक् नदी के तीर् पर् जाय्, कौनो पेड़ के जड़् पर् खीर् कै दोना ध के, हाय् मुँह् धोए के वदे नदी मे गयल्; तब् ले एहर् ओहे पेड़् पर् से एक् करइत् साँप् उतर् के, ऊ खीर् थोरऐक्[3] खैलेस्, और् ओ मे अपने मुह् से जहर्[4] उगिल् के, फर् ओही पेड़् पर् चढ् गयल्; तब् ले ऊ बेचारा ब्राह्मन् भुखायल् जलदी से आये के ओहे दोना के सब् खीर् खाय् गयल् और् थोरी वेर् मे जेहर् से बियाकुल् होय् के मुइ[5] गयल्॥

अब् एह् कथा मे ई बिचारल् चाही कि ओ करे मुअले के हत्या के के भइल्, ओहे गिरस्थ् के, कि ओकरे मेहरारू के, कि ओहे साँप् के॥

Notes: 1) 3. pl. 2nd pret. ind. of potent. pass. 2) for गृहस्थ्. 3) or थोरेक्, see § 291. 4) pers. زهر. 5) irregular conj. part. of the verb मरब् *to die.*

INDEX OF SUBJECTS.

Note: The numbers refer to the pages.

A.

D.

G.

H.

I.

Q.

R.

S.

ERRATA.

p. II. l. 20. extends *for* extents.

p. III. l. 22. Kachchh *for* Kachh.

p. III. l. 23. Kachchhí *for* Kachhí.

p. IV. l. 29. however *for* howerer.

p. VI. l. 2. eighthly *for* eightly.

p. VIII. l. 14. XXXVII *for* XXXV.

p. IX. l. 29. and the short *for* and of the short.

p. XVII. l. 32. válakko *for* valakko.

p. XXIV. l. 17. what *for* wbat.

p. XXV. l. 33. Práchyá *for* Práchá.

p. XXV. l. 34. Práchyá *for* Gauḍí.

p. XXXVII. l. 11. comes *for* come.

p. XXXVII. l. 20. Prakáṣ *for* Prakaṣ.

p. 17. l. 28. difficulty *for* difficully.

p. 56. l. 27. give thou *for* take thou.

p. 57. l. 5. सगड़् *for* सगल्.

p. 61. l. 33. मोटल् *for* मोटल्.

p. 64. l. 31. वईई or वऱ्हई *for* वहँइ or वऱ्हइ.

p. 65. l. 29. § 77 *for* § 74.

p. 70. l. 7. add: E. H. बइल् or बैल्.

p. 70. l. 10. दोन् *for* दोना.

p. 104. l. 34. वाउड़् *for* वउड़्.

p. 107. l. 6. पाछिल् *for* पछिल्.

p. 110. l. 24. चमोटा *for* चमोटो.

p. 110. l. 26. हिरनोटा *for* हिरणोटा.

p. 112. l. 23. गहुआई *for* गहुआइ.

p. 123. l. 34. चोलो *for* चोली.

p. 124. l. 10. बेटा *son for* बेटो *son*.

p. 141. l. 6. चलिय or चलिव *for* चलिय् or चलिव्.

ADDENDA.

p. 67. rule 119, 2. W. H. हुाटा *three and a half* for Pr. अड्डोट्ठ°, see § 416.

p. 88. rule 160. न्त् becomes न्द् in S., P., Mw. अंदो for अंतो suffix of pres. part., see § 301. Also P., S. पंज *five* for Pr. पंच, Skr. पञ्च, see p. 256.

p. 90. rule 172. W. H. हुाटा for *अड्डाटा *three and a half*, see § 416.

p. 90. add rule 172[a]. इ is elided; rarely; E. H. छाहै or चाहै *he desires*, Pr. इच्छाग्रइ, Skr. *इच्छायति, see p. 389, footnote.

p. 113. rule 227. The forms त्त and तन are preserved in the O. H. of Chand; e. g. वृड्डत्त *old age* Pr. R. 28, 38; प्रीतत्तन *friendship* Pr. R. 28, 56; कुसलत्तन *prosperity* Pr. R. 28, 38; वृढत्तन *old age* Pr. R. 28, 38.

p. 117. rule 239. In O. H. the suff. is इत; e. g. रगतेत *bloody* Chand Pr. R. 28, 39.

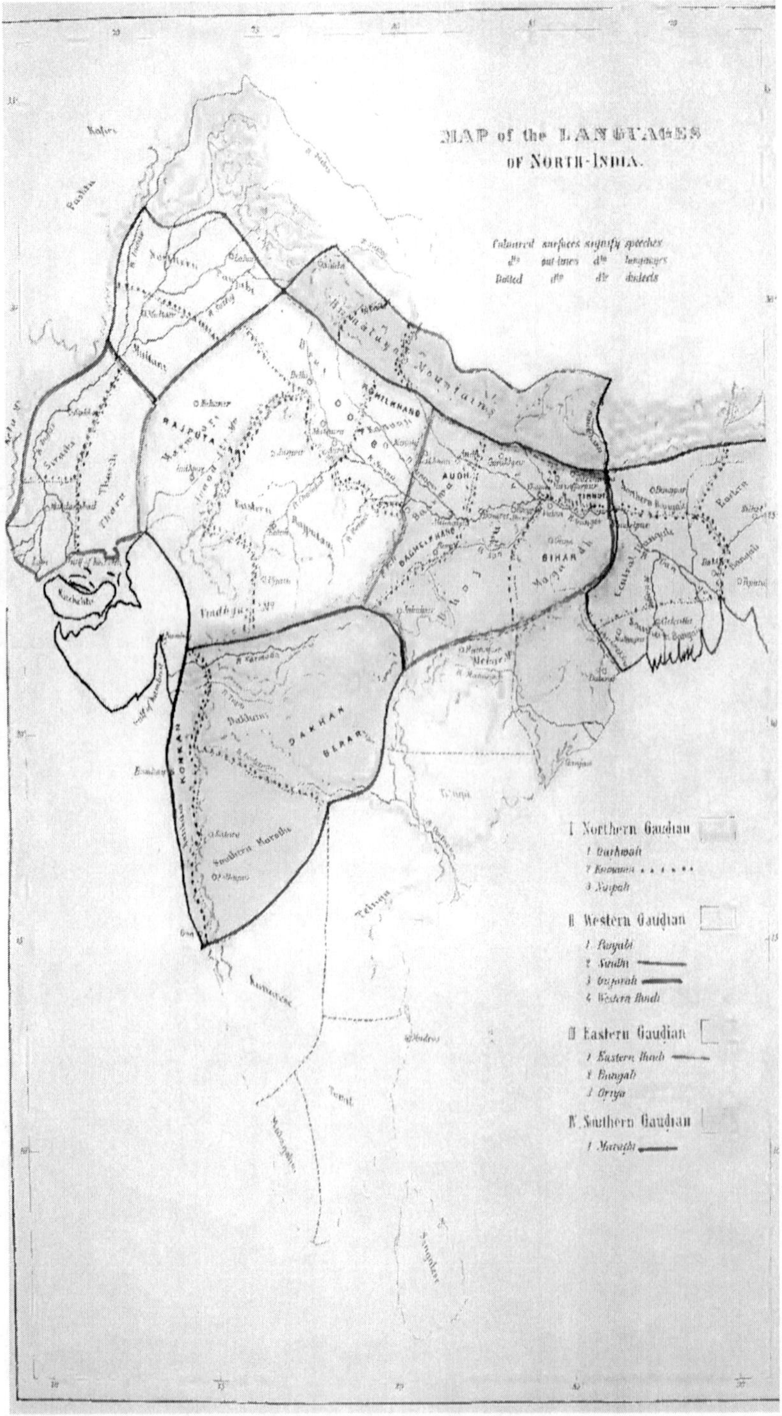

MAP of the LANGUAGES
OF NORTH-INDIA.
Coloured surfaces signify speeches
do out-lines do languages
Dotted do do dialects
I Northern Gaudian
1 Garhwali
II Western Gaudian
1 Panjabi
2 Sindhi
3 Gujarati
4 Western Hindi
III Eastern Gaudian
1 Eastern Hindi
2 Bangali
3 Oriya
IV Southern Gaudian
1 Marathi
Himalaya Mountains
RAJPUTA
ROHILKHAND
AUDH
BIHAR
DAKHAN
BERAR
KONKAN
Southern Marathi
Telugu
Tamil
Kanarese
Madras
Bombay

TABLE OF ALPHABETS.

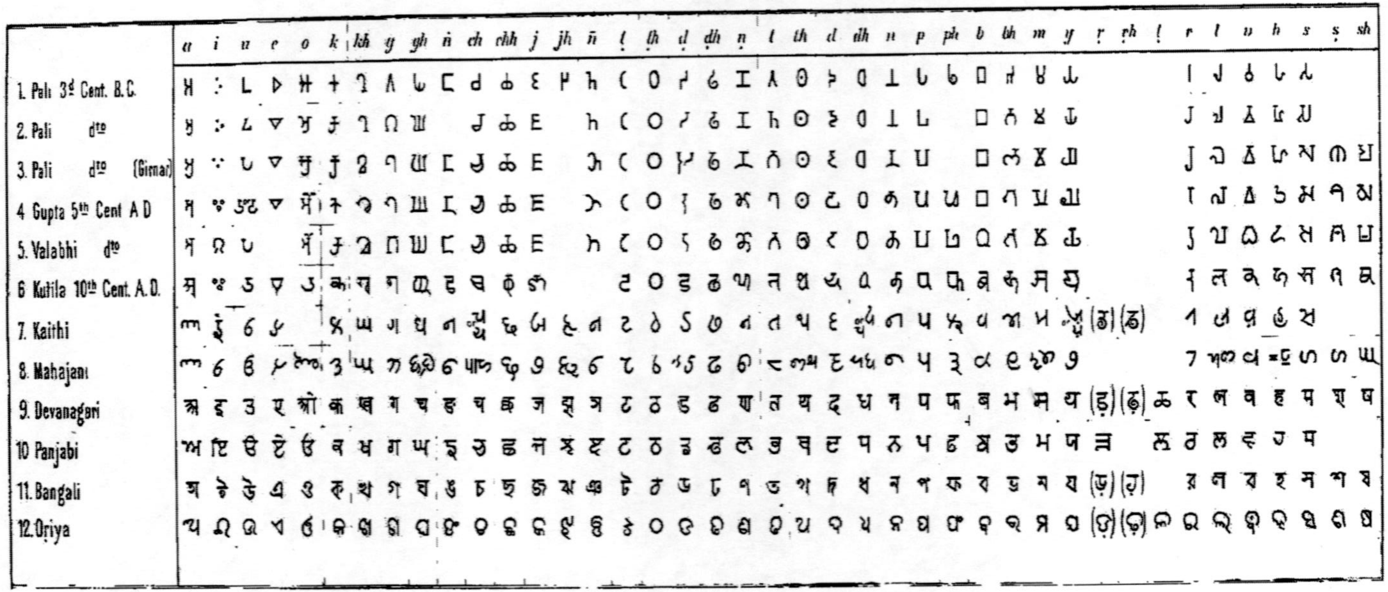